W9-BQZ-016

HANDBOOK OF POPULATION AND FAMILY ECONOMICS

VOLUME 1B

HANDBOOKS
IN
ECONOMICS

14

Series Editors

KENNETH J. ARROW
MICHAEL D. INTRILIGATOR

ELSEVIER
AMSTERDAM · LAUSANNE · NEW YORK · OXFORD · SHANNON · TOKYO

HANDBOOK OF POPULATION AND FAMILY ECONOMICS

VOLUME 1B

Edited by

MARK R. ROSENZWEIG
University of Pennsylvania

and

ODED STARK
University of Oslo and University of Vienna

1997

ELSEVIER

AMSTERDAM · LAUSANNE · NEW YORK · OXFORD · SHANNON · TOKYO

338.91
H236

ELSEVER SCENCE B.V.   *VOL. 1B*
Sara Burgerhartstraat 25
P.O. Box 211, 1000 AE Amsterdam, The Netherlands

ISBN Volume 1A: 0 444 82645 9
ISBN Volume 1B: 0 444 82646 7
ISBN Set (1A & 1B): 0 444 89647 3

© 1997 ELSEVIER SCIENCE B.V. All rights reserved.

No part of this publication may be reproduced, stored in a retrieval system or transmitted, in any form or by any means, electronic, mechanical, photocopying, recording or otherwise, without the prior written permission of the publisher, Elsevier Science B.V., Copyright & Permissions Department, P.O. Box 521, 1000 AM Amsterdam, The Netherlands.

Special regulations for readers in the U.S.A. – This publication has been registered with the Copyright Clearance Center Inc. (CCC), 222 Rosewood Drive, Danvers, MA 01923. Information can be obtained from the CCC about conditions under which photocopies of parts of this publication may be made in the U.S.A. All other copyright questions, including photocopying outside of the U.S.A., should be referred to the copyright owner, Elsevier Science B.V., unless otherwise specified.

No responsibility is assumed by the publisher for any injury and/or damage to persons or property as a matter of products liability, negligence or otherwise, or from any use or operation of any methods, products, instructions or ideas contained in the material herein.

This book is printed on acid-free paper.

PRINTED IN THE NETHERLANDS

INTRODUCTION TO THE SERIES

The aim of the *Handbooks in Economics* series is to produce Handbooks for various branches of economics, each of which is a definitive source, reference, and teaching supplement for use by professional researchers and advanced graduate students. Each Handbook provides self-contained surveys of the current state of a branch of economics in the form of chapters prepared by leading specialists on various aspects of this branch of economics. These surveys summarize not only received results but also newer developments, from recent journal articles and discussion papers. Some original material is also included, but the main goal is to provide comprehensive and accessible surveys. The Handbooks are intended to provide not only useful reference volumes for professional collections but also possible supplementary readings for advanced courses for graduate students in economics.

University Libraries
Carnegie Mellon University
Pittsburgh, PA 15213-3890

CONTENTS OF THE HANDBOOK

VOLUME 1A

Chapter 1
Introduction: Population and Family Economics
MARK R. ROSENZWEIG and ODED STARK

PART I: THE FAMILY

Chapter 2
A Survey of Theories of the Family
THEODORE C. BERGSTROM

Chapter 3
The Formation and Dissolution of Families: Why Marry? Who Marries Whom? And What Happens upon Divorce
YORAM WEISS

Chapter 4
Intrahousehold Distribution and the Family
JERE R. BEHRMAN

Chapter 5
Intergenerational and Interhousehold Economic Links
JOHN LAITNER

PART II: FERTILITY

Chapter 6
The Cost of Children and the Use of Demographic Variables in Consumer Demand
BERNARD M.S. VAN PRAAG and MARCEL F. WARNAAR

Chapter 7
The Economics of Fertility in Developed Countries
V. JOSEPH HOTZ, JACOB ALEX KLERMAN and ROBERT J. WILLIS

Chapter 8
Demand for Children in Low Income Countries
T. PAUL SCHULTZ

PART III: MORTALITY AND HEALTH

Chapter 9
New Findings on Secular Trends in Nutrition and Mortality: Some Implications for
Population Theory
ROBERT WILLIAM FOGEL

Chapter 10
Determinants and Consequences of the Mortality and Health of Infants and Children
KENNETH I. WOLPIN

Chapter 11
Mortality and Morbidity among Adults and the Elderly
ROBIN C. SICKLES and PAUL TAUBMAN

VOLUME 1B

PART IV: MIGRATION

Chapter 12
Internal Migration in Developed Countries
MICHAEL J. GREENWOOD

Chapter 13
Internal Migration in Developing Countries
ROBERT E.B. LUCAS

Chapter 14
Economic Impact of International Migration and the Economic Performance of
Migrants
ROBERT J. LALONDE and ROBERT H. TOPEL

Chapter 15
International Migration and International Trade
ASSAF RAZIN and EFRAIM SADKA

PART V: AGING, DEMOGRAPHIC COMPOSITION, AND THE ECONOMY

Chapter 16
The Economics of Individual Aging
MICHAEL D. HURD

Chapter 17
The Economics of Population Aging
DAVID N. WEIL

Chapter 18
Demographic Variables and Income Inequality
DAVID LAM

PART VI: AGGREGATE POPULATION CHANGE AND ECONOMIC GROWTH

Chapter 19
Population Dynamics: Equilibrium, Disequilibrium, and Consequences of Fluctuations
RONALD D. LEE

Chapter 20
Growth Models with Endogenous Population: a General Framework
MARC NERLOVE and LAKSHMI K. RAUT

Chapter 21
Long-Term Consequences of Population Growth: Technological Change, Natural
Resources, and the Environment
JAMES A. ROBINSON and T.N. SRINIVASAN

PREFACE TO THE HANDBOOK

When the idea for a compendium on economic demography was conceived, we had to persuade ourselves that there was a sufficient body of economics literature on population and the family to support a *Handbook;* that the compendium could be sensibly divided into main areas and well-defined chapter topics; that there was a group of scholars able and willing to take critical stock of each area in a coordinated enterprise; and that there was a reasonable likelihood that those assigned to write chapters would deliver drafts within a finite time. We believe that the resulting product – the *Handbook of Population and Family Economics* – shows that our original affirmative assessments of at least the first three of these ex ante conditions were correct, although we had not anticipated that our comprehension of many demographic events such as mismarriage, miscarriage, and overdue births would also be enriched by this experience. We are indebted to the *Handbook* chapter authors who were waiting (while updating) long and patiently for their fellow authors to complete the write-ups of their drafts. Our pinched nerves notwithstanding, we also thank the late-coming authors for finally heeding our pleas and noncredible threats, so that by the Spring of 1996, completed drafts of all the chapters were in hand.

At the outset it seemed to us that the task of providing a comprehensive reference source divided into survey chapters that summarize frontier areas of research, elucidate new theoretical developments, and review the existing evidence, would be made considerably easier if we could bring together the authors of the *Handbook* chapters at the stage at which detailed chapter outlines were in hand. Such a meeting would acquaint all authors with each other's planned work, assist in filling gaps, help achieve appropriate coverage, identify interconnections, and limit unwarranted duplications. We are indebted to the Ford Foundation and its Reproductive Health and Population Division for providing us, through a grant to Harvard University and the University of Pennsylvania, with financial support for our authors' conference. We believe that the conference was highly conducive to transforming the *Handbook* into a product more valuable than the sum of its parts. We are also grateful to Ann Facciola, Janet Conway, and Claudia Napolilli for competent assistance in coordinating the conference and subsequent author and editor communications. We will know that our efforts and theirs were worthwhile if the *Handbook of Population and Family Economics* contributes to increasing the population of economists involved in research on population and the family, and if the family of social science disciplines more readily adopts the thinking of economists on population and family issues.

MARK R. ROSENZWEIG
ODED STARK

3.4. Summary of wealth change   935
3.5. Evidence about the LCH based on consumption data   938
3.6. Tests of the bequest motive for saving   939
3.7. Summary of consumption and saving   947
4. Economic status of the elderly   948
    4.1. Introduction   948
    4.2. Income-based measures of economic status   948
    4.3. Consumption-based measures of economic status   954
    4.4. Distribution of economic resources   956
    4.5. Summary of economic status   958
5. Directions for future research   960
References   962

Chapter 17
The Economics of Population Aging   967
DAVID N. WEIL

1. Introduction   968
2. Population aging: facts and determinants   969
    2.1. Facts and forecasts on population aging   969
    2.2. Sources of aging: fertility and mortality   970
    2.3. Immigration   975
3. Aging, production, and consumption   977
    3.1. The effect of population aging on youth and old-age dependency   977
    3.2. Age structure, population growth, and dependency in stable populations   979
    3.3. Implications of changes in morbidity and mortality for support ratios   981
    3.4. Aging and sustainable consumption in a model with capital   983
    3.5. Aging and the labor market   989
4. Aging in a life-cycle model   994
    4.1. Demographic change in a two-period life-cycle model   995
    4.2. Aging and saving in partial equilibrium   996
    4.3. Aging and saving in general equilibrium   997
    4.4. Limitations of the life-cycle model   998
5. Social security and other government programs   1000
    5.1. Dependency ratios for government programs   1000
    5.2. Interaction of age structure, social security, and life-cycle saving   1001
    5.3. The response of social security to demographic change   1003
    5.4. Political economy of social security benefits and of increased aged population   1005
6. Within-family intergenerational relations and aging   1006
    6.1. Parent to child transfers   1007
    6.2. Child to parent transfers   1008
7. Conclusion   1009
References   1010

5.1. Social welfare transfers 840
5.2. Transfers and fertility 842
5.3. Comparing transfers and tax payments 844
6. Conclusions 846
References 847

Chapter 15
International Migration and International Trade 851
ASSAF RAZIN and EFRAIM SADKA

1. Introduction 852
2. Substitution and complementarity between labor mobility and good mobility 856
   2.1. Substitution 857
   2.2. Complementarity 861
3. Substitution and complementarity between labor mobility and capital
   mobility 865
4. Global population dispersion: the efficient volume of migration 868
5. Gains and losses from international migration 871
6. Migration in the presence of wage rigidity 873
   6.1. The wage flexibility benchmark 873
   6.2. Rigid wages 878
7. Income distribution and migration 881
8. Conclusion 884
Appendix 885
References 886

PART V: AGING, DEMOGRAPHIC COMPOSITION, AND THE ECONOMY

Chapter 16
The Economics of Individual Aging 891
MICHAEL D. HURD

1. Introduction 892
2. Retirement 892
   2.1. Overview of explanations 893
   2.2. The effect of social security on retirement 895
   2.3. The effect of pensions on retirement 902
   2.4. Models to explain retirement 905
   2.5. Empirical evidence on retirement 912
   2.6. Summary of retirement 919
3. Consumption and saving following retirement 919
   3.1. Introduction 919
   3.2. The life-cycle model 923
   3.3. Empirical findings about the LCH based on wealth data 931

2.6. Temporary, return and permanent migration   748
2.7. Family strategies   749
2.8. The contextual setting   753
2.9. Displaced persons   755
3. Effects of migration on production and inequality   756
3.1. Rural labor markets and agricultural production   756
3.2. Urban labor market issues   760
3.3. Dynamic models   768
3.4. Effects of migration upon income distribution   769
4. Policy issues and options   775
4.1. Direct controls on mobility   775
4.2. Influencing urban pay and labor costs   777
4.3. Rural development   778
4.4. On industrial location   780
4.5. Investing in infrastructure   782
4.6. The nature and dispersion of education   784
4.7. Structural adjustment and development strategies   785
5. Closing thoughts   785
References   787

Chapter 14
Economic Impact of International Migration and the Economic Performance of
Migrants   799
ROBERT J. LALONDE and ROBERT H. TOPEL

1. Introduction   800
2. Migration between source and receiving countries   801
2.1. Magnitude and characteristics of immigration   801
2.2. Economic incentives to immigrate   805
2.3. Estimating the determinants of immigration   807
2.4. Regulation of international migration   808
2.5. The impact of immigration regulations   810
2.6. Enforcing immigration controls and counting the undocumented   812
2.7. Emigration from the receiving country   814
3. Labor market adjustments to new immigration   817
3.1. Gains and losses from new immigration   817
3.2. Estimating the labor market effects of immigration   819
3.3. Econometric methods for estimating the effects of immigration   821
3.4. Econometric evidence of immigration's effects   824
4. Assimilation of immigrants   827
4.1. Estimates of assimilation   833
4.2. The impact of language proficiency   837
5. Transfers, taxes, and social welfare programs   840

CONTENTS OF VOLUME 1B

Introduction to the Series   v

Contents of the Handbook   vii

Preface to the Handbook   xi

PART IV: MIGRATION

Chapter 12
Internal Migration in Developed Countries   647
MICHAEL J. GREENWOOD

1. Introduction   648
2. What is migration?   650
3. Selected facts about internal migration in developed countries   651
   3.1. Cross-national comparisons of migration propensities   651
   3.2. Age/education and migration   655
   3.3. Trends in migration   656
4. The determinants of migration   658
   4.1. The importance of place characteristics: early contributions   659
   4.2. Gravity and modified-gravity models   663
   4.3. Distance   666
   4.4. Theoretical perspectives on migration   668
   4.5. Employment status and migration   681
   4.6. Personal characteristics and life-cycle forces in the decision to migrate   688
5. Conclusions   707
References   712

Chapter 13
Internal Migration in Developing Countries   721
ROBERT E.B. LUCAS

1. Introduction: outline and patterns   722
   1.1. Focus and outline of the review   722
   1.2. Concepts and patterns of migration   723
2. Factors affecting migration flows and selectivity   730
   2.1. Income streams: the basics   730
   2.2. Migration and job search   732
   2.3. Estimating responsiveness to labor market opportunities   738
   2.4. Networks and information   743
   2.5. The role of capital   746

Chapter 18
Demographic Variables and Income Inequality   1015
DAVID LAM

1. Introduction   1016
2. Age structure and income inequality   1017
   2.1. Decomposing the effects of age structure   1017
   2.2. Evidence on the effects of age structure on inequality   1022
   2.3. Direct effects of age structure on wages and inequality   1023
3. Marital sorting and inequality among married couples   1024
   3.1. Empirical evidence from the US   1027
   3.2. Empirical evidence from other countries   1029
   3.3. The role of assortative mating   1030
4. Household composition and income distribution   1031
5. Differential fertility, intergenerational mobility, and inequality   1035
   5.1. The mathematics of population growth and inequality   1036
   5.2. Differential fertility and intergenerational mobility   1038
   5.3. Welfare implications of endogenous fertility   1043
6. Effects of population growth on wages and inequality   1044
   6.1. Relative wages, factor shares, and income distribution   1044
   6.2. Empirical evidence on the effects of population growth on inequality   1046
7. Demographic change and trends in inequality in the US   1050
8. Summary and conclusions   1052
References   1054

PART VI: AGGREGATE POPULATION CHANGE AND ECONOMIC
GROWTH

Chapter 19
Population Dynamics: Equilibrium, Disequilibrium, and Consequences of
Fluctuations   1063
RONALD D. LEE

1. Introduction   1064
2. Population equilibrium   1064
   2.1. Classical population theory   1064
   2.2. Evidence for Classical theory   1066
   2.3. The behavior of the Classical population system   1075
   2.4. Modern theories of population equilibrium   1076
3. Population response to shocks   1078
   3.1. Short-run shocks   1079
   3.2. Long-run shocks   1086
4. The internal dynamics of population renewal: endogenous baby booms?   1089

4.1. Generational cycles	1090
4.2. Malthusian cycles	1092
5. Economic response to population fluctuations	1097
5.1. Consequences of fluctuating rates of population growth	1099
5.2. Compositional effects arising from age distribution fluctuations	1100
5.3. Behavioral effects of fluctuating age distributions	1105
6. Conclusions	1107
References	1109

Chapter 20
Growth Models with Endogenous Population: a General Framework — 1117
MARC NERLOVE and LAKSHMI K. RAUT

1. Introduction	1118
2. Models of economic growth with endogenous population	1124
2.1. Solow–Swan	1124
2.2. Niehans	1130
2.3. Malthus–Boserup	1132
2.4. Lucas and Romer: new directions in growth theory	1139
3. The microeconomics of endogenous population: fertility, mortality and investment in children	1141
3.1. Quality versus quantity: the Becker–Lewis model	1142
3.2. Parental altruism and investment in human capital	1147
3.3. Survival probability, fertility and investment in health care	1155
3.4. Transfers from children to parents and fertility: old-age security motive	1160
3.5. Two-sided altruism and transfers from children to parents	1168
4. Concluding remarks	1171
References	1171

Chapter 21
Long-Term Consequences of Population Growth: Technological Change, Natural Resources, and the Environment — 1175
JAMES A. ROBINSON and T.N. SRINIVASAN

1. Introduction	1177
1.1. Population past and population present: a review	1183
1.2. Growth, development, demography and resources: a perspective	1187
1.3. Our approach	1197
1.4. Overview of the paper	1200
2. Long-run development with exogenous population and exogenous technical change	1202
2.1. Neoclassical growth: infinitely-lived agents	1202
2.2. Neoclassical growth with finite lifetimes	1220
2.3. Neoclassical growth with resources	1228

PART IV

MIGRATION

3. Endogenizing population and technical change 1245
  3.1. Models of endogenous fertility and mortality with exogenous technical change 1246
  3.2. Natural resources in economies with endogenous population 1250
  3.3. Theories of endogenous technical change 1253
  3.4. Population and endogenous growth 1260
  3.5. Resources and endogenous growth 1269
  3.6. Endogenous population and growth in the presence of natural resources 1271
4. Assessment 1272
  4.1. Sustainable development 1272
  4.2. Discounting 1275
  4.3. Uncertainty 1278
  4.4. International issues 1279
5. Conclusions 1279
References 1283

Index to Volumes 1A and 1B 1299

Chapter 12

INTERNAL MIGRATION IN DEVELOPED COUNTRIES

MICHAEL J. GREENWOOD*

University of Colorado

Contents

1. Introduction	648
2. What is migration?	650
3. Selected facts about internal migration in developed countries	651
3.1. Cross-national comparisons of migration propensities	651
3.2. Age/education and migration	655
3.3. Trends in migration	656
4. The determinants of migration	658
4.1. The importance of place characteristics: early contributions	659
4.2. Gravity and modified-gravity models	663
4.3. Distance	666
4.4. Theoretical perspectives on migration	668
4.5. Employment status and migration	681
4.6. Personal characteristics and life-cycle forces in the decision to migrate	688
5. Conclusions	707
References	712

*I am indebted to Robert J. LaLonde, who did an unusually careful job of reading and commenting upon the manuscript, as did Gary Hunt, Philip Graves, Peter Mueser, and Donald Waldman. Each made a number of helpful suggestions. Their effort and eye for details helped me enormously. I am grateful to each of them.

Handbook of Population and Family Economics. Edited by M.R. Rosenzweig and O. Stark
© *Elsevier Science B.V., 1997*

1. Introduction

Residential mobility and migration are pervasive facts of life in most developed countries. Long and Boertlein (1976) estimate that as of 1970 the average American made almost 13 residential moves over the life course. Average residents of Britain and Japan were estimated to have made, respectively, eight and seven such moves. The US Bureau of the Census (1991) reports that between March, 1989, and March, 1990, 17.9% of the US population one year old and over changed houses and 6.6% migrated in the sense that they also changed their county of residence. In most advanced societies interregional migration is a major mechanism through which labor resources are redistributed geographically in response to changing economic and demographic forces.

As migration has become relatively commonplace, it has given rise to numerous policy concerns in both developed and developing countries. These concerns have run the gamut from too much regional in-migration (and how to control it) to too little (and how to encourage it) and from too little regional out-migration (and how to stimulate it) to too much (and how to dampen it). Not surprisingly, as these policy concerns have been raised, the migration literature has grown enormously, although few direct links have ever been drawn between policy tools, such as migrant subsidies and regional employment policies (Bartik, 1991), and internal migration.

The migration literature can be classified in a number of ways, but perhaps the most convenient classification scheme distinguishes two broad areas of research, one dealing with the determinants and one dealing with the consequences of migration. Of course, some studies treat both the determinants and consequences within the same framework. The vast majority of migration research concerns the determinants of migration. This orientation has been strengthened during the last 20 years by the availability of microdata, which at least until now have been used far more to study migration's determinants than its consequences.

The "determinants" of migration are the factors that affect migration, including characteristics both of places and of persons and their families. The term refers to the qualitative and the quantitative importance of each factor. Place characteristics are specific to a given area, such as employment and wage opportunities, the presence of family and friends, and location-specific amenities. Personal and family characteristics help shape individual and family responses to opportunities that may exist at different locations. The "consequences" of migration refer both to the performance of migrants in their new locations relative to a benchmark, such as their presumed performance in their former place of residence had they not moved, and to the impacts that migrants have on others in sending and receiving areas.

Traditionally, research on the determinants and consequences of migration has addressed several questions:

(a) Who migrates? Such characteristics as age, education, race, income, and marital status have been extensively studied for some time (Ravenstein, 1885; Thomas, 1938).

(b) Why do these people migrate? This question has led to numerous studies of the determinants of migration, where in certain cases the determinants have been inferred from largely descriptive studies (Ravenstein, 1885) and in other cases formal models of the migration decision process have been estimated (Greenwood, 1975a). A limited number of attempts have been made to analyze the determinants of migration in a laboratory experimental setting using techniques from cognitive psychology (Greenwood et al., 1994). Many determinants have been studied, such as wage differentials, job opportunities, unemployment rates, local public spending and its mix, and location-specific amenities.

(c) Where are the migrants coming from and where are they going? This question has led not only to detailed descriptions of the spatial patterns of migration flows, but also to a focus on how place characteristics have influenced the flows. Because many public agencies are concerned with future population levels, and because migration is an important mechanism through which population is redistributed geographically, the issue of where migrants are coming from and where they are going has led to substantial interest in forecasting the migration component of population change (e.g., Smith and Sincich, 1992).

(d) When do they migrate? The timing of migration flows has been studied, but not to the extent of the questions raised above. For example, as today's developed countries experienced their demographic transitions, which generally refer to changed birth and death rates, they almost certainly also experienced a migration transition of which rural-to-urban movement and perhaps international migration were major parts. Moreover, national business conditions affect different regions differently, triggering migration (Milne, 1993). Just as cohort effects have been found to be important in other areas of demographic research, they may also be important for migration, but this issue has been studied very little.[1]

(e) What consequences result from migration? This question has been addressed at two levels. The first deals with the migrants themselves, where the emphasis has been on the benefits to migrating, often measured in terms of earnings gains. Although migrant outcomes fit in a discussion of the consequences of migration, this literature has typically been discussed in the context of the determinants of migration, because rational individuals act on their expectations regarding various outcomes. The second deals with migration's impact on others in the origin and the destination. Do migrants depress local wages in receiving areas and displace local residents from jobs? To the extent that migrants tend to be young and well-educated, does migration deprive

---

[1] As pointed out by Greenwood et al. (1991), two aspects of the cohort effect seem particularly relevant – volume and timing. The volume of internal migration almost certainly changes as large cohorts, such as the baby boom, mature through those age classes with high migration propensities (Greenwood, 1988). However, the timing of migration may also be affected by cohort size, but this potentially important issue has been almost completely neglected.

source regions of critically needed human capital that ensures these regions of long periods of economic stagnation? This study treats the first type of consequence in some detail, but not the second, which although potentially important, has not been studied in sufficient depth regarding internal migration.

Many studies have aimed primarily at describing migration flows. Such a description of migration phenomena can provide a useful background for a discussion of the determinants and consequences of migration because if theories and empirical analyses of migration are any good, they ought to provide explanations of observed migration behavior. The present study is organized with this thought in mind.

Much literature has concerned migration in less-developed countries, as well as international migration. The literature on these topics has a decidedly different orientation than that concerned with internal migration in the US and other advanced industrial nations. For example, much of the literature concerned with less-developed countries focuses on rural-to-urban migration (Todaro, 1976; Stark, 1991). That concerned with international migration has many strands, with the so-called "brain drain" literature standing out, along with numerous studies dealing with immigrant assimilation or adaptation in the receiving country (Greenwood and McDowell, 1986). Issues concerning language abilities are much less important in the context of internal than international migration. Many noteworthy studies deal with these areas of migration research, but because they are featured elsewhere in this volume, they are not considered here. A sizable literature also concerns migration of the elderly, which because it is treated elsewhere in the volume is ignored in this paper.

2. What is migration?

In part because migration cannot be defined or measured as precisely as births and deaths, migration research has long been the stepchild of demographic research (Kirk, 1960). The United Nations manual, *Methods of Measuring Internal Migration* (1970), has served as the basis for several definitions of migration and migrants.[2] This document proposes the following definitions:

> A migration is defined as a move from one migration-defining area to another (or a move of some specified minimum distance) that was made during a given migration interval and that involved a change of residence. A migrant is a person who has changed his usual place of residence from one migration-defining area to another (or who moved some specified minimum distance) at least once during the migration interval (United Nations, 1970: p. 2).

---

[2] K.C. Zackariah prepared the first draft of the U.N. manual, and H.T. Eldridge, S. Kono, H.S. Shryock, and D.S. Thomas made contributions to the manual, which does not carry the author's names on the title page.

Shryock and Siegel suggest that in defining a migrant "the minimum distance might be set at the point at which commuting to work becomes so time-consuming and expensive as to require the substitution of a change of residence" (Shryock and Siegel, 1976: p. 374).

Migration may be defined and measured in many different ways, but obviously an operational definition must be developed if migrants are to be identified and the number of migratory moves is to be measured. A committee formed by the Population Association of America and made up of a number of migration experts defined migration as follows:

> Most statistical offices in the United States "define" *migration* as a relatively permanent change of residence that crosses jurisdictional boundaries (counties in particular), measured in terms of usual residence at a prior point in time, typically 1–5 years earlier. Local moves within jurisdictions are referred to as *residential mobility* (Population Association of America, 1988: p. 1).

If another word were substituted for "counties", this definition could apply to almost any country. However, certain operational definitions of migration are not defined on the basis of usual place of residence, but rather migrants are identified as persons who change the jurisdiction of their place of work.[3] Migration also may be defined in terms of a change of both place of residence and place of work.

In many instances the intercounty or interjurisdictional definition of migration is problematic because moves frequently cross the relevant political boundaries but remain in the same labor market and are thus more like residential moves than migration. Consequently, the US government, as well as the central governments of other nations, provide migration data for regions that approximate labor market areas (e.g., in the US, Metropolitan Statistical Areas and Bureau of Economic Analysis Economic Areas).

3. Selected facts about internal migration in developed countries

3.1. Cross-national comparisons of migration propensities

In most countries people migrate from one place to another in pursuit of increased utility resulting from better employment opportunities, higher wages, a preferred bundle of amenities, and many other factors discussed in more detail below (Greenwood, 1975a, 1985). Although differences between countries in internal migration rates are not extensively documented, certain developed countries, specifically

---

[3] The Social Security Continuous Work History Sample (CWHS) is an example of migration data formulated on a place-of-work basis. The US government no longer maintains the CWHS.

the US and Canada, have long been thought to have somewhat higher rates than others (Nam et al., 1990). Several problems have prevented comparisons of internal migration rates across countries and consequently have hindered efforts to explain cross-national differences in such rates.

International comparisons of internal migration rates are difficult to make for several reasons. First, various countries define migrants differently in terms of whose movement is being considered (e.g., total population versus noninstitutional population), in terms of the type of border they must cross (e.g., municipality, county, state, province), and in terms of the interval over which the movement occurs (e.g., one year, five years, since birth). Second, the method of measuring migration differs widely. In some countries censuses are the main source of information concerning migration, whereas in others population registers and other types of administrative records (e.g., tax records, family allowance records) are the major source. Third, the size and shape of the spatial areas between which migration is measured are not uniform either within or between countries. Migration is known to decline as distance increases. Thus, for larger spatial areas more internal moves will fail to cross a relevant boundary and therefore will not be reflected in the migration measure. Fourth, migration propensities are sensitive to national economic (Greenwood et al., 1986) and demographic (Greenwood, 1988) conditions, and consequently even if internal migration were measured over the same time interval in various countries, which often is not possible, interregional migration propensities could differ for behavioral reasons. These behavioral differences would be useful to study in a cross-national context if the other conditions noted above were met.

Three sources are particularly relevant for describing international differences in mobility and migration rates: (1) the work of Long at the US Bureau of the Census: Long (1988: Chapter 8), Long (1991, 1992), Long et al. (1988), and Long and Boertlein (1976); (2) a set of country studies in Nam et al. (1990); and (3) a series of country studies published under the auspices of the International Institute for Applied Systems Analysis during the late 1970s and early 1980s.[4] For comparative purposes, Long (1991) and Long and Boertlein (1976) are the most useful.

The most unambiguous method of making cross-national comparisons of mobility is to focus on residential moves. The obvious problem with this approach is that residential mobility includes more than what is commonly regarded as migration. Nevertheless, such measures are meaningful to compare, and based upon them rates of mobility vary widely across developed countries. Furthermore, residential mobility data for a handful of countries allow for certain distinctions that better reflect migration. These distinctions are of two types: (1) intraregional moves versus interregional

---

[4] The most relevant of these studies for developed countries are Rees (1979) concerning the United Kingdom, Termote (1980) concerning Canada, Koch and Gatzweiler (1980) concerning the Federal Republic of Germany, Sauberer (1981) concerning Austria, Nanjo et al. (1982) concerning Japan, Long and Frey (1982) concerning the US, Ledent (1982) concerning France, and Campisi et al. (1982) concerning Italy.

Table 1
Percentage of population residentially mobile in selected developed countries, circa 1971 and 1981

Country	Percent moving in one year		Percent moving in five years	
	1971	1981	1971	1981
Australia	NA	17.0	NA	47.1
Austria	NA	NA	NA	20.1
Belgium	NA	7.3	NA	NA
Canada	NA	NA	46.6	47.6
France	NA	9.4	NA	NA
Great Britain	11.8	9.6	NA	NA
Ireland	5.1	6.1	NA	NA
Israel	NA	NA	NA	29.8
Japan	12.0	9.5	NA	22.6
Netherlands	NA	7.7	NA	NA
New Zealand	15.3	19.4	37.5	45.3
Sweden	NA	9.5	NA	NA
Switzerland	NA	NA	NA	36.0
US	18.7	17.5	47.0	46.4

Source: Long (1991: Tables 1 and 4).

moves, and (2) moves that are short of some threshold distance versus moves that are at least as far as the threshold distance.

Examining 1980 or 1981 one- and five-year measures of residential mobility for 16 countries, Long (1991) shows that rates of movement are quite high for Australia, Canada, New Zealand, and the US (Table 1). A second group of developed countries that is far behind these four includes France, Great Britain, Israel, Japan, Sweden, and Switzerland. Belgium, Ireland, and the Netherlands have the lowest rates of residential mobility.[5] In an earlier paper, using data on mobility over a one-year interval, Long and Boertlein (1976) show that around 1970 a representative cohort would make 12.91 lifetime moves per person in the US, 8.22 in Britain, and 7.35 in Japan. They go on to argue that an average resident of Australia, Canada, and the US would probably make three to four times more moves over the life course than the average resident of Ireland.

As a means of disentangling migration from residential moves that do not involve migration, Long (1991) and Long and Boertlein (1976) distinguish between purely local moves, moves between areas within a state or province, and moves between states or provinces. Because both local areas (e.g., counties for the US, localities for Canada) and states/provinces differ in size and shape, the internal migration figures provided in Table 2 are not strictly comparable. Nevertheless, since they give a rough

---

[5] Observed differences could be due in part to differences in population age distributions. However, standardizing for age has little effect on comparative mobility rates.

Table 2
Percentage of population moving within and between local areas[a] in selected developed countries, circa
1971 and 1981

Country	Total		Within local areas		Between areas	
	1971	1981	1971	1981	1971	1981
One-year interval						
Great Britain	11.8	9.6	NA	NA	NA	NA
Ireland	5.1	6.1	3.1	3.2	1.2	2.1
Japan	12.0	9.5	8.3	6.9	3.7	2.6
New Zealand	15.3	19.4	NA	NA	NA	NA
US	18.7	17.2	11.4	10.4	6.5	6.2
Five-year interval						
Canada	46.6	47.6	23.8	24.9	18.6	20.2
New Zealand	37.5	45.3	NA	NA	NA	NA
US	47.0	46.5	26.2	25.1	19.2	19.5

[a]Local areas are counties in Ireland and the US, prefectures in Japan, and localities in Canada.
Source: Adapted from Long (1991: Table 4).

indication of short-distance versus long-distance moves, the measures reported in Table 2 come closer to reflecting migration. Based on one-year measures, the US stands out as having high rates. Based on five-year measures, the US and Canada have high internal migration rates, but roughly comparable data for other countries are not readily available.

Another method of making international comparisons of migration rates is to focus on distance moved. Unfortunately, as shown by Long et al. (1988), the appropriate measures can be developed for very few countries and for the countries for which such measures can be developed, the time-frame of migration differs somewhat. These authors report that per thousand population, 46 persons moved 50 km or more in the US (1975–1976), 24 in Sweden (1974), and 15 in Great Britain (1980–1981).

Why do residential mobility rates and rates of internal migration differ so widely across developed countries? Many factors that influence internal migration rates are discussed below, and in addition to these international differences in the underlying data and in the responsiveness to the various forces may be responsible for observed differences.[6] Moreover, Long and Boertlein (1976) suggest that countries like the US,

---

[6]The "demographic transition" refers to the changes that occur in birth and death rates as a country passes from a traditional to a modern society. Such a transition almost certainly also involves changes in the volume, composition, and average distance of migration (Zelinsky, 1971; Parish, 1973). Thus, differences across countries in internal migration rates could be due broadly to differences in the stage of development of the various countries.

Canada, and Australia (and presumably New Zealand) are nations of immigrants, which they feel may cause a "long-run dynamic" to develop that encourages long-distance movement. They also argue that these countries had histories in which a frontier played an important role and in which public policy actively encouraged movement to less densely populated regions. In his later paper, Long (1991) suggests that differences in housing opportunities may distinguish the US, Canada, Australia, and New Zealand. Housing markets are not as controlled in these countries, and the availability of land and building materials at low cost have encouraged the construction of new dwelling units and home ownership, which have conditioned the populations of these countries to move more frequently.

A distinct pattern is evident among the countries for which Long (1991) has computed rates of residential mobility and migration, as reported in Tables 1 and 2. The countries demonstrate a positive rank pattern between geographic size and mobility rate. For small countries the array of alternative destinations is more limited, particularly at longer distances, which are nonexistent. As a consequence of the shorter distances to alternative destinations, residents of smaller countries may find commuting to be a more viable substitute for migration. Migration in smaller countries also may be more inhibited by cultural factors. Moreover, whatever the size of the country, the primacy of the largest urban areas could be important. Apparently no formal tests have ever been performed to determine why migration rates differ across countries, and thus the various reasons remain speculative.

3.2. Age/education and migration

One of the most universal mobility relationships is that between age and migration. Migration propensities peak during the early to mid-twenties and then decline steadily, with a slight upturn at retirement age in some countries (Plane, 1993). Another important relationship, less-well documented than that between age and migration but no less universal, is that migration propensities rise with education.

For US flows between 1980 and 1985, Table 3 shows migration propensities cross classified by five age classes and six education groups. Except for the group with the least education, migration propensities are highest for the 25–29-year-old group and decline steadily thereafter. Data on US migration by single year of age indicate that the peak propensity often occurs in the 18–24-year-old group, usually at 22 or 23 years of age depending upon the specific year. Similar relationships have been observed for other countries, frequently peaking in the early twenties (e.g., the Netherlands, Vergoossen (1990); Japan, Otomo (1990); Canada, Ledent (1990)).

With one exception, for each age class migration propensities rise with education (Table 3). For the group with five or more years of college relative to that with 0–8 years of elementary school, migration propensities range from 4.6 times as high (25–29 years old) to 2.0 times as high (45–64 years old). Although the precise quanti-

Table 3
Propensities to migrate interstate in the US, 1980–1985, by age and education

Education	Age[a]				
	18–24	25–29	30–34	35–44	45–64
Elementary					
0–8 years	8.21	7.02	6.74	4.37	3.78
High school					
1–3 years	9.33	12.50	9.30	5.61	3.94
4 years	11.31	13.10	9.83	7.33	4.84
College					
1–3 years	10.12	15.67	11.60	10.75	6.84
4 years	24.13	25.32	16.54	12.97	7.19
5 years or more	29.04	32.24	21.67	14.06	7.71

[a]The base population is the relevant number of nonmovers over the 1980–85 period, plus out-migrants.
Age is defined as of 1985.
Source: Calculated from data presented in US Bureau of the Census (1987: Table 17).

tative relationships are no doubt somewhat different for other developed countries, the qualitative relationships are almost certainly similar to those for the US.[7]

3.3. Trends in migration

In part due to the strong relationship between age and migration, trends in the spatial distribution of population in the US have undergone dramatic changes during the last 25 years. Two trends particularly stand out. First, after many decades during which the West experienced the greatest volume of net in-migration, the South has, since about 1970, had a volume of net in-migration about twice that of the West. Second, during the 1970s the historical trend of migration out of nonmetropolitan areas and into metropolitan areas reversed such that population in nonmetropolitan America began to grow more rapidly than that in metropolitan America. This latter phenomenon was not unique to the US. Vining and Kontuly (1978) show that, during the 1970s, in 11 of 18 countries either the direction of the net population flow from less densely populated regions to the core regions reversed, or a sharp reduction occurred in the level of the net flow.

[7] For Canada, Ledent (1990: Table 3.5B) provides a table similar to Table 3 that indicates generally consistent migration propensities by age and education.

In the US the maturing of the baby boom through young and highly mobile age classes almost certainly played an important role in both the regional shift and non-metropolitan to metropolitan migration turnaround (Greenwood, 1988). Due to the baby boom, the number of persons at high risk to migrate increased greatly. Moreover, lagging employment opportunities in certain regions of the US combined with rapidly rising opportunities in other regions gave the baby boom an incentive to migrate (Greenwood and Hunt, 1984). Other developed countries also experienced baby booms coincident with that of the US, but regarding these countries few efforts have been made to link internal migration to the baby-boom phenomenon.

Whereas the maturing of the baby boom greatly increased the number of persons at high risk to make interregional moves in the US, at the same time an offset occurred when propensities to migrate declined secularly for those age classes with the highest migration propensities. For example, the annual propensity of persons 20–24 years of age to make an interstate move was 0.091 during 1960–61, 0.089 during 1970–1971, 0.058 during 1980–1981, and 0.059 during 1990–1991.[8] Virtually no formal modeling has been done to address such declines, but the underlying reasons are almost certainly related to major societal trends. One possible cause is the steady decline in marriage rates among the young, who have a high propensity to migrate due to marriage.[9]

Rogerson (1987) hypothesizes that declines in age-specific migration rates in the US are due to an Easterlin phenomenon. That is, large generations such as the baby boom have low average mobility due to relatively low expectations regarding future labor force participation and unemployment of the spouse. Moreover, Long (1988) argues that increased labor force participation of wives, slow economic growth during the 1970s, and difficulties in housing markets (e.g., high mortgage rates) reduced migration rates. These assertions remain untested hypotheses.

During the last 25 years internal migration rates have also fallen in several developed countries. For example, between 1970–1971 and 1985–1986, the Canadian interprovincial migration rate declined from 18.4 to 14.3 per thousand (Ledent, 1990). Between 1970 and 1985 the interstate migration rate in the Federal Republic of Germany fell from 18.5 to 10.5 per thousand (Friedrich, 1990), and during the same period the interprefectural rate in Japan declined from 41.1 to 25.9 per thousand (Otomo,

---

[8] The annual interstate migration propensity of the 30 to 34 year-old class was 0.059 during 1950–1951, declined to 0.038 during 1960–1961, rose to 0.055 during 1970–1971, and fell again to 0.035 during 1990–1991. Comparable propensities for the 35 to 44-year-old class fell gradually between the early 1950s and the early 1980s, but rebounded during the early 1990s. Plane and Rogerson (1991) track the migration propensities of various US birth cohorts over limited time intervals.

[9] Of married males 16 to 24 in 1980 and living with their wife, 14.9 percent made an interstate move between 1975 and 1980, but only 9.3% of other males in the same age class made such a move. A distinction should be made between the event of marriage and the state of marriage. The event of marriage encourages migration, but the state of marriage discourages it, ceteris paribus. See Greenwood (1981) for a more detailed discussion.

1990). The rate at which males changed their municipality of residence in the Netherlands between 1973 and 1983 declined from 53.8 to 38.7 per thousand (Vergoossen,
1990). Again, such declines have not been addressed in a rigorous way, but cohort and
period effects ought to be studied where appropriate data are available.

4. The determinants of migration

Many factors contribute to the decision to migrate. Differential characteristics of
sending and receiving regions provide a potential incentive for moving, and individual
and/or family traits help condition the responses to utility differentials that may arise
from these different characteristics. Given an individual's personal characteristics,
including accumulated job skills, general labor market conditions and employment
composition will help determine the probability of gaining employment during a period of job search. Prevailing conditions in land and housing markets may also be important, and state and local taxes and the associated availability of public goods may
be critical for certain potential migrants. Topological, climatological, and environmental amenities may enter into many decisions. Conceivably, the potential for natural (e.g., earthquakes in California) and technological (e.g., nuclear waste repositories)
hazards could affect migration decisions. Moreover, the values of such ameni-
ties/disamenities may be reflected at least partly in labor and land markets.

A number of life-cycle considerations – such as marriage, divorce, completion of
schooling, entry into the labor force, start of a career, birth, aging, and leaving home
of children, home ownership, and retirement – are critical in an individual's or a family's decision to migrate. Other personal circumstances, often related to the life cycle,
are also important, such as employment status, earnings, education, accumulated
skills, age, job tenure, sex, and health.

Many potentially important migration determinants have been studied very little to
date. For example, the influence of health on migration barely has been touched, and
the effects of institutional impediments such as employer-sponsored health insurance
are only just beginning to attract attention.[10] The influence of natural hazards like
earthquakes and the influence of man-made hazards like the presence of nuclear
wastes have been addressed infrequently. Moreover, subjective beliefs about risk may

---

[10] Holtz-Eakin (1993) uses data from the Panel Study of Income Dynamics to examine the influence of
nonportable health insurance on worker mobility. He finds that individuals with employer-provided health
insurance are less likely to switch jobs than those without it, but he suggests that such insurance may simply reflect better jobs. When he extends his study to include spousal insurance and also accounts for skills
of both spouses, he finds little evidence of "job-lock", even for those in poor health. Notwithstanding these
results, certain nonqualifying illnesses almost certainly inhibit mobility due to the nonportability of health
insurance. The value of the foregone fringe benefit would in many cases require a substantial compensa-
tory offset, which would make the marginal migrant (for whom the benefits of migrating just equal the
costs of doing so) require a higher wage payment.

influence migration decisions, but these types of influences rarely have been examined empirically.[11] The types of migration models typically estimated by economists and sociologists are not well-suited to studying the effects of risk perceptions on migration. At least one type of approach used in cognitive psychology and in some marketing studies may hold promise for analyzing such determinants of migration (Greenwood et al., 1991a, 1994).

Studies of the determinants of migration commonly have been formulated in the context of individual utility maximization, with the expected utility hypothesis at least implicitly underlying most studies. Some attention has also been given to the family or the household as the decision-making unit. Models based upon such behavioral foundations frequently have been estimated with aggregate data relating both to migrants and to the determinants of migration. Before the general availability of micro and longitudinal data, virtually all applied migration research was of necessity based on aggregate data. Although aggregate data were and are limiting in many respects, they did not prevent a boom in migration research during the 1960s and 1970s. Moreover, even in the presence of many microdata sets, aggregate data are frequently studied today. Not only are aggregate trends and tendencies of interest in their own right, but also for many countries such data are all that is available. Thus, because much still can be learned from studying aggregate data and because they will remain a major source of information concerning migration, some attention to the use of aggregate data is appropriate.

4.1. The importance of place characteristics: early contributions

Early papers dealing with the determinants of migration employed neither formal models of the migration decision process nor formal statistical techniques. Rather, these studies were mainly descriptive in style and inferential in tone; their findings were in certain instances powerful, insightful, and anticipatory of later migration research.

One of the earliest examples of a paper dealing with the determinants of migration is Ravenstein's (1885) "The Laws of Migration". Using the 1871 and 1881 census place-of-birth data, Ravenstein examined internal migration in the UK. After an exhaustive descriptive analysis, he listed seven conclusions that he called "laws". (1) Most migrants move only a short distance and then typically to major cities. (2) Rapidly growing cities are populated by migrants from nearby rural areas. In turn, the "gaps" left in the rural population are filled by migrants from more distant areas. (3) The process of dispersion is the inverse of the process of absorption and exhibits

---

[11] Risk in migration decisions has been addressed theoretically for some time (David, 1974; Stark, 1991), and search-theoretic models of migration are fairly common (Herzog et al., 1993). However, empirical studies directly addressing risk, such as Rosenzweig and Stark (1989), are unusual.

similar features. (4) Each main current of migration produces a compensating countercurrent. (5) Long-distance migrants tend to move to major cities. (6) Rural people have a higher propensity to migrate than urban people. (7) Women have a higher propensity to migrate than men. Although he did not formally or specifically adopt what was to become the "gravity law" of spatial interaction, Ravenstein clearly anticipated this law by recognizing that most migrants move only a short distance and that migrants tend to move to major cities.

Ravenstein leaves little doubt that he believed employment and wage opportunities were the major determinants of migration: "In most instances it will be found that they did so (leave their homes) in search of work of a more remunerative or attractive kind than that afforded by the places of their birth" (1885: p. 181) (parentheses are mine). Later he wrote that "the call for labour in our centres of industry and commerce is the prime cause of those currents of migration" (p. 198). He did, however, recognize that the motives for migration are "various" (p. 181). In a later paper by the same title, Ravenstein (1889) studied migration in several European countries, as well as the US and Canada. Again based on descriptive analysis, his conclusions were generally supportive of his earlier "laws", although he recognized that the rate of internal migration in the US was relatively quite high.

During the 1920s and especially during the 1930s, considerable interest was directed at migration phenomena in both the US and the UK, and the nature of this research began to take on a decidedly more formal tone, although descriptive analysis remained the primary research methodology. For example, Makower et al. (1938, 1939, 1940) published a series of papers in *Oxford Economic Papers* that was extremely insightful. These authors used data from the Oxford Employment Exchange, which reported the number of persons who entered the unemployment insurance system in various specific places other than Oxford and who were residing in Oxford in 1936.[12]

Two "incentives" to migrate received particular attention in the work of Makower et al.: unemployment differentials and distance. They defined the "relative unemployment discrepancy" as "the ratio of the difference between the unemployment rate in the county (or Division) and the unemployment rate in the whole country, to the unemployment rate in the whole country" (Makower et al., 1939: p. 81). They argued further that "the greater the mean deviation of relative unemployment rates ... the greater would be the total amount of migration measured as a percentage of the population of the whole country" (1939: p. 81). Makower et al. went on to show that "there was a very clear correspondence between variations in the relative unemployment of the county and variations in the gains and losses by migration" (1939: p. 82).[13]

---

[12] Thomas (1934, 1937) had previously used Employment Exchange data.

[13] "Gains and losses" refers to net internal migration (corrected for international migration).

Although Makower et al. are not credited with the development of the gravity law of spatial interaction, they clearly laid out the same concepts: "Quite a close relationship was found between discrepancies in unemployment rates and migration of labour where allowance was made for the size of the insured population and the distance over which migrants had to travel" (Makower et al., 1938: p. 118). These authors even computed a distance elasticity of migration, which they called the "coefficient of spatial friction": "an increase of distance by 1 per cent reduces migration by from 1.6 per cent to 2.1 per cent." (1938: p. 106).[14]

Makower et al. (1939, 1940) also considered the time lags inherent in migration, as well as the relationship between aggregate economic activity and migration. They concluded that the lag between "incentive to move and migration" was short, certainly not more than 18 months, but more likely about six months for Great Britain as a whole, and between zero and six months for migration to Oxford. Moreover, their analysis indicates that mobility declined during slumps and rose during recoveries and that moves over short distances were less sensitive to national economic conditions than moves over long distances.

At the same time considerable attention was being directed at US internal migration. In 1924 the Social Science Research Council appointed the Committee on Scientific Aspects of Human Migration. As an outgrowth of the Council's interest in migration, C. Warren Thornthwaite published *Internal Migration in the United States* (Philadelphia: University of Pennsylvania Press) in 1934, followed by Carter Goodrich et al.'s *Migration and Economic Opportunity* (Philadelphia: University of Pennsylvania Press) in 1936, and Dorothy Swaine Thomas's *Research Memorandum on Migration Differentials* (New York: Social Science Research Council) in 1938. At the time of their publication these were extremely useful analyses of US internal migration, though the methodologies remained descriptive in style. Particularly the work of Thomas on "migration differentials" confirmed much of the earlier work of Ravenstein. However, Thomas went well beyond Ravenstein by considering "family status differentials", "physical health differentials", "mental health differentials", "intelligence differentials", "occupational differentials", and "differentials in motivation and assimilation" in what is a comprehensive review of then existing migration literature.[15] Goodrich's work stressed the notion that migration was a response to changing job opportunities. This work also provided a useful description of patterns of

---

[14] Interestingly, Makower et al. started with individual records that indicated sex, age within broad age class (14–15, 16–18, 18–21, 21–65), industry of employment before and after the move, and county of origin. Today such microdata no doubt would be analyzed themselves, but these investigators aggregated the data by county of origin presumably because microdata were rare, techniques for their analysis were not yet developed, and consequently the econometric analyses of microdata were also very rare.

[15] In two appendices, Thomas provides annotated bibliographies that contain 119 American and English contributions and 72 German contributions to the migration literature. Her entries, which may have been influenced by her discipline (sociology) suggest that prior to her writing in the 1930s, migration research was primarily in the domain of sociology, which is a valid conclusion in any case.

US internal migration, beginning with data from the 1850 census, which was the first US census to provide migration data classified by place of birth (i.e., lifetime migration data).

The premier migration study conducted during the 1950s and early 1960s was also carried out at the University of Pennsylvania. The three-volume work, *Population Redistribution and Economic Growth United States, 1870–1950*, had a number of widely-recognized participants, including C.P. Brainerd, R.A. Easterlin, H.T. Eldridge, S. Kuznets, E.S. Lee, A.R. Miller, and D.S. Thomas.[16] The study, which was directed by Kuznets and Thomas, is a detailed, state-level analysis that like most earlier migration research is descriptive in style and inferential in tone. The basic notion that underlies the study is that "the distribution of a country's population at any given time may be viewed as a rough adjustment to the distribution of economic opportunities" (Kuznets and Thomas, 1957: p. 2). In this sense, the study is a logical extension of Goodrich's earlier work, which had the same type of theme. One of the main hypotheses of the study is that technological progress critically affected the sectoral and spatial distribution of economic activity. Moreover, the rapidity with which the changes occurred allowed little room for the vital processes of births and deaths to play an important role in adjusting population to altered economic opportunities. Migration had to provide the main impetus. Another important aspect of this study was its emphasis on the selective nature of migration, especially long-distance migration and migration between dissimilar places.

Data were clearly a problem that prevented migration research from blossoming. The availability of only lifetime migration data in the US Census was especially limiting. Not until 1940 did the Census include a question on past residence at a fixed date (1935), and not until 1950 did the Census report migration cross-tabulations by age.[17] Spatial detail at the county level required that migration be estimated by the survival method.[18] The resulting net migration data caused a strong orientation during the 1930s and 1940s toward migration of the rural-farm population. Although the creation of these net-migration data required some sophistication, analyses remained descriptive (Bernert, 1944a, b).

During the late 1940s, the Current Population Survey (CPS) began asking place of residence 1 year earlier, which resulted in an annual series of US migration data that could be disaggregated to the four Census regions. In many respects, the period of descriptive migration research reached its peak in 1964 with the publication of Henry S. Shryock, Jr.'s *Population Mobility within the United States* (Chicago: University of Chicago). This book provided a truly detailed descriptive analysis of existing CPS

---

[16] The three volumes are Lee et al. (1957), Kuznets et al. (1960), and Eldridge and Thomas (1964).

[17] Shryock (1964) provides a useful history of the collection and reporting of US migration data.

[18] The survival method of measuring internal migration refers to applying survival rates to a population from t to $t + 1$ and comparing the "expected" population, assuming zero net migration, to the "actual" population measured or estimated at $t + 1$. The difference is assumed to be due to net migration, but could be due to other factors as well.

data, as well as 1940 and 1950 Census data. However, even before this book was published, a new day had begun to dawn on migration research. The first survey of which this author is aware that yielded usable microdata on migration was conducted in 1960.

4.2. *Gravity and modified-gravity models*

During the 1960s, the main thrust of migration research began to take on a decidedly more formal tone that has continued to the present. Most of the research was not formal in a theoretical sense, but rather intuitively generated hypotheses were at first tested formally in an econometric sense with aggregate data, typically but not always with place-to-place migration data. These aggregate models of migration frequently were specified in the context of modified gravity models. The models are "gravity type" in that migration is hypothesized to be directly related to the size of relevant origin and destination populations, and inversely related to distance.[19] The models are "modified" in the sense that the variables of the basic gravity model are given behavioral content, and additional variables that are expected to importantly influence the decision to migrate are included in the estimated relationship.

Modified gravity models that become common in the migration literature beginning during the 1960s add several additional variables to those of the basic gravity model. Thus, we now commonly find studies of place-to-place migration that take the following form:

$$\ln M_{ij} = \ln \beta_0 + \beta_1 \ln D_{ij} + \beta_2 \ln P_i + \beta_3 \ln P_j$$
$$+ \beta_4 \ln Y_i + \beta_5 \ln Y_j + \sum_{n=1}^{m} \beta_{in} \ln X_{in} + \sum_{n=1}^{m} \beta_{jn} \ln X_{jn} + e_{ij}, \tag{1}$$

where the Y terms refer to income. Other variables that are commonly included (as

---

[19] During the 1940s Princeton astronomer Stewart noted that the distance to his students' home towns seemed to behave like the Newtonian law of gravitation. Thus, Stewart (1941) expressed the gravity law of spatial interaction as $f = GP_iP_j/D_{ij}^2$ where F = gravitational or demographic force, G = constant, P_i = population of origin i, P_j = population of destination j, and D_{ij} = distance between i and j. This relationship states that "demographic" force is directly related to origin and destination population size and inversely related to the square of the distance between them. If the square on the distance term is replaced by α and the relationship is placed in the migration context by substituting migration from i to j, M_{ij}, for F, we get $M_{ij} = GP_iP_j/D_{ij}^\alpha$. If this model is expressed in double-log form, it suggests that the population parameters are equal to 1.0, meaning that a 1% increase in origin or in destination population results in a 1% increase in migration from i to j. This assumption is clearly restrictive, and the population elasticities are subject to empirical tests. Thus, the gravity model can be written as $M_{ij} = GP_i^{\beta_1}P_j^{\beta_2}/D_{ij}^\alpha$. In this form, the values of β_1 and β_2 can be freely estimated, and the hypothesis that they are equal to 1.0 can be tested. This basic form of the gravity model was tested rarely because little additional effort was required to specify and estimate the more appealing modified gravity model.

reflected in "X" terms above) are unemployment rates, degree of urbanization, various climatological amenity variables, various measures of public expenditures and/or taxes, and many other factors. For certain variables, some models contain only origin characteristics, such as median age or median number of years of schooling, which are meant as proxies for the characteristics of the population from which the migrants are drawn. Modified gravity models hold an important place in the migration literature because their formulators tried to incorporate behavioral content in the context of the gravity-model approach. These efforts subsequently led to formal models of the migration decision process such as those reflected in many studies that incorporate microdata. Moreover, such models included a mix of disequilibrium and equilibrium notions that anticipated the later, more rigorous development of the equilibrium hypothesis as related to migration.

The connection between modified gravity models and the migration decision process has not always been tight. The dependent variable in modified gravity models is meant to proxy the probability of moving from i to j. However, the denominator of the dependent variable frequently has been population measured at the beginning or end of the migration interval. Such a measure falls short of reflecting the population at risk to make a move from i to j.[20]

Modified gravity models are frequently estimated in double logarithmic form, presumably because this functional form yields reasonably good fits and the coefficients obtained from it can be directly interpreted as elasticities of migration's response to changes in the various independent variables of the estimated models.[21] However, common use of the double-logarithmic functional form to estimate modified gravity models has led to a criticism by T.P. Schultz (1982), who argues for the adoption of nonlinear maximum likelihood logit methods over the double-log form of the model. In part his argument hinges on the geographic size of the regions for which migration is measured. If all regions had the same population and land area, migration and nonmigration probabilities would reflect the costs and benefits of the various locational choices. However, the regions of any country differ greatly in population and land area. A larger share of all moves will tend to occur within the boundaries of larger regions. Consequently, more nonmigration will appear to exist for such regions. The result is that nonmigration is spuriously correlated with origin population size and land area.

In the polychotomous logistic model the migration probabilities are expressed as ratios, and the probability of not migrating is used in the denominator of the expres-

---

[20] For example, beginning-of-period population includes persons who die during the period over which migration is measured, as well as those who emigrate from the country, and who are thus not available to be counted as migrants. The end-of-period measure includes in-migrants who were not at risk to be out-migrants from the area and also introduces simultaneity between migration and the population measure.

[21] Goss and Chang (1983) show considerable differences in the estimated coefficients of a migration model depending upon the precise nature of the functional form that is specified.

sion to normalize the "flows". That is, the dependent variable is $\ln[m_{ij}/(1 - m_{ij})]$, which is sometimes called the logarithm of the odds-ratio. Here m_{ij} refers to the probability of migration from i to j, and is thus measured as M_{ij}, or the actual number of movers from i to j divided by the population at risk to migrate from i. The model can be estimated in one of two ways that make sense in the migration context. First, again assuming the double-log form of the model, the log of the ratio of various destination-to-origin characteristics can be used. This approach, referred to as "uniform symmetric", implies that coefficients on variables for corresponding origin and destination characteristics are the same except for sign. Second, a two-step decision process can be assumed in which the decision maker first decides whether to migrate based on origin characteristics and then decides where to migrate based on destination characteristics and perhaps other variables (such as distance) that link the areas. In this case, origin and destination characteristics are introduced separately. In an analogous fashion, nested decision trees could be constructed for other levels of the decision process (e.g., to move, where to move, what house to select, etc.). Some dissatisfaction has been expressed with the notion that an individual can decide whether to move independently of where he/she might move. Thus, whether to move and where to move are seen as joint decisions and not discrete and independent decisions (Linneman and Graves, 1983).

Schultz sees the standard gravity approach as inefficient because it fails to incorporate information on the relative frequency of nonmigration $(1 - m_{ij})$. He argues, however, that "in the limit, as the unit of time diminishes over which migration is measured, differences between the two specifications of the migration model might be expected to diminish" (1982: p. 576). The reason is that the population at risk to migrate becomes a better measure of the nonmigrating population when the migration interval is very short. In any case, the logit approach provides a more natural transition from the gravity model to the more behaviorally-grounded modified gravity model.

Prior to 1975 virtually all migration research was based on aggregate data.[22] In addition to the problem noted above, modified gravity models were characterized by other problems and shortcomings frequently associated with the use of such data. Aggregate data often were used to proxy the characteristics of the population at risk to move, resulting in empirical estimates that did not reflect accurately the influence of personal characteristics on the decision to migrate. With some notable exceptions (e.g., DaVanzo, 1976b; Kau and Sirmans, 1977), studies of aggregate migration failed to account for different types of moves, such as primary (or new), return, and other repeat migration. Aggregate data also concealed differences in the underlying determinants of migration of various population subgroups, although stratification by age and race was not uncommon. Such data failed to account for the institutional population, of which the military was especially important, and they made the study of fam-

---

[22] My 1975 survey article in the *Journal of Economic Literature* reflects this orientation. Of the 251 publications cited in this paper, only three made direct use of microdata and none used longitudinal data.

ily migration decisions difficult. Another problem with modified gravity models was that the variables used to explain migration often were measured at the end of the migration interval and were thus subject to simultaneity bias (Greenwood, 1975c). During the 1970s, several simultaneous equations models were developed to explain the causes and consequences of migration within the same empirical framework, but for the most part during the last 10–15 years these models have not been further developed.[23]

4.3. Distance

One of the major implications of the gravity model approach is that place-to-place migration declines with distance. Modified gravity models arrive at a similar conclusion, but provide a behavioral basis for the results. That migration decreases with increased distance from the origin has been attributed to several factors, among which the following are most prominent: (a) distance is a proxy for the out-of-pocket money costs of moving, such as gasoline and moving vans. (b) Opportunity costs rise with distance in the sense that longer moves require more time, which in turn means more foregone earnings if the individual is not involved in a job transfer. (c) Opportunity costs rise with distance in a second sense in that the greater the distance of the contemplated move, the better are likely to be the foregone alternatives within a given distance (Wadycki, 1974).[24] (d) Information costs rise with distance, which in turn requires greater search costs to offset the greater uncertainty associated with more distant locations. (e) Distance serves as a proxy for the psychic costs of moving, which can be offset by making more frequent trips or trips of longer duration back to the origin, where each type of return trip raises the cost of moving as a positive function of distance (Schwartz, 1973). (f) If past migrants tended to move to nearby places, and if current migrants tend to follow past migrants, then current migrants tend to move to nearby places (Nelson, 1959; Greenwood, 1969). If a "migrant stock" or lagged migration variable is not included in the model, distance reflects the importance of relatives and friends as well as other forces.

For a number of reasons the deterring effects of distance are likely to decline over time. One set of reasons is related to the fact that over time the transportation and communications systems are improved and expanded, whereas another set is related to the fact that education and income levels of the population generally rise over time. By reducing transport costs, improvements in the transportation system encourage the flow of both commodities and resources, including labor. Improvements in the com-

---

[23] For simultaneous equations approaches to migration, see Muth (1971) and Greenwood (1975b). Mueller (1982) provides an overview of this literature.

[24] Whereas for Wadycki (1974) alternative opportunities intervene by being geographically closer than the chosen alternative, for Denslow and Eaton (1984) alternative opportunities intervene by being economically closer.

munications system encourage the transmittal of greater quantities of information at lower cost, including information relevant to migration decisions.

The term "distance elasticity of migration" refers to the percentage change in migration from *i* to *j* that results from a 1% change in the distance between *i* and *j*, other factors held constant. These elasticities typically range between about –0.1 or –0.2 to well over –2.0, depending upon the population subgroup under study, the type of migration flow studied, the time period over which migration is measured, the size, shape, and location of the geographic area used, and the explanatory variables included in the model. Distance elasticity estimates that have been obtained for the US are similar in terms of order of magnitude to those obtained for other countries.

Because most empirical work on place-to-place migration uses census data, only a few studies provide comparable cross-sectional estimates of distance elasticities for different points in time. These studies have tended not to focus on the temporal patterns, thereby not providing any statistical tests for the significance of observed differences over time. Observed temporal patterns are mixed. For example, Gallaway and Vedder (1971), provide US elasticities of interstate out-migration for 1920 and 1960 that show the absolute value of the distance coefficients declining for many midwestern and western states, but not for most eastern states. Denslow and Eaton (1984) show roughly comparable estimates for 12 selected states, but their elasticities are for each census from 1870 to 1970. For most but not all states, the absolute values of the distance elasticities decline over time.

Using annual interprovincial migration data for Canada, Courchene (1970) estimates distance elasticities for each year from 1952 to 1967. Toward the end of the period, his elasticities taper off from about –1.35 to around –1.10. Also studying Canada, Shaw (1985) estimates metropolitan-to-metropolitan migration models for four periods (1956–1961, 1966–1971, 1971–1976, 1976–1981). He adjusts his origin and destination wage variables for inflation (because at times he pools the data) and cost of living differences, among other factors. The estimated distance elasticity falls over time for each variant of his wage measures. For example, when the wage is adjusted for cost of living differences, the distance elasticity falls in absolute value from –0.602 (1956–1961) to –0.399 (1976–1981).

Several studies that examine the movement of persons from specific states or localities find that the absolute value of the distance elasticity rises with the distance of those places from other areas. Among studies of US migration patterns, this finding entails that western states and localities generally have considerably higher distance elasticities than states and localities located elsewhere in the country (Gallaway and Vedder, 1971; Greenwood and Gormely, 1971; Greenwood and Sweetland, 1972). Fotheringham (e.g., 1981) and others argue that estimates of distance-decay parameters, in addition to being functions of behavior relating to spatial interactions, are also functions of spatial structure, where spatial structure relates to the location, geographic size, and configuration of the regions that are the units of measurement. Using US Census data on migration for three periods (1955–1960, 1965–1970, 1975–1980),

Mueser (1989) provides direct evidence of the role played by spatial structure in estimated distance elasticities. He shows that distance elasticities differ systematically by origin and destination, with distance providing a less serious obstacle to migration between highly urbanized regions and between areas with high income.

4.4. Theoretical perspectives on migration

The theoretical perspective taken in almost all migration research conducted by economists prior to the late 1970s was that of a disequilibrium system.[25] The perspective is called "disequilibrium" because migration is assumed to be driven by the existence of a set of non-market clearing regional wages. Moreover, spatial variations in wages or earnings or income are assumed to reflect opportunities for utility gains. During more recent years, this disequilibrium perspective has been challenged by proponents of the "equilibrium" hypothesis, which assumes that spatial variations in wages are compensating and therefore do not reflect opportunities for utility gains.

Anticipating somewhat material that is more rigorously developed below, consider an indirect utility function (V) and a unit cost function (c):

$$V = f(w, r; a, \varphi), \tag{2}$$

$$c = g(w, r; a, \theta), \tag{3}$$

where w is the regional wage level, r is the regional rent level, a is a vector of location-specific amenities, and φ and θ are shifters for exogenous disturbances. The disequilibrium approach does not rely on amenities (a) and w and r adjust slowly to exogenous disturbances. In the equilibrium approach, migration is conditional on amenities. Moreover, this approach does not rely on long adjustments of w and r to disturbances, especially in the US where institutional and other impediments to factor mobility appear to be relatively low. Systematic long-term forces, such as rising real income in some or all locations, importantly underlie consumption amenity demand growth and provide the rationale for migration (Graves and Linneman, 1979). Thus, both the disequilibrium and equilibrium approaches assume that spatial variations in utility underlie migration decisions, but the differences spring from the source and persistence of these variations.

The perspective taken by the analyst not only shapes the precise form of the model that is specified and estimated, it also contributes importantly to the interpretation placed on the estimated coefficients of wage (or related) variables. This section develops the thinking underlying the disequilibrium perspective, including a discussion of

---

[25] Molho (1986) provides a survey of various migration models that reflect the disequilibrium perspective.

related empirical findings concerning wages. It then develops the equilibrium perspective and discusses associated empirical work.

4.4.1. The disequilibrium perspective

Underlying the disequilibrium perspective, at least implicitly, is the simple income–leisure model of labor economics wherein an optimizing agent maximizes a utility function with two arguments, income and leisure, subject to a full-income constraint. One implication of this model is that the individual will supply labor such that the marginal rate of substitution of consumption for leisure equals the wage rate, which in turn implies that individual labor supply is a function of the wage rate. If we abstract from mobility costs and accept many other assumptions that underlie this simple, yet powerful model, the individual is expected to offer his labor services in the market with the highest wage, which may require migration.

The human capital approach. The human capital approach added to the disequilibrium perspective. After the publication in 1961 of T.W. Schultz's classic paper in the *American Economic Review*, soon followed in 1962 by Becker's paper on investment in human capital and, in the same special issue of the *Journal of Political Economy*, by Sjaastad's paper on migration as an investment in human capital, migration research by economists really began to blossom. The human capital perspective provided a paradigm that caught the attention of economists and provided a convenient theoretical framework for their research.

The potential migrant will select that locality at which the real value of the expected net benefit that accrues to him from migration is greatest. The income that the individual expects to earn at each alternative destination enters importantly into his judgment concerning the benefits associated with each location. The relevant income measure for the individual to consider is the present discounted value of his expected future stream of net pecuniary returns.

Sjaastad was the first to actually apply the notion of investment in human capital to the decision to migrate. Let the present value of the earnings stream in locality j less that in i be

$$\sum_{t=1}^{n} (E_{jt} - E_{it}) / (1+r)^t,$$

where r is the internal rate of discount, which although written as a constant does not have to be constant. Let the present value of net costs associated with residence in this pair of localities be

$$\sum_{t=1}^{n} (C_{jt} - C_{it}) / (1+r)^t.$$

The summation is over the individual's remaining life. Then the present value of investment in migration from i to j (PV_{ij}) is

$$PV_{ij} = \sum_{t=1}^{n} \left[\frac{1}{(1+r)^t} \right] [(E_{jt} - C_{jt}) - (E_{it} - C_{it})]. \tag{4}$$

An individual residing in i will presumably select that destination for which PV_{ij} is maximized.

The disequilibrium perspective is clearly evident in Sjaastad's (1962) model of migration. In the human capital model, economic opportunity differentials represent potential for household utility gains that can be arbitraged by migration. For all intents and purposes, the human capital model was unrivaled for almost 20 years. Indeed, disequilibrium forces were presumed to be the primary drivers of migration long before Sjaastad provided the human capital explanation for migration. For example, the disequilibrium notion almost certainly underlies Hicks's contention that "differences in net economic advantages, chiefly differences in wages, are the main causes of migration" (1932: p. 76).[26]

The human capital model provided an appealing rationale for the presence of income variables in modified gravity models, as well as in other models of migration. Based on the disequilibrium perspective, in modified gravity models the origin wage or income variable is expected to take a negative sign, whereas the destination wage or income variable is expected to take a positive sign, as migrants move out of low-income areas and into high-income areas. A number of studies have tested Hicks's assertion regarding the importance of wages in explaining migration by examining the factors affecting interregional migration in the US and in many other countries. Based on aggregate data, empirical findings associated with income, earnings, and wage variables in modified gravity models have not been uniformly strong, although it is probably fair to conclude that the weight of available evidence favors Hicks's expected disequilibrium results, particularly for rural-to-urban migration that dominated movement at the time of his writing. Of course, the exact results are sensitive to many factors, such as the precise specification of the model, the country and period studied, the population subgroup under investigation, the type of functional form assumed, and

---

[26] Although both Hicks (1932) and Sjaastad (1962) recognized that disequilibrium and equilibrium forces are at work, they emphasized the disequilibrium forces (Hunt, 1993). Hicks thought that the attraction of high wages would cause a "gradual flow of labour" to these places (p. 73). He also believed that some regional differences would persist because of the "indirect attractions of living in certain localities" (p. 74). Sjaastad recognized a "non-money component ... reflecting preference" for a place of residence and even mentions such preference as reflecting "climate, smog, and congestion" (p. 86), of which at least climate is a key element of the equilibrium perspective.

the estimation technique employed. Moreover, income or wage measures have almost never been refined to reflect real consumption wages.[27]

Although the migration models of economists are typically formulated in the context of individual utility maximization, the data employed in estimating the models were for many years aggregate in the sense that they referred to mean income or earnings levels in sending and receiving regions. The influence of income on migration can be considered from two different perspectives, one consistent with aggregate income measures and one consistent with migrant-specific income measures. The first perspective involves the determination of whether migration occurs from low-to-high income or wage areas, and if it does, the magnitude of the relationship. The second perspective involves the determination of whether and to what extent migrants themselves benefit by moving. The latter type of study is considered in connection with the personal characteristics of migrants.

A finding common to a number of gross migration studies of both the US and Canada (Shaw, 1985) is that income (and job) opportunities provide a better explanation of in-migration than they do of out-migration. Several explanations have been offered for this finding.

(1) Perloff et al. (1960) argue that localities with attractive economic conditions draw sizable numbers of migrants from other localities, though only small numbers from any single locality. On the other hand, what is important in determining out-migration from a locality suffering from economic distress is the percentage of the labor force that is willing to leave in order to search for opportunities elsewhere. This percentage, argue Perloff et al., is sensitive to the personal characteristics of the residents of the locality. Like Perloff, Lowry (1966), in his study of (1955–1960) inter-metropolitan migration, concludes that the labor market characteristics of an origin locality make little difference to an individual who is contemplating a move to another metropolitan area. However, destination characteristics help determine the locality to which the migrant will move.

(2) O'Neill (1970) suggests that the role that consumption plays in migration may help account for the tendency for destination-income variables to provide a better explanation of migration than origin-income variables. If migration is a "normal (consumption) good", an increase in destination income increases both the potential

---

[27] The role of taxes and public services in migration decisions is not emphasized in this paper, which is not to say that the public sector is unimportant in this respect. Day (1992) uses panel data on Canadian provinces for the period 1962–1981 to show that the composition of government expenditures affects migration, with spending for health and education attracting migrants, but spending for social services discouraging their in-movement. Helms (1985), also using panel data, but for US states for the period 1965–1979, reports findings similar to those of Day. He concludes that the manner in which taxes are used is critical in determining state economic growth. States that allocated their tax revenues toward transfer payments found their growth performance significantly reduced relative to those that emphasized spending on education, highways, and health. Charney (1993) provides a survey of the literature on migration and the public sector.

investment gain from migration and the expected level of permanent income.[28] Both investment and consumption effects thus would lead to increased in-migration. An increase in origin income of the same magnitude, however, would lead to an equivalent fall in the potential investment gain, but the expected level of permanent income would rise. In this instance the investment and consumption effects would oppose each other, and the direction of the impact on out-migration would depend upon the relative magnitude of the two effects. Vanderkamp (1971) makes a similar point, but he emphasizes that potential migrants from high-income regions are better able to finance a move and possible return, which also tends to offset the negative expectation on the origin-income variable.

(3) Miller (1973) denies the validity of the finding that origin characteristics are relatively unimportant in explaining migration, arguing instead that the rate of growth of employment is the primary economic determinant of out-migration rates. He claims that the findings of Perloff et al., Lowry, and others are the result of a failure to control for differences in the population's propensity to migrate. Persons who have moved at least once have higher migration rates than those who have not moved at all. Thus, areas with high in-migration rates tend to have high out-migration rates. The conditions that promote out-migration are the same as those that discourage in-migration. Areas in which such conditions prevail have relatively few recent in-migrants and the population of such places tends to be relatively immobile (since the more mobile have presumably already left). The factors that encourage out-migration do not influence those left behind as strongly as they have influenced those who have already moved. Just the opposite situation exists in areas where conditions are attractive to migrants, because where in-migration rates are high, out-migration rates also tend to be high. Hence, localities with higher income levels, lower unemployment rates, and higher rates of employment growth tend to have relatively heavy out-migration, which is contrary to expectations, because they tend to have relatively heavy in-migration.

The income–distance trade-off. The so-called "income–distance trade-off" in modified gravity models has been used as a rough indication of the money and non-money costs of moving a given distance farther. The trade-off is the percentage increase in destination income required to offset a 10% increase in distance and is measured by the absolute value of the ratio of the estimated distance elasticity to the esti-

---

[28] O'Neill provides no underlying rationale for migration being a "normal (consumption) good". Because migration is a process, and not a good or a service, on the surface O'Neill's statement makes little sense. However, if we consider the "migration process" to be like the "buying process", then we can make the statement more meaningful. The buying process has the goal of acquiring a good or service. The migration process has the goal of acquiring a bundle of attributes including a job, a new location with its amenities, etc. The equilibrium proponents whose work is discussed below would argue that the underlying motivation for migration is location-specific amenities, demand for which will grow with rising real income. Day (1992) makes essentially the same point as O'Neill, but more correctly emphasizes the notion that increased wages increase the price of leisure, which causes a substitution of goods for leisure, but at the same time increases full income, which causes more consumption.

mated elasticity on destination income (times 10). Trade-off values are clearly sensitive to the variables included in the empirical model from which they are derived. Nevertheless, given the mean distance between regions and mean income levels in the data underlying the estimation, the trade-off values can be transformed into absolute figures: a move x miles (or kilometers) farther away is offset by y dollars (or other unit of currency). Thus, Sjaastad states that "the typical migrant would be indifferent between two destinations, one of which was 146 miles more distant than the other, if the average annual labor earnings were $106 (1947–1949 dollars) higher in the more distant one" (1962: p. 84).

For Canada, Courchene (1970) reports a series of annual regressions that allow the computation of the income–distance trade-off for several consecutive years. The trade-off value declines from 3.46 in 1952 to 1.46 in 1967, due both to a declining (absolute value of the) distance elasticity and to a steadily rising destination income elasticity. Mean values for distance and income are not reported, so absolute measures of the trade-off cannot be calculated. Courchene also notes that within broad age classes, the trade-off is higher for more educated migrants. For example, for persons 25–34 years of age with at least a high-school education, the value is 4.39, compared to a value of 2.88 for those with no more than an elementary school education.[29] The reason for this difference is that education increases the benefits of migration while it decreases the costs (by improving information about alternative destinations and decreasing the risk associated with movement over greater distances). Vanderkamp (1971) finds a distinct cyclical pattern in the trade-off (for primary migration), with the extra dollars necessary to compensate for another mile falling with low national unemployment and rising with high national unemployment. For a move of 1000 miles, an extra mile is offset by $0.36 during periods of low unemployment, but by $0.54 during periods of high unemployment.

4.4.2. The equilibrium perspective[30]

Due in part to the fairly consistent tendency for empirical studies based on aggregate data to fail to confirm the importance of wages or income in migration decisions, the equilibrium approach has been offered as an alternative to the traditional disequilibrium perspective described above. The equilibrium theorists begin by assuming that households and firms are in proximate equilibrium at any point in time. This assumption means that the marginal household and firm, while maximizing utility and profit, respectively, are spatially arrayed so as to receive zero consumer and producer surplus from their location. Thus, any movement from the general equilibrium configuration cannot improve utility or profit.

---

[29] The income elasticity here is for the ratio of the destination to origin income variables.

[30] This section of the paper has benefited greatly from numerous discussions with Philip Graves and Gary Hunt concerning the equilibrium approach. The section, with considerable modification, is primarily drawn from Graves and Greenwood (1987).

Household location decisions are modeled as follows:

$$U = (X_{tr}, X_{ntr}, a, h, s) \tag{5}$$

where X_{tr} is traded goods (available at a nationally-determined price in all locations), X_{ntr} is nontraded goods (having regionally-varying prices that depend on regional wage (w) and rent (r) levels), a is amenities that vary in nature regionally but are un-produced (e.g., climate), h is leisure, and s is residential land. The utility function given in Eq. (5) is maximized subject to the following full-income constraint:

$$w(a)T + I_0 = P_{tr}X_{tr} + P_{ntr}(a)X_{ntr} + w(a)h + r(a)s, \tag{6}$$

where T is total time available during the period, I_0 is nonlabor income (which is as-sumed to equal zero for simplification), and P_{tr} and P_{ntr} are the respective prices of traded and nontraded goods. Household income depends on amenities. This income is spent on the numeraire traded good (whose price does not depend on amenities) and on nontraded goods, leisure, and lot size (whose prices do depend on regional amenity levels).

Utility is made spatially invariant by migration. Any location offering extra-normal utility for whatever reason will experience in-migration until, in some combination, wages fall or rents rise sufficiently to eliminate the utility differential. Level sets in indirect utility space (e.g., V_0, V_1) demonstrate the ultimate equilibrium (Fig. 1). If amenities were distributed uniformly among regions (e.g., at a_0) the curve labeled $V_0(w, r; a_0)$ shows various combinations of wages and rents that would give house-holds equal satisfaction. If one region were to have differentially preferred amenities (e.g., a_1 in Fig. 1) the amenity-rich region must have, in equilibrium, some combina-tion of lower wages and higher rents. All points on the respective indirect utility curves $V_0(w, r; a_0)$ and $V_1(w, r; a_1)$ yield the same level of utility (U) in direct-goods space.

Since, with negligible transportation costs, the traded good is exchanged in national markets, the only source of variation in regional profit levels is from the cost func-tion.[31] Let the production function be specified as

$$X_i = X_i(N, L, X_{ntr}, X_{tr}; a), \tag{7}$$

where $N =$ labor, $L =$ land, and the i subscript refers to nontraded (ntr) or traded (tr) goods.[32] In practice, the amenities most relevant to production (e.g., access to raw

---

[31] This is not the case for the nontraded good, whose price is not determined by national markets due to transportation costs, which provide a degree of protection for producers of this good.

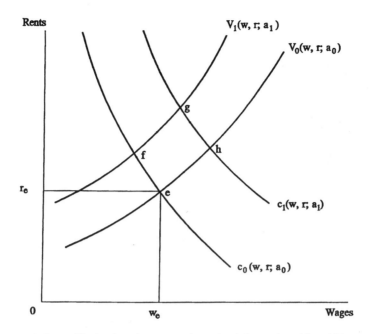

Fig. 1. Constant indirect utility levels and constant unit cost levels in a region with variable wages and rents.

materials, good harbors) may be different than those most relevant to consumption, but for convenience consumption and production amenities are included in the same vector (a). Hence, the unit cost function (assuming a linear homogenous production function) is

$$c_i = (w, r, P_{ntr}, P_{tr}; a). \tag{8}$$

The respective prices of traded and nontraded goods in equilibrium will equal their respective unit costs of production, and will thus be functions of w, r, and a. Taking the traded good's price to be the numeraire and solving for P_{ntr} in terms of w, r, and a, we simplify the unit cost functions to

$$c_i = c_i(w, r; a).^{33} \tag{9}$$

In equilibrium, profits must be the same in all locations. If no spatial variation in

---

[32] Capital could be included in Eq. (7), but is left out for expositional convenience, along with its price in Eqs. (8) and (9).

[33] See Roback (1982) for a more detailed development of this model.

production amenities existed, locations with high wages would have compensatingly lower rents, and conversely, as illustrated by c_0 in Fig. 1. The ubiquitous presence of production-enhancing amenities must result, in equilibrium, in compensation in either labor or land markets. If a production amenity were to exist in City A relative to an otherwise identical City B, the amenity would make City A more profitable. Firm expansion and relocation would increase demand for labor and industrial land in City A, whereas in City B the opposite would tend to occur. Wages and rents would rise in City A (equilibrium h) and would fall in City B until profits equilibrate between Cities A and B (c_1 compared to c_0 in Fig. 1).

Fig. 1 shows the unique equilibrium rent (r_e) and wage (w_e) level that would exist in a world of uniform production and consumption amenities. Because the various regions of many countries offer a diversity of amenity combinations, some affecting households (positively or negatively) and some affecting firms (positively or negatively), a wide diversity of possible equilibrium rent/wage combinations is likely. One of the major points made by the equilibrium theorists is that even in simple cases, neither producer nor consumer amenities can be valued solely in either land or labor markets. Both exclusively producer and exclusively consumer amenities will be undervalued, in terms of their true economic importance, by studies assuming capitalization in only one market. This position leads proponents of the equilibrium hypothesis to deny the validity of migration studies that account for wages or income, but fail to account for rents and location-specific amenities.

According to the equilibrium approach, changes in life-cycle factors or generally rising real incomes continuously change the demand for consumer amenities. Real incomes may rise due, for example, to persistent technical progress. Because amenities are not evenly distributed spatially, migration occurs and quickly reequilibrates households. Net in-migration to amenity-rich areas tends to drive down wages and drive up the prices of locally-produced goods and services and land, ceteris paribus. In amenity-poor areas, opposite patterns of change occur. Wages and local prices diverge across regions until they just compensate households for the differing amenity bundles that the various regions supply.

The equilibrium approach has another important facet. Following Rosen's (1979) paper on wage-based indexes of urban quality of life, a number of studies use the level of regional wages or rents to measure regional environmental quality, including the quality of the climate. Particularly noteworthy in this respect are studies by Roback (1982, 1988), Hoehn et al. (1987), and Blomquist et al. (1988). The assumption underlying these studies is that equilibrium prevails so that wage and rent differentials are compensating differentials and thus serve as accurate proxies for differentials in environmental quality. For equilibrium to prevail, regional markets must be efficient so that regional wages and prices quickly realign to clear such markets subsequent to any disequilibrating exogenous disturbances. The equilibrium proponents believe that at any point in time, it is highly likely that regional wages and prices have adjusted to their equilibrium values. Graves and Knapp clearly state this position:

> But is the world likely to be very far from an equilibrium in which utility is the same everywhere? We believe not, on the grounds that mobility in the United States is quite high and information about alternative locations is good (1988: p. 3).

In the equilibrium approach, regional differentials in wages and prices do not generally reflect utility differences that can be arbitraged through household migration. Only those noncompensating regional differentials that remain after controlling for amenity differentials across regions should represent utility differentials that would induce migration. As noted above, the implication of this view for migration analysis is that a properly specified migration equation should include both regional amenity and regional wage and rent variables. For this reason, proponents of the equilibrium hypothesis typically include a wide variety of regional amenities in their empirical models (Graves, 1979, 1980). Among the variables frequently included are climatological amenities (e.g., average temperature at some time during the year, average humidity, degree days) and topological amenities (e.g., the presence or absence of a sea coast, variety of terrain, national forest lands).

From an economist's perspective, an equilibrium process makes great sense. Without the operation of such forces, economists would be hard pressed to develop a reasonable theory to explain interregional movements and the adjustments that result therefrom. However, for the most part until recently tests of the equilibrium hypothesis in the context of the migration literature have not been fully convincing (Hunt, 1993). Empirical models have been poorly specified and have failed to include appropriate variables that nest disequilibrium and equilibrium forces in the same model. Moreover, the variables of the model often have been crudely constructed and have therefore failed to precisely measure what was intended. Time series data have almost never been used to test the relevant equilibrium hypotheses in spite of the fact that such data are essential if adjustments toward or to equilibrium are to be addressed. Finally, the problem of the endogeneity of wages or income (because they contain the effects of amenities as compensating differentials) has been addressed rarely. The same type of endogeneity problem also characterizes studies that use a measure of rents (e.g., Graves, 1983) to reflect the combined influence of various amenities. The basic idea here is that if consumption amenities are not included in the estimated model, the error term will pick up their effects and be correlated with w and r.

Three obvious empirical questions arise with respect to the equilibrium approach (Hunt, 1993). First, does interregional equilibrium, or something close to it, prevail in the US or in other areas of the world? If the system is typically far from equilibrium, the basic assumption underlying the approach would be invalid, and empirical models based on the approach would presumably fail. Second, when the system is shocked, how rapidly does it reestablish equilibrium wages and rents? If the system is slow to adjust, the disequilibrium framework assumes more appeal (Evans, 1990). Third, in migration decisions, how important are location-specific amenities compared to traditional disequilibrium-type variables like relative wage rates?

In the sense that variables that adequately reflect the two hypotheses are rarely nested in the same empirical model, the issues of whether and to what extent equilibrium prevails are almost never directly examined. Rather, the assumption of equilibrium is made, or its existence is inferred based on empirical results. An exception is a recent study by Greenwood et al. (1991b). These investigators develop a model of net migration that encompasses both equilibrium and disequilibrium components. The model is of the following form:

$$\ln[(NLF_{i,t-1} + ECM_{i,t})/NLF_{i,t-1}] = \ln \lambda_i + \lambda_1 RY_{i,t} + e_{i,t}, \tag{10}$$

where NLF refers to natural civilian labor force (exclusive of military personnel and their dependents, persons 65 and over, and immigrants), ECM is net economic migrants (including their dependents), $\ln \lambda_i$ represents a fixed-effect due to location-specific amenities, broadly defined (and perhaps other unmeasured and locationally invariant features, such as population characteristics), and $RY_{i,t}$ is relative expected income, measured by the relative wage bill divided by the natural labor force.

Instrumental-variables (to account for the endogeneity of RY) fixed-effects estimates of the model with time-series data for 51 US areas over the period 1971–1988 support the importance of both equilibrium and disequilibrium factors in migration. In the Greenwood et al. model, equilibrium is assumed to occur in an area when the measure of net economic migration equals zero. The equilibrium value of RY for each area is that value generating no net migration, which is the value that just offsets the impact of the estimated individual effect for each area. Solving their estimated model for the equilibrium condition of zero net migration, these authors demonstrate that some US states are not in equilibrium during 1980.[34] However, this finding can be demonstrated at a statistically significant level for only a few states. Indeed, errors generated in the estimation of compensating differentials by erroneously assuming regional equilibrium appear to be relatively minor, both quantitatively and qualitatively. Thus, the Greenwood et al. study suggests that the equilibrium approach must be taken seriously as a challenge to the disequilibrium approach.

The speed of adjustment to equilibrium is a second important issue about which little is known. The equilibrium theorists believe the adjustment is relatively rapid, but they assume this position rather than demonstrating it directly.[35] A recent study by

[34] The reason that 1980 was chosen is that Blomquist et al. (1988) assume equilibrium in 1980 and estimate compensating differentials. Thus, for 1980 the results from the two studies can be related.

[35] Some equilibrium theorists appear to be moderating their view on the speed of adjustment. For example, Graves and Mueser state that "the equilibrium model suggests that (a location with abundant amenities) would display gradual increases in rents and declines in wages. Observed positive migration would occur over an extended period" (1993: p. 82) (parentheses are mine).

Treyz et al. (1993) suggests that the adjustments to equilibrium in the US require considerable time. Given an exogenous shock, about 40% of the adjustment in relative employment opportunity occurs by three years and 80% by 20 years. The same type of conclusion is drawn by Eberts and Stone (1992). Pissarides and McMaster arrive at a similar position regarding Britain: "the adjustment is slow and the long run is a very long run indeed – even in the absence of exogenous shocks adjustment to it (long-run equilibrium) takes more than twenty years" (1990: p. 812) (parentheses are mine). Existing empirical studies do not suggest extremely rapid adjustments to equilibrium, even in the US, where institutional impediments appear to be lower than elsewhere, but the speed of adjustment to equilibrium remains a potentially fruitful topic for future research.

How important are regional amenities in migration decisions? In one of the most comprehensive empirical analyses of the influence of location-specific amenities on migration, Graves (1979) demonstrates that when income levels and unemployment rates are taken into account, climatological amenity variables are important in explaining age- and race-specific net population migration during the 1960s. Specifically, Graves studies the influence of heating degree days, cooling degree days, annual temperature variance, relative humidity, and wind speed. Each variable tends to be significant in the various equations for net white migration. Moreover, in the absence of the amenity variables, income is typically insignificant. But in the presence of the amenity variables, the income variable tends to have the expected sign, to take on statistical significance, and to exhibit a more plausible life-cycle pattern. In a later paper Graves (1983) suggests that gross contract rent may serve as a good proxy for a host of interrelated amenity variables in a net-migration equation. He interprets his positive and significant coefficients on the rent variable across various age groups as lending support to the equilibrium thesis.

Subsequent studies find amenities a less important determinant of migration. Using a data set that includes 18 annual observations on migration, employment, and earnings for each of 57 Bureau of Economic Analysis Economic Areas in the US, Greenwood and Hunt (1989) subject Graves's amenity hypotheses and his findings to further scrutiny. They show that with respect to their direct effects, at least, employment opportunities are far more important in explaining metropolitan migration than location-specific amenities. In the presence of a variable for employment change, amenity variables roughly comparable to those used by Graves are rarely significant. When the employment variable is excluded from the model, the amenity variables take on somewhat greater importance in explaining migration, but still the results are far less supportive of the amenities hypothesis than those provided by Graves.

To the extent that real income is rising over time, the importance of location-specific amenities in migration decisions should also increase over time. To test this hypothesis, Greenwood and Hunt (1989) use two alternative data sets to estimate a model of net metropolitan migration roughly comparable to that of Graves. In one case they estimate the model for each of 17 consecutive years, and in the other they estimate it for three periods of greater length. This first approach yields no support for the idea that the importance of location-specific amenities has been rising over time, and the second yields only modest support for the hypothesis.

The results developed by Greenwood and Hunt (1989) indicate that disequilibrium forces, specifically relative wages and employment opportunities, are important determinants of migration. Moreover, they show that the direct effects of equilibrium forces such as location-specific amenities do not appear to be as strong in explaining work force migration as they have proven to be in other studies of population migration (e.g., Graves, 1979). These findings not withstanding, location-specific amenities could still be important in explaining migration. Two possible explanations seem plausible. First, if the system is in interregional general equilibrium, no systematic migration occurs, although it did in the past in order to bring general equilibrium about. In this case, migration is not motivated by increasing utility or increasing profits. Second, if desirable places have lower wages due to the embedded values of their amenities, and if firms are attracted to areas with lower wages because of increased profitability associated with such locations, employment will grow most rapidly in amenity-rich areas. Jobs certainly attract migrants, and to the extent that these jobs are ultimately due to the amenities, amenities attract migrants in an indirect fashion.

Some empirical evidence exists in support of the first explanation. Roback (1982), for example, shows that a large fraction of observed regional wage differentials can be explained by local amenities. Moreover, following Graves, Porell (1982) has attempted to ascertain the relative importance of economic versus quality of life factors, as well as the trade-offs between the two, in explaining aggregate migration between 25 SMSAs over the 1965–1970 period. He concludes that "the regression results provide strong empirical support to the premise that both economic and QOL factors are important determinants of migration" (p. 152), which is the result arrived at more recently by Clark and Cosgrove (1991). However, somewhat in contrast to Graves's findings, Porell suggests that "migration is more responsive to marginal changes in economic factors than QOL factors" (p. 153) and "the results did not support the long-run equilibrium thesis of migration" (p. 156). Rather, Porell sees disequilibrium job incentives as encouraging migration to SMSAs that offer attractive amenity bundles.

Direct evidence concerning the second explanation mentioned above, namely that the influence of amenities is exerted through employment growth, is less plentiful. Much empirical research has focused on employment, but amenities have not received a great deal of attention as determinants of differential rates of employment growth. Some years ago Fuchs (1962) showed that manufacturing employment grew more rapidly in the South and West, and he speculated that one reason was the availability of sunshine and temperate climates. Greenwood and Hunt (1989) estimate very simple reduced-form equations for employment growth that present a generally negative picture regarding the second possible explanation. That is, the data reflect no particularly strong pattern of differential employment growth in amenity-rich areas.[36]

4.5. Employment status and migration

Three "channels" have been identified through which employment status, specifically unemployment, affects migration: (1) a region's unemployment rate relative to other regions; (2) personal unemployment; and (3) aggregate or national unemployment rates over the cycle. This order emphasizes the manner in which the literature developed rather than logic, which would place personal unemployment at the top of the list. All three channels, which reflect different hypotheses regarding unemployment's influence on migration, are rarely nested in the same model. Pissarides and Wadsworth (1989) is a possible exception.

4.5.1. Regional unemployment

Migration has been distinguished as "speculative", where it occurs in order for an individual to search for an acceptable employment opportunity, as opposed to "contracted", where the individual migrates with a job in hand (Silvers, 1977). Molho (1986) correctly notes that speculative migration is an intrinsic part of the job-search process, whereas contracted migration is the outcome of the search process. Although much migration is of the contracted type, such as job transfers, many analysts fail to distinguish between types, or cannot due to data shortcomings.[37]

In the process of searching for a new job, an individual will be influenced by expected income at alternative locations. Consequently, the values of alternative wage rates, as well as the corresponding probabilities of getting those wage rates, will enter the potential migrant's decision calculus. Both the unemployment rate (Todaro, 1969;

---

[36] For many years, employment has clearly grown more rapidly in the South and West. A number of studies address the issue of differential employment growth (e.g., Bartik, 1991, 1993; Crandall, 1993; Helms, 1985; Newman, 1983). Newman, for example, finds that corporate tax rate differentials, degree of unionization, and a favorable business climate (as measured by right-to-work laws) were important in attracting employment to the South.

[37] The US Annual Housing Survey has asked the main reason that the household head changed his/her previous residence. Sell (1983) uses the 1973–1977 surveys to determine the importance of job transfers, which averaged 600 000 per year over the period. Migration was defined as movement between metropolitan areas and metro to nonmetro, nonmetro to metro, and intrametro moves crossing a state line. Over 50% of the men aged 30–59 claimed to be involved in a job transfer (compared to taking a new job). Using the same data set, Long and Hansen (1979) show that 27.6% of the persons who migrated between states during the mid-1970s were involved in a job transfer and 23.4% moved to look for work. Whatever the shortcomings of the data, the job-transfer phenomenon appears to important and worthy of more attention than it has received.

Day, 1992) and the employment rate (Treyz et al., 1993) have been used as proxies for the probability of getting a job.

Numerous papers hypothesize that areas with high unemployment rates should have both more out-migration and less in-migration, other things being equal (Greenwood, 1975a). Somewhat surprisingly, perhaps, studies that have examined empirically the influence of unemployment rates on migration have found mixed results with some obtaining the anticipated signs and significant coefficients, whereas others obtain unanticipated signs or insignificant coefficients. Several examples of these various mixed findings are available. Gallaway et al. (1967), in their study of 1955–1960 US state-to-state migration, find that the unemployment-rate differential between the origin and destination state is positive and statistically significant, but when they examine out-migration from specific origin states to other states, they find that this differential is rarely significant. Rabianski (1971), studying US inter-SMSA migration over the same period, finds that the logarithm of the ratio of the destination to origin unemployment rate is negative, as anticipated, and statistically significant. However, also studying gross interstate migration over the 1955–1960 period, Wadycki (1974) finds a positive but statistically insignificant coefficient on the destination unemployment-rate variable.

For many years, one of the most perplexing problems in migration research, at least from the economist's perspective, was the consistency with which such conflicting results were uncovered in connection with the relationship between unemployment rates and migration. Several possible explanations have been offered for the failure of unemployment rates to influence migration in the expected direction and/or with the expected relative magnitude. However, until microdata were available to test certain of the hypotheses that were suggested, these explanations amounted to little more than speculation.

One of the intuitively most convincing explanations for the unanticipated results associated with unemployment rates is that they are caused by aggregating population subgroups whose motives for migration differ widely (Creedy, 1974). The unemployed are a small fraction of the labor force and an even smaller fraction of the population. Thus, studies of population migration and even those of labor force migration may not reflect the importance of unemployment because the unemployed are aggregated together with the employed and with individuals who are not members of the labor force. Since higher unemployment rates are likely to be of most concern to the unemployed and perhaps of little or no concern to those who have a job when they move, the effects of higher unemployment rates may well not be apparent in studies that attempt to explain population or labor force migration with aggregate data.

Fields (1976) argues that the reason for the unanticipated findings regarding unemployment-rate variables is the manner in which such rates are calculated. He suggests that variables relating to job turnover are more relevant than unemployment rates. The most important consideration, argues Fields, is that the unemployment rate pertains to the entire stock of workers and jobs, including experienced workers who are secure in their jobs. Potential migrants are presumably more concerned about the rates at which hiring for new jobs is taking place and hence are presumably more concerned about job turnover. Field's empirical results are much stronger in connection with job-turnover variables than with unemployment-rate variables. However, his results are based on aggregate data and consequently do not distinguish the employment status of potential migrants.

4.5.2. Personal unemployment

A convincing explanation for the frequent, unanticipated signs on variables for regional unemployment rates, along with supporting empirical results, required microdata. Herzog et al. (1993) provide a review of the literature dealing with the relationship between employment status and migration, as well as that between migration and employment status, and make a number of points regarding the need for microdata in this area of research. First, they argue that microdata allow the investigator to use in multivariate analysis a binary independent variable for employment status before a move, which permits the estimation of the effect of personal unemployment on migration under ceteris paribus conditions. Second, with microdata, personal characteristics can be measured and consequently the investigator need not rely on mean characteristics of different groups of potential migrants. Third, the aggregation problem noted above can be avoided because microdata allow the analysis of the appropriate research sample, which in this case is the labor force.

Before microdata were generally available, the typical procedure was to use area-wide characteristics, such as age and median number of years of schooling, as proxies for the characteristics of the population at risk to out-migrate. In a regression context, this procedure was thought to allow a determination of the relative importance of personal compared to place characteristics in migration decisions. In such regressions, variables relating to personal characteristics were frequently lacking significance and/or of unanticipated sign. Such findings are hardly surprising since the aggregate variables may be virtually uncorrelated with the migrant (or potential migrant) traits of concern. Moreover, the lack of true data relating to the personal characteristics of migrants and potential migrants led to a literature on the determinants of migration that was strongly oriented toward the study of place characteristics.

Navratil and Doyle (1977) were perhaps the first to use microdata to study the influence of personal unemployment on migration (Herzog et al., 1993). Using 1970 US Census microdata, they also examine the influence of aggregation on the estimated elasticities reflecting the determinants of migration. In one model they use average values of the personal characteristics of subclasses of in-migrants, along with a number of commonly used area characteristics. In a second model they use the actual personal characteristics of the individual in-migrants and almost the same area characteristics. The empirical results suggest "that the process of aggregation camouflages some of the personal characteristics which are important determinants of an individual's decision to migrate while it had only a marginal effect on the labor market characteristics of an area" (p. 1558). Moreover, 1965 personal unemployment encouraged migration of each group studied (black/white, by gender) over the 1965–1970 period. These findings underscore the importance of using available microdata. In short, the relative importance of personal compared to place characteristics (such as unemployment) cannot be directly established in the absence of information from microdata.

A major breakthrough in this area of migration research was a study by DaVanzo (1978) that provides a more direct test of Field's (1976) hypothesis that the migration response of the unemployed is likely to be more sensitive to the tightness of the labor market than the response of the employed. Her work also bears on the question of aggregation. DaVanzo's data, which are drawn from the Panel Study of Income Dynamics (PSID) and which relate to individual households, actually distinguish the employment status of the head of the household. She shows that families whose heads are looking for work are more likely to move than families whose heads are not looking. Moreover, the unemployed are more likely to move than the employed. Higher area unemployment rates encourage the out-migration of those who are unemployed, but exert little influence on those who have a job. These findings are important and were dependent upon the availability of microdata, and specifically longitudinal microdata. They could not have been derived, at least not with such great precision, with census data – not even with the census microdata files, because these data fail to report employment status before and after the move; they report only status at the time of the census and five years earlier.

Since the publication of DaVanzo's paper, several other contributions using US data have confirmed or refined her basic finding (Herzog et al., 1993). Using 1970 census microdata, Herzog and Schlottmann (1984) examine the relationship between unemployment and white male migration. Census data report employment status in 1965 and subsequent migration between 1965 and 1970. Controlling for several personal characteristics (age, education, marital status, and prior mobility, in addition to 1965 employment status) and place characteristics (unemployment rate and average earnings), these authors separately analyze the migration of professional and technical persons, persons with white-collar occupations, and those with blue-collar occupations. They find that individuals who were unemployed in 1965 were more likely to migrate than those who were not. Moreover, this relationship holds for each occupational group. Higher local unemployment rates also encourage out-migration. For blue collar workers, unemployment before migration increases the probability of unemployment after migration. While these results are meaningful, some caution should be exercised in interpreting them because as noted above the Census does not report employment status at the time of the move, but rather only in 1965 and 1970. Thus, a necessarily direct link need not have existed between 1965 employment status and 1965–1970 migration.

A number of studies dealing with the influence of unemployment on European migration have failed to confirm DaVanzo's findings for the US that the unemployed are particularly sensitive to local unemployment rates. Very little work concerning Europe has been done with micro- and longitudinal data, but four noteworthy studies, one concerning the Netherlands (Van Dijk et al., 1989), two concerning Great Britain (Hughes and McCormick, 1989; Pissarides and Wadsworth, 1989), and one concerning Sweden (Harkman, 1989), have appeared recently. In contrast to DaVanzo's use of longitudinal data, these studies all use non-longitudinal microdata, but recall that using the latter type of data Herzog and Schlottmann (1984) confirm DaVanzo's finding for the US.

As pointed out by Hughes and McCormick (1989), personal unemployment raises the propensity to migrate in the US, UK, and the Netherlands, although by considerably different relative magnitudes (i.e., 34% in the US, 93% in the Netherlands, and 181% in the UK). On the basis of logit regressions, we can also conclude that many forces work to influence migration in the same direction in the US, UK, the Netherlands, and Sweden. For example, other things being equal, increased age reduces migration and increased education raises it. However, with respect to local unemployment rates, the results are different.

Van Dijk et al. (1989) compare the determinants of labor force migration in the US and the Netherlands. These researchers interact their variable for employment status at the end of the period with the local unemployment rate and conclude that "estimates for these variables were insignificant for both countries; thus, the effect of local employment conditions on interregional migration is apparently unaffected by personal unemployment" (p. 81). This conclusion holds whether the personal unemployment is measured at the beginning or the end of the migration period. Pissarides and Wadsworth (1989) arrive at a similar conclusion concerning Great Britain.

DaVanzo's results for the US and those of others for the Netherlands and Great Britain could differ for several reasons. The periods over which migration is measured in the three countries are different, and, as shown by Sandefur and Tuma (1987), this could lead to somewhat different findings even if other conditions were the same. Furthermore, comparison of migration between 10 (Great Britain) or 11 (the Netherlands) regions of a country compared to 48 regions that comprise a small part of another country could cause problems. Institutional differences, such as between unemployment insurance programs, could also lead to different findings. Nevertheless, with respect to the local unemployment variable, the findings for the two European countries are different, whereas in other respects the results are similar.

Harkman's (1989) study of Sweden is based on data drawn from March, 1988, questionnaires given to individuals who were registered at Swedish employment agencies in March, 1987, and were unemployed at that time. Only persons aged 20–29 in 1988 were included in the sample. The logit regressions estimated by Harkman include age and sex, as well as several variables relating to unemployment compensation and one relating to duration of unemployment. His variable reflecting the local labor market situation is the ratio of job searchers to job vacancies in the region (relative to a comparable variable for Sweden). This variable proves to be insignificant in each migration equation. Thus, although Harkman's variable strictly speaking is not an unemployment rate, his findings also appear to fail to support those of DaVanzo.

In terms of understanding the relationship between personal unemployment, local unemployment rates, and the decision to migrate, DaVanzo's use of the PSID leads to the most convincing results. However, if her results do not hold for other countries, as suggested by available evidence for those countries, it would be interesting to know why.

Migration propensities of the employed and the unemployed may, among other factors, also differ due to the prior migration experience of the two groups. Schlottmann and Herzog (1981) use 1970 PUMS data to distinguish employment status in 1965 and whether potential migrants were at risk to be primary as opposed to repeat migrants. Primary migrants are defined as persons living in their state of birth in 1965, whereas repeat migrants are persons living in a state other than that of their birth in 1965. They study only white males between 19 and 70 years of age in 1965 who were in the labor force in 1970. Those attending college or in the armed forces in 1965 or 1970 are excluded from their sample. They show that the probability of interstate migration for persons unemployed in 1965 and at risk to make a primary move was 0.17, whereas those at risk to make a repeat move had a corresponding probability of 0.25. Corresponding probabilities for persons employed in 1965 are 0.06 and 0.13, respectively. Hence, previous migration experience encourages the movement of both employed and unemployed persons, and unemployed persons at risk to make either a primary or repeat move are substantially more likely to migrate than employed persons at risk to make the same type of move.[38]

Schlottmann and Herzog also find that for potential primary migrants, increased education encourages significantly more migration of the employed than the unemployed. For potential repeat migrants, but not for potential primary migrants, more education encourages unemployed persons to migrate. The propensity of the unemployed to migrate is not reduced by high state welfare levels, but is for states with high educational quality and access to manpower and vocational training programs. Higher area wages do not discourage the migration of unemployed persons who are potential primary migrants, but they do discourage potential repeat migrants.

The incidence of unemployment clearly declines with age. If migration propensities

---

[38] We saw previously that persons in their late teens and early twenties have a relatively high propensity to migrate and that the US population is highly mobile. Thus, a large number of the young persons in this sample who were living outside their state of birth could have moved with their parents. Consequently, some fraction of the repeat migrants could have been, for all practical purposes, primary migrants, but census data do not allow a cleaner distinction.

are higher for the unemployed, these propensities could correspondingly also decline with age. Schlottmann and Herzog find that for both the employed and unemployed, migration declines with age. They conclude that the "age selectivity of migration derives from factors other than an age-employment status phenomenon" (1981: p. 594).

To some extent, migration appears to be a function of the assets that a household has to cover the cost of moving. Lack of such assets may impede mobility. Thus, households whose head has been unemployed for some time may be less likely to move than those whose head has been recently unemployed. Not only are accumulated assets depleted during the period of unemployment, but also unemployment insurance benefits may expire. Using PSID data and analyzing the decision to migrate between 1977 and 1978, Goss and Schoening (1984) have specifically addressed this issue. In addition to a variable for the number of weeks that an unemployed worker has been searching for a job, Goss and Schoening include in their model variables for employment status, 1977 wage payments, years of education, age, prior migration, and home-ownership. The empirical results suggest that the probability of migrating declines with increased duration of unemployment. With US data from the Survey of Income and Program Participation (SIPP), Herzog et al. (1993) employ event history analysis and arrive at the same conclusion.

A factor complicating the relationship between local unemployment rates and migration is that as unemployment rates rise, relatively more individuals qualify for unemployment insurance benefits. Even if higher unemployment itself encourages more out-migration, increased unemployment insurance benefits may discourage it. This is the pattern observed empirically by Courchene (1970) for Canada and confirmed with microdata for Sweden by Harkman (1989). The relationship between unemployment duration and unemployment insurance benefits may also help explain Goss and Schoening's finding that the probability of migration decreases with increased duration of unemployment. Apparently microdata have not yet been used to study how the expiration, or impending expiration, of unemployment insurance benefits affect migration. Such a study would be worthwhile.

4.5.3. National unemployment

Much of the work on the relationship between national economic conditions and migration has concerned Canada (Milne, 1993), and especially Great Britain (Makower et al., 1939; Molho, 1984; Gordon, 1985; Pissarides and Wadsworth, 1989). Lack of good time-series data on migration has prevented the development of this area of research for the US, but a limited number of studies have appeared (Greenwood et al., 1986; Haurin and Haurin, 1988). Available evidence suggests that migration declines during national slumps and rises during recoveries (Makower et al., 1939; Molho, 1984; Gordon, 1985). However, for specific regions, the importance of the regional business cycle dominates that of the national cycle (Milne, 1993).

Swings in national economic conditions also help shape the propensity to migrate. Greenwood et al. (1986) show that when national employment is growing relatively rapidly in the US, the propensity to migrate in response to both employment and earnings opportunities is enhanced. Pissarides and Wadsworth (1989) demonstrate that in Great Britain the unemployed have a lower propensity to migrate when national unemployment is high.[39] Moreover, the impact of employed migrants on local jobs is greater when the national economy slumps (Greenwood et al., 1986), which may be due to the fact that during slumps migration is more highly selective of the best educated. A study that tracks the characteristics of migrants over the cycle would be worthwhile.

4.6. Personal characteristics and life-cycle forces in the decision to migrate

A number of life-cycle considerations are potentially important in an individual's or a family's decision to migrate. Among these are marriage, divorce, birth and aging of children, completion of schooling, military service, and retirement. Other personal characteristics, often related to the life cycle, are also potentially important. These circumstances include employment status, earnings, education, accumulated skills and training, job tenure, age, sex, and health.

4.6.1. Individual returns to migration

Because economists view expected utility differentials as the underlying motivating force for migration, and because these differentials are closely related to expected earnings or income, the questions of whether and to what extent migrants benefit economically from moving naturally arise. To address this question, the following simplified type of earnings model has been estimated:

$$\ln w = P\alpha + M\beta + (R\gamma) + \varepsilon, \tag{11}$$

where w is the hourly wage, P represents a vector of personal characteristics, including labor market experience; M is a vector of migration characteristics indicating migrant status, years since migration, and other features of migration discussed in more detail below; R is a vector of regional characteristics (placed in parentheses because it typically has not been included); and ε is the error term. Although many of the models

---

[39] Another possibility is apparent for the differences noted above in the responsiveness of the unemployed to local unemployment in the US compared to Europe. DaVanzo's (1978) PSID sample of migrants refers to 1971 and 1972 when the US was experiencing a major recovery, which could have enhanced the responsiveness of the unemployed to opportunities elsewhere.

discussed below differ in various ways from this model, Eq. (11) provides a good starting point for the discussion because it identifies the hypotheses of interest.

A number of potential problems may arise in the estimation of a model such as that given in Eq. (11). These problems include questions regarding the appropriate group of nonmigrants to use as the reference group, as well as a number of potential sources of bias in the estimated parameters, including selectivity bias.

Appropriate reference group. In assessing the monetary returns to migration, investigators have several choices regarding the reference-group earnings against which to compare those of the migrants: (1) the earnings of otherwise comparable individuals who remain in the origin locality; (2) the earnings the migrants would have made if they had not moved; (3) the earnings of those who stay in the origin locality if they had moved, and (4) the earnings of otherwise comparable individuals residing in the destination locality. The "outcome" of the migration decision, as measured by the investigator, could clearly be dependent upon which reference group is selected. A move that appears to be favorable from one perspective could well be unfavorable from the other. At least with respect to internal migration, those left behind at the origin have frequently been presumed to be the appropriate reference group. However, Morrison (1977) argues that "in making this comparison ... we cannot rule out the possibility that the migrant's advantage arises primarily from his access to a broader set of opportunities" (p. 65). He points out that one advantage of comparing migrants with otherwise comparable individuals at the destination is that at least the set of available opportunities is the same. DaVanzo and Hosek (1981) argue that the appropriate method is to compare post-move earnings of migrants with the earnings these individuals would have made had they not moved. They further argue that the earnings of otherwise comparable nonmigrants are not appropriate for this comparison. In practice, the appropriate reference group is shaped by the objective of the investigator and data availability, the latter of which frequently helps determine the former.

Some potential biases in estimation. The studies described above and others suggest that one of the most common findings derived from the estimation of migrant/nonmigrant earnings functions with microdata is that internal migrants tend to suffer earnings losses immediately after their move. This finding seems to hold for the US, Canada, and other countries. Furthermore, it holds whether migrants are compared with nonmigrants in the origin locality or with residents of the destination. The relationship is also true for international migrants, who are almost always benchmarked against residents of the destination. Several potential problems have been raised regarding the estimation of migrant earnings equations. Certain of these problems could cause a downward bias in estimates of the returns to migration, but certain of them could also cause an upward bias. Let us next consider some of these problems.

(1) The previous discussion of equilibrium forces in migration suggests that spatial earnings differentials are at least in part compensating differentials. Thus, measured earnings losses for internal migrants do not necessarily reflect lower utility for them. Amenity controls are almost never included in the earnings functions discussed in more

detail below.[40] Especially with many moves in the US occurring from high-wage, presumably amenity-poor areas of the North and East to relatively low-wage, presumably amenity-rich areas of the South and West, such factors should be given more attention.

(2) One possibility is that migrants give up "local capital" when they move. Some years are required to acquire an equivalent amount of local capital in the destination. Local capital may refer to many things, such as knowing one's way around the local job market, establishing contacts and references, owning a house, etc.

(3) Closely related to the concept of local capital is the notion that to the extent that migrants embody specific training and on-the-job experience, some part of their human capital is not transferable from firm to firm. Such individuals may require a catch-up period to make up for lost experience associated with a given job. Because many microdata sets do not include information on job tenure, it is often difficult to empirically pick up such effects, but this potentially could be a key determinant of the observation that migrants frequently suffer immediate earnings losses.[41]

(4) Some studies are based on data that have very limited time horizons of perhaps 5 years or less. Sizable returns to migration may accrue in the more-distant future, but these are not observed. Thus, measures of lifetime returns to migration are biased downward by the use of right-censored data that are too recent relative to the time of migration.

(5) The timing of the move could affect the subsequent returns to migration. That is, those who move during periods of high national unemployment may accept occupations that are not particularly well matched with their accumulated occupational skills, and they may also accept lower entry-level wage rates than otherwise. The effects of such decisions may linger for many years. Such "period effects" have not been given careful consideration in the context of estimates of the returns to internal migration. However, they have received some attention in the literature on US immigrant assimilation.

(6) Those who migrate more than once may have different earnings profiles than those who move only once. For example, new, return, and other repeat migrants appear to be influenced differently by the various determinants of migration. Not only may the determinants of migration differ by migrant type, but also the individual consequences may differ. If a person's local human capital does indeed affect the returns to migration, other things being equal, a return move should have a greater payoff

---

[40] Roback (1982, 1988) shows that the values of regional amenities are indeed embedded in regional earnings levels. She concludes that "the data strongly support the contention that utility income broadly measured to include amenities is equalized across regions. This in turn supports the claim that utility income is the most conceptually appropriate notion of income" (1988: p. 38).

[41] For example, Mincer and Jovanovic argue that their estimates "provide a complete though very rough decomposition of lifetime wage growth: about 25 percent of it is due to interfirm mobility; another 20–25 percent to firm-specific experience; and over 50 percent to general (transferable) experience" (1981: p. 43).

than an onward move. Moreover, the sooner the second move occurs, the greater this differential is likely to be.

Herzog et al. (1985) estimate separate earnings functions for primary and repeat migrants. These authors observe that repeat migrants are significantly older, better educated, and more concentrated in professional and technical occupations, and consequently have significantly higher earnings, than primary migrants, which is plausible. Moreover, using the logarithm of 1969 weekly earnings as their dependent variable, they find that repeat migrants "have significantly higher potential destination weekly earnings ($400.06 vs. $301.23)" (pp. 379–380) and that "among repeat migrants, potential earnings are also higher for those individuals choosing to move 'on' rather than 'back' ($415.11 vs. $365.79, respectively)" (p. 380).

Perhaps somewhat surprisingly, Herzog et al. find that in spite of embodying less human capital, primary migrants possess significantly more pre-move information than repeat migrants. In this study pre-move information is inferred from the error term in the earnings equation, where any shortfall of observed earnings below potential earnings is assumed to be due to incomplete information. Consequently, primary migrants have higher post-move reservation wages than otherwise comparable repeat migrants. Moreover, among repeat migrants, return migrants do not appear to have more pre-move information about post-move job search than those repeat migrants who move on. These investigators feel that their findings help explain earlier results that show return migrants to have lower expected earnings than nonreturn migrants (Kiker and Traynham, 1977).[42] They also claim that their results contradict the assertions of Kau and Sirmans (1977) and Miller (1973) that return migrants possess more and/or better knowledge than nonreturn migrants.

(7) Another possibility to explain the reduction in the post-move earnings of migrants relative to the benchmark group is that nonmonetary compensation plays an important role in many moves, but differences in nonpecuniary aspects of jobs in origins and destinations have not been given any attention in migrant earnings equations. Mathios (1989) shows that nonmonetary compensation is more important for more highly educated individuals. In his model, when he adds a vector of variables relating to job satisfaction (e.g., convenient hours, convenient location, job status, free time, liking for the job), for persons with 16 or more years of education, the adjusted R^2 in an earnings equations rises from 0.23 to 0.32 with an F-value of 12.6. Mathios argues that this relationship is plausible because better-educated, higher-income individuals "consume" more nonpecuniary job satisfaction than individuals with lower incomes, as long as job amenities are equivalent to normal consumption goods. Moreover, because marginal tax rates are positively related to income, but not to total compensa-

---

[42] Kiker and Traynham (1977) find that "in the year of out-migration, out-migrants who later return to the Southeast enjoy relatively greater earnings increases than do those who do not return. The relative improvement in the real earnings position of nonreturn migrant cohorts occurs only after the return migrants have moved back to the Southeast" (p. 4). These conclusions are based on data for the 1960s drawn from the Social Security One Percent Continuous Work History Sample.

tion (including nonpecuniary job attributes), a tax effect reinforces this income effect.[43]

Another factor of potential importance is state and local taxes, as well as variables relating to local public spending and its mix (Day, 1992).[44] Migrant earnings functions are frequently estimated with pretax earnings as the dependent variable and no controls for state and local taxes or public spending and its mix in the new locality relative to the old. Such functions should include these types of variables so as to better control for real consumption wages.

(8) Alfred Marshall in his *Principles of Economics* states that "the large towns and especially London absorb the very best blood from all the rest of England; the most enterprising, the most highly gifted, those with the highest *physique* and strongest characters go there to find scope for their abilities" (1948: p. 199). Presumably, by examining the earnings of otherwise comparable individuals who do not migrate, we take into account what an individual would have earned had he or she not moved. However, Morrison (1977) points out that whether migrants are compared with other individuals in the destination or those left behind in the origin, ambiguity remains: "whether the act of migration, by freeing an individual's energies, leads to subsequent observed improvements in his life; or whether, as a prism separates light, the act is merely selective of certain persons who would have improved their status irrespective of the decision to migrate" (p. 65). This is the issue of sample selection bias. Because this type of bias has the potential to play an important role in efforts to estimate the returns to migration, it requires a more detailed discussion.

Sources of sample selection problems. Sample selection problems arise from situations in which a population subgroup is not representative of the entire population whose behavior is under study. Stated more formally, the problem is one "of estimating a regression $E(y \mid x)$ when realizations of (y, x) are sampled randomly but y is observed selectively" (Manski, 1989: p. 343). Some unobservable variable may distinguish population subgroups. The natural temptation is to analyze only the subgroup for which data are available, but this procedure may result in parameter estimates tainted by "selectivity bias". Thus, if Eq. (11) were estimated by ordinary least squares with only those observations for which the dependent variable is measured, the resulting parameter estimates would be inconsistent.

Sample selection problems have many opportunities to arise in migration studies. Four sources are most likely to cause these problems: (1) sampling design/population

---

[43] Marginal tax rates are most relevant when an individual is moving up or down the income distribution. However, when the individual is moving across space and taking his/her income from one tax system to another, the average effective tax rate seems most relevant.

[44] Fox et al. (1989) and Herzog and Schlottmann (1986) use microdata to examine the influence of variables relating to the local public sector on migration. Several such variables prove to be significant determinants of individual migration. See Winer and Gauthier (1982) for a detailed study relating to Canada.

coverage, (2) panel attrition, (3) time-dependent disturbances, and (4) differential behavioral responses. The last of these is the typical source of sample selection bias.

(1) *Sampling design/population coverage.* The first possible problem originates in the data used to study migration. Due to sampling design or, if the data are from an administrative source, population coverage, the data may not be representative of the entire population. For example, migration data derived from US Internal Revenue Service files are selective of those with sufficiently high incomes that they are required to file an income tax return. Annual migration data for Canada derived from the Family Allowance System are selective of families with children. Many similar examples are available. This type of data shortcoming does not cause the usual sample selectivity problem, which refers to bias in the estimation of certain parameters. Rather, it leads to an inability to generalize from accurately estimated parameters.

(2) *Panel attrition.* Over time some attrition is almost certain to occur within any panel. Families move and are difficult or impossible to trace. Others do not wish to put up with the effort of being interviewed repeatedly. For others, payments to participants in the panel may become insufficient. Even though the lost panel members may be replaced with seemingly otherwise comparable individuals and families, systematic differences may well exist between those who remain in the panel and those who drop out. This will cause bias when the attrition is correlated with the dependent variables in migration studies. Some unobservable differences may distinguish the groups, such as attitudes in general or attitudes toward risk. An advantage of panel data is that fixed-effect estimates may remove this source of bias. Any investigator who uses panel data sets such as the PSID and the NLS should study what is known about panel attrition in the data set and understand how attrition problems might affect the particular study under consideration.[45]

(3) *Time-dependent selectivity problems.* A third potential source of sample-selection problems also arises from the data, but specifically from the time period of the sample. Time-dependent selectivity problems occur when migrants from different periods are compared. The idea is that the model applies over a span of years, but the disturbance term is time dependent (and perhaps a function of some latent, unobservable variable). Although this type of selectivity problem may occur in many contexts, two are particularly relevant to migration:

(a) *Secular problems.* The education and training received by individuals during one period may differ from the education and training received during a later period. Thus, estimates of the monetary returns to different cohorts of migrants may be tainted. This type of bias may be especially important in the study of the returns to different cohorts of immigrants, who may differ systematically not only in education, training, and other personal characteristics, but also in the self-selective nature of their decision to migrate.

---

[45] See, for example, Becketti et al. (1988).

(b) *Cyclical problems*. Little or no research has directly addressed the issue of changes in migrant quality over the business cycle, but such changes should occur. Migrants tend to be self-selected in the sense that they are typically of greater innate ability and possess greater motivation for personal achievement than otherwise comparable nonmigrants.[46] The self-selective nature of the migration decision should be more pronounced the greater the costs of migration, including the probability of finding a job and the costs of subsequent adjustment in the new occupational environment. During periods of relatively poor economic conditions, as indicated by slow national growth of job opportunities, the costs associated with migration are higher. These higher costs are due to more intensive job search activities, since access to entry-level jobs, as well as jobs providing specific skill training, is more difficult. On the contrary, during periods of more rapid national economic expansion, the probability of gaining access to jobs is increased and, consequently, the costs of migration are lower. Since the costs associated with migration are expected to be lower during a period of economic expansion, a lower degree of self-selection occurs in periods of relatively good economic conditions. In other words, when economic conditions are generally favorable, the average quality of the migrant flow is relatively lower. This lower quality may be manifested in labor force participation patterns or work motivation, as well as by general skill level. Virtually no research has ever addressed these issues.

(4) *Differential behavioral responses*. The fourth potential source of a selectivity problem is also behavioral and is analogous to the classic selectivity bias that motivated Heckman (1976), following Roy (1951), Lewis (1963, 1974) and Gronau (1974), to write about the problem. Heckman's concern dealt with the relationship between wage levels and female labor force participation. In the migration context at least three types of self-selection may occur:

(a) Persons who migrate may be selective of those individuals with the most favorable opportunities, as suggested by Marshall (1948). Rational economic agents select their chosen alternative because they have some basis for believing that it will yield a higher return than their other options. Consequently, those individuals who select a given alternative are not randomly drawn from the population as a whole. The fact that individual A migrates, whereas otherwise comparable B does not, suggests that an important difference exists between the individuals. These differences may be in the way they view costs. The differences may also be in the way they view future benefits, and therefore could be due to differences in discount rates. Individual A, for example, may be more highly motivated to invest in human capital formation, not only in migration, but in other forms as well. If such were the case, the earnings of the remaining cohort from which the migrant is drawn

---

[46] Chiswick (1978), for example, has shown that after several years most US immigrants catch and thereafter surpass the earnings of otherwise similar native-born Americans. Qualitatively similar results have been reported concerning US internal migration (Borjas et al., 1992a).

may not provide an accurate estimate of the earnings the migrant would have received in the absence of migration.[47] The resulting selectivity bias, if not properly taken into account, poses potentially serious problems in econometric attempts to estimate the returns to migration. Lewis (1974) points out that due to this type of problem the returns to nonmigrants are also biased.

(b) Among those who migrate, some stay in the new place whereas others move back to the origin or move on to a third location. If those who move back or move on are the economically least successful migrants, then the remaining migrants will bias upward any estimate of the returns to migration. The selectivity bias problem as associated with the remigration phenomenon is raised by Yezer and Thurston: "The departure of unsuccessful migrants from a destination leaves a residual of successful lifetime migrants. Calculation of the returns to migrations based on these individuals alone results in an upward bias" (1976: p. 702).[48] Although remigration selectivity is potentially important in assessing the returns to internal migration, it seems especially relevant in estimating the returns to international migration because the presumably less successful immigrants who later leave are lost completely from any data collection system in the original country of immigration.

(c) Individuals may sort themselves based on their productivity. Roy (1951) discussed such self-selection in terms of occupations (hunting and fishing), but the same argument can be made for region of residence as well as for occupation (Borjas et al., 1992b). The sorting could be based on the individual's absolute advantage in a region (and occupation) or on his comparative advantage, but the basic idea is that he would locate in the region and work in the occupation that yields the highest expected relative earnings.

Empirically accounting for sample selection bias. The effects of sample selection bias are similar to those caused by left-out variables. Controlling for these left-out variables yields consistent estimates. Although a number of econometric procedures are available to accomplish this control (Maddala, 1983), a frequently used approach is to estimate a first-stage (structural) probit in order to form an estimate of the missing expectations in the earnings equation. In the migration context, an exam-

---

[47] In the case stated here, the estimated returns are upward biased. However, Robinson and Tomes (1982) point out that this position implicitly assumes that one type of motivation (i.e., ability) is useful in every location. If the comparative advantage of various individuals differs for different jobs in different regions, self-selection could cause estimated returns to migration that are either biased upward or downward.

[48] In a comment on the Yezer and Thurston paper, DaVanzo (1977) argues that "differences between estimated returns to lifetime migration and recent migration are ... more likely to be due to unmeasured differences in the characteristics of 'lifetime' and 'recent' migrants, or to adjustments the migrants undergo after moving, than to a selectivity bias caused by the subsequent migration of disappointed migrants" (p. 391). Her reason for taking this position is that most return and repeat migration occurs relatively soon after the initial move, and therefore many such migrants will not even be picked up by census data that relate to a five-year interval.

ple of this probit would be to estimate a regression to predict migrant status (i.e., migrant/nonmigrant). A practical difficulty is identifying the earnings equation.

Empirical approaches to sample selection bias in migration studies can conveniently be grouped into two types of models: (1) two-region models, which may be models of (a) single selection, or (b) double selection; (2) multi-region models. The models are "two-region" models in the sense that the relevant regimes place the migrant in one region or somewhere else. This is the case, for example, when the regimes are "migrant" and "non-migrant" (or "mover" and "stayer"). These models sometimes are estimated separately with a number of different regions as the "base" region (Robinson and Tomes, 1982). The population is frequently disaggregate in some way, such as by labor market experience (Robinson and Tomes, 1982), age (Islam and Choudhury, 1990), or by whether the individuals made some other type change, such as an industry shift (Islam, 1985). Double-selection models distinguish those who move once (primary migrants) from those who move more than once (repeat migrants). Due to the greater econometric complexity, this type of model has been estimated rarely. Tunali's (1986) work on Turkey entails a model with double selection.

Empirical findings. Empirical studies aimed at assessing the monetary returns to migration can usefully be distinguished as those based on nonlongitudinal microdata and those based on longitudinal microdata (Antel, 1980). Findings based on aggregate data (Gallaway, 1969; Cox, 1971) are not discussed here.

Antel (1980) points out that studies based on nonlongitudinal microdata, which he refers to as "cross-sectional" studies, are characterized by two types of models:

$$w_i = \alpha_0 + \alpha_1 X_i + \alpha_2 M_{it} + \alpha_3 X_i \cdot M_i + (\alpha_4 + \lambda_i) + \varepsilon, \tag{12}$$

$$w_i = \beta_0 + \beta_1 X_i + \beta_2 D_i + \beta_3 O_i + (\beta_4 \lambda_i') + \varepsilon_i. \tag{13}$$

Here w_i is wage or earnings, X_i is a vector of personal characteristics (e.g., age, education, race), M_i is a dummy variable for migrant status, D_i is a dummy for current region of residence, O_i is a dummy for previous region of residence, perhaps region of birth, and λ_i and λ_i' are selectivity corrections, which may or may not be included in the estimated relationship. A mixed approach is also possible, where in Eq. (12) dummy variables are introduced for specific types of moves, such as rural to urban (possibly by various population sizes of the origin and destination region) and South to North.

The key difference between Eqs. (12) and (13) is that in Eq. (12) migrant status appears, whereas in Eq. (13) controls for destination and origin appear, but no migration indicator per se. In Eq. (12) migrants are benchmarked against nonmigrants. In Eq. (13) otherwise comparable persons in other regions are used as the control group. Antel points out that in Eq. (12) the economic performance of migrants and nonmigrants is in opposite directions. If migrants are gainers, nonmigrants must be losers.

However, in Eq. (13) economic performance is assessed in terms of region of current residence, where the control is the origin region. Early studies neither used the semi-log form of the model that has become standard procedure more recently, nor did they provide any corrections for selectivity bias.[49]

Proper estimation of individual returns to migration require microdata. One of the first studies to use this type of data to analyze such returns is Lansing and Morgan (1967), who use a model similar to Eq. (12) to compare the earnings of US migrants with those of nonmigrants in the receiving locality. They conclude that migrants in general tend to have lower earnings than nonmigrants.[50] Because more educated persons tend both to have higher earnings and to be migrants, these investigators hold education constant by stratifying their sample, but still conclude that the annual earnings of migrants are no higher than those of nonmigrants. The appropriate comparisons to make, argue Lansing and Morgan, are not those between migrants and nonmigrants in a given locality, but rather those between migrants from a given locality and otherwise similar individuals who have remained behind. To perform such a comparison, they estimate a regression for hourly earnings of heads of spending units who worked during 1959 as a function of a number of control variables (e.g., education, age, gender, race) and several dummy variables for different types of moves that indicate where or what type of place an individual grew up relative to where or what type of place he/she now lives. Based on their regression results and a comparison between migrants and those left behind, these investigators conclude that two of the historically dominant migration streams in the US have been profitable for the movers – movement out of the Deep South and movement off the farm.

Lansing and Morgan conjecture that the reason that persons who grew up in low-income localities may be at a permanent disadvantage relative to those who grew up in higher-income localities is that the quality of education received in the low-income localities may be correspondingly low. This view is similar to that expressed in the Coleman Report (Coleman et al., 1966: p. 41). However, Weiss and Williamson (1972), using a model like Eq. (13), conclude that inferiority of southern black schools can be discounted as a cause of poverty among black migrants to the North. Moreover, they argue that the overall effect of either northern or southern urban ghetto environments may be more harmful to blacks than a rural southern background.

---

[49] A semi-log functional form is often used to estimate wage or earnings equations, in part because earnings tend to be skewed to the right, due to the fact that earnings cannot be negative. Logging the dependent variable tends to make it normally distributed, which is usually a desirable property for estimation purposes. Moreover, as noted by Mincer (1974) and others, human capital theory implies an upward sloping and concave earnings–experience profile under the assumption that on-the-job training declines over one's working life. Concavity of the earnings profile is enhanced by the semi-log functional form.

[50] The data upon which this study was based were drawn from two national surveys conducted by the Survey Research Center at the University of Michigan, the first in 1960 and the second in 1965. Detailed data references are provided in Lansing and Morgan (1967).

Masters (1972) was one of the first to use the Public Use Microdata Sample (PUMS) of the US Census to study this issue. He adopts an approach similar to that of Lansing and Morgan along the lines of Eq. (12), comparing black in-migrants with black nonmigrants at the destination. He finds that lifetime male migrants from the US South to northern cities are better off than male nonmigrants residing in northern cities, although recent migrants generally fare worse than nonmigrants. Masters reports (without presenting his results) that when he compares black migrants with blacks who stayed behind, the net effect of migration, holding education constant, is to increase earnings by 15 to 20%.

A number of other studies have specifically examined migration from the South and migration off the farm. While all are not in agreement with the conclusions of Lansing and Morgan and of Masters that migrants are better off than those left behind, most are in agreement. Among the dissenters is Niemi (1973), who concludes that migration of blacks from the South offered little financial return, while migration of southern blacks to Atlanta offered potentially sizable returns. Laber (1972), on the other hand, finds that both blacks and whites benefit from migration out of the Southeast.

Along with Lansing and Morgan (1967) and Masters (1972), Wertheimer (1970) was one of the first to employ microdata to estimate an earnings function for migrants. In his study, which is similar in form to Eq. (12), he uses microdata from the Survey of Economic Opportunity to assess the returns to both South-to-North and rural-to-urban migration. He concludes that five years after moving, migrants have earnings equal to those of northern and urban nonmovers of the same education, age, race, and sex. Wertheimer estimates that most migrants who left the South earned approximately $800 per year more than they would have earned had they remained in the South. An interesting aspect of Wertheimer's findings is that this $800 per year earnings differential breaks down to no gain for the first five years after migrating, $1000 per year for the next 30 years, and $350 per year after that.[51] If Wertheimer is correct, migrants must have accepted immediate earnings cuts for greater growth of future earnings.[52] This type of finding has been common when a formal human capital approach has been employed to estimate the monetary returns to migration.

In addition to migrant earnings functions that have been estimated with microdata for the US, similar functions have been estimated for other developed and developing

---

[51] Master's (1972) results provide some confirmation of Wertheimer's in that he finds that recent black migrants from the South to northern cities fare worse than black nonmigrants in northern cities, but lifetime black migrants fare somewhat better than nonmigrants.

[52] Iden (1974) uses the same data set as Wertheimer to examine essentially the same issues. His conclusions are very similar, indicating "pronounced racial differences in the returns from migration. White migrants to southern metropolitan areas experienced higher earnings than their counterparts who migrated north. Nonwhites who migrated from the South earned substantially more than their counterparts who migrated to the urban South. Within the South, both white and nonwhite male migrants experienced the highest earnings in cities of intermediate size. Among migrants who left the South, whites earned more in large cities than in less urbanized areas, while the reverse was true for nonwhites" (pp. 177–178).

countries, such as Canada, Turkey (Tunali, 1986), and Venezuela (Falaris, 1987). In many respects the empirical findings for these countries are remarkably similar to those for the US.

For example, Marr and Millerd (1980) use microdata from the 1971 Canadian census to examine what they believe to be longer-term returns to migration, also using a model form like Eq. (12). Their definition of a migrant is somewhat different than that used in other studies, namely, anyone who in 1971 was living in a province different than that in which he or she received the highest level of schooling. It is this definition that Marr and Millerd feel allows them to interpret their empirical findings as reflecting long-term returns to migration. They estimate a standard earnings equation and conclude that interprovincial migrants received $532 more in 1971 than otherwise comparable nonmigrants. The $532 gain is statistically significant, but Marr and Millerd appropriately point out that they do not know whether the difference is due to migration or to unobservable characteristics of the migrants. Moreover, they examine migrants defined as individuals who changed provinces between 1966 and 1971 but did not return to the province where they completed their schooling. When these migrants are compared with individuals who in 1966 and 1971 lived in the same province as they finished school, Marr and Millerd find no significant return to migration. Thus, they conclude that positive returns to migration require a period of time. None of these early studies accounted for potential selectivity problems.

Nakosteen and Zimmer (1980, 1982) were among the first to provide selectivity-controlled estimates of the returns to migration. They use a switching regression model with endogenous switching. Their results provide evidence of selectivity bias in US data, but their use of the Social Security Continuous Work History Sample severely limited their ability to estimate a properly specified model. For example, they were unable to include education in their regressions.

A number of studies concerned with the US have, however, failed to uncover selectivity bias. Two examples are DaVanzo and Hosek (1981) and Borjas et al. (1992a). In certain studies selectivity bias may fail to appear because earnings are studied too soon after migration (DaVanzo and Hosek, 1981). Another potential problem is that the first-stage probit almost never contains information about alternative destinations for the potential migrant, which implicitly assumes that an individual is able to determine whether to migrate apart from where he or she might go. The failure to include such variables in the first-stage probit may make the predictions that come from it less precise, which in turn could obscure estimates in the second-stage regressions and result in a failure to reject the null of zero selection bias.

Several studies using Canadian data do, however, uncover evidence of selectivity bias. One of the most detailed studies to date of the selectivity bias issue is that by Robinson and Tomes (1982), who analyze microdata from the 1971 Canadian census. They follow the two-stage procedure suggested by Heckman (1976), where the first stage consists of estimating a reduced-form probit equation to correct their earnings equations for selectivity bias. The significance of the coefficient on the correction term is a measure of the degree of this bias. Their estimates are performed separately for each of two experience groups (5–20 years experience, 20 or more years experience) and each origin province. For the less-experienced group, their estimate of the sample selection bias term is generally negative, which suggests that "the people who actually moved out of origin b earned more, ceteris paribus, in their destination than the stayers in origin b would have done had they also moved" (1982: p. 491). For the more experienced group, no clear pattern of signs emerged. Perhaps more importantly, they argue that "the coefficient on the expected wage gain variable proved to be very sensitive to whether we correct for selection bias in estimating wage equations for movers and stayers" (1982: p. 497). That is, when these researchers ignored selectivity, they failed to measure a significant effect of potential wage gain on migration, but when they corrected for sample-selection bias, they found that potential wage gains significantly affected individual migration decisions. Islam (1985) and Islam and Choudhury (1990) also provide evidence of selectivity bias in Canadian data. The latter paper concludes that in the absence of a selectivity correction the income gains to migration are underestimated.

Models estimated with longitudinal microdata have generally taken one of the following forms:

$$w_{i,t} - w_{i,t-1} = a_0 + a_1 X_{i,t} + a_2 M_{i,t} + a_3 w_{i,t-1} + u_i, \tag{14}$$

$$w_{i,t} = b_0 + b_1 X_{i,t} + b_2 M_{i,t} + b_3 w_{i,t-1} + v_i, \tag{15}$$

$$\ln w_{i,t} = c_0 + c_1 X_{i,t} + \gamma_1 E_{i,t} + \gamma_2 E_{i,t}^2 + \delta_0 M_{i,t} + \delta_1 M_{i,t} \cdot T + \delta_2 M_{i,t} \cdot T^2 + (\sigma_1 \lambda_i'') + z_i. \tag{16}$$

Eq. (14) represents change in earnings or in the wage rate. Another form of this equation expresses $w_{i,t}$ as a function of $w_{i,t-1}$ and other variables, but does not difference on the left-hand side of the regression equation (Eq. (15)). Since in Eq. (14) earnings are typically differenced over a fairly short period of time, such as a year or two, the findings are best interpreted as short run. Moreover, since the emphasis of Eq. (14) is on changes from one period to another, the independent variables frequently are expressed as changes also. For example, change in marital status and change in employer are commonly used dummy variables that appear in regressions like Eq. (14).

In one sense, specifications similar to Eq. (14) have an econometric advantage. The differencing tends to eliminate (or control for, as in Eq. (15)) any individual fixed effects that are reflected in the error terms of regressions such as Eq. (12) that are based on nonlongitudinal data. These fixed effects could be correlated with various unobserved factors that affect the individual's propensity to migrate, such as ability, attitudes toward risk, and other factors that lead to selectivity problems in regressions like Eqs. (12) and (13). As a consequence, specifications (14) and (15) are not typically estimated with a selectivity correction.

Borrowing an approach that has been successfully implemented in the study of immigrant assimilation and applying it to internal US migration, Borjas et al. (1992a) set up a model like Eq. (16), where w is the hourly wage, X represents a vector of personal characteristics, E is labor market experience, M is a dummy variable distinguishing migrants from nonmigrants in the destination, T is years since migration, and z_i the error term. The basic idea underlying this model is that experience is not perfectly transferable between regions, which should result in a negative sign on δ_0, which indicates the migrant–nonmigrant earnings differential at the time of migration. If a period of catch-up occurs during which migrant earnings approach those of otherwise comparable individuals at the destination, δ_1 will have a positive sign. If the convergence of migrant and nonmigrant earnings slows with duration of the migrant's residence in the destination, δ_2 will have a negative sign.

Grant and Vanderkamp (1980) employ longitudinal microdata for the period 1965–1971 to estimate earnings functions like that in Eq. (15) for Canada. The dependent variable refers to 1971 (log) income (or alternatively earnings). According to Grant and Vanderkamp, the returns to early migrants are slightly positive, but those to more recent migrants are negative. Early long-distance migrants do slightly better than early short-distance migrants, but recent long-distance migrants suffer greater losses than recent short-distance migrants. These investigators speculate that long-distance migration involves more uncertainty, and consequently a transition period is required to catch up with and pass those who move over short distances.

Another important finding that supports Mincer's (1978) theory, which is described below, is that among long-distance migrants single males do the best, whereas married females suffer fairly large losses. Grant and Vanderkamp conclude that "the testing process and final estimates show that it is very difficult to detect a significantly positive effect of migration on income within a five-year time horizon. Within the first few years after a move there appears to be a strong negative impact of migration on the earnings level" (1980: p. 398). They go on to conclude that "the empirical results provide only weak support for the human capital model" (p. 400). Several additional studies that employ specifications (14) and (15) and relate to the US are discussed below in connection with family migration.

A number of more recent studies concerning US migration have also appeared. Many of these have partitioned the migrant population in one way or another, such as according to whether the move was a primary (presumably first-time) move or a repeat move (which is often distinguished as being a return or an onward move), as well as by gender and race (Krieg, 1990). Moreover, as noted above, the same type of approach that has been applied to immigrant assimilation has recently been applied to the earnings of young internal migrants in the US Using the 1970–1986 waves of the National Longitudinal Survey of Youth (NLSY), Borjas et al. (1992a) show that migrants initially earn 10% less than natives but catch up in about six years. When return migrants are eliminated from the sample, the initial disadvantage is about 11%, but the catch-up period is only three years. These authors also show that long-distance (interregional) migrants experience an initial disadvantage about twice that of short-distance (intraregional) migrants. Moreover, among interregional migrants those who moved to states with zero employment growth between 1980 and 1986 earned 22% less than otherwise comparable natives during their first two years in the new location, but those who moved to states whose employment grew by 32% over the same period experienced no disadvantage relative to natives. The earnings disadvantage may be less for those who move over short distances and to fast-growing areas because uncertainty is less, but the exact reason for the observation is not tested.

Sample selection does not appear to have been a problem in the Borjas et al. study. These authors report that their selection variable was not significant in the various second-stage regressions in which it was included. The inclusion of variables to control for compensating differentials would be an advance in estimating models like Eq. (16), but the application of the models of immigrant assimilation to internal migration is an advance in itself.

4.6.2. Family and life-cycle considerations

Based on a survey of 3991 household heads, 723 of whom were involved in a move during the last five years prior to the survey in the early 1960s, Lansing and Mueller (1967: p. 126) report that 24% of the most recent moves entailed a family reason. For example, 12% of the moves were to be closer to other family members, 4% due to health considerations, 3% due to marriage, and 2% due to divorce or separation. Moreover, 42% of return moves included a family reason, compared to 20% of other moves.[53]

Given their pivotal importance in research concerning the determinants of migration, life-cycle forces have been given far too little attention. Partly in connection with the development of microdata and the application of econometric techniques appropriate for their analysis, greater emphasis has been placed on various life-cycle and familial factors.

The influence of family ties on migration has been specifically analyzed by Mincer (1978), who shows that such ties result in negative personal externalities that are usually internalized by the family and that thus tend to discourage migration. "Tied persons" in the family are "those whose gains from migration are (in absolute value) dominated by gains (or losses) of the spouse" (p. 753). Presuming that their joint net returns to migrating from i to j exceed their joint net costs of migrating, a husband-wife family would presumably migrate from i to j. If, for example, the wife's expected earnings in j were less than in i, but the husband's were sufficiently greater in j than in i to offset these losses, the wife would be a "tied mover". On the other hand, if the husband's earnings gain in j were to fail to offset his wife's earnings loss in i, the couple would remain in i, and the husband would be a "tied stayer". Moreover, ac-

---

[53] Using data from the Annual Housing Surveys, Long and Hansen (1979) provide more recent detail that is roughly similar to that reported by Lansing and Mueller.

cording to Mincer such ties tend to reduce the employment and earnings of those wives who do migrate and to increase the employment and earnings of their husbands. Mincer goes on to show that increased labor force participation rates of women cause an increase in migration ties, which results in both less migration and more marital instability. Increased marital instability in turn encourages migration as well as increased women's labor force participation. More recently, Mont (1989) applies a search-theoretic approach to family migration decisions.

Several testable hypotheses emerge from Mincer's work. First, husband–wife families are less likely to migrate than unattached individuals. Second, when husband–wife families move, the husband's earnings will generally improve, but the wife, who is usually a tied mover, will work less and have lower earnings. Mincer's hypotheses regarding "second round" effects of increased female labor force participation on migration have apparently not been tested to date. That is, we do not know if increased female labor force participation initially results in less migration and more marital instability, with increased marital instability in turn resulting in increased female labor force participation and more migration. Long (1974) shows that much movement over both short and long distances is connected with marriage and establishment of households, but after these events married men are more residentially stable than unmarried men. Moreover, with the exception of 20–24-year-old men, those with working wives had lower rates of interstate movement than those with nonworking wives. However, those with working wives were more likely to move within a county. Long concludes that "having a wife who works may inhibit long-distance movement but appears to promote short-distance movement" (1974: p. 344). One problem with Long's findings, which he notes and addresses, is that employment status is defined at the end of the migration interval and could therefore be influenced by the movement that occurred.

Long's data indicate that a wife's labor force participation reduces the probability of family migration. If migration occurs, it reduces the wife's labor force participation. Does the wife's reduced labor force participation increase the probability of return or other repeat migration? This issue has apparently not been studied in the context of primary, return, and other repeat migration and would be interesting to address.

Some of the observed income differences between men and women could be due to career interruptions experienced by women when they move with their husbands. Wives may not be in a position to further their careers through migration in the same way that men do. Moreover, the career choices of women may be affected by the anticipation of migration. Long feels that women may choose occupations that are more easily transferable between regions, such as elementary school teaching, nursing, and secretarial work.[54]

---

[54] This point is similar to that made by McDowell (1982) in connection with academic women. McDowell argues that because they may anticipate a career interruption, due for example to child-bearing, academic women choose fields of specialization in which knowledge obsolescence is slow. After measuring the rate of knowledge obsolescence in different academic disciplines by observing the citation decay rate, he finds considerable empirical support for his hypothesis.

What is it about moves over longer distances that reduces the labor force participation of wives? The answer seems potentially to lie in one or more of three factors: (a) the characteristics of the wives and their families and any changes that might occur in these characteristics; (b) the characteristics of the places of origin and destination and any differences that might exist in these; and (c) information relevant to job search that is more costly to acquire at more distant locations. Some combination of these factors could also be responsible. For instance, better-educated individuals tend to move over greater distances. However, since better-educated women tend to have higher labor force participation rates, this factor should work against the observed relationship. Apparently no one has sought to determine whether better-educated wives experience less severe drops in their labor force participation as distance rises.

Factor (b) seems the least likely to provide an answer to the question posed above. Factor (c) appears to have more promise. Many of the intercounty, intrastate moves studied by Long could involve neighboring counties where job-market information is considerably cheaper to acquire than that relating to another state. If the wife tends to be a tied mover, her job search may be postponed until after the family is settled in its new location. However, we would expect that if, due to the move, fundamental changes did not occur in the underlying determinants of the wife's participation decision, eventually her participation would return to its initial level. It would be of great interest to know if wives who reduce their labor force participation immediately after a move eventually resume their participation, as well as the time and pace of the resumption.

In support of Mincer (1978), Graves and Linneman (1979) also find that the probability of moving is negatively related to marital status. However, Bartel's (1979) results do not reflect a strong marriage effect on migration. In her numerous regressions, her variable for marital status is almost always negative, but almost never significant.[55] Van Dijk et al. (1989) obtain a negative but insignificant effect for US couples without children, but a very strong negative effect associated with presence of children. For the Netherlands each variable is negative and significant. At least for the US, this finding demonstrates the need to include a variable for presence of children in the regression.[56]

---

[55] Bartel considers each individual as facing six probabilities (migrate and quit (P_1), migrate and be laid off (P_2), migrate and keep job (P_3), not migrate and quit (P_4), not migrate and be laid off (P_5), and not migrate and keep job (P_6)). Amemiya (1981) argues that "Bartel ignored the multivariate nature (as well as the multi-response nature) of the data and estimated each of the five probabilities P_1 thought P_5 separately by the univariate, dichotomous logit ML estimator" (p. 1526). Consequently, her procedure could result in the five estimated probabilities exceeding unity; moreover, she does not account for the correlation between the five dependent variables. Finally, Amemiya points out that if the work decision comes before the migration decision, a sequential model would be required.

[56] Bartel (1979) includes children in her regressions, but the variable is rarely significant in spite of the fact that she uses three data sets that pick up men at different ages that cover most of the working life. These findings may be due to her use of school-aged children only.

Sandell (1977), using a model like Eq. (15) above, provides further empirical evidence in support of Mincer's position. He shows that the wife's labor-market orientation is an important determinant of family migration decisions. Families with an employed wife have a significantly lower probability of migrating, as predicted by Mincer. Moreover, the wife's increased job tenure further reduces the probability of migrating. Family migration probabilities increase with the husband's education and decrease with his age. Migration tends to increase the earnings of the husband and to initially decrease those of the wife, but family earnings rise. This initial decrease in the wife's earnings is only temporary, however, and is in part due to a decrease in weeks worked.[57]

Also studying wage change with a specification like Eq. (14), Bartel (1979) stresses the importance of distinguishing between job transfers, quits, and lay-offs. Migration in connection with a job transfer benefits men in their twenties and thirties. Migration in connection with a quit benefits only young men. DaVanzo and Hosek (1981) corroborate Bartel's finding that the largest wage gains are enjoyed by those who migrate and stay with the same employer.

DaVanzo (1976a) finds that families with unemployed heads who are looking for work have a higher probability of migrating over a long distance (interdivisionally) than those with an employed head who is seeking a new job. DaVanzo (1978) also finds that families with heads who are unemployed but looking for a different job are highly responsive to the present value of wage differences. Families with heads who are employed but not looking for a different job are unresponsive to opportunities elsewhere. For families with an unemployed head, the income effect is negative, meaning that an increase in income due, for example, to a subsidy of some sort, will have the result of causing these families to stay rather than move.

Migration frequently occurs in connection with a change in life-cycle circumstances, such as at the completion of one's college education, at the time of marriage, and soon after retirement. Thus, examining the relationship between a given life-cycle characteristic and migration may obscure the relationship between changes in life-cycle characteristics and migration. Graves and Linneman (1979) and Linneman and Graves (1983), for example, provide evidence that changes in family composition, changes in family income, and changes in the family head's education all positively influence the probability of migration.[58]

---

[57] Antel (1980) indicates two problems with Sandell's study. First, his dependent variable is earnings change over the 1967–1971 period. The migration interval also includes 1971, which for some observations could include pre-move earnings. Second, Sandell does not distinguish his migrant groups as clearly as he might have because he fails to specifically identify moves that were both multiple and intrafirm.

[58] Hunt (1993) appropriately expresses caution about the findings of these studies because very few migrants are included in the sample. Of 1937 observations, only about 40 involved a move across a county line, half with a job change and half without one. Many studies based on microdata do not report the number of migratory moves, so it is difficult or impossible to determine the size of the sub-sample upon which the findings are based.

Employing the NLS panels of young men and young women, Maxwell (1988) provides direct evidence that changing marital status affects the returns to migration. She estimates an earnings function like Eq. (15), but introduces several innovative terms, such as whether an individual was married, separated, or remained married during the migration period. She also interacts these terms with migration status. She concludes that female migrants who remained married and who were presumably tied movers, suffer substantial earnings losses immediately upon migration. However, female nonmigrants who remained married and were presumably tied stayers, also suffer immediate losses, but these losses increase sharply over time, whereas the losses of the otherwise comparable migrants decline over time. Whether they migrate or not, divorce does not appear to affect the earnings of women, but for men the results are different. Three years after migrating, men who divorced earn considerably more, but after the same period those who do not migrate earn somewhat less. Maxwell speculates that nonmigrating, divorced men may be analogous to tied stayers, perhaps due to the presence of children in the area.

Time-varying household characteristics may be important determinants of migration not only in the current period, but also in the prior and following periods. Krumm and Kelly (1988) argue that focus on a single period may produce response estimates that are questionable. Their multinominal logistic parameter estimates indicate that the duration of certain household characteristics is important in the decision to migrate, and not simply their presence or absence. In the model developed by Krumm and Kelly these points are nicely illustrated by an increase in family size, which perhaps contrary to expectations results in a slight decline in migration responses. This finding appears to be due to families anticipating the need for more housing before actually realizing an increase in family size. Thus, before additional children arrive, they have moved into housing that accommodates their needs.

The empirical studies noted above have an important limitation. Migration is defined over a given period of time, and consequently the importance of life-cycle variables is assessed within a cross-sectional framework. A more complete treatment of life-cycle effects requires that migration be studied as an event that occurs in continuous time. Longitudinal data allow the development of an event history for an individual or family. Although some years ago DaVanzo (1982) wrote about event history analysis of migration data, this type of analysis has been slower to gain a foothold in migration research than in other areas of economic demography.

Few migration histories that allow event history analysis have been constructed. However, one of the earliest such data bases referring to the US was collected by the National Opinion Research Center in 1969, when retrospective life histories were gathered from a random national sample of 851 white men aged 30–39. Sandefur and Scott (1981) and Sandefur (1985) have used these data to study the effects of work careers and family life cycles on migration, concluding that when variables relating to such factors are taken into account, the inverse relationship between age and migration disappears. Herzog et al. (1993) have used event history analysis to study migration's role in the transition to employment, and Odland and Shumway (1993) have used it to examine the relationships between various life-cycle events and migration. More work of this sort is badly needed.

5. Conclusions

In the introduction several questions were posed regarding internal migration in developed countries. Who migrates? Why do they migrate? Where do the migrants come from and where do they go? When do they migrate? What consequences does migration have for the migrants themselves and others in origin and destination regions? During the last 30 years, firm answers have been provided to many of these questions, but at the same time new, narrower, and in certain ways more refined, interesting, and certainly more challenging questions have arisen.

Migration propensities appear to vary considerably across countries for reasons that are not always obvious. Moreover, estimated parameters that address the questions raised above, while generally in qualitative agreement, are quantitatively somewhat different across developed countries, even when the models and data are roughly comparable. With regard to internal migration, rigorous cross-national studies are virtually nonexistent, but differences in geographic size (and hence spatial distribution of economic opportunities) and culture are likely to importantly underlie observed differences.

Until about 20 years ago, aggregate data were almost exclusively used to study various migration phenomena. Such data embody a number of shortcomings that prevented the study of many important issues bearing on migration. The relatively recent availability of micro- and longitudinal data have had a major impact on four areas of migration research. First, such data have gone far toward clearing up earlier puzzles concerning the relationship between unemployment and migration. Second, these data have allowed the human capital model to be tested in the migration context by allowing the estimation of migrant earnings equations. Third, micro- and longitudinal data have permitted a clarification of the relationship between personal characteristics and the decision to migrate, and they have allowed a deeper understanding of the relationship between various life-cycle and familial factors and migration. Fourth, these data have permitted a detailed focus on different types of migrants, particularly primary, return, and other repeat migrants.

Researchers now know that local unemployment in the US has a significant influence on the migration decisions of the unemployed and those who are seeking new jobs, but has little influence on individuals who are secure in their jobs. However, they do not know why this relationship fails to hold for European countries. Moreover, they do not know with great confidence why some unemployed individuals are faster to migrate than others. To some extent, immediate migration could be discouraged if a person's spouse remains employed. What characteristics of a spouse's employment discourage migration? To what extent does it matter whether the party remaining employed is the husband or the wife? What role does the availability of unemployment insurance play in discouraging immediate migration? Institutional settings differ substantially by country, such as in the nature of unemployment insurance programs, and could cause differences in the response to personal unemployment. More cross-national work is needed in migration research.

The human capital model has provided a powerful analytical tool for the study of numerous important issues in labor economics. It is somewhat surprising that this model has not typically provided a comparably powerful explanation of migration. Whether migrants are compared to otherwise comparable individuals in the origin or the destination, they appear to suffer earnings losses for at least several years after migration. This finding has been verified repeatedly for the US and for other countries. Although several explanations have been offered for these findings, we still do not know enough about why they occur.

The most likely explanation for the apparent failure of the human capital model is that the model has not failed, but rather it has just not been properly or fully implemented. An immediate drop in earnings need not, and probably does not, mean a drop in lifetime utility. Job tenure should be an important argument in earnings equations, and yet this variable has rarely been included in migrant earnings equations. Except when job transfers are involved, migration entails a termination of job tenure and the monetary returns to that tenure. Little has been done to examine the characteristics of a migrant's job before and after a move. Consequently, little has been done to understand which specific aspects of a job are transferable to the new employment. Moreover, the nonmonetary aspects of jobs in the origin and destination have not been studied, although they have been shown to be important, at least for well-educated individuals. Although location-specific amenities have proven to be significant determinants of interregional migration, and although the values of such amenities are likely capitalized in wages and rents, controls for these factors have only recently been introduced into earnings equations. Frequently, state and local taxes, as well as state and local spending and its mix, are unaccounted for in spite of the fact that they have proven to be significant determinants of migration at both the micro level (Herzog and Schlottmann, 1986) and the macro level (Day, 1992). Furthermore, differences in leisure time (or work effort) are frequently not taken into account. Since this aspect of a job could be an important consideration in many migration decisions, especially where location-specific amenities are involved, leisure time should be taken into account specifically. Finally, depending upon the reference group's location, the absence of good price deflators (Shaw, 1985) could bias the interpretation of earnings variables in migration regressions, as well as in earnings regressions that account for migration.

Due to incomplete information and lack of perfect foresight, individuals obviously make mistakes in their choices regarding whether and where to migrate. Notwithstanding these mistakes, individuals presumably believe that their utility levels will improve through migration. The choices are frequently inherently risky, and although the expected utility model forms the basis for the typical migration model, risk has not been studied to a significant degree in this context. It is worthy of attention.

Many questions remain to be answered regarding the adaptation of migrants to the area of destination. Do those who are more likely to stay in a new region invest in skills and training that is more specific to the region and that thus makes them less likely still to migrate out? Do the involuntarily mobile adapt less well because they have had less time to plan for their move or to have participated extensively in job search activities? Are those who move over greater distances less likely to remigrate, and if so, why? How and why do the returns to those who move over greater distances differ from those who move over shorter distances? Although certain of these issues have been addressed with micro- and panel data, an adequate understanding of the answers has yet to be developed.

Selectivity problems are potentially quite important in a wide variety of migration studies. Yet only a few studies have made any attempt to correct for selectivity bias. Certain studies that have made such attempts have demonstrated that selectivity can obscure the true direct relationship between certain variables and migration, but not all studies arrive at this conclusion. Time-dependent selectivity has been ignored almost completely. Virtually nothing is known about changes in migrant quality (i.e., human capital embodied) over the business cycle. Longitudinal data could be used to address this issue. Although they have been given some attention in the literature on US immigration, cohort effects also have been ignored almost completely with respect to internal migration. Moreover, much remains to be learned regarding the selectivity associated with remigration decisions of both the return and onward types.

The finding that persons who are unemployed prior to an initial move are much more likely to return than those who are employed is fascinating. Another interesting observation is that better educated individuals are more likely than others to quickly move on. Among the unemployed, what characteristics increase the probability of a quick return? Among the better educated, what characteristics enhance the likelihood of a quick onward move? The use of longitudinal data to further study the sequence of moves would be welcome.

Some of the most important findings based on micro- and longitudinal data have concerned the relationships between personal, family, and life-cycle forces and the decision to migrate. Yet many of the most important unanswered questions also involve these relationships. We can say with some certainty that a wife's employment discourages family migration. Family migration also seems to negatively affect a wife's labor force participation and earnings, but we do not know much about the circumstances that affect this relationship. For how long are the wife's employment and earnings affected by migration? Are the relationships different for better-educated women? Do expected career interruptions influence the occupational choices of women? These interruptions could be due to child bearing, but they could also be due to migration. Are wives with occupations that are more easily transferred from place-to-place more likely to gain quick reemployment after a move without significant loss of earnings?

The influences of life-cycle changes on migration decisions have only barely been touched by researchers. The relationships between many such changes and migration therefore have remained undiscovered. Completion of education, birth and aging of children and the anticipation of these events, changing marital status and especially divorce, death of a spouse, acquisition of a home, and retirement are only a few potentially important life-cycle changes that are likely to importantly affect migration and about which much remains to be learned. The connection between divorce and migration seems particularly relevant (Grundy, 1985). To what extent do children affect the migration response associated with divorce? The relationships between health status and its changes and migration are also important, and except for a limited amount of research concerning the health status of retired migrants, little is known about this relationship.[59]

The effects of a period of military service have been studied from a number of perspectives. Participation in the military is an important life-cycle event and certainly involves migration. However, apparently no one has studied the possible effects of military participation on subsequent geographic mobility. A number of potential channels of influence could operate between military service and migration. For example, military participants have migration experience and knowledge of alternative areas. They are repeat migrants. Is their responsiveness to the various determinants of migration like that of other repeat movers with otherwise similar characteristics? Do military participants have post-military migration histories that differ in any substantive way from otherwise similar individuals from their "home" communities who do not serve in the military. The military is thought to provide a bridging environment for minorities that allows them increased occupational mobility. Does a similar effect operate through increased geographic mobility, which is clearly another avenue to increased economic opportunities? Do military retirement benefits influence migration?

Surprisingly little is known about the interactions between migration and fertility in the contemporary US or in other developed countries. As discussed in Zarate and de Zarate (1975), a sizable literature on this topic began developing in the 1930s, but was mainly focused on rural–urban migration. A good deal of more recent work has also focused on rural-to-urban migrants in less developed countries, and a few studies concentrate on US immigrants. However, in spite of the availability of more and better data in recent years, little has been done to study how the act of migration affects fertility in the US In their new settings do migrant fertility patterns reflect what they would have been in the former location? Alternatively, do migrants adapt in the sense that they assume patterns more like those of the receiving area? Do those who move

[59] Linneman and Graves (1983) study the relationship between changes in health status (as measured by increases or decreases in annual hours of illness experienced by the household head) and migration, but their results are inconclusive.

repeatedly have lower fertility than those who stay put or move only once? Do other changes associated with migration affect fertility? For example, if migrants really do experience earnings losses for a few years after a move, are these losses sufficient to negatively affect their fertility? In spite of lower fertility rates in the US and narrowing regional and rural–urban differentials in these rates, further study of the linkages between migration and fertility would be welcome.

Migration serves an equilibrating function in the economy, expediting the balancing of demand and supply forces within and across regions, and thus facilitating the operation of market economies. This facilitating role of migration has attracted the attention of policy makers. In a number of European countries, such as Great Britain, France, and the Netherlands, migration policy has been directly tied to regional development policy, whereas in others, such as Sweden, migration policy has been oriented toward improving the efficiency of the labor market (Klaassen and Drewe, 1973; Willis, 1974). In either case, a major objective has been to reduce unemployment. Subsidization of relocation expenses and employment information exchanges are the most common forms that migration policy has taken in Europe.

In the US, policy concerns regarding migration generally are passive, although this was not the case during the nineteenth century. These concerns have been directed toward both how various national, state, and local policies have affected in- or out-migration and how migration has affected the public sector of states and localities (Charney, 1993). During recent years, migration has been viewed as playing a role in state and local economic development efforts, but again this role has been seen as passive, where migration is regarded as a means of accommodating incremental employment. A policy concern that has arisen in this respect is whether the jobs created by economic development efforts go to previous residents or in-migrants (Bartik, 1993).

The quality of migration data has increased dramatically during the last 20 years and has allowed numerous important advances in migration research that otherwise would have been impossible. The availability of microdata and longitudinal data have been particularly noteworthy in this respect. In a certain sense, however, migration research has swung too far in the micro direction. Variables relating to the communities in which people live and to which they consider migrating have been shown to clearly affect migration, as well as the monetary returns to migration. Yet some investigators include only personal or family variables in their migration models, completely ignoring variables that are sometimes called "contextual". This type of omission is potentially serious. Notwithstanding these comments, microdata and longitudinal data will almost certainly provide the key resources for future advances in migration research by economists.

References

Addison, J.T. and P. Portugal (1989), "Job displacement, relative wage changes, and duration of unemployment", Journal of Labor Economics 7: 281–302.

Amemiya, T. (1981), "Qualitative response models: a survey", Journal of Economic Literature 19: 1483–1536.

Antel, J.J. (1980), "Returns to migration: literature review and critique", Rand note N-1480-NICHD (The Rand Corporation, Santa Monica, CA).

Bartel, A.P. (1979), "The migration decision: what role does job mobility play?", American Economic Review 69: 775–786.

Bartik, T.J. (1991), Who benefits from state and local economic development policies? (W.E. Upjohn Institute, Kalamazoo, MI).

Bartik, T.J. (1993), "Who benefits from local job growth: migrants or the original residents?", Regional Studies 27: 297–311.

Becker, G.S. (1962), "Investment in human capital: a theoretical analysis", Journal of Political Economy, Supplement, 70: 9–49.

Becketti, S., W. Gould, L. Lillard and F. Welch (1988), "The panel study of income dynamics after fourteen years: an evaluation", Journal of Labor Economics 6: 472–492.

Bernert, E.H. (1944a), "Volume and composition of net migration from the rural-farm population, 1930–40, for the United States, major geographic divisions and states" (US Department of Agriculture, Bureau of Agricultural Economics, Washington, DC).

Bernert, E.H. (1944b), "County variation in net migration from the rural-farm population, 1930–40" (US Department of Agriculture, Bureau of Agricultural Economics, Washington, DC).

Blomquist, G.C., M.C. Berger and J.P. Hoehn (1988), "New estimates of quality of life in urban areas", American Economic Review 78: 89–107.

Borjas, G.J., S.G. Bronars and S.J. Trejo (1992a), "Assimilation and the earnings of young internal migrants", Review of Economics and Statistics 74: 170–175.

Borjas, G.J., S.G. Bronars and S.J. Trejo (1992b), "Self-selection and internal migration in the United States", Journal of Urban Economics 32: 159–185.

Campisi, D., A. LaBella and G. Rabino (1982), "Migration and settlement: 17. Italy", Report RR-82-33 (Institute for Applied Systems Analysis, Laxenburg, Austria).

Charney, A.H. (1993), "Migration and the public sector: a survey", Regional Studies 27: 313–326.

Chiswick, B.R. (1978), "The effects of Americanization on the earnings of foreign-born men", Journal of Political Economy 86: 897–921.

Clark, D.E. and J.C. Cosgrove (1991), "Amenities versus labor market opportunities: choosing the optimal distance to move", Journal of Regional Science 31: 311–328.

Coleman, J.S. et al. (1966), Equality of educational opportunity (US Government Printing Office, Washington, DC).

Courchene, T.J. (1970), "Interprovincial migration and economic adjustment", Canadian Journal of Economics 1: 211–223.

Cox, D. (1971), "The effect of geographic and industry mobility on income: a further comment", Journal of Human Resources 6: 525–527.

Crandall, R.W. (1993), Manufacturing on the move (The Brookings Institution, Washington, DC).

Creedy, J. (1974), "Inter-regional mobility: a cross-sectional analysis", Scottish Journal of Political Economy 21: 41–53.

DaVanzo, J. (1976a), "Why families move: a model of the geographic mobility of married couples", Report R-1972-DOL (The Rand Corporation, Santa Monica, CA).

DaVanzo, J. (1976b), "Differences between return and nonreturn migration: an econometric analysis", International Migration Review 10: 13–27.

DaVanzo, J. (1977), "Migration patterns and income change: implications for the human capital approach to migration: comment", Southern Economic Journal 43: 391–393.

DaVanzo, J. (1978), "Does unemployment affect migration? – evidence from microdata", Review of Economics and Statistics 60: 504–514.

DaVanzo, J. (1982), "Techniques for analysis of migration-history data", Rand note N-1824-AID/NICHD (The Rand Corporation, Santa Monica, CA).

DaVanzo, J. and J.R. Hosek (1981), "Does migration increase wage rates? – an analysis of alternative techniques for measuring wage gains to migration", Rand note N-1582-NICHD (The Rand Corporation, Santa Monica, CA).

David, P.A. (1974), "Fortune, risk, and the microeconomics of migration", in: P.A. David and M.W. Reder, eds., Nations and households in economic growth (Academic Press, New York) pp. 21–88.

Day, K.M. (1992), "Interprovincial migration and local public goods", Canadian Journal of Economics 25: 123–144.

Denslow, D.A. and P.J. Eaton (1984), "Migration and intervening opportunities", Southern Economic Journal 51: 369–387.

Eberts, R.W. and J.A. Stone (1992), Wage and employment adjustment in local labor markets (W.E. Upjohn Institute, Kalamazoo, MI).

Eldridge, H.T. and D.S. Thomas (1964), Population redistribution and economic growth in the United States, III. Demographic analysis and interrelationships (The American Philosophical Society, Philadelphia, PA).

Evans, A.W. (1990), "The assumption of equilibrium in the analysis of migration and interregional differences: a review of some recent research", Journal of Regional Science 30: 515–531.

Falaris, E. (1987), "A nested logit migration model with selectivity", International Economic Review 28: 429–444.

Fields, G.S. (1976), "Labor force migration, unemployment and job turnover", Review of Economics and Statistics 63: 407–415.

Fotheringham, A.S. (1981), "Spatial structure and distance-decay parameters", Annals of the Association of American Geographers 71: 425–436.

Fox, W.F., H.W. Herzog, Jr. and A.M. Schlottmann (1989), "Metropolitan fiscal structure and migration", Journal of Regional Science 29: 523–537.

Friedrich, K. (1990), "Federal Republic of Germany", in: C.B. Nam, W.J. Serow and D.F. Sly, eds., International handbook on internal migration (Greenwood Press, New York) pp. 145–161.

Fuchs, V.R. (1962), "Statistical explanations of the relative shift of manufacturing among regions in the United States", Papers and Proceedings of the Regional Science Association 8: 106–126.

Gallaway, L. (1969), "The effect of geographic labor mobility on income: a brief comment", Journal of Human Resources 4: 103–109.

Gallaway, L.E. and R.K. Vedder (1971), "Mobility of native Americans", Journal of Economic History 31: 613–649.

Gallaway, L.E., R.G. Gilbert and P.E. Smith (1967), "The economics of labor mobility: an empirical analysis", Western Economic Journal 5: 211–223.

Goodrich, C. (1936), Migration and economic opportunity (University of Pennsylvania Press, Philadelphia, PA).

Gordon, I. (1985), "The cyclical interaction between regional migration, employment and unemployment: a time series analysis for Scotland", Scottish Journal of Political Economy 32: 135–158.

Goss, E. and H.S. Chang (1983), "Changes in elasticities of interstate migration: implication of alternative functional forms", Journal of Regional Science 23: 223–232.

Goss, E.P. and N.C. Schoening (1984), "Search time, unemployment and the migration decision", Journal of Human Resources 19: 570–579.

Grant, E.K. and J. Vanderkamp (1980), "The effects of migration on income: a micro study with Canadian data 1965–1971", Canadian Journal of Economics 13: 381–406.

Graves, P.E. (1979), "A life-cycle empirical analysis of migration and climate, by race", Journal of Urban Economics 6: 135–147.

Graves, P.E. (1980), "Migration and climate", Journal of Regional Science 20: 227–237.

Graves, P.E. (1983), "Migration with a composite amenity: the role of rents", Journal of Regional Science 23: 541–546.

Graves, P.E. and M.J. Greenwood (1987), "Two views of recent regional location patterns in the United States: competing models with non-competing implications", paper presented at the International Conference on Migration and Labor Market Efficiency, Knoxville, TN.

Graves, P.E. and T.A. Knapp (1988), "Mobility behavior of the elderly", Journal of Urban Economics 24: 1–8.

Graves, P.E. and P.D. Linneman (1979), "Household migration: theoretical and empirical results", Journal of Urban Economics 6: 383–404.

Graves, P.E. and P.R. Mueser (1993), "The role of equilibrium and disequilibrium in modeling regional growth and decline: a critical reassessment", Journal of Regional Science 33: 69–84.

Greenwood, M.J. (1969), "An analysis of the determinants of geographic labor mobility in the United States", Review of Economics and Statistics 51: 189–194.

Greenwood, M.J. (1975a), "Research on internal migration in the United States: a survey", Journal of Economic Literature 13: 397–433.

Greenwood, M.J. (1975b), "A simultaneous-equations model of urban growth and migration", Journal of the American Statistical Association 70: 797–810.

Greenwood, M.J. (1975c), "Simultaneity bias in migration models: an empirical examination", Demography 12: 519–536.

Greenwood, M.J. (1981), Migration and economic growth in the United States (Academic Press, New York).

Greenwood, M.J. (1985), "Human migration: theory, models, and empirical studies", Journal of Regional Science 25: 521–544.

Greenwood, M.J. (1988), "Changing patterns of migration and regional economic growth in the US: a demographic perspective", Growth and Change 19: 68–87.

Greenwood, M.J. and P.J. Gormely (1971), "A comparison of the determinants of white and nonwhite interstate migration", Demography 8: 141–155.

Greenwood, M.J. and G.L. Hunt (1984), "Migration and interregional employment redistribution in the United States", American Economic Review 74: 957–969.

Greenwood, M.J. and G.L. Hunt (1989), "Jobs versus amenities in the analysis of metropolitan migration", Journal of Urban Economics 25: 1–16.

Greenwood, M.J. and J.M. McDowell (1986), "The factor-market consequences of US immigration", Journal of Economic Literature 24: 1738–1772.

Greenwood, M.J. and D.P. Sweetland (1972), "The determinants of migration between Standard Metropolitan Statistical Areas", Demography 9: 665–681.

Greenwood, M.J., G.L. Hunt and J.M. McDowell (1986), "Migration and employment change: empirical evidence on the spatial and temporal dimensions of the linkage", Journal of Regional Science 26: 223–234.

Greenwood, M.J., J.R. Ladman and B.S. Siegel (1981), "Long-term trends in migratory behavior in a developing country: the case of Mexico", Demography 18: 369–388.

Greenwood, M.J., G.H. McClelland and W.D. Schulze (1994), "The effects of perceptions of hazardous waste on migration: a laboratory experimental approach", Unpublished paper.

Greenwood, M.J., P.R. Mueser, D.A. Plane and A.M. Schlottmann (1991a), "New directions in migration research: perspectives from regional science disciplines", Annals of Regional Science 25: 237–270.

Greenwood, M.J., G.L. Hunt, D. Rickman and G.I. Treyz (1991b), "Migration, regional equilibrium, and the estimation of compensating differentials", American Economic Review 81: 1382–1390.

Gronau, R. (1974), "Wage comparisons – a selectivity bias", Journal of Political Economy 82: 1119–1143.

Grundy, E. (1985), "Divorce, widowhood, remarriage and geographic mobility among women", Journal of Biosocial Science 17: 415–435.

Harkman, A. (1989), "Migration behavior among the unemployed and the role of unemployment benefits", Papers of the Regional Science Association 66: 143–150.

Haurin, D.R. and R.J. Haurin (1988), "Net migration, unemployment, and the business cycle", Journal of Regional Science 28: 239–254.

Heckman, J.J. (1976), "The common structure of statistical models of truncation, sample selection, and limited dependent variables and a simple estimator for such models", Annals of Economic and Social Measurement 5: 475–492.

Helms, L.J. (1985), "The effect of state and local taxes on economic growth: a time series–cross section approach", Review of Economics and Statistics 67: 574–582.

Herzog, H.W., Jr. and A.M. Schlottmann (1984), "Labor force mobility in the United States: migration, unemployment, and remigration", International Regional Science Review 9: 43–58.

Herzog, H.W., Jr. and A.M. Schlottmann (1986), "State and local tax deductibility and metropolitan migration", National Tax Journal 39: 189–200.

Herzog, H.W., Jr., R.A. Hofler and A.M. Schlottmann (1985), "Life on the frontier: migrant information, earnings and past mobility", Review of Economics and Statistics 67: 373–382.

Herzog, H.W., Jr., A.M. Schlottmann and T.P. Boehm (1993), "Migration as spatial job search: a survey of empirical findings", Regional Studies 27: 327–340.

Hicks, J.R. (1932), The theory of wages (Macmillan, London).

Hoehn, J.P., M.C. Berger and G.C. Blomquist (1987), "A hedonic model of interregional wages", Journal of Regional Science 27: 605–620.

Holtz-Eakin, D. (1993), "Job-lock: an impediment to labor mobility? Is health insurance crippling the labor market?", Public policy brief no. 10 (The Jerome Levy Economics Institute of Bard College, Annandale-on-Hudson, NY).

Hughes, G.A. and B. McCormick (1984), "Migration intentions in the UK: which households want to migrate and which succeed?", Economic Journal, Conference Papers, 113–123.

Hughes, G.A.K. and B. McCormick (1989), "Does migration reduce differentials in regional unemployment rates?", in: J. Van Dijk, H. Folmer, H.W. Herzog, Jr. and A.M. Schlottmann, eds., Migration and labor market adjustment (Kluwer, Dordrecht).

Hunt, G.L. (1993), "Equilibrium and disequilibrium in migration modelling", Regional Studies 27: 341–349.

Iden, G. (1974), "Factors affecting earnings of southern migrants", Industrial Relations 13: 177–189.

Islam, M.N. (1985), "Self-selectivity problems in interregional and interindustry migration in Canada", Environment and Planning A 17: 1515–1532.

Islam, M.N. and S.A. Choudhury (1990), "Self-selection and intermunicipal migration in Canada", Regional Science and Urban Economics 20: 459–472.

Kau, J.B. and C.F. Sirmans (1977), "The influence of information cost and uncertainty on migration: a comparison of migrant types", Journal of Regional Science 17: 89–96.

Kiker, B.F. and E.C. Traynham (1977), "Earnings differentials among nonmigrants, return migrants, and nonreturn migrants", Growth and Change 8: 2–7.

Kirk, D. (1960), "Some reflections on American demography in the nineteen sixties", Population Index 26: 307–313.

Klaassen, L.H. and P. Drewe (1973), Migration policy in Europe (Lexington Books, Lexington, MA).

Koch, R. and H.P. Gatzweiler (1980), "Migration and settlement: 9. Federal Republic of Germany", Report RR-80-37 (Institute for Applied Systems Analysis, Laxenburg, Austria).

Krieg, R.G. (1990), "Does migration function to reduce earnings differentials by race and gender?", Annals of Regional Science 24: 211–221.

Krumm, R.J. and A. Kelly (1988), "Multiperiod migration patterns: the timing and frequency of household response", Journal of Regional Science 28: 255–270.

Kuznets, S. and D.S. Thomas (1957), "Introduction", in: E.S. Lee, A.R. Miller, C.P. Brainerd and R.A. Easterlin, eds., Population redistribution and economic growth: United States, 1870–1950, Vol. I, Methodological considerations and reference tables (American Philosophical Society, Philadelphia, PA).

Kuznets, S., A.R. Miller and R.A. Easterlin (1960), Population redistribution and economic growth in the United States. II. Analyses of economic change (The American Philosophical Society, Philadelphia, PA).

Laber, G. (1972), "Returns to southern migration", Review of Regional Studies 3: 95–107.

Lansing, J.B. and J.N. Morgan (1967), "The effect of geographical mobility on income", Journal of Human Resources 2: 449–460.

Lansing, J.B. and E. Mueller (1967), The geographic mobility of labor (Survey Research Center, Ann Arbor, MI).

Ledent, J. (1982), "Migration and settlement: 15. France", Report RR-82–28 (Institute for Applied Systems Analysis, Laxenburg, Austria).

Ledent, J. (1990), "Canada", in: C.B. Nam, W.J. Serow and D.F. Sly, eds., International handbook on internal migration (Greenwood Press, New York) pp. 47–61.

Lee, E.S., A.R. Miller, C.P. Brainerd and R.A. Easterlin (1957), Population redistribution and economic growth in the United States, 1875–1950. I. Methodological considerations and reference tables (The American Philosophical Society, Philadelphia, PA).

Lewis, H.G. (1963), Unionism and relative wages in the United States (University of Chicago Press, Chicago, IL).

Lewis, H.G. (1974), "Comments on selectivity biases in wage comparisons", Journal of Political Economy 82: 1145–1155.

Linneman, P. and P.E. Graves (1983), "Migration and job change: a multinomial logit approach", Journal of Urban Economics 14: 263–279.

Long, L.H. (1974), "Women's labor force participation and the residential mobility of families", Social Forces 52: 342–348.

Long, L.H. (1988), Migration and residential mobility in the United States (Russell Sage Foundation, New York).

Long, L.H. (1991), "Residential mobility differences among developed countries", International Regional Science Review 14: 133–147.

Long, L.H. (1992), "Changing residence: comparative perspectives on its relationship to age, sex, and marital status", Population Studies 46: 141–158.

Long, L.H. and C.G. Boertlein (1976), "The geographical mobility of Americans: an international comparison", Current population reports, Special studies, Series P-23, no. 64 (Bureau of the Census, Washington, DC).

Long, L.H. and W.H. Frey (1982), "Migration and settlement: 14. United States", Report RR-82–15 (International Institute for Applied Systems Analysis, Laxenburg, Austria).

Long, L.H. and K.A. Hansen (1979), "Reasons for interstate migration: jobs, retirement, climate, and other influences", Current population reports, Series P-23, no. 81 (US Government Printing Office, Washington, DC).

Long, L.H., C.J. Tucker and W.L. Urton (1988), "Migration distances: an international comparison", Demography 25: 633–640.

Lowry, I.S. (1966), Migration and metropolitan growth: two analytical models (Chandler Publishing Company, San Francisco, CA).

Maddala, G.S. (1983), Limited-dependent and qualitative variables in econometrics (Cambridge University Press, Cambridge).

Makower, H.J., J. Marschak and H.W. Robinson (1938), "Studies in mobility of labor: a tentative statistical measure", Oxford Economic Papers 1: 83–123.

Makower, H.J., J. Marschak and H.W. Robinson (1939), "Studies in mobility of labor: analysis for Great Britain, Part I", Oxford Economic Papers 2: 70–97.

Makower, H., J. Marschak and H.W. Robinson (1940), "Studies in mobility of labor: analysis for Great Britain, Part II", Oxford Economic Papers 4: 39–62.

Manski, D.F. (1989), "Anatomy of the selection problem", Journal of Human Resources 24: 343–360.

Marr, W.L. and F.W. Millerd (1980), "Employment income levels of inter-provincial migrants versus non-migrants, Canada, 1971", in: J. Simon and J. DaVanzo, eds., Research in population economics, Vol. 2 (JAI Press, Greenwich, CT).

Marshall, A. (1948), Principles of economics (The Macmillan Company, New York).

Masters, S.H. (1972), "Are black migrants from the South to the northern cities worse off than blacks already there?", Journal of Human Resources 7: 411–423.

Mathios, A.P. (1989), "Education, variation in earnings, and nonmonetary compensation", Journal of Human Resources 24: 456–468.

Maxwell, N.L. (1988), "Economic returns to migration: marital status and gender differences", Social Science Quarterly 69: 108–121.

McDowell, J.M. (1982), "Obsolescence of knowledge and career publication profiles", American Economic Review 72: 752–768.

Miller, E. (1973), "Return and nonreturn in-migration", Growth and Change 4: 3–9.

Milne, W.J. (1993), "Macroeconomic influences on migration", Regional Studies 27: 365–373.

Mincer, J. (1974), Schooling, experience and earnings (National Bureau of Economic Research, New York).

Mincer, J. (1978), "Family migration decisions", Journal of Political Economy 86: 749–773.

Mincer, J. and B. Jovanovic (1981), "Labor mobility and wages", in: S. Rosen, ed., Studies in labor markets (University of Chicago Press, Chicago, IL) pp. 21–63.

Molho, I. (1984), "A dynamic model of interregional migration flows in Great Britain", Journal of Regional Science 24: 317–337.

Molho, I. (1986), "Theories of migration: a review", Scottish Journal of Political Economy 33: 396–419.

Mont, D. (1989), "Two earner family migration: a search theoretic approach", Journal of Population Economics 2: 55–72.

Morrison, P.A. (1977), "The functions and dynamics of the migration process", in: A.A. Brown and E. Newberger, eds., Internal migration: a comparative perspective (Academic Press, New York).

Mueller, C.F. (1982), The economics of labor migration (Academic Press, New York).

Mueser, P. (1989), "The spatial structure of migration: an analysis of flows between states in the USA over three decades", Regional Studies 23: 185–200.

Muth, R.F. (1971), "Migration: chicken or egg?", Southern Economic Journal 37: 295–306.

Nakosteen, R.A. and M. Zimmer (1980), "Migration and income: the question of self-selection", Southern Economic Journal 46: 840–851.

Nakosteen, R.A. and M. Zimmer (1982), "The effects on earnings of interregional and interindustry migration", Journal of Regional Science 22: 325–341.

Nam, C.B., W.J. Serow and D.F. Sly, eds. (1990), International handbook on internal migration (Greenwood Press, New York).

Nanjo, Z., T. Kawashima and T. Kuroda (1982), "Migration and settlement: 13. Japan", Report RR-82-5, (International Institute for Applied Systems Analysis, Laxenburg, Austria).

Navratil, F.J. and J.J. Doyle (1977), "The socioeconomic determinants of migration and the level of aggregation", Southern Economic Journal 43: 1547–1559.

Nelson, P. (1959), "Migration, real income and information", Journal of Regional Science 1: 43–74.

Newman, R.J. (1983), "Industry migration and growth in the South", Review of Economics and Statistics 65: 76–86.

Niemi, Jr., A.W. (1973), "Returns to educated blacks resulting from southern out-migration", Southern Economic Journal 40: 330–332.

Odland, J. and J.M. Shumway (1993), "Interdependencies in the timing of migration and mobility events", Papers in Regional Science 72: 221–237.

O'Neill, J.A. (1970), "The effect of income and education on inter-regional migration", Unpublished Ph.D. dissertation (Columbia University, New York).

Otomo, A. (1990), "Japan", in: C.B. Nam, W.J. Serow and D.F. Sly, eds., International handbook on internal migration (Greenwood Press, New York) pp. 257–274.

Parish, Jr., W.L. (1973), "Internal migration and modernization: the European case", Economic Development and Cultural Change 21: 591–609.

Perloff, H.S., E.S. Dunn, Jr., E.E. Lampard and R.F. Muth (1960), Regions, resources, and economic growth (Johns Hopkins University Press, Baltimore MD).

Pissarides, C.A. and I. McMaster (1990), "Regional migration, wages and unemployment: empirical evidence and implications for policy", Oxford Economic Papers 43: 812–831.

Pissarides, C.A. and J. Wadsworth (1989), "Unemployment and the inter-regional mobility of labour", Economic Journal 99: 739–755.

Plane, D.A. (1993), "Demographic influences on migration", Regional Studies 27: 375–383.

Plane, D.A. and P.A. Rogerson (1991), "Tracking the baby boom, the baby bust, and the echo generations: how age composition regulates US migration", Professional Geographer 43: 416–430.

Population Association of America (1988), Migration statistics in the United States, Report of the subcommittee on migration statistics of the committee on population statistics.

Porell, F.W. (1982), "Intermetropolitan migration and quality of life", Journal of Regional Science 22: 137–158.

Rabianski, J. (1971), "Real earnings and human migration", Journal of Human Resources 6: 185–192.

Ravenstein, E.G. (1885), "The laws of migration", Journal of the Royal Statistical Society 48: 167–235.

Ravenstein, E.G. (1889), "The laws of migration", Journal of the Royal Statistical Society 52: 241–305.

Rees, P.H. (1979), "Migration and settlement: 1. United Kingdom", Report RR-79-3 (Institute for Applied Systems Analysis, Laxenburg, Austria).

Roback, J. (1982), "Wages, rents, and the quality of life", Journal of Political Economy 90: 1257–1278.

Roback, J. (1988), "Wages, rents, and amenities: differences among workers and regions", Economic Inquiry 26: 23–41.

Robinson, C. and N. Tomes (1982), "Self-selection and interprovincial migration in Canada", Canadian Journal of Economics 15: 474–502.

Rogerson, P.A. (1987), "Changes in US national mobility levels", Professional Geographer 39: 344–351.

Rosen, S. (1979), "Wage-based indexes of urban quality of life", in: P. Mieszkowski and M. Straszheim, eds., Current issues in urban economics (Johns Hopkins University Press, Baltimore, MD) pp. 74–104.

Rosenzweig, M.R. and O. Stark (1989), "Consumption smoothing, migration, and marriage: evidence from rural India", Journal of Political Economy 97: 905–926.

Roy, A.D. (1951), "Some thoughts on the distribution of earnings", Oxford Economic Papers 3: 135–146.

Sandefur, G.D. (1985), "Variations in interstate migration of men across the early stages of the life cycle", Demography 22: 353–366.

Sandefur, G.D. and W.J. Scott (1981), "A dynamic analysis of migration: an assessment of the effects of age, family and career variables", Demography 18: 355–368.

Sandefur, G.D. and N.B. Tuma (1987), "How data type affects conclusions about individual mobility", Social Science Research 16: 301–328.

Sandell, S.H. (1977), "Women and the economics of family migration", Review of Economics and Statistics 59: 406–414.

Sauberer, M. (1981), "Migration and settlement: 10. Austria", Report RR-81-16 (Institute for Applied Systems Analysis, Laxenburg, Austria).

Schlottmann, A.M. and H.W. Herzog, Jr. (1981), "Employment status and the decision to migrate", Review of Economics and Statistics 63: 590–598.

Schultz, T.P. (1982), "Lifetime migration within educational strata in Venezuela: estimates of a logistic model", Economic Development and Cultural Change 30: 559–593.

Schultz, T.W. (1961), "Investment in human capital", American Economic Review 51: 1–17.

Schwartz, A. (1973), "Interpreting the effect of distance on migration", Journal of Political Economy 81: 1153–1169.

Sell, R.R. (1990), "Market and job transfers in the United States", in: J.H. Johnson and J. Salt, eds., Labour migration: the internal geographical mobility of labour in the developed world (David Fulton Publishers, London) pp. 17–31.

Shaw, R.P. (1985), Intermetropolitan migration in Canada: changing determinants over three decades (NC Press Ltd., Toronto).

Shryock, H.S. (1964), Population mobility within the United States (University of Chicago Press, Chicago, IL).

Shryock, H.S., J.S. Siegel and Associates (1976), The methods and materials of demography (Academic Press, New York).

Silvers, A. (1977), "Probabilistic income maximizing behaviour in regional migration", International Regional Science Review 2: 29–40.

Sjaastad, L.A. (1962), "The costs and returns of human migration", Journal of Political Economy, Supplement 70: 80–89.

Smith, S.K. and T. Sincich (1992), "Evaluating the forecast accuracy and bias of alternative population projections for states", International Journal of Forecasting 8: 495–508.

Stark, O. (1991), The migration of labor (Basil Blackwell, Inc., Cambridge, MA).

Stewart, J.Q. (1941), "An inverse distance variation for certain social influences", Science 93: 89–90.

Termote, M.G. (1980), "Migration and settlement: 6. Canada", Report RR-80-29 (Institute for Applied Systems Analysis, Laxenburg, Austria).

Thomas, B. (1934), "The movement of labour into South-East England 1920–32", Economica N.S. 1: 220–241.

Thomas, B. (1937), "The influx of labour into London and the South East 1920–36", Economica N.S. 4: 323–336.

Thomas, D.S. (1938), Research memorandum on migration differentials (Social Science Research Council, New York).

Thornwaite, C.W. (1934), Internal migration in the United States (University of Pennsylvania Press, Philadelphia, PA).

Todaro, M.P. (1969), "A model of labor migration and urban unemployment in less developed countries", American Economic Review 59: 138–148.

Todaro, M.P. (1976), Internal migration in developing countries (International Labour Office, Geneva).

Treyz, G.I., D.S. Rickman, G.L. Hunt and M.J. Greenwood (1993), "The dynamics of US internal migration", Review of Economics and Statistics 75: 209–214.

Tunali, I. (1986), "A general structure for models of double selection and an application to a joint migration/earnings process with remigration", in: R.G. Ehrenberg, ed., Research in labor economics (JAI Press, Greenwich, CT) pp. 235–283.

United Nations (1970), Methods of measuring internal migration, Manual VI (United Nations, New York).

US Bureau of the Census (1991), "Geographical mobility: March 1987 to March 1990", Current population reports, Series P-20, no. 456 (US Government Printing Office, Washington, DC).

Vanderkamp, J. (1971), "Migration flows, their determinants and the effects of return migration", Journal of Political Economy 79: 1012–1031.

Van Dijk, J., H. Folmer, H.W. Herzog, Jr. and A.M. Schlottmann (1989), "Labor market institutions and the efficiency of interregional migration: a cross-nation comparison", in: J. Van Dijk, H. Folmer, H.W. Herzog, Jr. and A.M. Schlottmann, eds., Migration and labor market efficiency (Kluwer, Dordrecht) pp. 61–83.

Vergoossen, D. (1990), "The Netherlands", in: C.B. Nam, W.J. Serow and D.F. Sly, eds., International handbook on internal migration (Greenwood Press, New York) pp. 287–304.

Vining, Jr., D.R. and T. Kontuly (1978), "Population dispersal from major metropolitan regions: an international comparison", International Regional Science Review 3: 49–73.

Wadycki, W.J. (1974), "Alternative opportunities and interstate migration: some additional results", Review of Economics and Statistics 56: 254–257.

Weiss, L. and J.G. Williamson (1972), "Black education, earnings, and interregional migration: some new evidence", American Economic Review 62: 372–383.

Wertheimer, R.F., III (1970), The monetary rewards of migration within the US (The Urban Institute, Washington, DC).

Willis, K.G. (1974), Problems in migration analysis (Lexington Books, Lexington, MA).

Winer, S.L. and D. Gauthier (1982), Internal migration and fiscal structure (Canadian Government Publishing Centre, Ottawa).

Yezer, A.M.J. and L. Thurston (1976), "Migration patterns and income change: implications for the human capital approach to migration", Southern Economic Journal 42: 693–702.

Zarate, A. and A.U. de Zarate (1975), "On the reconciliation of research findings of migrant–nonmigrant fertility differentials in urban areas", International Migration Review 9: 115–156.

Zelinsky, W. (1971), "The hypothesis of the mobility transition", Geographical Review 61: 219–249.

Chapter 13

INTERNAL MIGRATION IN DEVELOPING COUNTRIES

ROBERT E.B. LUCAS*

Boston University

Contents

1. Introduction: outline and patterns   722
    1.1. Focus and outline of the review   722
    1.2. Concepts and patterns of migration   722
2. Factors affecting migration flows and selectivity   730
    2.1. Income streams: the basics   730
    2.2. Migration and job search   732
    2.3. Estimating responsiveness to labor market opportunities   738
    2.4. Networks and information   743
    2.5. The role of capital   746
    2.6. Temporary, return and permanent migration   748
    2.7. Family strategies   749
    2.8. The contextual setting   753
    2.9. Displaced persons   755
3. Effects of migration on production and inequality   756
    3.1. Rural labor markets and agricultural production   756
    3.2. Urban labor market issues   760
    3.3. Dynamic models   768
    3.4. Effects of migration upon income distribution   769
4. Policy issues and options   775
    4.1. Direct controls on mobility   775
    4.2. Influencing urban pay and labor costs   776
    4.3. Rural development   778
    4.4. On industrial location   780
    4.5. Investing in infrastructure   782
    4.6. The nature and dispersion of education   784
    4.7. Structural adjustment and development strategies   785
5. Closing thoughts   785
References   787

*I am very grateful to Sharon Russell and Oded Stark for many detailed comments on an earlier draft.

Handbook of Population and Family Economics. Edited by M.R. Rosenzweig and O. Stark
© *Elsevier Science B.V., 1997*

1. Introduction: outline and patterns

1.1. Focus and outline of the review

It is 20 years since Simmons, Diaz-Briquets and Laquian wrote:

> The movement of peoples in developing countries has been intensively studied, and in recent years the results of these studies have been thoroughly reviewed. One needs good justification for preparing yet another review... (Simmons et al., 1977: p. 5].[1]

However in the last decade, a substantial literature on the economics of internal migration in the developing countries has appeared, and on this the present review focusses. This literature encompasses theoretical contributions which, not surprisingly, have moved in parallel with the broader evolution of mainstream microeconomic theory: from simple human capital models with known alternative opportunities, through treatment of uncertainty and search, to asymmetric information and strategic behavior. The associated empirical evidence undoubtedly lags behind, yet at least some strands have been subjected to extensive and increasingly sophisticated testing. Meanwhile policy issues have remained at the fore, and experiences with migration related policies have received much attention in the literature of recent years.

This chapter reviews some of the principal contributions addressing each of these three spheres: theory, empirical evidence and policy experience, focussing in particular upon the more recent literature. The balance of the introduction is taken up with a brief review of some basic concepts and patterns of internal migration. The remainder of the chapter is then divided into four. Section 2 is about the causes of migration – earnings opportunities and job search, information and financing, family strategies and the contextual setting, and displaced persons. Section 3 takes up the economic consequences of internal migration – the direct and indirect effects of rural emigration on rural production, the overall effects upon national product in the light of various market pathologies, and the much disputed consequences for income inequality. In the light of the foregoing sections, Section 4 turns to a review of the literature on policy experiences, and Section 5 offers a few closing thoughts.

---

[1] Many of the prior surveys have adopted fairly specific themes. For instance, Krugman and Bhagwati (1976), Yap (1977) and Schultz (1982a) examine the estimation of migration functions; Lucas (1976) considers theories of labor market pathologies in relation to migration, while Todaro (1976b, 1980) focusses upon the Todaro hypothesis; Todaro (1984) and Williamson (1988) are concerned with urbanization in LDCs; and various policy themes and stylized facts are reviewed in Simmons et al. (1977), Abumere (1981) and Oberai (1983).

1.2. Concepts and patterns of migration

It will be useful, at the outset, to establish some of the broad patterns which characterize internal migration within the developing countries. Our knowledge of these patterns is, however, restricted by the nature of the data available. This section therefore
opens with a discussion of the data base and the limitations which this imposes upon
analyses of these patterns. Rural-to-urban migration has dominated both policy concerns and economic analysis, and some stylized facts surrounding these movements
are addressed in the following subsection. The remaining subsections take up rural–
rural movements which dominate the volume of migration but have generated comparatively little interest, then temporary and circular migration on which the statistical
base is exceedingly poor.

1.2.1. The data base

The movement of peoples may take many forms: moving house within an urban area,
the wanderings of nomads, commuting to work, visiting relatives or friends, or relocating dwelling between regions. Our interest in any one form varies with the issues at
stake: movements within a town may be of interest for urban planning but less so for
an overall employment strategy.

Census and sample survey data normally report only a limited range of population
movements. One limitation is the number of movements documented per person. Full
life mobility histories are rarely gathered. More typically a census or survey may record place of birth as well as place of enumeration, though occasionally a place of prior
"residence" is reported. Such limited mobility records can hide a good deal of movement in the presence of step and circular migration, both of which appear to be common in LDCs according to our restricted evidence.

A second source of limitation is in the degree of disaggregation when reporting
"place" of current or prior residence. Frequently only a broad region is coded, perhaps
together with some indication as to whether the residence is in a rural or urban zone.
Naturally this precludes estimation of the extent of, for instance, rural–rural mobility
within a region.

The picture is also complicated by difficulties in distinguishing birthplace, home,
domicile and work place. With more frequent births under medical supervision in
LDCs, birthplace and initial home are probably increasingly separated (Schultz,
1982a). The distinction between "home" – in the sense of a place to which one owes
allegiance – and where one happens to be living is, perhaps, particularly sharp in some
portions of the developing world. And transport improvements are permitting more
extensive commuting, even in the developing countries, with a resultant separation of
job location from residence, though largely ignored in dualistic models (Connell et al.,
1976).

A part of the distinction between home and domicile is tied up with the intent to stay. In empirical work, most economists prove unwilling to trust self-reported intent to stay – an intent which may or may not be realized. There probably are behavioral differences between sojourners and settlers, for instance with respect to duration of optimal job search, forms and location of investments, and conjugal separation. But these differences prove difficult to investigate without reliance on reported intent. Yet documentation on actual return and onward migration is very partial (Nelson, 1976).

Some portions of the literature on migration in developing countries have come to focus more upon family strategies. In empirical work, this raises the difficult question of an appropriate definition of a family. Joint decisions involving immediate family members, and even unrelated persons not dwelling together, may not be uncommon. This may be particularly prevalent in those developing countries where the agricultural cycle normally involves rotation of family members between multiple dwellings (Lucas, 1985), and where kinship ties extend commitments well beyond the immediate family (see the discussion of shadow households in Caces et al. (1985)).

These various conceptual difficulties render interpretation of any observed migration patterns sensitive to the concepts used. What appear to be some of the emerging patterns?

1.2.2. Urbanization

Much of the policy interest in internal migration derives from concern, or even alarm, with respect to the rate of growth in urban populations and that of the larger cities in particular. Some data on the rates of urban transition and urban population growth are therefore reviewed first in this subsection, followed by evidence on the contribution of migration to urban population growth. The subsection closes with a few stylized facts on the selectivity of rural–urban migration with respect to age, gender and other personal characteristics – facts which will prove useful in subsequent sections but which are also relevant to considerations of the role of migration in promoting urbanization.

Rates of LDC urban population growth. International comparisons of urban population growth are hampered by the lack of a uniform minimum size for urban settlement definitions, and even by the practice in some contexts of defining a market town as rural, irrespective of size, if it happens to be in a predominantly rural region (see Todaro, 1984).

Based on each country's own definitions of urban areas Table 1 shows the intercensal rates of urban population growth and of urban transition for Africa, Asia[2] and for South America (including Central America and the Caribbean).

There is no clear trend in overall LDC urban growth in the second half of this century. South America does display a systematic trend toward slower urban population

---

[2] Japan is excluded from the urban population growth rates but not from the urban transition measures.

Table 1
Urban population growth and rate of urban transition

	Overall LDC	Africa	Asia	South America
Urban annual population growth rate (%)				
1950–1960	4.87	4.72	5.01	4.57
1960–1970	3.59	4.92	3.07	4.27
1970–1980	3.90	4.83	3.78	3.74
1980–1990	4.68	5.08	5.17	3.12
1990–2000	4.04	4.95	4.30	2.53
% of population residing in urban areas				
1950	17.0	14.5	16.4	41.5
1960	22.1	18.3	21.5	49.3
1970	24.7	22.9	22.9	57.3
1980	28.9	27.8	26.3	65.0
1990	37.1	33.9	34.4	71.5
2000	45.1	40.7	42.7	76.4

Source: United Nations (1991).

growth, but this is not true for Africa, and Asia shows no monotonic pattern. On the other hand, there has been a fairly steady rise in the proportion of population residing in urban areas, both overall in the developing countries and within each of the three continents reported in Table 1.

Williamson (1988) argues that this rate of urban transition is not unusual by European historical standards, though he also maintains that LDC city growth is exceptionally rapid in historical perspective.

Between 1875 and 1900, currently developed countries' urban share rose from 17.2 to 26.1 percent, about the same increase which took place in the Third World between 1950 and 1975, 16.7 to 28 percent...Between 1875 and 1900, city populations in the currently developed countries rose by about 100 percent; between 1950 and 1975, city populations in the Third World increased by 188 percent. (Williamson, 1988: pp. 428–429.)

The common concern with the speed of metropolitan growth in the developing countries must however be seen in perspective. The rate of population growth in the LDC cities (both overall and within each of our three continental regions) has actually been slower, for the most part, than has urban population growth. This is brought out in Table 2, in which the city population growth rates are derived from the populations of 173 urban agglomerations comprising one million or more inhabitants in 1990.

A similar reservation must also be expressed with respect to the pattern noted by Preston (1979: p. 201), "The general relationship between city size and city growth rates in developing regions is U-shaped". Preston (1979) reports, for 792 LDC cities,

Table 2
LDC city and urban intercensal growth rates

	Annual population growth %							
	Overall LDC		Africa		Asia		South America	
	Urban	City	Urban	City	Urban	City	Urban	City
1950–1960	4.87	4.49	4.72	4.57	5.01	4.23	4.57	5.15
1960–1970	3.59	3.99	4.92	4.90	3.07	3.70	4.27	4.41
1970–1980	3.90	3.40	4.83	4.19	3.78	3.22	3.74	3.53
1980–1990	4.68	3.36	5.08	4.18	5.17	3.30	3.12	3.17
1990–2000	4.04	3.26	4.95	4.34	4.30	3.41	2.53	2.39

Source: United Nations (1991).

population growth between the latest two censuses according to city size at the earlier census. Some of Preston's measures are summarized in the top panel of Table 3. The U-shape noted by Preston is apparent in the overall measures: the largest and the smaller cities grow most rapidly. However this U-shape appears to be a chance result of aggregating across quite different patterns within each of the four LDC regions reported in Table 3: only within East Asia is such a U-shape sustained. Moreover the smaller UN sample of 173 urban agglomerations shows the medium size cities with populations in 1980 between one and two million growing more rapidly than the largest cities since 1970, as may be seen from the lower panel of Table 3.

To sum up: urban population growth in the LDCs is high, though the transition to an urban population is not proceeding especially rapidly by historical standards. Although much of the policy concern focusses upon metropolitan growth, and on the

Table 3
LDC city population growth by city size

City size in 1000	Population growth rate %				
	Overall LDC	Africa	Latin America	East Asia	South Asia
4000+	3.89	2.66	4.55	3.58	2.95
2000–3999	3.20	–	–	1.73	4.66
1000–1999	3.08	2.61	3.73	2.32	3.55
500- 999	3.20	3.42	4.38	2.18	3.80
250- 499	3.81	4.45	3.90	3.67	3.40
100- 249	3.95	4.70	3.60	3.61	3.70
	Overall LDC				
	1950–1960	1960–1970	1970–1980	1980–1990	1990–2000
4000 +	4.59	4.02	3.31	3.07	2.84
2000–3999	4.68	3.92	3.30	3.21	3.26
1000–1999	4.22	4.02	3.59	3.81	3.75

Sources: Preston (1979) and United Nations (1991).

larger metropolises in particular, the LDC cities are not growing as rapidly as the broader urban areas, nor is it true that the largest cities are outgrowing the medium size cities, at least in proportional rates of growth.

The role of migration in LDC urban growth. How large is the contribution of rural–urban net migration to the high growth in LDC urban populations? Reported urban population growth may be decomposed into three contributing factors: natural population increase among indigenous urban inhabitants; the rate of migration into the urban sector; and the rate of reclassification of areas as urban zones. Todaro (1984: Table 4), reports a partial breakdown of intercensal, urban population growth with most of the evidence drawn from the 1960–1970 period. Only for 29 developing countries do census data permit any breakdown, and even then the role of migration and reclassification must be combined as a residual. The sample average contribution of migration plus reclassification amounts to 41.4% of total urban population growth in these 29 developing countries: natural, annual population growth amounts to 2.53%, while migration plus reclassification add a further 1.79%.[3]

> Urban growth is currently exceptionally rapid in developing countries, but the explanation is not to be found in unusually rapid changes in the urban proportion produced by rural–urban migration but in the rapid changes in total population to which those proportions are applied... This point is readily overlooked in the midst of scholarly and political concern with internal migration. (Preston, 1979: p. 198.)

In view of the last remark, is the policy concern over rural–urban migration misplaced? The answer is surely no. The policy issues surrounding rural–urban migration transcend urban population growth alone. Such issues as the efficiency of labor use and consequences of migration for overall poverty are of paramount importance, even beyond any considerations of pressures on infrastructure stemming from rapid urban growth. Moreover, even if the principal concern remains that of urban population pressures, there are at least three reasons why migration rates are of critical importance: (i) although the estimated contribution of rural–urban migration to urban population growth may be smaller than that of natural urban population growth, the role of migration is still substantial; (ii) it could prove more cost-effective to tackle urban population expansion through policies directed at rural–urban migration than through attempts to promote family planning; (iii) the selectivity of rural–urban migration may result in an understatement of the ultimate contribution of migration to urban population growth as revealed by the simple decompositions into natural growth, migration and reclassification considered so far, for as the next subsection discusses, rural–urban migrants are predominantly in higher fertility age ranges.

---

[3] In a similar breakdown for a sample of 20 developed countries, Todaro finds the absolute contribution of the residual migration plus reclassification is smaller, though this represents a much higher relative contribution to the slower urban expansion in these developed countries.

Selectivity in rural–urban migration. Rural-to-urban migration in developing countries, as in the developed regions, is dominated by young adults;[4] higher levels of
schooling completion are positively correlated with the probability of migrating to
town, though the educated comprise a minority of migrants from most areas; and there
are gender biases in urban immigration – with more male urban migrants in Africa
and Asia, and more female migrants in Latin America, though obviously there are
exceptions within these regions.[5]

Characterizing the selectivity of migration in this fashion may help in framing
questions, but ultimately one wishes to know why migration is selective upon particular characteristics. The latter cannot be determined from a single equation, reduced-
form analysis of regression upon personal characteristics alone. A structural, behavioral model is required. Indeed within such a framework, many personal characteristics – such as the extent of schooling and marital status – are endogenously determined together with the migration decision.

1.2.3. The importance and neglect of rural–rural migration

The extent of rural–rural migration is not well documented, particularly when this
involves intra-regional movements. Where analysis proves possible, the rate of rural–
rural migration typically proves far higher than of rural–urban migration (Connell et
al., 1976).

For instance, Skeldon (1986) notes that just over 30% of India's population in the
1981 census report a previous place of residence different from their place of enumeration. Of those who moved in the ten years prior to this census, the composition of
movements is:[6]

	%
Rural–rural	57.4
Rural–urban	19.5
Urban–urban	15.2
Urban–rural	7.9

If rural–rural migration is so much more common than rural–urban migration, why
does the former remain relatively neglected in theoretical modelling, empirical analy-

---

[4] Todaro (1984) notes that the high rates of natural population increase among urban dwellers are
attributable in part to the age structure of the urban population, and to some extent this profile is kept younger
through more frequent arrival of young migrants. In this sense, as Todaro notes, the contribution of rural–
urban migration to urban population growth is understated by simply counting the numbers arriving.

[5] For surveys of the "non-rigorous descriptive literature" (Todaro, 1976b: p. 65), establishing these
patterns, see Brigg (1971), Herrick (1971), Byerlee (1974), Connell et al. (1976), Todaro (1976b), Simmons et
al. (1977).

[6] See also Lucas (1985) on Botswana and Lucas and Verry (1990) on Malaysia.

sis and in policy discussion? A part of the answer lies in the lack of data, though this, in itself, is also a reflection of lack of attention. Part of the answer derives from the visibility of urban population growth. In addition, the early dualistic development models envisioned a rather homogeneous rural sector, within which migration was seen to confer no real benefit. In point of fact intra-rural migration may have many properties in common with rural–urban migration: it can enhance income opportunities, may involve a transition from family to wage labor, may involve a shift from one line of production to another (between subsistence and cash crops, or simply between crop types), and may offer opportunities for family risk-spreading, no less than does rural–urban migration (Ahluwalia, 1978; Kikuchi and Hayami, 1983; Rosenzweig and Stark, 1989).

1.2.4. Notes on temporary and circular migration

Circular migration – returning to an initial residence – can normally only be detected in specialized surveys, since initial residence and place of enumeration do not differ. In consequence, the extent of circular migration, in the developing world or elsewhere, is not always appreciated.

Nelson (1976) examines some of the survey evidence available on circular and temporary migration (onward movement to another place) and detects some broad regional differences:

> In most of Latin America the great bulk of migrants to the cities have left the countryside permanently. They may move on to different cities and they may return to their place of origin to visit relatives and friends, but few come back to rural areas to stay. In contrast, much rural-to-urban migration in Africa and parts of Asia is temporary. (Nelson, 1976: p. 721.)

One of the most detailed examinations is by Lee (1980) based on census data as well as a specialized survey in South Korea. The 1970 Census of Korea asked place of usual residence five years ago, as well as place of birth. Based on this, Lee finds that 9.1% of in-migrants during the 1965–1970 period are persons returning to their province of birth. Although this portion is not negligible, at least the Korean case hardly lends support to the idea that much rural-to-urban migration is temporary. Moreover, Lee finds that only 5.2% of inter-district migrants in Korea are persons returning to their province of birth and for inter-community migrants this fraction drops to 4.1%. Whether this declining fraction with level of disaggregation reflects differences in behavior among the different migrant groups or a constant rate of return to one's initial province, but not necessarily to one's initial community, is unclear.[7]

---

[7] See Hugo (1982) on circular migration in Indonesia and Stichter (1985) on Africa. For data on rate of urban-to-rural migration, some of which is no doubt circular, see Skeldon (1986) on India, Lucas and Verry (1990) on Malaysia, and Pessino (1991) on Peru.

Later sections of this chapter take up some of the causes and consequences of temporary and return migration. However, even at this stage of depicting stylized facts, it is worth reproducing Nelson's account of a stylized life history, compiled from a number of case studies (notably in East Africa):

> a young man who has completed his primary education moves to the city. There he stays with friends or relatives for a few years and earns cash for his own immediate needs and for future marriage payments, as well as to help pay younger siblings' school fees and contribute to general family funds … when the migrant wants to marry he will return to his homeplace. If he has access to land or alternative ways to make a living he will stay for a time. Later, growing pressures for cash to build a house, buy or improve land or stock, and pay school fees and taxes may drive him back to the city, leaving his wife in charge of the home plot. … After a few years the migrant may feel his interests at home need more constant attention. He may also have obligations to his aging parents…. One or more further cycles may follow. Eventually he will return to the country home permanently, either because he can afford to retire or because he has lost his job in the city. (Nelson, 1976: p. 723.)

It is clear from Nelson's account that cyclical movements can be quite complex, even though many individuals may fulfill only some stages of this stereotype pattern. Few statistical surveys are designed to disentangle full migration histories of return or step migration. As a result, statistical documentation of the patterns and selectivity in cyclical and step movements remains poor. Nonetheless portions of this chapter will address statistical evidence on at least some of the elements emerging from the case study material – on such issues as remittances to the rural home, the role of rural property and familial separation.

2. Factors affecting migration flows and selectivity

2.1. Income streams: the basics

Migrants obviously move for many reasons. The notion that migrants often move to gain access to a higher income stream has a very long history in the economics literature. Sjaastad (1962) formalized this idea by hypothesizing that whether an individual elects to move is influenced by the present value of the difference in income streams between alternative locations, minus any initial or subsequent, financial or psychic costs of moving. To the extent that costs are incurred at an early stage, migration is then a form of investment.

One common corollary, drawn from this human capital model of migration, is an explanation for the higher rate of migration amongst the young. Given a longer life horizon, the present value of any given stream of income differences is greater for the

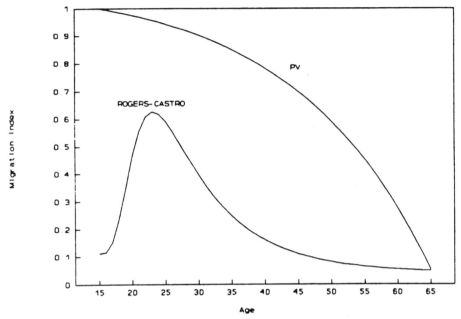

Fig. 1. Model of urban migration by age.

young, offering an enticement to move which diminishes with age. To the extent that the young have a higher discount rate than have older persons, this frequently made assertion may, of course, not hold.

Such a simple view does not do well in depicting a typical age profile of migrants (Schultz, 1982a). Fig. 1 shows the present value (PV) of the difference between an urban income which is a constant multiple of rural income, irrespective of age, assuming a constant discount rate and fixed retirement at age 65.[8] The other curve in Fig. 1 is derived from the model of migration according to age fitted by Rogers and Castro (1984).[9]

The Rogers–Castro curve obviously picks out the peak of migration in early adult years, whereas the simple human capital model does not. In other words, the narrowing life span to retirement may help to explain the diminishing rate of migration with age, but other factors must enter the story to gain a more realistic picture as to why migration at first rises than falls away very quickly after the early twenties – a pattern common to both developed and developing countries.

[8] See Schwartz (1976) for a discussion of the context in which employment opportunities are also affected by age.

[9] This is the Rogers and Castro seven-parameter model, applied to mean parameter estimates for males in Japan, Sweden and the UK. For details on the nonlinear estimation methods used, see Rogers and Castro (1984: Appendix A).

2.2. Migration and job search

2.2.1. The Todaro hypothesis and theoretical extensions

In the first two decades following World War II, policy advice in the newly independent, developing countries, as well as conventional wisdom in the emerging field of development economics, followed earlier Soviet models, in focussing upon the transfer of labor from agriculture to industry as a concomitant of growth. That this transfer continued despite burgeoning shanty towns and even open, urban unemployment became both a pressing policy concern (in part because of the potential for political instability) and an intellectual puzzle.

Todaro (1969) offers a simple but powerful hypothesis. The essential idea is that urban jobs are more attractive than rural employment; entry to the better urban activities is somehow constrained; and search for urban job openings can be more effectively conducted in close geographical proximity. As a result, urban migration is induced as an investment in job search for the attractive, urban opportunities.[10]

Todaro's statement of the migration decision is actually a restatement of the model in Sjaastad (1962), in which Todaro replaces Sjaastad's known urban incomes by their expected values in computing present values, though Todaro continues to assume rural incomes are risk free.

Todaro also makes some strong, simplifying assumptions about the process of urban job search: formal sector wage jobs are the goal of rural–urban migrants; wages in the urban formal sector are exogenous and maintained above clearing by unspecified institutional forces; job search is conducted from a state of open, urban unemployment; workers are risk neutral and derive no utility from leisure. Together these permit expected utility from urban earnings to be expressed as proportional to the going urban wage multiplied by the probability of employment.

Blomqvist (1978) actually identifies two separate formulations of the Todaro hypothesis, distinguished by the determination of the latter element – the probability of employment. According to Blomqvist, Todaro's (1969) specification of the employment probability is determined in a short-run, dynamic setting, such that

$$p = (g+t)\frac{e}{u}, \tag{1}$$

where p is the probability of obtaining a job, g is the proportional rate of new job creation; t is the proportional rate of job turnover, e is the level of employment and u is the level of unemployment.

[10] As usual, these ideas had their precedents. Indeed, in the *Wealth of Nations*, Smith (1812: p. 215) had rather a clear statement of the basic ideas; Frank (1968) addresses a number of these issues in an African context; and Wellisz (1968) develops a more general model.

In other words, Eq. (1) specifies the relevant employment probability as the number of job openings occurring within any period, relative to the number of persons unemployed. In contrast, Harris and Todaro (1970) assume that every urban job turns over in each period and no new jobs are created. In this essentially static case, the probability of employment is simply the fraction of the urban labor force in formal employment, since the chances of obtaining an urban job are equal for all urban workers (who are assumed homogeneous), irrespective of prior employment status:

$$p = \frac{e}{(e+u)}. \tag{2}$$

Few theories in economics have been the subject of such widespread acceptance in policy circles, of empirical challenges, and of theoretical extensions. Each of these will be dealt with in various sections of this chapter, but the present section focusses upon the job search process, at first reviewing theoretical extensions then turning to empirical evidence.

The Harris–Todaro simplifying assumption of a random job lottery with replacement in each period is patently unrealistic. Fortunately, the assumption of this specific form of job turnover can be relaxed to some extent without significantly altering the model. Specifically, Stiglitz (1974) shows that exactly the same expression for the expected urban wage is derived from two alternative approaches, when job openings are created only through exogenous turnover: (a) a random selection from the urban pool of unemployed, resulting in a Poisson distribution of duration of unemployment; and (b) a queue for jobs organized in order of arrival in the urban sector.

Harris and Sabot (1982) expound a theoretical framework which relaxes two other assumptions in the Harris–Todaro stylized job search process – the assumptions of a single urban wage and of perfect information about job opportunities (see also Stark, 1982). Harris and Sabot depict workers confronted by a continuous probability distribution of alternative urban wages, though what sustains this exogenous distribution is explicitly omitted from consideration. At first the actual distribution is unknown and decisions are based upon a subjective distribution. Sampling of job offers, which is assumed to take time, enhances information, and subjective estimates of the available opportunities converge towards the objective distribution. Perhaps the main contribution of this framework is that an increase in the variance of urban wages extends the average duration of optimal job search and hence exacerbates unemployment. The decision to migrate is thus enhanced not only by a greater expected urban wage but also by a lower spread in urban wages.

The appearance of higher moments in the distribution of incomes as an additional explanatory term is a feature to which later sections of this chapter return – in considering risk aversion, the role of relative deprivation as a determinant of migration decisions, and the consequences of aggregating individual decisions. Indeed the manifold potential roles for the variance and other moments of the income distribution in influencing migration flows raises an issue, which has not been adequately addressed in empirical testing, of discerning among these alternative explanations.

In the Harris–Todaro model an equilibrium, with no incentive to further rural–urban migration, occurs when the rural wage equals the expected urban wage. Comparisons of rural and urban pay are thwart with many difficulties – including skill differentials, adjustments for cost of living, property components in income of the self-employed, and complexities in contractual terms both in urban and rural areas (Squire, 1981; Kannappan, 1985). Nonetheless it seems the earnings gap is large: Gregory (1975) estimates that nominal manufacturing wages average 37% higher than agricultural wages for unskilled laborers in a sample of 23 LDCs (see Squire, 1981: Table 30). If this estimate is approximately correct then equilibrium in the Harris–Todaro model would require an unemployment rate of some 27%. Yet open unemployment rates in LDCs very rarely attain such extreme levels, even in the urban sector (see Todaro, 1984: Table 5); the poor cannot finance a protracted job search while jobless. Two responses are possible to such rough calculations: one is that a zero migration rate does not prevail and therefore a wage–unemployment equilibrium should not be anticipated; alternatively a number of commentators have suggested that some reformulation of the Todaro model is warranted.

Todaro's model was in part a response to observations on migration into Nairobi. That same city prompted a path-breaking ILO employment mission focussing considerable attention on the operations of the informal labor market (ILO, 1972). Fields (1975) combines these two, remodelling Todaro's formal sector job search, financed in part by participation in the informal sector (see also Stiglitz, 1974). In addition, Fields hypothesizes that even rural residents who conduct an urban job search from their rural base have some chance of finding an urban formal sector job, though their chances of success are lower than for persons who move into town to search (which is quite consistent with the spirit of Todaro's original model). Another realistic alternative is to allow for risk aversion on behalf of migrants.

Suppose, for instance that the objective of a family is to assign some portion of family members (ϕ) such as to maximize

$$p\omega(\phi[w_1 - c] + [1 - \phi]w_r) + [1 - p]\omega(\phi[w_2 - c] + [1 - \phi]w_r), \tag{3}$$

where p is the probability of obtaining a formal sector urban job, ω is the family's utility function, w_1 is the urban formal sector wage, w_2 is the urban informal sector wage, w_r is the rural wage and c is the cost of migrating.

If the utility function takes a simple logarithmic form, then using the first-order condition with respect to ϕ it can be shown that $\phi > 0$ if and only if

$$pw_1 + [1 - p]w_2 - c > w_r. \tag{4}$$

It follows that when $w_2 = c = 0$, equilibrium with positive assignment of some family members to town in this case of risk aversion requires $pw_1 > w_r$.

Each of these modifications allows more realistic calculations of equilibrium unemployment rates in the extended Todaro framework. These extensions also raise important empirical questions about the nature of the urban informal sector and its role in the job search process – questions to which the next section turns.

2.2.2. Evidence on job search and the informal sector

At least four aspects of initial job placement and job mobility amongst rural–urban migrants have been subjected to empirical examination: the duration of initial unemployment among migrants; the frequency with which migrants find an urban job prior to actual relocation; the extent of subsequent mobility from the informal into the formal sector; and the income gap between the urban formal and informal labor markets.

Duration of initial unemployment. If a scenario is envisioned in which the only period of unemployment is an initial one after arrival in town, then the fraction of time a migrant will be employed is equal to one minus the duration of initial search relative to time until withdrawal from the labor force. Ignoring discounting and assuming a constant urban wage, the expected wage in town is then the prevailing wage multiplied by one minus the duration of initial unemployment relative to remaining work life (Stiglitz, 1974). However, the initial duration of unemployment suffered by migrants is of general interest even beyond this particularly simple formulation. Are migrants in fact unemployed for long periods upon arrival? Do migrants suffer more extensive periods of unemployment than urban residents who lose their jobs?

In the context of Botswana, Lucas (1985) estimates logistic functions for the probability of being in employment (either wage or self-employment) in town. This probability does rise with duration in town, a rise which tapers off. However, the magnitude of this rise is both small and statistically insignificant (perhaps in part because the data measure time elapsed in town in years, thus not permitting a distinction within the first year). Moreover one cannot discern from such estimates whether any tendency for employment to rise is a cohort effect or the consequence of reverse migration by those failing to obtain a job.

In a sample of 1406 male migrants into Delhi (both from rural and other urban locations), Banerjee (1991) finds the average completed spell of unemployment is only 17 days. The distribution of these spells is (Banerjee, 1991: Table 1):

Duration of initial unemployment	%
Prearranged job	17.3
Less than 2 days	28.9
3–7 days	17.4
8–15 days	13.7
16–30 days	10.5
30–90 days	8.4
More than 90 days	3.8

Thus, more than 80% of migrants experience some initial open unemployment, but by the end of the first month only 12% have not found a job. Again, Banerjee notes that these estimates may be biased downwards to the extent that unsuccessful job seekers have returned from Delhi and hence are omitted from the sample. Moreover, India has enjoyed quite low rates of open unemployment (see Fallon, 1983). Studies for a few other LDCs, summarized in Yap (1977: Table 3), also suggest that more than three-quarters of migrants who stay in town have found work within 3–6 months.

Frequency of urban jobs arranged prior to migration. In a series of studies, based on his Delhi sample, Banerjee (1983, 1984b, 1991) examines whether or not migrants report having identified their initial urban job prior to arrival in town.

> Of those who entered the informal wage sector, 12 per cent had prearranged their urban jobs (in the sense that they had received firm commitment of employment from the employer), and 42 per cent had migrated on the suggestions of urban-based contacts ... [N]early three-quarters of the non-wage sector entrants expected to set up such activities on arrival in the city ... [A] majority of formal sector entrants too had ... lined up their jobs from the rural area. (Banerjee, 1983: pp. 411, 419.)

It is difficult to reconcile this with the evidence on initial unemployment, summarized in the previous paragraph, derived from the same survey. Two possibilities for reconciliation are that migrants arrive before their prearranged urban jobs are ready or that a substantial fraction of purported prearranged jobs fail to materialize.

Banerjee (1991) reports probit estimates of migrating with or without a prearranged job, based upon these data. According to these estimates, the probability of finding an urban job before relocation rises with the level of education, with age, and with desire for a non-manual job. In other words, a strategy of migrating to seek an urban job – the Todaro scenario – is more common among young, uneducated, manual workers. Interestingly, Banerjee also finds the chance of identifying an urban job prior to moving is lower if the migrant owns any rural land. This Banerjee suggests may reflect dominance in the ability of land owners to finance an initial job search over any difficulties of being an absentee land owner. Alternatively, land may provide a valuable source of insurance, rendering risk averse potential migrants more willing to undertake a risky move to town if they possess land.

Informal–formal sector mobility. Fields' (1975) extension of the Todaro hypothesis suggests that initial urban informal sector employment is used to finance search for formal sector entry. Is such mobility observed in practice?

Cole and Sanders (1985) note that most migrants into Mexico City have little education and consequently the authors assume these migrants must be unable to transfer to the formal sector. They consequently argue that any observed positive correlation between modern urban sector growth and more rapid rural-to-urban migration is the consequence of an indirect effect: formal sector growth stimulates demand for the services and goods produced in the informal sector, and expansion in the latter stimulates migration. However this hardly constitutes a direct test. Moreover, Santiago and Thorbecke (1988), in reviewing time-series data on sectoral pay and employment in Puerto Rico, report a decline in informal sector pay and employment associated with expansion in the formal sector[11] (see also Stark, 1982).

Banerjee (1984b) reports that in his survey of male migrants in Delhi, "Only 24 per cent of those who entered the informal sector on arrival and 6 per cent of the non-wage workers had found their way into the formal sector by the time of the survey" (p. 414). On the other hand, this rate is slightly higher for those who had been in Delhi longer – just over 29% of those who entered the informal sector on arrival are in the formal sector after five years, whereas this averages only 10% for those arriving in the last two years. The chances of transfer from the informal to the formal sector are thus not negligible in this context, and are somewhat greater among men who have been in town longer, though yet again the latter may reflect selective, return migration by those failing to transfer.

Informal–formal sector pay comparisons. Fields' extension of the Todaro hypothesis assumes that pay is greater in the formal sector, thus prompting search for these more attractive alternatives even while employed in the informal sector. Two studies of Bangkok (Chiswick, 1977; Teilhet-Waldorf and Waldorf, 1983) and two of Kuala Lumpur (Mazumdur, 1981; Blau, 1986) present seemingly contradictory evidence, asserting that pay is greater in the informal sector, at least for the unskilled. However at least three difficulties plague any such comparisons. The first is the definition of income from self-employment in the informal sector: as Blau (1986) notes, capital employed in such activities generally remains unknown, and even whether income refers to gross output or to value added is not always clear. A second difficulty stems from potential selection bias: for instance Blau (1985) concludes that in urban areas of Malaysia, ignoring self-selection as between wage and self-employment overstates relative earnings in the latter. The third difficulty raises a much more general and murky issue, namely the definition of the informal sector. Thus, both Blau (1986) and Teilhet-Waldorf and Waldorf (1983) assume that self-employment and the informal sector are synonymous, even though the self-employed typically include many professionals.

Summing up: Is the Todaro hypothesis refuted? Several of the contributions under the four prior headings depict their results as refutations of the Todaro hypothesis. Is this appropriate?

---

[11] On the other hand, Portes and Benton (1984) emphasize some of the data limitations in measuring informal sector growth, and argue that the relative magnitude of formal sector employment growth is normally exaggerated.

The evidence is really too limited to draw any strong conclusions. Such as it is, it seems the average duration of initial unemployment may not be very long, that a substantial portion of migrants have identified their job prior to moving, and by no means all informal sector entrants subsequently transfer to the formal sector. This scenario does not fit well with the Todaro or Harris–Todaro models.[12]

These models are intentionally stated in stylized, exaggerated form. Much of what matters in these hypotheses survives this subsequent evidence: even in low-unemployment India, more than 80% of Delhi's male migrants experience some initial open unemployment, and 24% of those entering the informal sector transfer to the formal sector. This evidence is thus quite consistent with a substantial portion of urban migrants relocating to enhance their chances of finding a better urban job, though this may be a more common strategy among the young and unskilled. Nor need a "better urban job" be confined to the formal wage sector; more lucrative opportunities in the urban self-employment sector may also be more readily sought after arrival in town. Indeed, the Todaro hypothesis may even be inverted, suggesting an investment in menial, urban wage jobs as a path to subsequent transfer to the urban self-employment sector (see Blau, 1986: Table 3). What ultimately matters in the Todaro idea (and its subsequent extension in the Harris–Todaro model) is that entry into low (or no) pay activities may be a worthwhile investment in local search for better opportunities – and this is not convincingly contradicted by the evidence.

2.3. Estimating responsiveness to labor market opportunities

The direct evidence with respect to job search and transition by migrants is suggestive but inconclusive in regard to the Todaro hypothesis. Other forms of evidence on the effect of labor market opportunities on the decision to migrate are abundant. The purpose of the present section is to sketch some of these under three headings: (a) One branch of the literature addresses aggregate evidence on industrial job creation and urban population growth, and this is taken up first. (b) Some of the difficulties in specifying and estimating migration decision equations, incorporating earnings differentials, as well as a synopsis of the results, are given under the second heading. (c) Lastly the subset of migration equation estimates which incorporate employment probabilities as well as earnings is summarized.

2.3.1. Industrial employment and urban population growth

Hoselitz (1953) notes an empirical regularity in the small ratio of industrial employment to urban population in developing countries, relative to ratios observed historically in the now developed economies. "Hoselitz's thesis has encouraged the view

---

[12] See Fields (1989) for extensions of the Harris–Todaro model incorporating some of these stylized facts.

...[of] urbanization without industrialization ... the problem took on alarmist dimensions ... [and] fresh new tests of the Hoselitz hypothesis have gained high research priority" (Williamson, 1988: p. 440).

Much of this evidence is cast in growth form. Preston (1979) detects no decline in the ratio of industrial employment to urban population in the LDCs as a whole from 1950 to 1970. However, using World Bank data from the 1960s, Berry and Sabot (1984) show that, in historical perspective, LDC urban population growth is indeed rapid despite small rates of industrial employment growth. Becker et al. (1986) argue that not only has India's manufacturing employment growth (in the factory sector) been slower than urban population growth, but when "organized" urban employment growth slowed during the 1970s, urban population growth accelerated. Becker and Morrison (1988) find that urban population growth in sub-Saharan Africa exceeds the growth in manufacturing employment. Moreover, in regression estimates of urban population growth in that region, Becker and Morrison report a positive but quite small (instrumented) effect of urban modern sector employment.

Whether one should be alarmist about such findings is far from obvious. The shadow cost of marginal industrial jobs cannot be deduced from this evidence. Certainly the mere observation that much of the urban population, and even a growing fraction, is not employed in the formal industrial sector need not imply a zero marginal product. Any tendency to translate the Hoselitz thesis, or a growth variant of this thesis, into a statement about over-urbanization is misplaced.

Whether rapid urban growth accompanies slower industrial growth because of an induced supply of labor or, for instance, as a result of intersectoral demand is not identified in a single equation model. One method adopted to disentangle some of these links is simulation with spatial computable general equilibrium (CGE) models. Such models can be useful in quantifying the contribution of alternative policies and exogenous trends in promoting city growth (Collier, 1979; Becker et al., 1986). But this genre of models is ultimately driven by their construction: they are not appropriate grounds for classical statistical tests.

2.3.2. Estimating responsiveness to earnings differentials

A key component in constructing spatial CGE models is the elasticity of labor supply to geographic earnings differentials. The literature reporting estimates of this responsiveness is vast and no attempt is made here to review all of these contributions. Rather, the focus here falls upon some of the econometric problems associated with specifying and estimating this responsiveness.

For simplicity, suppose that the probability μ of person a, observed at random, choosing location i, is

$$\mu_i^a = \mu(W^a, C^a, A^a, \varepsilon^a), \tag{5}$$

where W^a is a vector of discounted wage streams available to a in various locations, C^a is a similar vector of discounted costs incurred in relocating, A^a is some vector of a's personal attributes, and ε^a is a stochastic term reflecting a's idiosyncratic tastes. Two principal routes are adopted to estimation of such equations – distinguished by whether aggregate or micro data are used.

A stylized representation of a macro migration equation estimate might be written

$$m_{ji} = m(w_i, w_j, d_{ji}, A_j, \xi),$$ (6)

where m_{ji} is the fraction of j's population migrating to i, w_i and w_j are the mean wages in i and j respectively, d_{ji} is the distance from j to i, A_j is a vector of average personal attributes among j's population, and ξ is a stochastic disturbance.

Two aspects of Eq. (6) as an approximation to Eq. (5) are worth emphasizing. One is the use of proxy variables. In particular, the typical macro migration equation includes only current earnings as a proxy for the discounted stream of future earnings at the time of migrating. Also distance is normally seen as a proxy for transition costs, assumed to vary directly with transportation costs, psychological costs of removal to an unfamiliar milieu, and costs of information acquisition.

The second aspect is that Eq. (6) includes only mean values for earnings and personal characteristics. If both Eqs. (5) and (6) are strictly linear, Eq. (6) can then simply be viewed as derived from the expected value of Eq. (5). If Eq. (6) is nonlinear, however, as when estimating a logit form to avoid dependent variable truncation for instance, this simple transition is incomplete. In particular, if Eq. (5) is nonlinear then taking expected values would introduce higher moments of the explanatory variables, and omission of these terms may result in omitted variable bias (see Lucas, 1975).

A substantial number of macro migration equations, similar to Eq. (6) have been estimated for developing countries. Most are cross-sectional, using different regions of origin and destination as observations.[13] Some, but not all, instrument the earnings terms to correct for simultaneity bias. As Yap (1977) notes in reviewing the earlier contributions in this sphere, most estimates find a positive effect for destination wage, a negative effect for origin wage, and a negative effect for distance.

With the advent of specialized sample surveys, micro estimates of migration decision equations similar to Eq. (5) have proliferated in more recent years. In these, the dependent variable is usually a dummy variable, for the mover–stayer distinction, or polytomous if more than one destination is distinguished. The principal difficulty which such estimates present is in the measurement of earnings at the alternative locations. For stayers, the wage they would receive elsewhere is not directly observed; for migrants, earnings prior to migration are not usually reported, nor is potential pay in

---

[13] For early examples see, for instance, Beals et al. (1967), Sahota (1968), Greenwood (1971), Levy and Wadycki (1974).

rejected locations directly observed.[14] Macro estimates effectively bypass this difficulty by assuming that each person's pay in any given location is the mean pay actually observed there. A number of micro studies attempt to improve on this by estimating an earnings equation in alternative locations, thus at least projecting average pay according to a subset of personal characteristics. In itself, this approach raises three additional problems. (i) Some identifying restrictions are necessary to distinguish the set of personal characteristics entering the earnings prediction equation from those conditioning taste or otherwise entering the migration decision equation. (ii) Unbiased estimation of the earnings equations requires correction for sample selection, since not everyone earns. Typically this is achieved through a subsidiary probit estimate of the chances of earning, from which a hazard rate is computed and included in the earnings equation. This again requires some identifying restrictions on the set of personal characteristics included in the probit equation for earners. (iii) Finally there is a potential problem of positive or negative selection in migration; movers may differ systematically from stayers in ways not reflected in measured characteristics alone. They may, for instance, be more enterprising, more willing to take risks, or brighter. Conversely, migrants may differ from the indigenous population at destination in unmeasured ways.

There has been a fairly steady rise in the degree of sophistication in dealing with these issues. Perhaps one of the most comprehensive is Falaris (1987).[15] Falaris estimates a nested logit model, with choice of state nested within regional choice in Venezuela. The estimation procedure allows for selection correction for choice of state (and region) in estimating earnings equations for each state, as well as for correlation between the errors in the earnings equation and in the stochastic utility function for any given individual. Falaris finds significant positive selection in six out of the 17 state earnings equations estimated, implying that in these six cases the people who chose to go to (including remaining in) these six states receive higher wages than would observationally equivalent people drawn at random from the population. Unobserved similarities are also found between states within the regional groupings adopted, indicating a gain in efficiency in specifying a nested logit model. However, "the main results of the structural estimates are that wages and distance are important determinants of migration (with positive and negative coefficients, respectively, as expected). If a state is the individual's origin, this increases the relative probability of choosing it over another state" (Falaris, 1987: pp. 440–441).

Despite the refinements, the chief messages from the results have thus not altered our understanding, even in comparison to macro estimates. Whether further effort in refining our estimation techniques will pay off in terms of removing biases and in-

---

[14] If information on migrants is in the form of absentees, then even current pay may be unknown. Some studies bypass the difficulty by looking at push factors alone, but this may well lead to specification bias (see, for instance, Nabi, 1984).

[15] See also Hay (1980) on Tunisia, Tunali (1985) on Turkey, Vijverberg (1989) on Cote d'Ivoire, and Pessino (1991) on Peru.

creasing precision is obviously unknown. A systematic comparison of the improvements to date, from any given data set, may be worthwhile. On the other hand, perhaps the balance of effort should shift toward formulating and testing newer hypotheses.

2.3.3. Estimates incorporating unemployment

Surprisingly few estimates of migration decision functions incorporate measures of unemployment. Again, those that do may be divided according to their use of macro and micro data.

Falaris (1979) finds that employment rate measures at origin and destination have no significant effect on migration in a two-stage least squares model of inter-regional migration in Peru.[16] However, from three-stage least squares estimates of inter-regional migration in Mexico, Greenwood (1978) reports that rising employment levels (given earnings) both deter out-migration and accelerate in-migration, though reductions in the level of unemployment accentuate only the latter effect.[17] Schultz (1982b) finds, for Venezuelan males with less than secondary schooling, that migration is affected by the wage gap but not by employment probabilities. However, for males with more education, Schultz finds that the elasticity of migration with respect to employment is greater than with respect to wages. Moreover, at least three studies based on inter-regional aggregate migration data estimate that higher unemployment rates at destination deter migration, given earnings differentials.[18] In Tanzania, Barnum and Sabot (1977) estimate a positive role for urban job probability, whether constrained to interact with urban wage to form the expected wage or not. Salvatore (1980) finds the difference between unemployment rates at origin and destination affects south to north migration within Italy.[19] Banerjee and Kanbur (1981), formulate the urban risk variable as the open unemployment rate relative to the employment rate and detect a negative effect upon urban migration in the 1961 census of India.

Lucas (1985) applies micro data to estimate a multinomial logit model of migration decisions in Botswana, incorporating both earnings and employment at origin and destination. As with the micro data studies incorporating earnings alone, prediction equations are estimated for earnings and for employment probabilities in the alternative locations. Earnings and employment probabilities at origin and in town are included separately, without constraining them to be symmetric or to enter in the form of expected earnings. Four separate migration equations are estimated, for four regions of origin. Tests on the estimated parameters fail to reject a hypothesis of symmetry – higher home earnings and employment probabilities have an equal and opposite

---

[16] See also Fields (1982).

[17] See also Greenwood et al. (1981).

[18] In addition, Cole and Sanders (1983) proxy unemployment by labor force participation measures in Mexico, which offers a fairly indirect test of the Todaro hypothesis, though they interpret their results as consistent with the Todaro hypothesis.

[19] See also Salvatore (1981).

effect upon migration in comparison to urban earnings and employment probabilities. Moreover, the implied number of additional adult migrants resulting from creation of one extra urban job exceeds one. Whether the additional migrants are simply adult family members accompanying the migrant with no intent to enter the urban labor force cannot be distinguished.[20] In addition, these results emphasize the problem of rural income risk, to which later sections of this chapter return.

2.4. Networks and information

A substantial amount of evidence indicates an empirical regularity: persons having access to kinship and other networks at a place of destination are more likely to choose that place.

> Destination contacts have a positive effect on migration to a specific area, when contacts are measured by the presence of parents in the city, ... by potential ethnic contacts, ... by language similarity between areas .. or by the stock of persons in the destination who had migrated earlier from the home area. (Yap, 1977: pp. 248–249.)[21]

However, several interpretations of these regularities are possible. For instance, having personal contacts may diminish the psychic costs of relocating, may lower the financial costs of resettling (by the common practice of initial accommodation with friends or relatives), or may speed the process of job search (Yap, 1977). More generally, networks may enhance information available to potential migrants and reduce the risk associated with the urban prospect (see, for instance, Goodman, 1981; Taylor, 1986).

The lack of complete information certainly raises an interesting issue, for Sjaastad's human capital model is couched in terms of known and certain alternatives, while the Harris–Todaro model introduces uncertainty but retains complete information about wages and the chances of employment. Does adding more complete information about earnings opportunities and the risks of unemployment enhance or deter migration? It is not clear. The answer depends very much upon whether uninformed perceptions are biased upwards and skewed towards smaller subjective risks (see Harris and Sabot, 1982).

Not surprisingly, given this ambiguity and the difficulty in disentangling the role of information from other factors, the evidence in this sphere is difficult to interpret. An observation that the educated tend to be less deterred by distance in migrating (Levy

---

[20] Ultimately labor force participation is difficult to measure in any context, but perhaps especially so in low-income countries where family enterprises are common.

[21] Yap also cites the sources of evidence in support of these statements. See also Ritchey (1976).

and Wadycki, 1974) has been interpreted as a reflection of easier access to distant information for the literate (Schwartz, 1973). There are other reasons why the educated may be less deterred by distance, including access to capital to finance such moves (to be taken up in the following section), and perhaps the lack of nearby jobs for the educated – the greater the degree of specialization, the larger the market necessary to secure a match (Yap, 1977).

Caces et al. (1985) report a multinomial logit analysis of intent to move to Manila, to Hawaii or to stay at home, for a sample of adults in the Ilocos Norte province of the Philippines. Included in the explanatory variables are dummies for the existence of friends or relatives in the two destinations. The estimates show a positive effect of relatives in either Manila or Hawaii in attracting more migrants to the respective destination.[22] The cross effect – contacts in Manila affecting migration to Hawaii or vice versa – the authors dub a "competing auspices" effect. This effect proves negative (although statistically insignificant) in both cases, the cross effects not being constrained to be equal. However, as Caces et al. note, the cause of these effects is unclear if only because the presence of family in Hawaii renders access to a US visa considerably easier. Taylor (1986), similarly estimates a multinomial logit model for internal migration, international migration or remaining in the home village for a sample of 423 adults from two villages in Mexico. Taylor finds that having kin (son, daughter, sibling, or parent of household head) at destination increases the chances of international migration but not of internal migration. Taylor interprets this as a reflection of the higher risk inherent in international migration and the importance of kinship networks in reducing the effective risk, though presumably an alternative interpretation may again stem from ability to enter the US legally.

Banerjee (1984b) reports that 27% of his sample of male migrants in Delhi indicate having no prior information about employment opportunities before moving although 85% had relatives or friends there. This is one of the few studies that attempts to incorporate direct data on job information, and the result suggests that having a contact in town is no guarantee of possessing specific information, although of course more general information about the job market could still have been transmitted.

One of the most interesting recent models incorporating information generation and migration is that of Pessino (1991). The idea is that distant information is less readily available and all information can take time to acquire. Initial moves from villages are thus often to nearby towns, about which information is available. In the town the migrant learns of other opportunities more distant from his or her initial home, resulting in the frequently observed step migration. Once again these ideas prove difficult to distinguish empirically, and the connection with the interesting evidence from Peru presented by Pessino is not transparent.

If differential information were available among potential migrants – perhaps enhanced by contacts at destination, perhaps affected by distance – what would be the

---

[22] For related evidence on Mexican emigration, see Taylor (1986).

policy implication? Yap (1977: p. 250) suggests that "... redirection from larger to smaller cities may be feasible if wage incentives are supplemented by advance information and assistance in moving". Fuller et al. (1985) report on an experiment, offering more information about opportunities in towns, other than Bangkok, to residents of a set of villages in Thailand. From the villages where additional information was provided, migration to the smaller towns increased, whereas no such increase occurred from other, control villages. On the other hand, no reduction in the rate of migration to Bangkok from the better informed villages was observed. In other words, total migration was increased, not diverted from the capital to smaller towns, as a result of the additional information.

The foregoing literature on networks and information addresses information available to migrants about jobs. However this is only one side of the story. Modern labor economics also focusses upon the asymmetry in information about skills or productivity – information possessed by workers about themselves but not readily seen by a potential employer. In a series of theoretical contributions, Katz and Stark address these issues within the context of migration, showing that both extent and selectivity in migration may be affected (Katz and Stark, 1986b, 1987, 1989; Stark, 1991a). In particular, these models assume that the skill of each worker is known at the place of origin but not at destination. Risk neutral employers at the place of potential destination attribute to each migrant, irrespective of individual skill, the average skill of all those who actually migrate.[23] If wage offers at destination then reflect this estimated skill, the consequence of asymmetric information is to lower destination wage offers by most for the most highly skilled. The consequences for the extent and selectivity of migration depend upon the resulting shape of the skill–wage profile at destination and origin. If these profiles are nonlinear, then multiple equilibria may exist and generalizations become difficult (Katz and Stark, 1987). On the other hand, if the skill–wage profiles are linear in both locations, and if low-skill workers would migrate under symmetric information, then adding asymmetric information rotates the destination wage profile downwards at higher skill levels – more skilled migrants are attributed with only the average skill of their migrating compatriots who include the least skilled.[24] Adding asymmetry then clearly lowers the average skill level of migrants and reduces the volume of migration. Katz and Stark also explore the effects of eventual discovery by destination employers of migrants' true skills and of pre-migration signalling by migrants. Somewhat surprisingly, the addition of eventual discovery may benefit low skilled workers:

> ... one would have thought that eventual discovery will lower the benefits to those who have most to hide, namely the workers with low skill levels. However, this does not happen in our case since the workers with higher skill levels attracted by

---

[23] For an extension to risk averse employers, see Katz and Stark (1987).

[24] Sufficient conditions for linearity are spelled out in Stark (1991a).

eventual discovery provide a benefit to low-skill workers by raising the pre-discovery wages (Katz and Stark, 1987: p. 724.)

Stark (1991a) considers a signalling model where the costs of signalling true skill are fixed. If this cost is too high to warrant signalling by low-skill workers but sufficiently low to encourage signalling by high-skill workers then a U-shape pattern emerges. Low-skill workers migrate without signalling, no migration occurs among those with intermediate skills, and migration plus signalling is undertaken by the highly skilled.[25] This pattern essentially corresponds to the rural–urban selectivity, noted by Connell et al. (1976), drawing disproportionately upon primary and secondary school graduates with a (weak) dip among middle school leavers in between. However, as with much of the labor market literature on asymmetric information, these theories await more rigorous testing.

2.5. The role of capital

So far, in this chapter, the focus in discussing the determinants of migration has fallen largely upon the earnings of labor. This section now takes up two aspects related to capital: the financing of migration and the issue of tied rents received from capital.

2.5.1. Financing migration

Although largely neglected in the estimation of migration equations, the human capital framework emphasizes the discounted stream of incomes in alternative locations and hence the fact that migration is a form of investment. The supply curve of loanable funds shifts from family to family (see Becker's Woytinsky Lecture reproduced in Becker, 1975). This need not be a reflection of imperfect capital markets, but simply of variations in collateral possessed, or in the opportunity cost of marginal use of funds. Yet it seems likely that imperfections in capital markets compound these differences in low-income countries where financial markets are less complete.

   Whatever the cause, differences in the supply of loanable funds enable varying degrees of investment in the more expensive forms of migration. From their survey of village studies, Connell et al. (1976) detect a U-shape pattern in out-migration from LDC villages with higher propensities to move among the rich and poor. In the context of India they note:

   Sons, and to a lesser extent daughters, of successful farmers move to ... urban employment; sons, or often families, of labourers move temporarily, as often to the village as to the city (Connell et al., 1976: p. 24.)

---

[25] This result can also be extended to the case where signalling costs diminish with skill levels.

The possibility of a quadratic relation between income and propensity to migrate is taken up in two multivariate analyses, with conflicting results. Despite the suggestion by Connell et al. of a dip in migration rates among middle income groups in India, Banerjee and Kanbur (1981) find that migration by men from rural areas of one state to urban areas of another state of India, prior to the 1961 Census, initially rises with rural income then turns down at higher incomes. In contrast, Stark and Taylor (1991), in their multinomial logit analysis of migration among 423 adults from the Patzcuaro region of Mexico in 1983, find no statistically significant pattern with respect to the influence of family income on the propensity for internal migration. This last result could partly reflect including education as an explanatory variable: the wealthy are better educated, and there is evidence that educated migrants more readily take on more expensive moves to town (Levy and Wadycki, 1974). Any effects of access to cheaper funds on the propensity to migrate thus remain to be disentangled in the empirical literature. Simple correlates of the type noted in Connell et al. are clearly insufficient: any pattern detected might then reflect differential gains in earnings according to education level, more and better use of information, contacts in town among the educated/wealthy and hence cheaper settling in costs, variations in the degree of subjective risk aversion across wealth classes, or indeed differences in the supply of funds for education and hence migration.

2.5.2. Tied rents

These complexities are compounded by the role of personal and family assets in influencing the migration decision, for the composition of these assets and the distribution of ownership rights, and not just the level of assets may matter.

Early views of the peasant household within development economics focussed upon the tendency to share in output from the family plot. It was assumed that selfish individuals would therefore compare their income at home, the average product under equal sharing, with an outside wage in deciding whether to migrate.[26] Presuming the outside wage reflects marginal product, this leads to an equilibrium with surplus labor allocated to peasant farming. The weak link in these early depictions is now understood to be the implicit role assigned to capital (see Stiglitz, 1969). Suppose that the individual is able to rent out his or her portion of the capital upon leaving the family farm, for a rent equal to the marginal product that the land would generate if he or she remained at home. Even the selfish person will then balance only the marginal product

---

[26] Bhattacharyya (1985) finds a positive coefficient on the average product of labor in agriculture, given a negative role for local wages, in estimating an aggregate rural-to-urban migration function for India. This he interprets as reflecting the selfish family's interest, rather than the individual's, in making the migration decision, on the grounds that if the migrant had stayed at home he or she would have consumed the average product. An alternative interpretation might derive from the role of greater average product in enabling costly migration to be financed.

of his/her own labor at home against the outside wage.[27] Surplus labor does not persist. On the other hand, if no market for renting out or selling land exists, if the individual would be denied rights to all or some portion of the land upon departure, or if the marginal product of the assets would be less in the absence of the individual, the rents are effectively tied to presence. In the extreme case, when no rent would be generated upon departure, if the household shares equally while together and the individual acts selfishly, the average product wage returns. Indeed even if the division of property rights generates a rent to the individual, but a rent less than the marginal product of the land, then surplus labor remains (Manove et al., 1987).

There are circumstances, in developing countries, under which individuals indeed lose their right to assets upon departure. For instance, under tribal land schemes in Africa, it is not uncommon to reassign land which is not operated by a person or family. Similarly, members of cooperatives may not have the right to compensation to their implicit portion of the assets upon withdrawal. To what extent individual households operate in this fashion is much more difficult to detect.

A second class of cases must be distinguished, namely the instance when the marginal product of a locally specific asset is affected by the presence of a particular person or persons. For instance, knowledge about the idiosyncrasies of family land may result in a potential rent to outsiders which is less than the marginal product of the land to the specific family, assuming that no device exists for perfect transmission of knowledge. (For evidence in an Indian context, see Rosenzweig and Wolpin (1985)). More generally, any locally specific knowledge, which cannot be marketed while absent, tends to tie an individual to a particular place (Jagannathan (1987) refers to local contacts and other investments in local information as social assets). This more general form has not been subject to systematic tests.

2.6. Temporary, return and permanent migration

Explanations for temporary, and especially circular migration may broadly be divided into two. The first provides a link with the foregoing section on capital, for temporary migrants are often characterized as target savers with a specific investment in mind (including marriage or education of children, as well as saving for a home, land, item of capital, or retirement) (Nelson, 1976). Such target savers are viewed as intending to return from the outset, perhaps because of a preference for living at home, or because the cost of living is lower in the rural area of origin (see Fan and Stretton, 1985). A second explanation postulates that return migrants may not have intended a temporary move: these migrants may include those whose perceptions of the destination failed to materialize, those who proved unlucky in their gamble for a job, or whose tastes changed to the detriment of living in the destination area. Distinguishing between

---

[27] This assumes constant returns to scale so that Euler's theorem holds.

these two major alternatives presents a major challenge to empirical research – a challenge not yet successfully taken up.

More attention has been given to the target saver model. Beringhaus and Seifer-Vogt (1988) develop a stochastic, dynamic programming model of a target saver migrant with incomplete information. An intent to be a temporary migrant may be transformed into a decision to remain permanently, in this model, if the host conditions render achieving the target impossible. This may well be mitigated in practice by learning and target adjustment on behalf of the migrant, but this is explicitly omitted from the model of Beringhaus and Seifer-Vogt. Galor and Stark (1990) model an interesting consequence of target saving. They hypothesize that migrants who are more likely to return to their initial lower income s ting will have higher savings propensities, while in the host context, than do mi ants who are less likely to return or, for that matter, than do identical natives. If return migration then does not materialize, high saving migrants accumulate more capital than the native born.

The statistical evidence on the causes of temporary migration is sparse. In his study of urban-to-rural return migration in Korea, Lee (1980: p. 148), concludes that "repulsion from the city rather than attraction in the rural origin is more important", though this is founded upon reasons stated by returnees. Blejer and Goldberg (1980) find that most migrants returning from Israel do so after only a very short stay, and that unemployed immigrants and those withdrawing from the labor force as discouraged workers are most likely to return home. Despite the lack of systematic evidence, it does seem likely that in other contexts target savings represent an important component in the story, and surely so for international guest workers (Nelson, 1976; Lucas, 1988).

2.7. Family strategies

Much of the literature on migration in LDCs treats urban unemployment risk explicitly, but typically abstracts from rural risks. In most developing countries, this seems perverse. Droughts, floods, pests and world price fluctuations may well render agriculture a far riskier proposition than making a living in town (Stark and Levhari, 1982). Explicit crop insurance rarely exists in developing countries, in part because of the moral hazard involved. Instead, rural families seek alternative modes of insuring their incomes. One device for reducing the variance in family incomes is diversifying across alternative sources of income which are not highly, positively correlated. For instance, placing some family members in town and pooling village and town incomes may offer insurance both for the urban migrants and for those who stay in the village, if an enforceable mechanism for pooling is established. Indeed, risk averse families may gain from such a strategy, and hence migration may be observed, even if the mean and variance of incomes is identical in town and countryside and if no net transfer occurs – transfers between village and town occur according to the state of nature in any given period but balance each other on average. This idea of families straddling the rural–urban divide is noted in a number of case studies (amongst others, see Corner (1981) on Kedah district, Malaysia; Curtain (1981) on Papua New Guinea; Shaw (1988) on Calcutta and Oberai et al. (1989) on Bihar, Kerala and Uttar Pradesh).

Lucas and Stark (1985) and Stark and Lucas (1988) estimate remittance functions for households in Botswana during a year of drought, in part to test for the presence of such insurance provision.[28] The incidence of drought is beyond the control of the family, and hence involves no moral hazard. Families living in the worst drought hit villages are not observed systematically receiving more remittances than others. Nor are low-income families. It therefore seems that pure altruism is not the major motive for remitting. However, families with more cattle and with larger cropping lands, in drought areas, do receive larger remittances. This is quite consistent with rural households assigning members to town in order to insure against investing in risky assets at home.

Lucas and Stark also explore another family understanding through their estimates of remittance equations. Remittances from all absentees are greater, the higher is the education achieved by the migrant. However, among the family's own young members (most notably females), likely to have been educated by the family, the rise in remittances with education is even greater. This suggests the possibility of an understanding that the family educates its young members in return for subsequent repayment. More generally, though not tested by Lucas and Stark, it seems plausible that education is part of an intertemporal arrangement; the family educates members in order for them to migrate and gain urban entry, ultimately to repay the family from town and hence finance subsequent education of younger family members (see Connell et al., 1976; Katz and Stark, 1985b).

A difficulty with such intertemporal understandings within the family, whether with respect to initial urban risk and continuing rural insurance or with respect to initial schooling, is enforcement after the educated urban migrant has passed the initial risky phase. To some extent, trust, tradition and altruism make the family a natural enforcement unit. Elder members of the family may also threaten to disinherit those who cheat. In support of this, Lucas and Stark report that families with larger cattle herds (the main form of hereditary wealth in Botswana) receive larger remittances from sons eligible to inherit, than from others.

Rosenzweig and Stark (1989) investigate another form of insurance sought by rural families through migration, namely intra-rural migration for marriage. Across six villages in central India, pairwise village correlations in monsoon rainfall, real agricultural profits and real agricultural wages over a ten-year interval are shown to decline significantly with distance between villages. In other words, risk spreading would be

---

[28] Intra-household transfers are not taken up systematically in this chapter, since they are dealt with in Chapter 12 of this volume.

possible by diversifying income sources across villages, especially villages far apart. Nonresident in-laws are a major source of income transfers during episodes of shortfall in India. Thus, placing in-laws in distant villages offers the potential for effective insurance. After noting the commonality of inter-village marriage, over a mean distance of 30 kilometers, Rosenzweig and Stark examine the extent of consumption smoothing achieved by individual households over a ten-year interval. The variance in household consumption is positively associated with the variance in profits from own land, indicating less than perfect smoothing. However, an interaction between this variance in profits and number of married women present, and a further interaction with marital distance, both prove to reduce the variance in consumption, which is consistent with consumption smoothing through migration for marriage. Rosenzweig and Stark also find that an increase in variance of profits on own land, instrumented to purge for the effects of moral hazard, is associated with an increased number of outmigrants and with marriage distance. On the other hand, greater inherited wealth is associated with shorter marital distance, perhaps reflecting the lesser need for insurance.

Behrman and Wolfe (1985) examine another aspect of marriage in relation to migration, namely the search for husbands in Nicaragua.[29] Micro data are deployed to estimate the micro decision among females in relation to labor market differentials, the demographic marriage market (the probability of a male companion) and the economic marriage market (the expected earnings of a companion). Options with respect to the explanatory variables are examined for three locations – Managua, other urban areas, and rural areas. For each location a prediction equation is estimated to provide measures on the three sets of explanatory variables. The problem of identifying separate effects is severe, for it is not obvious which explanatory variables can reasonably be excluded from the various prediction equations. As a result, the predicted values are highly collinear. In response, Behrman and Wolfe present estimates both including and excluding employment probabilities. When these are excluded, the labor market variables play an insignificant role, while both the demographic and economic marriage market variables prove statistically significant (though not always with the anticipated sign). If employment probabilities are incorporated, then the influence of the labor market in the migration decision is estimated to be greater.

As noted in the section on stylized facts, in Latin America rural–urban migrants are more likely to be female than male. This is also true in the Philippines, in which context Lauby and Stark (1988) offer an explanation rooted in a risk reduction strategy pursued by the rural family, rather than in an individual decision derived from either the job or marriage markets for women. In particular, Lauby and Stark argue that, at least in the Philippine context, although female migrants' earnings may be lower than

---

[29] Stark (1988) develops a number of interconnections between the labor market, migration and marriage, including the simultaneity of these decisions for an individual, some consequences of joint decisions of couples, and potential effects upon the stability of marriages.

males' they are also more secure, and that daughters remit more than sons from a given level of earnings. Placing daughters in town may thus offer greater security to the rural family than having sons migrate.

Rural families apparently can insure their incomes to some extent by placing either sons or daughters in town and by intra-rural marriage of children. It is then natural to proceed beyond considering the allocation of a given number of family members to inquire into the implications for family size. Katz and Stark (1985a) consider several comparative statics effects on the demand for children, precisely in a context where the family pursues a migration strategy to enhance utility derived both from income per member and from lower risk in this income stream. In general it proves difficult to sign effects, given potentially opposing forces. For instance, if the income of a child-migrant increases:

- the returns to an additional child are increased leading to a substitution effect enhancing the demand for children;
- family income is raised and, assuming diminishing absolute risk aversion, the income effect reinforces the increased demand for children to the extent that concern for higher mean family income dominates;
- but if concern to reduce risk in family income dominates, then the income effect works in the opposite direction – higher income reduces risk aversion and hence reduces the demand for child-migrants as insurance;
- the child-migrant is individually better off and may be tempted to break any implicit contract to support the rural family, presumably reducing the demand for children, though this may be more than offset to the extent that the child's altruism toward the family is a normal good.

These components also act in the same direction if the risk in the child-migrant's income is reduced.[30]

Stark (1991b) notes several additional factors which may complicate this picture. The potential for migration can, for instance, increase the demand for children to enhance the bargaining position of the family vis-à-vis its migrant members: a larger pool of migrant members increases the credibility of threat to disinherit individuals and diminishes capacity for children to collude. Moreover, as Stark argues, if the core family receives declining marginal support for money invested in each migrant member, there is again an incentive to think of a large family.

Ultimately, signing the combined effect from such changes must consequently fall to empirical evidence. Such investigations must face a difficult problem in time, for any change in an urban migrant's income would only be realized through newborn family members with at least a 15-year lag.

Finally, under this heading of family strategies, the issue of conjugal separation – migration by one marital partner alone – is addressed. Single men apparently domi-

---

[30] Katz and Stark (1986d) extend this analysis to the case when the decision by the child whether and how much to remit is endogenous to the analysis.

nate rural-to-urban migration in Africa and Asia (Todaro, 1976b). Among those who are married, it is common to leave wives at home in the village. Usually this is part of a temporary migration pattern, with visits or more permanent return by the husband, or subsequent urban settlement by the wife and children (Nelson, 1976). Often the period of separation is depicted as a source of hardship for the wives in particular (Colfer, 1985), though it is not always clear they are economically worse off if they receive some remittances from an absent husband, or are able to increase their control over, and share of, the rural generated income.

Banerjee (1984a) notes, from his sample of male migrants in Delhi, that 30% of married rural-to-urban migrants are not living with their wives, while this is true for only 7% of inter-urban migrants. Focussing on the rural–urban migrants exclusively, Banerjee estimates a linear probability function, with the dependent dummy variable indicating whether the wife is with the husband or not. Banerjee finds that conjugal separation declines with the level of education of the migrant, a U-shaped pattern is found with respect to duration of residence in Delhi, and an inverse U-shape for age when first moved. The turning point in the quadratic on duration of residence is estimated to occur after 60 years and the positive portion is therefore irrelevant. Whether the tendency for longer term residents to have their wives with them reflects subsequent reunification in town, higher return migration by men separated from their wives, or a secular trend cannot be discerned from these results. The inverse U with respect to age at time of arrival also does not turn down until age 66. Conjugal separation is thus less likely to occur the younger is the male upon arrival in town, which could reflect a pattern of younger arrivals finding an urban bride, of adopting urban attitudes, or of accumulating sufficient savings to bring a village bride to town.

The theoretical literature on family strategies – linking migration with such issues as fertility, education, marriage, inheritance, and risk spreading – has proved very fruitful in the last few years. However the empirical literature still offers no more than a few isolated examples. Replication or rejection of results in other contexts should be a high research priority. In so doing, it may prove fruitful to explore the implications of estimating a fully simultaneous model in which the multiple implications of a family migration strategy are treated as endogenous in an intertemporal framework, though the resultant identification problem will no doubt prove difficult (Moreland, 1982).

2.8. The contextual setting

Much of the early economics literature on migration decisions focussed exclusively upon the individual potential migrant. The preceding section reviews some of the more recent literature emphasizing the role of family strategies in shaping the nature and extent of migration. A substantial sociological literature emphasizes yet a third level of factors, namely the influence of the sending community upon migration decisions.[31]

This is particularly true with respect to case studies on the variation in impact of rural development programs on placement of family members outside of the village. Several contributors agree that variations in the contextual setting of these programs cause substantial differences in responses (Brown and Sanders, 1981; Harbison, 1981; Hugo, 1981a; Roberts, 1982, 1985).

Findley (1987) estimates a binary logit equation on migration decisions of individuals in the Ilocos Norte region of the Philippines, including a number of indices representing the contextual setting. These indices include previous community migration, a community development index, accessibility to town, measures of community agricultural commercialization and municipal facilities available. Findley finds little direct effect from these measures, but they do prove statistically significant in interaction with a vector of family characteristics, though not all coefficients have signs consistent with the author's priors.

Many of these contextual variables may have effects readily interpreted within the models of economists, acting for instance through information availability (prior migration and access to town), tightness and risks in the local labor market (commercialization and community development), and costs of relocating (access to town again). Nonetheless these measures are not often included in empirical studies of migration by economists (see, however, Connell et al., 1976).

An exception to this comparative neglect is the recent literature on relative deprivation. Stark (1984) hypothesizes that the village represents a stable reference group for rural–urban migrants, at least initially. A person who is poor relative to his home village reference group may elect to migrate to town in order to improve his ranking relative to the home group. On the other hand, a person who is even poorer, yet relatively well off compared to others from his particular village, may not move for the same level of gain, if his utility is sufficiently strongly influenced by his ranking relative to his reference group. This framework offers an interesting dynamic feature; removal of the relatively deprived from a community lowers the relative position of some of those remaining, which may consequently engender further migration. Over time, also, the reference group of migrants is likely to shift to their urban setting, but this may not worsen the migrant's sense of well-being if the reference group is formed from other urban migrants from a similar setting, for with the continued inflow of migrants earlier migrants are usually those who are better off. Nonetheless the change in reference group could leave the migrant more deprived relative to this new group and Stark and Yitzhaki (1988) accordingly distinguish between weak and strong

---

[31] Brown and Jones (1985) interact the coefficients of a fairly standard macro regional migration equation with the map coordinates at origin, for intercantonal migration in Costa Rica. The coordinate effects are used to map spatial variations and the authors argue that the observed geographic differences can be related to the contextual development patterns.

conditions for migration, the former referring to cases in which an absolute gain in income may occur but the migrant is relatively deprived by migration, or vice versa.

Stark and Taylor (1991) include a measure of relative deprivation in a multinomial logit equation for individuals' decisions to stay at home, to emigrate, or to relocate internally from 61 village households in Mexico.[32] The relative deprivation index is found to affect emigration from Mexico significantly but not internal migration, which the authors assume reflects the likelihood of shifting reference group under internal migration but not in relation to foreigners in the emigrant's host country.

2.9. Displaced persons

Extreme instances of the relevance of contextual settings in affecting migration are the flight of refugees and of displaced persons moving within international borders.[33] The number of migrants designated to be internally displaced persons has risen sharply in recent years, as individuals and families flee from violence and ecological disasters. According to the *World Refugee Survey 1992* even a partial list of the internally displaced includes 23 million people, and the total number is undoubtedly much higher.[34] To what extent the sharp increases in reported numbers represent a real rise or a change in recognition is unclear. Indeed, although international legal definitions of refugees and displaced persons exist, there is frequent dispute as to which term applies in a specific context and statistical information on the internally displaced is fragmentary.

Despite the apparent growing number of displaced persons, economists have had almost nothing to say about them. To some extent this is because the movement of displaced persons is perceived as a political rather than an economic problem, though disentangling the two is not always easy (Barnum, 1976). An exception is the study of interregional migration in Colombia by Schultz (1971), which reports estimates of macro, net, migration equations incorporating both a measure of local wage and of the rate of local politically motivated homicide from 1958 to 1963. Both prove significant in affecting rural out-migration. In fact in separate estimates for various gender–age groups, the only category for whom out-migration is not increased significantly by heightened rural violence are males age 17 to 21 – the violence makers.

Gottschang (1987) looks at the movement of eight million people from Heboi and Shandong provinces of China to Manchuria from 1890 to 1946. The flow of migrants

---

[32] The index of relative deprivation adopted for a person with income y is the product of $[1 - \Phi(y)]$ – the fraction of population in the reference group having incomes greater than y – and of $E\{\psi - y \mid \psi > y\}$ – the mean income of persons with income greater than y.

[33] For a survey of the literature on international refugees in Sub-Saharan Africa (both the major source and host of refugees), see Russell et al. (1990).

[34] See US Committee for Refugees (1992: p. 34).

is shown to rise during years of disaster (some of which are ecological) in the sending area, but this effect is not statistically significant.

3. Effects of migration on production and inequality

Models embedding migration, and most notably rural–urban migration, in a general equilibrium framework are distinguished by three main dimensions: by their assumptions about rural and urban labor market operations, by treatment of the short and long runs, and whether they are static or dynamic. The following two sections deal with static models, both short and long run, focussing upon rural labor market issues and agricultural production in Section 3.1 then turning to urban labor market pathologies in Section 3.2. In both instances, evidence with respect to some of the distinguishing features is dealt with, as well as the basic theoretical ideas including the ranking of policy instruments. Section 3.3 covers dynamic models incorporating migration and Section 3.4 then turns to the much disputed effects of rural–urban migration upon income inequality.

3.1. Rural labor markets and agricultural production

If all markets were perfect then labor migration, and rural–urban migration in particular, would simply reflect an efficient transfer of resources. In practice, trade barriers imposed by LDCs normally offer higher effective protection to industry than to agriculture. This may well translate into an incentive for an excess allocation of labor to industry, as compared to the Pareto optimum, unless the industrial protection can be justified by some other form of market failure. Although the distorting effects of trade protection are both common and major factors in affecting the inter-sectoral allocation of labor, they are rarely discussed within the migration literature (Lipton, 1977). Rather the chief departures from perfect markets examined in labor migration theory are various pathologies arising in the labor markets themselves. Typically, this takes the form of examining a single departure from perfect markets at a time, studying its comparative statics effects, and ranking optimally applied policy instruments.

The earlier literature typically assumes perfect urban labor markets and considers various potential failures in the rural labor markets. A full treatment of this literature on rural labor markets in developing countries is well beyond the scope of this chapter. This material is well summarized elsewhere (see Rosenzweig, 1988). Nonetheless at least some of the important dimensions, insofar as they impinge upon migration in particular, are worth sketching briefly here. In particular, three potential problems are summarized: "surplus" rural labor, sharecropping, and nutrition wages. This section also discusses some of the potential long-run effects of rural out-migration upon agricultural production through induced changes in technology and investments.

3.1.1. Surplus labor

Both families and collectives share incomes, though not necessarily equally. In the early theory of both peasant households and of collectives, equal sharing was thought to give rise to a market failure.[35] It does not. Rather, the source of any market failure stems from the absence of transferable property rights, tying individuals to specific locations in a manner which may be neither efficient nor equitable (see Section 2.5.2 of this chapter). In this event, establishing transferable property rights normally represents the first-best solution. In the event that the associated administrative costs prove prohibitive, or if the distributional consequences are unacceptable (as perhaps in enclosure of communal land), then some form of urban employment subsidy may be warranted.

Testing for whether surplus rural labor exists, in the sense of exhibiting a lower (social) marginal product than in town, is complicated by several factors.[36] (i) The marginal product of labor in LDC agriculture is highly seasonal. The marginal product foregone with the withdrawal of a migrant then depends in part upon whether the migrant is able to return temporarily during peak seasons (Connell et al., 1976). Indeed, in some contexts, urban employers have organized hiring accordingly around peak seasons, in an attempt to reduce the opportunity cost and hence the supply price of migrants (Lucas, 1987). (ii). Departure of a migrant may induce remaining family members to work additional hours (see Sen, 1966) and the evidence summarized in Rosenzweig (1988). In this case, output foregone upon departure is not appropriately measured while holding all other labor inputs constant. However, the leisure foregone by remaining family members clearly represents an opportunity cost to migration not reflected by comparing marginal products alone. (iii). Out-migration is selective. Measuring the marginal product of a typical rural laborer may thus misrepresent the output foregone upon migrant withdrawal.

3.1.2. Sharecropping

Various forms of share-tenancy continue to be common in many developing countries.[37] By sharing a fixed fraction of output with the landlord, a share-tenant receives only a fraction of his or her marginal product. It is as if the tenant's income were taxed, and the result is to discourage labor supply to share-tenancy. Several models consequently depict an inefficient allocation of labor between share-tenancy and elsewhere. Although these models do not explicitly address the implications for migration,

[35] For a review of the literature on collectives, see Bonin and Putterman (1987).

[36] Unfortunately most of the early tests for surplus labor ask whether the private marginal product of labor in agriculture is positive. This is hardly the point; the marginal product of labor in agriculture can be below that in industry even if positive.

[37] Not only is share-tenancy common in arable farming, but in parts of Africa animal husbandry is organized on a very similar basis (see Hertel, 1977).

they are nonetheless of relevance for the implication is that excess migration occurs from areas where share-tenancy is common. It is therefore worth briefly pausing to outline some of these issues with respect to efficiency of labor use under share-tenancy.

One argument is that, in the absence of complete insurance markets, share-tenancy offers a device for risk-sharing between risk averse tenants and (perhaps) risk neutral landlords. If the only source of uncertainty is in the level of agricultural output, then share-tenancy offers no additional protection as compared to some combination of fixed rent leases and fixed wage labor operation by the landlord, the former leaving the tenant as sole bearer of all risks, the latter leaving the landlord as residual risk taker.[38] Rural wage labor markets are also uncertain, and share-tenancy may then represent an efficient mechanism for sharing the combined risks from production and wage income (Newbery and Stiglitz, 1979). A second argument stems from the fact that wage labor needs to be monitored, while sharecroppers have an incentive to work hard given that they receive a portion of their production. Given the real costs required to supervise wage workers, share-tenancy may well again represent an efficient arrangement, obviating any need to discuss excess rural out-migration (Lucas, 1979). Eswaran and Kotwal (1985) extend this to a model in which the landlord also possesses asymmetric information with respect to management decisions, and share-tenancy represents a Pareto-efficient exchange of supervision and managerial talent.

3.1.3. The nutrition wage

Several models of rural–urban migration incorporate urban unemployment. Few address rural unemployment. Whether this is appropriate probably varies with the context, for extensive rural unemployment is not ubiquitous.[39] Nonetheless a substantial literature exists on the nutrition variant of efficiency wage theory, with particular reference to rural labor markets (Leibenstein, 1957; Rodgers, 1975; Bliss and Stern, 1978; Weiss, 1990). The essential idea is that labor costs may be minimized by setting a wage above labor market clearing, since the effort workers are able to deliver may be enhanced by better nutrition affordable at higher wages, particularly in very low income regions. With resulting unemployment in rural areas, the concept of surplus rural labor is resurrected, though in another guise. Indeed, in this context, migration from rural to urban areas could actually serve to increase rural output, for with fewer rural inhabitants to feed, nutrition among those remaining in the rural areas could rise, permitting higher levels of effort (Rosenzweig, 1988). Yet whether the first-best pol-

---

[38] This assumes constant returns to scale, so that there is no difficulty in dividing plots between alternative modes of production.

[39] Measured rural unemployment rates are very sensitive to the definition of unemployment adopted, especially where part-time and seasonal work are common. Rural unemployment rates may also be sensitive to proximity to urban areas (permitting more effective urban search from a rural base). See Bardhan (1977) and Rosenzweig (1988) on India, Lucas and Verry (1990) on Malaysia, Dickens and Lang (1991) on Sri Lanka.

icy prescription is to promote migration depends critically upon whether nutrition wage issues are of relevance in the urban sector too.

The usual recommendation in terms of policy prescriptions is some form of wealth redistribution, since non-labor incomes can raise nutrition, permit payment of lower wages, and enhance employment levels (Dasgupta and Ray, 1987). However, wealth redistribution, whether in the form of land reform or food aid, is notoriously difficult to effect, as is the alternative of subsidizing rural wage employment.

How relevant are nutrition wage theories in practice? Reviewing the evidence, Rosenzweig (1988: p. 720), concludes "... it is unclear if the model has any relevance to any known population on this planet". For instance, one of the more common pieces of evidence cited in favor of the nutrition wage hypothesis is that permanent agricultural workers are sometimes paid higher wages if they have larger families and hence more dependents to share their food. Alternatively, one can imagine that workers with larger families might be more responsible, work more diligently and thus merit higher pay. But causality may easily run in the opposite direction: higher wages may encourage higher fertility levels (Rosenzweig, 1988). Moreover, at least in parts of India, permanent laborers are apparently often paid higher wages if they have larger families who help during peak seasons (Lucas, 1982).

3.1.4. Remittances, risks and new technologies

The short-run impact of rural emigration addresses only a part of the potential effect of out-migration upon agricultural production. Section 2.7 on family strategies outlines how placing family members in town or in more distant rural areas, can help to spread risks. The additional security may encourage adoption of riskier techniques in agriculture, resulting in productivity gains through technical progress (Stark, 1978). Moreover, investments made possible by migrants' remittances, or merely by the higher earnings of migrants, can increase output per worker in agriculture through capital deepening.[40]

There is far less evidence on the long-run effects of rural out-migration upon agriculture than on the short-run issue of surplus labor. Rempel and Lobdell (1978) argue that net remittances are too small to have much effect on enhancing rural productivity, and that remittances are in any case not normally spent on productive investments. Similarly, Banerjee (1984c) notes that of male migrants in Delhi whose families have undertaken some agricultural improvement, "only" two-thirds are remitting, though no control group is analyzed to see if this rate of improvement is abnormal. As Stark (1980a) notes, however, no remittances need occur to encourage investments and adoption of more productive techniques: the insurance provision, additional income of family members, and possibly the relaxation of a binding cash constraint on the

---

[40] Katz and Stark (1986a) consider the migration implications of a case when the returns to such investments increase with the scale of investment.

household, can induce these changes even without remittances; remittances spent on housing and schooling are productive investments; and anyway the additional income from remittances is fungible, and investments may well increase even if the actual cash remitted is not invested.

As a result, the long-run effects of out-migration upon rural production are difficult to test empirically. Lucas (1987) applies annual time-series data to estimate arable production functions and cattle accumulation equations for several countries in southern Africa. Included in the explanatory variables is the accumulated earnings of migrant mine workers, which in all but one case prove to increase both crop output and cattle herd size significantly. Thus, although migrant withdrawal is shown to diminish crop output in the short run, investments made possible by migrants' earnings may at least help to offset this in the long run.

3.2. Urban labor market issues

In discussing urban labor market pathologies it will be useful to distinguish between models in which the failure of labor markets to clear is a result of policy intervention and those in which private wage setting mechanisms are the underlying cause.

3.2.1. Models with government intervention

First-best solutions. The basic tenets underlying the Todaro hypothesis have already been described. Harris and Todaro (1970) set this hypothesis, of migration induced by more effective job search, within a general equilibrium model. The Harris–Todaro model depicts a static, short-run equilibrium for a two-sector, small, open economy. The rural labor market is presumed to be perfect but the urban wage is set by government at a level above clearing. For the moment, we may refer to this as a minimum wage. Since the only imperfection introduced into this model is the minimum wage, the first-best policy, ignoring distributional issues, is to remove the minimum wage restraint.

What are the consequences of lowering the minimum wage without removing the restraint entirely? In the short run, lowering the urban minimum wage obviously stimulates urban employment and hence urban output in this model. The induced change in rural production is ambiguous. Whether rural production expands or contracts depends in the short run solely upon whether the rural wage is lowered or raised. In the static equilibrium, migration equates the rural wage and the expected urban wage, but the latter has two components, the minimum wage and the probability of urban employment, and whether the expected urban wage moves in the same direction as the minimum wage depends upon the elasticity of demand for urban labor.[41] Thus,

---

[41] For an elegant diagrammatic exposition see Corden and Findlay (1975).

if the rural wage (w_r) equals the urban minimum wage (w_u) multiplied by the probability of an urban resident holding a job as given in Eq. (2), then

$$w_r = w_u \frac{e_u(w_u)}{1 - e_r(w_r)}, \tag{7}$$

where e_u and e_r indicate urban and rural employment respectively and the total labor force is normalized to equal one. Differentiating with respect to the urban minimum wage and rearranging gives

$$\frac{\partial w_r}{\partial w_u} = \frac{(1 - e_r)e_u(1 + \eta_u)}{(1 - e_r)^2 - w_u e_u e'_r}, \tag{8}$$

where η_u is the urban elasticity of demand for labor and e'_r indicates the derivative of e_r with respect to w_r. The denominator and the first two terms in the numerator in Eq. (8) are positive. Consequently whether w_r (and hence rural employment) rises or falls with w_u depends upon the sign of $(1 + \eta_u)$. If urban employment is wage inelastic then lowering the minimum wage creates few additional urban jobs. The combined effect of a lower wage and few extra jobs discourages migrants, reduces rural–urban migration, and rural output expands together with urban output. On the other hand, if urban employment is wage elastic then rural production falls with a declining minimum wage. Indeed, despite the expansion in urban production, total production may even decline. As one should expect from the general theory of the second best, although removing the minimum wage unambiguously enhances production, the effect of lowering the minimum wage depends upon the context.

In the long run, when capital is mobile between sectors, imposition of an urban minimum wage can even serve to increase urban production. Corden and Findlay (1975) illustrate this point by considering a fixed coefficient technology. Imposition of a minimum wage does not then reduce employment with the initial capital. The higher wage with initial full employment attracts migrants, and the reduction in rural labor leaves some agricultural capital idle. Both capital and migrants are consequently diverted from the rural to urban sectors and urban output expands. Nonetheless, the first-best solution is to remove the minimum wage.

Drazen (1986) presents a model in which removal of a minimum wage may not be first-best (irrespective of capital mobility). The Harris–Todaro model assumes complete information. Drazen depicts a scenario of asymmetric information, in which the quality of the pool of urban arrivals is positively affected by the average urban wage. No atomistic firm is willing to raise its wage to the social optimum level since free-riding firms also benefit from the enhanced pool attracted by these pay increases. Thus, Drazen maintains, a minimum wage regulation may be desirable to circumvent the externality, despite the induced migration and resultant unemployment. As Drazen notes, this failure arises only if employers cannot write a binding contract offering a higher wage conditional upon applicants passing a test. Whether such pathologies are sufficiently common, and whether policy makers are sufficiently astute in setting minimum wages, to justify the common regulations, are not obvious.

In practice, minimum wage regulations are not the only means by which policy-makers impose a floor on wages. Public sector hiring, whether in public services or state owned enterprises can have a very similar effect. For instance, if public sector pay is higher than in the private sector, and if government is unwilling or unable to hire all comers at going public pay levels, then open unemployment and induced migration for public sector job search may ensue. Indeed, given the difficulties of enforcing minimum wage laws and the comparatively large public sector employment in many developing countries, the effects of public sector hiring may be far more influential. Whether the public sector pays more or less than the private sector, for similar employees, seems to vary from one LDC to another (Heller and Tait, 1984). Standard human capital earnings equations are found to exhibit positive coefficients on appended public sector dummy variables, at least in some contexts (see Lindauer and Sabot (1983) on Tanzania, Lucas and Verry (1990) on Malaysia). However, as always, unmeasured attributes could underlie these results: government may hire the brightest among those with equal quantities of schooling. Moreover, such earnings equations do not reflect differences in job content and prospects (Robinson, 1990). In principle, if public sector pay does induce urban unemployment and migration out of productive rural activities, then lower pay levels represent the first-best solution. However adjusting to lower levels may prove politically impractical. In consequence, a very wide range of alternative policy instruments has been explored in the literature. Chief amongst these are wage subsidies.

Wage subsidies. Application of even the best feasible wage subsidy to the urban sector alone may reduce total production in the Harris–Todaro model. Ignore, for the moment, issues of financing this subsidy. In the short run, a wage subsidy to the urban sector lowers labor costs, expanding urban employment and hence urban output. At the same time take-home pay for urban workers remains unchanged. Combined with higher initial urban employment levels, this induces additional migration resulting in diminished rural production, which may more than offset the expansion in urban production and may even increase the rate of urban unemployment.[42] The transfer of labor from rural to urban production lowers the returns to capital in the countryside while raising returns in town. In the long run, capital is transferred out of agriculture,

---

[42] On the short-run production effect, see Harris and Todaro (1970). The conditions under which the unemployment rate is raised have been disputed (Zarembka, 1970; Todaro, 1976a; Blomqvist; 1978). For a resolution, see Arellano (1981), who shows that the formulation of migrant supply responses to urban job creation (given wages) is critical. See also Stark et al. (1991).

lowering the rural wage and, since take-home pay is fixed in town, equilibrium occurs at a higher rate of unemployment.[43]

Continuing to ignore the problem of financing wage subsidies, Bhagwati and Srinivasan (1974) show that a first-best solution can be achieved by applying an equal rate of wage subsidy to both sectors.[44] For migration to cease in the absence of unemployment requires that take-home pay in both sectors equal the minimum wage. For the marginal product of labor to be equal everywhere also requires that labor costs be the same in both sectors, and an equal wage subsidy must close the gap between pay and costs.

Unfortunately this delightfully simple solution is rendered impractical by the need to finance a universal subsidy and by the difficulties of administering a rural wage subsidy.

Ranking policy instruments. A series of contributions evaluate two related issues when first-best policy options are not available and an urban minimum wage restriction prevails: ranking the distortionary effects of various forms of taxation just sufficient to finance optimal wage subsidies; and the social welfare ranking of policy instruments other than wage subsidies (Khan, 1980; McCool, 1982; Bennett and Phelps, 1983; Lundborg, 1990).

Among the policy instruments considered within this literature are production subsidies, trade taxes (with and without consideration of consumer losses), and taxation of urban incomes (as a form of migration tax). Both the short-run and long-run implications of such instruments, applied at their second-best optimal rates, have been considered. Unfortunately the consequences of applying taxes to finance optimal wage subsidies and of using corrective policy instruments other than wage subsidies prove sensitive to several factors. These factors include: the factor intensities of the two (or more) sectors; which good is imported and the elasticities in demand for exports and supply of imports; and since consumer prices are affected by some of the policies, it matters whether the minimum wage is defined in terms of agricultural goods, urban goods or nominal values. Not only is the order of social welfare ranking affected by these factors, but in some instances whether a tax or subsidy is to be recommended depends upon assumptions with respect to these elements.

The model of Bennett and Phelps (1983) is particularly interesting in depicting the rural household straddling the urban divide through migration: when nominal wages

---

[43] See Corden and Findlay (1975). Khan (1980) shows that, in this long-run model, a sufficient condition for the existence of an equilibrium is that the rural sector be more capital intensive than the urban sector, which seems unlikely.

[44] The large country case is analyzed in Srinivasan and Bhagwati (1975). Anand and Joshi (1979) reanalyze the small country case, in the context of a Benthamite social welfare function, when revenue constraints prohibit achieving equal take-home pay in both sectors. Shukla and Stark (1990) combine the small country case with urban agglomeration externalities. Obviously equal wage subsidies to both sectors do not prove to be the first-best solution in any of these situations.

increase less than in proportion to the cost of living, a devaluation proves less costly in its effect upon rural employment per urban job created, than do (unproductive) urban public works, an urban employment subsidy, an import tax on the urban good or an export tax on the rural good. What seems to drive this result is the effective cut in real wages as a result of the devaluation, a resulting loss in real urban incomes provided the urban demand for labor is inelastic (thus making urban migration less attractive), and an elastic demand for rural exports (given the small country assumption). On the other hand, if the real urban wage is rigid, then devaluation has no effect upon urban employment in the Bennett–Phelps model. Clearly the responsiveness of wages to cost-of-living changes is a crucial element (a common result in the analysis of real effects of devaluation), and the next section turns from government administration of wage setting to private determination.

3.2.2. Models with wage setting by unions and firms

Two models of unregulated, non-clearing, private sector, wage setting are covered in this section: collective bargaining and efficiency wages. The literature on efficiency wages has not really addressed migration considerations directly. Nonetheless, efficiency wage models and their policy implications are of quite direct relevance in the present context. Policy recommendations must depend upon an understanding of any market forces which sustain urban formal sector wages in the presence of open unemployment or of competition from low-wage informal sector jobs. At the moment, the various efficiency wage models probably offer the most popular explanations for this phenomenon, and as such deserve attention here.

Collective bargaining. Calvo (1978) suggests that LDC trade unions act to maximize the product of urban employment and the difference between urban and rural wages. Two scenarios are posited. The first is similar to the McDonald and Solow (1981) monopolistic framework, in which the union sets wages and employers determine the employment level accordingly. The second approach envisions a Nash equilibrium, permitting firms to react. In both scenarios, because of the assumed union objective, urban wages exceed rural wages in equilibrium and open urban unemployment provides a migration equilibrium.

In Calvo's models, neither a wage subsidy (in one or both sectors) nor an income (migration) tax is capable of achieving a first-best solution in which output is maximized and unemployment disappears. In essence, unions care about after-tax pay of members, and, by always seeking to sustain a gap between rural and urban take-home pay, thus prevent full employment from being reached.

Calvo's model does not appear to have been tested empirically, although as Calvo notes:

> ... the existence of an entity acting as [a trade union] is not strictly necessary for this model to have empirical relevance. Similar situations may arise in the absence

of a [trade union] if, for example, the government happens to be concerned, for political or other reasons [with] the welfare of urban workers and/or ... the attractiveness of the city. (Calvo, 1978: p. 80.)

Certainly urban-rural wage differentials appear to be more ubiquitous than organized labor. More generally, inter-industry wage differentials, which cannot be explained by differences in collective bargaining, persist – a point which has attracted the attention of efficiency wage testers.

Efficiency wage models. At present, the most widely accepted explanations for non-clearing wage setting by profit maximizing employers are several variations on the efficiency wage model. In brief, labor costs are hypothesized to fall as wages rise over an interval of lower wages, after which labor costs rise with wages. Employers pick the wage which minimizes labor costs. Several reasons are offered for the U-shape pattern of labor costs against wages, in addition to the nutrition wage variant which has already been discussed: shirking may be averted by the threat of losing above market wages; costly turnover of employees may be reduced by offering higher wages; or the average quality of job applicants may be improved by offering higher wages only up to a point, after which high wage offers attract at least some less qualified applicants hoping not to be screened out.[45]

If payment of efficiency wages in the urban formal sector, but not elsewhere, is the source of persistent wage differentials between town and village, or indeed between the formal and informal urban sectors, what are the policy implications? There are no easy answers. As Weiss notes:

For the incentive model, one might consider direct subsidies to the industrial sector ... [However] it is not uncommon for different efficiency wage models to have opposite policy implications... While it is clear that the market equilibrium is unlikely to maximize aggregate output, it is by no means clear whether any particular policy intervention will do more good than harm. (Weiss, 1990: p. 102.)[46]

Testing for the general relevance of efficiency wage models proves difficult, as does identifying which variant underlies the effect. Krueger and Summers (1988) demonstrate that inter-industry wage differentials within the US cannot be adequately explained by the extent of union organization or threat, by measured human capital of employees, by unmeasured attributes of employees (examined through a fixed effects model), or by compensating variations. As Krueger and Summers conclude, this at

[45] See Stiglitz (1974, 1976) and Weiss (1990). Katz and Stark (1987) note that the lack of specific information about potential employees, and hence the relevance of wage setting to the quality of applicants, may be particularly acute among (international) migrants.

[46] Most efficiency wage models call for some form of wage subsidy. On the other hand, a wage tax may be called for in the context of the wage-sorting variant. See Weiss (1990).

least leaves room for the unexplained, residual inter-industry variation in wages to reflect some form of rent sharing and efficiency wage payments in particular. Similar evidence is reported for some developing countries (Gatica et al., 1990; Romaguera, 1991). In fact, the inter-industry structure of wages is remarkably similar across developed and developing countries, which may offer some support to an efficiency wage view (Lang and Dickens, 1992). However there are skeptics. Moll (1992) argues that inter-industry wage differentials are highly correlated between black and white workers in South Africa, and that in the South African context it is difficult to envision voluntary rent sharing with black employees, but Moll's evidence does not contradict the possibility of efficiency wage payments to prevent shirking by both races.

Brief mention may also be made of a common argument that transnational corporations pay above market clearing wages in the developing countries. Again, this literature has not been specifically tied to migration considerations, but is of quite direct relevance in weighing policies to redress the inefficient division of labor and hence migration between sectors. For instance, Lim (1977) reports that in Malaysian industry, foreign owned enterprises pay higher basic wages and higher shift premia, both on average and in regressions controlling for sectoral capital intensity. In principle this could reflect some form of efficiency wage premium paid by transnationals (who may possess less complete information about local employees). However Lim's evidence is drawn from enterprise level data which do not report skills or personal characteristics of employees. The only test of a foreign ownership wage premium based upon earnings equation estimates for individuals appears to be for the Tanzanian manufacturing sector by Knight and Sabot (1983). Knight and Sabot also find a positive effect associated with a foreign ownership dummy, but the effect is both small and statistically insignificant. Indeed, even had Knight and Sabot found a significant positive effect, one could not be sure if this really reflected unmeasured personal characteristics – especially if foreign companies hire the best and the brightest: thus, Knight and Sabot do find that foreign companies in Tanzania pay higher returns to both education and experience.

In sum, appealing as the efficiency wage arguments may be, evidence of their importance (in the developing world or elsewhere) is difficult to glean. Distinguishing which variant on efficiency wages is responsible for wages sustained above full employment clearing levels is even more difficult, and unfortunately this matters to appropriate directions for policy design. Recommending policy action to counter any associated misallocation of labor, including excessive or inadequate rural–urban migration, would therefore seem premature.

3.2.3. The shadow wage of urban labor

A very common form of (implicit) employment subsidy in developing countries is public sector staffing in excess of the cost minimizing criterion indicated by the prevailing wage. To ask whether this is inappropriate, and more generally to evaluate both public and private projects, as well as to choose an optimal production technique, requires some measure of the shadow wage of labor (Aharoni, 1986).

Harris and Todaro (1970) maintain that despite persistent urban unemployment, the shadow cost of urban labor equals the going wage. If the urban unemployment rate is not altered by the creation of an additional urban job, it follows that $1/p$ additional workers must join the urban labor force, where p is the (constant) proportion of the urban labor force employed. Assuming further that the social cost of labor withdrawn from the rural sector is the rural wage, w_r, the opportunity cost of an additional urban job λ is simply:

$$\lambda = \frac{w_r}{p}. \tag{9}$$

However, from the Harris–Todaro migration equilibrium condition – that the rural wage equals the expected urban wage as in Eq. (5) – it follows that λ equals the urban wage.

Foster (1981) places this result in a broader context, suggesting that job search in the Harris–Todaro model may be seen as one form of rent seeking.[47] When rent seeking is competitive, Foster argues that the value of any good equals the cost of resources used both in production and in associated rent seeking, and "there should be no correction to the factor cost of a project to account for changes in rents" (Foster, 1981: p. 177). Heady (1981) also shows that the Harris–Todaro result is robust to some alternative job search scenarios, incorporating a potential spell in the informal sector, given risk neutral utility maximization by workers.

Other generalizations do cause a breakdown in the simple Harris–Todaro shadow price rule. If creation of an additional urban job lowers the urban unemployment rate, thus within the Harris–Todaro framework raising the rural wage, then the shadow urban wage is below the going urban wage (Heady, 1981). In particular, in a world of heterogeneous households, some are more likely to migrate than others. For additional migrants to be tempted to migrate requires lowering the unemployment rate, and inframarginal (prior) migrants gain (Scott et al., 1976). If workers are risk averse, then less rural–urban migration is induced by urban job creation and the shadow cost of an urban job is below the going wage (Katz and Stark, 1986c). Even under risk neutrality, among the additional migrants tempted into town with the creation of one extra job, the job recipient receives a higher income and the rest receive lower incomes than previously. Under a diminishing marginal propensity to consume, Katz and Stark (1986c) show that the increase in consumption by the lucky migrant is outweighed by greater austerity for the unlucky migrants. In a society where savings are at a pre-

---

[47] Whether job search really represents directly unproductive rent seeking may be disputed if sorting into matching jobs is important.

mium, the additional savings thus resulting from the urban job again lowers the shadow cost of that job (Stark, 1981).

Obviously, the Harris–Todaro rule also requires modification if either the urban or rural wage is not equal to the marginal social value of production. This depends critically upon the nature of any distortions in these labor markets (Stiglitz, 1982). A wedge may also be driven between wage and social marginal product by distortionary taxes, including those imposed to finance wage (or other) subsidies. Indeed, in general when first-best solutions are not achieved, the costs of additional job creation are complex (Khan, 1980; Stiglitz, 1982).

3.3. Dynamic models

Essentially all of the general equilibrium models reviewed thus far are static. The transfer of labor from one sector to another may involve migration, if those sectors exhibit different geographic dispersion, but the focus is upon comparative statics once migration is complete. In contrast, the on-going flow of migrants is inherently dynamic (Lucas, 1976; Blomqvist, 1978).

A small number of dynamic growth models incorporating migration and urban unemployment have appeared. Robertson and Wellisz (1977), Jha and Lachler (1981) and Das (1982) all consider the steady state of a two-sector growth model, in which migration continuously equates the rural wage with the urban wage multiplied by the fraction of the urban labor force employed. Das shows that the second-best optimal savings rate (assuming that no policy action to achieve full employment is implemented) is greater than it would be under the full employment golden rule. Essentially this is because the higher savings finance additional capital which increases the demand for labor and reduces unemployment. Despite the urban unemployment, Das shows that the constrained optimal allocation of capital does not necessarily require a greater fraction of investment allocated to the urban sector than would the golden rule, since rural investments also help to limit migration. Jha and Lachler (1981) design an optimal vector of linear taxes on urban wages, on capital income and income from land, subject to a social welfare function in the steady state. In this model, government also controls the allocation of capital between the two sectors, and one of the chief results is that optimal investment per unit of labor is higher in the rural sector than in town. In part, however, it seems this result is driven by the inclusion of the gap between rural and urban income as an argument in the social welfare function.

Bartlett (1983) also considers a two-sector growth model, but examines the consequences of adopting the Todaro (1969) variant on the probability of obtaining a job, given by the rate of new job openings (job growth plus turnover) relative to urban unemployment (see Eq. (1) and Blomqvist (1978)). Bartlett shows that the steady-state equilibrium indeed exhibits positive unemployment despite job growth. However this equilibrium is generally unstable: a small drop in urban job creation tends to diminish urban migration, ceteris paribus; but the resulting downward pressure on rural wages is shown to more than offset this effect, resulting in a greater rise in migration than in urban job creation and hence exploding levels of unemployment.[48] Day et al. (1987) consider the possibility that such instability may offer a further explanation for return migration flows.

3.4. Effects of migration upon income distribution

This section is organized according to two measures of inequality adopted in the literature.[49] The first recognizes three groups – migrants, stayers, and the indigenous population at destination – and considers the effects of rural–urban migration upon average wages or incomes of these three. The second set of measures considered in the literature is concerned with the size distribution of income, and notably measures of poverty and inequality within the rural sector.

3.4.1. Mean incomes of movers, stayers and destination population

As a reference point consider a very simple model with two homogeneous factors, labor and capital, producing a rural good and an urban good under constant returns to scale. Capital is immobile between sectors, and commodity prices are determined on the world market for this small open economy. Local labor markets are competitive, but initial wages are higher in the urban than in the rural sector.[50] Fully informed migrants presumably gain by moving to town. Under these conditions, the consequent withdrawal of labor from the rural sector and the increased supply of labor to the urban sector tend to close the wage gap between town and countryside. Migrants and rural stayers gain, initially better off urbanites lose.

These clear-cut predictions are quite sensitive to the assumptions on which they are founded. For instance, suppose that the rural sector produces more than one good (either two crops or a single crop with rural manufacturing will suffice). The Rybczinski theorem states that, given the assumptions listed above, in the long run, no change in real wage occurs as a result of the change in endowment of labor caused by out-migration: as labor leaves, the rural sector shifts mix of production away from labor-intensive activities (Johnson, 1967). The converse shift occurs in town and together these shifts may remove (or at least diminish) the tendency for migration to close an initial wage gap.

Returning to models with one good per sector, consider the implications of recognizing labor heterogeneity. Suppose skilled migrants move to town. Whether the wage

---

[48] See also Neary (1981) and Amano (1983).

[49] For a discussion of the connections between migration and class, see Keyfitz (1982).

[50] Factor price equalization through trade is prevented by complete product specialization.

of unskilled migrants is thereby raised or lowered depends upon whether skilled and unskilled workers are complements or substitutes. Thus the consequences for those left behind depend upon their skill mix, the skills of migrants, and the state of technology. Stayers' wages may either be lowered or raised by emigration, even though migration tends to close the wage gap for the migrating skill group.

Labor earnings are only one component in income. In a one-good, two-factor context, the departure of workers lowers the returns to sector-specific capital. The direction of this effect is less obvious in a three-factor model: the effects upon the returns to capital may depend upon the skill mix of movers (McCulloch and Yellen, 1976). Migrants may also transfer some capital with them, or alternatively may invest in the rural sector even after departure (Berry and Soligo, 1969). Indeed, a family with migrants in town may well be induced to invest, either in physical capital or in riskier technologies, even if the migrant does not actually remit for investment (Stark, 1980a). Thus, the effect of migrant departure on both the return to and the amount of capital in the rural sector depend upon the circumstances. Similarly, there may be a net flow of remittances either to rural stayers or to migrants, though in fact either group can benefit from remittances at key times without being a net recipient on average.

So far, it has been assumed that all goods are traded. The addition of nontraded goods (or domestic goods which are imperfect substitutes for foreign goods – the Armington assumption) renders some commodity prices endogenous to the migration process, affected both by shifts in the mix of commodities supplied and changes in consumer incomes. To the extent that rural and urban dwellers consume different bundles of goods, these endogenous changes in consumer prices alter the real mean incomes of these groups.

Although this sketches only some of the elements of the story (the myriad permutations of less than perfect labor markets are omitted, for instance), it should suffice to indicate that the direction of effect of migration on mean real wages and incomes of both stayers and urbanites is ambiguous. If theory is ambiguous in its predictions, what does the evidence show?

At least three branches of the literature address empirical aspects of the effects of migration on mean incomes: estimates of wage gains to migrants, evidence on the effects of migration on average wages at origin and destination, and CGE models permitting simulation of the general equilibrium consequences of migration.[51]

Estimating wage gains to migrants. As already pointed out, wages received by migrants prior to moving can only be recorded through panel tracer studies (which are both expensive and difficult) or through recall (which may be unreliable). In the absence of such data, estimation of the incremental wage resulting from migration re-

---

[51] A related literature addresses the issue as to whether regional income disparities widen or narrow as development proceeds. See Williamson (1965) and Gilbert and Goodman (1976).

quires imputation of the unknown wage prior to moving. Four broad approaches to imputation of the wage gain may be identified in the LDC literature.

One approach is to estimate an earnings equation pooling observations on rural stayers and on migrants, and test whether a dummy for migrants has a positive effect. Using this approach Yap (1976), for instance, estimates a 51% gain in average monthly income for migrants from rural Northeast Brazil, who have been in urban areas of Brazil less than four years, and an even larger gain for those living longer in town. Yap also reports no significant gain in average monthly income for rural–rural migrants.[52] This simple approach imposes an assumption that it is appropriate to pool movers and stayers – that the returns to education and other estimated coefficients are identical in town and countryside. There is also the difficulty that the migration dummy may be correlated with unobserved attributes which distinguish movers from stayers.

A second approach recognizes these last two difficulties. Separate earnings equations are estimated for various locations, allowing for sample censoring, as a result of location choice. The approach of Falaris (1987) has already been discussed in connection with micro estimates of the decision to migrate. To recapitulate, Falaris finds significant positive selection in six of the 17 earnings equations estimated for the states of Venezuela – workers in these six states receive higher earnings than would observationally equivalent people drawn at random from the population. Pessino (1991) is able to take this a step further, since her data for Peru indicate both current and last place of residence. In particular, Pessino allows different parameters in the earnings equations of movers and stayers, in Lima, other urban areas, and rural areas of Peru, while making sample selection adjustment for censoring on migrant status.[53] Among the rural stayers Pessino again finds significant selection, but in this case it is negative – rural stayers earn less than observationally equivalent movers would have earned had they stayed. The converse holds for stayers in Lima, perhaps partly reflecting a discouraged migrant phenomenon. Pessino imposes no cross-equation constraints on the sample selection effects, and finds no statistically significant selection among the migrants.

A third approach uses non-tracer panel data. The Living Standard Survey for Cote d'Ivoire includes a sample of persons working in rural areas in 1985 but who had migrated by the 1986 survey round. In these data Vijverberg (1989) finds an observed wage of migrants, prior to migrating, higher than that predicted from an estimated

[52] Ward and Sanders (1980) conclude that urban migrants in Ceara state in Northeast Brazil are worse off than if they had not migrated. However these results are difficult to interpret since the urban sample is truncated to include only the poor, whereas the rural sample is not.

[53] DaVanzo and Hosek (1981) estimate a closely related switching model using panel data in the US, and compare these results to those derived from the approach described in the previous paragraph – incorporating a migrant dummy in pooled estimates. DaVanzo and Hosek find that their switching model gives implausibly large estimates of the gains to migration and the authors consequently express doubts about the reliability of the switching approach.

wage equation, and conversely an observed wage for stayers which is lower than predicted, and Vijverberg concludes there is consequently positive selection.[54]

In contrast to simply including a dummy for migrants in an earnings equation, the
latter two approaches permit the extent of wage gain to vary according to both measured attributes of migrants and according to unobserved effects. The few results available suggest that selection effects do matter, both in obtaining unbiased estimates of
the effects of measured attributes (though the extent of bias is not explored) and in the
unobserved effects (which vary in sign between studies). A fourth, fixed-effects approach bypasses some of the issues arising from unobserved differences when comparing wages of separate individuals in alternative locations. The first round of the Malaysian Family Life Survey reports earnings of household members recalled over the
interval of a decade. Trzcinski and Randolph (1991) use this information to estimate a
multinomial logit model of upward, downward and no relative earnings mobility,
though the results prove difficult to interpret. Trzcinski and Randolph find no significant upward mobility in relative earnings as a direct result of rural–urban migration.
On the other hand, they do find significant downward mobility as a result of urban–
rural movement. Complicating the interpretation of both of these effects is the inclusion of a dummy variable for change of occupation which increases both the chance of
upward and downward mobility significantly. As the authors note, presumably most
rural–urban and urban–rural migrants change occupation, but the estimated model
does not include an interaction term between job change and migration status so it is
difficult to disentangle the separate effects. Whether the significant downward movement in relative earnings with rural–urban migration results, for instance, from retirement of target savers to their home village also cannot be discerned, for it is not clear
how many are returning nor is an interaction with age included in the model.

No matter which of these four approaches is adopted, a number of difficulties certainly remain. Data problems include the major difficulties in measuring earnings,
particularly in rural areas and urban informal markets in LDCs as discussed in an earlier section, and the index number problems inherent in measuring cost-of-living differences. There are also other sources of sample censoring. Only those people observed to be earning are included, yet correction for this is not always made even in
the recent contributions. Perhaps most important of all, no correction is made for return migration: though understandable given data limitations, this may prove a serious
source of bias. Migrants with the lowest gains (having proved unlucky in the urban
job lottery, ill informed about opportunities, or whose gains evaporate upon complete
information revelation and their subsequent removal from the "averaging pool") may
be censored from the migrant sample by virtue of having returned.

---

[54] From the standard errors reported in Vijverberg (1989: Table 1), it seems these differences are not,
however, statistically significant. Moreover, it is surprising to note from Vijverberg's data that both observed
and predicted wages of stayers are higher than for migrants, indicating that the more productive workers, as
measured by observed personal characteristics, apparently remain at home in this context.

The effect of migration on origin and destination wages. In a number of contexts, the effects of inter-regional migration upon average wages, expected wages, or incomes at origin and destination are explored using time-series data. The results are mixed.

Greenwood et al. (1981) estimate a simultaneous structural model of inter-state migration in Mexico from 1960 to 1970, using three-stage least squares. In the equation for change of earnings, the rate of in-migration proves to have a statistically significant, positive effect, while out-migration has no effect. The positive effect of in-migration upon wages, Greenwood et al. attribute to enhanced demand for local (nontraded) goods dominating the effects of increased labor supply, but the data do not permit this plausible argument to be tested. Garcia-Ferrer (1980) reports similar results for inter-provincial migration in Spain, though in this case the dependent variable is change in income and out-migration is also estimated to lower income growth significantly. Salvatore (1980) estimates a structural model of South–North migration in Italy from 1952 to 1976. In this model, migration helps to close the regional gap in unemployment rates through its effect on labor force growth, and the wage differential is also closed indirectly by migration through the pressure of reduced differences in unemployment. Lucas (1987) estimates a model of inter-regional migration within southern Africa, from 1946 through 1978, and finds that migration to South Africa's mines significantly increased estate wages in both Mozambique and Malawi (leading to political pressure to curtail migration from Malawi).

All of these studies suffer from a common problem, inherent in the data. Suppose that a high wage recipient leaves. It is quite possible that the average wage falls, even though wages of each remaining person rises. The population for which average earnings are reported shifts over time as migration proceeds. Whether this leads to over- or underestimates of the change in wages for stayers, depends upon whether migrants receive below or above average initial pay. Not much can be done about this when only aggregate data are available, and cross-sectional micro data do not permit exploration of wage changes, though panel data could be used to explore this effect.

CGE models. Spatial CGE models can be used to simulate the general equilibrium effects of migration (or exogenous parameters causing migration) upon incomes of various household categories. The results are, of course, entirely driven by the construction of the model. For instance, Becker et al. (1986) assume an exogenous rural–urban wage gap, irrespective of migration in India. Combined with an assumption of zero unemployment, this means that the gap between urban and rural employment income per capita is fixed. Adelman and Robinson (1978) also allow for no unemployment in their model of Korea, but allow wage differentials to vary. In this latter model, migration has a major effect in reducing the income differential between town and countryside, in part because migration improves the terms of trade in favor of agriculture. In turn, the increased relative price of agricultural goods stems from assumptions (a) that imported food is not a perfect substitute for domestically produced food (b) that the effect of reduced output of food, resulting from departure of rural labor, outweighs reductions in demand for food, given consumption patterns of urban workers.

3.4.2. Inequality within the rural sector

A number of critics of the rural–urban migration transformation assert that departure increases rural poverty and sharpens income disparities within the rural sector. "Migration proceeds out of inequality and further establishes this inequality".[55] On the other hand, the Adelman and Robinson (1978) CGE model for Korea, for instance, depicts rural–urban migration as a major equalizer both overall and within the rural sector. A number of elements may be distinguished in this general debate.

An important component is the income classes from which migrants originate. As noted already, there is some evidence both from village studies (Connell et al., 1976) and from econometric estimates (Banerjee and Kanbur, 1981) to indicate a non-monotonic relationship between propensity to migrate and income – albeit with conflicting results on the signs of the quadratic form. On the other hand, Adelman and Robinson assume migration occurs only from the landless, smallest and small land-owning families: members of medium and high income farming families are taken not to migrate at all. Presumably this has a major effect on the Adelman–Robinson simulated reductions in rural inequality.

A second component is the selectivity in migrant streams. Hance writes:

> ... there can be little doubt that migration does have the effect of draining away from the rural areas, either temporarily or permanently, some of the strongest, most able, most energetic young men. (Hance, 1970: p. 196.)

The point seems well established, at least in the sense of higher out-migration propensities of the young and the better educated. Whether it is true with respect to unobservable characteristics is less clear, as discussed here in the context of estimating gains to migrants. Yet, assuming that the general point is correct, it does not automatically follow that departure of the "strongest, most able, most energetic young men" necessarily lowers the productivity and earnings of those left behind (Lipton, 1980).

A third, potentially major factor is the role of remittances. Lipton (1980) draws upon an extensive set of village studies to argue that:
- Net remittances from town to village are small.
- Wealthy rural families are better able to educate their children who then migrate and remit.
- Wealthy rural families are able to finance more distant (particularly international) migration which is more lucrative.
- The children of the wealthy are more likely to retain their rural ties and to remit.

Stark et al. (1986, 1988) take issue with Lipton. They develop a method for examining

---

[55] Connell (1981: p. 254). See also Lipton (1980) and Schuh (1982).

the impact of remittances on the Gini coefficient of income distribution and examine evidence with respect to this from two villages in Mexico. The overall result is that remittances reduce village inequality in this context. However there are contrasting effects of internal and international migration. Internal migration, within Mexico, from one of the two villages generates remittances which increase the Gini coefficient, in large part because of the high returns to education of the wealthy internal migrants. From this same village there is a long history of migration to the US and here remittances from the US prove equalizing. From the other village, where less international migration occurs, remittances from internal migrants prove equalizing, though remittances from the US serve to sharpen inequality. In other words, as more families have members who migrate either internally or internationally, the remittances from this respective direction of migration help to diminish inequality.

The results of Stark et al. underscore the complexity of effects to be anticipated when examining the impact of remittances on rural income inequality. Allowing for induced changes in other income sources would complicate this picture further. In the end, there seems little reason to presume a universal pattern will emerge. The effects of rural–urban migration upon rural inequality probably are quite varied.

4. Policy issues and options

There are few economic policy instruments which do not affect, or whose efficacy is not altered, by migration. In order to keep the discussion tractable, this section therefore focusses upon classes of policies intended to act fairly directly upon internal migration. Most of these policies are aimed at reducing rural–urban migration. It should be emphasized at the outset of this section on policy issues, that this may not be desirable, for there are many reasons to believe that migration – including rural–urban migration – may prove socially beneficial.

The section begins with a review of experience with direct controls upon mobility before turning to incentives. Sections 4.2 and 4.3 address policies affecting urban pay and rural development (including rural settlement schemes) respectively. Section 4.4 outlines some issues arising from attempts to influence the spatial dispersion of industry, including the role of agglomeration economies. Section 4.5 then turns to the related issue of the interaction between migration and the spatial distribution of investments in infrastructure and other public programs, while discussion of the nature and dispersion of education is treated separately in Section 4.6. Finally, Section 4.7 turns to a brief deliberation on the role of migration in structural adjustment programs.

4.1. Direct controls on mobility

Many municipal governments in developing countries at first reacted to increased migration as if it were an invasion to repel (Simmons, 1981: p. 89).

In a few contexts, authorities have resorted to direct controls upon mobility, requiring permits for transport, settlement or acceptance of a job (see Simmons, 1981; Oberai, 1983). How effective such policies prove to be depends critically upon the ability and willingness of the state to enforce controls, as well as upon the real interest of the state in implementing such a policy. Certainly, the potential for rural–urban migration to enhance urban profits may result in political pressure from the capitalist class not to limit migration; this theme is developed in Stark (1980b).

In Jakarta in 1970, migrants were required to register and deposit their return fare, but vagrants and unlicensed hawkers who were transported out of the city soon reappeared (Simmons, 1981). This was true also of forced slum clearance in Delhi during the emergency declared by Mrs. Gandhi. In South Africa, job permits, settlement restrictions and curfews, have been used in attempts to restrict movement of the black population into designated white areas. Despite the willingness of the South African government and police to use extreme measures, including destruction of unapproved housing and forcible relocation to the "homelands", some migration has persisted even in this context. Communist China has required removal certificates from place of origin, documentation of job offers, check points on the transport systems, and forced rustication. "...During the period from 1969–73, between 10 and 15 million urban secondary school leavers were resettled in rural areas".[56] Li (1989) describes the compulsory relocation that occurred to the Northern Provinces of China, partly for security reasons, but also observes that even in this context there was some return migration – both legal and illegal. As Oberai notes:

> However, many researchers have observed that the Chinese programmes were remarkably successful in transferring population to the rural areas.... This may have helped the authorities to check problems of urban unemployment and poverty ... but if so it was largely accomplished by instituting laws and administrative procedures that restrict freedom of movement to a degree unknown in most other nations. (Oberai, 1983: p. 12.)[57]

Thus, direct restrictions upon mobility either prove ineffective or require Draconian enforcement measures, incurring a cost in civil liberties most nations are fortunately unwilling to tolerate.

---

[56] Oberai (1983: p. 12). Forced rustication also occurred on a massive scale in Cambodia under the Khmer Rouge.

[57] Goldstein (1990) disagrees with this perception of success in the Chinese context. He argues that it is erroneous to conclude that "... the Chinese have found a way to achieve high levels of urbanization while also controlling migration to urban areas and rapid urban growth" (Goldstein, 1990: p. 698). Rather, Goldstein depicts a scenario in which improvements in transport and communication have extended the urban hinterland in China.

4.2. Influencing urban pay and labor costs

There is a good deal of evidence to suggest that higher urban earnings act as a significant attraction to migrants. The most effective mechanisms for affecting take-home pay depend upon the source of any downward wage rigidity. Reducing the real minimum wage or public sector pay, in any context, normally proves politically difficult, though failing to increase nominal levels in the face of inflation may be easier. Moreover, showing wage restraint under conditionality imposed by multilateral lenders can permit shifting of some political blame. On the other hand, it is not obvious how often minimum wage laws are the major force in preventing wage flexibility: enforcement is far from uniform and, as Henderson (1986) notes, to the extent that urban migration is biased toward skilled workers, the minimum wage may not be binding on migrants. Where collective bargaining is the major source of the rural–urban wage gap, regulating the collective bargaining process may prove effective in restraining urban wage pressures. Certainly several developing countries have acted to restrain union formation and collective bargaining, though concerns for induced migration are probably not the main root cause for these restraints. A third alternative is an income tax on urban wage income, though evasion and informal sector non-wage employment impose limits on the potential of this as an instrument.

Subsidies to promote urban employment are common in the developing countries.

Slowly the attitude towards migrant squatters and slum dwellers in many developing countries, particularly in Asia, is changing from a punitive to a more tolerant one. A number of measures have now been taken to accommodate migrants in urban areas and promote their welfare.... In order to provide employment, governments have introduced urban public works programmes, promoted the expansion of the construction industry, and legislated on small-scale enterprises. Instead of discouraging hawkers, vendors and family enterprises, many countries have provided them with various types of assistance. (Oberai, 1983: p. 23.)

To this list should be added the common practice of over-staffing in the public enterprises and civil service. Thus, payment of overt wage subsidies is rare, in part because of the difficulties in financing and administering these as already discussed. Rather, subsidies are more typically offered to promote production in certain labor-intensive activities or to promote investment (through cheap loans, diminished collateral requirements, or accelerated depreciation) in such activities (offset by induced adoption of more capital intensive techniques). An alternative to subsidies is a reduction in payroll taxes, such as social security contributions often imposed on the organized urban sector alone, though again this raises a major issue of revenue.[58]

---

[58] Other forms of labor market regulation may act very much like wage taxes though without generating any revenue. For instance, several developing countries require government permission to retrench workers, resulting in a diminished willingness to hire. See Fallon and Lucas (1991, 1993).

From the discussion in Section 3.2 it should be clear that the problem of financing such subsidies or tax cuts is not their only drawback. Enacted in isolation, these well-meant attempts to promote urban employment can readily exhibit detrimental side effects – potentially reducing total production and exacerbating urban unemployment.

4.3. Rural development

The message that promoting rural employment opportunities can play a key role in stemming the rate of rural–urban migration now seems widely accepted. However, for such policies to succeed they must be sensitive to the underlying causes of migration. Thus, expanding the number of vulnerable jobs may achieve less than reducing the vulnerability of existing jobs. Consequently, acting upon appropriate rural employment strategies proves difficult in practice.

4.3.1. Intent versus reality in rural development

Findley (1981) distinguishes two sets of characteristics of rural development strategies. The first set includes several elements which often prove to reduce the demand for agricultural laborers: subsidized mechanization, research and development in labor displacing crop types[59], pricing policies favoring cash crops and commercial farming, and irrigation schemes which favor larger farmers (whose increased output may depress prices for smallholders). Indeed, irrigation schemes more generally can increase the demand for hours of work and permanent labor, yet diminish the total number of agricultural laborers employed. Findley proceeds to describe a number of contexts in which attempts to promote rural development by strategies exhibiting some of these elements have resulted in accelerated out-migration either to town or to other rural areas.

On the other hand, the intent of integrated rural development schemes, Findley argues, is to focus upon employment creation and human resources more generally. However, even the evidence on the effect of integrated rural development schemes upon out-migration is mixed. A number of the elements in such integrated schemes – such as improved transport and rural schooling to be discussed later in this section – can act to promote migration.

A common component in integrated rural development schemes is a rural works program. Narayana et al. (1988), in a CGE simulation for India, find that a rural works program to build productive rural infrastructure in the off-season can be very effective in reducing rural poverty, if "carried out efficiently, targeted effectively and financed

---

[59] See Becker et al. (1986) for a CGE simulation of the migration consequences of labor saving technical progress during the green revolution in India. Yet precisely which aspects of the green revolution were labor displacing and which employment enhancing is still disputed.

in a way that does not jeopardize long-term growth" (Narayana et al., 1988: p. 131). These latter qualifications are far from trivial.

The benefits to rural development schemes – whether integrated or otherwise – ought not to be judged solely by their effects upon rural out-migration. It has also become apparent from widespread experience that rural development, even if it serves to augment rural employment and incomes, may fail to stem the flow of rural–urban migration. Some reasons ought to be apparent from the foregoing discussion in this chapter. For instance, a rise in rural incomes may principally serve to finance more migration. A rise in rural mean income accompanied by greater risk can also accelerate rural out-migration, both because the rural income stream may look less attractive to risk averse households and because of the desire to purchase insurance by placing members in town. A rise in rural mean income accompanied by a more unequal distribution of income increases relative deprivation which once again can serve to accelerate migration.

An understanding of how any given rural development package will affect out-migration requires both a good sense of the motives underlying family migration decisions and of precisely how these components are likely to be altered by the proposed strategy. Various packages affect employment, incomes (both absolute and relative) and the risks associated with these in very different ways. The consequences for migration decisions of changes in levels and riskiness of incomes and employment are unlikely to be uniform across families, irrespective of family size, composition, endowments of physical and human capital, and contextual setting (Peek and Standing, 1979).

4.3.2. Rural settlement schemes

Rural settlement schemes, involving the establishment of new or much expanded farming communities, exist in a wide range of developing countries.[60] The objectives of such programs are often multidimensional, perhaps aiming to enhance incomes of the chosen settlers, to promote regional development for defense or strategic purposes, to diminish population pressure either in areas of settlers' origin or of their alternative migration choices, or to remove political dissidents to remote locations. As a result an appropriate criterion for evaluating success is not always apparent (Bahrin, 1981).

Nonetheless, there is some agreement that most programs prove extremely expensive for each person settled. Not surprisingly, Bahrin (1981) identifies selection of site, selection of settlers, magnitude of investment and quality of management as key elements in whether settlement schemes prove productive. Even when schemes offer

---

[60] For general reviews see Peek and Standing (1979), Bahrin (1981) and Oberai (1988). On the FELDA schemes in Malaysia see Chan (1981); James (1983) and James and Roumasset (1984) examine the pioneer settler schemes in the Philippines; and Gillespie (1983) looks at the effect of Paraguay's farm colony promotion on urbanization.

settlers higher than average incomes, the extent of income gain remains unclear, for at least in some contexts initial settlers are not chosen from the rural poor (James and Roumasset, 1984; Lucas and Verry, 1990). Thus James (1983) notes that income generated, for a given investment, is far higher on privately financed settlement schemes in the Philippines, but this is largely because the publicly financed schemes are settled by families with lower initial assets and skills. Moreover, even if initial settlers gain, there is some evidence to suggest that the children of settlers fair less well (Chan, 1981) as do any second-wave settlers (James and Roumasset, 1984).

4.4. On industrial location

Almost all developing countries adopt policies intended to influence the location of industrial production. Again the objectives of this can be multidimensional, but often an intent to relocate production rather than labor is a key component.

To the extent that agglomeration production economies exist, internal to a given location but external to the firm, too little rather than too much concentration of industrial production tends to result from private decisions of firms. Each firm fails to take account of external benefits to other producers in their location decision. The evidence on the extent and nature of such agglomeration externalities in developing countries is exceedingly thin (see, however, Shukla, 1984). Wheaton and Shishido (1981) examine cross-country patterns in city population concentration (measured by the square of city relative to total population) against non-agricultural GNP per capita (interpreted as a proxy for market size). They find that concentration at first rises then declines as income rises. It is very difficult to interpret these results in terms of agglomeration externalities: actual concentration surely fails to optimize with respect to these effects at every level of development; moreover, whether per capita or absolute incomes should be used as proxies for market size, and indeed whether the domestic market alone is relevant to the more open economies, may be disputed. Henderson (1986) presents more direct evidence by estimating cost functions for several manufacturing industries in Brazil. Henderson finds that costs decline with the level of employment in the same industry in the same location, but do not decline with local population: this suggests that economies are driven by within-industry production externalities rather than by size of local market or other benefits of urban size.[61]

Shukla and Stark (1985, 1990) undertake a ranking of optimally applied policy instruments when agglomeration production externalities exist. The first paper considers a model with two factors of production but with external benefits driven by the level of employment alone. In the context of a log-linear production function, Shukla and Stark demonstrate that an optimal production subsidy is more expensive to finance

---

[61] Henderson also finds that economies of scale are biased against low-skill workers, offering a partial explanation for relatively high demand for skilled workers in areas of industrial concentration.

than either a capital or labor subsidy, presumably because the external benefit is factor rather than output driven. More surprisingly, numerical simulations suggest that a capital subsidy is cheaper than an employment subsidy, despite modelling the externality as driven by employment, though this may reflect the higher total cost of the optimal employment subsidy resulting precisely from the need to raise employment levels to take advantage of the externality. The second paper, Shukla and Stark (1990), simplifies to one factor of production, but adds the complication of urban unemployment and migration according to the static Harris–Todaro expected wage rule. Simulations in this context show that, for plausible parameter values, the cost of a wage subsidy package is lower if optimally designed to take account of known urban agglomeration economies, rather than applying a uniform subsidy to both urban and rural areas.

Even if other elements dictate wider dispersal of industrial production – perhaps considerations of external diseconomies of overcrowding, or of regional development for strategic reasons – any agglomeration economies call for some concentration (Linn, 1982). Accordingly, industrial location policies frequently focus upon the development of select growth centers.[62] Hansen (1981) argues that by the 1970s the experience of the 1950s and 1960s led to considerable pessimism with the potential for select growth center development. Hansen maintains that the cumulative failure of these experiences is one of application rather than of principle, a result of political pressures dominating economic considerations, but the failures are no less real for this.

The basis for Hansen's expression of pessimism is not obvious. As Modi (1982) notes, there has been almost no systematic analysis of the cost–benefit ratios of the widespread and continuing use of incentives to affect industrial dispersal in the LDCs. Both Modi (1982) and Murray (1988) describe the range of financial policy instruments deployed in these attempts, including direct relocation assistance, investment tax credits, income and property tax exemptions, and loan guarantees for construction and housing. As Modi (1982) notes, many of these options favor capital and indeed overt employment subsidies do not appear to be common, but this may not be inappropriate in the light of the ranking in Shukla and Stark (1985). Murray parametrizes restricted cost functions for Korean manufacturing and uses these to simulate which instruments are likely to be more effective in lowering costs and hence redirect location decisions. Murray concludes that credit guarantee schemes are very cost effective. However, this conclusion is derived in a context in which access to credit is argued to be a major constraint on small and medium sized firms, with no allowance for the costs of default. Moreover, no explicit account is taken of agglomeration economies nor of any factor bias inherent in these. Nonetheless, Murray's contribution is to be

---

[62] See, however, Hackenberg (1980) on the penetration of rural areas by urban-like forms of production and infrastructure.

lauded as representing one of the few systematic empirical contributions in this sorely neglected field.[63]

4.5. *Investing in infrastructure*

The location of infrastructure may affect migration patterns both indirectly and directly. For instance, besides using financial instruments to promote select growth centers, many LDCs also attempt to influence the distribution of production activities through investments in infrastructure. The distribution of infrastructure whose output is directly consumed – water supply, electricity, health care, schooling, transport, etc. – may also shape decisions with respect to place of residence (Mills and Becker, 1986). Yet there exists surprisingly little evidence on either count.

The effects of improved rural transportation seem to have attracted the most attention. Whether easier and cheaper transportation between town and countryside promotes or diminishes outward movement is not obvious (Connell et al., 1976). Improved transport permits easier marketing of products in town but also heightens competition from goods imported from town: the effects on relative prices of local goods, whether this favors more labor-intensive activities, and hence the consequences for rural employment are therefore ambiguous. Moreover, better transportation diminishes the cost of an initial move to town and of subsequent visits home, thus encouraging outward movement; but better transportation also enhances the potential for commuting and access to urban facilities for village dwellers. Improved rural transportation facilities may also facilitate movements of labor within the rural sector which in turn can affect rural–urban movements in a number of ways: cheaper (or easier) movement of labor from village i to village j may encourage greater movement to town from j; ability to move labor between rural locations at non-synchronous peak demands can leave the rural area more responsive to vagaries that do not co-vary strongly across villages, thus substituting for rural–urban migration for insurance purposes; and improved intra-rural transport can enhance the returns on rural capital (notably on trucks or other vehicles), perhaps encouraging rural–urban migration for capital accumulation.

Not surprisingly the evidence on the migration consequences of improved rural transportation is mixed. Findley (1981) summarizes much of the LDC case study material and concludes that extending rural road networks tends to increase departure in the short run but deter out-migration in the longer run through enhanced commuting and local development. Hugo (1981b) examines the case study materials for Indonesia and concludes that improved road transport has probably increased the extent of population mobility, though it may have enhanced circular migration while discouraging long-distance, more permanent moves. Udall (1981) estimates the reduced form of

---

[63] See, however, Tolley and Thomas (1987).

a two-equation model with number of family members migrating and family consumption as dependent variables, using Colombian household data. Included in the explanatory variables are both distance to town and a measure of frequency of bus service. Udall finds that out-migration increases with distance to town and with frequency of bus service, but an interaction effect between the two proves negative. The combined effect is such that increasing bus service enhances migration to town from nearby villages but discourages movement from more remote areas, though one can only speculate on the underlying causes of this observed pattern.

The interaction between the housing market and migration decisions remains comparatively neglected, at least in the developing countries. In the transition economies of central Europe, this interaction is proving problematic. Given the frequent absence of private property rights to housing combined with almost no mortgage financing, the housing market is extremely thin. This is rendering relocation of workers even more difficult during anticipated major structural adjustments. Either a rental or selling housing market must deepen, commuting increase, or location of jobs will be an important component in restructuring and in the definition of comparative cost advantage (Lee et al., 1992). Richardson (1987) includes the incremental capital cost of urban housing in a cost analysis of LDC urbanization. Housing costs should, however, only be viewed as part of the shadow cost of urban job creation if the two projects – job creation and additional housing – are considered totally inextricable, and then the joint output must be included on the benefit side.

One of the most interesting, recent analyses of the interaction between migration and infrastructure in a developing country context is that of Rosenzweig and Wolpin (1988). The authors point out that in evaluating the benefits to subsidized local public programs, the fact that the composition of the local population may be affected, precisely through the attraction of the subsidy to select migrants, is usually neglected (see also Schultz, 1988). Rosenzweig and Wolpin distinguish between family inputs to human capital generation which exhibit properties of a public good versus expenditures which benefit a specific individual. Programs subsidizing the latter tend to attract families with high propensities to spend on children, but this may be either in the form of higher fertility or of higher expenditures per child. Subsidizing family "public" good inputs also attracts families with high propensities to spend but in this case the benefits are not diluted by larger family size: larger families and those tending to spend more per person are attracted. In the light of this, Rosenzweig and Wolpin look at the effects of a child health care program, from 1968 to 1974, in one village in Candelaria, Colombia, on selectivity of migrants from surrounding villages without a similar program.

> ...in-migrants were evidently drawn from the low tail of the family size distribution, were of relatively high income and, within income groups, had children whose nutritional status was lower than that of observationally-identical members of the resident population. As a consequence, evaluations of the program inatten-

tive to migration selectivity based on differences in program exposure across children born prior to the program were shown to significantly overestimate the impact of the program. (Rosenzweig and Wolpin, 1988.)

Subsequently, however, Pitt et al. (1992) have shown that government decisions with respect to location of public programs, such as health care and schooling, are also significantly shaped by the composition of the local population. It remains to explore the simultaneity of these two threads, when location of programs is affected by population composition and population composition is affected by program sites through induced migration.

4.6. The nature and dispersion of education

Evaluating rural education exhibits similar difficulties. Measuring the returns to rural education among those who elect to remain in the rural areas offers a biased picture in view of the selectivity of out-migration (Schultz, 1988). Indeed, there appears to be such widespread agreement about the incidence of rural education having a major effect on the propensity to migrate, that rural education programs cannot be appropriately evaluated without taking the consequences of induced migration into account.[64]

Yet almost all of the statistical evidence on the effects of rural education upon departure focusses upon quantity rather than quality or content of education, whereas the important decisions at the margin may be investments in upgrading quality (Behrman and Birdsall, 1983). Indeed, partly in response to the induced rural–urban migration, a number of developing countries design rural, vocational curricula in the hope both of raising productivity in agriculture relative to that in town, as well as of changing tastes with regard to rural life. There is some evidence to indicate that even conventional primary schooling does raise productivity in agriculture (Lockheed et al., 1980). Whether rural vocational training enhances this effect is much disputed, and certainly the case study evidence on whether the rural-relevant education diminishes out-migration is mixed (Findley, 1981).

Migration for education, though usually at higher levels of schooling or college, is not uncommon in developing countries. This may either take the form of individual children moving (often to stay with kin), or of families relocating to take advantage of better educational facilities (Henderson, 1986). On the other hand, older children in

---

[64] Speare and Harris (1986) note that in Indonesia the much higher rate of rural–urban migration among those with post-primary education is difficult to explain in terms of relative earnings alone. Speare and Harris suggest that this may simply be a reflection of the skill mix of jobs created in town, resulting in migration of the better educated without necessarily raising their rural–urban earnings differential. Alternatively, the non-monetary advantages of urban jobs – both job security and working conditions more generally – may be a source of attraction for the more highly educated.

rural areas may commute substantial distances to attend school, raising difficult empirical issues of appropriately measuring access to schooling facilities.

4.7. Structural adjustment and development strategies

Differing levels of effective protection offered to various production activities can have a profound effect upon the spatial distribution of the demand for labor and hence labor migration (Rehnberg, 1977; Kelley and Williamson, 1984). This is true not only of policies affecting the domestic terms of trade between agriculture and industry. Protection offered to mineral extraction or other natural resource based activities also generates location-specific labor demands. Moreover the intensity of agglomeration economies associated with various industries affects the degree of population concentration likely to be induced by any given structure of protection.

Conversely, structural adjustment resulting from an episode of trade liberalization involves some degree of labor migration. Indeed, the speed with which labor migration is induced may be an important component in the speed of structural adjustment, though this is not necessarily an argument for slow reform (Mussa, 1986).

Despite the potential importance of this interaction between structural adjustment and labor migration, little empirical evidence exists on the subject. A few spatial CGE models are used to simulate the consequences for rural–urban migration of changing the terms of trade between agriculture and industry,[65] though such models are usually not founded upon direct econometric evidence and none adequately incorporates issues of lags in adjustment.

5. Closing thoughts

Our ideas and information about internal migration in developing countries have grown substantially in the last decade or so. Yet the dominant policy concern continues to be containment of rural–urban migration. This concern may well be misplaced. The transition to a more highly urban population is not proceeding at a particularly alarming rate. Rather the rapid LDC urban population growth is driven largely by high overall population growth. Moreover, answers to the narrower question as to whether too much labor is being transferred to the urban sector are far from clear-cut. Major elements of urban bias do exist in many contexts, although there has been a heightened awareness of the benefits to some forms of rural development schemes.

---

[65] Becker et al. (1986), for instance, simulate the consequences for Indian urban population growth of a shift in the world terms of trade between agriculture and industry. In this context, only a tiny effect is found, though this is largely because India's production decisions were largely insulated from world prices, precisely by her trade protection strategy, at least until very recently.

Despite many claims to the contrary the basic ideas of the Harris–Todaro frame-work survive in essence if not intact after prolific modifications and some testing. Nonetheless we surely reached rapidly diminishing returns to further modifications to and extensions of the Harris–Todaro model quite some time ago. This is true also of the empirical literature estimating the responsiveness of migration flows to earnings differentials. Despite increasing refinements in estimation techniques, the basic mes-sages seem to remain the same.

On the other hand, our understanding of factors determining the urban component of those earnings differentials remains poor. Efficiency wage stories now dominate the world of theory, but little evidence has been compiled either in favor of or to contra-dict these ideas. Indeed it is not yet clear how they may be tested even in principle.

In spite of the importance of rural development as a counter force to urban job creation, implementing "appropriate" forms of rural development has proved far more difficult and contentious. We have gained some understanding of the complexity of raising the demand for labor or laborers in agriculture. Yet whether additions to rural incomes discourage or permit more rural–urban migration is not everywhere apparent. The potentially important role of rural risks in promoting migration for insurance is also now recognized, though quite how these risks may effectively be reduced through policy measures is not obvious.

Despite the ubiquitous adoption of policies to promote industrial dispersal, either in select growth centers or, perhaps less often, through "rurbanization", almost no quan-tification exists of any net benefits from moving capital rather than people. Even the responsiveness of industry to fiscal incentives to relocate has hardly been touched upon.

The literature on the interconnections between the location and nature of infrastruc-ture and public programs on the one hand and migration on the other hand is only slightly richer. There is very little evidence on the effect of such investments on the decisions of potential migrants to relocate or not. Moreover, the evaluation of such investments may be biased if the consequences of induced migration are ignored.

Indeed in general terms it is probably fair to say that economists have been largely preoccupied with the migration of labor. Movements of families or parts of families to gain access to (better) schooling, health facilities, or other publicly provided services has therefore often been of peripheral concern.

The growing literature on family strategies and migration has more recently wid-ened this circle of reference for economists. The interactions between migration, fer-tility, marriage, and family structure have begun to be explored. Within other disci-plines similar issues were raised at a much earlier stage. Thus far, the contributions by economists in these spheres seem promising. Still, our tests of any resultant hypothe-ses have normally been conducted in one context at best. Replication or refutation of these ideas in other spheres must be high on our agenda.

Exploration of family risk spreading strategies has led economists to follow some earlier sociologists in rejecting the sharp urban–rural development distinctions of the early dual growth models. Such evidence as we have suggests that a view of families straddling at least these two sectors is both more accurate and more illuminating.

The bulk of internal migration in the Third World is rural–rural and not rural–urban. Our early focus on dual models blinded economists to the feasible diversification within the rural sector, resulting in almost total neglect of the predominant mode of internal migration. Similarly, though for different reasons, circular and temporary migration have hardly been studied except in the context of micro case studies. Statistical testing of hypotheses on the causes and consequences of this apparently common phenomenon will require more specialized surveys.

Thus, while our ideas and (to a lesser extent) our information about internal migration in the developing countries have been considerably enriched in recent years, a great deal remains to be done. There are major policy areas, touching more or less directly upon migration, where almost no systematic empirical knowledge has yet been amassed.

References

Abumere, S.I. (1981), "Population distribution policies and measures in Africa south of the Sahara: a review article", Population and Development Review 7: 421–433.

Adelman, I. and S. Robinson (1978), "Migration, demographic change and income distribution in a model of a developing country", in: J.L. Simon, ed., Research in population economics, Vol. 1 (JAI Press, Greenwich, CT).

Aharoni, Y. (1986), The evolution and management of state owned enterprises (Ballinger, Cambridge, MA).

Ahluwalia, M.S. (1978), "Rural poverty and agricultural performance in India", Journal of Development Studies 14: 298–323.

Amano, M. (1983), "On the Harris–Todaro model with intersectoral migration of labour", Economica 50: 311–325.

Anand, S. and V. Joshi (1979), "Domestic distortions, income distribution and the theory of the optimal subsidy", The Economic Journal 89: 336–352.

Arellano, J.-P. (1981), "Do more jobs in the modern sector increase urban unemployment?", Journal of Development Economics 8: 241–247.

Bahrin, T.S. (1981), "Review and evaluation of attempts to direct migrants to frontier areas through land colonization schemes", in: Population distribution policies in development planning, Population studies no. 75 (Department of International Economic and Social Affairs, United Nations, New York).

Banerjee, B. (1983), "The role of the informal sector in the migration process: a test of probabilistic migration models and labour market segmentation for India", Oxford Economic Papers 35: 399–422.

Banerjee, B. (1984a), "Rural-to-urban migration and conjugal separation: an Indian case study", Economic Development and Cultural Change 32: 767–780.

Banerjee, B. (1984b), "Information flow, expectations and job search: rural-to-urban migration process in India", Journal of Development Economics 15: 239–257.

Banerjee, B. (1984c), "The probability, size, and usefulness of remittances from urban to rural areas in India", Journal of Development Economics 16: 293–311.

Banerjee, B. (1991), "The determinants of migrating with a pre-arranged job and of the initial duration of urban unemployment: an analysis based on Indian data on rural-to-urban migrants", Journal of Development Economics 36: 337–351.

Banerjee, B. and S.M. Ravi Kanbur (1981), "On the specification and estimation of macro rural–urban migration functions: with an application to Indian data", Oxford Bulletin of Economics and Statistics 43: 7–29.

Bardhan, P.K. (1977), "On measuring rural unemployment", Journal of Development Studies 14: 342–352.

Barnum, H.N. (1976), "The relationship among social and political variables, economic structure, and rural–urban migration", Economic Development and Cultural Change 24: 759–764.

Barnum, H.N. and R.H. Sabot (1977), "Education, employment probabilities and rural–urban migration in Tanzania", Oxford Bulletin of Economics and Statistics 39: 109–126.

Bartlett, W. (1983), "On the dynamic instability of induced-migration unemployment in a dual economy", Journal of Development Economics 13: 85–96.

Beals, R.E., M.B. Levy and L.N. Moses (1967), "Rationality and migration in Ghana", Review of Economics and Statistics 49: 480–486.

Becker, C.M. and A.R. Morrison (1988), "The determinants of urban population growth in sub-Saharan Africa", Economic Development and Cultural Change 36: 259–278.

Becker, C.M., E.S. Mills and J.G. Williamson (1986), "Modeling Indian migration and city growth, 1960–2000", Economic Development and Cultural Change 35: 1–33.

Becker, G.S. (1975), Human capital, 2nd edn. (University of Chicago Press, Chicago, IL).

Behrman, J.R. and N. Birdsall (1983), "The quality of schooling: quantity alone is misleading", American Economic Review 73: 928–946.

Behrman, J.R. and B.L. Wolfe (1985), "Micro determinants of female migration in a developing country: labor market, demographic marriage market and economic marriage market incentives", in: T.P. Schultz and K.I. Wolpin, eds., Research in population economics, Vol. 5 (JAI Press, Greenwich, CT).

Bennett, J. and M. Phelps (1983), "A model of employment creation in an open developing economy", Oxford Economic Papers 35: 373–398.

Beringhaus, S. and H.G. Seifer-Vogt (1988), "Temporary versus permanent migration: a decision theoretical approach", Journal of Population Economics 1: 195–211.

Berry, A. and R.H. Sabot (1984), "Unemployment and economic development", Economic Development and Cultural Change 33: 99–116.

Berry, R.A. and R. Soligo (1969), "Some welfare aspects of international migration", Journal of Political Economy 77: 778–794.

Bhagwati, J. and T.N. Srinivasan (1974), "On reanalyzing the Harris–Todaro model: policy rankings in the case of sector-specific sticky wages", American Economic Review 64: 502–508.

Bhattacharyya, B. (1985), "The role of family decision in internal migration: the case of India", Journal of Development Economics 18: 51–66.

Blau, D.M. (1985), "Self-employment and self-selection in developing country labor markets", Southern Economic Journal 52: 351–363.

Blau, D.M. (1986), "Self-employment, earnings, and mobility in Peninsular Malaysia", World Development 14: 839–852.

Blejer, M.I. and I. Goldberg (1980), "Return migration-expectations versus reality: a case study of western immigrants to Israel", in: J.L. Simon and J. DaVanzo, eds., Research in population economics, Vol. 2 (JAI Press, Greenwich, CT).

Bliss, C.J. and N.H. Stern (1978), "Productivity, wages and nutrition", Journal of Development Economics 5: 331–398.

Blomqvist, A.G. (1978), "Urban job creation and unemployment in LDCs: Todaro vs. Harris and Todaro", Journal of Development Economics 5: 3–18.

Bonin, J.P. and L. Putterman (1987), Economics of cooperation and the labor-managed economy (Harwood Academic Press, New York).

Brigg, P. (1971), Migration to urban areas, Staff working paper no. 107 (World Bank, Washington, DC).

Brown, L.A. and J.P. Jones (1985), "Spatial variation in migration processes and development: a Costa Rican example of conventional modeling augmented by the expansion method", Demography 22: 327–352.

Gottschang, T.R. (1987), "Economic change, disasters and migration: the historical case of Manchuria", Economic Development and Cultural Change 35: 461–490.

Greenwood, M.J. (1971), "A regression analysis of migration to urban areas of a less developed country: the case of India", Journal of Regional Science 11: 253–262.

Greenwood, M.J. (1978), "An econometric model of internal migration and regional economic growth in Mexico", Journal of Regional Science 18: 17–31.

Greenwood, M.J., J.R. Ladman and B.S. Siegel (1981), "Long-term trends in migratory behavior in a developing country: the case of Mexico", Demography 18: 369–389.

Gregory, P. (1975), "The impact of institutional factors on urban labor markets", World Bank studies in employment and rural development no. 27 (World Bank, Washington, DC).

Hackenberg, R.A. (1980), "New patterns of urbanization in Southeast Asia: an assessment", Population and Development Review 6: 391–419.

Hance, W.A. (1970), Population, migration, and urbanization in Africa (Columbia University Press, New York).

Hansen, N. (1981), "A review and evaluation of attempts to direct migrants to smaller and intermediate-sized cities", in: Population distribution policies in development planning, Population studies no. 75 (Department of International Economic and Social Affairs, United Nations, New York).

Harbison, S.F. (1981), "Family structure and family strategy in migration decision making", in: G.F. De Jong and R.W. Gardner, eds., Migration decision making: multi-disciplinary approaches to microlevel studies in developed and developing countries (Pergamon Press, New York).

Harris, J.R. and R.H. Sabot (1982), "Urban unemployment in LDCs: towards a more general search model", in: R.H. Sabot, ed., Migration and the labor market in developing countries (Westview Press, Boulder, CO).

Harris, J.R. and M.P. Todaro (1970), "Migration, unemployment and development: a two-sector analysis", American Economic Review 60: 126–142.

Hay, M.J. (1980), "A structural equations model of migration in Tunisia", Economic Development and Cultural Change 28: 345–358.

Heady, C.J. (1981), "Shadow wages and induced migration", Oxford Economic Papers 33: 108–121.

Heller, P.S. and A.A. Tait (1984), Government employment and pay: some international comparisons, Occasional paper no. 24 (IMF, Washington, DC).

Henderson, J.V. (1986), "Urbanization in a developing country: city size and population composition", Journal of Development Economics 22: 269–293.

Herrick, B.H. (1971), "Urbanization and urban migration in Latin America: an economists' view", in: F. Rabinovitz and F. Trueblood, eds., Latin American urban research (Sage Publications, Beverly Hills, CA).

Hertel, T.W. (1977), "The system of mafisa and the highly dependent agricultural system", Rural sociology report series no. 11 (Ministry of Agriculture, Gaborone, Botswana).

Hoselitz, B.F. (1953), "The role of cities in the economic growth of underdeveloped countries", Journal of Political Economy 61: 195–208.

Hugo, G.J. (1981a), "Village-community ties, village norms, and ethnic and social networks: a review of the evidence from the Third World", in: G.F. De Jong and R.W. Gardner, eds., Migration decision making: multi-disciplinary approaches to microlevel studies in developed and developing countries (Pergamon Press, New York).

Hugo, G.J. (1981b), "Road transport, population mobility and development in Indonesia", in: G.W. Jones and H.V. Richter, eds., Population mobility and development: Southeast Asia and the Pacific, Development studies monograph no. 27 (Australian National University, Canberra).

Hugo, G.J. (1982), "Circular migration in Indonesia", Population and Development Review 8: 59–83.

International Labour Office (ILO) (1972), Employment, income and equality: a strategy for increasing productive employment in Kenya (International Labour Office, Geneva).

Jagannathan, V. (1987), The logic of unorganized markets (Oxford University Press, Oxford).

James, W.E. (1983), "Settler selection and land settlement alternatives: new evidence from the Philippines", Economic Development and Cultural Change 31: 571–586.

James, W.E. and J. Roumasset (1984), "Migration and the evolution of tenure contracts in newly settled regions", Journal of Development Economics 14: 147–162.

Jha, R. and U. Lachler (1981), "Optimum taxation and public production in a dynamic Harris–Todaro world", Journal of Development Economics 9: 357–373.

Johnson, H.G. (1967), "Some economic aspects of the brain drain", Pakistan Development Review 7: 379–409.

Kannappan, S. (1985), "Urban employment and the labor market in developing nations", Economic Development and Cultural Change 33: 699–730.

Katz, E. and O. Stark (1985a), "Desired fertility and migration in LDCs: signing the connection", in: Proceedings of the Florence General Conference (International Union for the Scientific Study of Population, Liege).

Katz, E. and O. Stark (1985b), "A theory of remittances and migration", Discussion paper series, no. 18 (Harvard University Migration and Development Program, Cambridge, MA).

Katz, E. and O. Stark (1986a), "Labor migration and risk aversion in less developed countries", Journal of Labor Economics 4: 134–149.

Katz, E. and O. Stark (1986b), "Labor mobility under asymmetric information with moving and signalling costs", Economics Letters 21: 89–94.

Katz, E. and O. Stark (1986c), "On the shadow wage of urban jobs in less-developed countries", Journal of Urban Economics 20: 121–127.

Katz, E. and O. Stark (1986d), "On fertility, migration and remittances", World Development 14: 133–135.

Katz, E. and O. Stark (1987), "International migration under asymmetric information", The Economic Journal 97: 718–726.

Katz, E. and O. Stark (1989), "International labor migration under alternative informational regimes: a diagrammatic analysis", European Economic Review 33: 127–142.

Kelley, A.C. and J.G. Williamson (1984), What drives Third World city growth? (Princeton University Press, Princeton, NJ).

Keyfitz, N. (1982), "Development and the elimination of poverty", Economic Development and Cultural Change 30: 649–670.

Khan, M.A. (1980), "The Harris–Todaro hypothesis and the Heckscher–Ohlin–Samuelson trade model: a synthesis", Journal of International Economics 10: 527–547.

Kikuchi, M. and Y. Hayami (1983), "New rice technology, intrarural migration, and institutional innovation", Population and Development Review 9: 247–257.

Knight, J.B. and R.H. Sabot (1983), "The role of the firm in wage determination: an African case study", Oxford Economic Papers 35: 45–66.

Krueger, A.B. and L.H. Summers (1988), "Efficiency wages and the inter-industry wage structure", Econometrica 56: 259–293.

Krugman, P and J. Bhagwati (1976), "The decision to migrate: a survey", in: J.N. Bhagwati, ed., The brain drain and taxation: Vol. II. Theory and empircal evidence (North-Holland, Amsterdam).

Lang, K. and W.T. Dickens (1992), "Labor market segmentation, wage dispersion and unemployment", Working paper no. 4073 (NBER, Cambridge, MA).

Lauby, J. and O. Stark (1988), "Individual migration as a family strategy: young women in the Philippines", Population Studies 42: 473–486.

Lee, O.-J. (1980), Urban-to-rural return migration in Korea (Seoul National University Press, Seoul).

Lee, E. (Chief of Mission) (1992), Economic transformation and employment in Hungary (International Labour Office, Geneva).

Leibenstein, H. (1957), Economic backwardness and economic growth (Wiley, New York).

Levy, M.B. and W.J. Wadycki (1974), "Education and the decision to migrate; an econometric analysis of migration in Venezuela", Econometrica 42: 377–388.

Li, R.M. (1989), "Migration to China's northern frontier 1953–82", Population and Development Review 15: 503–538.

Lim, D. (1977), "Do foreign companies pay higher wages than their local counterparts in Malaysian manufacturing?", Journal of Development Economics 4: 55–66.

Lindauer, D.L. and R.H. Sabot (1983), "The public–private wage differential in a poor urban economy", Journal of Development Economics 12: 137–152.

Linn, J.F. (1982), "The costs of urbanization in developing countries", Economic Development and Cultural Change 30: 625–648.

Lipton, M. (1977), Why poor people stay poor: a study of urban bias in world development (Temple Smith, London).

Lipton, M. (1980), "Migration from rural areas of poor countries: the impact on rural productivity and income distribution", World Development 8: 1–24.

Lockheed, M.E., D.T. Jamison and L.J. Lau (1980), "Farmer education and farm efficiency: a survey", Economic Development and Cultural Change 29: 37–76.

Lucas, R.E.B. (1975), "The supply of immigrants function and taxation of immigrants", incomes: an econometric analysis", Journal of Development Economics 2: 289–308.

Lucas, R.E.B. (1976), "Internal migration and economic development: an overview", in: A. Brown and E. Neuberger, eds., Internal migration (Academic Press, New York).

Lucas, R.E.B. (1979), "Sharing, monitoring and incentives: Marshallian misallocation reassessed", Journal of Political Economy 87: 501–521.

Lucas, R.E.B. (1982), "Labour in four districts of India", Mimeo., Report submitted to the International Labor Office, Geneva.

Lucas, R.E.B. (1985), "Migration amongst the Batswana", The Economic Journal 95: 358–382.

Lucas, R.E.B. (1987), "Emigration to South Africa's mines", American Economic Review 77: 313–330.

Lucas, R.E.B. (1988), "Guest workers, circular migration and remittances", in: D. Salvatore, ed., World population trends and their impact on economic development (Greenwood Press, Westport).

Lucas, R.E.B. and O. Stark (1985), "Motivations to remit: evidence from Botswana", Journal of Political Economy 93: 901–918.

Lucas, R.E.B. and D.W. Verry (1990), Human resource-led growth, Mimeo. (ILO-ARTEP, New Delhi).

Lundborg, P. (1990), "Rural–urban migration and the transition from traditional to modern agriculture", Journal of Development Economics 33: 287–307.

Manove, M., G.F. Papanek and H.K. Dey (1987), "Tied rents and wage determination in labor abundant countries", Mimeo. (Boston University, Boston, MA).

Mazumdar, D. (1981), The urban labor market and income distribution, a study of Malaysia (Oxford University Press, Oxford).

McCool, T. (1982), "Wage subsidies and distortionary taxes in a mobile capital Harris–Todaro model", Economica 49: 69–79.

McCulloch, R. and J.L. Yellen (1976), "Consequences of a tax on the brain drain for unemployment and income inequality in less developed countries", in: J.N. Bhagwati, ed., The brain drain and taxation: theory and empirical evidence (North-Holland, Amsterdam).

McDonald, I.M. and R.M. Solow (1981), "Wage bargaining and employment", American Economic Review 71: 896–908.

Mills, E.S. and C.M. Becker (1986), Studies in Indian urban development (Oxford University Press, New York).

Modi, J.R. (1982), "Narrowing regional disparities by fiscal incentives", Finance and Development 19: 34–37.

Moll, P.G. (1992), "Industry wage differentials and efficiency wages: a dissenting view with South African evidence", Mimeo. (Economics Department, University of Cape Town, Cape Town).

Moreland, R.S. (1982), "Population, internal migration, and economic growth: an empirical analysis", in: J.L. Simon and P.H. Lindert, eds., Research in population economics, Vol. 4 (JAI Press, Greenwich, CT).

Murray, M.P. (1988), Subsidizing industrial location: a conceptual framework with application to Korea, World Bank occasional papers, New series, no. 3 (World Bank, Washington, DC).

Mussa, M. (1986), "The adjustment process and the timing of liberalization", in: A.M. Choksi and D. Papageorgiou, eds., Economic liberalization in developing countries (Oxford University Press, New York).

Nabi, I. (1984), "Village-end considerations in rural–urban migration", Journal of Development Economics 14: 129–145.

Narayana, N.S.S., K.S. Parikh and T.N. Srinivasan (1988), "Rural works programs in India: costs and benefits", Journal of Development Economics 29: 131–156.

Neary, J.P. (1981), "On the Harris–Todaro model with intersectoral capital mobility", Economica 48: 219–234.

Nelson, J.M. (1976), "Sojourners versus urbanites: causes and consequences of temporary versus permanent cityward migration in developing countries", Economic Development and Cultural Change 24: 721–757.

Newbery, D.M.G. and J.E. Stiglitz (1979), "Sharecropping, risk sharing and the importance of imperfect information", in: J.A. Roumasset, J.-M. Boussard and I. Singh, eds., Risk, uncertainty and agricultural development (Agricultural Development Council, New York).

Oberai, A.S. (1983), "An overview of migration-influencing policies and programmes", in: A.S. Oberai, ed., State policies and internal migration: studies in market and planned economies (Croom Helm, London).

Oberai, A.S. (1988), "An overview of settlement policies and programs", in: A.S. Oberai, ed., Land settlement policies and population redistribution in developing countries: achievements, problems and prospects (Praeger, New York).

Oberai, A.S., P.H. Prasad and M.G. Sardana (1989), Determinants and consequences of internal migration in India: studies in Bihar, Kerala and Uttar Pradesh (Oxford University Press, Delhi).

Peek, P. and G. Standing (1979), "Rural–urban migration and government policies in low income countries", International Labour Review 118: 747–762.

Pessino, C. (1991), "Sequential migration theory and evidence from Peru", Journal of Development Economics 36: 55–87.

Pitt, M.M., M.R. Rosenzweig and D.M. Gibbons (1992), "The determinants and consequences of the placement of government programs in Indonesia", Mimeo. (Brown University, Providence, RI).

Portes, A. and L. Benton (1984), "Industrial development and labor absorption: a reinterpretation", Population and Development Review 10: 589–611.

Preston, S.H. (1979), "Urban growth in developing countries: a demographic reappraisal", Population and Development Review 6: 195–215.

Rehnberg, R.D. (1977), "Agricultural price policy and rural-to-urban migration: the recent South Korean experience", Journal of Developing Areas 11: 509–518.

Rempel, H. and R.A. Lobdell (1978), "The role of urban-to-rural remittances in rural development", Journal of Development Studies 14: 324–341.

Richardson, H.W. (1987), "The costs of urbanization: a four-country comparison", Economic Development and Cultural Change 35: 561–580.

Ritchey, P.N. (1976), "Explanations of migration", Annual Review of Sociology 2: 363–404.

Roberts, K.D. (1982), "Agrarian structure and labor mobility in rural Mexico", Population and Development Review 8: 299–322.

Roberts, K.D. (1985), "Household labour mobility in a modern agrarian economy: Mexico", in: G. Standing, ed., Labour circulation and the labour process (Croom-Helm, London).

Robertson, P. and S. Wellisz (1977), "Steady-state growth of an economy with intersectoral migration", Oxford Economic Papers 29: 370–388.

Robinson, D. (1990), Civil service pay in Africa (International Labour Office, Geneva).

Rodgers, G.B. (1975), "Nutritionally based wage determination in the low-income labour market", Oxford Economic Papers 27: 61–81.

Rogers, A. and L.J. Castro (1984), "Model migration schedules", in: A. Rogers, ed., Migration, urbanization, and spatial population dynamics (Westview Press, Boulder, CO).

Romaguera, P. (1991), "Wage differentials and efficiency wage models: evidence from the Chilean economy", Working paper no. 153 (Kellog Institute, Notre Dame, IN).

Rosenzweig, M.R. (1988), "Labor markets in low-income countries", in: H. Chenery and T.N. Srinivasan, eds., Handbook of development economics, Vol. I (North-Holland, Amsterdam).

Rosenzweig, M.R. and O. Stark (1989), "Consumption smoothing, migration and marriage: evidence from rural India", Journal of Political Economy 97: 905–926.

Rosenzweig, M.R. and K.I. Wolpin (1985), "Specific experience, household structure and intergenerational transfers: farm family land and labor arrangements in developing countries", Quarterly Journal of Economics 100 (Supplement): 961–987.

Rosenzweig, M.R. and K.I. Wolpin (1988), "Migration selectivity and the effects of public programs", Journal of Public Economics 37: 265–289.

Russell, S.S., K. Jacobsen and W.D. Stanley (1990), International migration and development in sub-Saharan Africa, World Bank Africa Technical Department series, Discussion paper 101 (World Bank, Washington, DC).

Sahota, G.S. (1968), "An econometric analysis of internal migration in Brazil", Journal of Political Economy 76: 218–245.

Salvatore, D. (1980), "A simultaneous equations model of internal migration with dynamic policy simulations and forecasting: Italy, 1952–76", Journal of Development Economics 7: 231–246.

Salvatore, D. (1981), "A theoretical and empirical evaluation and extension of the Todaro migration model", Regional Science and Urban Economics 11: 499–508.

Santiago, C.E. and E. Thorbecke (1988), "A multisectoral framework for the analysis of labor mobility and development in LDCs: an application to postwar Puerto Rico", Economic Development and Cultural Change 37: 127–148.

Schuh, G.E. (1982), "Outmigration, rural productivity, and the distribution of income", in: R.H. Sabot, ed., Migration and the labor market in developing countries (Westview Press, Boulder, CO).

Schultz, T.P. (1971), "Rural–urban migration in Colombia", Review of Economics and Statistics 53: 51–58.

Schultz, T.P. (1982a), "Notes on the estimation of migration decision functions", in: R.H. Sabot, ed., Migration and the labor market in developing countries (Westview Press, Boulder, CO).

Schultz, T.P. (1982b), "Lifetime migration within educational strata in Venezuela: estimates of a logistic model", Economic Development and Cultural Change 30: 559–593.

Schultz, T.P. (1988), "Heterogeneous preferences and migration: self-selection, regional prices and programs, and the behavior of migrants in Colombia", in: T.P. Schultz, ed., Research in population economics, Vol. 6 (JAI Press, Greenwich, CT).

Schwartz, A. (1973), "Interpreting the effect of distance on migration", Journal of Political Economy 81: 1153–1169.

Schwartz, A. (1976), "Migration, age and education", Journal of Political Economy 84: 701–719.

Scott, M.F., J.D. MacArthur and D.M.G. Newbery (1976), Project appraisal in practice (Heinemann, London).

Sen, A.K. (1966), "Peasants and dualism with and without surplus labor", Journal of Political Economy 74: 425–450.

Shaw, A. (1988), "The income security function of the rural sector: the case of Calcutta, India", Economic Development and Cultural Change 36: 303–314.

Shukla, V. (1984), "The productivity of Indian cities and some implications for development policy", Ph.D. dissertation (Princeton University, Princeton, NJ).

Shukla, V. and O. Stark (1985), "On agglomeration economies and optimal migration", Economics Letters 18: 297–300.

Shukla, V. and O. Stark (1990), "Policy comparisons with an agglomeration effects-augmented dual economy model", Journal of Urban Economics 27: 1–15.

Simmons, A.B. (1981), "A review and evaluation of attempts to constrain migration to selected urban centres and regions", in: Population distribution policies in development planning, Population studies no. 75 (Department of International Economic and Social Affairs, United Nations, New York).

Simmons, A., S. Diaz-Briquets and A.A. Laquian (1977), Social change and internal migration: a review of research findings from Africa, Asia and Latin America (International Development Research Centre, Ottawa).

Sjaastad, L.A. (1962), "The costs and returns of human migration", Journal of Political Economy 70 (Supplement): 80–93.

Skeldon, R. (1986), "On migration patterns in India during the 1970s", Population and Development Review 12: 759–779.

Smith, A. (1812), The wealth of nations (Cadell and Davies, London).

Speare, Jr., A. and J. Harris (1986), "Education, earnings, and migration in Indonesia", Economic Development and Cultural Change 34: 223–244.

Squire, L. (1981), Employment policy in developing countries: a survey of issues and evidence (Oxford University Press, Oxford).

Srinivasan, T.N. and J. Bhagwati (1975), "Alternative policy rankings in a large, open economy with sector-specific, minimum wages", Journal of Economic Theory 11: 356–371.

Stark, O. (1978), Economic-demographic interactions in agricultural development: the case of rural-to-urban migration (UN Food and Agricultural Organization, Rome).

Stark, O. (1980a), "On the role of urban-to-rural remittances in rural development", Journal of Development Studies 16: 369–374.

Stark, O. (1980b), "On slowing metropolitan city growth", Population and Development Review 6: 95–102.

Stark, O. (1981), "On the optimal choice of capital intensity in LDCs with migration", Journal of Development Economics 9: 31–41.

Stark, O. (1982), "On modelling the informal sector", World Development 10: 413–416.

Stark, O. (1984), "Rural-to-urban migration in LDCs: a relative deprivation approach", Economic Development and Cultural Change 32: 475–486.

Stark, O. (1988), "On marriage and migration", European Journal of Population 4: 23–27.

Stark, O. (1991a), "International labor migration under alternative informational regimes: supplement to chapter 11", in: O. Stark, ed., The migration of labor (Blackwell, Oxford).

Stark, O. (1991b), "Fertility, drought, migration and risk", in: G. Gaburro and D.L. Poston, eds., Essays in population economics (Casa Editrice Dott. Antonio Milani, Padova).

Stark, O. and D. Levhari (1982), "On migration and risk in LDCs", Economic Development and Cultural Change 31: 191–196.

Stark, O. and R.E.B. Lucas (1988), "Migration, remittances and the family", Economic Development and Cultural Change 36: 465–481.

Stark, O. and J.E. Taylor (1991), "Migration incentives, migration types: the role of relative deprivation", The Economic Journal 101: 1163–1178.

Stark, O. and S. Yitzhaki (1988), "Labor migration as a response to relative deprivation", Journal of Population Economics 1: 57–70.

Stark, O., M.R. Gupta and D. Levhari (1991), "Equilibrium urban unemployment in developing countries: is migration the culprit?", Economics Letters 37: 477–482.

Stark, O., J.E. Taylor and S. Yitzhaki (1986), "Remittances and inequality", The Economic Journal 96: 722–740.

Stark, O., J.E. Taylor and S. Yitzhaki (1988), "Migration, remittances, and inequality: a sensitivity analysis using the extended Gini index", Journal of Development Economics 28: 309–322.

Stichter, S. (1985), Migrant laborers (Cambridge University Press, Cambridge).

Stiglitz, J.E. (1969), "Rural–urban migration, surplus labour, and relationships between urban and rural wages", Eastern Africa Economic Review 1: 1–27.

Stiglitz, J.E. (1974), "Alternative theories of wage determination and unemployment in LDCs: the labor turnover model", Quarterly Journal of Economics 88: 194–227.

Stiglitz, J.E. (1976), "The efficiency wage hypothesis, surplus labor, and the distribution of income in LDCs", Oxford Economic Papers 28: 185–207.

Stiglitz, J.E. (1982), "The structure of labour markets and shadow prices in LDCs", in: R.H. Sabot, ed., Migration and the labor market in developing countries (Westview Press, Boulder, CO).

Taylor, J.E. (1986), "Differential migration, networks, information and risk", in: O. Stark, ed., Migration, human capital and development (JAI Press, Greenwich, CT).

Teilhet-Waldorf, S. and W.H. Waldorf (1983), "Earnings of self employed in an informal sector: a case study of Bangkok", Economic Development and Cultural Change 31: 587–607.

Todaro, M.P. (1969), "A model of labor migration and urban unemployment in less developed countries", American Economic Review 59: 138–148.

Todaro, M.P. (1976a), "Urban job creation, induced migration and rising unemployment: a formulation and simplified empirical test for LDCs", Journal of Development Economics 3: 211–226.

Todaro, M.P. (1976b), Internal migration in developing countries: a review of theory, evidence, methodology and research priorities (International Labour Office, Geneva).

Todaro, M.P. (1980), "Internal migration in developing countries: a survey", in: R.A. Easterlin, ed., Population and economic change in developing countries (University of Chicago Press, Chicago, IL).

Todaro, M.P. (1984), "Urbanization in developing nations: trends, prospects and policies", in: P.K. Ghosh, ed., Urban development in the Third World (Greenwood Press, Westport).

Tolley, G.S. and V. Thomas, eds. (1987), The economics of urbanization and urban policies in developing countries (World Bank Symposium, Washington, DC).

Trzcinski, E. and S. Randolph (1991), "Human capital investments and relative earnings mobility: the role of education, training, migration, and job search", Economic Development and Cultural Change 40: 153–168.

Tunali, I. (1985), "Isolating the use of a decision on the outcome: some formal illustrations and evidence from a joint migration earnings structure", Paper presented at the 1985 Winter meetings of the Econometric Society.

Udall, A.T. (1981), "Transport improvements and rural outmigration in Colombia", Economic Development and Cultural Change 29: 613–629.

United Nations (1991), World urbanization prospects (UN Department of International Economic and Social Affairs, New York).

US Committee for Refugees (1992), World refugee survey (US Committee for Refugees, Washington, DC).

Vijverberg, W.P.M. (1989), "Labor market performance as a determinant of migration", World Bank, living standards measurement study, Working paper no. 59 (World Bank, Washington, DC).

Ward, J.O. and J.H. Sanders (1980), "Nutritional determinants and migration in the Brazilian northeast: a case study of rural and urban Ceara", Economic Development and Cultural Change 29: 141–163.

Weiss, A. (1990), Efficiency wages: models of unemployment, layoffs and wage dispersion (Harwood, New York).

Wellisz, S. (1968), "Dual economies, disguised unemployment and the unlimited supply of labour", Economica 35: 22–51.

Wheaton, W.C. and H. Shishido (1981), "Urban concentration, agglomeration economies, and the level of economic development", Economic Development and Cultural Change 30: 17–30.

Williamson, J.G. (1965), "Regional inequality and the process of national development: a description of the patterns", Economic Development and Cultural Change 13: 3–45.

Williamson, J.G. (1988), "Migration and urbanization", in: H. Chenery and T.N. Srinivasan, eds., Handbook of development economics, Vol. I (North-Holland, Amsterdam).

Yap, L.Y.L. (1976), "Rural–urban migration and urban underemployment in Brazil", Journal of Development Economics 3: 227–243.

Yap, L.Y.L. (1977), "The attraction of cities: a review of the migration literature", Journal of Development Economics 4: 239–264.

Zarembka, P. (1970), "Labor migration and urban unemployment: comment", American Economic Review 60: 184–186.

Chapter 14

ECONOMIC IMPACT OF INTERNATIONAL MIGRATION AND THE ECONOMIC PERFORMANCE OF MIGRANTS

ROBERT J. LALONDE

Michigan State University

ROBERT H. TOPEL*

University of Chicago

Contents

1. Introduction	800
2. Migration between source and receiving countries	801
2.1. Magnitude and characteristics of immigration	801
2.2. Economic incentives to immigrate	805
2.3. Estimating the determinants of immigration	807
2.4. Regulation of international migration	808
2.5. The impact of immigration regulations	810
2.6. Enforcing immigration controls and counting the undocumented	812
2.7. Emigration from the receiving country	814
3. Labor market adjustments to new immigration	817
3.1. Gains and losses from new immigration	817
3.2. Estimating the labor market effects of immigration	819
3.3. Econometric methods for estimating the effects of immigration	821
3.4. Econometric evidence of immigration's effects	824
4. Assimilation of immigrants	827
4.1. Estimates of assimilation	833
4.2. The impact of language proficiency	837
5. Transfers, taxes, and social welfare programs	840
5.1. Social welfare transfers	840
5.2. Transfers and fertility	842
5.3. Comparing transfers and tax payments	844
6. Conclusions	846
References	847

*The authors thank the National Science Foundation for financial support. LaLonde expresses appreciation to the University of Chicago Graduate School of Business for its support; Topel is grateful to the Bradley Foundation at the Graduate School of Business' Center for the Study of the Economy and the State for financial support. The authors have benefited from comments by Oded Stark and by participants at the 39th North American Regional Science Association Meetings.

Handbook of Population and Family Economics. Edited by M.R. Rosenzweig and O. Stark
© *Elsevier Science B.V., 1997*

1. Introduction

Empirical research on the economic impact of international migration has proliferated during the last two decades (Greenwood and McDowell, 1986). This occurred at a time when in many developed countries immigration became an increasingly important determinant of population growth. In principle, these countries should benefit from immigration because the resulting labor supply shift leads to increased returns to capital and to other productive factors. These welfare gains also apply to native workers when their skills complement those of immigrants. Nevertheless, every developed country regulates the flow and composition of its immigrant population. Their intent is to mitigate the adverse effects that these population flows have on the distribution of income and on the costs of social welfare systems. If immigrants tend to be relatively unskilled, their presence may lower unskilled natives' earnings and increase the demands on government transfer programs – including those providing health and education services.

In the following section of this chapter, we begin by documenting the numbers and characteristics of international migrants to selected developed countries. We next survey some of the economic factors motivating international migration. We find empirical research on the determinants of international migration lags far behind work on the determinants of domestic migration. In light of this, we devote a larger portion of this section to examining how developed countries' regulatory polices affect the composition of their immigrant populations.

Section 3 examines the impact of immigration on the receiving country's labor markets. We begin by explaining why most research on this question has concentrated on its "distributional" rather than its "efficiency" consequences. We then develop an econometric model that relates increased immigration to the labor market outcomes of different demographic groups. Finally, we survey the existing evidence which shows that immigrants usually have relatively modest impacts on the receiving country's labor market.

In Section 4, we examine the extent to which immigrants "assimilate" to the receiving country's labor market. This question is important for two reasons. First, as immigrants spend time in the receiving country's labor market, they acquire skills that are specific to that country. As a result, although they arrive relatively unskilled, with the passage of time they become less similar to the most unskilled native workers, and more like skilled ones. Consequently, an immigrant cohort's adverse impact on the welfare of unskilled natives should be larger in the short run than in the long run. Another reason that immigrant assimilation is important is that persons' use of social welfare programs usually depends on their earnings. Although many immigrants arrive relatively unskilled, if they quickly acquire country-specific skills that significantly raise their earnings, they may make relatively little use of government transfer programs.

Finally, in Section 5, we survey several studies of immigrants' effects on the social welfare system. We begin by documenting immigrants' use of this system and show

how their use of it rises with time spent in the receiving country. This finding is somewhat puzzling because, as documented in Section 3, immigrants' earnings usually rise during this period, thereby making it less likely that they would be eligible to participate in many social welfare programs. We next discuss immigrant fertility and how it might be linked to use of the social welfare system. Finally, we conclude this section with some calculations comparing the benefits natives receive from immigrants' tax payments to the costs of their claims on the social welfare system. These calculations suggest that, at least in the US, natives derive modest pecuniary benefits from immigration.

Before beginning our discussion of migration to developed countries, we should note that this chapter focuses heavily on the experiences of Australia, Canada, and the US. This emphasis reflects the large share of recent empirical research devoted to the labor market consequences of immigration in these countries. However, as we observe in the following section, immigrants now constitute significant percentages of many European countries' work forces. Their increased visibility in these countries has led governments to reexamine their regulatory policies and also has spawned new research.[1] Nevertheless, we believe that the questions that have informed research on Australian and North American immigration, and the research strategies used to address them, also are relevant for assessing the European experience.

2. Migration between source and receiving countries

2.1. Magnitude and characteristics of immigration

In most developed countries, immigrants account for a relatively small percentage of the labor force. Even in the US, which is often called a "nation of immigrants", the percentage of foreign-born persons in the work force (8% in 1990) is comparable to the percentages in countries such as Sweden, France, and Germany, and is substantially below the percentages in countries such as Switzerland, Canada, and Australia (Simon, 1989). However, the flow of new immigrants into developed countries has increased of late, which has raised new concerns about the economic effects of immigration on receiving countries.

As shown by panel A of Table 1, the flow of immigrants into the US accelerated during the 1970s and recent figures indicate that this acceleration continued during the 1980s (Abowd and Freeman, 1991). This increased flow has caused the percentage of foreign-born persons in the US to rise, after declining during the early postwar period.

---

[1] For example, see "Europe Tries to Shut the Floodgates", Financial Times, June 3, 1993, p. 3; "French Parliament to Debate Bill to Curb Immigration," Agence France Presse, June 15, 1993; "Anti-Immigration Debate Opens", Associated Press, June 15, 1993.

Table 1

Stock of immigrants in selected countries

A: Stock and flow in Australia, Canada and the US[a]

Year	Percentage of population foreign-born			Percentage of population arriving during previous decade		
	Australia	Canada	US	Australia	Canada	US
1950	9.8	14.7	6.9	–	4.7	0.7
1960	16.8	15.6	5.4	–	11.0	1.5
1970	NA	15.3	4.7	–	7.9	1.7
1980	21.8	16.1	6.8	–	6.7	2.7

B: Stock of foreign persons in selected European countries

Country	Total foreign (%)	From outside European Union (%)
Germany	6.9	5.1
France	6.3	4.0
Italy	1.4	1.1
Spain	1.2	0.5
Sweden	10.0	NA
United Kingdom	4.3	2.9

[a]The 1950 figure for Australia is from 1947; the 1950 figure for Canada is from 1951; the 1960, 1970 and 1980 figures for Australia and Canada are from 1961, 1971 and 1981, respectively, the 1980 figures for the US include estimates of the undocumented population.
Source: Abowd and Freeman (1991: p. 4, Table 1); Bloom and Gunderson (1991: p. 327, Table 12.2); Gregory et al. (1991: p. 387, Table 15.1). Source for (B): Zimmerman (1994), except for Sweden (Wadensjö, 1994).

By 1990, immigrants comprised more than 8% of the US working-age population (Meisenheimer, 1992). Panel A also indicates that immigration is an even more important factor in Australia and Canada, where immigration stocks and flows are greater than in the US. Indeed, current immigration to Australia and Canada is comparable in magnitude to the rates experienced in the US at the turn of the century. Panel B of Table 1 underscores the point that immigrants also play a significant role in northern European labor markets. Further, the table shows that the immigrant population in those countries is not simply from other countries in the European Union.

Traditional analyses of the economic impact of immigration assume that immigrants are unskilled prime-aged adults (Reder, 1963). This view is only roughly consistent with the facts. In most developed countries the percentage of foreign-born working-age persons between the ages of 25 and 44 is modestly larger than the corresponding percentage for the native population (Simon, 1989: pp. 31–38). According to the November 1989 US Current Population Survey (CPS), 48% of male US immi-

Table 2

Education attainment of natives and immigrants in the US, Canada and Australia
(years of completed schooling in 1980)

	Australia	Canada	US
Natives	11.6	11.3	12.7
All immigrants	11.7	11.7	11.7
By area of birth			
Asia	12.9	13.6	14.6
Africa	13.1	14.0	15.3
Europe	11.4	10.9	12.1
Latin America	12.1	12.1	9.4

Source: Borjas (1991b: p. 64, Table 1.10).

grants fell into this age category, compared with 44% of male natives (Meisenheimer, 1992: p. 6). The percentage of recent immigrants in this age category is slightly larger.

While immigrants are younger than the native-born working-age population, they are not necessarily less educated. As shown by Table 2, average schooling levels among Australian, Canadian, and US immigrants are similar to the corresponding levels for natives. The small difference in schooling levels between immigrants and natives in the US is accounted for by the large number of immigrants from Latin America, mainly Mexico, where schooling levels are low. Immigrants to the US from other parts of the world are as educated as natives, and they have more schooling than immigrant populations in Australia and Canada.

Instead of characterizing the immigrant populations in developed countries as unskilled, it is better to characterize them as having a more unequal distribution of skills than natives.[2] For example, Table 3 shows that a larger proportion of US immigrants than natives has fewer than eight years of schooling. Yet equal percentages are college graduates. Among Asians, who comprise a growing fraction of US immigrants, the proportion with fewer than eight years of schooling is more than double the figure for natives. But half of Asian immigrants are college graduates, compared with only a third of natives. This diversity of skills means that gross statistics on immigration flows will be poor indicators of the effects of immigration on labor supply and on natives' welfare. We elaborate on this point below.

Perhaps the most striking difference between the immigrant and native populations is in their geographic distributions (Stark, 1991: Chapter 3). Immigrants are much

[2] Further, some immigrant skills may be less valuable in the host country. Proficiency in the source country's language is an obvious example. Some occupation-specific skills, say, knowledge of Indian law, also are imperfectly portable. Thus, among the highly skilled, those with portable skills (doctors) are more likely to migrate than those with country-specific ones (lawyers).

Table 3
Educational attainment of US natives and immigrants
(percentage of men 25–54 years old in category, November 1989)

	Years of completed schooling				
	8	9–11	12	13–15	16+
US-born					
All	4	9	38	21	27
Asians	5	6	32	22	34
Blacks	8	17	41	22	13
Hispanics	12	18	39	21	11
Whites	3	8	38	21	30
Foreign-born					
All	23	8	25	15	28
Asians	12	3	23	14	49
Blacks	6	10	43	11	30
Hispanics	43	12	24	13	9
Whites	7	6	28	19	39

Source: Meisenheimer (1992: pp. 7, 9, Tables 4 and 5).

more concentrated in large metropolitan areas. This is especially true in the US. The 25 largest metropolitan areas in the US contain 40% of the native population, but 75% of the immigrant population. About 40% of US immigrants reside in just six metropolitan areas: New York, Los Angeles, Chicago, Miami, San Francisco, and Houston (LaLonde and Topel, 1991a: p. 170). This geographic concentration may cause the costs and benefits of immigration to be similarly concentrated in particular areas or among particular groups of natives.

Immigrants' geographical concentration depends on their skills and ethnicity. Highly educated immigrants are less likely to reside in the large population centers. Similarly, US immigrants from English speaking countries, such as Great Britain, are no more geographically concentrated than the native population (Bartel and Koch, 1991: p. 123). But immigrants from southern European countries, such as Italy and Greece, are as geographically concentrated as their counterparts from Asia and the Americas. This tendency for less-skilled immigrants to reside in "enclaves" suggests that there are benefits from living among persons of similar ethnicity or who speak the same language. The data also suggest that these benefits are greatest among the least skilled.

Geographic concentration of immigrants does not diminish with time in the host country (LaLonde and Topel, 1991a). Thus an increase in immigration to a particular area has an enduring impact on the area's ethnic composition and on its labor force. This lasting impact occurs because new arrivals tend to remain in ethnic enclaves, and

also because *future* immigrants are more likely to flow toward existing enclaves. Thus new immigration can have a "multiplier" effect on local labor supply.

While immigrant populations are geographically concentrated, immigrants are not immobile. In the US, immigrants' internal mobility is comparable to that of natives (Bartel and Koch, 1991: pp. 125–126). This mobility does little to dissipate their geographic concentration, however, because immigrants tend to move among ethnic enclaves. Because of this pattern of mobility, the existence of an enclave in a locale is a better predictor of where immigrants reside, and where they might move, than are other measures of prevailing economic conditions.

2.2. *Economic incentives to immigrate*

...[R]ecent researches are indicating more and more clearly that differences in net economic advantages, chiefly differences in wages, are the main causes of migration. (J.R. Hicks, 1963: p. 76.)

Economists and demographers have developed a variety of theories to explain the population movements observed above. The most basic model posits that international migration is driven by differences in the net present value of earnings between the sending and receiving countries (Sjaastad, 1962; Todaro, 1969). An implication is that as living standards in the source and receiving countries converge, the flow of immigration between them should decline. Hence, immigration from Western Europe to North America has declined during the postwar period. Another implication is that immigrants should be young, because they have a longer time horizon over which to realize the gains from moving. As we have observed above, this prediction also is consistent with the facts.

This model also predicts the relative skills of migrants from a source country. Skilled persons are more likely to migrate if the difference between their expected earnings in the receiving and source countries exceeds the corresponding gain for the less-skilled. In turn, these relative gains depend on the returns to skills in the sending and receiving countries. A receiving country with a compressed earnings distribution is less likely to attract high-skilled immigrants than a receiving country with similar average earnings, but greater earnings inequality. Thus Germany and Sweden, with a relatively narrow income distribution, attract few skilled immigrants, while the US, with much greater returns to skill, attracts more. Borjas (1987b) finds empirical support for this model.

Of course, factors other than earnings differences influence migration decisions. The theory can be broadened to explain why migration sometimes fails to occur even when substantial earnings differences exist, or why migration will continue even without such differentials. For example, income uncertainty in the receiving country may deter risk-averse persons from migrating, even if expected earnings gains are

positive (David, 1974). Even more important, family ties and cultural differences between source and receiving countries raise the costs of immigration. Therefore, ethnic enclaves in the receiving country encourage new migrants.[3]

This observation also points to the important role of the family in migration decisions. If the current generation altruistically values the utility of their offspring, then utility-maximizing migration decisions will be dynastic. It may pay the current generation to migrate even if the change in their own wealth is small or negative, because their descendants will be better off in the receiving country. These gains depend on the extent to which first and second generation migrants "assimilate" into the receiving country's labor market (Chiswick, 1978a; Borjas, 1985; LaLonde and Topel, 1991b, 1992). Evidence on assimilation is presented below.

The idea that immigration results from a family's optimizing decisions also has implications for which family members will migrate, for the sequence of migration among family members, and for patterns of remittances to the home country. So long as the family can induce income transfers among its members, it will send abroad the members that maximize the family's net wealth (Mincer, 1978). In such instances, even nonmigrant family members benefit from the migrants' earnings gains.

Other explanations for remittances do not depend on a model of familial optimization. Instead, one alternative explanation suggests that altruism toward family members back home motivates remittances. This view predicts that these transfers will be larger when family members' incomes are low. A second explanation suggests that remittances constitute immigrants' savings or investments in the source country, such as in land, a taxicab, or a house. It is reasonable to expect that it is more advantageous for the immigrant to remit to a trustworthy family member, who will effectively manage the investments, than to a third party (Stark, 1991: Ch. 16).

Evidence of the sizable impact that remittances can have on source countries is found in official statistics showing, for example, that in 1980 remittances equaled total exports in Pakistan, and were equal to 60% of exports in Egypt, Turkey, and Portugal (Stark, 1994). Evidence of their impact on households is found in a study by Funkhouser (1992) on El Salvadorian immigrants to the US. He found that these immigrants remitted an average of $140 per month back to their families in El Salvador. This amount was more than two times what these immigrants would have earned had they not migrated. Moreover, sustained payments at this level would quickly reimburse their families for the estimated $1600 cost of migration.

---

[3] Another extension of the theory turns on whether persons' well-being depends in part on interpersonal comparisons they make between themselves and others in their community. If people derive satisfaction not only from their absolute well-being, but also from their relative standing in their community, they may migrate so as to improve that standing or perhaps change their "reference" community. As a result, the outcomes of these interpersonal comparisons may generate migration even when it would not have been generated by prevailing earnings differences. So "relative deprivation", as measured, for example, by the difference between their source country earnings and the median earnings in their community, would predict migration flows (Stark, 1991).

That migration decisions are often made by families is suggested by the apparent existence of "tied" or "chain" migration, where one family member's immigration is accompanied, either simultaneously or later, by others. In this instance, the decision to move depends on the net utility gain for the family as a whole rather than for an individual. The "tied" decision clearly affects the type of selection that occurs in the sending country's population: some individuals migrate as part of a family who otherwise would stay, and some stay even though the individual gains to migration might be large. The result is that there will be less systematic sorting on individual talent, and so greater heterogeneity of talent in the immigrant population. For example, income equality and low returns to skill in Sweden raise the possibility of a "brain drain" in which the most talented individuals may leave. The importance of this effect is reduced, however, when families migrate together. So long as the talents of individual family members are imperfectly correlated, there will be less selection on talent in the pool of movers (Borjas and Bronars, 1991).

2.3. Estimating the determinants of immigration

These theories have been implemented in a number of empirical studies of *internal* migration; that is, of movements among locales in a particular country. The goal in these studies is to estimate the determinants of migratory behavior: who moves and who stays among a population of potential migrants? We are not aware of any work that directly estimates the determinants of international migration decisions. The reason is that large usable micro-data sets on both individual immigrants *and* nonimmigrants from a source country are rarely available. For example, data that could be used to model immigration decisions among, say, Mexicans, should include a contemporaneous sample of persons who immigrated from Mexico to the US, as well as a representative sample of Mexicans from the nonimmigrant population. Researchers have collected such data in a few Mexican villages, but representative samples of Mexican migrants and nonmigrants are unavailable (Stark, 1991: Ch. 9).

Internal migration studies can still be informative about some of the economic factors that affect decisions to move. Using micro-data on individuals, these studies relate migrant status to a list of observable personal, family, and socio-economic characteristics. As one might expect, efforts to estimate "structural" models normally include some estimate of the potential earnings gain from migration among the explanatory variables.

As noted by Greenwood (1983) and many others, this approach has some obvious difficulties. Even when both "movers" and "stayers" are observed, micro-data will (at most) report a person's earnings in the receiving or in the source country, but not in both. So the potential earnings gain from migration, or its proxy, must be imputed from observable information. In the most sophisticated studies, econometricians estimate the earnings potential of nonmigrants in the receiving country from the observed

earnings distribution of immigrants with similar observed characteristics such as age, years of schooling, or marital status. This approach is not very satisfying because if the two groups are really the same, they should presumably exhibit the same migratory behavior. So, for consistency, one must assume that the difference between the groups' migratory behavior depends on unobserved characteristics.

Studies that push ahead in spite of these difficulties account for differences between immigrants' and nonimmigrants' unobserved characteristics using the econometric approaches developed in the sample selection literature (Heckman, 1978, 1979). These approaches effectively identify the unobserved differences between migrants' and nonmigrants' characteristics using either problematic exclusion restrictions or nonlinear functional forms to relate individuals' characteristics to the probability of migration (Stark, 1991: Ch. 9). Other studies estimate "reduced form" models that relate persons' decisions to migrate to a vector of exogenous characteristics. Such models are informative for predictive purposes, but cannot test the importance of earnings differentials in explaining international migration flows.

2.4. Regulation of international migration

Along with economic incentives, the regulatory apparatus that restricts emigration from source countries and immigration into receiving countries also determines the magnitude and composition of international migration. Perhaps because of customs in democratic countries or because of existing international treaties, countries usually do not restrict the exit of their citizens to the same extent that they restrict entry of noncitizens (ILO, 1980). Nevertheless, restrictive emigration policies have limited emigration from many former eastern bloc and less-developed countries. A recent illustration of the impact of emigration restrictions was seen in the movement of approximately one-half million persons to Israel in a span of less than three years after the former Soviet Union relaxed its emigration controls (Flug and Kasir, 1993).

Policy makers have established immigration restrictions to achieve a variety of economic, political, and social objectives. For example, during the early 1920s US policy makers came to believe that recent immigrants were less skilled than those from earlier cohorts. The evidence was a change in the relative contributions of various source countries to the immigrant population; recent arrivals were predominantly Southern and Eastern Europeans instead of the Western Europeans who dominated immigration flows in the middle and late nineteenth century. In addition to any ethnic concerns that this shift may have caused, it also raised fears that new arrivals were adversely affecting the welfare of unskilled natives, with whom they competed in the labor market (Douglas, 1919).

To limit these effects and maintain the ethnic composition of the population, Congress established "national origins" quotas that restricted the flow of immigrants from the Eastern Hemisphere and required that the ethnic composition of new arrivals con-

form to the 1920 US population.[4] The number of slots or "visas" available each year ranged from more than 65 000 for persons from the United Kingdom to 100 for persons for all Asian countries, including China. These policies remained in place until Congress passed the Immigration Reform Act of 1965. Consequently, it is not surprising that during this period only a small percentage of US immigrants were of Asian descent.[5]

Current immigration controls in developed countries usually restrict flows to three categories of persons. These controls allow entry because (i) persons have close relatives in the receiving country, (ii) they have skills that immigration authorities determine are "scarce", or (iii) they are political refugees. Definitions of these categories differ widely. For example, until recently it was much easier to qualify as a political refugee in Germany and Sweden than in the US.[6] Within each of the three categories, the extent of the rationing varies substantially among countries. For example, during 1992 and 1993, Australia, the developed country with the largest share of foreign-born persons, allowed 80 000 persons to permanently immigrate. Of these, 56% were allowed to enter because of family ties, 30% because of their skills, and 13% because of their status as refugees (Minister for Immigration, 1992). By contrast, the US has no restrictions on the entry of spouses and their young children, nor are there specific quotas on the number of persons entering as refugees. But the annual quota for the Eastern Hemisphere is set at 270 000, about 80% of which is accounted for by families of current US residents. The rest are admitted for their skills. The quota for the Western Hemisphere is rationed on a first-come first-served basis (US INS, 1990).

Because immigration authorities in developed countries usually set binding annual quotas, rationing is the rule. There are, however, many ways to allocate the available slots. One (unused) method is an auction, in which rights to immigrate would go to those most willing to pay. Assuming that willingness to pay and productivity are correlated, an auction would select those who will be most productive among any given class of potential entrants. As a result, it would achieve the goals of skill-based quotas, while raising revenue for the receiving country. In practice, immigration authorities do sometimes "sell" rights to immigrate. In the US and Canada potential immigrants can receive a visa by investing a specified amount or by creating a certain number of jobs. Between 1987 and 1992, approximately 10 000 persons and their dependents entered Canada annually under these criteria (IC, 1992: various issues, Table S1). But the main method of rationing slots is by rules: the US, Canada, and Australia admit most immigrants based on either family ties or on an evaluation of skills.

---

[4] For a survey of the political, economic, and demographic forces that led the US Congress to enact immigration restrictions beginning with the 1917 literacy tests and culminating with the 1929 National Origins Act, see Goldin (1993).

[5] For a description of postwar immigration policy in Europe, especially Germany, see Zimmerman (1994).

[6] The German government has recently changed these laws.

The Canadian and Australian systems are instructive in showing how policies might alter the characteristics of the immigrant pool. Applicants are awarded points based on their education, labor market experience, age, language proficiency, and family ties. Those with point totals that exceed a threshold are admitted. Both the points awarded for individual characteristics and the threshold can vary from year to year, depending on policy goals. The idea is to admit persons who are most likely to assimilate and to succeed in the receiving country's labor market.

2.5. *The impact of immigration regulations*

In principle, immigration controls could be more important than economic incentives in determining the flow and composition of immigrant populations. But whether attempts to regulate the quantity and quality of immigrants have the desired effects is an open question. Do skill-based quotas and point systems really raise immigrant "quality"? What are the effects of family unification criteria on the size and quality of immigrant flows? Do immigration quotas really bind, or are they largely offset by illegal immigration? Recent research has tackled these questions with some success.

Consider the impact of skill-based controls. Many countries have periodically altered their policies in hopes of raising immigrants' average skill levels. For example, after Canada liberalized its immigration polices in 1956, the numbers of unskilled immigrants arriving from Southern and Eastern Europe expanded substantially. In response, the government began to screen the skills of potential immigrants from that part of Europe. Several years later they extended the policy to all potential immigrants except dependents of Canadian residents.

Borjas (1991b) compared the characteristics of US and Canadian immigrants in order to evaluate the impact of these controls. He found that Canadian immigrants of the 1960s and 1970s were more educated. The difference was attributable to source countries: a larger portion of US immigrants came from source countries with low educational levels, such as Mexico. Within source countries, however, average schooling levels differed little between the two countries. Borjas also concluded that Canada's skill-based system did not prevent the same deterioration of immigrants' relative skills that occurred in the United States, a country without such controls. Between 1970 and 1980, the earnings of new arrivals relative to natives fell in both countries by approximately 15 percentage points. This decline can be attributed to a change over time in the source countries from which the US and Canada draw their immigrants (LaLonde and Topel, 1992). Together, these conclusions suggest that skill-based immigration controls are less effective than policy makers might hope in altering the skill levels of their immigrant population.

Family unification policies have implications for current and future immigrant flows, as well as for average immigrant "quality". For example, under US law, naturalized citizens can more easily sponsor a relative's immigration to the US. Because an

immigrant can become a US citizen after being a permanent resident for five years, this regulation can produce "chain" migration. Once granted a visa to the US, a new immigrant creates a set of potential future immigrants through family ties.

The dramatic rise in the number of Asian immigrants arriving in the US during the 1970s and 1980s illustrates this point. As noted above, prior to 1965, immigration from Asia to the US was severely limited. After that, US policy shifted to emphasize family reunification and, to a more limited extent, labor market skills (Chiswick, 1986). The initial impact of the new reunification policies was slight because the stock of Asians in the US was small. But the small initial flow of immigrants admitted for their skills had a multiplier effect on later immigration due to family reunification. Further, because the skills of family members are only imperfectly correlated, those admitted for family reasons were less skilled, on average, than the initial wave of Asian immigrants (Chiswick, 1986).

Borjas and Bronars (1991) provide somewhat broader evidence on the role of chain migration. Using the public use files of the US Census for 1970 and 1980, they studied the incidence of immigrants from the same household who arrived in different years. Despite some substantial data limitations,[7] they found evidence of chain migration. The strongest connections are for close relatives such as spouses and children. Among immigrants who had resided in the US for 0–5 years, 18% of the 1970 respondents and 27% of the 1980 respondents lived with an immigrant who arrived before they did. The corresponding figures for persons with 5–10 years residency are 14% and 22%. These proportions differ widely among source countries. Forty percent of Mexicans who arrived in 1975–1980 lived with a Mexican immigrant who had arrived before 1975. Among Filipinos the proportion was 43%, but among immigrants from Canada or the UK the figure was only 9%.

Census data provide some evidence of the extent of chain migration, but they do not allow us to gauge the size of the "multiplier" effect that is implied by family unification policies. It would be useful to know how many expected future immigrants will be generated by the admission of one current immigrant.

To address this issue, Jasso and Rosenzweig (1986) analyzed INS records of legal immigrants who arrived in the US in 1971. They found that about 40% of the 1971 immigrants were naturalized within ten years. This proportion varied widely among source countries. Immigrants from source countries in which English was the official language were more likely to become naturalized citizens. Persons from countries with high per capita incomes, were close to the US, or had low literacy rates where less likely to become naturalized. The tendency for the naturalization rates to vary among groups indicates that the "multiplier" is likely to vary according to the relative economic and social conditions in the source countries.

---

[7] For example, the Census only records the date of arrival in five-year intervals, so some chain migrants who arrived at different times will fall in the same interval. This leads to an understatement of the extent of chain migration in Census data.

To examine this possibility, Jasso and Rosenzweig estimated the following model:

$$I_t^i = \delta_0^i + \delta_{T+2.5}^i N_{5t} + \delta_{T+7.5}^i N_{10t} + \cdots + \sum_l \delta_l^t X_{lt} + \varepsilon_t^i. \tag{1}$$

According to Eq. (1), the flow of legal immigrants arriving in the US from source country t under visa category i depends on the number naturalized citizens, N_{jt}, that arrived from source county t, j years in the past, and a vector of source county characteristics, X_t. The estimated parameters indicated that, holding constant source country characteristics, most chain migration occurs when immigrants have been in the US between five and ten years. Further, the long-run multiplier implies that each naturalized citizen brings in about 1.5 subsequent immigrants. However, because less than half of immigrants become naturalized citizens, the overall immigration multiplier is less than one. Accordingly, the authors concluded that their findings for the 1971 cohort implied that "chaining" resulting from US policy's emphasis on family reunification was unlikely to lead to an immigration "explosion" in the US.

2.6. Enforcing immigration controls and counting the undocumented

Studies of the impact of Canada's skill-based immigration controls raise doubts about whether policies can greatly affect the skill composition of immigrants. The US experience raises an even more fundamental question about whether these controls can even limit the *quantity* of immigrants. There is substantial evidence that a large portion of US immigrants entered the country illegally. This evidence includes Census counts of foreign-born persons, mortality and birth statistics for different ethnic groups, and border control reports showing as many as one million apprehensions annually along the US–Mexican border.

The most direct evidence of a large undocumented US population is found in the Census. The Census does not ask foreign-born persons whether they legally entered the country. But because the number of foreign-born counted in the Census substantially exceeds the numbers legally admitted into the US, some respondents must be illegal. Warren and Passel (1987) estimate that, despite their illegal status, about two million undocumented persons responded to the 1980 Census. As shown by Table 4, this figure constitutes more than one-quarter of the nonnaturalized foreign-born population.

Warren and Passel's study also indicates that most undocumented aliens in the United States are from Mexico. As shown by Table 4, Mexicans accounted for nearly 55% of the undocumented Census respondents. No other source country accounted for more than 3%. Further, unlike other immigrant groups, undocumented aliens account for nearly half of the Mexican foreign-born population (as measured by the sum of legal and illegal aliens plus naturalized citizens). For all other source countries combined the corresponding figure is only 16%.

Table 4
Estimates of 1980 foreign-born population from Census and INS records
(total entered US since 1960 in 1000s)[a]

Country or area of birth	Undocumented aliens	Census aliens	I-53 aliens	Naturalized citizens (revised)
All countries	2057	7440	5383	1627
North and South America	1608	4215	2608	497
Mexico	1131	2326	1195	42
El Salvador	51	89	38	NA
Haiti	44	77	33	NA
Europe	150	1239	1089	551
United Kingdom	38	219	181	NA
Asia: East, South and Near East	213	1787	1574	541
Iran	58	112	55	NA
Africa	65	147	82	32

[a]The five countries listed in the table are the source countries with the largest number of undocumented persons in the 1980 US census.
Source: Warren and Passel (1987: pp. 378–381, Tables 1 and 2).

The accuracy of these estimates depends on whether the Census was as successful in enumerating the undocumented population as it was enumerating the legal population. Because it is unlikely that the percentage of uncounted undocumented persons was as small as the percentage (1%) of uncounted persons in the legal population, Warren and Passel's estimates likely understate the true 1980 undocumented population.

Additional evidence on the size of the undocumented population can be derived from the death and birth figures compiled by *Vital Statistics of the United States*. Assume that death and birth figures in *Vital Statistics* are accurate. The number of recorded "events" (deaths or births) is

$$R_i = r_c * P_i + r_u * U_i. \tag{2}$$

In Eq. (2), R_i is the number of events for age group i, P_i and U_i are the numbers of persons in the counted and uncounted populations, and r_c and r_u are the death rates of those populations. If the two populations have the same death rates, the uncounted population among group i is equal to

$$U_i = R_i/r_c - P_i. \tag{3}$$

So Eq. (3), which combines information from *Vital Statistics* and the Census, provides an estimate of the uncounted population of type i. This estimate will be too large if, as seems likely, the uncounted population's death rate exceeds that of the counted population.

Using this framework, Borjas et al. (1991) estimated that the 1980 Census missed approximately 700 000 Mexican-born persons. Not surprisingly, most of the un-counted were young adults, between 15 and 34 years old. Using the same approach for births, they estimated that 40% of the uncounted were women. This percentage was only slightly below the proportion of women among the counted population. Adding the estimated 700 000 illegals to the 1.1 million undocumented Mexican-born persons counted in the Census yields an estimate of 1.8 million undocumented Mexican-born persons in the US.

These calculations also suggest that Warren and Passel's figures understate the en-tire undocumented population, perhaps by as much as 40%. If other ethnic groups were undercounted to the same extent as were the Mexican-born aliens, then the US was home to approximately three million undocumented persons in 1980. That figure equals approximately 20% of the US immigrant population.

Additional evidence about the numbers and characteristics of the US's undocu-mented population resulted when Congress granted many of them amnesty as part of the Immigration Reform and Control Act (IRCA) 1986. The Act allowed undocu-mented aliens to become legal permanent residents if they could show either that they had (i) resided continuously in the US for more than four years or (ii) worked for more than 90 days as an agricultural worker during 1986. Under this program, ap-proximately three million aliens applied for amnesty. Records of these applicants show that more than 80% were from Mexico and other Latin American countries. By contrast, 5% were from Asia and only 1% were from Europe. At the time of their ap-plication, this group was much more likely to be employed than either natives or other foreign-born workers. However, these persons worked predominantly in low-skilled blue-collar production or services occupations (Tienda et al., 1991).

The experience of the US with its undocumented population demonstrates that immigration controls cannot be costlessly established and enforced. Annual quotas and skill-based evaluations of potential immigrants may be of little importance with-out mechanisms to ensure that they actually restrict immigration. Therefore, as part of the IRCA, US policy makers augmented resources available for enforcing its immi-gration controls. This legislation substantially increased the funding of border control activities and for the first time imposed sanctions on employers who knowingly hired undocumented aliens. Such legislated provisions increase the likelihood that authori-ties can limit the flow and composition of the immigrant population. Yet little is known about the effectiveness of these programs, or whether their benefits warrant their additional costs (Ethier, 1986).

2.7. Emigration from the receiving country

Policy makers establish immigration controls to reduce the flow of immigrants into the receiving country. But immigrants often return to their home country, which means that even binding quotas may overstate the effects of immigration on the population and labor force.

There are several different explanations for return migration to the source country that yield different predictions about the durations of migrants' stays in the receiving country and whether high- or low-skilled workers are more likely to emigrate. The most straightforward explanation of emigration parallels that of immigration: migrants return when the present discounted value of earnings in the receiving country is less than that in the source country. There are two ways that this relation could hold. First, migrants might learn that they are not as productive in the receiving country as they had anticipated and accordingly they revise downward their expectations of future earnings. Second, conditions in the source country might have unexpectedly improved, making life back home more attractive.

In many cases we might expect the less successful or less-skilled migrants to be most likely to return home. But whether the unskilled or skilled are more likely to return also depends on changes in the distribution of earnings in the source and receiving countries. For example, market reforms in the source country that substantially increased earnings inequality would likely encourage skilled more than unskilled migrants to return home. Likewise, trends toward greater income equality in the receiving country are more likely to encourage skilled immigrants to leave.

Among alternative explanations of emigration is its role in managing the family's optimal income insurance. In this case, families that desire greater income insurance are more likely to have a family member migrate. When conditions at home change so that the variance in the family's income declines, the demand for such insurance diminishes and the migrant is likely to return home. Another explanation turns on the "possibility that consumption at home is preferable to consumption abroad" (Stark, 1994: p. 8). In this case, immigrants return home when their savings are sufficiently high. When this case holds, we expect that more skilled immigrants would have shorter stays in the host country than their less-skilled counterparts. Finally, a related explanation holds that some immigrants arrive in the host country intending to return once they acquire skills that make them more productive back home.

Many countries collect statistics both on immigrant arrivals and on departures. For these countries it is easy to compute emigration rates. For example, Australian statistics covering the period 1959–1982 indicate that the ratio of departures to arrivals was approximately 0.22 for English speaking immigrants and 0.04 for immigrants from Southern Europe (Beggs and Chapman, 1991: p. 371). These figures indicate that an immigrant group's ethnicity may determine whether statistics on "gross" flows adequately characterize their impact on a receiving country's population.

The US stopped collecting information on emigrants in 1957. Historical statistics indicate that nearly one-third of US immigrants subsequently emigrate. This fraction is based on the ratio of the 15.7 million persons admitted between 1908 and 1957 and the 4.8 million persons who departed during the same time period. These figures suggest that current statistics on the "gross" flow of legal and illegal US immigrants, such as those shown in Table 1, may be substantially larger than the "net" flow of this population.

Absent statistics on emigration rates from the US, there is no straightforward way to estimate net immigration rates. However, because of this issue's policy significance, several studies have inferred US emigration rates from other data. The strategy compares estimates of the foreign-born population in two different years, but adjusts for expected mortality and the number of new arrivals between the two years. More formally, the number of emigrants from group i, E_i, is given by

$$E_i = P_{t,i} - D_i + I_i - P_{t',i}. \tag{4}$$

In Eq. (4), $P_{t,i}$ and $P_{t',i}$ are the number of foreign-born persons in years t and t'; D_i is an estimate of the number of deaths occurring between years t and t' for persons in group i; and I_i is the number of new immigrants arriving during that time period.

Warren and Peck (1980) used this strategy to estimate the number of emigrés who left the US between 1960 and 1970. They used Census data to estimate the number of foreign-born persons, standard mortality tables to estimate death rates by age and gender, and INS figures on legal immigration to estimate immigration flows. Based on this strategy, they estimated that 1.1 million of the 13.4 million immigrants in the US during the 1960s emigrated by 1970. More importantly, they found that recent immigrants were much more likely to emigrate than earlier arrivals. For example, 18% of the immigrants who arrived between 1960 and 1970 left before the decade was over. The figure for those who arrived before 1960 was only 5%. Extrapolating over arrival cohorts and ignoring any possible "cohort effects" in propensities to leave, these estimates imply that about one-third of all new arrivals will leave the US within 40 years. This is roughly the same as the figures from INS data covering the first half of the twentieth century.

Borjas and Bratsberg (1993) extended the Warren and Peck analysis to cover immigrants who arrived during the 1970s. They find very similar results. Together, these studies indicate that a substantial number of immigrants – say 30–40% – eventually remigrate. This means that current INS quotas overstate the effect that legal immigration has on the size of the labor force.

Given the magnitude of remigration, it may be as important for policy purposes to know *who* stays as to know just how many stay. As one might expect, there is some evidence that remigration rates differ by country of origin – for example, Mexicans are more likely to leave the US than Asians.[8] But the main interest of policy makers

---

[8] Borjas and Bratsberg also show that Asian immigrants were less likely than other immigrants to remigrate. They estimate that only 4% of the Asians who arrived in the US between 1975 and 1980 had left by 1980. Jasso and Rosenzweig (1982) find similar evidence in their analysis of INS records. This finding implies that average remigration rates may decline, because the Asian share of all immigrants to the US has been rising.

may be in the skills of those who stay and leave. Just as there is little direct evidence about which types of workers choose to emigrate from source countries, there also is little direct evidence about whether it is high- or low-skilled workers who choose to return home (Ramos, 1992).

3. Labor market adjustments to new immigration

The immigration flows described in the previous section increase labor supply in the receiving country. The consequent increase in employment, if it takes place, raises total output and per capita income of natives, but it also redistributes income among factors of production. Indeed, redistribution seems to be the central issue for policy makers. Most of the policy debate about immigration relates to its effects on income distribution. Accordingly, this section develops both a theoretical framework and an empirical strategy for assessing the distributional gains and losses associated with immigration.

3.1. Gains and losses from new immigration

To see how these distributional consequences arise, consider a country whose aggregate production is subject to constant returns to scale. Then a proportional increase in all inputs (including capital) will leave per capita income unchanged and will not affect the distribution of income among factors. By contrast, immigration has important effects because it increases the relative supply of some types of workers, changing factor proportions and relative prices. Consider Fig. 1, which shows a marginal productivity schedule for a given type of native labor. If immigration raises labor supply by dL units, then workers' wages must fall. Area T in the figure is a transfer of income from these workers to capital, consumers, and other factors. Area I is the income received by new immigrants, and area W is the surplus – received by consumers (including the native workers), capital and other factors – caused by the increase in labor supply. By the usual calculations for small changes in supply, the amount of this surplus is

$$W = 0.5Y(1/\eta)(dL/L)^2, \tag{5}$$

where Y is native workers' aggregate earnings and η is the elasticity of demand for their services.

This simple analysis has several implications. First, on net, natives gain from immigration. Second, as shown by Eq. (5), natives' gain is larger (i) the more inelastic the demand native workers, and (ii) the larger the total income, Y, they earn. For example, consider immigration policies that could admit either skilled (denoted by s)

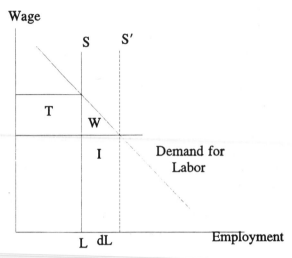

Fig. 1. Gains and losses from new immigration.

workers who would earn wages in the highest quintile of the wage distribution, or unskilled (denoted by u) workers whose wages would fall in the lowest quintile. Which group produces a larger surplus for natives? When these groups are of equal size and skilled workers command higher wages, $Y_s > Y_u$, other things the same, the skilled immigrants produce the larger surplus by a factor proportional to their productivity. Further, econometric studies of labor demand (Hamermesh, 1986) suggest that skilled workers are more inelastically demanded, which also favors admission of skilled individuals. Consistent with this result, we noted above that Australia and Canada ration immigration using point systems that are meant to favor skilled persons.

Another, perhaps more important, implication of Eq. (5) is that immigration redistributes income. In Fig. 1, area T is a transfer of income from the native workers to other factors. Some algebra shows that this transfer equals

$$T = Y(1/\eta)dL/L = 2W(dL/L)^{-1}. \tag{6}$$

Eq. (6) makes two important points. First, welfare gains and income transfers of immigration go together. Second, for reasonable values of dL/L, Eq. (6) states a practical theorem of welfare economics: rectangles are bigger than triangles. That is, income transfers from immigration exceed the net welfare gains.

This result explains why distributional effects are at the center of policy debates over immigration controls, and it also explains the positions taken by various groups. Labor unions commonly advocate stronger immigration controls because immigrants are thought to compete with blue-collar workers. Owners of capital advocate more open immigration policies.[9] And, in light of policy concerns over income inequality, evidence that new immigrants compete in the labor market with less-skilled natives strengthens arguments for immigration controls or redistributive polices meant to off-set the effects of immigration. As a result, a key empirical issue is how immigration affects labor market outcomes of natives, especially less-skilled natives.

A similar analysis can be used to assess the allocative and redistributional effects of immigration on the country of origin. Although there is less empirical evidence about the importance of immigration on source countries' economies, there are instances where these effects may be substantial. For example, during the 1970s, the number of Jamaican immigrants to the US was equal to 7.3% of the 1970 Jamaican population. In cases such as these, the "leftward" shift in the supply of labor is associated with an increase in the marginal product of labor and a decrease in the marginal product of capital. As a result, nonmigrants' wages rise in the source country and the returns to capital decline. Therefore, emigration from the source country involves a transfer of income from other productive factors to workers. If migrants remit some of their earnings back home, this redistribution likely is reinforced.

3.2. Estimating the labor market effects of immigration

Attempts to estimate increased immigration's distributive effects treat it as an exoge-nous shift in the supply of labor. Then wage adjustments among native workers de-pend on own and cross-wage elasticities of labor demand – that is, how well immi-grants substitute for natives – and on elasticities of native labor supply. These issues are closely related to ones that arise in more traditional empirical studies of labor de-mand (Hamermesh, 1986). Therefore, the methodology used to study the impact of immigration draws heavily on that literature.

The sizes and geographic distributions of immigrant populations also have impli-cations for empirical methods. As indicated above, in most industrialized countries immigrants constitute relatively small percentages of the population and total labor force growth. This means that immigration flows are unlikely to have large effects on these countries' aggregate wages and labor force participation rates. In the United States, for example, new immigration increased aggregate labor supply by about two million persons during the 1970s. This shift is fairly small in comparison to the 20 million new workers who entered the labor force because of the baby boom and in-creased participation of women. In this environment, effects of immigration on wages or other employment outcomes are likely to be small and difficult to detect from ag-gregate time-series data.

Yet immigrant populations are highly concentrated in particular geographic areas and industries. We noted earlier that new immigrants to the US locate in a small num-

---

[9] In the US, the Wall Street Journal editorializes for open immigration policies.

ber of immigrant "enclaves", where substantial populations of previous immigrants and natives of similar ethnicity already reside. This means that immigration will have a larger impact on overall labor supply in these areas. For example, during the 1970s new immigration increased total labor supply in metropolitan Los Angeles by over 30%. That increase constituted two-thirds of total labor force growth over the decade. The corresponding figures for Miami were 38% and 37%, respectively. These shifts are large enough that immigration may have important effects on wages within a geographic market, at least in the short run, when other factors of production are inelastically supplied. Further, the wage and employment effects of immigration should be largest among natives whose skills substitute well for those of immigrants. Young Hispanics in Los Angeles or young blacks in Miami are prime candidates.

Although their industrial concentration is less pronounced, immigrants are somewhat more concentrated than natives in low-wage industries. For example, in 1980, 38% of US apparel industry employees and 16% of restaurant employees were immigrants (Altonji and Card, 1991). As with their geographic concentration, this may lead to lower wages for natives in these industries, as well as mobility of natives to other industries in which immigrant concentration is lower.

In light of these facts, attempts to estimate labor market adjustments to immigration exploit variation in the fractions of immigrants across local labor markets and industries (Grossman, 1982; Borjas, 1987a; LaLonde and Topel, 1991a; Altonji and Card, 1991). One approach is to compare the fraction of recent immigrants in a locale with the wages or participation rates of some target population that might be affected by immigration. Young unskilled natives or other (recent) immigrants are examples.

Altonji and Card (1991: p. 220) find that less-skilled US natives who reside in metropolitan areas with large immigrant shares have lower labor force participation rates, employment–population ratios, and weeks worked in the previous year than similarly skilled natives in other cities.[10] Their results suggest that a 10% increase in the supply of immigrants would lower these employment related outcomes by approximately 2%. By contrast, their evidence on a connection between immigration and wages is mixed, but Grossman (1982) and Borjas (1987a) find that natives' wages are not significantly lower in cities with high percentages of immigrants. In fact, Borjas finds that black and Hispanic natives have slightly higher wages when they live in areas with large concentrations of Hispanic immigrants. But Grossman and Borjas, as well as LaLonde and Topel (1991a: p. 175) all find that US immigrants' weekly wages are substantially lower when they reside in cities with a large fraction of other immigrants. Borjas

---

[10] Altonji and Card define lesser skilled natives as white males with less than 12 years of completed schooling, and white females and blacks with less than 13 years of completed schooling. LaLonde and Topel define recent immigrants as those who had arrived in the US within ten years of the Census.

(1987a: p. 391) finds that this relationship is especially strong among Hispanic immigrants: a 10% increase in their supply to a locale lowers their wages by 10%.[11]

These results suggest that increased immigration modestly reduces the labor market opportunities of natives and significantly reduces the earnings of other immigrants. Yet these findings are subject to several criticisms. One is that the underlying economic model strains credulity. In order for native wages to be lower in cities with large immigrant populations, the price of their skills must be lower than elsewhere. These price differences are difficult to square with a long-run equilibrium of the labor market with geographically mobile workers. At best, one might argue that these "snapshots" obtained from cross-sectional comparisons reflect short-run equilibrium adjustments to recent changes in the pace of immigration.

But if this criticism is correct, why is there a cross-sectional relationship between immigrant shares and, for example, immigrant wages? One possibility is selection bias. If less-skilled immigrants tend to gather in cities with large immigrant enclaves, then immigrant wages are lower in areas with large immigrant shares. However, this relationship has nothing to do with wage adjustments to changes in supply. For example, LaLonde and Topel (1991a) report that immigrant wages are 64% lower than those of white males in cities with large immigrant shares in the local labor force, but only 28% lower in cities with small immigrant shares. These differences are much too large to attribute to equilibrium wage adjustments. Extending this argument further, if the average skills of natives are also lower in these locales, then it will look in cross-sectional data as if immigration adversely affects natives.

Two approaches to this selection bias problem have been used in the literature. Using Census data for the US, the first approach examines the relationship between the relative earnings of different immigrant and native groups and their relative shares in a locale's population. By looking for evidence of labor market substitution among natives and immigrants within a locale this approach circumvents some of the difficulties associated with "across-city" comparisons. The second approach examines the relationship between *changes* in labor market outcomes and *changes* in the fraction of immigrants in a locale. This approach seeks to eliminate selection effects associated with immigrant enclaves by "differencing out" city-specific effects.

3.3. Econometric methods for estimating the effects of immigration

Before summarizing the results from studies adopting these methods we present some details of the econometric strategies. We begin by assuming that immigration repre-

---

[11] In her study of the wage impacts of late nineteenth- and early twentieth-century immigration into the US, Goldin used a similar empirical strategy and found that the wage growth of low skilled workers was significantly depressed in cities that experienced the largest growth in the fraction of foreign-born persons. By contrast, wage growth of higher skilled workers in those cities was relatively unaffected by these demographic changes (see Goldin, 1993).

sents an exogenous shift in labor supply to geographically distinct labor markets. The key idea is that immigrants and other identifiable groups form input aggregates that substitute imperfectly in local production. Then wage adjustments to changing supply will vary among different native and immigrant groups.[12]

To formalize these ideas, consider a concave local production function that combines immigrant or native labor, M_{ck}, separately from capital and materials, N_{cl},

$$Q_c = Q(\theta_c g(M_{c1}, ..., M_{cK}), \alpha_c h(N_{c1}, ..., N_{cL})). \tag{7}$$

In Eq. (7), Q_c refers to total output produced in locale c and M_{cj} is total human capital supplied by group j in locale c. Each member of group j supplies one unit of relevant human capital. The number of different groups included in $g(\cdot)$ reflects judgments about substitution possibilities among different labor aggregates. Thus some natives who are thought to be close substitutes for immigrants – for example, young native Hispanics or immigrants from earlier arrival cohorts – should be included as separate factors.

The form of $Q(\cdot)$ imposes several additional restrictions that facilitate the interpretation of the resulting parameters in the model. First, a reasonable assumption about $g(\cdot)$ is that it has constant returns to scale: a doubling of all labor quantities within a locale should leave relative wages unchanged. Second, the (weak) separability assumption between labor and other inputs implies that changes in these other inputs do not change relative wages. The advantage of this assumption is that (hard to obtain) measures of local capital stocks can be ignored.[13] Finally, we capture the effects of shifts in local labor demand through the locale-specific parameters θ_c and α_c. This specification implies that local demand shifts also leave relative wages unchanged.

Given these assumptions, the wage of group j workers at locale c is their marginal product of labor or

$$W_{cj} = Q_1(\cdot)\theta_c g_j(M_{c1}, ..., M_{ck}). \tag{8}$$

In Eq. (8), subscripts to functions denote partial derivatives with respect to the indicated argument. At this stage, the relationship between wages and the labor aggregates M_{ck} depends on the functional form given to $Q(\cdot)$. Grossman (1982) assumed that local output is generated by a translog production function, whereas Borjas (1987a) assumed a generalized Leontief production function. LaLonde and Topel (1991a) adopt another form by first expressing the log wage of group j workers in locale c as

$$w_{cj} = \ln(Q_1(\cdot)\theta_c) + \ln g_j(M_{c1}, ..., M_{ck}). \tag{9}$$

---

[12] Our discussion follows LaLonde and Topel (1991a).

[13] A weaker assumption is that capital is perfectly mobile among locales, so that it has a fixed price.

The first term on the right-hand side of Eq. (9) is an area-specific term that is independent of j and is fixed for all labor inputs within a locale. The second step in their specification replaces $\ln(Q_1(\cdot)\theta_c)$ with an area-specific fixed effect, β_c, and expands $\ln g_j(M_{c1}, \ldots, M_{ck})$ to first order in logs to arrive at

$$w_{cj} = \beta_c + \sum_i \gamma_{ji} \ln M_{ci}. \tag{10}$$

Finally, to complete the empirical specification, they allow individuals to contribute different amounts of human capital to the labor aggregate M_j. Accordingly, an individual l's stock of human capital, m, depends on his characteristics, X, according to

$$m_{cjl} = \exp\{X_{cjl}\delta + \varepsilon_{cjl}\}.$$

Among the characteristics included in X are years of schooling, potential labor market experience, marital status, and the number of children in the household. For immigrants, X also includes years in the receiving country and the immigrant's source country. With these assumptions, the log wage of individual l is:

$$w_{cjl} = \beta_c + X_{cjl}\delta + \sum_i \gamma_{ji} \ln M_{ci} + \varepsilon_{cjl}. \tag{11}$$

The controls in Eq. (11) for city "fixed effects" (β_c) explicitly address the ambiguities associated with comparisons between labor market outcomes and immigration levels across locales. Unobserved differences across areas in average immigrant "quality" are subsumed into β_c. Second, controlling for city-specific effects implies that estimates of γ_{ji} are unaffected by differences in demand conditions, local amenities, or the cost of living across markets, so long as these conditions have factor-neutral effects on relative wages within a locale. So demand-induced shifts in the flow of immigrants to a locale are not an issue unless they have differential effects on particular immigrant or native groups.

The assumptions associated with this model imply that the parameters γ_{ji} ($i = 1,2, \ldots, k$) in Eq. (11) are "elasticities of complementarity" that satisfy $\sum_i \gamma_{ji} = 0$ because of constant returns to scale. The only restriction implied by economic theory is $\gamma_{jj} < 0$ – an increase in the supply of group j workers reduces their wage. However, we expect $\gamma_{ij} < 0$ (for $i \neq j$) when recent immigrants are close labor market substitutes with group i and $\gamma_{ij} > 0$ when they are labor market complements with group i (Hamermesh, 1986).

This interpretation of the parameters γ_{ji} assumes that other inputs to local production are held fixed. As we noted above, this assumption might be misleading if other factors are highly mobile in response to immigration. For example, when immigration changes factor ratios and wages, existing workers may either reduce (or increase) their participation in the labor market or migrate to (or from) areas with lower immigrant concentrations and with higher (lower) wages. These labor supply responses reduce the effects of immigration on local wages. More generally, the parameters γ_{ji} subsume the adjustments of other factors that may occur in response to immigration. By Le-Chatlier's Principle, labor demand is more elastic – the effects of immigration on wages are smaller – when other factors can freely adjust. In the extreme, local wages are unaffected by immigration, even in the short run, because other factors adjust rapidly, leaving factor ratios unchanged.[14]

These considerations indicate that the γ_{ji}'s capture the net changes in the relative earnings of different native and immigrant groups *within* a locale. These adjustments are generated by changes in relative factor shares. Because of constant returns to scale, the estimable substitution parameters are $\gamma_{ji} - \gamma_{ki}$, $j = 1, ..., k - 1$. If changes in the stocks of immigrants do not affect the wages of prime age natives denoted by k, then $\gamma_{ki} = 0$. In this case, $\gamma_{11} < 0$ implies that in a locale with a large share of recent immigrants, wages of these immigrants will be low relative to the earnings of other workers in that area. Further, because the cross-substitution effects γ_{ji} (for $j \neq i$) typically will be nonzero, an increase in the supply of all immigrants may have a larger negative impact on immigrant earnings than would be implied by the own substitution effects (γ_{jj}) alone. Even though the estimated area effects, β_c, subsume wage adjustments for each locale, it is still true that an increase in the supply of all immigrant groups likely reduces immigrant and other native groups' wages relative to those of prime-aged natives. These relative wage adjustments also can be evaluated from Eq. (11).

3.4. Econometric evidence of immigration's effects

LaLonde and Topel (1991a) use this model to evaluate the effects of immigration to the US. They estimate relative wage adjustments among five immigrant cohorts – defined by year of entry to the US – as well as among young black and Hispanic natives. Their rationale is that the effects of immigration on wages should be largest among immigrants themselves: the best substitute for an immigrant is another immigrant. This means that wage adjustments among immigrant cohorts will form reasonable upper bounds for the effects that immigration may have on natives.

Estimates of these effects are shown in Table 5. The first row shows that higher immigration modestly lowers the wages of more recent immigrant cohorts (those in the US for less than five or ten years), but it has little if any effect on other groups, including young natives. For example, a doubling of the relative fraction of new immigrants to a locale would lower the wages of new immigrants by less than 3%, and

---

[14] One might argue that factor mobility simply spreads the effects of immigration across a broader geographic area. But the economy-wide effects of immigration on wages are likely to be small: recall that immigration flows are minor in comparison to overall labor supply, at least in a country like the US. In other words, either immigration affects labor market outcomes within local labor markets, or it is unlikely to have any appreciable effects.

Table 5
Impact of immigration on labor market outcomes in the US
(percentage change due to doubling of recent immigrants)

	0–5	6–10	11–15	Hispanics	Blacks
Wages	−0.032	−0.021	−0.010	+0.007	−0.010
Earnings	−0.026	−0.018	−0.010	+0.015	−0.006

Source: LaLonde and Topel (1991b: Tables 6.7, 6.9, 6.10).

of young black natives by less than 1% relative to other natives. As seen in the table's second row, because the results for earnings are similar to those for wages, immigration primarily affects wages and not employment rates or hours worked. If increased immigration simultaneously reduced wages and hours and weeks worked, the earnings estimates should exceed (in absolute value) the wage estimates. In fact, the two sets of estimates are identical.

An advantage of this framework is that the parameters in Eq. (11) can be estimated from a single cross-section. Yet the existence of even modest wage adjustments in the cross-section may be surprising because the mobility of natives or other productive factors should arbitrage long run wage differences. As a result, Eq. (11) may underestimate the true effects of immigration on wages and employment. An alternative is to estimate within-locale *changes* in relative wages that are caused by *changes* in immigration flows. If cross-sectional data are available at two points in time, this "differencing" method eliminates the biases associated with city-specific effects in Eq. (11).

Differencing Eq. (11) over time is equivalent to

$$w_{cjlt} = \beta_{cj} + \beta_t + X_{cjlt}\delta + \sum_i \gamma_{ji} \ln M_{cit} + v_{cjlt}, \tag{12}$$

where t indexes different years. In Eq. (12), differences in groups' relative earnings across areas are subsumed in the β_{cj}'s, which vary by area and group (but not by year). The parameters γ_{ij} are identified from within-area-group *changes* in relative immigrant shares over time. For example, $\gamma_{11} < 0$ implies that new immigrants' wages will decline relative to other workers when their share of the work force increases.

LaLonde and Topel (1991a) find that the estimates from Eq. (12) are nearly identical to those generated by the cross-section model Eq. (11). They conclude that the effects of immigration on wages and employment are modest. Consistent with this, Altonji and Card (1991: p. 221) find that differencing reverses the negative relationship between employment outcomes and the fraction of immigrants across cities. This reversal indicates that immigrant concentrations are larger in cities where unskilled native participation rates are lower for reasons other than immigration flows. Accordingly, they conclude that there is "little evidence that inflows of immigrants are associated with large or systematic effects on employment or unemployment rates of less-skilled natives". They also find that wages are only weakly related to a locale's immigrant concentration.

A shortcoming of the differencing approach is that the change in the fraction of immigrants in a locale may be determined by transitory changes in that locale's demand for immigrant labor. This would bias least squares estimates of wage adjustments. In an attempt to deal with this possibility, Altonji and Card use the fraction of immigrants in a locale in the first cross-sectional year as an instrument for the change in the fraction of immigrants between the two cross-sections. This procedure yields a much larger negative relationship between immigration and unskilled natives' wages. Although the standard errors associated with their estimates are large, their results suggest that a 10% increase in the fraction of immigrants to a locale will reduce the wages of less-skilled natives by 10%.

This estimate aside, most studies in the literature find only small effects of immigration on labor market outcomes of natives. As mentioned above, one explanation for these findings is that native workers and other factors may be geographically mobile. An area can more easily absorb immigrants if natives are elastically supplied to the area. A historical example of this effect is the acceleration of black migration from the rural south to the urban north after the US Congress tightened immigration controls during the early 1920s. Reder (1963) has observed that "the broad outline of the temporal pattern of rural to urban migration of Negroes is what would be expected if Negroes and immigrants were close labor market competitors". Thus the 1920s immigration controls probably had little effect on unskilled native and immigrant living standards in urban areas, because they encouraged domestic migration among natives. In recent times, Filer (1992) finds that net migration among US natives tends to be away from areas of high immigration concentration. Although native migrants (in industrial countries) are often more skilled than immigrants, and therefore less likely to be close labor market substitutes, Filer's results provide one explanation for why most studies find so little effect of immigrants on labor market outcomes.

These considerations about the migratory patterns of immigrants and natives underscore the potential value of studies of specific events in which the flow of immigrants to a locale might be characterized as an exogenous shift in labor supply (Butcher and Card, 1991). An example of such an event is the migration that followed Fidel Castro's April 1980 proclamation allowing Cubans who wanted to emigrate to leave the country. During the following three months, more than 125 000 persons arrived in Miami, Florida, where ethnic Cubans previously constituted 27% of the city's population. One-half of these new arrivals, known as the Mariels, settled permanently in Miami, thereby increasing the city's labor force by 7% and the Cuban labor force by 20%. Moreover, because these new arrivals were relatively unskilled, the unskilled work force increased by an even larger amount. Yet despite this sudden supply shock, Card (1990) found no evidence that the wages and unemployment rates of Miami's unskilled blacks, other blacks, non-Hispanic whites, non-Cuban Hispanics or even

Cubans were affected by the new arrivals.[15] Only the Cubans' wages declined relative to other workers, but this decrease resulted from the "dilution" of this group's work force with the relatively unskilled Mariel immigrants. One explanation offered by Card for these findings is that after 1980 there was a marked slowdown in the migration of natives into the Miami area compared to other cities in the region.

An example of a similar migratory event in Europe occurred when 900 000 repatriates reentered France from Algeria during the year following March, 1962.[16] These relatively high-skilled persons increased the French labor force by 1.6%, with substantially larger concentrations in low-wage areas of Southern France. Hunt (1992) examined the effects of Algerian repatriates on regional unemployment rates and earnings.[17] Her results suggest that the Algerian repatriates had a greater adverse effect on the labor market opportunities of French natives than did the Marielitos in Miami. She found that doubling repatriates' share of an area's work force raised the locale's unemployment rate by approximately 0.3 percentage points and reduced its average earnings levels by 1.3%.[18] Further, she found no evidence that the adverse wage and unemployment effects were dampened by nonimmigrant migration.

4. Assimilation of immigrants

Do immigrants easily assimilate to their host country? The term "assimilation" can mean many things. At one extreme it may refer to the ability of immigrants to adopt the culture, values, and traditions of the host country; that is, to become American or French or Japanese, as the case may be. Whether immigrants assimilate in this sense can have important social and public policy implications. For example, proponents of greater immigration controls often point to the costs of ethnic and cultural heterogeneity in a society, which are alleged to degrade the social cohesiveness of the host country. Thus the Japanese government views its opposition to immigration as an effort to protect Japanese culture, and they point to the alleged costs of ethnic diversity in the US to buttress their view. Immigration controls in Australia and Israel, as well as incipient nationalist movements in Europe also reflect this "cultural" view of assimilation.

[15] Card used data from the 1980 Census and the outgoing rotation groups of the 1979–1985 Current Population Survey to estimate annual wages, unemployment, and employment–population ratios of different ethnic groups in Miami.

[16] Another example of such a repatriation occurred when 600 000 ethnic Portuguese returned to Portugal from Africa between 1974 and 1976. See Carrington and deLima (1994).

[17] Hunt's population and employment data for 88 French departments came from the 1962 and 1968 Censuses, published by Institut National de la Statistique et des Etudes Economiques (INSEE). Her earnings and occupation data were departmental averages from private and semi-private employers' tax reports, as provided by the tax service.

[18] Such a doubling corresponds to approximately a 1.6 percentage point increase in the share of repatriates in a locale's labor market.

A narrower, but quantifiable, definition of assimilation is based on the relative earning power of immigrants. Do immigrants earn less than natives? If so, does their earnings disadvantage dissipate over time? There are reasons to believe that this pattern of "earnings assimilation" should be the typical pattern. Many skills that command a price in the labor market are specific to a particular country. Examples include language, institutional knowledge, job-related skills in particular industries or occupations, and even culture. Almost by definition, new immigrants have fewer of these country-specific skills than do otherwise similar natives. This means that new immigrants arrive with a human capital "deficit" that reduces their earning power relative to ethnically similar natives.

But the gap should narrow over time. Immigrants who expect to remain in the host country have strong incentives to invest in human capital. The usual life-cycle reasoning (e.g., Ben-Porath, 1967) indicates that these investments are greatest soon after arrival, and they diminish with time. Time in the labor market is also an aid to search and matching, so we expect that job mobility is high among new arrivals. Then productivity rises with time in the host country because immigrants sort themselves to jobs in which earnings are greatest (Chiswick, 1978b; DeFreitas, 1981).

Even with this narrower, but quantifiable, definition based on earnings, assessing the extent of assimilation depends on how it is defined. For example, the popular idea that the United States is an ethnic "melting pot" suggests that immigrant earnings should be compared to those of a typical native, independent of ethnicity. Then a measurable definition of assimilation is the rate of convergence between immigrants' and natives' wages. Yet it is known from cross-sectional data that earnings differences among ethnic groups exist even in the native population. For example, native Hispanics and blacks typically earn less than whites and Asians. In this sense, it is obvious from the earnings distribution of *natives* that complete assimilation does not occur.

This point can have important policy implications. If, for example, Mexican immigrants to the US never achieve the melting pot ideal of catching up with a representative native, then increased flows of Mexican immigrants will inevitably increase overall income inequality. Ethnicity and culture aside, proponents of immigration controls argue that rising inequality can itself undermine "social cohesion". Rising inequality also places greater burdens on social welfare systems (see Section 5). Without assimilation, those additional social burdens will persist long after immigration occurs.

But the failure of the "melting pot" experiment doesn't mean that earnings assimilation is unimportant. Not only do new immigrants earn less than the average native, they also earn less than natives of similar ethnicity and less than ethnically similar *immigrants* from earlier arrival cohorts. These groups provide alternative, and probably superior, benchmarks for assessing the importance of earnings assimilation and post-immigration human capital growth. With these benchmarks, for example, Mexican immigrants can be said to assimilate if their earnings converge toward those of native Hispanics, even if they do not converge to the earnings of an average native.

To show how these definitions differ and underscore the measurement difficulties associated with them, we outline an empirical model of immigrant and native wages. Let immigrant wages depend on a vector of observed human capital-related characteristics, X, and unobserved factors:

$$w_{it} = X_{it}\beta_t + e_{it}. \tag{13}$$

In Eq. (13), w_{it} is the log wage of an immigrant from cohort i in year t, where cohort represents the period in which immigration occurred. For example, Canadian and US Census files define time in the host country in discrete intervals. The 1980 US Census records immigrants as having arrived during one of four five-year intervals between 1960 and 1979, a ten-year interval between 1950 and 1959, or prior to 1950. Accordingly, w_{it} refers to wages of immigrants in one of these intervals at calendar time t.

We model the unobserved factor in Eq. (13) as

$$e_{it} = u_i + b_{it} + a_{it}. \tag{14}$$

The first component, u_i, denotes the mean value of unobserved skills in cohort i. Parameter b_{it} is a time effect that accounts for the impact of time t labor market conditions on the wages of cohort i immigrants, so changing market conditions may have differential effects across groups. The main parameter of interest is a_{it}, which denotes the cohort's average (receiving) country-specific accumulated human capital. If human capital accumulates with time in the host country, then $a_{it'} - a_{it} > 0$ for $t' > t$. Alternatively, earnings assimilation occurs if the regression-adjusted earnings of new immigrants are less than those of a cohort that arrived, say, ten years earlier; $a_{it} < a_{i-10,t}$.

We define natives' wages similarly to those of immigrants:

$$w_{nt} = X_{nt}\Theta_t + u_n + b_{nt}. \tag{15}$$

In Eq. (15), natives wages depend on their observed characteristics, X_{nt}, on their fixed unobserved characteristics, u_n, and on year effects b_{nt}. We allow observed characteristics to have different effects on immigrant versus native wages. For example, returns to schooling may be lower among immigrants because of differences in the quality of schools, or because skills learned in the sending country are not perfectly portable.

This framework incorporates the various definitions of earnings assimilation. Consider the melting pot view, where the empirical issue is whether immigrant and native wages converge. Relative immigrant wage growth from year t to t' is

$$(w_{it} - w_{it'}) - (w_{nt} - w_{nt'}) = \ \Theta_t[(X_{it} - X_{it'}) - (X_{nt} - X_{nt'})] + [(\beta_t - \beta_{t'})(X_{it'} - X_{nt'})]$$

$$+ X_{nt'}[(\beta_t - \beta_{t'}) - (\Theta_t - \Theta_{t'})] + (X_{it} - X_{it'})(\beta_t - \Theta_t)$$

$$+ [(b_{it} - b_{it'}) - (b_{nt} - b_{nt'})] + (a_{it} - a_{it'}). \tag{16}$$

Eq. (16) indicates that host-country-specific human capital accumulation is only one of several factors affecting immigrants' relative wage growth. First, as indicated by the first term on the right-hand side of Eq. (16), the time-varying observable characteristics of immigrants and natives may change in different wages. Second, if immigrants have less experience than natives, their earnings should grow more rapidly than natives' because they are on a steeper portion of their experience–wage profiles. Third, relative returns to immigrants' observed characteristics may change. Fourth, immigrants' and natives' returns to observable characteristics may differ. Finally, as indicated by the second-to-last term in Eq. (16), market conditions may affect immigrants and natives differently. The upshot is that immigrant earnings may not grow relative to natives', even if assimilation, in the sense of rising a_{it}, is important.

An alternative to measuring new immigrant earnings relative to natives' is to measure them relative to those of earlier arrivals. The inter-cohort difference between immigrants' wages in year t is

$$(w_{it} - w_{i't}) = (X_{it} - X_{i't})\beta_t + (u_i - u_{i'}) + (b_{it} - b_{i'i}) + (a_{it} - a_{i't}). \tag{17}$$

Differences between cohorts' wages may arise from differences in the accumulated stocks of country-specific skills and from any of three other factors. First, successive cohorts' observable characteristics, X, may differ; second, their unobserved characteristics may differ; and finally, economic conditions may have differing effects on cohort wages.

The implication of Eq. (17) is that assimilation cannot be identified from a single cross-section without additional restrictions on the model. The differences between the cohorts' observable characteristics pose no problem because they can be accounted for using a standard wage regression. Evidence that earlier immigrant cohorts earn more than recent cohorts is consistent with assimilation, but it also can be explained by a decline in unobserved skills between successive immigrant cohorts, u_i, or by the differing effects of economic conditions, b_{it}. So an identifying assumption must be that successive cohorts have the same average value of unobserved characteristics (that are orthogonal to X) and that current economic conditions affect all cohorts equally.

This identification problem can be resolved partly by comparing two immigrant cohorts' relative wage growth using cross-sectional data from different years. Subtracting the relative wage growth of cohort i' from that of cohort i, we have

$$(w_{it} - w_{it'}) - (w_{i't} - w_{i't'}) = \beta_t[(X_{it} - X_{i't}) - (X_{i'} - X_{i'i'})]$$

$$+ (\beta_t - \beta_{t'})(X_{it'} - X_{i'i'}) + [(b_{it} - b_{i'i}) - (b_{i't} - b_{i't'})]$$

$$+ [(a_{it} - a_{it'}) - (a_{i't} - a_{i't'})]. \tag{18}$$

Because the unobserved characteristics are fixed, they do not affect wage growth. Instead, the relative wage growth between cohorts depends on changes in time-varying characteristics, on the effects of changing demand conditions, and on differing rates of accumulation of country-specific skills. Relative assimilation is identified so long as time-varying effects of market conditions, b_{it}, affect both cohorts in the same manner. Further, if one of the two cohorts has been in the receiving country for many years, it may be safe to assume that they are no longer acquiring country-specific human capital (i.e., $a_{i't} = a_{i't'}$). Then regression-adjusted relative wage growth of immigrant cohort i measures the rate of assimilation between years.

This procedure for identifying assimilation rates amounts to using cross-sections from at least two different years to construct a panel of immigrant cohorts. An alternative way to represent this estimator is in a diagram. As shown by Fig. 2, the two solid lines depict the regression-adjusted earnings growth of the 1960 and 1970 immigrant cohorts. The way the lines are drawn, both cohorts' wages grow at similar rates with time in the host

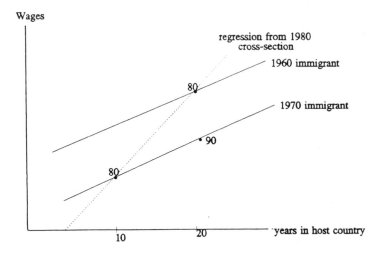

Fig. 2. Cross-sectional and synthetic panel estimates of immigrant assimilation.

country, but the 1970 cohort are less skilled than their 1960 counterparts. Ideally we would like to measure directly the rate of assimilation for immigrants during the second decade in the host country. This estimate corresponds to the rate associated with the points labeled 80 and 90 on the line depicting the 1970 immigrants' wage growth. However, when we have only a single cross-section, say from the 1980 Census, our best estimate of immigrants' assimilation rates corresponds to the greater slope of the dashed line in Fig. 2. The bias associated with this estimate arises because the 1970 immigrant cohort is less skilled than the 1960 immigrant cohort.

Although the procedure represented by Eq. (18) is an improvement over using a single cross-section, two interpretive problems remain. First, implicit in expression (18) is the assumption that unobserved immigrant skills, u_i, do not change. However, as discussed in Section 2, indirect evidence suggests that many US immigrants return to their source countries. This would not be a problem if return migrants were a random sample of each cohort. But theory suggests otherwise. For example, emigrés may have been less successful than their counterparts who remained in the host country, so the distribution of u_i is left-truncated. Then average skill levels rise with time in the host country, which the model will attribute to assimilation. The empirical importance of this problem depends on whether many members of the original cohort emigrate and on the skill composition of those who leave. As observed above, this problem may be important among Latin American immigrants to the US, but probably less so among Asian immigrants.

It is worth observing that true panel data on immigrants will still not resolve the interpretive problems associated with synthetic panel estimates of assimilation. With true panel data such as the Panel Study of Income Dynamics (PSID) in the US or the Socio Economic Panel in Germany differencing an individual's earnings between different years eliminates the cohort effect defined in Eq. (14). However, if immigrants emigrate when their assimilation rates are low (high), then these fixed effects estimates of immigrant assimilation will be too high (low). Nevertheless, one advantage of true panel data is that we can observe which immigrants remain in the host country and which emigrate. This advantage enables us to obtain unbiased estimates of assimilation rates for immigrants who remain in the host country (Pischke, 1992).

A second interpretive problem with panel estimates of assimilation arises because immigrant cohorts who have been in the host country longer include a larger fraction of persons who migrated as children (Friedberg, 1992). Unless immigrants who have been in the host country for a long time migrated as children, they now would be retired and have no labor market earnings. This source of selection causes the cohort effects, u_j, to change over time in a way that is similar to how it changes when less-skilled members of an immigrant cohort emigrate from the host country. Because the cohort effects change, in principle, we cannot be certain that the panel estimates have "differenced" them away. If t and t' are not too many years apart, this source of bias is not likely to be significant. However, if immigrants who arrive as children experience a different assimilation process compared with those who arrive as adults, estimated assimilation rates generated from Eq. (18) may be misleading. We suspect that policy makers and analysts are more interested in knowing assimilation rates for immigrants who arrived as adults than the rates for those who arrived as children and were educated in the host country's school system.

A third interpretive problem with panel estimates of assimilation turns on the identification of the time effects, $[(b_{it} - b_{i't}) - (b_{i't} - b_{i't'})]$. LaLonde and Topel (1992) argue that because the wage distribution in industrialized countries has been widening, identification of this effect is crucial (Juhn et al., 1993; Davis, 1992). Because relative wages of less-skilled workers have fallen *in general*, the wages of immigrant also will decline because they typically are less skilled than a representative native. If this effect is ignored, longitudinal estimates of immigrant assimilation will be biased downward.

To deal with this last problem, LaLonde and Topel argue that recent immigrants' wage growth should be compared to the wage growth either of immigrants of the same ethnicity who have been in the US for more than 30 years, or ethnically similar natives. For example, LaLonde and Topel estimate that because of the rise in US wage inequality, the average 1979 wage of recent Mexican immigrants relative to natives was 8% lower than the average 1969 relative wages of their newly arrived counterparts. Therefore using growth in natives' wages to measure changes in demand conditions would cause estimates of the rate that Mexican immigrants acquired US-specific human capital to be too low.

4.1. Estimates of assimilation

Both definitions of assimilation motivated Chiswick's (1978a) influential study of immigrant assimilation in the US. Using a single cross-section from the 1970 US Census, and controlling for workers' years of schooling, potential labor market experience, marital status, and region, Chiswick found that immigrants' relative wages rose with time spent in the US. Despite arriving with lower earnings and having lower estimated returns to schooling, Chiswick estimated that immigrant earnings surpassed those of a comparable white native after 13 years in the US. Moreover, after examining the separate assimilation paths of immigrants from a number of different English speaking and non English speaking countries, Chiswick concluded that "an earnings cross-over at 10–15 years appears to be quite robust" (Chiswick, 1978a: p. 919).

Chiswick's results suggest that immigrants acquire a significant amount of country-specific human capital during their first decade in the United States. When compared to earlier immigrant cohorts, his results indicate that new immigrants' (those in the US for less than five years) earnings rose by 11% relative to immigrants with the same observed characteristics who had been in the US for 30 or more years. However, because these results are derived from cross-sectional data, this estimate of the rate of assimilation may be too large, resulting from lower unobserved skills among recent immigrant arrivals.

This concern about the reliability of cross-sectional estimates of assimilation is particularly relevant when studying immigration to Australia and North America. As shown by Table 6, during the postwar period immigrants' countries of origin changed. During the 1950s, approximately 60% of immigrants to the US were from Europe, compared with only 6.2% from Asian countries. Twenty years later these percentages had changed so that less than 20% of immigrants to the US were from Europe and 36% were from Asia. Similar changes in the contributions of different source countries also occurred in Australia and Canada. The implication of these figures is that cross-sectional estimates of assimilation compare immigrant cohorts with substantially different labor market skills upon arrival in the receiving country (Borjas, 1991a). For example, European immigrants include many persons from the northwestern part of the continent, who arrive in the US with high levels of education and English language proficiency. By comparison, immigrants from Latin America and Asia arrive with substantially poorer skills. Thus, cross-sectional comparisons among immigrant cohorts from different years leads to comparisons between relatively skilled European immigrants and less-skilled immigrants from Latin America and Asia.

Although it is clear that the skills of recent immigrants to the US have declined over time, it is not so clear that this has led to biased estimates of the rate of assimilation. Some of Chiswick's specifications include crude controls for immigrants' source country, years of schooling, and experience, so the changing observable characteristics of immigrant cohorts will not bias his estimate of assimilation. Still, declines in unobserved skills may occur "within" an educational-experience-source country category. For example, Mexican immigrants who arrived in the US between 1975 and 1979 with six years of schooling and ten years of potential experience may be less skilled than observably similar Mexicans who arrived a decade earlier.

Both Borjas (1985) and LaLonde and Topel (1992) examined the importance of this possibility using two cross-sections derived from the 1970 and 1980 US Censuses.

Table 6
Region/country of origin of immigrants to the US

Region/country of origin	1951–1960 (%)	1961–1970 (%)	1971–1980 (%)
Europe	59	37	18
United Kingdom/Germany	22	13	4
Asia	6	13	36
Americas	33	48	43
Canada	11	9	3
Mexico	13	13	14

Source: Chiswick (1986: p. 170, Table 1).

But they reached different conclusions. Although Borjas found some evidence of immigrant assimilation, he concluded that "the strong assimilation rates measured in the cross-section may be partly due to a precipitous decline in the 'quality' of immigrants admitted to [the US] since 1950". As a result, cross-sectional estimates overstate the rate of assimilation "by as much as 20 percentage points in some immigrant cohorts" (p. 484). Further, the rate of immigrant wage growth relative to natives was "greatly overestimated by cross-section analysis".

By contrast, LaLonde and Topel acknowledged that the average skill of immigrants had declined substantially, but argued that there was "no important evidence of declining immigrant 'quality' within the groups that we studied". They point to evidence in both their own and in Borjas's study, showing that there was no decline in the educational attainment of successive immigrant cohorts within ethnic groups. Lack of change in *observable* skills makes it less plausible that there were important declines in *unobservable* skills within an ethnic category. More to the point, they found that both cross-sectional and "panel" estimates of assimilation were similar. Provided researchers control for immigrants' education, experience, and ethnicity, LaLonde and Topel conclude that estimates of immigrant assimilation from a cross-sectional data set may be reliable estimates of the amount of assimilation likely to be observed in a panel.

LaLonde and Topel's results indicate that immigrants acquire significant amounts of county-specific human capital during the first ten years in the US. They also find that the rate of assimilation is positively correlated with the gap between a newly ar-

Table 7
Rates of US immigrant assimilation[a]

Ethnic groups	(1)	(2)	(3)	(4)	(5)
Europeans and Canadians	0.09	0.08	0.08	−0.05	–
	(0.02)	(0.03)	(0.03)	(0.02)	–
East Asians	0.24	0.25	0.24	−0.33	−0.07
	(0.03)	(0.03)	(0.09)	(0.02)	(0.03)
Mexicans	0.17	0.22	0.21	−0.22	−0.11
	(0.03)	(0.03)	(0.09)	(0.02)	(0.02)
Other Latin American and Caribbean	0.23	0.24	0.19	−0.22	−0.20
	(0.03)	(0.03)	(0.09)	(0.03)	(0.03)

[a]Column (1), log wage differences for ethnic natives; column (2), initial gap with ethnic natives. The rates of assimulation in columns (3), (4) and (5) are relative to: column (3), ethnic natives 1980 cross-section; column (4), old immigrants 1980 cross-section; column (5), old immigrants 1970–80 panel. Estimates control for years of completed schooling, a quartic in experience, and interactions between schooling and experience. Additional controls do not affect the results. Assimilation rates estimate the effect of the first ten years' US experience on wages, measured relative to observationally identical ethnic natives and ethnic immigrants who have been in the US for more than 30 years. Standard errors are in parentheses.
Source: LaLonde and Topel (1991b: Table 2).

rived cohorts' wages and those of ethnically similar natives. As shown by Table 7, skills associated with their first ten years in the US raises European and Canadian immigrants' wages by 8%, compared with a 20% rise in Mexican and East Asian immigrants' wages. These results hold both when using only the cross-section (columns (1) and (2)) and when using the panel (column (3)). However, as shown by column (4), Mexican and East Asian immigrants begin work in the US with a larger wage gap between themselves and natives of the same ethnicity.

The foregoing rates of assimilation indicate that immigrants will "catch up" with *ethnically similar* natives who have similar levels of education within 10–20 years. But immigrant earnings will *not* approach those of the median native. For example, earnings of Mexican immigrants will approach those of Hispanic natives. But, as shown by column (5) of Table 7, Hispanic natives earn less than an otherwise observationally equivalent native of European ancestry. In the US, the melting pot analogy is incomplete, as is indicated by persistent earnings differentials among members of ethnic groups who are natives (Glazer and Moynihan, 1963).

There are fewer studies that examine immigrant assimilation in other developed countries. Those that exist for Australia, Canada, Germany, and the United Kingdom suggest that years spent in these countries yield substantially smaller returns than estimates for US immigrants. Chiswick and Miller (1993) find that a year of experience in Australia raises immigrant earnings by approximately three-tenths of a percent. Baker and Benjamin (1994) report low, if not negative rates of assimilation for several early immigrant cohorts in Canada. Pischke (1992) and Chiswick (1980) find no evidence of immigrant assimilation in Germany and the United Kingdom.

One potential explanation for these findings is that new immigrants to these countries have skills that are more similar to natives' than is the case for immigrants in the US. US studies suggest a negative relationship between estimated assimilation rates of a given immigrant cohort and that cohort's skills relative to natives (Duleep and Regets, 1992). One interpretation of this finding is that immigrants who arrive in the receiving country at a significant earnings disadvantage to natives are more likely than other immigrants to lack the country-specific skills of the native population. For these disadvantaged migrants, time in the receiving country provides them with an opportunity to acquire these skills. By contrast, new immigrants who can earn as much as natives likely arrive with these country-specific skills, and therefore do not earn any returns by gradually acquiring them during their stay in the receiving country.

Several studies of immigrant assimilation outside the US find some support for this explanation. For example, after accounting for Canadian immigrants' changing ethnic composition and for their age at migration, Baker and Benjamin report that five years of experience in Canada raised the earnings of immigrants arriving between 1971 and 1975 by 5%, and between 1976 and 1980 by 6%. Similarly, Schmidt (1992), using the same data used by Pischke in the study cited above, reports that a year of experience in Germany for Turkish, Greek, and Italian immigrants raised their earnings by nearly

1%.[19] One characteristic of the more recent immigrants to Canada and the Turkish, Greek, and Italian immigrants to Germany is that, when compared to other immigrant groups, their initial earnings were lower relative to natives. In Canada this decline in the relative earnings of new immigrants tracks the shift in immigrant composition away from Northwestern European countries and toward Asian countries.

4.2. *The impact of language proficiency*

New immigrants acquire a variety of social and cultural "skills" that facilitate their assimilation into the receiving country's labor force. Among these skills, the one that has received the most attention in the literature is language proficiency. If a person's language skills are an important component of his or her work-related human capital, immigrants' earnings should depend on their language skills upon arrival in the receiving country and on the rate that these skills improve over time. This conjecture suggests immigrants' proficiency in the dominant language of the receiving country should account for a portion of their earnings and of its rise with time since migration.

The extent that greater language proficiency leads to increased earnings depends on how production is organized, on the nature of the product, and on the share of consumers that speak the dominant language. If all output consisted of standardized products produced in one-person firms using only labor, communication skills would be less important and measures of language proficiency would not be strongly related to earnings. However, when production requires communication among workers and capital, or when consumers demand customized products, those lacking proficiency in the receiving country's language are likely to have lower earnings (McManus, 1985). As a result, theory not only predicts that language-deficient immigrants have lower earnings, but that these earnings differentials would vary among workers according to their occupation and industry. Further, the presence of large numbers of language deficient immigrants may affect equilibrium occupation and industry wage differentials (Kossoudji, 1988).

Most available data sources for studying language proficiency and earnings only contain individuals' self-reported assessments of their ability to speak the receiving country's language (Bloom and Grenier, 1991). For example, the US, Canadian, and Australian censuses inquire about the "mother tongue", the "language spoken at home", and, if the respondent speaks a language other than English (or in Canada, French) at home, whether they speak English "very well", "well", "not well", or "not

---

[19] Although Pischke (1992) finds little evidence among several econometric specifications that German immigrants assimilate, he does report that when he used native blue-collar workers as this "base" group, he generated nearly the same assimilation rates that Schmidt found for Greek, Italian, and Turkish immigrants. Because immigrants from these groups are nearly always blue-collar or low-skilled workers, this choice of a base group makes some sense.

at all". For these countries, there also are some special surveys, such as the 1976 US Survey of Income and Education (SIE), that contain more detailed information on immigrants' language skills (McManus et al., 1983: Appendix). However, even when using these sources, researchers usually must evaluate an immigrant's language proficiency by relying on respondents' (or interviewers') assessments of their spoken English. Most available data sources not only lack objective measures of language skills, but even lack self-assessments of respondents' ability to write or read the receiving country's language.

Although the available measures of immigrants' language skills have obvious shortcomings, these measures have the expected correlations with other determinants of individuals' human capital. In their studies of immigrants' language skills and earnings in Australia, Canada, Israel, and the US, Chiswick and Miller (1992, 1993) report that after controlling for differences among observed characteristics, immigrants' language proficiency increased with years of schooling and years in the receiving country and was lower when immigrants had migrated at older ages, married abroad, or lived in an area with a high concentration of persons of similar ethnicity. In a separate paper, Chiswick (1991) reports these same patterns hold even among a sample of apprehended illegal immigrants awaiting deportation from the US.

Studies that use these measures of language proficiency usually find that they are significant determinants of immigrants' earnings. As shown by Table 8, US immigrants' earnings are strongly correlated with their ability to speak English. Chiswick and Miller (1992: pp. 264, 275) report that in 1980 there was a 46% earnings differential between US immigrants who were fluent and those reporting themselves as "English language deficient". This difference falls to approximately 17% after they accounted for the standard variables in an earnings equation. These authors' studies of language acquisition by Australian, Canadian, and Israeli immigrants yielded similar, but somewhat smaller, effects of language proficiency on earnings (Chiswick, 1993; Chiswick and Miller, 1993).

This regression-adjusted language earnings premium suggests that a US immigrant who was fluent in English earned approximately $4500 (1992$) more annually than

Table 8
Earnings of US natives and immigrants by English fluency
(median weekly earnings in dollars, males 25–54 years old in November 1989)

Age	Native-born	Immigrants who speak English		
		At home	Well, but not at home	Not well
25–34	455	482	409	221
35–44	575	622	506	239
45–54	582	739	506	286

Source: Meisenheimer (1992: pp. 16–17, Tables 10 and 12).

an observationally equivalent immigrant who spoke English either "not well" or "not at all". Likewise, despite using different econometric approaches and a different data set, McManus (1985) and Kossoudji (1988) each arrived at a similar conclusion for Hispanic immigrants. They found that earnings of the typical non-English speaking Hispanic (male) immigrant would rise by approximately $5000 (1992$) if he became fluent in English. Kossoudji reports that about one-third of this gain results because fluent immigrants are more likely to be employed in higher-paid managerial and professional occupations, while the remaining two-thirds of this gain occurs as a result of increased earnings within occupations.

Although many studies find that immigrants with greater language proficiency have greater earnings, they agree less on how much their acquisition of these skills accounts for the rates of assimilation observed above. Chiswick and Miller (1992) using US Census data and Tainer (1988) using the SIE report that including measures of language proficiency in an earnings equation reduces estimated assimilation rates by less than 25%. Likewise, these authors find that similar measures of immigrants' language proficiency have approximately the same effect on estimated assimilation rates of Australian, Canadian, and Israeli immigrants. Further, these measures of language proficiency only explain a fraction of the earnings differences between immigrants and natives. These findings suggest that immigrant assimilation is explained largely by the acquisition of other country-specific skills. By contrast, studies such as those by McManus et al. (1983) and McManus (1985) reach the opposite conclusion. Using different econometric specifications applied to the same data, they each report that once they account for an Hispanic immigrant's language deficiency, neither ethnicity nor time in the US are statistically significant determinants of earnings.

Understanding the connection between language proficiency and earnings growth is important because there may be considerable gains associated with improving immigrants' language skills. For example, McManus' and Kossoudji's studies suggest that the lifetime earnings losses to non-English speaking Hispanic immigrants' may amount to as much as $90 000. Therefore, if it costs less than that amount to make such an immigrant fluent, paying for such training may be privately beneficial. Further, if an immigrant cannot borrow from family members, or does not have sufficient access to capital markets or to existing public-sector sponsored educational loan programs, it also may be socially beneficial for governments to subsidize this training. However, this $90 000 estimate has another interpretation. It may underscore the high costs incurred by adults, as compared to those incurred by children, when they learn a new language.

Chiswick and Miller (1992) offer another argument as to why these estimates may not reflect the gains associated with becoming fluent in English. But rather than disputing the foregoing interpretations of these estimates, they argue that they are biased because measures of language proficiency are endogenous in an earnings equation. Immigrants "become fluent in English if their unobserved skills are more highly rewarded when they are fluent" (p. 266). They note that the gains to fluency are greater for more educated persons. Educated people are likely to invest more in improving their English skills. Because returns to proficiency are greater for observed skills such as education, it seems likely that these returns also would be greater for larger endowments of unobserved skills. As a result, measures of language proficiency likely are correlated with the error term in the earnings equation.

The authors attempted to address this problem by instrumenting their measures of language proficiency. Their instruments included immigrants' veteran status, number and age structure of their children, whether they were married abroad, and local concentration of "minority language" speakers. The validity of their procedure depends on whether they are uncorrelated with the unobserved characteristics in the immigrants' earnings equation. This caveat aside, the instrumental variable estimates yielded substantially larger estimated premiums for immigrants proficient in the dominant language in Canada, Israel, and the US, while yielding lower premiums for similar immigrants in Australia (Chiswick and Miller, 1993). Results such as these underscore the potential importance of endogenous language proficiency in earnings equations and of their sensitivity to the instrumental variables used in the analysis.

5. Transfers, taxes, and social welfare programs

Recent waves of immigrants to Western Europe and the US have included a large number of unskilled, and thus low income, families. Aside from their impact on the wage distribution, these immigrants raise additional concerns in countries with generous social welfare systems. One obvious problem is that generous transfer programs are most attractive to the least skilled, so the composition of immigrants is affected. For example, Sweden – with the most generous income-support programs in the world – received about 80 000 immigrants annually in the early 1990s. This flow represents 1% of the Swedish population, and many of the immigrants are relatively unskilled refugees from the Middle East. This effect can only worsen with Sweden's planned entry into the European Community, which will allow free labor mobility among member states.

The other problem is that participation of immigrants in social welfare programs places a burden on native taxpayers. As one extreme example, California taxpayers bear the medical costs of childbirth for illegal Mexican immigrants, whose US-born children are automatically citizens. The incentives for Mexican women to give birth in the US are huge. Should immigrants' use of these services exceed the taxes they pay plus their contribution to consumers' surplus, then receiving country policy makers have a strong incentive to restrict the flow of low-skilled immigrants into their country.

5.1. Social welfare transfers

In addition to reducing the benefits that natives receive from a given flow of immigrants, the presence of a social welfare system also increases the numbers of low-skilled persons and may reduce the numbers of high-skilled persons migrating to the receiving country. Because the social welfare system creates a minimum living standard, low-skilled persons' expected income in the receiving country may rise above their expected labor market earnings. As a result, because the benefits from migration are more likely to exceed their costs, these persons have a greater incentive to migrate to the receiving country (Borjas and Trejo, 1992). By contrast, these incentives do not affect the migration rates of high-skilled persons because their high receiving country earnings would likely make them ineligible for transfer payments. Instead, their migration rates might decline if the receiving country supported a generous social welfare system with high tax rates. Again, Sweden is a good example.

Studies of 1970 and 1980 US Census data support the contention that immigrants make substantial use of the receiving country's social welfare system. As shown by Table 9, in 1970 approximately the same percentages of immigrant and native households received either Aid to Families with Dependent Children (AFDC), Supplemental Security Income, or general assistance. In 1980, the percentage of immigrants receiving transfers exceeded the native percentage by nearly one point. Moreover, the table suggests that immigrant households' use of the social welfare system increases with time in the US. In both 1970 and 1980, immigrant households whose head reported being in the US for no more than five years were usually less likely to receive welfare payments than other immigrant households.

However, as the discussion of assimilation rates indicated in the previous section, cross-sectional comparisons of participation in transfer programs will understate the growth in the proportion of families receiving assistance. Recent arrivals are less skilled, so they have higher participation rates in these programs than earlier cohorts. The importance of this point is clear from Table 9, which shows that in 1970 approximately 6.0% of immigrant households whose head had been in the US no more than ten years received welfare payments. But by 1980, 9.7% of a comparable sample households whose head now had been in the US for 11–20 years received welfare payments. These figures suggest that the percentage of immigrant households receiv-

Table 9
Welfare participation of US immigrants
(percentage of households receiving payments)[a]

Census year	Natives	Immigrants	Years in the US			
			0–5	6–10	1–20	20+
1970	6.1	5.9	5.5	6.5	5.0	6.2
1980	7.9	8.8	8.3	8.4	9.7	8.5

[a]Percentages of immigrant and native households with head 18 years and over that received Aid to Families with Dependent Children, Supplemental Security Income, or general assistance in the year prior to the Census.
Source: Borjas and Trejo (1991: p. 198, Table1).

ing welfare jumped by more than 60% during the decade. This is more than twice the growth rate for native households.

The figures in Table 9 highlight two points about the costs of immigration to native taxpayers. First, new US immigrant households are more likely to receive welfare payments than their earlier counterparts. Second, the longer immigrants remain in the US, the more likely they are to use the social welfare system. Borjas and Trejo (1991) find that the first result is due to the changing ethnic composition of immigrants to the US. As observed in Section 2, recent immigrants to the US are less likely to come from European countries, and more likely to come from Asia and Latin America. Immigrants from these regions are much more likely to reside in households receiving welfare. For example, in 1980, 29% of Vietnamese-headed households, 18% of Cuban-headed households and 12% of Mexican-headed households received welfare. By contrast, the percentages of German-headed and British-headed households that received welfare were 4.7 and 5.4% respectively.

Borjas and Trejo estimated the probability that immigrant households received welfare while holding constant years in the US, ethnicity, and other demographic characteristics. Using a logit framework, they found that after including controls for ethnicity (white, black, Hispanic, or Asian) immigrant households were *less* likely to receive welfare than ethnically similar native households (see also Blau, 1984; Tienda and Jensen, 1986). However, the probability that a household would receive welfare rose by approximately 0.15 percentage points for each year that they spent in the United States. These results indicate that not only do changes in the ethnic composition of immigrants account for the higher percentages of immigrant households receiving welfare, but that these percentages are likely to grow as they spend time in the United States. Combining these results, Borjas and Trejo predict that immigrant welfare recipiency will eventually exceed that of natives.

Rising welfare recipiency appears inconsistent with earnings assimilation among immigrants, since participation in social welfare programs usually requires low income. One explanation for this paradox is that legal barriers initially exclude new immigrants from receiving welfare payments. For example, immigrants in principle may be deported from the US if they become public charges during the five-year period before they become eligible to apply for US citizenship, though this policy is rarely enforced.

5.2. Transfers and fertility

Another possible explanation for the rising percentages of immigrants receiving welfare turns on the close connection between eligibility for these programs and the presence of dependent children. For example, low-income persons obviously receive AFDC only if they have dependent children. Likewise, families' eligibility for Medicaid, the US program that provides health care services to low-income persons, is significantly more likely if there are unborn or infant children in the household. Finally, families with children are considerably more likely to use the public school system. So higher fertility among less-skilled immigrants could explain rising participation rates in welfare programs.

The importance of assessing this possibility for the US is underscored because immigrants have increasingly arrived from source countries with substantially higher average fertility rates. These rates probably overstate the fertility rates of those women who emigrate. Women who migrate probably have lower fertility than those who remain in the source country. Further, fertility among immigrants may converge to that among natives as part of the assimilation process. The counter argument is that the act of immigration may postpone fertility, so that child-bearing increases once women are settled in the receiving country.

These hypotheses about immigrant fertility suggest that direct comparisons between the numbers of children ever born to immigrant and native women may create a misleading impression about the differences between these women's fertility levels. Large cross-sectional data sets such as the Censuses report the number of children ever born at a point in time. For younger women this date is before they have completed their child-bearing years, so the data are censored. If immigration delays child bearing, the difference between native and immigrant fertility would be understated. Comparisons of the number of children ever born to older immigrant and native women do not suffer from these shortcomings because these groups have completed their child bearing. By following older cohorts over time we may estimate whether immigrants' fertility rates converge or diverge from those of natives.

Although these comparisons are informative for predicting the likely fertility patterns of recent immigrant cohorts, care is required when extrapolating past immigrant fertility patterns to those of recent cohorts. For example, to the extent that these patterns depend on economic conditions, extrapolations should account for the differing "time" effects that influenced the fertility behavior of each arrival cohort. One way to control for these effects is to condition on the fertility patterns of native cohorts, especially natives with the same ethnicity as immigrants.

A more important problem with using the fertility patterns of past immigrants to project the pattern for recent arrivals is that immigrants' ethnic composition changes with time. In the US, the older immigrant cohorts are from source countries with low average fertility rates compared to the those of new arrivals. Therefore, the differences between their and natives' fertility levels and as well as growth may not provide a reliable basis for estimating the completed fertility differences between new arrivals and similarly aged natives. An improvement upon such estimates involves comparing the fertility patterns of past immigrants from the same source countries.

Blau (1992) accounted for these effects in her analysis of immigrant and native fertility in the United States. She found that even immigrants who arrive from source countries with high fertility rates have comparable fertility levels to natives. According to the 1980 US Census, the number of children ever born to immigrants who had arrived in the US during the previous decade was only 0.1–0.2 children larger than the numbers born to similarly aged natives. Earlier immigrant cohorts reported fewer children compared with natives, and immigrants generally had fewer children than ethnically similar natives. To be sure, the fertility rates of immigrants groups are correlated with the average fertility rates in their countries of origin. This correlation is especially strong for immigrants who had married prior to arriving in the United States. But the fertility rates of recent immigrants are much lower than those of their source countries.

At least for the US, these findings imply that immigrant fertility rates do not portend substantially higher participation in social welfare programs. Nevertheless, Blau found that immigrants fertility rates rise relative to natives during their first decade in the United States. Following the cohort of immigrants who arrived between 1965 and 1970, the immigrant–native difference in number of children born increased by 0.5 children between 1970 and 1980. Should this trend continue, by 1990 the average immigrant will bear 0.7 more children than a comparable native.

Because the presence of more dependent children increases a household's likelihood of receiving social welfare transfers, Blau's findings are consistent with those of Borjas and Trejo showing that immigrants "assimilate" toward the social welfare practices of ethnically comparable natives. However, it is unclear whether increased immigrant fertility, both within and across cohorts, explains a significant portion of immigrants increased use of the US social welfare system. What is clear is that although US immigrants have increasingly arrived from countries with high fertility rates, their fertility behavior in the US is fairly similar to that of natives.

5.3. Comparing transfers and tax payments

A comprehensive estimate of the benefits of immigration should include the costs of immigrant participation in the full range of income-support programs. These include transfers from the unemployment insurance and social security systems, public health insurance, and the public schools. Simon (1984) provides such an estimate for a sample of 15 000 immigrant households from the 1976 Survey of Income and Education. As shown by column (1) of Table 10, families headed by immigrants who arrived in the US between 1965 and 1975 received less from the social welfare system than other immigrant or native households. The reason is that these families are headed by younger persons, who are less likely to be eligible for Social Security and Medicare.[20] However, as shown by the table, immigrants receive as much if not more than natives from the other transfer programs.

---

[20] Social Security provides retirement benefits and Medicare provides health care services to older Americans. US immigrants' parents are not eligible to receive payments under these programs.

Table 10

Annual benefit to natives from immigration

(transfer payments received and taxes paid by US immigrant and native families)[a]

Cohort arrival dates	Public transfers			(4) Estimated taxes paid ($)	(5) Net taxes (4) − (1) ($)	(6) Net benefit (5) − $282 ($)
	(1) Total ($)	(2) SSA ($)	(3) Other ($)			
1970–1974	1414	72	1342	3048	1634	1352
1965–1969	1941	200	1741	3552	1611	1329
1960–1964	2247	414	1833	4064	1817	1535
1950–1959	2292	500	1792	3927	1635	1353
Natives	2279	902	1377	3201	922	–

[a]Total transfers per family include unemployment and workmen's compensation, veteran's benefits, public welfare, Supplementary Security Income, Aid to Families with Dependent Children, food stamps, Social Security, and estimated costs for Medicare (at $592 per patient year), Medicaid (at $126 per patient year) and schooling for children aged 5–17 (at $1302 per child year). SSA includes both Social Security and Medicare payments. The figures in the table are in $1975 per family. To convert them to 1993 dollars, multiply by 2.7.

Source: Simon (1974: pp. 58, 65, Tables 1 and 4).

While immigrants appear to make substantial use of the US social welfare system, an equally important consideration is whether the tax payments associated with their incomes exceed these costs. Existing micro-data sets do not report individuals' tax payments. But, as shown by column (5) of Table 10, estimates based on their reported incomes indicate that, on balance, immigrants who arrived in the US prior to 1975 paid more in taxes than they collected from social welfare programs. Notice that the same also is true for natives. Natives' net taxes must be positive, because tax payments must also pay for the provision of public goods, such as national defense, international affairs, or general science, and for other government services. Simon estimates that 20% of natives' tax payments cover expenditures on public goods. By definition, the presence of immigrants does not affect the usage of these services, but the number of immigrants may affect usage of and therefore expenditures on other government services. We can estimate these government expenditures per family by subtracting the government's per-family expenditures on public goods, $640 (= 0.2 × $3201), from natives' net taxes, $922, to arrive at $282. We then compute the net benefits (column (6)) that natives received from an immigrant family in a given arrival cohort by subtracting this figure from immigrants' net taxes.

As the final column of Table 10 shows, immigrants' net tax payments exceed the costs associated with their use of the social welfare system by approximately $1400 per family. The main source of this surplus is due to current immigrants contributions to Social Security, which is a transfer to older natives. Overall, during the mid-1970s a cohort of 500 000 immigrant families transferred approximately $0.7 billion (1975$) annually to natives.

These calculations indicate that policy concerns about the effect of immigration on social welfare costs may be unwarranted. However, two considerations suggest that they overstate the benefits associated with more recent US immigration. First, the calculations assume that average immigrant skills have not declined. We know that they have, and that recent immigrant cohorts have higher poverty rates. For example, the percentage of new immigrant arrivals with incomes below the poverty line rose from 18.4% in 1970 to 29.4% in 1980 (Borjas, 1990). This change occurred during a period when the poverty rates for both white and minority US natives declined. Therefore, the net benefits associated with immigrants who migrated after 1975 may be substantially smaller than for those who arrived in the US prior to that year.

A second reason why the figures in Table 10 overstate the net benefits to natives from recent immigration is that they do not take into account that a cohort's use of the social welfare system rises with time in the US. The growth in welfare payments received by the 1970–1974 cohort between 1975 and 1985 will be larger than indicated by the difference between payments received by the 1970–1974 and 1960–1964 cohorts in 1975. Further research is required on the forthcoming 1990 Census and other micro-data sets to assess the importance of these considerations.

6. Conclusions

Studies of the labor market impact of immigration find generally that increased immigration has only a modest impact on the distribution of income. However, most of these adverse affects fall on immigrants themselves. Recent immigrants to a locale depress the earnings of other new immigrants in the area, but they have little measurable effect on the employment and earnings prospects of natives. These effects might be small as a result of the effects that immigrants have on local labor demand or of changes in natives' migration patterns. In the former case, there is little reason to expect large effects from immigration on natives' income distribution. In the latter case, such migratory behavior would imply that any adverse impact of immigration on natives is not isolated to a locale, but is spread more widely across the economy.

The literature on assimilation has several implications for studies of the labor market impact of immigration. First, there is evidence of a significant amount of immigrant assimilation in the US data, although there is less evidence of it in Australian, Canadian, and European data. This result implies that the adverse effects that US immigrants have on wages lessen as they spend more time in the US. Second, this assimilation does not mean that immigrants' wages approach those of the median native. Instead, it implies that their earnings approach those of comparably skilled, and ethnically similar natives within a generation. Finally, one reason that there may be less evidence of immigrant assimilation outside the US is that the US receives a more heterogeneous pool of immigrants. Indeed, within the US there is less evidence of assimilation among groups that arrive with skills that are similar to the typical native. Years of experience in the host country may be particularly valuable to the unskilled as they acquire country-specific skills that their more skilled counterparts already have. This result suggests that because in recent years immigrants to the US (and Canada) have become less skilled compared to the native population, the process of assimilation will be a more important part of the immigrant experience in the years ahead.

References

Abowd, J.M. and R.B. Freeman (1991), "Introduction and summary", in: J.M. Abowd and R.B. Freeman, eds., Immigration, trade, and the labor market (University of Chicago Press, Chicago, IL) pp. 1–25.

Altonji, J. and D. Card (1991), "The effects of immigration on the labor market outcomes of less-skilled natives", in: J.M. Abowd and R.B. Freeman, eds., Immigration, trade, and the labor market (University of Chicago Press, Chicago, IL).

Baker, M. and D. Benjamin (1994), "The performance of immigrants in the Canadian labor market", Journal of Labor Economics 12: 369–405.

Bartel, A. and M. Koch (1991), "Internal migration of US immigrants", in: J.M. Abowd and R.B. Freeman, eds., Immigration, trade, and the labor market (University of Chicago Press, Chicago, IL).

Beggs, J. and B. Chapman (1991), "Male immigrant wage and unemployment experience in Australia", in: J.M. Abowd and R.B. Freeman, eds., Immigration, trade, and the labor market (University of Chicago Press, Chicago, IL) pp. 369–384.

Ben-Porath, Y. (1967), "The production of human capital and life cycle earnings", Journal of Political Economy 75: 352–365.

Blau, F. (1984), "Use of transfer payments by immigrants", Industrial and Labor Relations Review 37: 222–239.

Blau, F. (1992), "The fertility of immigrant women: evidence from high-fertility source countries", in: G. Borjas and R. Freeman, eds., Immigration and the workforce: economic consequences for the United States and source areas (University of Chicago Press, Chicago, IL) pp. 93–134.

Bloom, D. and G. Grenier (1991), "The earnings of linguistic minorities: French in Canada and Spanish in the United States", Working paper no. 3660 (NBER, Cambridge, MA).

Bloom, D. and M. Gunderson (1991), "An analysis of earnings of Canadian immigrants", in: J.M. Abowd and R.B. Freeman, eds., Immigration, trade, and the labor market (University of Chicago Press, Chicago, IL) pp. 321–342.

Borjas, G.J. (1985), "Assimilation, changes in cohort quality, and the earnings of immigrants", Journal of Labor Economics 3: 463–489.

Borjas, G. (1987a), "Immigrants, minorities, and labor market competition", Industrial and Labor Relations Review 40: 382–392.

Borjas, G. (1987b), "Self-selection and the earnings of immigrants", American Economic Review 77: 531–553.

Borjas, G. (1990), Friends or strangers: the impact of immigrants on the US economy (Basic Books, New York).

Borjas, G. (1991a), "Immigrants in the US labor market: 1940–80", American Economic Review 81: 287–292.

Borjas, G. (1991b), "Immigration policy, national origin, and immigrant skills: a comparison of Canada and the United States", Working paper no. 3691 (NBER, Cambridge, MA).

Borjas, G. and B. Bratsberg (1993), "Who leaves? The outmigration of the foreign-born", Mimeo. (University of California at San Diego, San Diego, CA).

Borjas, G. and S. Bronars (1991), "Immigration and the family", Journal of Labor Economics 9: 123–148.

Borjas, G. and S. Trejo (1991), "Immigrant participation in the welfare system", Industrial and Labor Relations Review 44: 195–211.

Borjas, G. and S. Trejo (1992), "National origin and immigrant welfare recipiency", Working paper no. 4029 (NBER, Cambridge, MA).

Borjas, G., R. Freeman and K. Lang (1991), "Undocumented Mexican-born workers in the United States: how many, how permanent", in: J.M. Abowd and R.B. Freeman, eds., Immigration, trade, and the labor market (University of Chicago Press, Chicago, IL) pp. 77–100.

Butcher, K. and D. Card (1991), "Immigration and wages: evidence from the 1980s", American Economic Review 82: 292–296.

Card, D. (1990), "The impact of the Mariel boatlift on the Miami labor market", Industrial and Labor Relations Review 40: 382–393.

Carrington, W.S. and P. deLima (1994), "Large-scale immigration and labor markets: an analysis of the retornados and their impact on Portugal", Unpublished working paper (Johns Hopkins University, Baltimore, MD).

Chiswick, B. (1978a), "The effect of Americanization on the earnings of foreign born men", Journal of Political Economy 86: 897–921.

Chiswick, B. (1978b), "A longitudinal analysis of the occupational mobility of immigrants", in: B.D. Dennis, ed., Proceedings of the 30th Annual Winter Meetings (Industrial Relations Research Assocation, Madison, WI) pp. 20–27.

Chiswick, B. (1980), "The earnings of white and coloured male immigrants in Britain", Economica 47: 81–87.

Chiswick, B.R. (1986), "Is the new immigration less skilled than the old?", Journal of Labor Economics 4: 168–192.

Chiswick, B. (1991), "Speaking, reading, and earnings among low-skilled immigrants", Journal of Labor Economics 9: 149–170.

Chiswick, B. (1993), "Hebrew language usage: determinants and effects on earnings among immigrants in Israel", Mimeo. (University of Illinois at Chicago, Chicago, IL).

Chiswick, B. and P. Miller (1992), "Language in the immigrant labor market", in: B. Chiswick, ed., Immigration, language, and ethnicity: Canada and the United States (AEI Press, Washington, DC).

Chiswick, B. and P. Miller (1993), "The endogeneity between language and earnings: an international analysis", Journal of Labor Economics, in press.

David, P.A. (1974), "Fortune, risk, and the microeconomics of migration", in: P.A. David and M.W. Reder, eds., Nations and households in economic growth (Academic Press, New York).

Davis, S. (1992), "Cross-country patterns of change in relative wages", in: 1992 NBER macroeconomic annual (MIT Press, Cambridge, MA).

DeFreitas, G. (1981), "Occupational mobility among recent black immigrants", Proceedings of the Thirty-third Annual Winter Meetings (Industrial Relations Research Association, Madison, WI) pp. 41–47.

Douglas, P. (1919), "Is the new immigration more unskilled than the old?", Journal of the American Statistical Association, 393–403.

Duleep, H.O and M.C. Regets (1992), "The elusive concept of immigrant quality", Mimeo.

Ethier, W. (1986), "Illegal immigration: the host-country problem", American Economic Review 76: 56–71.

Filer, R. (1992), "The impact of immigrant arrivals on migratory patterns of native workers", in: G. Borjas and R. Freeman, eds., Immigration and the workforce: economic consequences for the United States and source areas (University of Chicago Press, Chicago, IL).

Flug, K. and N. Kasir (1993), "The absorption of immigrants in the labor market", Mimeo. (Research Department, Bank of Israel).

Friedberg, R. (1992), "The labor market assimilation of immigrants in the United States: the role of age at arrival", Mimeo. (Brown University, Providence, RI).

Funkhouser, E. (1992), "Mass emigration, remittances, and economic adjustment: the case of El Salvador in the 1980s", in: G. Borjas and R. Freeman, eds., Immigration and the workforce: economic consequences for the United States and source areas (University of Chicago Press, Chicago, IL) pp. 135–176.

Glazer, N. and D. Moynihan (1963), Beyond the melting pot: the Negroes, Puerto Ricans, Jew, Italians, and Irish of New York City (MIT Press, Cambridge, MA).

Goldin, C. (1993), "The political economy of immigration restriction in the United States, 1890–1921", Working paper no. 4345 (NBER, Cambridge, MA).

Greenwood, M. (1983), "The economics of mass migration from poor to rich countries: leading issues of fact and theory", American Economic Review 73: 173–177.

Greenwood, M.J. and J.M. McDowell (1986), "The factor market consequences of US immigration", Journal of Economic Literature 24: 1738–1772.

Gregory, R.G., R. Anstie and E. Klug (1991), "Why are low-skilled immigrants in the United States poorly paid relative to their Australian counterparts?", in: J.M. Abowd and R.B. Freeman, eds., Immigration, trade, and the labor market (University of Chicago Press, Chicago, IL) pp. 385–406.

Grossman, J. (1982), "The substitutability of natives and immigrants in production", Review of Economics and Statistics 64: 596–603.

Hamermesh, D.S. (1986), "The demand for labor in the long run", in: O. Ashenfelter and R. Layard, eds., Handbook of labor economics, Vol. 1 (Elsevier, Amsterdam) pp. 429–471.

Heckman, J. (1978), "Dummy endogenous variables in a simultaneous equation system", Econometrica 46: 931–959.

Heckman, J. (1979), "Sample selection bias as a specification error", Econometrica 47: 153–161.

Hicks, J.R. (1963), The theory of wages, 2nd edn. (Macmillan, London).

Hunt, J. (1992), "The impact of the 1962 repatriates from Algeria on the French labor market", Industrial and Labor Relations Review 45: 556–572.

IC (Immigration Canada) (1992), Immigration statistics (Minister of Supply and Services, Ottawa, Canada).

International Labor Organization (1980), Migrant workers: summary of reports on Conventions Nos. 97 and 143, and Recommendations Nos. 86 and 151, International Labor Conference, 66th Session, Information and Reports on the Application of Conventions and Recommendations (ILO, Geneva).

Jasso, G. and M.R. Rosenzweig (1982), "Estimating the emigration rates of legal immigrants using administrative and survey data", Demography 19: 279–291.

Jasso, G. and M.R. Rosenzweig (1986), "Family reunification and the immigration multiplier: US immigration law, origin-country conditions, and the reproduction of immigrants", Demography 23: 291–311.

Juhn, C., K. Murphy and B. Pierce (1993), "Wage inequality and the rise in returns to skill", Journal of Political Economy 101: 410–442.

Kossoudji, S. (1988), "English language ability and the labor market opportunities of Hispanic and East Asian immigrant men", Journal of Labor Economics 6: 205–228.

LaLonde, R. and R. Topel (1991a), "Labor market adjustments to increased immigration", in: J.M. Abowd and R.B. Freeman, eds., Immigration, trade, and the labor market (University of Chicago Press, Chicago, IL).

LaLonde, R. and R. Topel (1991b), "Immigrants in the American labor market: quality, assimilation, and distributional effects", American Economic Review 81: 297–302.

LaLonde, R. and R. Topel (1992), "The assimilation of immigrants in the US labor market", in: R. Freeman and G. Borjas, eds., Immigration and the workforce: economic consequences for the United States and source areas (University of Chicago Press, Chicago, IL).

McManus, W. (1985), "Labor market costs of language disparity: an interpretation of Hispanic earnings differences", American Economic Review 75: 818–827.

McManus, W., W. Gould and F. Welch (1983), "Earnings of Hispanic men: the role of English language proficiency", Journal of Labor Economics 1: 101–130.

Meisenheimer, J. (1992), "How do immigrants fare in the US labor market", Monthly Labor Review, December: 3–19.

Mincer, J. (1978), "Family migration decisions", Journal of Political Economy 86: 749–773.

Minister for Immigration (1992), "Local government and ethnic affairs", Media release MPS 28/92 (Parliament House, Canberra, ACT 2500, Hon Gerry Hand, MP).

Pischke, J.-S. (1992), "Assimilation and the earnings of guestworkers in Germany", Mimeo. (Zentrum für Europäische Wirtschaftsforschung).

Ramos, F. (1992), "Outmigration and return migration of Puerto Ricans", in: G. Borjas and R. Freeman, eds., Immigration and the workforce: economic consequences for the United States and source areas (University of Chicago Press, Chicago, IL) pp. 135–176.

Reder, M. (1963), "The economic consequences of increased immigration", Review of Economics and Statistics 45: 221–230.

Schmidt, C.M. (1992), "Country-of-origin differences in the earnings of German immigrants", Mimeo. (University of Munich, Munich).

Simon, J. (1984), "Immigrants, taxes, and welfare in the United States", Population and Development Review 10: 55–70.

Simon, J. (1989), The economic consequences of immigration (Basil Blackwell, Cambridge).

Sjaastad, L.A. (1962), "The costs and returns of human migration", Journal of Political Economy 70(S): 80–93.

Stark, O. (1991), The migration of labor (Basil Blackwell, Cambridge).

Stark, O. (1994), "Frontier issues in international migration", Presented at the Annual Bank Conference on Development Economics, World Bank, Mimeo. (Hebrew University of Jerusalem, Jerusalem).

Tainer, E. (1988), "English language proficiency and the determination of earnings among foreign-born men", Journal of Human Resources 23: 108–122.

Tienda, M. and L. Jensen (1986), "Immigration and public assistance participation: dispelling the myth of dependency", Social Science Research 15: 372–400.

Tienda, M., G. Borjas, H. Cordero-Guzman, K. Neuman and M. Romero (1991), "The demography of legalization: insights from administrative records of legalized aliens", Final report to ASPE (Department of Human Services).

Todaro, M.P. (1969), "A model of labor migration and urban unemployment in less developed countries", American Economic Review 59: 138–148.

US INS (US Department of Labor, Immigration and Naturalization Service) (1990), Annual report of the immigration and naturalization service (US Government Printing Office, Washington, DC).

Wadensjö, E. (1994), "The earnings of immigrants in Sweden", Mimeo. (University of Stockholm, Stockholm).

Warren, R. and J. Passel (1987), "A count of the uncountable: estimates of undocumented aliens counted in the 1980 United States census", Demography 24: 375–393.

Warren, R. and J.M. Peck (1980), "Foreign-born emigration from the United States", Demography 17: 71–84.

Zimmermann, K. (1994), "European migration: push and pull", Presented at the Annual Bank Conference on Development Economics, World Bank, Mimeo. (University of Munich, Munich).

Chapter 15

INTERNATIONAL MIGRATION AND INTERNATIONAL TRADE

ASSAF RAZIN and EFRAIM SADKA*

Tel-Aviv University

Contents

1. Introduction   852
2. Substitution and complementarity between labor mobility and good mobility   856
   2.1. Substitution   857
   2.2. Complementarity   861
3. Substitution and complementarity between labor mobility and capital mobility   865
4. Global population dispersion: the efficient volume of migration   868
5. Gains and losses from international migration   871
6. Migration in the presence of wage rigidity   873
   6.1. The wage flexibility benchmark   873
   6.2. Rigid wages   878
7. Income distribution and migration   880
8. Conclusion   884
Appendix   885
References   886

*We gratefully acknowledge the competent research assistance of Bernhard Bohm and Mischa Schamschule from the Institute for Advanced Studies in Vienna, Austria. We also thank Juan Dolado, Riccardo Faini, Elhanan Helpman, T.N. Srinivasan, Oded Stark and Andreas Woergoetter for useful comments and suggestions. Some of the work on this chapter was carried out while the authors were visiting at the Institute for Advanced Studies, Vienna, and the Institute for International Economic Studies, University of Stockholm.

Handbook of Population and Family Economics. Edited by M.R. Rosenzweig and O. Stark
© *Elsevier Science B.V., 1997*

1. Introduction

The study of international trade and international migration occupies a relatively small part of the traditional economic analysis. Conventionally, international trade theory tends to ignore international migration, which essentially changes the distribution and the size of national communities. Similarly, the literature on international migration typically abstracts from the effects of labor migration on international flows of goods, services and capital and often considers the movement of labor akin to the movement of goods. This chapter, which combines elements from these seemingly disjoint parts of the literature and presents them in a consistent analytical framework, lays the ground for an integration of the two disciplines into a unified treatment.

International migration is driven by a multitude of factors: social, political, religious, ethnic and economic. Some of these elements mainly push people to migrate from their country of origin (e.g. religious persecution) and others mainly attract the migrants to their country of destination (as the "land of unlimited opportunities"). Occasionally, countries impose strict restrictions on the exodus of people (e.g. the former Communist bloc countries). And, very often potential destination countries impose strict entry requirements (quotas and others, as is the case with the United States and Canada). The observed patterns of international migration reflect a combination of these factors and barriers.

In Razin and Sadka (1995a) we provide a brief survey of the major migration patterns over the last two centuries. The flows of people from the "old world" of Europe to the "new world" of the Americas and Australia in the second half of the nineteenth century and early in the twentieth century stand out as major international migration waves that accelerated over time. Great Britain has been a primary source of the registered out-migration from Europe throughout this period although its share petered down gradually. Germany supplied a sizable share of the migrants early in this period but its share came down to almost zero at the end. The decline in emigration from Germany may be explained by the 1871 unification of Germany, which brought about national health insurance (Krankenversicherung) in 1883, and old age benefits (Pensionsversicherung) in 1889. Interestingly enough, the Italian unification which was not accompanied by such provisions was associated with acceleration of emigration. Portugal, Spain and Italy started out very low, but then eventually became major suppliers at the end of the nineteenth century and the beginning of the twentieth century.

Among the leading destination countries for the European migrants, the United States stands out as the largest destination country throughout that period, absorbing between approximately 60 to 80 percent of the registered migrants.[1] In fact, net mi-

---

[1] Hatton and Williamson (1992) provide the following historical perspective: "In the century following 1820, an estimated 60 million Europeans set sail for labor-scarce New World destinations. About three fifths of these went to the United States. By comparison, earlier migration from labor-abundant Europe had been a mere trickle and other nineteenth century emigrations from, for example, India and China were also relatively modest. The only comparable intercontinental migration was the black slaves from Africa to the

gration contributed a significant share of the total growth of the white population in the United States. For instance, net migration accounted for between 32 and 43% of the total increase in the white population during 1880–1910. Nevertheless, the combined share of the United States and Canada, another significant destination country declined while that of South America and Australia rose. After World War II, both the magnitude and the source composition of immigration to the United States changed significantly. The share of Europe as an origin of migrants declined significantly. In its stead, Latin American and Asian countries became a major source.

In the period after World War II, a clear increase can be detected both in inter-European migration (especially from the relatively poor South to the relatively rich North) and in migration from North African and Mediterranean countries to Europe. At the receiving end, the developed countries of North-West Europe stand out. In 1950, France had the largest absolute number of foreigners (1.76 million). In 1983, with the Federal Republic of Germany at this time already well established as an economic superpower, migrants were mostly attracted to Germany. (Percentage-wise though, Luxembourg had always been exceptionally high in this regard.) Noteworthy is the fact that in the North-West European countries, except for France and the Netherlands, the percentage of foreigners in employment is higher than in the population. This arises from foreigners having, on average, fewer dependents than the native-born.

With the new world order that followed the collapse of Communism, flows of migrants can be expected from the former Eastern bloc to Western countries which are willing to accept migrants (such as some European countries and Israel). This kind of migration very much resembles the South-North (and West) migration in post World War II Europe.

Intertwined with international migration is international trade. The international migration of people can often substitute for both international movements of capital and international trade in goods and services. However, in many important cases international migration is a complement to international flows of capital or commodities. Although economic motives can by themselves generate various patterns and magnitudes of international flows, political conflicts and ethnic rifts quite often play a key role. Historically, political factors served to halt trade among hostile nations and drive them on a track of economic self-sufficiency (autarky) in preparation for military conflicts.

Over the years, one can detect a clear trend of growth in the volume of international trade. This may be due to several factors:
- technological improvements lowered both the money and time costs of transportation;

Americas and the Caribbeans. Indeed, it was only in the 1840s that the movement of Europeans into North America exceeded the Africans, and it was not until the 1880s that the cumulative total of Europeans exceeded African immigration".

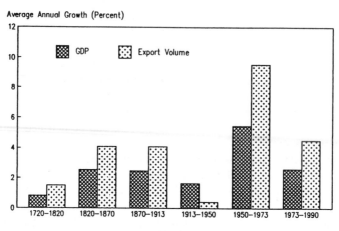

Fig. 1.

– output growth reinforced international trade (especially, via intra-industry trade);
– the public at large and policy-makers in particular have become increasingly aware of the mutual gains from trade and have gradually been pushing for removal of trade barriers.

The surplus in the current account of the balance-of-payments, which is equal to net trade flows (i.e., exports minus imports) obviously cannot measure the volume of trade. For instance, when trade is balanced (and the surplus is nil), it obviously does not follow that there is no trade. For this reason, it is customary to measure the volume of trade by gross trade flows, i.e., by the *sum* of exports *and* imports. Alternatively, one can look just at exports *or* imports in order to infer trends over time or to compare different countries. (Of course, for the world as a whole, either the sum of exports or the definitionally equal sum of imports can serve as a measure).

Fig. 1 depicts the growth rates of exports, and gross domestic products (GDP) for the six major industrialized countries, from the eighteenth century on. Throughout this period, exports grew much faster than GDP, except for the period covering the two world wars, which was much influenced by political conflicts and protectionist attitudes. Note that high growth rates of exports are accompanied by high growth rates of GDP. For instance, the exceptionally high growth rate of GDP in the 1950s and 1960s (about 6% annually) occurred when exports grew at an even higher rate (about 10% annually). In contrast, the inter world war period is marked by a very low growth rate of both exports and GDP. This casual observation may suggest a positive interaction between trade liberalization and economic growth.

Until the last two decades, international capital flows had ups and downs. There were quite sizable flows during the gold standard period. The international flows of capital shrank during the two world wars period and the Bretton-Woods era of fixed exchange rates and capital controls that began in 1944 and lasted until 1973. More recently, with the liberalization of the international capital markets, international capital movements picked up considerably. In economies that are open to international flows of capital, *net* capital flows are accounted for by the difference between national saving and investment. Net capital flows are measured by the current account deficit (or surplus) in the balance of payments: net exports – by surpluses; and net imports – by deficits. Of course, net capital flows (or current account deficits and surpluses) understate the scope of international capital movements. They do not fully measure flows of capital into and out of a country. Typically, removal of barriers to international capital movements is followed by a *two-way* increase in capital flows. These are not necessarily reflected in the *net* exports or imports of capital.

The volume of international capital movements is commonly measured by the *sum* of capital exports and capital imports and is divided by GNP (or GDP). Considering the seven major industrial countries (the G-7) one can detect a dramatic increase in capital movements from the early 1970s through the late 1980s. In the United Kingdom and Japan, gross capital flows (as percentages of GNP) rose about fivefold during the two decades: from 6.4 to 32.6 in the United Kingdom, and from 3.3 to 19.5 in Japan. In the United States and Germany, the ratio of gross capital flows to GDP more than doubled during the period. In fact, in recent years the degree of integration of capital markets (as measured by gross capital movements) has grown more rapidly than the degree of integration of goods markets, as measured by the gross volume of trade in goods and services (that is, exports plus imports). At the same time, cross-country interest-rate differentials, among the G-7 and other countries which liberalized international capital flows, narrowed down considerably.

These stylized facts and trends serve as a background for the topics and issues examined in this chapter, which is organized as follows. Section 2 explains how different trade models account for either substitution or complementarity patterns between labor mobility and commodity trade, and what are the key elements in the models responsible for the contrasting predictions on the direction and magnitude of international trade. In Section 3 we analyze some dissimilarities between capital mobility and labor mobility, which can break down the substitution between the flows of labor and capital driven by the underlying international distribution of relative endowments. The remaining sections deal with a variety of related normative issues associated with migration. We begin in Section 4 with a benchmark framework in which all people are treated alike. This framework enables us to characterize the global dispersion of population. Section 5 identifies welfare gains and losses to the major participants in the migration process. Continuing with this line of inquiry the last two sections analyze some important anti-migration forces. Section 6 considers a two-skill model within which we examine the role of wage rigidity in explaining resistance towards in-migration. Section 7 considers the social burden brought by migration onto the modern welfare state, as another important anti-migration force. Section 8 concludes our survey.

2. Substitution and complementarity between labor mobility and good mobility

Autarky results in different countries typically having different commodity and factor prices. Think of protectionist pre World War II Western Europe vis-à-vis the American market; or the former East-European bloc vis-à-vis the industrialized countries. For instance, Table 1 highlights the wage gap between Eastern Europe (with hourly wages below 1 US$) and the industrialized countries (with hourly wages typically above 10 US$). If barriers to labor mobility are removed or eased up, workers can be expected to migrate from low-wage countries (e.g., Eastern Europe) to high-wage countries (e.g. Western Europe).

A crucial question for migration policy is whether trade in goods can narrow the wage gap, thereby reducing pressures for labor migration. Put differently: is trade in goods a substitute or a complement to labor mobility?

To analyze the interaction between trade in goods and labor mobility, we shall employ a standard international trade model with two factors (labor and capital), two goods (exportables and importables), and possibly different technologies in the two

Table 1
Wage gaps and population (1990)

	Wage per hour (US$)	Population (millions)
Eastern Europe		
Poland	0.7	38
Hungary	0.7	11
Czechoslovakia	0.8	16
Bulgaria	0.2	9
Rumania	0.6	23
Yugoslavia	1.1	24
USSR (European)	0.9	222
Eastern Europe (total)	0.9	343
Industrialized countries		
Germany (West)	11	61
France	8	56
Italy	11	57
UK	8	57
EC (total)	9	340
EFTA (total)	13	25
Western Europe (total)	10	365
USA	13	250
Canada	13	27
Australia	14	17

Source: Layard et al. (1992).

countries.[2] Our starting point will be a set of assumptions that nullify all forces that can generate either commodity trade, or labor mobility. By relaxing these assumptions, one at a time, we allow room for commodity trade and incentives for labor mobility. We can then also study their interaction. Following Markusen (1983), we initially assume that:

(i) The two countries have the same relative endowments of capital and labor.
(ii) The two countries have the same technologies.

We further assume that:

(iii) There are constant returns-to-scale in production.
(iv) The two countries have the same homothetic preferences.

Under these assumptions, there will be no commodity trade between the two countries and no cross-country factor price differentials that can lead to international factor mobility.

2.1. Substitution

We relax assumption (i) and assume that the two countries differ only in their relative factor endowments. Suppose initially that labor and capital are internationally immobile. Let there be two goods – exportables (x) and importables (y), two factors – labor (L) and capital (K), and two countries – home (H) and foreign (F). This, of course, is the familiar Heckscher–Ohlin–Samuelson model of international trade. Suppose, for concreteness, that good x is more labor-intensive than good y (in both countries, since they have identical technologies). By this we mean that when both industries are faced with the same factor prices, industry x will employ a higher labor/capital ratio than industry y. Formally

$$\frac{a_{Lx}}{a_{Kx}} > \frac{a_{Ly}}{a_{Ky}} \tag{1}$$

for all factor price ratios, where a_{ij} is the unit input requirement of factor i in the production of good j, and where $i = L,K$ and $j = x,y$. By the factor price ratio we mean the ratio of wage to the rental price of capital.

Suppose that country H is more abundant in labor (relative to capital) than country F, that is

$$\frac{\overline{L}^{H}}{\overline{K}^{H}} > \frac{\overline{L}^{F}}{\overline{K}^{F}}, \tag{2}$$

---

[2] See Ethier (1985) for an earlier survey of these issues.

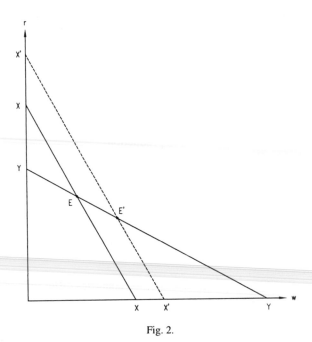

Fig. 2.

where $\bar{L}^i$ and $\bar{K}^i$ are the endowments of labor and capital, respectively, in country i, and where $i = $ H,F.

Suppose that good y is the numeraire with its price set to unity in both countries and denote by p^i, r^i and w^i the price of good x, the rental price of capital and the wage rate in country i, respectively, where $i = $ H,F.

First, observe the quite intuitive result due to Stolper and Samuelson (1941): an increase in the wage–rental ratio (w/r) raises the unit cost of the labor-intensive good (x) relative to the unit cost of the capital-intensive good (y) and must therefore raise the relative price (p) of the labor-intensive good.

To demonstrate graphically this result refer to Fig. 2.[3] For a fixed p, the line XX represents the zero-profit locus for industry x, given by $P = ra_{Kx} + wa_{Lx}$. The slope of this line is a_{Lx}/a_{Kx}. The line YY is the analogous locus for industry y, given by $1 = ra_{Ky} + wa_{Ly}$. Its slope is a_{Ly}/a_{Ky}. The point of intersection between these two loci (point E) yields the equilibrium factor prices for the given price ratio p. Now, if p rises, the zero-profit locus for industry x shifts outward from XX to $X'X'$. The new

[3] This graphic exposition is strictly correct for fixed unit-input-requirement coefficients (the a'_{ij} s). But it provides a linear approximation around the equilibrium factor-price point also for variable unit-input-requirements.

factor-price equilibrium is a point E', in which the wage rate (w) is higher and the rental price of capital (r) is lower. Conversely, an increase in w/r raises p.

Now, consider the autarky equilibrium in the two countries. Since country H has a higher relative endowment of labor than country F, it is straightforward to show (see below) that under autarky, labor will be relatively less expensive in country H, i.e.

$$\frac{\overline{w}^H}{\overline{r}^H} < \frac{\overline{w}^F}{\overline{r}^F}, \tag{3}$$

where $\overline{w}^i$ and $\overline{r}^i$ are the autarky prices of labor and capital, respectively, in country i and where $i = $ H,F. Hence, by the Stolper–Samuelson theorem, the autarkic price of good x is lower in country H than in country F. Thus, when trade is allowed, good x will be exported from country H to country F until commodity prices are equalized across countries. Of course, good y will be exported from country F to country H. The common equilibrium price of x in both countries will be higher than the autarkic price of x in country H and lower than the autarkic price of x in country F. This is the essence of the Heckscher–Ohlin–Samuelson proposition.

To complete the proof of the Heckscher–Ohlin–Samuelson proposition, it remains to show that Eq. (2) implies Eq. (3), that is: the country with the higher initial labor–capital ratio will have, under autarky, a lower wage–rental ratio. This result follows from the Rybczynski proposition which asserts that at a given factor price ratio, a higher labor–capital endowment ratio results in a higher x to y output ratio (where good x is more labor-intensive than good y). To see this refer to Fig. 3. The line LL describes the locus of output pairs (x, y) that yield full employment of labor, given by $\overline{L} = xa_{Lx} + ya_{Ly}$. The slope of this line is a_{Lx}/a_{Ly}. Similarly, the line KK represents full employment of capital, given by $\overline{K} = xa_{Kx} + ya_{Ky}$. Its slope is a_{Kx}/a_{Ky}. The equilibrium pair of outputs is at point E. Now, suppose $\overline{L}$ rises. This shifts outward the labor full-employment line from LL to $L'L'$. The new pair of equilibrium outputs is point E' with a higher x/y ratio. Hence, at the given autarky price ratios of country F (namely, $\overline{w}^F/\overline{r}^F$ and $\overline{p}^F$), country H has an excess supply of good x and an excess demand for good y (because demands in the two countries are derived from the same homothetic preferences). This implies that at an autarky equilibrium in country H we must have

$$\overline{p}^H < \overline{p}^F \quad \text{and} \quad \overline{w}^H/\overline{r}^H < \overline{w}^F/\overline{r}^F.$$

Thus, we have shown that Eq. (2) implies Eq. (3).

One can also calculate the *factor content* of the trade in goods. Denote by Q_i^j and C_i^j, respectively, the output and the consumption of good $i = x,y$ in country $j = $ H,F. This concept refers to the implicit net import of labor and capital embodied in the net import of goods x by a country. Specifically, denote by M_L^H and M_K^H, respectively, the

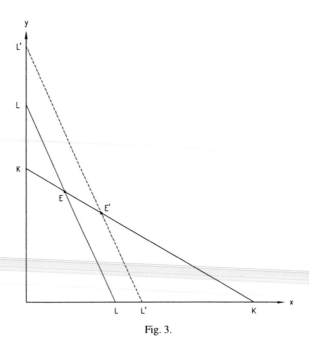

Fig. 3.

net labor and capital imported by country H from country F. One can show (see the Appendix) that

$$M_L^H = s^H(\overline{L}^H + \overline{L}^F) - \overline{L}^H \tag{4}$$

and

$$M_K^H = s^H(\overline{K}^H + \overline{K}^F) - \overline{K}^H, \tag{5}$$

where s^H is the share of country H in world-wide income.

Eqs. (4) and (5) give a simple measure of the factor content of trade which depends only on initial factor endowments and the cross-country distribution of world income. Since country H exports good x which is labor-intensive and imports good y which is capital-intensive, the factor content of its net imports follows a similar pattern: the labor component is negative while the capital component is positive. That is, country H implicitly exports labor and imports capital via its net imports of goods. This measure can also be empirically computed.

The summary of the key proposition derived from this trade model, known as the Heckscher–Ohlin–Samuelson proposition, is that in the absence of international factor mobility, each country will export the good which is intensive in its abundant factor; and that goods mobility equalizes not only commodity prices but also factor prices across countries. Thus, when free commodity trade takes place, it will at the same time nullify any incentive for factors to move from one country to another.

Now suppose that commodity trade is not allowed. In this case, factor mobility can fully substitute for commodity trade. In the above set-up, labor from the labor-abundant country (country H) will be employed in country F and/or capital will move in the opposite direction until factor prices are equalized. It then follows from the Stolper–Samuelson proposition, that commodity prices will also be equalized across countries. In this case, commodity trade becomes redundant (see Mundell, 1957). In fact, using the measure of factor content of trade, we can calculate the magnitude of the factor mobility that is needed to substitute for trade in goods. The magnitude of this mobility is given by Eqs. (4) and (5) which describes the implicit factor content which is embodied in the trade in goods.

In both cases, with either commodity trade and no factor mobility, or factor labor mobility and no commodity trade, the *same* international allocation of consumption obtains (even though patterns of production and trade differ). Thus, if the only difference between the two countries lies in their relative labor abundance, then commodity trade and labor (or capital) mobility are perfect substitutes. Thus, when both free commodity trade and factor mobility are possible, there is a complete indeterminancy between the two modes of international flows.

2.2. Complementarity

Let us now reinstate assumption (i) about identical relative endowments across countries, but relax assumption (ii). That is, suppose that technologies are not identical. For simplicity and concreteness, suppose that country H has a more productive technology for producing good x than country F, in a Hicks-neutral sense, that is,

$$G_x^H(K_x, L_x) = \alpha G_x^F(K_x, L_x), \quad \alpha > 1, \tag{6}$$

and that the technologies for producing y are identical, that is,

$$G_y^H(K_y, L_y) = G_y^F(K_y, L_y), \tag{7}$$

where G_j^i is the production function of good j in country i, and where $j = x,y$ and $i = H,F$.

In this case we show that trade in goods does not suffice to equalize factor prices. Indeed, under free trade the wage in the home country, which technologically is superior in the labor-intensive good, is higher than in the foreign country; and the opposite holds true with respect to the rental price of capital:

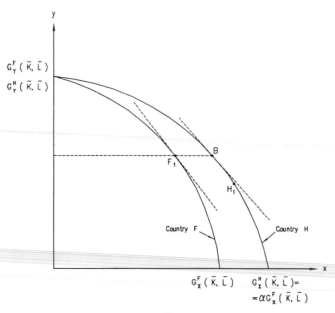

Fig. 4.

$$w^H > w^F \quad \text{and} \quad r^H < r^F. \tag{8}$$

To see this, we plot the production possibility frontiers for the two countries in Fig. 4. Note that the frontier for H is achieved by pulling the frontier for F to the right by the multiplicative factor α. Thus, the slope at B, for instance, is 1^α times the slope at F_1. It is important to notice that F_1 and B represent the same point (say, point F_2) on an identical contract curve in an identical Edgeworth Box of the two countries (Fig. 5). (The two countries have the same Edgeworth Box because they have the same factor endowments; and they have the same contract curve because their technologies differ only by a Hicks-neutral multiplicative coefficient). Thus, if both countries produce at the same point in the Edgeworth Box (say, point F_2 in Fig. 5, corresponding to F_1 and B in Fig. 4), then they cannot have the same commodity price ratio, which is required under free trade (recall that the commodity price ratio is equal to the slope of the production possibility frontier). Hence, with equal commodity prices, required under free trade, country H must produce less y (and more x) than country F. Thus, suppose that country H is at H_1 and H_2 in Figs. 4 and 5, respectively, while country F is at F_1 and F_2 in Figs. 4 and 5, respectively.

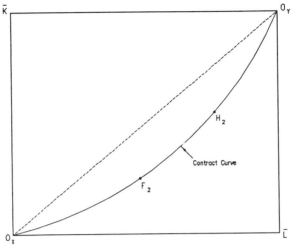

Fig. 5.

Since the two countries have the same (homothetic) demand patterns, while country H produces a higher x to y ratio than country F, it follows that under free trade, country H exports good x (in which she enjoys a superior technology) and imports good y. Given the convex shape of the contract curve, it follows that the factor price ratio w/r is higher in country H than in country F. Since both countries produce good y with the same technology and under the same price (namely, unity), it follows that Eq. (8) holds. Thus, commodity trade does not equalize factor prices.[4] Furthermore, depending on demand patterns and the degree of factor substitution in production, it may well be the case that free commodity trade widens, rather than narrows, the factor price differentials.

Now, suppose that factor mobility (labor and capital) is allowed alongside trade in commodities. Labor will move from country F to country H, and capital will move in the opposite direction. By the Rybczinski proposition, at the initial commodity trade price, there will be an excess supply of good x in country H, and an excess supply of good y in country F. Exports of x from country H, and its imports of y, will further rise. Indeed, country H with its superior technology will specialize in production of good x. Thus, factor mobility reinforces trade in commodities. In this setup of international technological differences in certain industries, factor mobility and commodity trade complement each other.

Alternatively, complementarity between commodity trade and labor mobility can also be generated by external economies-of-scale. Being external to the individual

---

[4] Strictly speaking, factor price equalization can still result from free trade, if the latter leads to complete specialization in at least one of the two countries. We are indebted to Lars Svensson for this point.

firm, economies of scale still preserve perfect competition. Suppose for concreteness that there are external scale economies in the production of good x. If countries differ in absolute size, but have identical relative factor endowments, Markusen (1983) showed that the larger country will export good x. As this good is more labor-intensive, the relative price of labor (w/r) in the free commodity trade equilibrium is higher in country H. Allowing labor to move from country F to country H will further increase the excess supply of good x in country H, via both the Rybczinski effect and the external-scale-economies effect, thereby generating an even higher volume of trade.

In a recent study on East–West migration, Layard et al. (1992) emphasize the role of trade in goods as an alternative to labor migration: "Given the difficulties posed by the prospect of very large-scale migration from East to West, and the risk that such large-scale migration could actually leave worse-off the remaining population in the East, we need to ask what alternatives are available. Ideally, policy should try to bring good jobs to the East *rather than* Eastern workers to the West. International trade ... *can* act as a substitute for migration. A free trade pact that ensures Eastern European countries access to the Western European market is the best single migration policy that could be put in place. In the amazing post-war reconstruction of Western Europe, the openness of the US market was a crucial factor. Western Europe now has the opportunity of providing a similar service to the East."

The gains from trade in goods notwithstanding, we have pointed out that such trade can be a complement to labor mobility. It does not necessarily equalize wages and may even widen the wage gap, thereby generating more incentives for labor migration, in the presence of technological advantage of one country over the other. Note also that the productivity advantage could merely reflect some superior infrastructure (roads, telecommunication systems, ports, energy, etc.) which is certainly the case in the East–West context. Thus, important elements of migration policy should be investment in infrastructure (possibly funded by foreign aid) and direct foreign investment, which tends also to diffuse technology and raise productivity. Once productivity gaps are narrowed down, trade in goods can further alleviate the pressure for labor migration.

In view of the empirical falsification of the factor price equalization theorems,[5] Davis (1992) introduced Hicks-neutral differences in technology across countries, uniform over all industries. He tested the hypothesis concerning convergence of relative industry wages across countries. The evidence found "strongly rejected the hypothesis of increasing uniformity across countries in the relative industry wage structure", despite the ongoing trend of trade liberalization.

---

[5] Leamer (1984: p. 11) reports that a sample of 32 countries' hourly wages in agriculture range from $0.46 in India to $2.04 in Denmark. As he puts it: "Part of these differences might be explained by skill differences, but agricultural wages seem unlikely to include a reward for skills that is sufficiently variable to account for the data... This observation encourages a search for assumptions that do not necessarily imply factor price equalization".

3. Substitution and complementarity between labor mobility and capital mobility

Classical economic setups suggest that factors of production will move, when not constrained, from locations where their marginal product is low to other locations where their marginal product is high. Thus, with frictionless factor mobility, eventually each factor of production generates the same marginal product wherever it is employed. In fact, with identical constant-returns-to-scale technologies everywhere and with two factors (capital and labor), it suffices that one factor is freely mobile to equalize the marginal product of every factor everywhere.

To see this, consider the familiar scissors diagram (Fig. 6), in which the schedules portraying the marginal product of capital for the two countries (home and foreign) that comprise the world economy, are depicted originating at opposite ends. Following MacDougall (1960), suppose that originally the world allocation of capital is at *A*, with the home country having a higher marginal product of capital than the foreign country. Now suppose that labor is internationally immobile but capital is internationally mobile. Capital will then flow from the foreign country to the home country

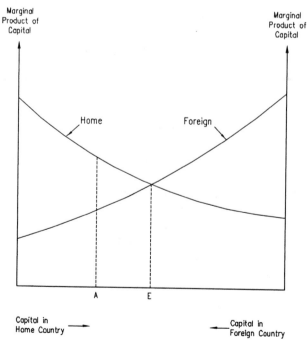

Fig. 6.

until the marginal product of capital is the same in the two countries. This occurs at point E. With constant-returns-to-scale technologies, the marginal product of each factor depends only on the capital–labor ratio. Thus, originally the home country had a lower capital–labor ratio than the foreign country. The subsequent inflow of capital, that equalized the marginal products of capital, brings about an identical capital–labor ratio in the two countries. But this implies that the marginal products of labor are equalized as well. Thus, even if labor were allowed to migrate from one country to another, it will not do so. We can alternatively look at the mobility of labor in the opposite direction (that is, from the home country to the foreign country). By a similar argument, this would lead to equal marginal products of capital, in addition to equal marginal products of labor.

In the real world, intercountry differentials in marginal products are enormous. For instance, the real wage in the United States is about 15 times higher than the real wage in India (see Summers and Heston, 1988). An explanation for the difference, which comes readily to mind, is the marked difference in skills or the human capital between American workers and Indian workers. But after correcting for the skill differences (based on estimates by Krueger (1968)), Lucas (1990) finds that the wage per effective unit of labor (adjusted for human capital) in the United States is still three times higher than the wage per effective unit of labor in India. Obviously, Indian labor can by no means freely enter the United States, so as to eliminate this wage differential. But when labor has a higher marginal product in the United States and the constant-returns-to-scale identical technology assumption largely holds, capital has a higher marginal product in India. According to Lucas's calculations, the marginal product of capital in India should be five times higher than the marginal product of capital in the United States. Why then does not capital flow from the United States and other rich countries into India, or other less developed countries?

To some extent, one may possibly resolve the puzzle by resorting to technological risks (see, for instance, Grossman and Razin, 1984), economic distortions (see, for instance, Bhagwati and Srinivasan, 1983), political and social unrest, and the like. Lucas, however, suggested an alternative explanation based on a mechanism which is central to the new developments in growth theory.[6] According to this explanation, there is no difference in the marginal product of capital between the United States and India. Instead, there is a productivity difference that is generated by an external economy effect of human capital: investment in human capital does not only augment the effective labor supply of the worker who made the investment, but also contributes positively to the productivity of all other workers and capital.

The existence of an external productivity effect suggests that even though capital has no incentive to move from the rich countries to the poor countries, labor nevertheless has an incentive to move from the poor countries with low levels of human capital

---

[6] These developments endogenize the long-run growth rate through dynamic increasing returns (see, for instance, Romer, 1986).

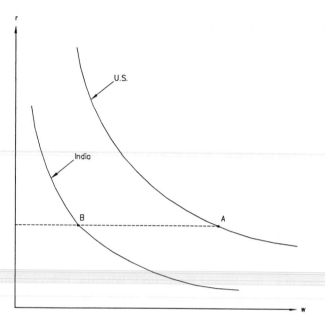

Fig. 7.

to the rich countries with high levels of human capital.[7] Lucas's explanation can be diagrammatically represented via factor-price frontiers drawn in Fig. 7, with the rental price of capital (r) plotted on the vertical axis and the wage rate (w) on the horizontal axis. The external productivity effect moves the factor price frontier outward. Thus, the United States and India can have the same rental price of capital even though Indian wage per effective unit of labor is only one-third of that of the United States. The latter could be at a point such as A on its factor price frontier while the former would be at point B.

The human-capital based model (and particularly the external-productivity effect) is a "bad news" for those who are looking for convergence in long-run productivity levels among countries (see Baumol, 1986). Migration of skilled workers will tend to increase the diversity in the level of per capita income across countries. With fixed (pecuniary) costs of migration (under the same proportional income differentials across countries) skilled labor has a stronger incentive to migrate than unskilled labor, thereby generating larger income diversity. (On the other hand, the time cost of migration is relatively higher for skilled labor, thereby mitigating the incentive to migrate.)

---

[7] A similar observation about the direction of migration is made also by Galor and Stark (1991) in an overlapping generations model with immobile capital.

4. Global population dispersion: the efficient volume of migration

Welfare analysis mandates a distinction between labor mobility and migration. Labor mobility refers to the mobility of a factor of production (indistinguishable from other factors such as capital), without the mobility of the consumption entity embodied in labor. The mobile labor continues to belong to his or her original country even though he or she exports labor services. Thus, labor mobility creates no new welfare issues since the set of people over which the social welfare function is defined does not change as a result of international labor mobility. However, matters differ if labor migration is perceived not merely as an export of labor services but also as a change in the consumption of national communities, because a migrant no longer belongs to the origin country community and becomes a resident in the destination country community.

It is instructive to begin with a benchmark framework in which all people are treated alike. Suppose a country can freely choose the number of its citizens or residents from a global pool of people. What is then the efficient level of migration?

This issue is tantamount to another set of well-dealt issues in the local public finance literature (e.g., Berglas and Pines, 1983; Wildasin, 1986) and also in the economic geography literature (e.g., Krugman, 1991). The simple idea underlying the determination of efficient population size is that there are factors that confer advantages to size and other factors that generate disadvantages to size. An efficient size is obtained when the two groups of factors are balanced. To the first group belong commonly mentioned increasing returns to scale and public goods (that are jointly consumed by all members of the community and hence their cost can be shared). To the second, belong: diminishing marginal productivity of labor due to the existence of some fixed factors of production such as land; costs of transportation from the marketplace or the place of production to the place of consumption and congestion effects in the consumption of public goods or utilization of public inputs.

The interaction between these two groups of factors an be captured by a model in which there is just one force pushing for a larger size and another force pushing in the opposite direction. Suppose that there is a pure public good that generates an advantage to larger size and a fixed factor of production (say, land) that causes labor to have a diminishing marginal product, thereby generating a disadvantage to larger size. To simplify, suppose that all individuals are alike and, in addition to the public good, there is only one other good which is privately consumed. To sharpen the analysis, assume that the world economy can be divided up into any number of countries at negligible cost.

Formally, the efficient population size is obtained by maximizing the common utility level

$$u(G,c), \tag{9}$$

subject to the resource constraint

$$F(T,n) \geq nc + G, \tag{10}$$

where G and c are, respectively, public good consumption and private consumption, $F(\cdot,\cdot)$ is a constant-returns-to-scale production function, T is the fixed endowment of land, and n is the size of population. The resource constraint simply states that total output (namely, $F(T, n)$) must be divided between public good consumption (namely G) and total private consumption (namely nc). The determination of the efficient population size is graphically depicted in Fig. 8. For each given population size (n), we first find the optimal levels of private and public consumption and, consequently, utility. The optimal allocation is, of course, governed by the familiar Lindahl–Samuelson rule which states that the sum over the population of the willingness to pay for the public good (that is, nu_G/u_c, where u_G and u_c are the marginal utilities of public consumption and private consumption, respectively) is equal to the marginal cost of producing the public good (that is, one):

$$nu_G/u_c = 1. \tag{11}$$

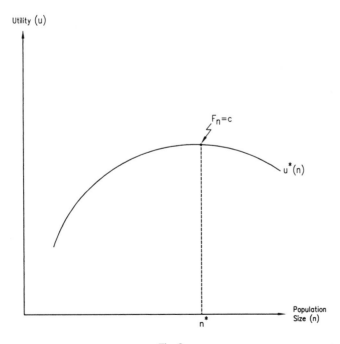

Fig. 8.

The maximized level of utility (for a given n) is now a function of n (namely, $u = u^*(n)$). The curve $u = u^*(n)$ is shown in Fig. 8. Its slope is equal to $u_G(F_n - c)$, where F_n is the marginal product of labor. The explanation for this equality is straightforward: an additional person contributes her marginal product to society, but takes out her private consumption, leaving a net contribution of $F_n - c$ to the rest of the society, expressed by $u_G(F_n - c)$ in utility terms.

Notice that the additional person takes out from the society's consumption only her *private* consumption, because, by definition, she is a free rider on the collectively consumed public good. Since the marginal product is diminishing (due to the fixed endowment of land), then the net contribution to the rest of the society of an additional person must be first positive, and then negative. The efficient population size is obtained when the marginal product of labor equals private consumption. This occurs at point n^* in Fig. 8, where

$$F_n = c. \tag{12}$$

An interesting implication of this rule, which determines the efficient population size, is that each person privately consumes only her marginal product. Thus, the entire land rent is left to finance public consumption. Thus, a country which has an efficient population size, provides public consumption at a level which is fully covered by a 100% tax on land rents (the so-called Henry George rule).[8]

An interesting modification of the model allows the government to distinguish between the native-born population and the migrant population. Suppose that the government wishes to maximize the utility of a representative native-born individual. The would-be migrant will come if and only if the bundle of public good and a private good consumed in the destination country does not yield lower utility than her reservation utility that she enjoys in the source country.

In this case, the efficient level of migration is obtained by maximizing

$$u^v(G, c_v), \tag{13}$$

subject to the resource constraint

$$F(T, n_v + n_M) \geq n_v c_v + n_M c_M + G, \tag{14}$$

and the reservation utility constraint

$$u^M(G, c_M) \geq \bar{u}^M, \tag{15}$$

[8] See George (1914). A modern treatment is provided by Stiglitz (1977).

where u^v is the utility function of a native-born person; u^M is the utility function of a migrant; c_v is the private consumption of a native-born person; c_M is the private consumption of a migrant; $\overline{u}^M$ is the reservation utility of a migrant; n_v is the (fixed) number of native-born persons; n_M is the number of migrants.

The control variables in this simple model are G, c_v, c_M and n_M. In this case, it will still be efficient to attract migrants (by public and private consumption provision) up to the point where the marginal product of a migrant worker is equal to her private consumption, that is,

$$F_n = c_M. \tag{16}$$

Similarly, the Lindahl–Samuelson rule for the efficient provision of public goods still holds:

$$n_v(u_G^v/u_c^v) + n_M(u_G^M/u_c^M) = 1. \tag{17}$$

That is, the sum of the measures of willingness to pay over the *entire* population (native-born individuals and migrants) is equal to the marginal cost of the public good.

The only notable deviation is, however, with respect to the Henry George rule. Consider the case in which the reservation utility of the migrants is low enough, so that at the efficient level of migration they enjoy a lower level of private consumption than do the native-born individuals (that is, $c_M < c_v$). In this case, the government will not tax away all the land rent, but rather leave some of the land rent at the hands of the native-born individuals, so that they can privately consume more than the migrants can consume. We thus conclude that if migrants have a relatively low reservation utility, there is likely to be a stronger constituency advocating migration than if migrants consume as much as the native-born individuals.

5. Gains and losses from international migration

In this section we follow Bhagwati and Srinivasan (1983) in identifying who gains and who loses from international migration and by how much.

The scissors diagram in Fig. 9 describes the allocation of labor between two countries: A Source Country (SC) and a Destination Country (DC). We assume that workers may migrate from one country to another and that migrants own no capital. Suppose that the initial allocation of labor is at point A where the DC marginal product of labor (which is equal to the real wage) is higher than the SC marginal product of labor. If free migration of labor is possible, labor will migrate from the SC to the DC until the marginal products of labor are equalized at point B. The migrants earn a higher wage in the DC. Their net gain is represented by the area *FNMK*. Output in the DC is

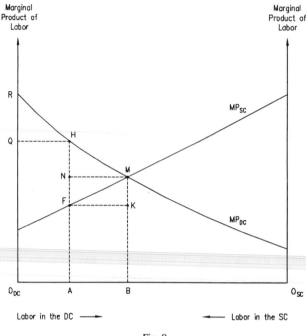

Fig. 9.

increased by the area *AHMB*, of which a sum represented by the area *ANMB* is paid to the migrants in wages. Thus, the net gain to the native-born in the DC is represented by the area *NHM*. Output in the SC falls by the area *AFMB*, of which the sum represented by the area *AFKB* was initially paid in wages to those who migrated. The net loss to the residents of the SC, the so-called "those left behind", is the area *FMK*. Worldwide, there is a positive net gain which is represented by the area *FHM*. But, as we have just seen, not all groups gain. The migrants and native-born in the DC gain, but those left behind in the source country lose. If we distinguish between wage earners and landlords (or capitalists), then native-born wage earners in the DC lose, landlords in the DC gain, the left-behind wage earners in the SC gain and landlords in the SC lose. Evidently, in the DC, native-born wage earners lose less than what the landlords gain, so that a compensation scheme could be devised so as to make both native-born wage earners and landlords better-off. In principle, there exists also a bilateral transfer from the DC to the SC which can make everyone better off. Furthermore, looking only at the gain to the migrants, it still exceeds the loss to those left behind. Therefore, the migrants themselves can compensate (for instance, by remittances) those left behind.

Alternatively, the government in the SC may impose an implicit emigration tax on the migrants. This tax can take the form of denial to entitlement programs that were paid for in the past by the migrants (old age or retirement benefits). In other cases, due to capital and foreign exchange controls, the migrants may not be able to realize the full value of their assets left behind.

Hamilton and Whalley (1984) attempted to quantify the implications of barriers to labor mobility between high-wage and low-wage countries. They point out that the efficiency gains of the removal of immigration barriers are substantial. They suggest that the issue may be much more important to LDCs than the more conventional trade issues raised in the North–South debate.

6. Migration in the presence of wage rigidity

In the preceding section we saw how migration, which typically shifts workers from economies with low productivity of labor to economies with high productivity of labor, can, accordingly, raise global output. We also showed that the destination country stands to gain from immigration, which tends to increase the consumption of its native-born population (output, minus wage payments to migrants). However, certain sectors in the destination country (namely, native-born workers that are a substitute for migrants) actually lose; but there exist certain redistribution mechanisms that can make all sectors in the destination country better off.

Nevertheless, in practice, one may often find a widespread resistance to guest workers or migrants in the destination country. In the remainder of this chapter we highlight two *economic considerations* that may explain the reasons behind such resistance. This section introduces wage rigidity as an anti-migration force. The next section describes how an income distribution system which is typical in a modern welfare state can also create anti-migration forces. These two sections draw on Razin and Sadka (1994, 1995b).

When wages are rigid (due to unionism, search costs, efficiency wage elements, etc.) migration may well lower the *total* share of the native-born population (skilled labor, unskilled labor, capital, etc.) in the domestic output. Furthermore, while with flexible wages we show that the gain from migration is minuscule, with wage rigidity our calculations suggest a substantial loss to the native-born population as a result of migration. Also, with wage rigidity, migration induces a misallocation of investment between human and physical capital.

6.1. The wage flexibility benchmark

Following Saint-Paul (1994), we assume a stylized economy in which there are only two types of labor productivity: "low" and "high". While a high-productivity worker provides one efficiency unit of labor, the low-productivity worker provides only ρ (<1) efficiency units of labor. Every person can acquire education which makes her a high-productivity worker (denoted "skilled" worker). With no education she remains a low-productivity worker (denoted "unskilled" worker). There is a continuum of individuals varying in the cost (c) of acquiring education (due to innate ability or family surroundings). We assume that the distribution of these costs in the native-born population is uniform over the interval $[0, \bar{c}]$. For notational ease, we normalize the size of the native-born population to one.

Each individual can either invest in human capital (through education) or in physical capital (which yields a return r). There exists therefore a cut-off cost level, c^*, such that all those with education-cost below c^* invest in human capital and become skilled workers, while all the rest remain unskilled. Denoting the wage per efficiency unit by w, the cut-off cost level is determined by an equality between the marginal return and marginal opportunity cost (via an alternative investment in physical capital) to education:

$$(1+r)c^* = [(1-u_1) - \rho(1-u_2)]w, \tag{18}$$

where u_i is the unemployment rate among workers of type i (where $i = 1$ denotes "skilled" and $i = 2$ denotes "unskilled"). Notice that in calculating the return to education, one must take into account the differential wage and the probability of attaining employment for skill level i (namely, $1 - u_i$). Note also that unemployment vanishes ($u_1 = u_2 = 0$) with wage flexibility. The symbols u_1 and u_2 are included here in order to better connect with the next subsection which introduces wage rigidity and unemployment.

The proportion (x) of skilled workers in the total population is given by

$$x = c^* / \bar{c}. \tag{19}$$

Therefore, a total of

$$\int_0^{c^*} (c/\bar{c}) \, dc = (c^*)^2 / 2\bar{c} \equiv H \tag{20}$$

is invested in human capital.

Denoting by I the initial endowment of a representative native-born individual, the endogenously determined stock of physical capital (K) is given by

$$K = I - H. \tag{21}$$

Finally, we specify a standard Cobb–Douglas production function for the GDP of this economy with constant returns to scale:

$$Y = AK^{\alpha}L^{1-\alpha}, \tag{22}$$

where

$$L = x(1 - u_1) + \rho(1 - x)(1 - u_2) + \rho m \tag{23}$$

is the input of labor in efficiency units. (Notice that the two types of labor are assumed, for simplicity, to be perfect substitute in production.) The proportion of unskilled migrants in the native-born labor force is denoted by m. Assuming that capital does not depreciate, $Y + K$ is available for consumption at the end of the production process.[9] The wage rate (w) and the return to capital (r) are given by the standard marginal productivity conditions:

$$w = (1 - \alpha)A(K/L)^{\alpha} \tag{24}$$

and

$$r = \alpha A(L/K)^{1-\alpha}. \tag{25}$$

With wage flexibility (the market-clearing case), there is no unemployment, that is, $u_1 = u_2 = 0$. Given the proportion of migrants (m), Eqs. (18)–(25) determine the equilibrium levels of w_F, r_F, c_F^*, x_F, H_F, K_F, Y_F, and L_F as functions of m. (The subscript F stands for the "Flexible" wage case.)

The aggregate consumption of native-born workers (who, by assumption, own all the domestic stock of physical capital) provides an indicator (W) for the welfare of the native-born population. This indicator is our primary concern here. W is equal to GNP (that is, GDP, minus wage payments to foreign labor), plus the underpreciated stock of physical capital. Thus, the change of welfare due to migration is given by

$$\Delta W_F = \Delta Y_F + \Delta K_F - w_F(m)\rho m, \tag{26}$$

where $\Delta Z = Z_F(m) - Z_F(0)$ and $Z_F = W_F, Y_F, K_F$.

Graphically, ΔW can be illustrated with the help of the marginal product of labor schedule in Fig. 10. Accordingly, let the schedule denoted by MP_L describe the marginal product of labor at the pre-migration stock of capital (that is, $K_F(0)$). Suppose for a moment that migration does not change the stocks of physical capital (K_F) and human capital (x_F). In this case we obtain, as in the preceding section, the standard measure of the gains from migration, which is represented by the area of the triangle ABC.

Obviously at this stage there is also a change in the functional distribution of income between capital and labor. The wage rate (w) declines and therefore wage pay-

---

[9] To sharpen the analysis, human capital is assumed to depreciate fully.

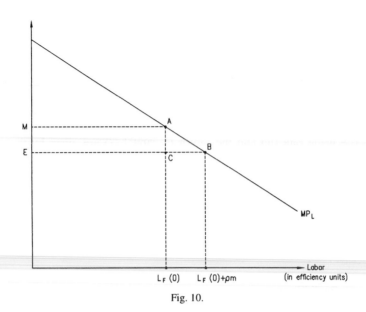

Fig. 10.

ments to native-born workers fall by the area of the rectangle *EMAC*. The return to capital (r) rises and thus the total return to capital increases by the area of the trapezoid *EMAB*. The area of the triangle *ABC* represents the net gain to the native-born population. This *functional* redistribution of income also changes the *size* distribution of income. To see this, notice that the unskilled workers own more physical capital than the skilled workers because all have the same initial endowment but the unskilled workers retain all of their initial endowment in the form of physical capital, while the skilled workers invest part of it in human capital. Also, within the group of skilled workers, the more able workers (those with a lower cost of education, c) own more physical capital than the less able workers. Accordingly, the curve *ABEF* in Fig. 11 depicts the ownership of physical capital as a function of the individual cost of acquiring education (c). Thus, while the decline in the wage rate (w) affects the labor income of all native-born workers in the same proportion, the rise in the return to physical capital (r) has a differential effect on the native-born workers according to their ownership of physical capital, as described in Fig. 11.

Now let the stocks of physical and human capital adjust to the change in factor prices. Since the wage per an efficiency unit of labor falls, the return to human capital falls as well and therefore investment is shifted from human capital to physical capital. As a result, the MP_L curve in Fig. 9 rises and the supply of effective labor falls. The additional adjustment must raise the total gain from migration (over the standard measure of gain), accruing to *both* native-born individuals *and* migrants because the

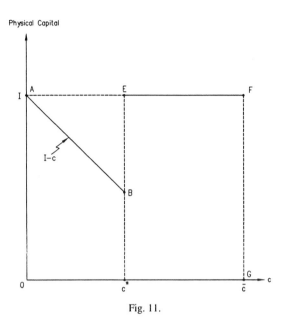

Fig. 11.

underlying competitive allocation is Pareto-efficient (for every exogenously given level of migration).

However, the gain to the native-born workers which is the focus of our attention here (as measured by Eq. (26)) may actually fall by this adjustment in the stocks of physical and human capital, because of the familiar terms-of-trade effect. The initial (pre-adjustment) decline in w lowers the return to human capital and increases the return to physical capital. As a result, the induced adjustment in the allocation of investment raises the stock of physical capital and lowers the stock of human capital. Consequently, the ratio of physical capital to labor (in efficiency units) rises and w rises as well. Thus, the capital stock adjustments lead to a deterioration in the terms of the trade of the destination country; that is, the wage paid on imports of labor services (of the migrants) increases. This wage increase may actually more than offset the efficiency gain resulting from the adjustments in the capital stock. Nevertheless, altogether the destination country must gain from migration because the classical gains-from-trade argument is still valid.

Table 2 illustrates the magnitude of the gains from migration. It turns out that the standard gain which accrues to the native-born workers for fixed K, H and x (the familiar triangle *ABC* in Fig. 10) is quite small: A migration of the size of 10% of the native-born population generates a gain to the native-born population amounting to 0.045% of their consumption. The induced shift of investment from human to physical capital actually reduces this gain in our setup, but not by much, to 0.044%.

Table 2
Gains from migration: flexible wages[a,b]

Percentage of migrants in the native-born population	Standard gain	Gain from the reallocation of investment between human and physical capital	Total gain
2	0.0019	−0.0001	0.0018
4	0.0075	−0.0001	0.0074
6	0.0166	−0.0003	0.0163
8	0.0290	−0.0004	0.0286
10	0.0446	−0.0006	0.0440

[a]The gain is measured as a percentage of the aggregate consumption of the native-born population which is equal to $GNP + K$.
[b]The parameter values are: $\alpha = 0.33, \rho = 0.75, \overline{c} = 2, I = 1, A = 1$.

6.2. Rigid wages

Consider now some imperfections in the labor market which prevent wages from fully adjusting downward so as to fully clear the market in the wake of migration. Consequently, migration must create unemployment among the native-born workers. There are quite a few attempts in the literature to model imperfections in the labor market and the reason for persistent unemployment (e.g., Layard and Nickell, 1990; Pissarides, 1990). To sharpen the analysis we make the extreme assumption that wages are frozen at their pre-migration market-clearing levels.

Strictly speaking, it does not matter in this model whether migrants are skilled or unskilled since the various labor types are assumed to be perfect substitutes. All that matters is how much labor in efficiency units has been brought in with migration. Nevertheless, as a matter of interpretation, we assume that the migrants are all unskilled and that they replace only unskilled native-born workers, since skilled workers have typically some advantage in the job market over unskilled workers.

In this case, we have $u_1 = 0$ and w_R is fixed at the pre-migration wage level, that is $w_R = w_F(0)$. (The subscript R stands for the "Rigid" wage model.) Thus, for any given level of m, Eqs. (18)–(25) determine $u_{2R}, r_R, c_R^*, x_R, H_R, K_R, Y_R$ and L_R as functions of m. In essence w and u_2 change roles between the flexible and rigid wage models. In the flexible wage model, $u_2 = 0$ and w is determined by the market-clearing condition in the labor market. In the rigid wage model, w is fixed (at the pre-migration, flexible wage equilibrium level) and u_2 is equal to the excess supply of labor.

Schedule MC in Fig. 12 describes the marginal product of labor for the pre-migration stock of capital ($K_R(0)$). Pre-migration GNP is thus measured by the area $OMCD$. If K and x were fixed, migration will reduce GNP to an amount represented by the area *OMCTA*, creating a loss which is measured by the area of the rectangle *ATCD*. However, since unemployment among the unskilled workers rises, the expected return to education must rise as well (see Eq. (18)). Hence, a chunk of investment switches from physical to human capital. Thus, K must fall and x must rise, which leads to an even further increase in unskilled labor unemployment. The marginal product of labor schedule shifts downward to *NB* and the post-adjustment GNP is measured by the area *ONBGQ*. Thus, the fall in K and the increase in x induce an additional loss in GNP by an amount which is measured by the sum of the areas *NMCB* and *QGTA*. In addition, aggregate consumption of the native-born population falls also by the amount in which K falls. (Recall that aggregate consumption of the native-born population is equal to GNP, plus the undepreciated capital stock owned by the native-born population.)

It is useful to compare the two cases: the flexible and the rigid wage cases. In the former case, the migration per se (even before adjustment in the allocation of investment between human and physical capital) raises the welfare of the native-born population. In the absence of market-distortions, the induced adjustment in the two forms of capital (that is, a shift from human to physical capital resulting from the wage decline) further enhances world-wide efficiency. However, the native-born population may not enjoy any part of this global efficiency gain because it may be more than offset by the deterioration in the terms of trade (that is, the rise of the wage paid to mi-

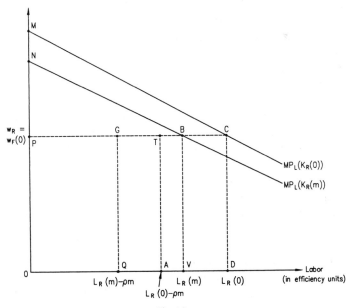

Fig. 12.

Table 3
Losses from migration: rigid wages[a,b]

Percentage of migrants in the native-born population	Loss from substitution of domestic labor by foreign labor	Loss from reallocation of investment between human and physical capital	Total loss
2	0.60	0.07	0.67
4	1.19	0.16	1.35
6	1.79	0.25	2.04
8	2.40	0.33	2.73
10	2.98	0.45	3.43

[a]The loss is measured as a percentage of the aggregate consumption of the native-born population which is equal to $GNP + K$.
[b]The parameter values are: $\alpha = 0.33, \rho = 0.75, \overline{c} = 2, I = 1, A = 1$.

grants). In the case of wage rigidity, however, the migration per se lowered the welfare of the native-born population, since foreign labor merely drove out domestic labor. The induced reallocation of investment from physical to human capital further reduces the welfare of the native-born population. Indeed, the additional investment in human capital is a total loss, in the sense that even a penny of the investment is not recovered. Nevertheless, the private net yield to the individual making the investment is positive, thereby producing the (socially wrong) market incentive for such an investment.

It turns out that the extra loss in the aggregate consumption of the native-born population, due to the reallocation of investment between human and physical capital, relative to the loss that results from the mere substitution of native-born workers by migrants is quite substantial. Table 3 illustrates the relative magnitudes of these two components of the loss. When migrants make up 10% of the native-born population, the loss due to the reallocation of investment is about as much as 1/7th of the total loss. Our sensitivity analysis suggests that when the share of capital in GDP (namely, α) is lowered from 1/3 to 1/4, the standard loss rises from 2.98% of consumption to 3.3% and the total loss rises from 3.43% to 3.97%. Thus, the relative importance of the loss due to the reallocation of investment rises from 1/7th to 1/6th of the total loss. An increase in the productivity gap between skilled and unskilled labor (that is, a decline in ρ) also raises the relative importance of the loss due to the reallocation of investment from physical to human capital: from 14% to 18% of the total loss.

7. Income distribution and migration

Income distribution makes a developed welfare state more attractive to poor migrants from the less developed countries, even when these migrants do not qualify for all the ingredients of the entitlement programs. Therefore, migration has a strong implication for the welfare of the native-born residents in the destination country. A recent study by Borjas (1994) uses the 1970, 1980, and 1990 Public Use Samples of the US Census to trace the evolution of immigrant participation in welfare programs during the past two decades. The data indicate that foreign-born households in the US accounted for 10% of households receiving public assistance by 1990 and for 13% of total cash assistance distributed, even though they constituted only 8% of all households in the US.[10] We now introduce into the model income distribution policies in order to demonstrate these considerations.[11] For the sake of simplicity we consider the flexible wage case only.

Suppose that the government levies an egalitarian income tax. Many studies (for instance, Mirrlees, 1971) suggest that a best egalitarian income tax may be approximated by a linear tax. We therefore introduce into our model an income tax with a flat rate (t) and a lumpsum cash demogrant (β). If all families are of similar size and age structure, the uniform demogrant may capture also free provisions of public services such as health, education, etc.

We continue to assume that the individual labor supply is fixed, so that the income tax per se does not distort the individual labor-supply decisions. However, we do endogenize migration decisions by assuming that migration depends on international net-income differentials. Specifically, suppose that there is a (given) net wage rate (w^*) for unskilled labor in the source country which is below the net income of unskilled workers in the destination country when there is no migration. Unskilled labor then migrates from the source country to the destination country until this gap is closed:

$$(1-t)\rho w + \beta = w^*. \tag{27}$$

An income tax (which is levied also on capital income) typically distorts investment decisions between physical and human capital, because investment in human capital (i.e. the cost of acquiring education) is not tax-deductible, while investment in physical capital is deductible, via the standard depreciation allowances (see Nerlove et al., 1993).[12] In order to focus on migration and income distribution, we therefore ab-

---

[10] LaLonde and Topel (1994) also observe that "because the social welfare system creates a minimum living standard, low-skilled persons expected income in the receiving country may rise above their expected labor market earnings. By contrast, the incentives do not affect the migration rates of high-skilled persons because their high receiving country's earnings would likely make them ineligible for transfer payments". They also look at the 1970 and 1980 US Census data and find support to the contention that immigrants make substantial use of the receiving country's social welfare system.

[11] Wildasin (1991) examines analytically similar issues, but he focuses on the functional distribution of income (between labor and land rent).

[12] In our model physical capital does not at all depreciate, so that no depreciation allowance is warranted.

stract from this distortion by assuming that the cost of education is tax-deductible. Thus, Eq. (18) which determines the cutoff cost level ($c*$), now becomes

$$[1 + r(1-t)]c* - tc* = (1-\rho)w(1-t),$$

which can be rewritten as

$$c*(1+r) = w(1-\rho),$$

so that the tax does not affect investment decisions at all, and we are back to Eq. (18) (with, obviously, $u_1 = u_2 = 0$).

The other equations of the flexible wage model (namely, Eqs. (19)–(25)) remain also intact. However, we have to add now a budget constraint for the government. Since the income tax is levied on both labor and capital income and on both native-born and migrant workers, it follows that the entire GDP (namely, Y) is subject to the tax. As the cost of investing in human capital is tax-deductible and the demogrant is paid to both native-born individuals and migrants, the government budget constraint is

$$t(Y - H) - \beta(1 + m) = 0. \tag{28}$$

The disposable income or consumption of a native-born individual with an education-cost level of c is given by[13]

$$v(c) = \begin{cases} w(1-t) + tc + \beta + (I-c)[1+r(1-t)] & \text{for } c \le c*, \\ \rho w(1-t) + \beta + I[1+r(1-t)] & \text{for } c \ge c*. \end{cases} \tag{29}$$

The government is free to set its income redistribution policy variables (t and β) in any desirable way which is compatible with its budget constraint. To fix ideas, suppose that the government wishes to offset the adverse effect of migration on the disposable income of native-born unskilled individuals. Specifically, suppose that a native-born unskilled worker enjoys a disposable income (or consumption) of $\bar{v}$ when migration is not allowed and the government is inactive ($t = \beta = 0$). Thus, when migration is allowed, the government chooses t and β so as to maintain: $v(c) \ge \bar{v}$ for all $c \ge c*$.

Employing (29), we thus write

$$\rho w(1-t) + \beta + I[1+r(1-t)] = \bar{v}. \tag{30}$$

---

[13] The reader can verify that total consumption of native-born individuals, that is,

$$\int_0^{\bar{c}} v(c)(1/\bar{c}) \, dc,$$

is equal to GNP, that is, $(Y - w*m)$, plus the stock of physical capital, that is, K. This, of course, follows from Walras's Law.

The model is now fully determined. Eqs. (18)–(25), (27), (28) and (30) can be solved for the 11 endogenous variables: w, r, c^*, x, H, K, Y, L, m, t and β. Given the policy that renders unskilled labor indifferent to migration, we simulate the model in order to examine the effect of migration on skilled labor.

The results are described in Fig. 13 where w^* is taken to be just 0.5% below the pre-migration and absent-government wage of unskilled labor in the destination country. (The other parameters in the model are as in Tables 2 and 3). Without migration the cutoff cost-of-education level is $\bar{c}^*$ and the curve $v(c)$ is described by *ABE*. Naturally, given the egalitarian ownership of initial endowment (I), disposable income declines monotonically (and linearly) in the cost of acquiring education for those who choose to acquire education, and then remains flat for unskilled labor of various cost levels (i.e., for $c \geq c^*$). Allowing free migration and a compensating policy towards unskilled labor, the number of migrant workers reaches about 12% of the number of native-born workers. The cutoff cost-of-education level shifts inward to c^*. (This is because w falls and r rises.) The disposable-income schedule becomes *GPBE*. Thus, all the pre-migration skilled workers lose and some of them (those at the high end of the cost-of-education distribution among the pre-migration skilled labor, that is, those with a c-level between c^* and $\bar{c}^*$, choose to become unskilled. Thus, with the present redistribution policy, migration is *Pareto-inferior* for all the native-born population. The reason for this result is straightforward: the migrants are net beneficiaries of the

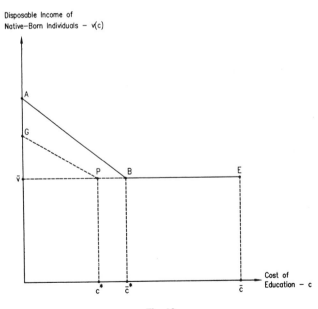

Fig. 13.

tax-transfer system and this is not offset by the traditional gains from trade, shown in Section 6 to be minuscule. Certainly in this case, one can find no Pareto-improving government policy with free migration.

8. Conclusion

Persistent wage differentials are the major driving force behind international migration. These differentials may be either narrowed or (possibly) widened by international trade in goods depending on either international factor endowment differentials or technological gaps across countries. International capital movements (foreign direct investment) can serve as an additional alternative for labor migration. However, when investment in human capital generates external economies which are locked within national borders, this alternative mechanism fades away and capital flows and skilled labor flows will reinforce each other.

When the welfare of both the native-born population and the foreign-born population counts equally in the receiving country, the efficient volume of migration is determined by an equality between the marginal productivity of labor and private consumption. This equality generates the so-called Henry George rule: a 100% tax on land rent and pure profits exactly supports the efficient size of government. A notable deviation from this extreme rule is when the receiving country does not treat the welfare of native-born and foreign-born alike and when the migrant's opportunity cost is relatively low. In this case, the government will not tax away all the land rent so that the native-born will consume more than the migrants. The lower is the migrant's reservation utility, the more likely it is that there will be a larger constituency among the native-born advocating migration.

Evidently, just like any trade activity in well-functioning markets, migration tends to generate gains to all parties involved: the migrants as well as the native-born population. But typically these gains tend to be rather low. However, when the labor market is mal-functioning, migration tends to exacerbate the imperfections in the market. Consequently, it may lead to losses to the native-born population which can be quite sizable. Yet another problem raised by migration is the toll it imposes on the welfare state. Being unable to perfectly exclude migrants from various entitlements' programs and public services, the modern welfare state finds it more costly to run its various programs. These costs can give rise to anti-migration forces, since they cannot be offset by the relatively small gains from trade that are traditionally associated with immigration. These economic considerations may help explain why there is strong resistance to migration. Thus, immigration could be more beneficial to the native-born population when the labor markets are better-functioning and the welfare programs are less comprehensive.

Appendix: Factor content of trade

In this appendix we derive Eqs. (4) and (5) which express the factor content of trade. Denoting by Q_i^j and C_i^j respectively, the output and the consumption of good $i = x, y$ in country $j = H, F$, we can calculate the net import vector of country H by

$$M^H \equiv \begin{Bmatrix} M_x^H \\ M_y^H \end{Bmatrix} = \begin{Bmatrix} C_x^H & -Q_x^H \\ C_y^H & -Q_y^H \end{Bmatrix} \equiv C^H - Q^H.$$

Full-employment in country $i = H, F$ requires that

$$AQ^i \begin{bmatrix} \overline{L}^i \\ \overline{K}^i \end{bmatrix} \equiv \overline{V}^i,$$

where

$$A = \begin{bmatrix} a_{Lx} & a_{Ly} \\ a_{Kx} & a_{Ky} \end{bmatrix}$$

is the unit-input-requirement matrix. (Note that the matrix A is the same for the two countries because trade has equalized factor prices, the arguments of the a_{ij} coefficients). From the assumption of identical homothetic preferences it follows that

$$C^H = s^H (Q^H + Q^F) = s^H (A^{-1}\overline{V}^H + A^{-1}\overline{V}^F) \equiv s^H A^{-1}\overline{V},$$

where s^H is the share of country H in worldwide income and $\overline{V} \equiv \overline{V}^H + \overline{V}^F$ is the world factor endowment vector.

Hence,

$$M^H = C^H - Q^H = s^H (A^{-1}\overline{V}^H + A^{-1}\overline{V}^F) - A^{-1}\overline{V}^H.$$

Therefore, the factor content of the net import flows which is AM^H can be expressed as

$$AM^H = s^H \overline{V} - \overline{V}^H = s^H \begin{bmatrix} \overline{L}^H + \overline{L}^F \\ \overline{K}^H + \overline{K}^F \end{bmatrix} - \begin{bmatrix} \overline{L}^H \\ \overline{K}^H \end{bmatrix},$$

which is Eqs. (4) and (5) in matrix form.

References

Baumol, W.J. (1986), "Productivity growth, convergence and welfare: what the long-run data show?" American Economic Review 76: 1072–1085.

Berglas, E. and D. Pines (1983), "Clubs, local public goods, and transportation models: a synthesis", Journal of Public Economics 15: 141–162.

Bhagwati, J.N. and T.N. Srinivasan (1983), "On the choice between capital and labor mobility", Journal of International Economics 14: 209–221.

Borjas, G. (1994), "Immigration and welfare, 1970–1990", Working paper no. 4872 (NBER, Cambridge, MA).

Davis, S.J. (1992), "Cross country patterns of change in relative wages," in: O.J. Blanchard and S. Fisher, eds., NBER macroeconomics annual (MIT Press, Cambridge, MA).

Ethier, W. (1985), "International trade and labor migration", American Economic Review 75: 691–707.

Galor, O. and O. Stark (1991), "The impact of differences in the levels of technology on international labor migration", Journal of Population Economics 4: 1–12.

George, H. (1914), Progress and poverty (Doubleday, New York).

Grossman, G.M. and A. Razin (1984), "International capital movements under uncertain", Journal of Political Economy 92: 286–306.

Hamilton, B. and J. Whalley (1984), "Efficiency and distributional implications of global restrictions on labor mobility: calculations and policy implications", Journal of Development Economics 4: 37–60.

Hatton, T.I. and J.G. Williamson (1992), "International migration and world development: a historical perspective", Historical paper no. 41 (NBER, Cambridge, MA).

Krueger, A.O. (1968), "Factor endowments and per capita income differences among countries", Economic Journal 78: 641–659.

Krugman, P. (1991), Geography and trade (MIT Press, Cambridge, MA).

LaLonde, R.J. and R.H. Topel (1994), "Economic impact of international migration and the economic performance of migrants", Mimeo. (University of Chicago, Chicago, IL).

Layard, R. and S. Nickell (1990), Unemployment (Oxford University Press, Oxford).

Layard, R., O. Blanchard, R. Dornbusch and P. Krugman (1992), East–west migration (MIT Press, Cambridge, MA).

Leamer, E.E. (1984), Sources of international comparative advantage (MIT Press, Cambridge, MA).

Lucas, Jr., R.E. (1990), "Why doesn't capital flow from rich to poor countries?" American Economic Review, Papers and Proceedings, 80: 92–96.

MacDougall, G.D.A. (1960), "The benefits and costs of private investment from abroad: a theoretical approach", Economic Record 36: 13–35.

Markusen, J.R. (1983), "Factor movements and commodity trade as complements", Journal of International Economics, May: 341–356.

Mirrlees, J.A. (1971), "An exploration in the theory of optimum income taxation", Review of Economic Studies 38: 175–208.

Mundell, R.A. (1957), "International trade and factor mobility", American Economic Review 47: 321–335.

Nerlove, M., A. Razin, E. Sadka and R. von Weizsacker (1993), "Comprehensive income taxation, investments in human and physical capital, and productivity", Journal of Public Economics 50: 397–406.

Pissarides, C. (1990), Equilibrium unemployment theory (Basil Blackwell, Oxford).

Razin, A. and E. Sadka (1994), "Resisting migration: the problem of wage rigidity and the social burden", Working paper no. 4903 (NBER, Cambridge, MA).

Razin, A. and E. Sadka (1995a), Population economics (MIT Press, Cambridge, MA).

Razin, A. and E. Sadka (1995b), "Resisting migration: wage rigidity and income distribution", American Economic Review, Papers and Proceedings, 85.

Romer, P.M. (1986), "Increasing returns and long-run growth", Journal of Political Economy 94: 1002–1037.

Saint-Paul, G. (1994), "Unemployment, wage rigidity and returns to education", European Economic Review 38: 535–544.

Stiglitz, J.E. (1977), "The theory of local public goods", in: M. Feldstein and J. Inman, eds., The economics of public services (Macmillan, London) pp. 274–344.

Stolper, W.F. and P.A. Samuelson (1941), "Protection and real wages", Review of Economic Studies 9: 58–73.

Summers, R. and A. Heston (1988), "A new set of international comparisons of real product and price levels: estimates for 130 countries, 1950–1985", Review of Income and Wealth 34: 1–25.

Wildasin, D.E. (1986), Urban public finance (Harwood, New York).

Wildasin, D.E. (1991), "Income redistribution and migration", Working paper no. 2 (Center for Economic Studies, University of Munich, Munich).

PART V

AGING, DEMOGRAPHIC COMPOSITION, AND THE ECONOMY

Chapter 16

THE ECONOMICS OF INDIVIDUAL AGING

MICHAEL D. HURD*

University of New York at Stony Brook

Contents

1. Introduction   892
2. Retirement   892
   2.1. Overview of explanations   893
   2.2. The effect of social security on retirement   895
   2.3. The effect of pensions on retirement   902
   2.4. Models to explain retirement   905
   2.5. Empirical evidence on retirement   912
   2.6. Summary of retirement   919
3. Consumption and saving following retirement   919
   3.1. Introduction   919
   3.2. The life-cycle model   923
   3.3. Empirical findings about the LCH based on wealth data   931
   3.4. Summary of wealth change   935
   3.5. Evidence about the LCH based on consumption data   938
   3.6. Tests of the bequest motive for saving   939
   3.7. Summary of consumption and saving   947
4. Economic status of the elderly   948
   4.1. Introduction   948
   4.2. Income-based measures of economic status   948
   4.3. Consumption-based measures of economic status   954
   4.4. Distribution of economic resources   956
   4.5. Summary of economic status   958
5. Directions for future research   960
References   962

*Financial support from Rand and from the National Institute of Aging is gratefully acknowledged.

Handbook of Population and Family Economics. Edited by M.R. Rosenzweig and O. Stark
© *Elsevier Science B.V., 1997*

1. Introduction

Two of the most important economic decisions individuals and couples must make late in life are when to retire and, following retirement, how much to consume. These choices, along with public programs such as Social Security and Medicare and family transfers, determine in an important way economic status during retirement. The broad outline of this chapter is to review the economic models that explain retirement and consumption and saving, and then to discuss the empirical evidence about the models. The discussion will be the context of data from the United States because US data are much more extensive than data from other countries, and, consequently, more empirical research has been done based on US data. Then evidence about the economic status of the elderly, including levels and trends, is reviewed. The chapter concludes with a discussion of unanswered research questions and directions for future research.

2. Retirement

Research on retirement aims to explain individual decision-making, but it should also be able to explain two striking facts. The first fact is the large decline between 1965 and 1985 in the labor force participation rate of older males (Table 1).[1] The trend is particularly notable because of the increases in life expectancy at age 65 (Table 2). The two trends taken together imply adults have spent increasing fractions of their lives in retirement.[2] The second fact, as shown in Fig. 1, is that labor force participation rates of men and women fall at age 62 and 65. This is seen more clearly in Fig. 2 which has retirement hazard rates: the probability of leaving the labor force at age t conditional on being in the labor force at age $t - 1$.[3] The spikes in the retirement hazard rate at age 62 and 65 are not consistent with gradually changing tastes for leisure, which would produce a smooth upward trend in the retirement hazard rates. A major aim of the research on retirement behavior has been to understand the determinants of the trend to earlier retirement and the determinants of the spikes in the retirement hazard rates.

---

[1] Participation by older women has been roughly constant, the result of two opposing changes: there has been a long-term trend toward increasing participation by younger women, and a trend toward increasing retirement among older female workers.

[2] There have been similar trends, both in retirement and in life expectancy, in other developed countries.

[3] The hazards are calculated as $1 - (p_t/p_{t-1})$ where p_t is the participation rate at age t. Although the retirement hazards are calculated from cross-section data, similar patterns are found in panel data.

Table 1
Labor force participation rates (percentage)

	55–59	60–64	65–69	70–74	75+
Men					
1957	91.4	82.9	52.6	a	a
1965	90.2	78.0	43.0	24.8	14.1
1970	89.5	75.0	41.6	25.2	12.0
1975	84.4	65.5	31.7	21.1	10.1
1980	81.7	60.8	28.5	17.9	8.8
1985	79.6	55.6	24.5	14.9	7.0
1990	79.8	55.5	26.0	15.4	7.1
1994	76.9	52.8	26.8	15.8	8.6
1995	77.4	53.2	27.0	16.8	7.6
Women					
1957	38.2	30.3	17.5	a	a
1965	47.1	34.0	17.4	9.1	3.7
1970	49.0	36.1	17.3	9.1	3.4
1975	47.9	33.2	14.5	7.6	3.0
1980	48.5	33.2	15.1	7.5	2.5
1985	50.3	33.4	13.5	7.6	2.2
1990	55.3	35.5	17.0	8.2	2.7
1994	59.2	37.8	17.9	8.7	3.5
1995	59.5	38.0	17.5	9.3	2.9

[a]Not available.
Source: Labor Force Statistics Derived from the CPS (1948–1987). US Department of Labor, Bureau of Labor Statistics, #2307, August, 1988. Employment and Earnings, January, 1991, 1995 and 1996.

2.1. Overview of explanations

Before discussing models and empirical findings based on the models, some overall trends in participation and possible explanations are reviewed. The main explanations depend on Social Security, private pensions, wealth, wage rates and medical insurance.

According to Ransom and Sutch (1988) the decline in participation began with the introduction of the Social Security system in the late 1930s. Furthermore, as shown in Table 3, Social Security benefits are the most important income source for most of the elderly. For example, in 1992 48% of the households with an elderly person had at least 60% of their income from Social Security, and 13% of the households had all of their income from Social Security. Although other economic resources such as private pensions and assets are undoubtedly important determinants of retirement for some workers, the income figures suggest that Social Security is the most important determinant for most workers.

Table 2
Actual and projected life expectancy at age 65

	Men	Women
1900	11.4	12.0
1910	11.4	12.1
1920	11.8	12.3
1930	11.8	12.9
1940	11.9	13.4
1950	12.8	15.1
1960	12.9	15.9
1970	13.1	17.1
1980	14.0	18.4
1990	14.8	18.8
2000	15.3	19.4
2010	15.8	19.8
2020	16.2	20.2
2030	16.7	20.7
2040	17.1	21.2

Source: Bell et al. (1992).

This supposition is strengthened by the change in real Social Security benefits over time which coincided with the fall in participation. Fig. 3 shows median real Social Security benefits for couples and singles receiving benefits. The increase is particularly large for couples: 42% from 1971 to 1990. As it relates to retirement, however, the figure is somewhat misleading because the median is taken over all recipients, not just recent retirees. Thus, it does not show the change in incentives facing a worker who is thinking of retiring. Fig. 4 shows full benefit levels among newly retired workers: between 1970 and 1979 real benefits rose by about 40% among men. It would not be surprising if the increase had an important effect on the trend toward early retirement.

The availability of private pensions has increased over time. Fig. 5 shows the percentage of the elderly with pension income. In 1971 about 23% of couples had pension income, and this increased to 41% by 1990. Yet the level of real pension benefits among these couples who received pension income was roughly constant, and actually declined among singles (Fig. 3).[4] While the wider availability of pension income may have induced some earlier retirement it seems doubtful that it could be the major explanation of the fall in participation.

Although wealth is difficult to measure, there has been some increase in wealth holdings over time. For example in 1971, 49% of the elderly had income from assets, while in 1992 56% had asset income (Table 3). Yet, because asset holdings are highly

---

[4] The decline is related to the high rate of inflation during the 1970s, which is shown at the bottom of the figure. Few private pensions are completely indexed, and many pensions are not indexed at all.

Table 3
Relative importance of income from Social Security, private pensions and
assets: distribution of aged units (65 or over) (1992)

Percent of income	Social Security	Private pensions or annuities	Assets
0	7	68	44
1–19	9	14	33
20–59	36	16	18
60–79	16	1	3
80–99	19	0	1
100	13	0	0
All	100	100	100

Source: Grad (1994).

skewed, assets could not be an important determinant of retirement for most: in 1992 77% of the elderly had less than 20% of their income from assets (Table 3).

Other determinants of retirement are thought to be wage rates, health and the availability of health insurance. Because wage rates have been roughly stable over the last 20 years, they probably have not had a large effect on the trends in participation: but in any event, they are accounted for in the retirement models outlined here. The increases in life expectancy at age 65 indicate that health has been improving, so health changes could not be responsible for the fall in participation. Because of data limitations knowledge of the effects of health insurance is very limited. Furthermore, because of two interacting long-term trends, it is difficult to understand even the qualitative effects. The major source of health insurance for the elderly (Medicare) because available in 1965, which is roughly coincident with the decline in participation. Thus, its availability could have allowed some to retire who were covered by employer-provided health insurance on the job. However, medical costs were much lower in the 1970s than today, so it is hard to see how medical insurance per se could have been an important determinant of the fall in participation in the 1970s.

2.2. The effect of social security on retirement

To understand how the Social Security system could affect retirement, some of the important features of the Social Security system are briefly reviewed.

As originally conceived, Social Security was to be one of three sources of retirement income, the others being private pensions and savings. As we have seen, however, for many of the retired, Social Security benefits are the primary income source. This is partly due to the large changes of between 1968 and 1972 in the Social Security benefit schedule, the function relating lifetime earnings to Social Security benefits. Holding earnings constant, benefits were increased in 1968, 1970, 1971 and 1972, increasing money benefits of a retired person by 72%. Over the same period the CPI

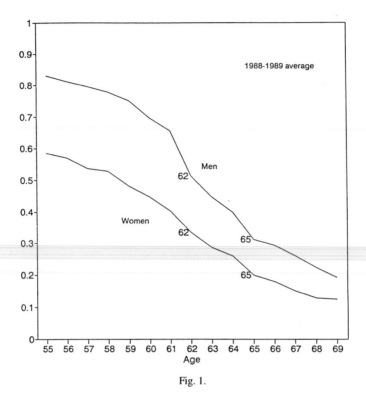

Fig. 1.

increased by 28%. In addition, earnings were increasing, so that benefits were calculated on a rising earnings base. The additional taxes on the earnings were much less than the additional Social Security wealth resulting from the taxes because the retirees in the 1970s were still benefiting from the startup and changes in the system. Most of their benefits were windfall gains. As a result, real average Social Security benefit awards (benefits at retirement) rose by 51% between 1968 and 1977. That is, on average, retiring workers in 1977 had benefits 51% higher than retiring workers in 1968 even though the 1977 workers retired at younger ages. It is certainly plausible that these large increases in benefits were responsible for at least part of the fall in labor force participation.

The discussion will describe the system as it was in the 1970s because most of the empirical research used the Retirement History Survey (RHS), a panel data set that covers 1969–1979. The description is meant to illustrate the main features of the program as they related to the retirement decision at that time. Since then the system has been changed many times, but most of the changes are rather small quantitative changes, which have not changed its basic character.

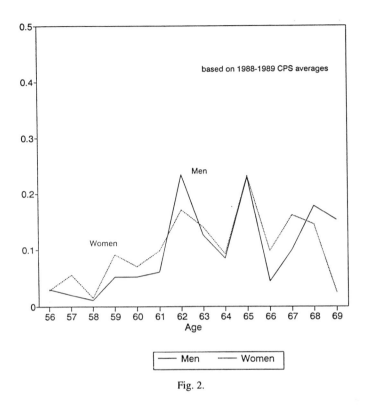

Fig. 2.

Primary Insurance Amount (PIA), which is a function of lifetime contributions to the Social Security system, is the retirement benefit a qualified worker would receive were he to retire at the normal retirement age, currently age 65. A worker has the option of taking benefits as early as age 62; however, his benefit is reduced by about 7% for each year of retirement before 65 to a maximum of 20% for retirement at 62. This reduction is roughly actuarially fair for males at an interest rate of 4%. That is, the year's benefit gained by retiring a year early is about equal to the expected present value of the foregone gain from retiring a year later, which is 0.07 × (expected present value of a year's benefit). Once benefits are set, they do not change in real terms unless the retiree returns to work; should he return to work his benefits will be recalculated to reflect any new contributions and any benefits lost while working. Because of rising wages and a generous benefit schedule, the increase in the expected present value of Social Security benefits (Social Security wealth) from an additional year's work was substantially greater for older workers during the 1970s than the marginal

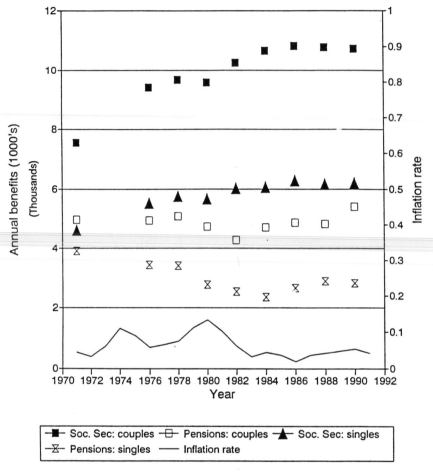

Fig. 3.

Social Security taxes; thus, the Social Security system implicitly increased the compensation from working between 62 and 65 (and, of course, at earlier ages).

If, after benefits are drawn, the retiree has earnings, they are subject to an earnings test: annual earnings above an exempt amount ($2520 in 1975, indexed) were effectively taxed (at a 50% rate in the 1970s) through a reduction in Social Security benefits. However, on eventual complete retirement, benefits were recalculated to take account of any previous reduction in benefits. To the extent that the recalculation was actuarially fair, which was the aim of the recalculation, the expected present value of Social Security benefits was not reduced either by the reduction in benefits for early

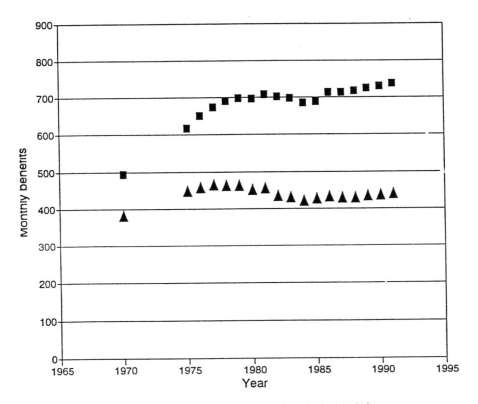

Source: Social Security Administration, 1993, and author's calculations

Fig. 4.

retirement or by the earnings test. However, after age 65, benefits were increased by only 1% per year of work (rather than 7% before 65), which encouraged retirement at 65: thus, after 65 the earnings test is a true tax.

Two kinds of budget constraints show some of the features of the Social Security system: an annual budget constraint (Fig. 6) that gives within-year labor–consumption tradeoffs for someone aged 62–64 when there is no saving or dissaving; and a lifetime budget constraint (Fig. 7) that gives tradeoffs between years of retirement and lifetime income. The slope of the annual budget constraint was reduced by the earnings test to half the wage rate between *A* and *B* (Fig. 6). This caused a kink at earnings of $2520 in 1975. However, in view of the pay back at eventual retirement of benefits lost

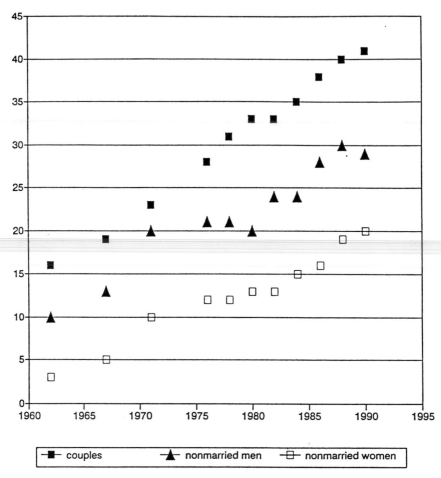

Fig. 5.

through the earnings test, workers may act as if the annual budget constraint is a straight line. It is, of course, an empirical matter whether workers view the earnings test as a tax or simply as deferred compensation. If they view it as a tax, they will tend to choose hours at A. The questions is whether one year's benefit is greater or less than the expected present value of 7% of a year's benefit.

Suppose, for example, that the interest rate is zero and there are two types of workers: unhealthy, who will live for 11 years and healthy, who will live for 21 years. For unhealthy workers the gain from delaying retirement is 0.7 of a year's benefit (7% of the benefit for ten years); yet he loses a year's benefit from the delay for a net loss of

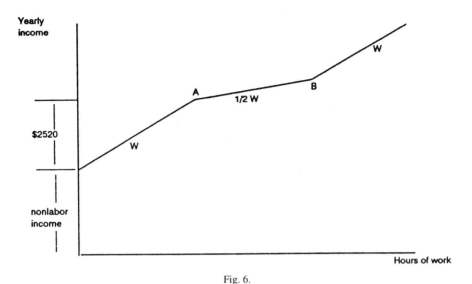

Fig. 6.

0.3 of a year's benefit. This type of worker would see a convex kink at age 62 and tend to retire at 62. A healthy worker will gain 1.4 of a year's benefit from delaying retirement (7% of a year's benefit for 20 years). Such a worker will see a concave kink at 62, and tend not to retire at 62.

Apparently many who work part-time after retirement choose hours close to the exempt amount in the earnings test, viewing the kink in Fig. 6 to be convex. For example, 27% of post-retirement working males in the RHS have annual earnings within 10% of the exempt amount (Burtless and Moffitt, 1984, 1985). This produces a sharp peak at the exempt amount in the distribution of earnings. Of course, the peak could stem from the reluctance of workers to reveal to an interviewer that they have earned more than the exempt amount; but taking the results at face value indicates that after retirement part-time work was often chosen to avoid the earnings test.

The lifetime budget constraint in Fig. 7 is drawn as if the wage were constant over the lifetime to highlight the effects of Social Security. Until 62 the slope is the total lifetime compensation from a year of work, including any accrual to Social Security at 62. The budget constraint is drawn for someone whose expectation of life is substantially above average. Thus, delaying retirement after 62 causes lifetime income to increase at a greater rate than before 62. At age 65, the budget constraint is flattened because at 65 someone loses about 6% of Social Security wealth per year. The loss could be even greater than earnings in which case the constraint would have a negative slope. The kinks at 62 and 65 should cause few workers to retire at 62 and many to retire at 65.

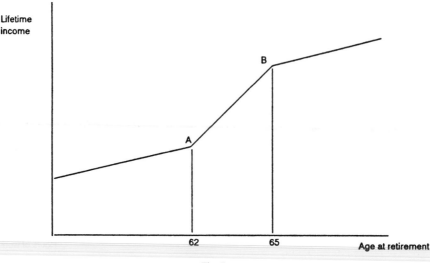

Fig. 7.

The lifetime budget constraint is drawn under the assumption that an individual may transfer resources across years, so that he can choose his annual consumption independently from his retirement age. But if Social Security benefits are large, individuals may reach retirement age with few private resources; then, consumption cannot be chosen independently from retirement because consumption must be financed by the flow of Social Security benefits, which do not begin until retirement. For example, someone on the basis of lifetime wealth and the wage rate may desire to retire at 61; but if he cannot finance consumption at 61 he will wait to retire at 62. He is liquidity constrained (Crawford and Lillian, 1981; Hurd and Boskin, 1984; Burtless and Moffitt, 1986). A liquidity constraint could induce people to retire at 62.

2.3. The effect of pensions on retirement

Private pension coverage grew rapidly from 1950 to 1970 with more modest increases in later years. In 1984 about half of the workers in the private sector had pension coverage (Clark et al., 1988; Clark and McDermed, 1990). Some 83% of all workers in the public sector had pensions (Andrews, 1985). The growth in pensions is expected to continue (Andrews and Chollet, 1988), so understanding their influence in retirement is important.

Most pensions are either defined contribution (DC) pensions or defined benefit (DB) pensions. As the name suggests a defined contribution pension plan is described by the contributions the worker and the firm make to the plan: typically the plan will specify that the firm will contribute some fraction of the worker's earnings to purchase financial assets. The assets will finance the retirement of the worker; but the benefit level will depend on the investment performance of the assets. The worker bears considerable investment risk under a DC plan. A DB plan is described by the retirement benefits the worker will have. Typically benefits are a function of years of service at a particular firm, age at retirement and earnings with the firm. For example, a DB plan might specify that if normal retirement (say, 65) is taken, the monthly benefit is proportional to the average of the last three years' earnings times the years of service. In this example, the worker bears "earnings risk": should his real earnings fall toward the end of his work life, he could lose substantial pension wealth.

DC plans are becoming more common: in 1977 22% of large plans were DC; in 1983, 29% were DC. Yet, because DB plans tend to cover larger establishments, the fraction of covered workers in DC plans was just 17% in 1983 (Clark et al., 1988). Both types of plans have incentive effects on retirement: DC plans increase the compensation from working and they may induce the same kind of liquidity effects as Social Security; DB plans can have large and complicated incentive effects that need to be described in more detail.

The most commonly used valuation of a pension plan (for purposes of evaluating their effects on workers) is the expected present value (EPV). The EPV varies widely with the age of the worker, the retirement age, discount factors (interest rate and mortality rate) and the details of the DB plan. Consider, for example, pension plans with ten-year vesting, which were typical during the 1970s and early 1980s. A worker who leaves the firm with less than ten years of service has no pension claim; at ten years he becomes vested. Therefore, EPV is zero before vesting, and jumps to some positive number at vesting. Annual pension accrual is the change in EPV associated with a year's work, and it is used as a measure of compensation in addition to earnings. Pension accrual is zero before vesting. One might think accrual is large during the vesting year, but this is usually not the case: a vested worker who leaves a firm at, say, 35 would normally have to wait until age 65 to receive pension benefits; the benefits, based on only ten years of service, would be small and they would be discounted 30 or more years by the nominal interest rate and the mortality rate. At other ages, however, the accrual rate can be very large, and in most plans it is negative after age 65.

The accrual rate can alter retirement because a worker would not want to retire during, or in the years just before, a year when the accrual rate is large (Lazear and Moore, 1988), and he would be inclined to retire in the year before the accrual rate becomes negative. There are thousands of DB plans each of which has different implicit accrual rates; furthermore, workers under a particular plan will have different accrual rates because of differing work histories (Ellwood, 1985; Kotlikoff and Wise, 1987b). Some plans encourage early retirement and some encourage late retirement (Mitchell and Fields, 1985; Gustman and Steinmeier, 1989).

Fig. 8 has an example of accrual rates in a DB plan. The plan is that of a "large Fortune 500" firm engaged in sales (Kotlikoff and Wise, 1989). The figure shows the pension accrual rate of a male manager who joined the firm when he was 20. At vesting (age 30) pension accrual jumps from zero to $1008, which is just 2.1% of earnings in the vesting year. Until the worker reaches his 50s, the pension accruals are too small to be seen in the figure. At age 55, however, accrual is $168 000, 1.6 times earnings in that year. The accrual rate is so large because of special early retirement pension benefits that become available to workers if they remain with the firm until 55. Pension accrual becomes negative at age 61 because, for this example, the worker would have 30 years of service: the provisions of the plan provide no additional benefits for more than 30 years of service, yet about 2% of EPV is lost at 61 because at that age the mortality rate of males is about 0.02. At 66 the sum of accrual from pension and Social Security is $40 300, which is 45% of annual earnings. The implicit wage rate at age 66 is, therefore, only about 55% of the nominal wage rate. It is not surprising that few workers who face such compensation schedules work past 65.

The accrual path in Fig. 8 is typical of workers in the firm, although actual magnitudes vary with earnings, age of hire and years of service. For example, a male manager hired at age 40 has a pension accrual at age 55 of 71% of earnings. Accrual is negative after age 65, but it is a smaller fraction of earnings than what is shown in Fig. 8, and could be expected to have a smaller effect. This means that if we want to estimate utility function parameters we must know the details of the incentives facing each worker, not simply the plan rules.

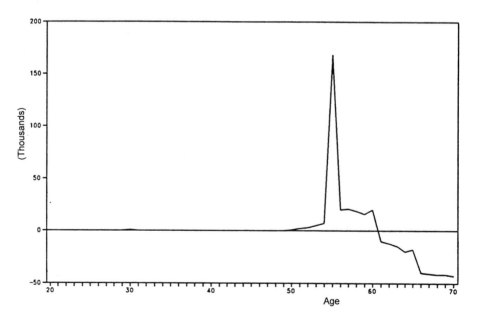

Fig. 8.

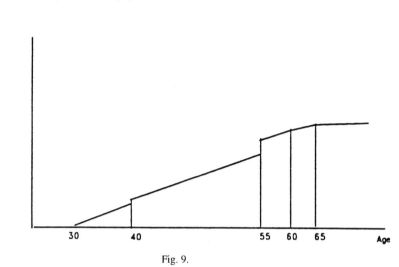

Fig. 9.

An approximate lifetime budget constraint associated with this plan is shown in Fig. 9 (not to scale). The constraint should concentrate retirement at 55, 60 and at 65. It should be clear that to estimate the parameters of a utility function defined over lifetime income and years of retirement is complicated, requiring detailed knowledge of pension plans. As Kotlikoff and Wise (1989) say, "…estimation of the effects of pension plans on labor force participation of older workers can only be done by taking account of the precise provisions of individual plans". The incentive effects can be large, and they may concentrate retirement more than Social Security. Their effects depend on the exact history of individual workers. It should be emphasized again that there are thousands of DB plans which may have quite different incentives from the plan underlying Figs. 8 and 9. For example, the budget set in Fig. 9 has only one non-convex region (near age 55); other plans could have several non-convex regions. This complicates estimation greatly because an estimation algorithm has to check conditions for global maximization, not just local maximization, and this requires specification of a utility function. For examples of other plans, see Mitchell and Fields (1985).

2.4. Models to explain retirement

Consider a single person who works full-time. Suppose that part-time jobs are not available, that there is no uncertainty about the future and that the annual wage, I, is fixed. The lifetime utility maximization problem is

$$\max_{L} U(c, L)$$

subject to $c = (N - L) + w$, where c is some measure of lifetime consumption, L is years of leisure, N is the number of years to live and w is wealth. In this formulation an individual demands lifetime consumption and years of leisure just as in any other simple utility maximization problem, and the solution would give L as a function of I and w. If we add the assumption that the utility function is indexed by age such that tastes for leisure increase with age,[5] then the retirement age is determined by the demand for L: the individual will first work and then consume leisure. Alternatively we could have the realistic assumption that it is costly to leave and then re-enter the labor force, which would cause anyone working to continue to work until the desired retirement age.

Under the first assumption we can write that the retirement age of a worker is a function of I, N, w and age with the expectation that it is increasing in N, decreasing in w, and increasing in age. Given observations on workers, the ages at which they retire, their annual wages, their initial wealth, and their remaining years of life, we could estimate the retirement age demand function in a rather straightforward way. The results would show how retirement age varies with wages and income, so we could recover income and substitution effects.

This specification and estimation strategy has a number of defects. First, neither Social Security nor pensions appears in the problem, yet, as we have seen, they are important resources for the elderly. Second, the budget set is in fact not linear because Social Security and pensions induce kinks, flat places, nonconvexities and possibly even discontinuities. Furthermore, there is some evidence that real wages decline with age causing further nonlinearities in the budget set. Third, the model says nothing about decision making within a time period: it simply assumes that someone either works full-time or not at all each time period. While it is true that many workers move from full-time work to complete retirement, not all do. The availability of part-time work should influence the retirement age: as tastes increase for leisure, workers should increasingly desire part-time work rather than full-time, and if it is available they will tend to stay in the labor force longer. Fourth, the models do not incorporate uncertainty, yet workers face uncertainty from health, future wage rates and so forth that should influence their retirement decision. Fifth, the model allows workers to choose years of work freely; but there is some casual evidence of employer pressure on workers to retire.

2.4.1. Nonlinearities in the budget set

To account for Social Security, pensions and other nonlinearities in the budget set, it is necessary to assume something about a utility function. This is because some of the nonlinearities cause the budget set to be nonconvex so that utility must be compared globally. For example, we must be able to say whether utility will be higher from retir-

---

[5] That is, the marginal rate of substitution (MRS) of for increases with age.

ing at 62 or at 67, not just at 62 or 63. Given a utility function, the model would specify that workers choose years of work to maximize utility; thus years of work would be found by comparing (numerically) utility over all possible retirement ages rather than being expressed in a demand function.

An unavoidable weakness of this approach is that the budget set must be forecast over future years; that is, we must say what wage rates, wealth, Social Security benefits, pensions and so forth would be over all possible retirement ages to accomplish the utility comparisons. We almost never have good data on which to make such forecasts. In particular for those who retire we do not observe what they would have earned had they continued to work, yet these potential earnings influence the probability of retirement at all earlier ages. A typical approach is to forecast wage paths at the individual level from observed individual wage rate rates and estimates of wage growth rates (Gustman and Steinmeier, 1986).

2.4.2. Full-time and part-time work

A more realistic model of work choice near the end of worklife has two kinds of jobs: full-time and part-time. Beyond the difference in annual hours of work, such jobs are different because a part-time job typically has lower hourly pay than a full-time job. For example, wage rates decline substantially when the elderly change jobs and reduce hours: 25% in Gordon and Blinder (1980); 30% in Gustman and Steinmeier (1984).

This complicates the analysis considerably because now the choices are over hours per year in each year and years of work. But the analysis is simplified if we assume for the moment that annual hours of each type of job are fixed and given, so that the lifetime utility maximization is in the choice of the number of years to work full-time and the number to work part-time. If we assume that with age tastes shift toward leisure, then workers will choose to work full-time for a number of years, then part-time, and then to retire completely. They will not choose part-time work followed by full-time work. This reduces the utility maximization problem to one of choosing the number of years to work at each type of job, not the sequence.

Suppose that the lifetime utility function is

$$U(c, L, n_f, n_p), \tag{1}$$

where c is some measure of lifetime consumption, L is years of leisure, n_f is years of full-time work and n_p is years of part-time work. The time constraint is

$$L + n_f + n_p = N,$$

where N is years of life. For a given number of years of full-time work, n_f^*, the utility function can be rewritten as

$$U(c, N - n_f^* - n_p, n_f^*, n_p) = V(c, n_p; n_f^*).$$

That is, lifetime utility is just a function of c and n_p, conditional on n_f^*. The lifetime budget constraint is shown in Fig. 10 with indifference curves of three individuals who have different tastes. The kink at full-time work in the figure (n_f^*) is partially due to lower annual earnings from a part-time job: thus the gain in lifetime consumption from a year of part-time work is less than the gain from a year of full-time work. But the kink is made sharper by the empirical fact that part-time work almost always pays less per hour than full-time work, 35–50% less. Most likely, this is at least partly responsible for the empirical finding that the majority of full-time workers move directly from full-time work to complete retirement with no intervening spell of part-time.

Individual 1 with V_1 would like to work negative part-time years, so the solution shown in the figure cannot be the solution to the (constrained) utility maximization problem. It is reasonable to assume that the marginal rate of substitution of n_p for consumption increases in n_f^*: if someone works more years at full-time, the value of a year of part-time leisure increases relative to consumption causing the slope of an indifference curve in Fig. 10 to increase. Thus if full-time years are reduced below n_f^* there will be two effects: the kink point will move down, and the indifference curves will rotate clockwise causing the tangency point of an indifference curve to move up. If full-time years are reduced sufficiently, individual 1 will reach a kink point like individual 2.

Conditional on n_f^*, individuals 2 and 3 are maximizing utility with individual 2

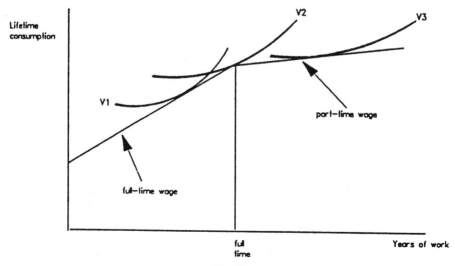

Fig. 10.

choosing zero years of part-time work and individual 3 working some part-time. However, we cannot tell whether the choices are optimal over all values of n_f^*. For example, reducing n_f^* moves the kink point to the left and also reduces the slopes of the indifference curves of individual 2. This could cause individual 2 to reach a position like individual 3. To find which is better, we would need to compare global utility levels using Eq. (1). Thus, a complete solution would result from solving the constrained maximization problem given some value for n_f^*, and then searching over all values of n_f^* to find the value that maximizes Eq. (1).

The estimation of this system requires a specification of the utility function, observations on years of full-time and part-time work, the annual wage from each type of work, and on other individual-level variables such as rights to Social Security, pensions, wealth and so forth. What makes the estimation difficult even in this simplified model is that typically we have no observations on annual earnings from part-time work for those who do not work part-time. We can only construct part of the budget constraint, that part corresponding to full-time work; yet the probability that someone will choose the kink point depends on the part-time wage as well as the full-time wage.

In principle this is a standard problem in sample selection, which could be solved by making some distributional assumptions about the part-time wage. However, a part-time wage is observed for just a small fraction of the population, and the population is rather heterogeneous: the difference between the full-time wage and the part-time wage surely varies substantially across classes of workers, and the difference is rarely observed among some classes because few ever work part-time. Take as a specific example, a worker in a fast-food restaurant and an engineer. Fast-food restaurants usually offer part-time work at the same hourly wage rate as full-time work. Thus, the kink in Fig. 10 is only caused by the reduction in annual hours. A full-time engineer probably has better alternatives for part-time work than in a fast-food restaurant, yet they are unlikely to pay as well as full-time work. Because few engineers work part-time near the end of work-life, we can only bound the part-time hourly wage rate of an engineer by the wage rate in a fast-food restaurant and the engineer's observed full-time hourly wage rate. This is not much information on which to base estimation.

A more realistic model allows annual part-time hours to be chosen. That is, the model offers the choice of a full-time job with fixed hours and annual earnings, and a part-time job with flexible hours and an hourly wage rate which is less than the implicit wage rate on the full-time job. An annual budget constraint is shown in Fig. 11. It consists of a line with a slope equal to the part-time wage, and a single point F.

Because of the nonconvexity, the solution requires the specification of a utility function to compare utility from full-time work with the optimal choice from part-time. Yet, the figure is misleading because it implies that annual consumption is the same as annual income. The actual tradeoff is between hours of leisure and lifetime consumption opportunities as measured by wealth. The optimal choice requires that the marginal utility of leisure equals the marginal utility of wealth. If lifetime utility is

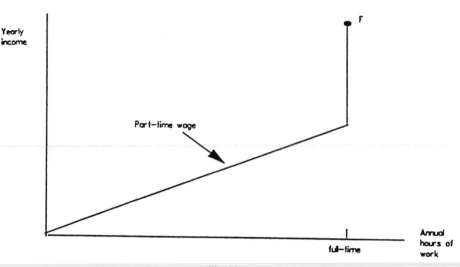

Fig. 11.

time separable, the marginal utility of leisure within a time period is not affected by the leisure choices at other time periods; however, the marginal utility of wealth is affected. For example, the marginal utility of wealth of someone with a long expected worklife is less than of someone with a short expected worklife simply because lifetime wealth is greater. This means that finding the optimal annual hours of work in any particular year requires finding the optimal annual hours in all years, and implicitly the year of retirement. Even this, however, is only one side of the problem because the marginal utility of wealth in any year depends on the level of consumption in that year, which, in turn depends on consumption in all other years. Thus, the complete solution must be over the choice of leisure in all years and the choice of consumption in all years. Needless to say the data and computational requirements are exceptionally great, and there is no successful estimation of such a model.

2.4.3. Uncertainty

Workers face uncertainty with respect to future health, marital status, wages, job security, interest rates, inflation and so forth. We would like to take uncertainty into account because it probably affects the retirement decision. For example, if a worker has a DB pension plan that is heavily dependent on final year's salary, but not indexed after retirement, the worker can reduce total exposure to risk by delaying retirement. If we had measures of the variance in inflation rates we could, at least in principle, estimate risk aversion by observing how the retirement age varies with the variance in inflation.

The general framework for modeling and estimating the effects of uncertainty is stochastic dynamic programming. In this framework someone maximizes expected lifetime utility by planning a sequence of decisions, but with the knowledge that later decisions can be altered as new information is obtained. For example, on the basis of current health status and information about the distribution of the future states of health, a worker will plan a sequence of actions such as a retirement age and saving levels. Yet, only today's action need be taken, and that action is taken knowing that tomorrow's action will probably be modified due to an updating on actual health status and to new information about the distribution of future health status.

While it is straightforward to write down the general form of a stochastic dynamic programming model, the informational requirements for estimation are substantial. It requires the specification of a utility function because the solution involves utility comparisons over different actions. It requires specifying what elements of the environment are stochastic, and the distributions of those elements. Furthermore, because the relevant distributions are those believed by the decision-maker, they are not necessarily the distributions in some population. For example, the distribution of health status in the population may not be the distribution that is used by an individual in making decisions. This is particularly true when there is heteroscedasticity in beliefs, which there almost surely is: a healthy person undoubtedly has a different distribution of future health outcomes than an unhealthy person.

Examples of stochastic dynamic programming models of retirement are Rust (1989), Berkovec and Stern (1991), Lumsdaine et al. (1992) and Rust and Phelan (1993). Each makes different assumptions, so it is not obvious how to compare the results. A more direct comparison can be made with a simplified model that still retains some stochastic elements. This is the model of Stock and Wise (1990a, b). In this model a worker chooses the year to retire to maximize expected utility where the expectation is with respect to the distributions of the stochastic variables of the problem in the base year. This sounds very much like a stochastic dynamic programming model, but there is a difference: in this model the worker makes the calculations as if there will be no new information about the distributions between the base year and a later year; in the stochastic dynamic programming model the individual knows at the base year (when the decision in being made about whether to retire) that new information will be available in the following year that can be used to reoptimize. This is, of course, more realistic: it recognizes that individuals can reoptimize and that they know they will be able to reoptimize. Being able to reoptimize means that often the best decision is to wait until new information becomes available. For example, the expected lifetime utility of someone in poor health may be maximized by retiring in the base year: that is, the certain path of retiring in the base year may produce a higher expected utility than any other sequence of (certain) retirement decisions where the expectation is taken with respect to the distribution of health outcomes in the base year. Yet, if the individual knows that new information about his health will be revealed during the year it may be worthwhile to delay retirement to find if his health recovers.[6]

Lumsdaine et al. (1992) compare the fit of a stochastic dynamic programming model with the fit of the model of Stock and Wise. They find little difference between them. This suggests that the data are not good enough to support the increased complexity and informational requirements of a stochastic dynamic programming model in the sense that little is gained by using this more complicated model. However, estimation of stochastic dynamic programming models is in its beginning stages, and greater success can be expected particularly when the HRS data become available.

2.5. Empirical evidence on retirement

Most people who study retirement behavior probably believe that increases in Social Security benefits increase retirement probabilities; yet there is little agreement on the magnitudes of the effects. For example, Mitchell and Fields (1982) conclude from their review of the literature on retirement, "Clearly, no empirical conclusions can be drawn about the effects of Social Security on retirement". Partly this is due to differences in definition: retirement has been defined to be permanent departure from the labor force (Hurd and Boskin, 1984); self-assessed retirement (Hausman and Wise, 1985); a "sudden and discontinuous drop in hours of work" (Burtless and Moffitt, 1985); and leaving a firm (Mitchell and Fields, 1983; Stock and Wise, 1990a, b). Partly it is because the description of the economic environment is complicated by variation in the availability, quality, and wages of jobs. For example, there is good evidence that if older workers want to reduce hours of work, they must take a pay cut (Gustman and Steinmeier, 1984, 1985; Rust, 1990). This leads to complicated behavior. Although gradual change with age in work effort would be expected, many workers switch from full-time work to complete retirement: Rust estimates that 75% of the transitions in the RHS are from full-time work to no work; according to the data in Berkovec and Stern (1991) among men over 55 in the National Longitudinal Survey, 67% of the transitions are from full-time work to no work. Based on the RHS, Quinn et al. (1990) estimated that among men who leave their full-time career jobs 73% leave the labor force completely, 15% move to part-time employment, and 12% go on to further full-time employment. A rough estimate would be that about 83% eventually leave full-time employment for complete retirement.[7] These kinds of complications make modeling of the retirement process difficult, and lead different researchers to use different models, depending on the data set and what aspect of the problem is to be emphasized.

---

[6] This argument requires the realistic assumption that "unretirement" is costly.

[7] The calculation assumes that the fraction moving from any full-time job to part-time is 0.15, which is the fraction that move from a full-time career job to a part-time job.

2.5.1. Effects of social security on retirement

As we have seen the provisions of the Social Security typically cause the budget set to be nonlinear. A straightforward way around the difficulties caused by a complicated budget constraint is simply to ask how retirement hazards at each age vary with some measure of Social Security entitlement. Thus, in a thought experiment, we would observe how the retirement decisions of 62-year-old workers vary with potential Social Security benefits, the benefits they would receive were they to retire at that age. This is a reduced-form approach that has the virtue of minimal information requirements: no attempt is made to construct the complex budget constraint that arises from the Social Security rules, pension rules and job availability. Furthermore, it does not require the specification of a utility function, and in some applications requires no distributional assumptions. It shares the general disadvantage of reduced-form estimation in that the results may not give good predictions of the reaction to changes in all the provisions of Social Security.

Table 4 has some examples of retirement hazards from the RHS (Hurd and Boskin, 1984). In 1971 the retirement hazard at age 62 of male workers with Social Security wealth of $15 000–20 000 and assets of $10 000–25 000 was 0.10. In the same year among males in the same asset category but with Social Security wealth of $20 000–25 000 the hazard was 0.21. In this comparison, as in the other three in the table, higher Social Security wealth is associated with higher retirement probabilities. The four comparisons are examples of 21 similar comparisons, 17 of which show that higher Social Security wealth is associated with higher retirement probabilities. The outcome of the thought experiment is that people with higher levels of Social Security wealth tend to retire earlier.

Although these results are suggestive, they do not control for other determinants of retirement. A natural extension is to specify that the hazards at each age depend on economic variables such as asset categories, wage rates (adjusted for any Social Security accumulation associated with work), health, mandatory retirement and interactions. Estimation shows that, as in Table 4, higher Social Security wealth is associated

Table 4
Retirement hazard rates of men at age 62 (percentage)

Year	Social Security wealth in 1969 ($ ×1000)	Assets in 1969 ($ ×1000)	
		$10–25	$25–45
1971	15–20	10	10
	20–25	21	13
1972	15–20	9	16
	20–25	29	35

Source: Hurd and Boskin (1984).

with higher hazard rates (Hurd and Boskin, 1984). Under the assumption that the results are reduced-form response parameters, the effects of Social Security changes on labor force participation can be found from simulations. A $10 000 change in Social Security wealth (mean wealth of $25 000) would cause participation to fall by about 0.06 at age 65, with somewhat larger decreases at earlier ages. According to the results, the increases in Social Security in the early 1970s accounted for the fall in labor force participation during that period.

These estimated effects of Social Security on retirement are higher than many others. For example, changing the definition of retirement from a labor force definition to a self-assessed definition and changing the statistical specification to include an individual effect reduced the impact of Social Security by about half (Hausman and Wise, 1984). The comparison is only approximate because the definition of retirement is different, the statistical models are different, and the models are complicated enough that the parameters cannot be interpreted directly. Their implicit magnitudes are only revealed through simulations. These problems are found throughout the literature on retirement, and they make the determination of a consensus very difficult.

These are examples of reduced-form estimation; that is, they neither try to find an underlying utility function nor to model the details of the decision-making process. Although they may give good estimates of the effect of some measure of Social Security entitlement on retirement, they cannot directly give estimates of the effect of altering details of the program. For example, the age of entitlement to full Social Security benefits is scheduled to rise from age 65 to 67 beginning in the year 2000. In the reduced form any effect on retirement can only come through changes in Social Security wealth or benefits, but the actual effects will probably be different from a Social Security wealth effect, at least partly coming from a movement in the kink in the budget constraint in Fig. 7. Structural-form estimates are needed to find the effects of changing the details of the program.

The aim of structural-form estimation is to estimate the parameters of an appropriate utility function. In a typical specification lifetime utility is time separable, which simplifies the problem greatly: at any age only the present and future budget sets matter, not the decisions that led to the budget set. Within a time period, utility depends on goods and leisure. Retirement occurs at the age when the lifetime utility associated with retirement becomes greater than the lifetime utility associated with continued work. As discussed earlier, if the budget set is not convex, the evaluation of the utility from work will require the evaluation of many future alternatives. For example, it may be better to retire today than to retire next year, but it may be even better to retire in five years. Evaluation of all the alternatives, not just today and next year, would find that the best choice is not to retire today.

Given the entire budget set, the estimation proceeds by finding the parameter values that produce the best match between actual retirement behavior and predicted retirement behavior. Although the concept is fairly straightforward, the execution is complicated. For example, the actions taken in one time period will affect the budget set in another time period: someone who loses Social Security benefits through the earnings test will have different Social Security benefits in later years than some who did not.

This kind of estimation method was used by Burtless and Moffitt (1984, 1985) to study retirement in the RHS. Because their definition of retirement was a "sudden and discontinuous drop in hours" the results are not directly comparable to others based on other definitions. From simulations, the results imply that a reduction of Social Security benefits of 20% would increase worklife by 0.2 years, and it would decrease the probability of retirement (a sharp drop in hours) by age 62 from 0.26 to 0.25, and the probability of retirement by age 65 from 0.61 to 0.59. These responses are interpreted by Burtless and Moffitt to be small, and indeed they are if they are used to estimate permanent departure from the labor force. For example, a linear extrapolation implies that eliminating Social Security entirely would increase labor force participation at 61 by 0.05. This is small compared with actual changes in participation: between 1970 and 1980 participation of 61-year-old males fell by 0.12. Because anyone who permanently leaves the labor force has a sharp drop in hours, but not necessarily the reverse, the estimated effects on participation would be even smaller than in the example given here.

All the results discussed are based on models that make no attempt to describe the complete economic environment facing a worker of retirement age, especially the drop in wages that seems to accompany the movement from full-time to part-time work (about 25–30%). In principle this is important. If we assume that the wage is constant, the high observed rate of switching from full-time work to retirement implies flat indifference curves: small changes in the budget constraint produce large movements in desired work. But retirement may equally well be due to a combination of moderately curved indifference curves and a discontinuous budget constraint. If the part-time wage is sufficiently low, the worker will remain at his full-time job even though he would prefer to reduce hours at the full-time wage rate. Eventually he may retire completely without ever having taken part-time work.

To estimate a full-scale intertemporal model that will take this into account requires detailed information on the choices that are available every year. For example, the decision of a worker to retire next year and take a part-time job with earnings of $10 000 will affect his labor–leisure choice this year through the marginal utility of wealth. Because the estimation proceeds by comparing utility levels over all possible alternatives in all years, it requires information on all possible choices whether taken or not. This method has the advantage of producing a complete (although estimated) description of the economic environment and an estimated utility function. Taken together they can be used to simulate the effects of changing the details of the Social Security program, of pension plans or of wage paths. The disadvantage is that it requires vast amounts of information, most of which is not known and must be estimated. Gustman and Steinmeier (1986) estimated this kind of model over the RHS data. Simulations which are based on comparing the estimated utility levels of different choices of retirement age produce the peak at age 62 in the retirement hazard shown in Fig. 2. The peak is caused by the slopes of the indifference curves interacting with the within- and across-period budget constraints, not by any age dummy variables. This provides strong confirmation that the peak is due to Social Security. The only other simulation in Gustman and Steinmeier that gives any evidence about the effects of Social Security comes from simultaneously eliminating pensions, Social Security and mandatory retirement. These changes increase labor force participation at age 66 by about 0.14. This is a substantial change, which, if it were due solely to Social Security, would be fairly close to the results of Hurd and Boskin (adjusting for the larger change in Social Security). It is not evident, however, how much is caused by the elimination of Social Security and how much by the other factors. Thus, no comparison with other results or with observed labor force participation can be made.

Rust and Phelan (1993) specify and estimate over the RHS data a stochastic dynamic programming model of retirement behavior. Limitations of the RHS data necessitate several undesirable simplifications. First, lacking good pension data they delete workers with pensions from their data set. Of course this eliminates any possibility of finding the effects of pensions on retirement, but it makes the sample unrepresentative of the population: workers with pensions have higher incomes and wealth than workers without pensions. Still, even for such a selected sample, it is interesting and useful to find the effects of Social Security on retirement. Second, because it is hard to estimate consumption they assume that consumption equals income.[8] But this surely influences the estimated effects of the liquidity constraint on retirement before 62: no worker, whether wealthy or not, would want to retire at, say, 61 unless nonlabor income is reasonably high because consumption cannot be financed out of capital. Despite these limitations their model has the realistic features that workers can choose full-time or part-time work, or complete retirement, and it makes mortality, health status, marital status and earnings stochastic. Because the future Social Security benefits of a worker depend on future earnings, Social Security benefits at retirement are also stochastic. The estimated model is able to explain the observed spikes in retirement hazard rates at 62 and 65: they are produced by a combination of incentives caused by the Social Security program and health insurance in an environment of substantial risk of large medical outlays. The approach is promising, but the data limit what can be achieved.

2.5.2. Effects of pensions on retirement

Even though the RHS is not well suited for investigating the effects of pensions on retirement because it does not have the necessary pension detail, many studies based on the RHS have found that pension eligibility increases retirement (Gordon and Blinder, 1980; Fuchs, 1982; Burtless and Moffitt, 1984, 1985; Anderson et al., 1986).

---

[8] Consumption is very difficult to measure either directly or as the change in wealth.

To obtain the pension detail necessary to go beyond this, research has been based on special data sets obtained from firms. Some of the data are not publicly available, and in some cases even the name of the firm is private information. This, of course, makes it impossible to reproduce results and for other researchers to try alternative ways of constructing variables and to test other functional forms. Nonetheless, because pensions present workers with such strong incentives to retire, empirical work using pension data is very promising. It may even help establish the quantitative effects of Social Security on retirement because, in principle, findings based on pension data about the position and shape of indifference curves could be used to predict reactions to changes in Social Security.

Data from private firms has one serious drawback, however: because they are based on the firm's records they typically have little information on the household. Unless the workers are given special questionnaires, there will be no data on assets, spouse's earnings and personal characteristics. In some cases, an approximation to Social Security benefits can be calculated from the firm's earnings records, but this will not include earnings from previous employers. The influence of some important variables, which can be studied in the RHS, will, of necessity, be ignored.

In 1965 United Auto Workers, aged 59–64, were offered a special supplemental early retirement pension benefit. The incentives induced by the pension program were large: the expected present value of the pension stream conditional on early retirement was $18 965 on average; at normal retirement (age 65) the pension was worth just $8660 on average. This is a large pension loss especially when compared with earnings gain: for example, total earnings from age 62 to 65 averaged $22 000. A worker facing these incentives would be advised to consider early retirement because his effective earnings from three years of work were cut from $22 000 to $10 305, a loss of 53%. Because the supplemental benefit varied with years of service, workers with similar wages and other determinants of retirement can have very different rewards from continued work. The program offered a good opportunity to estimate the reaction to the incentives.

Direct estimation of the probability of early retirement implied that the program was responsible for an increase of about 0.20 in the probability of early retirement (Burkhauser, 1979). This is a large effect as can be seen by comparing it with observed retirement hazards and labor force participation rates. In the population in 1970 the probability of early retirement (before 65) conditional on working at age 61 was about 0.21. Increasing that probability by 0.20 implies that the average participation rate of 62–64 year-olds, which was about 69% in 1970, would fall to about 48%. This is about what the change in participation of 60–64-year-olds was from 1960 to 1980, years of rapid change of the Social Security system.

Some information has already been given in Fig. 8 and the related discussion about the pension plan of a "large Fortune 500" firm (Kotlikoff and Wise, 1987a, 1989). If a worker is vested (ten-year vesting) he has strong financial incentives not to retire before 55; he could be expected to retire from ages 55 to 60 or possibly at 65. Table 5

Table 5
Separation hazard rates (percentage leaving firm)

Age	8–10 YOS[a]	11+ YOS		
	1980	1981	1982	1983
52	3	5	5	5
53	0	4	4	4
54	4	3	4	2
55	5	11	12	10
56	4	12	14	10
57	2	9	12	11
58	5	10	14	12
59	2	11	20	10
60	4	17	29	17
61	0	17	32	18
62	8	36	48	31
63	14	37	54	37
64	11	29	49	26
65	25	53	58	45

[a]YOS, years of service. 8–10 YOS is not vested.
Source: Kotlikoff and Wise (1989).

has the retirement hazards of workers in that firm by years of service and by calendar year and age. Among those with 8–10 years of service (not vested by the convention of Kotlikoff and Wise), the hazards are essentially flat until 62 when Social Security apparently induces some retirement. The hazard increases at 65 due to a combination of pension and Social Security incentives. The pattern among vested workers is very different: the hazard rates are much higher at all ages due, no doubt, to the wealth effects of the pension and to the effects of other unmeasured wealth variables that are positively correlated with pension eligibility. At age 55 the hazards increase substantially and remain approximately constant until 62 (with possibly an additional increase at 60 and 61). At 62 the hazards roughly double and increase again at 65.

The variation in these hazards is strong evidence that workers respond to the incentives of pension plans. The hazards also show a large effect that is surely due to Social Security: there is no other explanation for the jump in the hazard at 62 because the firm's pensions plan has no special incentives at that age, and there is no mandatory retirement.

One striking aspect is the difference in the hazards in 1982 from the hazards in 1981 and 1983. The explanation is that the firm offered, in 1982 only, an early retirement bonus. The bonus varied from three months salary for retirement at age 55 to 12 months salary at 60; between 60 and 65 it was probably 12 months salary. (Not enough information is given to be definite.) Especially at ages 60 and above, this is a strong incentive. For example, it reduced the annual earnings of a 60-year-old worker who planned to retire at 62 by 50%. The workers responded accordingly: the greatest differences by age in the hazards are at ages 59 and over.

To quantify the effects of the plan requires the estimation of a retirement model. Because the budget constraint is not convex (Fig. 9), the model should be based on a utility function; then, retirement would be chosen such that lifetime utility is maximized. However, a number of important explanatory variables such as Social Security benefits are not recorded in the data, and have to be estimated and forecast. Other variables such as earnings have to be forecast outside the sample period. In common with the models based on utility comparisons that have already been discussed, the informational requirements are substantial.

Stock and Wise (1990a, b) find that pensions have strong effects of retirement as would be suggested by Table 5. Workers seem to know the provisions of pensions and respond to the implicit incentives. Although Social Security benefits must be roughly estimated because complete data on work histories is lacking, Social Security nonetheless also has strong effects on retirement.

2.6. Summary of retirement

Important advances in the study of retirement behavior have come from placing the analysis and estimation in a dynamic framework and from modeling the incentives produced by the complex Social Security law and pension provisions. Workers seem to be quite sensitive to variations in the budget constraint induced by pensions, and by extension they should be sensitive to variations caused by the Social Security system. Yet, most models, although not all, find rather small effects from Social Security. However, this may be caused by estimation error on many of the variables that must be used but which are not directly observable. We need new and better data, in particular population representative data that integrate information on pensions and on Social Security. We need data that have observations on individual expectations of future events so that we can better estimate stochastic dynamic models. Several new data sets that will meet these requirements are discussed below.

3. Consumption and saving following retirement

3.1. Introduction

On reaching retirement, people have three broad types of income to support them in retirement. The first is interest or dividend income from assets which is almost universally a nominal return (not indexed).[9] The second is payments that continue for life:

---

[9] Dividends are informally indexed as they can be increased in response to an increase in nominal profit.

annuities broadly speaking such as Social Security, private (job-related) pensions, and privately purchased annuities. Some annuities are indexed for inflation in which case they are referred to as real annuities; others are not indexed and are called nominal annuities. In practice some private pensions are partially indexed on an ad hoc basic, particularly when inflation is high, so they are a mix of the two types. A third kind of income is income-in-kind. The most important sources are implicit income from owner-occupied housing and access to the Medicare–Medicaid system.

For most people wealth consists of financial assets and housing equity. The ability to convert both kinds of wealth to consumption, of course, increases the consumption opportunities beyond an income measure, so a complete evaluation of the economic status of elderly households should take into account both income and wealth.

In the 1983 Survey of Consumer Finances (SCF) mean wealth of the elderly, as measured by financial wealth, real estate, housing and other miscellaneous wealth, was \$118 700, and in the 1984 Survey of Income and Program Participation (SIPP) it was about \$90 800.[10] At a real interest rate of 3% the assets accounted for approximately \$3000 per year which is only about 18% of the average household income of the elderly in 1983 (\$16 386). However, should an elderly person consume part of the wealth as he ages, the wealth could make a much higher contribution to consumption. Suppose, for example, a 70-year-old woman chose a flat consumption over 15 years, which is about her life expectancy. At a real interest rate of 3%, she could consume \$8300 per year (1983\$)from the wealth. This is about 51% of average income in 1983. Of course, a flat consumption path is probably not optimal (she might live to 86), but the example implies that income alone does not adequately describe the opportunity set of an elderly person.

Because consumption opportunities are not completely measured by either income or wealth, it is common to aggregate both types of resources either by finding a wealth equivalent of each annuity income stream or by finding the annuity value of wealth.

As a simple example, consider a one-year annuity that will be sold to N individuals. Suppose the probability of dying during the year is λ and the interest rate is r. The survivors will be paid the interest and principal. Given that there will be about $N(1 - \lambda)$ survivors, each survivor will be paid

$$\frac{N \times (1 + r)}{N \times (1 - \lambda)} \approx (1 + r + \lambda)$$

at the end of the year. That is, the rate of return on the annuity will be $r + \lambda$. Therefore, a one-year annuity that pays A will cost

---

[10] These figures exclude a few asset categories such as consumer durables.

$$Ae^{-r-\lambda} \approx A(1-\lambda)\, e^{-r}$$

$$= A \times \text{(probability of living for a year)} \times \text{(interest rate discounting)}.$$

This is the expected present value of the annuity, the wealth equivalent of the annuity.

The generalization to the wealth equivalent of an annuity stream $\{A_t\}$ is the expected present value of the stream, where the expectation is with respect to the random event of dying:

$$w = \int A_t a_t\, e^{-rt}\, dt.$$

r is the interest rate, and a_t is the probability of living at least to t.

The annuity value of wealth (annuitized wealth) is the annuity that could be purchased in an actuarially fair annuity market. The constant annuity that could be purchased with w is

$$A = \frac{w}{\int a_t\, e^{-rt}\, dt}.$$

The denominator is the discounted probability of living.

If utility only depends on consumption, an actuarially fair annuity will generally increase utility because it increases the rate of return on assets. The reasoning is as follows. In the absence of annuities, the budget constraint on a consumption path $\{c_t\}$ is

$$w = \int c_t\, e^{-rt}\, dt,$$

in which w is initial wealth. Let $\{c_t^*\}$ be another consumption stream defined by $\{c_t^* a_t\} = \{c_t\}$. Because $a_t < 1\ \forall t > 0$, $c_t^* > c_t$, except at $t = 0$. Let $\{A_t\} = \{c_t^*\}$ be an annuity stream and suppose it is priced to be actuarially fair. Then it will cost

$$\int A_t a_t\, e^{-rt}\, dt = \int c_t^* a_t\, e^{-rt}\, dt = \int c_t a_t\, e^{-rt}\, dt = w.$$

That is, $\{c_t^*\}$ satisfies the budget constraint and provides greater consumption than $\{c_t\}$.[11] Thus, it will increase utility.

---

[11] Although $\{c_t^*\}$ may satisfy the lifetime budget constraint, it may not satisfy a liquidity constraint that wealth be non-negative at all times, not just at the end of life. This issue is discussed later.

An example is when $a_t = e^{-\lambda t}$, which implies that the conditional mortality rate (the mortality hazard rate) which is $-(1/a_t)(da_t/d_t)$ is equal to λ. The budget constraint becomes

$$\int c_t \, e^{-(r+\lambda)t} \, dt \, ,$$

so that the mortality risk with actuarially fair annuities acts exactly like an increase in the interest rate. In that the annuitants are lenders, an increase in the interest rate must increase utility.

An example of aggregating income and wealth to form a complete picture of the resources available to the elderly is given in Table 6.

The table has fully inclusive average net wealth from the 1979 Retirement History Survey (RHS). The ages of most of the heads of households were 68–73 in 1979, so the table shows wealth near the beginning of retirement. In fact, future earnings accounted for only 3% of wealth, so, practically speaking, the sample had retired by 1979. Financial wealth includes stocks and bonds, savings accounts and so forth. Flows (all but the first three entries) are converted to stocks through actuarial discounting, either real or nominal depending on the flow. SSI is Supplemental Security Income, a means-tested old-age welfare program. Transfers includes transfers from relatives and children. Medicare and Medicaid is the expected present value of the per household transfer through the Medicare and Medicaid program evaluated at cost (the market value). The average wealth levels are reasonably high and consistent with independent measures of income and wealth. However, most people would be surprised

Table 6
Average wealth and distribution (1979)[a]

	Mean wealth	Percentage
Housing	26.9	18
Business and property	11.6	8
Financial	22.5	15
Pensions	18.0	12
SSI, welfare and transfers	2.3	2
Medicare and Medicaid	17.7	12
Social security	44.0	30
Future earnings	3.9	3
Total	146.7	100

[a]Wealth in thousands of 1979 dollars. Based on 6610 (1979) observations from the RHS. Farm families and farm wealth excluded.
Source: Hurd and Shoven (1985).

at how little saving there is in the conventional form of financial, business and property wealth: about 23% in 1979. Adding in housing equity to find the fraction of saving that takes place at the household level brings this to 41%. Pensions and Social Security, which are savings done by firms and society on behalf of the household, accounted for 42%.

3.2. The life-cycle model

The main theoretical model for analyzing consumption and saving after retirement is the life-cycle hypothesis of consumption (LCH). Under the LCH individuals and couples are forward looking in their consumption and savings decisions; they optimize over their lifetimes (although, of course, distant events may be discounted so heavily that for practical purposes they do not matter); and they are uncertain about their date of death. The leading alternative is the LCH augmented by bequest motive for saving: a couple (or individual) gains utility from the knowledge that if both die, someone whose welfare they care about will receive their bequeathable wealth as a bequest. It may appear that a bequest motive changes the LCH only marginally; but, in fact, it changes the implications of many economic models and the effects of policy. For example, it bears on the neutrality of government policy in models with overlapping generations (Barro, 1974). It makes important predictions about the effects of changes in Social Security: for example, if the elderly have a strong bequest motive, increases in Social Security will be saved.

When the age of death is certain, a condition of utility maximization in the absence of a bequest motive is that wealth be zero at the age of death. When the age of death is uncertain, but the maximum age to which anyone can live is known, wealth must be zero by the maximum age; that is, an individual should plan his consumption path so that he would hold no wealth by the maximum age. Wealth must decline at some age, but that age is not known and it could be much greater than the retirement age.

Study of the LCH augmented by the bequest motive has been stimulated by three findings. (1) Simulations of life-cycle earnings, consumption and savings with "reasonable" utility function parameters generate much less household wealth than total wealth, implying that a substantial fraction of household wealth is inherited (White, 1978; Darby, 1979). Given that the date of death is uncertain, large inheritances and bequests are not necessarily evidence for a bequest motive, but they are consistent with it. (2) Kotlikoff and Summers (1981, 1988) estimated from calculations of the earnings and consumption paths of representative consumers that about 80% of household wealth was inherited. Again, this is not necessarily inconsistent with the LCH, but such a large fraction suggests a bequest motive may be important. (3) Cross-section data on wealth holdings by age sometimes show that wealth increases with age, implying that the elderly save as they age rather than dissave as required by the LCH (Lydall, 1955; Projector and Weiss, 1966; Projector, 1968; Mirer,

1979; Blinder et al., 1983; Menchik and David, 1983). Because the LCH predicts that wealth should decline with age (although the age when this starts is not known), this finding has been the most damaging to the LCH: for example, "Perhaps the most decisive attack on the life-cycle theory of savings came from the direct examination of the wealth–age profile itself" (Kurz, 1985). To be able to determine the age at which wealth should decline under the LCH (no bequest motive) and to find the influence of a bequest motive, some assumptions about the form of the lifetime utility function and the economic environment must be made.

3.2.1. Consumption by singles

Suppose that individuals maximize in the consumption path $\{c_t\}$ lifetime utility (Yaari, 1965):

$$\int_0^N u(c_t)\, e^{-\rho t} a_t\, dt + \int_0^N V(w_t)\, e^{-\rho t} m_t\, dt. \tag{2}$$

The first term in lifetime utility is the expected discounted utility from consumption: $u(\cdot)$ gives the utility flow from consumption; ρ is the subjective time rate of discount, a_t is the probability of being alive at t; N is the maximum age to which anyone can live, so that $a_N = 0$. The second term in the lifetime utility function is the expected discounted utility of bequests. $V(\cdot)$ is the utility from bequests; w_t is bequeathable wealth at t, and m_t is the probability of dying at t.

Because in this formulation utility does not depend on leisure, the model is only valid after retirement. Furthermore, it is only valid for a single person: a utility model for couples is much more complicated because it should include the utility flows when both spouses are alive, when only one spouse is alive and a utility from bequests. Such a model for couples is given below.

The constraints on the maximization of utility are a given level of initial bequeathable wealth, w_0, a constraint that w_t be non-negative (to prevent someone from dying in debt), and the equation of motion of bequeathable wealth.

$$\frac{dw_t}{dt} = rw_t - c_t + A_t,$$

in which r, the real interest rate, is constant and known and A_t is annuities at time t.

It was argued above that in the absence of a bequest motive annuitizing wealth increases utility. The reasoning implies that no one should have bequeathable wealth: all wealth should have been annuitized. In fact almost no one buys annuities in the US because the conditions which lead to a utility increase from annuities are not satisfied. First, neither privately purchased annuities nor life insurance are actuarially fair: typically they have a load factor of about 35% (Friedman and Warshawsky, 1987). This means that it is costly to choose the consumption path independently from the annuity path, which reduces the attractiveness of annuities. Second, almost all annuities are job related, either private or government pensions or Social Security. Furthermore, for most people, Social Security is the largest part of job-related pensions; yet, the benefit stream from Social Security cannot be used as collateral for a loan. Whether the benefit stream from a private pension could be used as collateral would depend on the detail of the particular pension program.[12] This makes it difficult to separate the consumption path from the annuity path, because a substantial fraction of the elderly have low levels of bequeathable wealth, requiring consumption to be approximately equal to annuities. For example, in 1988, 45% of those aged 75 or over received more than nine-tenths of their income from Social Security, pensions or other annuities (Grad, 1990). Thus, their consumption paths will have to follow closely their annuity paths.

Utility maximization implies that

$$\frac{du_t}{dt} = u_t(h_t + \rho - r) - h_t V_t$$

when $w_t > 0$ and $c_t = A_t$ when $w_t = 0$.[13] u_t is the marginal utility of consumption at time t; h_t is mortality risk, the probability (density) of dying at t given survival to t; and V_t is the marginal utility of wealth as a bequest.

Consider first the case with no bequest motive ($V_t = 0$). The mortality hazard rate, h_t, increases approximately exponentially. Therefore, regardless of the value of $r - \rho$, $du_t/dt > 0$ at some age and it will remain positive at all greater ages. Because the utility function is strictly concave, this implies that $dc_t/dt < 0$ at all greater ages.

The equation in marginal utility can be integrated to

$$u_t = u_{t+h} \frac{a_{t+h}}{a_t} e^{h(r-\rho)} + \int_t^{t+h} V_s \, e^{(s-t)(r-\rho)} \frac{m_s}{a_t} \, ds \qquad (3)$$

over an interval $(t, t + h)$ in which w_t is positive. This is an Euler equation: it requires that consumption be transferred from t to $t + h$ such that the marginal utility from consumption at t equals the expected marginal utility from consumption at $t + h$, where part of the expected marginal utility comes from a bequest between t and $t + h$.

If V_s were zero (no bequest motive)

$$u_t = u_{t+h} \frac{a_{t+h}}{a_t} e^{h(r-\rho)} \approx u_{t+h} \, e^{h(r-\rho-h_t)}.$$

If $\rho > r$, then $u_t < u_{t+h}$; that is, marginal utility will increase with age, which implies, under the usual assumption about the concavity of $u(\cdot)$ ($u'' < 0$), that consump-

---

[12] For example, future TIAA-CREF annuity benefits cannot be used to secure a loan.
[13] See my 1989 paper for details about the solution.

tion will fall with age. If $\rho < r$, the age at which marginal utility will begin to rise and consumption fall is found from

$$h_t = r - \rho.$$

For example, if $r = 0.03$ and $\rho = 0$, consumption will begin to fall at about age 66 for males and age 74 for females.

The path of wealth depends on the level of consumption which depends on the entire annuity path. Suppose that $A_t = A$, a constant, which is a correct assumption for the majority of the elderly in the US. Then, if consumption declines with age, wealth must also decline. If dw_t/dt were positive and dc_t/dt negative, then

$$\frac{d^2 w_t}{dt^2} = r \frac{dw_t}{dt} - \frac{dc_t}{dt} > 0.$$

This implies that dw_t/dt would remain positive for all future ages, violating a terminal condition that anyone who lives to the greatest age possible (age $= N$) will consume all of his bequeathable wealth; that is, $w_N = 0$. Therefore, the LCH makes the strong prediction that, in the absence of a bequest motive for saving, wealth should begin to fall at some age and that it will continue to fall at all greater ages. A reasonable guess would be that the wealth of retired single men would begin to fall by their 60s or possibly earlier, and of retired single women by their early 70s or earlier.

If $du_t/dt > 0$, the effect of a bequest motive is to flatten the path of u_t because V_t is positive. A flatter path of u_t implies a flatter consumption path. As illustrated in Fig. 12 a flatter consumption path means that initial consumption will be reduced, causing wealth to decline more slowly. The reasoning is as follows: Suppose initial consumption were not reduced. Then the consumption path with a bequest motive $\{c_t | V_s > 0\}$ would be greater at all ages than the consumption path without a bequest motive $\{c_t | V_s = 0\}$ because at any level of consumption $\{c_t | V_s > 0\}$ must have a larger slope. That is, if $\{c_t | V_s > 0\}$ is ever greater than $\{c_t | V_s = 0\}$ it will remain greater at all future ages. However, $\{c_t | V_s = 0\}$ satisfies the constraint that bequeathable wealth at N be zero, implying that $\{c_t | V_s > 0\}$ will cause its associated wealth path to become negative. Therefore, $\{c_t | V_s > 0\}$ will initially be less than $\{c_t | V_s = 0\}$ and bequeathable wealth will decline more slowly under a bequest motive. This result is very reasonable because a bequest motive means that wealth enters the lifetime utility function, so that at any age more wealth should be held. In fact the result holds under more general conditions such as uncertainty about future health status (Hurd, 1987).

Further analysis is very difficult without some restriction on the form of V_t. It is assumed that $V_t = \alpha$, a constant. This assumption may be defended in several ways. First, in other work it was found that the strength of the bequest motive did not seem to depend on the wealth level (Hurd, 1987). Second, variations in the level of wealth

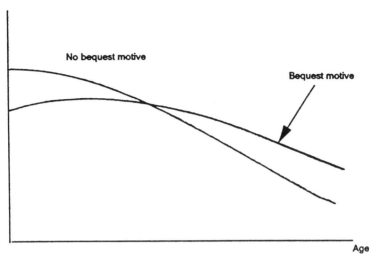

Fig. 12.

cause only small variations in the level of the wealth of the heirs; therefore, the marginal utility of wealth to the heirs will roughly be constant over variations in wealth of the older generation, so we would expect the marginal utility of bequests to be constant. Third, the observed variation within a family in actual bequests suggests that parents do not bequeath according to the economic status of their children: the rule is that all children receive the same bequest (Wilhelm, 1991). Apparently the marginal utility of bequests from the point of view of the parents does not depend on the economic status of the children. This is consistent with a constant marginal utility of bequests.

Even with the assumption that $V_s = \alpha$, the situation has only been analyzed when $\rho > r$, the subjective rate of discount is greater than the interest rate. Then, unless bequeathable wealth is very high compared with annuity wealth, the consumption and wealth paths eventually decline. Typical wealth and consumption paths are in Fig. 13. Initial wealth, w_0, is entirely consumed by T. Then consumption follows the path of annuities, $\{A_t\}$. Therefore, a declining wealth path is consistent with the strict LCH and the LCH augmented by a bequest motive. The LCH is not consistent with increasing wealth at all ages.

3.2.2. *Consumption by couples*

This model is not appropriate for couples because it does not specify what happens when just one of the spouses dies. An extension to couples is the following (Hurd, 1995).

Let the expected lifetime utility of a retired couple be given by

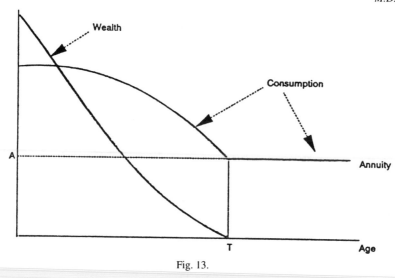

Fig. 13.

$$\int_0 U(C_t)\, e^{-\rho t} a_t\, dt + \int_0 M(w_t)\, e^{-\rho t} p_{mt}\, dt + \int_0 F(w_t)\, e^{-\rho t} p_{ft}\, dt + \int_0 V(w_t)\, e^{-\rho t} m_t\, dt,$$

$$(4)$$

where $U(\cdot)$ is the utility from consumption by the couple, ρ is the subjective discount rate of the couple, a_t is the probability that both spouses will be alive at t, $M(\cdot)$ is the widower's utility of wealth, P_{mt} is the probability (density) that the husband becomes a widower at t, that is, the probability that the wife dies at t and the husband is still alive at t, $F(\cdot)$ is the widow's utility of wealth, P_{ft} is the probability (density) that the wife becomes a widow at t, $V(\cdot)$ is the utility from bequests (outside the household), w_t is bequeathable wealth at t, m_t is the probability (density) that the surviving spouse dies at t.

This objective function has the same structure as in the single's problem: the couple derives utility from consumption, which is the first term in Eq. (4), and this continues as long as both are alive. The couple also gets utility from "bequests". The utility from bequests is in three parts: utility of wealth should the husband become a widower, utility of wealth should the wife become a widow, and utility from a true bequest outside the household when the last survivor dies.

In this formulation assets transferred to the surviving spouse on the death of the other spouse are not true bequests. The surviving spouse is simply the continuation of the household, and his or her welfare influences the consumption decisions of the couple through the second and third terms of the lifetime utility function of the household (Eq. (4)). Any desire to leave a true bequest influences consumption decisions through $V(\cdot)$ and through the consumption decisions the surviving spouse might make, that is, through the utility of wealth of each surviving spouse, $M(\cdot)$ and $F(\cdot)$.

Suppose the couple maximizes expected lifetime utility (Eq. (4)) subject to the equation of motion of wealth,

$$\frac{dw_t}{dt} = rw_t - C_t + A_t,$$

where r is the real rate of interest, assumed to be fixed and known, and A_t is annuities, including Social Security and other pensions. Other restrictions on the maximization are that initial bequeathable wealth, w_0, is given and that bequeathable wealth must be nonnegative. The nonnegativity condition means that the couple cannot die in debt.

The solution to the utility maximization problem at $t = 0$ when all couples are alive ($a_0 = 1$) satisfies the equation of motion of marginal utility,

$$\frac{du_t}{dt} = U_t(h_t + \rho - r) - (M_t\phi_t + F_t\mu_t), \tag{5}$$

in which U_t is marginal utility of consumption by the couple, h_t is the couple's mortality risk (the probability density that one of them will die at t given that neither has died before), M_t is the marginal utility of wealth of the widower and F_t is the marginal utility of wealth of the widow. ϕ_t is the mortality risk of the wife and μ_t is the mortality risk of the husband. If the surviving spouse optimizes his or her lifetime utility, M_t and F_t will be determined by the solution to the single's problem as outlined in Section 3.2.1. The last term in Eq. (5) is composed of two parts: the marginal utility of wealth of the widower times the probability he becomes a widower (the wife dies), and the marginal utility of wealth of the widow times the probability she becomes a widow (the husband dies). Therefore, the last term is the expected marginal utility of wealth of the household in the event that one or the other of the spouses dies. This solution is similar to the solution of the single person's utility maximization problem:

$$\frac{du_t}{dt} = u_t(h_t + \rho - r) - h_t V_t.$$

V_t is the marginal utility of a bequest and h_t is the probability (density) that the single person will die at t and leave the bequest. $H_t V_t$ corresponds to the last term of Eq. (5). In the case of the couple the wealth goes to the surviving spouse; in the case of the single person the wealth goes to the heir.

Because of time separability of utility, the couple maximizes Eq. (4) starting from any arbitrary date. That is, as long as the couple is alive, we can put $t = 0$ and solve the utility maximization problem forward from that date. At a later time either both spouses are alive, the husband only is alive, the wife only is alive, or both have died, so the probabilities of these outcomes must sum to one. That is,

$$a_t = 1 - b_t - f_t - \int_0^t m_s \, ds.$$

If t becomes small the probability that both will die between 0 and t goes to zero. Therefore, in a small interval of time a bequest takes place through the surviving spouse, not through the simultaneous deaths of both spouses: one spouse must die in order that the probability the other spouse will die and leave a bequest becomes positive.

The relationship between h_t, ϕ_t and μ_t can be found as follows. Let h_{t0} be the probability density that one spouse or the other or both die at t given that both are alive at $t = 0$.

$$a_t = 1 - \int_0^t h_{s0} \, ds.$$

Let ϕ_{t0} be the mortality risk of all females alive at $t = 0$, and μ_{t0} the mortality risk of males. Then

$$h_{t0} = -\frac{da_t}{dt} = \frac{db_t}{dt} + \frac{df_t}{dt} + m_t.$$

Under the assumption that the mortality risk of the husband and of the wife are independent, the probability that the husband only is alive at t is given by

$$b_t = \int_0^t \phi_{s0} \, ds \left[1 - \int_0^t \mu_{s0} \, ds \right].$$

Similarly,

$$f_t = \int_0^t \mu_{s0} \, ds \left[1 - \int_0^t \phi_{s0} \, ds \right].$$

Then,

$$\frac{db_t}{dt} = \phi_{t0} \left[1 - \int_0^t \mu_{s0} \, ds \right] 1 - \int_0^t \mu_{s0} \, ds - \mu_{t0} \int_0^t \phi_{s0} \, ds \rightarrow \phi_0 \quad \text{as } t \rightarrow 0.$$

This says that the rate of flow of husbands to widowers is given by the mortality risk of wives. In a similar way

$$\frac{df_t}{dt} \rightarrow \mu_0.$$

Then,

$$m_t = \mu_t b_t + \phi_t f_t \rightarrow 0 \quad \text{as } t \rightarrow 0 \quad \text{because } b_t \text{ and } f_t \rightarrow 0.$$

Finally, $h_{t0} \rightarrow \phi_0 + \mu_0$ as $t \rightarrow 0$.

In Eq. (5), $h_t + \rho$ will be larger than r if the couple is sufficiently old because both ϕ_t and μ_t increase approximately exponentially. Therefore, in the absence of the second term in Eq. (5), U_t would be increasing. The second term flattens the path of U_t and could even cause it to fall. Thus, with the usual assumption that $U(\cdot)$ is concave, the second term flattens the path of consumption, which would otherwise be declining, and could even cause the path to rise. This "bequest" motive (to leave wealth to the surviving spouse) has the same effect on the consumption path of a couple as it does on the consumption path of a single person. Beyond the fact that the consumption path is flattened, the path of marginal utility is not easy to analyze because neither M_t nor F_t could be expected to be constant as bequeathable wealth varies.

The equation of motion of marginal utility (5) can be integrated over a small interval $(0, t)$ to give

$$U_0 \approx U_t a_t \, e^{(\rho-r)t} + \int_0^t M_s \phi_s \, e^{(r-\rho)s} \, ds + \int_0^t F_s \mu_s \, e^{(r-\rho)s} \, ds. \tag{6}$$

The interpretation of this equation is that the reallocation of consumption from $t = 0$ to t will result in a loss of utility at $t = 0$ of U_0; the offsetting gain is composed of three parts: the discounted increase in utility should the couple live, the discounted increase in utility should the wife die between 0 and t, and the discounted increase in utility should the husband die between 0 and t. The approximation ignores a second-order term which is the utility from true bequests should both spouses die between 0 and t, but this term goes to zero as t goes to zero much faster than the other three terms because the probability density goes to zero. Thus, the first-order conditions imply an Euler condition: marginal utility at $t = 0$ equals the expected discounted marginal utility in all future periods.

The true bequest motive (bequeathing to heirs outside of the household) operates through M_s and F_s: a bequest motive will increase the marginal utility of wealth of both the widower and the widow. This increases the right-hand side of Eq. (6) which requires that U_0 be increased. That, in turn, requires that C_0 be decreased with the result that more wealth will be held. Thus, the effect of a true bequest motive on a couple is the same as on a single: consumption will be lower and wealth higher.

3.3. Empirical findings about the LCH based on wealth data

The objective of studying how wealth varies by age in cross-section is to find how individuals accumulate or decumulate wealth as they age. It was indicated earlier that a number of earlier studies found wealth to increase with age in cross-section. However, this has not been found in a number of recent studies. Table 7 has cross-section wealth by age from four data sources, normalized so that wealth at 55–64 is 1.00. In these data, wealth declines with age, as required by the LCH. It is not clear why these results differ from the earlier results. One explanation is that in some earlier studies there was too much aggregation by age (Wolff, 1988). For example, in the 1983 SCF (with high income supplement) if all the age intervals above 64 are combined into a single category of 65 and above, wealth will seem to increase with age: mean wealth of 55–64-year-olds is $202 000 and of those 65 and over is $250 000 (Avery and Elliehausen, 1986). As Table 7 shows, however, wealth declines after age 69.

Regardless of whether wealth actually declines with age in cross-section, as in these data, there are a number of barriers to interpreting cross-section wealth paths as the wealth paths of individuals. (1) Cohort wealth effects: suppose individuals save as they age (wealth increases with age) at all ages. Because older cohorts had lower lifetime wealth than younger cohorts, in cross-section they may have less wealth than younger cohorts. Thus wealth would appear to fall in cross-section supporting the LCH, even though individuals were not consuming according to the LCH. (2) Cohort-specific lifetime shocks: events that affect cohorts differently could make wealth comparisons across age invalid. For example, the oldest cohorts have the largest windfall gains from Social Security. If during their working lives they saved under the assumption they would have modest Social Security benefits, they would have reached retirement with more wealth than the younger cohorts. Even controlling for lifetime earnings, one could find rising wealth after retirement with age. (3) Retirement: it is difficult to control for retirement in cross-section. It would not be surprising to find increasing wealth with age if some individuals are working, even though retired indi-

Table 7
Relative bequeathable wealth

Age	Data set			
	1962 SFCC	1979 ISDP	1983 SCF	1984 SIPP
55–64	1.00	1.00	1.00	1.00
65–69	1.00	0.85	1.27	0.96
70–74	0.96	0.81	0.84	0.79
75–79	0.89	0.62[a]	0.69	0.69[a]
80+	0.67	0.62[a]	0.52	0.69[a]

[a]75 or over.
Sources: 1962 SFCC (Survey of Financial Characteristics of Consumers) and 1983 SCF (Survey of Consumer Finances): Wolff (1979; 1988); ISDP (Income survey Development Program) and 1984 SIPP (Survey of Income and Program Participation): Radner (1989).

viduals dissave. But even the cross-sectional wealth of retired persons would not follow the wealth path of any individual if wealth itself has an influence on retirement: the more wealthy members of a cohort will retire earlier, so that the wealth of retired persons will decline in cross-section. (4) Differential mortality: the wealthy live longer than the poor: wealth in cross-section could rise, even though individuals dissave.

It may be that these theoretical objections to interpreting cross-section wealth trajectories as individual wealth trajectories are not empirically important. However, that appears not to be the case. It was the correction for cohort effects that led Mirer (1979) to find increasing wealth with age: wealth declined with age in the raw data. An adjustment for permanent income (cohort effects) caused an estimate of the wealth path to decline with age rather than increase with age in King and Dicks-Mireaux (1982). Shorrocks (1975) found that wealth increased with age in raw data, but fell when a correction was made for differential mortality. Using panel data from the NLS, Jianakoplos et al. (1989) investigated the effects of adjusting for cohorts and differential mortality. They could compare the cross-section wealth paths with the wealth paths of individuals. They conclude that "There does not appear to be any systematic differences between cross-section and cohort age–wealth profiles which could be used to correct the cross-sectional profiles". That is, cross-section wealth paths cannot be used to give evidence about the LCH because one cannot recover wealth paths of individuals or even of cohorts; yet, it is these paths that need to be observed.

The alternative to cross-section wealth comparisons is to observe wealth changes of individuals in panel data. Indeed Jianakoplos et al. (1989) conclude that "... there are no substitutes for panel data in the analysis of household life-cycle wealth accumulation and portfolio allocation". It should be noted, however, that if the panel is short, macroeconomic shocks which affect the wealth of everyone in the panel could lead to incorrect conclusions about desired wealth change. For example, if rates of return happen to be especially large during the years of the panel, wealth may increase at the individual level even though the individuals planned consumption levels such that wealth would decrease. Similarly, if inflation happened to be especially high, real wealth could decline even though individuals anticipated that it would increase. It is reasonable to suppose, however, that if the panel is sufficiently long, the actual rates of return will average out to the anticipated rate, and that average wealth change will equal anticipated wealth change.

Table 8 has ten-year (1969–1979) real wealth changes from the RHS. They were calculated by compounding observed two-year wealth changes of retired individuals and couples, so that in each two-year period composition is held constant. The changes that exclude housing wealth are more representative of desired wealth change because of large, surely unanticipated, increases in housing prices, mainly between 1975 and 1979.[14] They show total dissaving over ten years of about 36% for singles and 15% for couples, corresponding to annual rates of dissaving of 4.5% for singles and 1.6%

[14] During the years of the RHS (1969–1979) real housing prices increased by 22.7% (Poterba, 1989).

Table 8
Ten-year wealth changes in the RHS (percentage)

Housing wealth	Singles	Couples	All
Included	−22.4	−2.0	−13.9
Not included	−36.4	−14.5	−27.3

Source: Hurd (1987).

for couples. The median age of single persons in the ten years of the RHS is about 65. At a dissaving rate of 4.5% per year it takes about 15 years to decumulate half of initial wealth. Most of the singles are females who had a life expectancy at age 65 of about 18 years; were the rate of decumulation to remain constant at 4.5% per year, at age 83 they would still have about 44% of initial wealth. However, the LCH suggests and the data seem to confirm that as the individuals age and mortality increases, the rate of decumulation increases: except for the period from 1977 to 1979, when it seems a macroeconomic shock caused wealth to increase by 1%, the rate of wealth decumulation increased in each two-year period from 1969–1977, as the sample aged.

The rate of decumulation by couples is less than by singles. An explanation is that the expected lifetime of their household (time until both die) is greater than the expected lifetime of a single person. To see how this could affect wealth change consider an extreme case in which there are complete returns to scale in household consumption: that is, two can, indeed, live as cheaply as one. Then the appropriate mortality rate for the couple to use in its consumption calculations is the probability that both members of the household will die, which is very much lower than the probability that either will die. Therefore, the desired consumption path of the couple could still be rising at age 65 whereas the desired consumption of either a single male or female could be falling. The result could be a flat or slowly falling wealth path of the couple until one spouse dies. Then the survivor would switch to the more steeply falling path of a single. If returns-to-scale in consumption is somewhat less than complete, a similar result would obtain. However, it should be noted that the result depends on the returns-to-scale assumption. Consider the opposite assumption of no returns to scale whatsoever: the couple's utility is just the sum of the utility of the husband and of the wife. If both have the same utility function, the optimal allocation in each time period is that both consume the same amount. Except for mortality discounting, this will be the same amount as what will be consumed by the surviving spouse. Thus, consumption by the couple could be as much as twice the consumption by a single person. Then, holding wealth constant, the rate of wealth decline will be greater among couples than among singles. The conclusion is that although couples seem to dissave more slowly than singles, it is not necessary under the LCH that they do.

The importance of differential mortality can be found by comparing the rates of dissaving in Table 8 with rates calculated over all retired couples and over all retired

Table 9
Average bequeathable wealth change in panel data

Data set	Annual rate of wealth change (%)	Source
1963, 1964 Federal Reserve[a]	−1.2[b]	Mirer (1980)
NLS mature men	−5.0	Diamond and Hausman (1984)
RHS 1969–1979 (singles)	−4.5	Hurd (1987)
RHS 1969–1979 (couples)	−1.6	Hurd (1987)
SIPP 1984, 1985 (singles)	−3.9	Hurd (1991)
SIPP 1984, 1985 (couples)	−1.8	Hurd (1991)

[a]Survey of Financial Characteristics of Consumers and Survey of Changes in Family Financing.
[b]Median wealth change.

singles in successive cross-sections of the RHS. This calculation follows a cohort, but it does not hold composition constant because some spouses and some singles died between surveys. Because couples have considerably more wealth than singles the surviving spouse will tend to increase the wealth of all singles in subsequent surveys. Because the poorer tend to die earlier than the more well-to-do, the wealth of the survivors (both couples and singles) will tend to be higher in the later surveys.

According to this calculation real nonhousing bequeathable wealth of couples remained roughly constant over the ten years of the RHS, rather than declining by 14.5% as in Table 8 (Hurd, 1990a); real nonhousing bequeathable wealth of singles increased by about 12%, rather than declining by 36.4%. That is, not controlling for differential mortality causes a change in the fundamental conclusion of the data analysis: the elderly seemed to save, not dissave.

A decrease in nonhousing bequeathable wealth after retirement of a similar magnitude to Table 8 is found by Bernheim (1987) using a different subsample from the RHS. He also shows the importance of controlling for retirement: both for singles and for couples cross-section regressions of wealth on age have positive coefficients on age; the same regressions over retired observations have negative coefficients on age.

Dissaving by the retired elderly is found in other panel data: Diamond and Hausman (1984) in the NLS found rates of dissaving after retirement that are higher than in the RHS, about 5% per year (Table 9). Mirer (1980) used a one-year panel from the 1963 and 1964 Federal Reserve wealth surveys to study wealth change of retired elderly. The median rate of dissaving was 1.2% per year. In the SIPP, the rates of dissaving are remarkably similar to the rates in the RHS (Table 9).

3.4. Summary of wealth change

The discussion of consumption and saving began with the observation that the increase in wealth with age in cross-section has been most damaging to the LCH. A number of recent studies, however, have shown this observation to be wrong for two reasons. First, wealth, in fact, seems to decline with age in cross-section; apparently the earlier studies did not have enough age detail to show that wealth eventually falls. Second, whether or not wealth increases with age in cross-section has little relevance for testing the implications of the LCH anyway; it would simply be coincidence if the cross-section wealth paths were the same as individual wealth paths, or even had the same slope. This conclusion is supported by empirical findings from panel data in which the difference between cross-section wealth paths and individual wealth paths can be studied.

The available evidence from panel data on average wealth change among the elderly seems to support the LCH. However, this says nothing about the diversity of behavior, and certainly there is a great deal of ex post variation in observed saving rates across individuals. Detailed examination of asset holdings in panel data support the view that considerable variation is due to observation error (Rust, 1990). Of the remaining variation, some probably results from taste differences, not only for bequests but in time rates of discount and risk aversion. Some variation is likely due to differences in initial conditions: for example, all individuals could have the same utility function parameters including the bequest motive parameter, yet the wealthy would save and the poor dissave (Hurd, 1989). Panel data offer the hope of finding if there is substantial variation in saving for bequests, and whether the variation is due to tastes or to wealth levels, but we are far from having a good understanding of the amount and causes of the variation.

According to the LCH the consumption path will vary with mortality risk; but because the magnitude of the variation depends on unknown parameters such as the risk aversion parameter, intended bequests cannot be identified in consumption and wealth data simply from the variation in their paths as mortality risk varies. In particular, very slowly declining wealth paths could be consistent with the LCH. However, some authors, while admitting that the elderly dissave, say that rate of dissaving is too low to be consistent with the LCH (Modigliani, 1986, 1988; Bernheim, 1987; Kotlikoff, 1988; Kotlikoff and Summers, 1988). It is difficult to assess what the appropriate rate of dissaving should be in the LCH model. Suppose for example that the instantaneous utility function is

$$u(c) = \frac{1}{1-\gamma} c^{1-\gamma}.$$

When there is no bequest motive, the optimal consumption path satisfies

$$\frac{dc_t}{dt} \frac{1}{c_t} = \frac{1}{\gamma}(r - \rho - h_t).$$

If γ, the risk aversion parameter, is large, consumption will be practically flat. Take that extreme case, and assume a real interest rate of 3% and a maximum age of 105.

Table 10
One-year wealth change (%) by age and health status[a]

Age range	Health status				Number of observations
	Poor	Average	Very good	All	
Singles					
65–69	−3.5	−2.8	5.7	−0.1	370
70–74	−12.3	−4.4	−2.9	−4.8	405
75+	−9.5	−6.2	−3.2	−6.0	548
All	−9.2	−4.7	−0.1	−3.9	1323
Couples					
65–69	−0.1	1.5	5.6	2.3	298
70–74	−11.9	−5.2	−2.0	−5.9	238
75+	−5.4	−2.8	−5.6	−3.7	206
All	−5.9	−1.8	1.9	−1.8	742
All					
65–69	−1.1	−0.2	5.7	1.3	668
70–74	−12.1	−4.8	−2.5	−5.3	643
75+	−7.5	−4.8	−3.6	−5.1	754
All	−7.3	−3.2	0.7	−2.9	2065

[a]Retired singles and couples. Health status: "Poor" means at least one family member reported poor health; "Very good" means all family members reported very good to excellent health; "Average" is all others.
Source: 1984 SIPP, Waves 3, 4 and 7.

Then, wealth at age 85 would be about 65% of wealth at age 65, an average rate of dissaving of about 2% per year. This is certainly consistent with observed rates of dissaving.[15]

Although the results discussed support the LCH, Table 10 gives evidence that the LCH is not a complete description of consumption and saving after retirement. It shows one-year real wealth changes of retired individuals and couples by self-assessed health status. The table shows increasing rates of dissaving with age as required by the LCH. The rate of dissaving is higher among singles than among couples, which is similar to what is found in the RHS. However, what is striking is the strong interaction between health status and the rate of dissaving. Those in poor health dissaved at a rate of 7.3% per year whereas those in very good health actually saved. A similar pattern is found holding age constant.

---

[15] The rate of wealth decumulation increases with age. With less risk aversion than the extreme case, the rate of decumulation predicted by the LCH could be rather small at younger ages observed in panel data sets.

There are a number of explanations for this pattern. The most obvious is, of course, that those in poor health have higher medical expenses. But the pattern is also consistent with the LCH. Self-assessed health is a strong predictor of mortality outcome, so those in poor health may believe their life expectancy is reduced: under the LCH they will have higher consumption than those who believe their life expectancy is greater. The pattern could also be explained by underlying heterogeneity in tastes. For example, individuals with higher subjective time rates of discount will both invest less in their own health and save less. Thus, ceteris paribus, they will have worse health and dissave at a greater rate. We do not have adequate data to quantify these explanations but the implication is that the LCH does not provide a complete description of saving behavior among the elderly.

3.5. Evidence about the LCH based on consumption data

Consumption data offer a more promising way to estimate parameters associated with the LCH and to test for the presence of a bequest motive than wealth data: the rate of change of consumption depends directly on current mortality rates and the degree of risk aversion, whereas the rate of change of wealth depends on the level of consumption, which depends on the entire time path of mortality rates. The importance of annuities (mainly Social Security) further complicates estimation based on wealth: they enter the utility maximization problem as a flow, not a stock of wealth. Because the optimal level of the consumption path depends on the entire path of annuities, the rate of change of wealth depends on the entire time path of annuities. However, the rate of change of consumption does not depend on annuities as long as a boundary condition on wealth is not binding, which greatly simplifies estimation. As we have seen, annuities are important for the elderly: in 1986 57% of the elderly (age 65 and over) received more than half of their money income from Social Security.

Although data on consumption offer, at least in principle, a more direct test of the LCH than data on wealth, consumption is difficult to measure even in surveys that are specifically designed to determine consumption such as the Consumer Expenditure Survey (CES). Table 11 has average after-tax income and consumption by age from the 1984–1986 CES. The table shows that households on average dissaved, yet we know from the national income and product accounts that households actually saved. That is, the overall levels of income and/or consumption are mismeasured, making it difficult to have confidence in any conclusions based on the levels of consumption. Even so, the pattern of saving by age is consistent with what is predicted by the LCH: for example, the rate of dissaving increases with age from 55–64 to 75 or over.

A different method of using consumption data depends on panel data. The LCH predicts that at advanced ages the level of consumption will decline as individuals age. The RHS has measures of consumption that cover about 34% of total consumption (Hurd, 1992b). Table 12 shows the percentage change in real consumption by retired

Table 11
After-tax income, expenditures and saving rates: United States[a]

Age	1986			1985			1984			Average saving rate
	(1)[b]	(2)	(3)	(1)	(2)	(3)	(1)	(2)	(3)	
Under 25	11.5	14.1	−22.6	10.9	13.8	−26.6	11.5	13.5	−17.4	−22.2
25–34	23.5	23.9	−1.7	23.1	23.3	−0.9	21.7	22.3	−2.8	−1.8
35–44	31.1	31.2	−0.3	29.6	29.6	0.0	27.5	28.2	−2.5	−1.0
45–54	30.1	32.2	−7.0	30.4	30.9	−1.6	27.6	28.7	−4.0	−4.2
55–64	25.5	24.8	2.7	24.6	24.8	−0.8	23.7	23.4	1.3	1.1
65–74	16.7	17.5	−4.8	17.2	17.9	−4.1	14.8	15.8	−6.8	−5.2
75+	11.7	12.2	−4.3	11.6	13.0	−12.1	11.0	11.1	−0.9	−5.8
All	23.2	23.9	−3.0	22.9	23.5	−2.6	21.2	22.0	−3.8	−3.1

[a]Income and expenditures in thousands of dollars. Saving rates in percent. Based on 1984, 1985 and 1986 Consumer Expenditure Surveys.
[b](1) After tax income; (2) Expenditures; (3) Saving rate.
Source: Bureau of Labor Statistics (1989).

couples and singles as measured by those components.[16] Because these are changes in panel data, the entries hold the composition of the sample constant. Consumption declined in every two-year period and the total decline over the ten years was about 38%. This is consistent with the LCH.

3.6. Tests of the bequest motive for saving

Although the evidence on wealth change is consistent with the LCH it does not rule out the possibility that people save to leave a bequest. The empirical implication of a bequest motive for saving is that declining consumption and wealth trajectories will be flattened, not that they will necessarily slope upward.

One way to test for a bequest motive is to compare the consumption level of someone who has children or close relatives with the consumption of someone who does not. A measure of the difference in their bequest motives would be the difference in the consumption or wealth trajectories of the two individuals. This kind of test has the appealing characteristic of being based on observed behavior. It does not depend on whether people actually give bequests, which because of uncertainty about the date of death, would happen anyway, or on whether they say they would like to give bequests. The test depends on whether the desire to give bequests leads to differences in consumption and wealth trajectories.

---

[16] In testing for age effects that could shift consumption between measured and unmeasured components, no such effects could be found.

Table 12
Consumption change in RHS (percentage of initial consumption)

Year	Singles	Couples	All
1969–1971	−2	−2	−2
1971–1973	−6	−5	−5
1973–1975	−21	−21	−21
1975–1977	−0	−5	−3
1977–1979	−5	−6	−6
1969–1979	−35	−39	−38

Source: Hurd (1992b).

Similar trajectories could mean that there is no difference in how much each cares about the welfare of his heirs. However, it could also mean they care differently, but the bequest motive is not operable: as in ordinary demand analysis, the optimum can be a corner solution. Someone may care about the welfare of his heirs, but when he weighs the utility of his own consumption against the utility from a bequest, he may choose the same consumption path as someone who has no heirs. That is, desired bequests could be zero even though someone has heirs he cares about; his bequest motive is not operable (Able, 1987; Hurd, 1987). In an economy in which incomes rise with each generation, it would not be surprising to find that each older generation has no desire to leave a bequest simply because it anticipates the succeeding generation will have adequate consumption without a bequest. In this setting bequests will be accidental, the result of uncertainty about the date of death, even though the older generation cares about the welfare of the younger generation.

A test based on the difference between paths cannot distinguish between an inoperable bequest motive and no bequest motive whatsoever. Whether this is important depends on the how the results are to be used. In some circumstances it is not important to distinguish between them: for example, the effects of a marginal change in a policy may be well approximated by assuming that no one switches from having an inoperable bequest motive to having an operable bequest motive, which is the same as assuming that those with an inoperable bequest motive have no bequest motive at all. The effects of a large change in policy, however, may not be well approximated by this assumption.

In that much of the discussion of a bequest motive concerns intergenerational transfers from parents to children, a natural way to classify elderly individuals by the strength of a bequest motive is by whether or not they have children. A test based on wealth comparisons requires panel data: it would not make sense to compare the wealth of two individuals of the same age in cross-section because one person expended an unknown amount on child raising, and, furthermore, we know from the labor supply literature that family earnings vary by the number of children. Therefore, variation in wealth by parental status is to be expected even in the absence of a be-

Table 13
Average annual real wealth change (%)[a]

	Singles		Couples	
	RHS	SIPP	RHS	SIPP
Children	−4.8	−2.6	−1.7	−4.5
No children	−3.9	−3.2	−0.2	−0.2
Support for bequest motive	No	Yes	No	No

[a]Retired singles and couples. RHS, bequeathable wealth excluding housing. 1984 SIPP waves 4 and 7, bequeathable wealth including housing.
Sources: RHS, Hurd (1987); SIPP, Wang (1991).

quest motive, and, indeed such variation is observed in the RHS. For example, in the 1975 RHS, childless couples had about $15 000 more in bequeathable wealth than parents.

Table 13 shows the change in bequeathable wealth among retired singles and couples over the ten years of the RHS, and over one year in the SIPP. As the last row shows, the bequest motive is not supported according to this test: parents should dissave at a greater rate than nonparents, but they only do in one case out of four.

The table does not control for differences in the levels of bequeathable wealth or annuities that could vary systematically over parents and nonparents and which could influence the rates of dissaving. To control for them and simultaneously to get evidence about the magnitude of mortality risk aversion the model of consumption by singles over wealth data in the RHS was estimated (Hurd, 1989). It was assumed that

$$u(c_t) = \frac{c_t^{1-\gamma}}{1-\gamma}.$$

This is the constant relative risk aversion utility function. γ is the coefficient of risk aversion because it determines the reaction to variation in mortality risk: from the equation of motion of marginal utility,

$$\frac{dc_t}{dt}\frac{1}{c_t} = \frac{1}{\gamma}(r-\rho-h_t) = \frac{r-\rho}{\gamma} - \frac{1}{\gamma}h_t.$$

Thus, if γ is large the consumption path will be unaffected by changes in h_t, mortality risk. If γ is small, the rate of decline of consumption will increase in h_t, which will cause wealth to be decumulated more rapidly. It was also assumed that $V_t = \alpha$, a constant, the justification of which has already been discussed. With these assumptions and the other conditions discussed above, the consumption path is implicitly defined by

$$c_t = A_T, \quad t \geq T,$$

$$c_0^{-\gamma} = c_t^{-\gamma} a_t \, e^{t(r-\rho)} + \alpha \int_0^t e^{(r-\rho)s} m_s \, ds, \quad t < T,$$

$$w_T = w_0 \, e^{rT} + \int_0^T (A_s - c_s) \, e^{(T-s)r} \, ds,$$

$$w_T = 0 \quad \text{(defines } T),$$

and the wealth path by

$$\frac{dw_t}{dt} = rw_t - c_t + A_t.$$

Thus wealth is implicitly defined as

$$w_2 = f(w_0, \{A\}, \{a\}, \theta),$$

where $\theta = (\gamma \, \rho \, \alpha)'$, the parameter vector.

This model was estimated over two-year panel data from the 1969–1979 RHS. Econometric identification of α comes from the assumption that

$$\alpha = \begin{cases} 0 & \text{if no children,} \\ 1 & \text{if children.} \end{cases}$$

Estimation was by nonlinear two-stage least squares:

$$\min_\theta [w_2 - f(\theta)' \, X(X'X)^{-1} X' [w_2 - f(\theta)].$$

w_2 and f are n-vectors of second-period wealth and predicted second-period wealth. X is an $n \times 15$ matrix of observations on income from wealth. The estimated coefficients and standard errors were

γ	ρ	α
1.12	−0.011	6.0×10^{-7}
(0.07)	(0.002)	(32×10^{-7})

Number of observations = 5452

The risk aversion parameter is small, which means that the slope of the consumption path is rather sensitive to variations in h_t. α is interpreted as the marginal utility of bequests; it is not statistically significant, and its effect on the paths of consumption and wealth is small. This should be expected as its econometric identification comes from differences in the wealth paths of parents and nonparents, and we have already seen that the paths do not differ.

The conclusion is that the estimates support the LCH: singles react to variations in mortality risk, and furthermore, as measured by differences in the behavior of parents and nonparents, the bequest motive is unimportant.

An alternate way to find the influence of a bequest motive comes from estimation over consumption data because a strong bequest motive will flatten the consumption path. Table 14 shows the average change in consumption in RHS panel data. On average consumption declined. Among singles consumption by parents declined less than consumption by nonparents, which supports that bequest motive, yet the changes among couples does not support it. In neither case is the difference statistically significant.

The conclusion from these empirical results is they offer no support for an operable bequest motive.

My outline of the bequest motive does not distinguish among different reasons for desiring to leave a bequest. It is most commonly thought that bequests are due to altruistic motives: people care about the welfare of their heirs (Becker, 1981). The theory says that a child's utility is an argument of the parents' utility function. Because bequests increase a child's utility, they increase the parents' utility, and, therefore, parents desire to leave bequests. This implies that wealth enters the lifetime utility function of the parents because it produces positive utility at death (Yaari, 1965). Under rather general circumstances this will cause parents to hold more wealth, ceteris paribus, than they would otherwise. In particular, as we have seen, they will reduce present consumption at the expense of future consumption, so that a declining consumption path will be flattened. The reduction in present consumption will reduce the rate of wealth decumulation.

Table 14
Average partial consumption (1969 dollars per week)[a]

Consumption	Singles		Couples	
	Children	No children	Children	No children
First period	21.35	22.72	38.58	37.89
Second period	20.26	21.44	36.22	35.95
Change	−0.59	−1.28	−2.37	−1.93
Support for bequest motive	Yes		No	

[a]This measure of consumption is about 34% of total consumption.
Source: Hurd (1992b).

An alternative to altruistic bequests is that parents use the promise of a bequest to induce desirable behavior by their children. In the extreme version of this theory, parents care about the attention children give them, but not about the welfare of their children. Parents make an implicit promise of a bequest to influence their children to provide attention, and bequests are simply the realization of those promises. That is, bequests are in exchange (payment for) attention. Notice that the desire for attention itself is not enough to produce exchange-motivated bequests. For example, if the parents pay for each unit of attention upon receipt, the purchase of attention is little different from the purchase of consumption goods, and in the absence of taste changes with age, the path of observed consumption and wealth should not be altered by the desire for attention. That is, there is no good reason to suppose that the allocation of wealth between present and future consumption should be altered because parents can purchase attention from their children.

If payment for attention is made in the form of a promise of a bequest, and the amount of attention depends on bequeathable wealth, the parents' utility function can be rewritten so that bequeathable wealth is an argument of the utility function. Then, just as in the case of an altruistic bequest motive the consumption and wealth paths will be flattened. Therefore, the two types of bequest motives cannot be distinguished by studying consumption or wealth change.

In the analysis of Bernheim et al. (1985), bequests are exchange motivated, and parents hold bequeathable wealth with an implicit promise to bequeath the wealth if their children perform adequately. However, strategic considerations enter the parents' decision about how much wealth to hold because they could secretly disinherit even a well-performing child or consume the wealth themselves. Bernheim et al., therefore, call this a strategic bequest motive.

The empirical support for exchange-motivated bequests is mixed. Tomes (1981) did not find a positive relationship between bequests and a measure of attention, and, therefore, concluded that "this result presents prima facia evidence against the pure 'child-services' model of inheritance". However, Cox (1987) found patterns of inter vivos transfers that are more consistent with exchange-related motives than with altruistic motives. Wilhelm (1991) used income tax data, which was linked across generations (Estate-Income Tax Match), to study the division of the estates of the wealthy (about the top 2.8% of wealth holders) as a function of the economic status of their children. Estates were exactly equally divided among their children in 68% of the estates and within 5% of equal division in 79% of the cases. Even when there was unequal division, the allocation of the estate did not compensate the less well-to-do child: if anything, a greater share went to the child with the greatest resources. Obviously these findings are evidence against the altruistic bequest motive: division should be equal only by chance and the largest share should go to the least well-off child. Less obviously the findings are evidence against the strategic bequest motive: variation in the economic resources of children should vary their willingness to supply attention; when parents maximize attention subject to a total level of bequests, the bequest to each child will vary.

Both the altruistic and strategic bequest motives should alter the shape of the consumption path. Wealth itself produces utility: in the case of the altruistic bequest motive it is because of the knowledge that after death wealth will increase the welfare of the heirs, and, in the case of the strategic bequest motive, wealth will increase the attention of the heirs. Therefore, both types of bequest motive will flatten the consumption path, reducing the rate of wealth decumulation after retirement. However, as we have seen, in the RHS there is no systematic difference between the consumption paths of retired parents and nonparents, and both retired parents and nonparents decumulate wealth at about the same rate, and in the 1984 Survey of Income and Program Participation (SIPP) there is no systematic difference in the rates of decumulation of wealth by parents and nonparents. These findings provide no evidence that a bequest motive, altruistic or strategic, influences the saving behavior of retired elderly. Bernheim et al. found empirical support for exchange-motivated bequests by studying the attention paid to parents by their children. The relationship between bequeathable wealth and the attention paid by children to their parents is, in the framework of the strategic bequest motive, generated by the choices of both parents and children. Parents reach retirement age with endowments of bequeathable wealth and annuity wealth (mostly Social Security and pensions). Children have a "supply of attention" schedule that gives attention as a function of a possible bequest. Knowing this schedule, parents consume in such a way as to maximize utility from both consumption and attention. These choices produce observed attention and bequeathable wealth. The objective of the empirical investigation is to find the children's structural "supply of attention" schedule.

Based on the RHS, Bernheim et al. estimated that attention as measured by telephone calls and visits by children increases in bequeathable wealth but not in annuity wealth, and they interpret this as support for the strategic bequest motive. Their model and findings have been widely cited in connection with a strategic bequest motive, and their empirical results probably constitute the most important evidence in support of it. Indeed, Bernheim et al. conclude that "... the strategic motive is central to the economic analysis of bequests" (1985: p. 1075).

However, Hurd and Wang (1991) argued that the functional form used by Bernheim et al. is not appropriate, and, in fact, will tend to produce a positive relationship between bequeathable wealth and attention even when none exists. When they re-estimated the model using a more flexible functional form, and using more years of the RHS, they did not find a positive relationship between bequeathable wealth and attention by children. They concluded that the RHS data offer no support for the strategic bequest motive.

In another test of the bequest motive, Bernheim (1991) pointed out that an individual could be "over-annuitized" in the sense that mandatory saving through the Social Security program and through private pensions could cause someone to hold too large a fraction of total resources in annuities. Therefore, someone with a bequest motive would want to reduce annuities, which are not bequeathable. This can be done by pur-

Table 15
Ratio of annuitized wealth to total wealth (%)

	Single men	Single women	Couples
1962	27	24	34
1983	35	50	38

Source: Survey of Consumer Finances (Auerbach et al., 1992).

chasing term life insurance with part of the annuity income flow, effectively converting part of the annuity into a bequest. Bernheim found empirical support for this idea in the RHS: those with particularly high Social Security wealth relative to bequeathable wealth apparently hold, ceteris paribus, more life insurance.

While the finding gives qualitative support to a bequest motive, its quantitative importance is doubtful, and, furthermore, it is hard to square the finding with other data. Table 15 shows that over time the ratio of annuitized wealth to total wealth among the elderly has increased, particularly for singles. This would have been mainly caused by large increases in Social Security benefits, and some increase in job-related pensions. We would expect that life insurance holdings would have increased to de-annuitize some of the increase in annuity wealth; yet, according to Auerbach et al. (1992) the "Amount of insurance protection ... declined by more than half for those aged 65 and above between 1962 and 1983".

In absolute level, the insurance value of life insurance holdings among the elderly is small. Table 16 shows the face value of life insurance as a ratio to total resources, including annuity wealth, in the SCF and in the RHS. The ratio is greatest in the RHS were it is 6.4% of total resources among 65–69-year-olds. Yet, this ratio overstates the amount of de-annuitization because life insurance typically has a cash value which is somewhat less than the face value. The cash value is bequeathable wealth, so the insurance value is only the difference between the face value and the cash value. The insurance component ranges from 3.4% to 1.4% of total resources among couples and from 1.1% to 0.8% among singles. Because some of the insurance among couples is to provide wealth for the surviving spouse, which is not really a bequest, the figures for singles are more pertinent, and they show small levels of insurance compared to total resources.

Possibly a more revealing comparison is between life insurance and earnings, which is traditionally insured by life insurance. Table 17 has data from the 1979 RHS when the heads of the households would have been 68–73. The net premium value is an estimate of the cash value of the life insurance, and the difference between the face value and the net premium value is the insurance value. This is less than estimated future earnings, which implies that the desire to insure against future earnings adequately explains insurance holdings at least as far as average levels are concerned. Particularly for singles the average insurance value is small, so that even if it were to

Table 16
Ratio of value of insurance to total resources[a]

	Age					
	65–69		70–74		75–79	80+
	SCF	RHS[b]	SCF	RHS[b]	SCF	SCF
Couples						
Face value	3.1	6.4	4.5	6.4	2.1	2.2
Insurance value	2.3	2.4	3.4	2.4	1.4	1.6
Human capital		2.0		2.0		
Singles						
Face value	1.6	1.6	1.4	1.6	1.1	1.3
Insurance value	1.1	0.8	0.9	0.8	0.8	0.9
Human capital		1.0		1.0		

[a]Total resources are the sum of bequeathable wealth and annuitized wealth. Insurance value is the face value of insurance less the cash value. Human capital is the expected present value of earnings.
[b]Ages 68–74.
Sources: SCF: 1983 Survey of Consumer Finances (Auerbach et al., 1992); RHS, author's calculations from 1979 Retirement History Survey.

represent desired de-annuitization in response to a bequest motive, this measure of the bequest motive is not important quantitatively.

3.7. Summary of consumption and saving

A critical prediction of the LCH is that, at advanced ages, the elderly will dissave, and the panel data discussed consistently finds that the elderly dissave. Dissaving is, how-

Table 17
Life insurance, future earnings and social security wealth (thousands of 1984 dollars)

	Couples	Singles
Life insurance		
Face value	13.4	2.9
Net premium value[a]	8.5	1.8
Insurance value	4.9	1.1
Future earnings	8.2	2.4
Social Security wealth	87.2	38.4

[a]Estimated saving component of life insurance.
Sources: Hurd and Shoven (1985); Hurd (1991).

ever, a necessary condition but not a sufficient condition. For example, the elderly could dissave even if they have an operable bequest motive: they would just dissave at a slower rate. Because a bequest motive predicts a slower rate of dissaving, the test discussed is based on a difference between parents and nonparents. No evidence is found in support of an operable bequest motive. However, this test is incomplete because there are other flows of actual and potential support that it does not take into account. If there are substantial amounts of inter vivos giving, the rate of consumption by parents will appear to be greater than it actually is, and could even be greater than the rate of consumption by nonparents. This is particularly true if children provide insurance against low asset levels should the elderly parents live substantially past their life expectancies. This insurance need not take the form of reverse money flows (from the children to the very aged parents) but it could take the form of joint residency. Its importance in very old age is shown in Table 25: about one-third of very old widows live with family members.

The younger generation could also provide support to very old parents in the form of time help that would substitute for purchases of help. The anticipation of such help may allow parents to consume financial assets more rapidly than they otherwise would, which would at least partly vitiate the test of the bequest motive. These objections to the test of the bequest motive suggest that we need to understand better the forms in which intergenerational transfers happen. However, this will require better data than we have had.

4. Economic status of the elderly

4.1. Introduction

It has been well documented that the economic status of the elderly has improved over the last 25 years, both absolutely and relative to the nonelderly (Hurd, 1990a; Radner, 1993). Increased Social Security benefits have been an important component of the improvement, particularly at the lower part of the income distribution, with the result that the poverty rate of the elderly has fallen sharply. Over about the same period, private pensions grew substantially, also making a contribution to the improved economic status of the elderly.

This section will review the changes in the economic status of the elderly, and outline the difficulties of using income to make welfare judgements. It will conclude with the prediction that poverty rates among the elderly will continue to decline.

4.2. Income-based measures of economic status

Most of the discussion will use income as a measure of economic status both because

Table 18
Money income, 1990 (thousands) and income ratio

	Mean household	Median household	Adjusted median[a]
Elderly	26.4	18.1	14.8
All	40.8	29.9	21.6
Income ratio	0.65	0.60	0.69

[a]Family unit income adjusted for size by poverty scale.
Source: Radner (1993).

it is the most widely used measure and because few measures based on wealth and income are available. As we have seen, however, income is only a partial measure of economic status in that it ignores the potential of wealth for consumption.

The first two columns of Table 18 show money income of aged households, of the entire population and the income ratio. The ratio of the means is greater than of the medians because income is more unequally distributed among the elderly than in the population: in 1990 the respective Gini coefficients were 0.465 and 0.426 (Bureau of the Census, 1991). The last column has family unit median income adjusted for family unit size. Family unit income differs from household income because a unit could be a single person living with relatives whereas that individual would be part of a household under the Census definition.

The adjustment for unit size is made by the implicit scaling of the poverty line index. According to that scaling an elderly couple needs 26% more income than a single elderly person to achieve the same level of well-being. This implies large returns-to-scale in consumption. It is well known that this scale is rather arbitrary. Other scales based, say, on observed budget shares typically have smaller returns-to-scale. Their use would increase the ratio of the income of the elderly to income of the population. Except where noted later, all the scaling for family unit size will be based on the poverty scale.

It should be noted at the outset that none of the comparisons take into account variation in "need" by age. The most prominent difference in need is in the consumption of medical services. Most people believe that if the elderly faced the same prices as the nonelderly and had the same economic resources, the elderly would choose a different consumption bundle which would include more medical services. In traditional utility terms, this implies that on average the elderly have a different utility function from the nonelderly. In this situation, income is not a good welfare measure, so we could not say that the elderly have lower welfare than the nonelderly even if their incomes were lower. Nonetheless, our means-based transfer system and our tax system are based on income comparisons, so society at least believes income is a good measure of relative welfare levels. Of course, it has the further advantage of being observable.

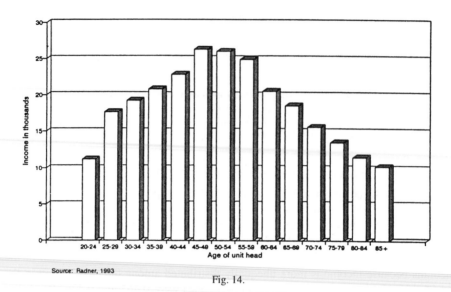

Source: Radner, 1993

Fig. 14.

Among the elderly variation in income by age is substantial as shown in Fig. 14. The median income of the oldest-old (85 or over) is just a little over half the income of 65–69-year-olds. Over the entire population income is highest at age 45–49. This is a somewhat younger age than would be found in panel data, but, of course, the figure includes cohort effects. An implication is that Fig. 14 cannot be used to study income over the life cycle without making adjustments for cohort and other effects.

Table 19 has annual percentage changes in real income between 1967 and 1990. In each of the four time periods covered in the table, the income of the elderly increased,

Table 19
Annual percent change in real median family unit income adjusted for size

	Under age 65	65 or over
1967–1972	3.1	4.9
1972–1979	1.1	1.9
1979–1984	−0.3	3.4
1984–1990	1.0	0.9
1967–1990	1.2	2.6
Total change (%) 1967–1990	31.8	82.8

Source: Radner (1993).

and in all but the last period, increased faster than income of the nonelderly. What is particularly striking is the difference in income growth from 1979–1984. During that period, the unemployment rate was high and inflation increased coinciding with the second oil shock. As a result, the real incomes of the nonelderly fell modestly. Few elderly work, however, so they were unaffected by the high rate of unemployment, and on average they are not vulnerable to inflation because a good deal of their income is indexed (Hurd and Shoven, 1985). This explains why their real income did not fall, but it does not explain why their real income rose. The remarkable increase was mainly due to increasing real Social Security benefits among newly retiring workers during the 1970s. In addition, new benefits in the late 1970s and early 1980s were increasing because double indexing was still applicable to workers who were over age 62 in 1978. As retirees with higher benefits became more numerous in the elderly population, average income levels increased.

The different rates of annual income growth in Table 19 cumulate to rather large income changes over the period: between 1979 and 1984 the income of the nonelderly fell by about 1.5% whereas the income of the elderly grew by 18.5%. Over the 23-year period covered in the table, income of the nonelderly increased by 31.8% and of the elderly by 82.8%.

Fig. 15 shows the ratio of the median income of elderly family units adjusted for family unit size to the median income of the entire population. It shows large increases until about 1984; since then it has been roughly constant. Because of indexing, Social

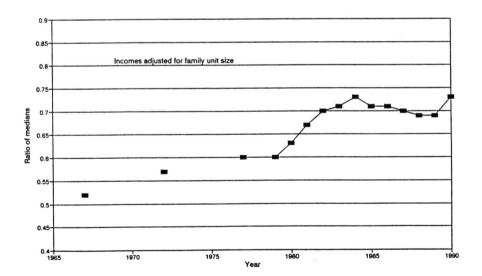

Fig. 15.

Table 20
Effects of adjustments to mean cash income

	Elderly	Nonelderly	Income ratio
Pre-tax cash income	26.4	40.9	0.65
+ capital gains	27.2	42.1	0.65
− taxes	23.7	33.1	0.72
+ government noncash income			
Excluding Medicare	24.0	33.5	0.72
+ imputed rent	27.4	35.5	0.77
+ employer provided health			
Insurance	27.8	37.3	0.75
+ Medicare	30.8	37.3	0.82

Source: Radner (1993).

Security will not have the large effects on the ratio as it did in the past unless there are substantial changes in productivity.

Money income is a partial measure of economic resources because it does not account fully for wealth, which, as described, appears to be slowly consumed. In addition, the income measures discussed do not include any accounting for taxes and non-cash income. Table 20 shows the effects of a number of adjustments to income. The aim of the adjustments is to find more accurate measures of economic resources. The base income is the usual Census measure, and in this table there is no adjustment for household size.

Adding in capital gains to cash income increases the mean income of the elderly by about $800 and of the nonelderly by about $1100: the income ratio is unaffected. Because the elderly have much lower tax rates accounting for taxes increases the ratio considerably to 0.72. The elderly have higher rates of home ownership and larger home equity, so imputing income to owner-occupied housing increases the ratio by 0.05.

Many would stop before accounting for Medicare. Surely, however, Medicare has some value to the recipients even if they may value it at less than cost. The measure shown here is the fungible value, which was developed by the Census.

The estimated fungible value depends on family income, the cost of food and housing needs, and the market value of the medical benefits. If family income is not sufficient to cover the family's basic food and housing requirements, the fungible value methodology treats Medicare or Medicaid as having no income value and assigns a value of zero. If family income exceeds the cost of food and housing requirements, the fungible value of Medicare and Medicaid is equal to the amount income exceeds food and housing requirements (up to the amount of the market value of the medical benefits). (Bureau of the Census, 1991.)

Although the fungible value is not based on any theory, it has some plausibility, and it has the favorable quality of assigning less value to medical benefits to the very poor than to the well-to-do. As the table shows it increases mean income of the elderly by about $3000, increasing the income ratio to 0.82.

Many people object to including any value for noncash medical benefits in income comparisons. In my view, however, the problem is not in valuing noncash transfers, whether for medical services, housing or food, but in the implicit utility comparisons:

> It should be emphasized that the full income comparisons are not utility comparisons. The adjustment for nonmoney transfers puts a monetary value on the transfers to an individual that yield a monetary measure of the economic position of the individual. It aims to answer the question: what money income would make the individual as well off as the combination of actual money income and nonmoney income transfers? Although actual measurement may pose difficulties, the concept is clear, simple, and well-supported in economic theory. The main difficulty arises in comparing incomes (whether adjusted for income-in-kind or not) across individuals or households because the comparison of income is not a welfare comparison. The utility functions of the individuals would have to be the same to make a utility comparison; but it is unreasonable to suppose they are, especially in the case of a comparison between the elderly and nonelderly because of different needs, in particular different medical needs. The important issue is not, as some people believe, the valuation of nonmoney transfers, but rather the use of an income measure to make cross-person or cross-household welfare comparisons. (Andrews and Hurd, 1992.)

According to this reasoning, we either should not make income comparisons across different groups or we should use full-income measures.

The income ratios in Table 20 are not adjusted for family size. A rough adjustment using the poverty line scale would increase the ratio from 0.75 to 0.92 (before Medicare) or 0.82 to 1.01 (after Medicare).

According to validation studies the elderly underreport their income by much more on average than the nonelderly, principally because a higher fraction of their income is from assets. Adjustments in the income ratio due to underreporting of income range from 9 to 20% (Radner, 1993). Applying the 9% figure to the pre-Medicare ratio (but with scaling for family size) would increase the income ratio to $1.09 \times 0.75 = 1.01$.

The literature has many other methods of scaling for family size. Table 21 has examples of two. The budget share method is based on estimates of returns-to-scale in consumption based on observed expenditures as family composition varies.[17] According to the budget share a couple requires 37% more consumption than a single person,

---

[17] The estimate in the table is from Van der Gaag and Smolensky (1982).

Table 21

Income of the elderly relative to the nonelderly, 1979: effects of scaling for household size and adjusting for nonmoney income

	Index			
	Household	Poverty line	Budget share	Per capita
Pre-tax money income	0.52	0.64	0.84	0.90
Pre-tax money income plus employer benefits and income-in-kind less taxes	0.65	0.80	1.04	1.14

Source: Hurd (1990a).

compared with 26% in the poverty scale. This difference is typical, and implies that the poverty scaling understates the relative income of the elderly.

The second line of the table has approximately the same adjustments to income as are given in Table 20. The table makes evident that the method of accounting for family size affects the income ratio at least as much as the method of adjusting income for noncash income and taxes.

4.3. Consumption-based measures of economic status

An alternative to an income measure of economic status is a consumption measure. It has the important advantage that people save during their working lives at least partially to finance their retirement years. If utility depends on consumption, income will overstate utility among the nonelderly and understate utility among the elderly.

Table 22 has average after-tax income, consumption, and the saving rate from the

Table 22

After-tax income and consumption measures of relative economic status:
1984–1986 consumer expenditure surveys

Age	After-tax income (1000s)	Consumption (1000s)	Saving rate	Relative income	Relative consumption	Scaled income	Scaled consumption[a]
65–74	16.23	17.07	−5.2	0.72	0.74	0.82	0.84
75+	11.43	12.10	−5.8	0.51	0.52	0.63	0.65
All ages	22.43	23.13	−3.1	1.00	1.00	1.00	1.00

[a]Poverty scaling.
Source: Bureau of Labor Statistics (1989) and author's calculations.

Table 23
Consumption measure of relative economic status: 1984–1986
consumer expenditure surveys and 1984 SIPP[a]

Age	Income (1000s)	Consumption (1000s)	Saving rate	Relative consumption	Scaled consumption[b]
65–74	16.23	18.13	−0.12	0.86	0.97
75+	11.43	15.05	−0.32	0.72	0.90
All ages	22.43	20.99	0.05	1.00	1.00

[a]Consumption by elderly is income plus observed wealth decumulation in 1984 SIPP, waves 4 and 7 (Hurd, 1991). Saving rate of "All ages" is from the National Income and Product Accounts.
[b]Poverty scaling.
Source: Bureau of Labor Statistics (1989) and author's calculations based on 1984 SIPP.

1984, 1985 and 1986 Consumer Expenditure Surveys (CES), and income and consumption ratios, and income and consumption ratios scaled for household size. The saving rate by the elderly is negative, implying that they consumed part of their assets each year. However, the saving rates of the elderly and of the entire population are not very different so the difference between the income ratio and the consumption ratio is rather small. But, it is clear from the table that either income and/or consumption is not accurately measured: the saving rates out of disposable income were positive (about 6%) over those years, not negative.

A different way of measuring consumption is to find rates of dissaving by the elderly from micro panel data and to apply those rates to the income entries in Table 22. Table 9 gives some examples of real saving rates out of wealth from four data sets. The observed rate of dissaving as measured in the Survey of Income and Program Participation (SIPP) is used because it covers all the elderly not just the limited age range of the Retirement History Survey (RHS).[18] The average rate of dissaving over all the elderly in the SIPP was 2.9% per year, which is a somewhat lower rate than in the RHS.[19] The rates of dissaving out of assets imply large rates of dissaving out of income, −12% for 65–74-year-olds and −32% for those 75 or over.

Table 23 uses observed income in the CES. For the elderly, saving rates are derived from SIPP. For the total population, the after-tax saving rate (6.4% in 1985) comes from the national income and product accounts (Bureau of the Census, 1992). Thus consumption is derived from income and the saving rate, rather than measured directly as in Table 22. This method produces much larger differences between the income ratios and the consumption ratios because it decreases consumption by the entire population and increases consumption by the elderly substantially. Scaling for household size makes the ratio of consumption close to 1.0.

[18] The maximum age range of the RHS sample is 58–74.
[19] The RHS saving rate does not include housing wealth, which was affected by extraordinary increases in housing values from 1975–1979. The SIPP rate does include housing wealth.

Table 24
Poverty rates (%)

	1970	1979	1985	1990
All	12.6	11.7	14.0	13.5
65 or over	24.6	15.2	12.6	12.2

Source: Bureau of the Census (1992).

4.4. Distribution of economic resources

Fig. 14 showed that even among the elderly there is considerable variation in income by detailed age class. And, as previously mentioned the Gini coefficient of income is higher among the elderly than the nonelderly. Here, we concentrate on the poverty rate as a measure of distribution both because it is of substantial policy interest and because it is the most intensively studied aspect of income distribution.

Table 24 shows the remarkable change in the poverty rate of the elderly since 1970: it is now about half the 1970 rate. The decline happened even as the poverty rate of the entire population increased. Social Security is substantially responsible for the difference: Social Security benefits comprise the greater majority of the income of the poor and near poor, so that if Social Security benefits were at their 1970 levels many more elderly would be in poverty.

Fig. 16 shows the age distribution of poverty in 1967 and 1990. With almost no exception the poverty rates of those over 40 declined even as the poverty rates of those under 40 increased. In particular the poverty rate of families with young children has increased substantially: in 1990 24% of children under five lived in families in poverty (Radner, 1993).

Among the elderly the poverty rate increases with age. This is partly a composition effect, a reflection of the higher fraction of widows among the oldest-old. Table 25 shows poverty rates of married couples and of nonmarried women, most of whom are widows, and the number in each group. The poverty rates are remarkably constant with age. The average poverty rate of all elderly increases with age because a large fraction of the oldest-old are nonmarried women, the result of the higher mortality risk of men and the age difference between husbands and wives.[20] The table also shows the poverty rates of the families in which the elderly live if they live with other family members. From this table we do not know the actual economic circumstances of the elderly person because we cannot observe any intra-household transfers. The low poverty rates certainly suggest, however, that the possibility of living with family members is an economic resource that needs to be accounted for, particularly for very elderly widows.

---

[20] 18% of the oldest-old are nonmarried men. Their poverty rate increases with age, and at 85 or over is about the same as that of nonmarried women 85 or over.

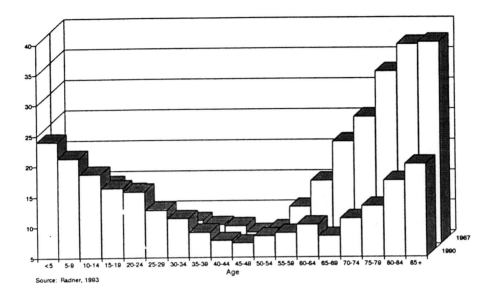

Source: Radner, 1993

Fig. 16.

Poverty rates are substantially affected by transfers. Table 26 shows the effects of a number of adjustments to income. As before the fungible value method is used to account for Medicare and Medicaid. Because low-income families gain rather small amounts of income according to this method, the poverty rate falls by much less than it would if market valuation of Medicare and Medicaid were used. The most important adjustment is imputing an income to home equity. Overall the poverty rate of the elderly falls by about 3.3 percentage points compared with 1.2 percentage points over the

Table 25
Poverty rates, 1988 (percentage)

	Married couples			Unmarried women		
	65–74	75–84	85+	65–74	75–84	85+
Number (thousands)	6205	2475	334	4792	4077	1280
All	5	6	6	21	23	21
Live with other family members	7	8		14	9	9
Live with no family members	4	6	6	23	27	28
Percent living with family members	19	12	13	28	27	36

Source: Grad (1990).

Table 26
Poverty rates 1990 (%): alternate income definitions

Age	Money income		Money income plus cash and noncash transfers				
	Pre-tax	After-tax + capital gains	Medicare	+ means-tested cash transfers	+ Medicaid	+ means-tested noncash transfers	+ imputed return on home equity
All	13.5	14.7	14.3	13.2	12.4	11.0	9.8
Under 18	20.6	21.8	21.5	20.2	18.7	15.8	14.9
Under 6	23.0	23.9	23.7	22.3	20.3	17.2	16.6
18–24	15.9	17.5	17.3	16.3	15.5	14.3	13.6
25–44	10.4	11.3	11.1	10.3	9.7	8.6	8.1
45–64	8.6	9.9	9.5	8.6	8.2	7.6	6.0
65 or over	12.2	13.7	12.1	10.7	10.4	9.5	6.2
65–74	9.7	11.2	9.7	8.4	8.2	7.3	4.9
75 or over	16.0	17.4	15.7	14.2	13.9	12.9	8.2

Source: Bureau of the Census (1991).

total population. After all of these adjustments, the poverty rate of the elderly was 6.2% compared with 9.8% over the entire population.

4.5. Summary of economic status

On average the economic status of the elderly has improved greatly over the past 25 years. Since about 1985, however, it has changed only marginally, at least partially because real Social Security benefits of the newly retiring remained almost constant during the decade. Among the elderly there are large differences in economic status that are not summarized by measures such as the mean and median. The poverty rate of elderly widows is still high, although valuing noncash income would certainly reduce it substantially. However, we can expect the poverty rate of the elderly to decline over time even if the overall economic status of the elderly remains roughly constant because the Social Security increases of the late 1970s should in the rather near future reduce the poverty rate of the oldest-old. Consider, for example, a husband who retired at age 62 in 1980. His wife (same age) will be 85 in 2003, and should she be a widow could have a widow's benefit based on his initial 1980 Social Security benefit. An 85-year-old in 1993 was 62 in 1970: initial benefits increased by about 40% between 1970 and 1980. In that the poor depend almost exclusively on Social Security and SSI, increases of 40% can lift many from poverty.

An example of the ultimate effects can be found through simulations. A model of consumption by singles and by couples was used to forecast the consumption, income and wealth paths of the 1979 RHS sample (Hurd, 1989, 1991, 1992a). The initial conditions were the incomes and wealth from the data. Then the initial conditions were updated according to the growth in economic resources between 1979 and 1984 as measured in the SIPP. Because the RHS cohort was 60–65 in 1971, it would mostly have retired before the large increase in Social Security benefits during the 1970s. The cohort just five years younger was 60–65 in 1976 when initial Social Security benefits were about 25% higher in real terms.

Table 27 compares wealth and income in the 1979 RHS and the 1984 SIPP. All entries are in 1984 dollars. The main differences are in nonhousing bequeathable wealth of couples, asset income of couples and of singles, earnings, and particularly Social Security benefits. They increased 30% among couples and 23% among singles. In the simulations these increases will propagate through the elderly population eventually reaching the oldest-old. Then poverty rate comparisons will show the results of changing initial conditions to the level of the SIPP.

Table 28 has poverty rates of singles and couples. There are two measures, one based on income and one on consumption. Because the model predicts declining wealth with age, consumption is greater than income so the consumption-based poverty rate is less than the income-based poverty rate. The differences are substantial among couples because they had considerable wealth; the differences were moderate among singles because they had little. Updating to the SIPP initial conditions decreased the poverty rate of couples by 2.8 to 4.1 percentage points. The change is rather small because few couples depend substantially on Social Security. Among

Table 27
Wealth and income comparison: 1979 RHS and 1984 SIPP (1984$)

	Couples, 68–74		Singles, 68–74	
	1979 RHS	1984 SIPP	1979 RHS	1984 SIPP
Wealth (thousands)				
Housing equity	51.0	49.1	23.8	26.0
Nonhousing bequeathable	78.0	93.9	27.0	29.8
Total	129.0	143.0	50.8	55.8
Income				
Social Security	6637	8595	3865	4741
Other real pensions	2011	2209	1058	960
Nominal pensions	1775	1857	631	676
Asset and property	3665	4514	1331	2136
Earnings	4365	3711	1033	900
Other	328	800	440	690
Total	18780	21685	8358	10101
Number of observations	3348	744	2883	870

Source: Hurd (1991).

Table 28
Predicted poverty rates as measured by income or consumption

Initial conditions	Couples		Singles	
	Income measure	Consumption measure	Income measure	Consumption measure
1979 HRS	11.3	5.3	38.5	27.7
1984 SIPP	7. 2	3.5	26.3	19.3

Source: Hurd (1992).

singles, however, the changes are large, up to 12.2 percentage points. This happens because the increase in Social Security is large, and, furthermore, it affects the entire income distribution.

These results and examination of the rates of increase of Social Security and pension benefits indicate that the economic status of the elderly should improve slowly as the increases propagate through the system. Social Security benefits of the oldest should continue to increase and more of the elderly will have pension income. We can anticipate further reductions in the poverty rate of the elderly.

5. Directions for future research

At a number of points it is indicated that data limitations prevented further progress. For example, no data set has had both detailed Social Security earnings records from which to construct Social Security entitlement, and detailed pension information from which to construct the incentives caused by defined benefit plans. Furthermore the economic environment has changed since the RHS was conducted, so that we would not necessarily expect the same behavioral response today. For example, health care costs have risen at a much faster rate than the CPI or incomes: in 1970 per capita health care costs were $960 per year (in 1985 dollars); in 1991, they were $2266, also in 1985 dollars, an increase of 134% in real terms. It would be surprising if the effect on retirement of both worker's and retiree's health insurance is not different today than in the early 1970s when the RHS data were gathered.

We will have available, however, two new data sets specifically designed to study the economics of aging. These are the Health and Retirement Survey (HRS) and the survey of the Asset and Health Dynamics of the Oldest-Old (AHEAD). Both are large biennial panels that are representative of the population except for oversampling of blacks and Hispanics.

At baseline the target age of the HRS was 51–61, so it will gather data as workers retire. It has detailed information about Social Security earnings histories, pensions, health insurance, and personal characteristics such as health status, income and assets.

The AHEAD is representative of the population age 70 or over at baseline. It has information similar to the HRS but with more emphasis on health status. Both surveys have family rosters that link the extended family to the respondents, so that we will be able to study intergenerational transfers, and the role of the extended family as a resource. Both surveys have innovative questions about the respondent's subjective probability distributions of events such as survival, inflation and medical expenses. These should assist considerably in the estimation of stochastic dynamic models.

In the area of retirement research, our knowledge of the demand side of the market is very limited. By the demand side, is meant, broadly speaking, the nature and availability of jobs for workers nearing retirement. For example, as workers age, they may find that a job that was not overly stressful becomes too stressful, leading eventually to retirement. Workers may wish to reduce hours gradually, but if part-time jobs have low pay, they will retire. Although discrimination by age is not legal, employers undoubtedly have ways of encouraging the retirement of older workers who have become less productive. The importance of the demand side comes from the observation that with the aging of the population, policies to encourage later retirement may be useless if employers do not want to retain older workers, or if the workers find the jobs overly stressful.

Most of the retirement studies have focussed on the retirement choice of either a male worker or a female worker. But there is ample evidence that when both spouses work, they coordinate their retirements (Hurd, 1990b). This implies, for example, that the structure of the husband's defined benefit pension plan will affect the retirement of the wife. The HRS has work-related data on both spouses, so we will be able to estimate joint retirement models.

In principle, workers choose a retirement plan and a savings plan as part of their life-cycle decisions. Yet, it is quite standard to take wealth as given in models to explain retirement. For example, the levels of individual retirement accounts along with accumulations in defined contribution plans are typically used as explanatory variables in retirement models. We are not used to studying the effects of anticipated retirement on saving before retirement. Integrating these two decisions in a single estimable model will be facilitated in the HRS because of measures of anticipated retirement: in particular the HRS asks workers their subjective probability of working past age 62 and 65.

In the area of consumption and saving following retirement there are still some unanswered questions about the basic descriptive facts. For example, can we verify in the AHEAD that the elderly dissave? Is the rate of dissaving related to health status? Does the rate of dissaving accelerate with advanced age as predicted by the LCH? What is the extent of transfers of time and money between the generations, and is it large enough to cause a reinterpretation of the bequest motive?

Then, we would aim to explain these facts, which will require modelling and estimation. We need to broaden our understanding of the economic determinants of intergenerational transfers, and in particular the relationship between bequests and inter vivos giving: they undoubtedly substitute for each other to some extent, yet they are not the same. Due to the increasing fraction of the population that is very old, greater numbers will be impaired and in need of care: the provision of help will strain the resources of society. A substitute for societal resources is time help from the extended family including joint living arrangements. This will be an important research topic.

Many models have assumed that individuals are alike, yet observed behavior, particularly saving behavior, varies substantially across individuals. Furthermore, they give widely varying answers to questions about "tastes" and expectations. Both the HRS and AHEAD have a number of questions that are meant to get at heterogeneity in tastes, and they will be included in behavioral models.

Economists have mostly relied on behavior to infer expectations. But in my view such data are not sufficiently strong to advance our knowledge of decision-making under uncertainty. We need independent observations on expectations (subjective probability distributions) at the individual level, so that we will be able to assess the individual's view of the risk in particular situations. For this reason subjective probabilities will become important variables in the estimation of stochastic dynamic models of decision-making.

References

Abel, A.B. (1987), "Operative gift and bequest motives", American Economic Review 77: 1037–1047.

Anderson, K.H., R.V. Burkhauser and J.S. Butler (1984), "Work after retirement: a hazard model of labor market reentry", IRP discussion papers, WP #768-84.

Andrews, E. (1985) The changing profiles of pensions in America (Employee Benefit Research Institute, Washington, DC).

Andrews, E. and D. Chollet (1988), "Future sources of retirement income: whither the baby boom", in: S.M. Wachter, ed., Social security and private pensions (D.C. Health and Co, Lexington, MA) pp. 71–95.

Andrews, E.S. and M.D. Hurd (1992), "Employee benefits and retirement income adequacy: data, research, and policy issues", in: Z. Bodi and A.H. Munnell, eds., Pensions and the economy: sources, uses, and limitations of data (University of Pennsylvania Press, Philadelphia, PA) pp. 1–30.

Auerbach, A.J., L.J. Kotlikoff and D.N. Weil (1992), "The increasing annuitization of the elderly--estimates and implications for intergenerational transfers, inequality, and national saving", Presented at the NBER Summer Institute, July.

Avery, R and G. Elliehausen (1986), "Financial characteristics of high income families", Federal Reserve Bulletin, March: 163–277.

Barro, R.J. (1974), "Are government bonds net wealth", Journal of Political Economy, 82: 1095–1117.

Becker, G.S. (1981) A treatise on the family (Harvard University Press, Cambridge, MA).

Bell, F., A. Wade and S. Goss (1992), "Life tables for the United States social security area 1900 – 2080", Acturial study no. 107 (Social Security Administration, US Department of Health and Human Services, Washington, DC).

Berkovec, J. and S. Stern (1991), "Job exit behavior of older men", Econometrica 59: 189–210.

Bernheim, B.D. (1987), "Dissaving after retirement: testing the pure life cycle hypothesis", in: J. Shoven, ed., Issues in pension economics (University of Chicago Press, Chicago, IL).

Bernheim, B.D. (1991), "How strong are bequest motives? Evidence based on estimates of the demand for life insurance and annuities", Journal of Political Economy 99: 899–927.

Bernheim, B.D., A. Shleifer and L.H. Summers (1985), "The strategic bequest motive", Journal of Political Economy 93: 1045–1076.

Blinder, A.S., R.H. Gordon and D.E. Wise (1980), "Reconsidering the work disincentive effects of social security", National Tax Journal 33: 431–442.

Blinder, A.S., R.H. Gordon and D.E. Wise (1983), "Social security, bequests and the life cycle theory of saving: cross-sectional tests", in: F. Modigliani and R. Hemming, eds., The determinants of national saving and wealth (St. Martin's Press, New York) pp. 89–122.

Boskin, M.J. and M.D. Hurd (1985), "Indexing social security benefits: a separate price index for the elderly?", Public Finance Quarterly 13: 436–449.

Bureau of Labor Statistics (1989), "Consumer expenditure survey: integrated survey data 1984–86", Bulletin 2333 (US Department of Labor, Washington, DC).

Bureau of the Census (1991), "Measuring the effect of benefits and taxes on income and poverty 1990", Current population reports, Series P-60, no. 176-RD (US Government Printing Office, Washington, DC).

Bureau of the Census (1992), Statistical abstract of the United States 1992, 112th edn. (Bureau of the Census, Washington, DC).

Burkhauser, R.V. (1979), "The pension acceptance decision of older workers", Journal of Human Resources XIV: 63–75.

Burtless, G. and R.A. Moffitt (1984), "The effect of social security benefits on the labor supply of the aged", in: H.J. Aaron and G. Burtless, eds., Retirement and economic behavior (Brookings Institution, Washington, DC) pp. 135–171.

Burtless, G. and R.A. Moffitt (1985), "The joint choice of retirement age and postretirement hours of work", Journal of Labor Economics 3: 209–236.

Burtless, G. and R.A. Moffitt (1986), "Social security, earnings tests, and age at retirement", Public Finance 14: 3–27.

Clark, R.L. and A.A. McDermed (1990), The choice of pension plans in a changing regulatory environment (American Enterprise Press, Washington, DC).

Clark, R.L., S.F. Gohmann and A.A. McDermed (1988), "Declining use of defined benefit pension plans: is federal regulation the reason?", Working paper no. 119 (Department of Economics, North Carolina State University, Raleigh, NC).

Cox, D. (1987), "Motives for private income transfers", Journal of Political Economy 95: 508–546.

Crawford, V. and D. Lilien (1981), "Social security and the retirement decision", Quarterly Journal of Economics XCVI: 509–529.

Darby, M.R. (1979), Effects of social security on income and the capital stock (American Enterprise Institute, Washington, DC)

Diamond, P.A. and J. Hausman (1984), "Individual retirement and savings behavior", Journal of Public Economics 23: 81–114.

Ellwood, D.T. (1985), "Pensions and the labor market: a starting point (the mouse can roar)", in: D.A. Wise, ed., Pensions, labor, and individual choice (University of Chicago Press, Chicago, IL) pp. 19–49.

Fields, G.S. and O.S. Mitchell (1984), Retirement, pensions and social security (MIT Press, Cambridge, MA).

Friedman, B.M. and M. Warshawsky (1988), "Annuity prices and saving behavior in the United States", in: Z. Bodie, J.B. Shoven and D.A. Wise, eds., Pensions in the U.S. economy (National Bureau of Economic Research, Chicago University, Chicago, IL) pp. 55–77.

Fuchs, V.R. (1982), "Self-employment and labor force participation of older males", Journal of Human Resources XVII: 339–357.

Gordon, R. and A. Blinder (1980), "Market wages, reservation wages and retirement", Journal of Public Economics 14: 277–308.

Grad, S. (1990), Income of the population 55 or older, 1988 (US Department of Health and Human Services, Social Security Administration, Washington, DC).

Grad, S. (1994), Income of the population 55 or older, 1992 (US Department of Health and Human Services, Social Security Administration, Washington, DC).

Gustman, A.L. and T.L. Steinmeier (1984), "Partial retirement and the analysis of retirement behavior", Industrial and Labor Relations Review 37: 403–415.

Gustman, A.L. and T.L. Steinmeier (1985), "The effect of partial retirement on the wage profiles of older workers", Industrial Relations 24: 257–265.

Gustman, A. and T.L. Steinmeier (1986), "A structural retirement model", Econometrica 54: 555–584.

Gustman, A.L. and T.L. Steinmeier (1989), "An analysis of pension benefit formulas, pension wealth, and incentives from pensions", in: R. Ehrenberg, ed., Research in labor economics, Vol. 10 (JAI Press, Greenwich, CT) pp. 53–106.

Hausman, J.A. and D.A. Wise (1985), "Social security, health status, and retirement", in: D.A. Wise, ed., Pensions, labor, and individual choice (National Bureau of Economic Research, Chicago University, Chicago, IL) pp. 159–181.

Hurd, M.D. (1987), "Savings of the elderly and desired bequests", American Economic Review 77: 298–312.

Hurd, M.D. (1989), "Mortality risk and bequests", Econometrica 57: 779–813.

Hurd, M.D. (1990a), "Research on the elderly: economic status, retirement, and consumption and saving", Journal of Economic Literature XXVIII: 565–637.

Hurd, M.D. (1990b), "The joint retirement decision of husbands and wives", in: D. Wise, ed., Issues in the economics of aging (University of Chicago Press, Chicago, IL) pp. 231–254.

Hurd, M.D. (1991), "The income and savings of the elderly", Final report to AARP Andrus Foundation, Typescript (SUNY, Stony Brook, NY).

Hurd, M.D. (1992a), "Forecasting the consumption, income and wealth of the elderly", Final report to the Social Security Administration, Typescript (SUNY, Stony Brook, NY).

Hurd, M.D. (1992b), "Wealth depletion and life-cycle consumption by the elderly", in: D. Wise, ed., Topics in the economics of aging (University of Chicago Press, Chicago, IL) pp. 135–160.

Hurd, M.D. (1995), "Mortality risk and consumption by couples", Presented at the IFS-Bank of Portugal Conference on the Microeconomics of Saving and Consumption Growth, Lisbon, November.

Hurd, M.D. (1996), "The effect of labor market rigidities on the labor force behavior of older workers", in: D. Wise, ed., Papers in the economics of aging (University of Chicago Press, Chicago, IL) in press.

Hurd, M.D. and M.J. Boskin (1984), "The effect of social security on retirement in the early 1970s", Quarterly Journal of Economics 98: 767–790.

Hurd, M.D. and J.B. Shoven (1985), "Inflation vulnerability, income, and wealth of the elderly, 1969–1979", in: M. David and T. Smeeding, eds., Horizontal equity, uncertainty, and economic well-being (University of Chicago Press, Chicago, IL) pp. 125–172.

Hurd, M.D. and D. Wang (1991), "Some doubts about the empirical relevance of the strategic bequest motive", Presented at the NBER Summer Institute, July.

Jianakoplos, N.A., P.L. Menchik and F.O. Irvine (1989), "Using panel data to assess the bias in cross-sectional inference of life-cycle changes in the level and composition of household wealth", in: R.E. Lipsey and H. Stone Tice, eds., The measurement of saving, investment and wealth (University of Chicago Press, Chicago, IL) pp. 553–640.

King, M. and L. Dicks-Mireaux (1982), "Asset holdings and the life-cycle", The Economic Journal 92: 247–267.

Kotlikoff, L.J. (1988), "Intergenerational transfers and savings", Journal of Economic Perspectives 2(2): 41–59.

Kotlikoff, L.J. and L. Summers (1981), "The role of intergenerational transfers in aggregate capital accumulation", Journal of Political Economy 89: 706–732.

Kotlikoff, L.J. and L. Summers (1988), "The contribution of intergenerational transfers to total wealth: a reply", in: D. Kessler and A. Masson, eds., Modelling the accumulation and distribution of wealth (Oxford University Press, New York) pp. 53–67.

Kotlikoff, L.J. and D.A. Wise (1987a), "Pension backloading, wage taxes, and work disincentives", Working paper no. 2463 (NBER, Cambridge, MA).

Kotlikoff, L.J. and D.A. Wise (1987b), "The incentive effects of private pension plans", in: Z. Bodie, J.B. Shoven and D.A. Wise, eds., Issues in pension economics (National Bureau of Economic Research, Chicago University, Chicago, IL) pp. 283–336.

Kotlikoff, L.J. and D.A. Wise (1989), "Employee retirement and a firm's pension plan", in: D. Wise, ed., The economics of aging (University of Chicago Press, Chicago, IL) pp. 279–330.

Kurz, M. (1985), "Heterogeneity in savings behavior: a comment," in: K. Arrow and S. Honkapohja, eds., Frontiers of economics (Basil Blackwell, Oxford) pp. 307–327.

Lazear, E. and R. Moore (1988), "Pensions and turnover", in: Z. Bodie, J. Shoven and D. Wise, eds., Pensions in the U.S. economy (University of Chicago Press, Chicago, IL) pp. 163–188.

Lumsdaine, R., J. Stock and D. Wise (1992), "Three models of retirement: computational complexity vs. predictive validity", in: D. Wise, ed., Topics in the economics of aging (University of Chicago Press, Chicago, IL).

Lydall, H. (1955), "The life cycle, income, saving, and asset ownership", Econometrica 23: 985–1012.

Menchik, P.L. and M. David (1983), "Income distribution, lifetime savings, and bequests", American Economic Review 73: 672–690.

Mirer, T. (1979), "The wealth–age relation among the aged", American Economic Review 69: 435–443.

Mirer, T. (1980), "The dissaving behavior of the retired aged", Southern Economic Journal 46: 1197–1205.

Mitchell, O.S. and G.S. Fields (1982), "The effects of pensions and earnings on retirement: a review essay", in: R. Ehrenberg, ed., Research in labor economics, Vol. 5 (JAI Press, Greenwich, CT) pp. 115–155.

Mitchell, O.S. and G.S. Fields (1983), "Economic incentives to retire: a qualitative choice approach", Working paper no. 1096 (NBER, Cambridge, MA).

Mitchell, O.S. and G.S. Fields (1984), Retirement, pensions and social security (MIT Press, Cambridge, MA).

Mitchell, O.S. and G.S. Fields (1985), "Rewards for continued work: the economic incentive for postponing retirement", in: M. David and T. Smeeding, eds., Horizontal equity, uncertainty, and economic well-being (National Bureau of Economic Research, Chicago University, Chicago, IL) pp. 269–286.

Modigliani, F. (1986), "Life cycle, individual thrift, and the wealth of nations", American Economic Review 76: 297–313.

Modigliani, F. (1988), "The role of intergenerational transfers and life cycle saving in the accumulation of wealth", The Journal of Economic Perspectives 2: 15–40.

Myers, D.A., R.V. Burkhauser and K.C. Holden (1987), "The transition from wife to widow: the importance of survivor benefits to the well-being of widows", Journal of Risk and Insurance 54: 752–759.

Poterba, J.N. (1989), "Comment on aging, moving and housing wealth", in: D. Wise, ed., The economics of aging (University of Chicago Press, Chicago, IL) pp. 48–55.

Projector, D. (1968), Survey of changes in family finances (Board of Governors, Federal Reserve Board, Washington, DC).

Projector, D. and G. Weiss (1966), Survey of financial characteristics of consumers (Board of Governors, Federal Reserve Board, Washington, DC).

Quinn, J., R. Burkhauser and D. Myers (1990), Passing the torch: the influence of economic incentives on work and retirement (Upjohn Institute, Kalamazoo, MI).

Radner, D.B. (1989), "The wealth of the aged and nonaged, 1984", in: R.E. Lipsey and H. Stone Tice, eds., The measurement of saving, investment and wealth (University of Chicago Press, Chicago, IL) pp. 645–684.

Radner, D. (1993), "An assessment of the economic status of the aged", Publication no. 13-21776 (Social Security Administration, Washington, DC).

Ransom, R. and R. Sutch (1988), "The decline of retirement in the years before social security: U.S. retirement patterns 1870–1937", in: R. Ricardo-Campbell and E. Lazear, eds., Issues in contemporary retirement (Hoover Institution Press, Stanford, CT).

Rust, J.P. (1989), "A dynamic programming model of retirement behavior", in: D. Wise, ed., The economics of aging (University of Chicago Press, Chicago, IL) pp. 359–398.

Rust, J.P. (1990), "Behavior of male workers at the end of the life-cycle: an empirical analysis of states and controls", in: D.A. Wise, ed., Issues in the economics of aging (University of Chicago Press, Chicago, IL) pp. 317–379.

Rust, J.P. and C. Phelan (1993), "How social security and Medicare affect retirement behavior in a world of incomplete markets", Typescript (University of Wisconsin, Madison, WI).

Shorrocks, A.F. (1975), "The age-wealth relationship: a cross-section and cohort analysis", Review of Economics and Statistics LVII: 155–163.

Stock, J.H. and D.A. Wise (1990a), "The pension inducement to retire: an option value analysis", in: D.A. Wise, ed., Issues in the economics of aging (University of Chicago Press, Chicago, IL).

Stock, J.H. and D.A. Wise (1990b), "Pensions, the option value of work and retirement", Econometrica 58: 1151–1180.

Tomes, N. (1981), "The family, inheritance, and the intergenerational transmission of inequality", Journal of Political Economy 89: 928–958.

Van der Gaag, J. and E. Smolensky (1982), "True household equivalence scales and characteristics of the poor in the U.S.", Review of Income and Wealth 28: 17–28.

Wang, D. (1991), "Savings of the elderly and the bequest motive", Unpublished Ph.D. dissertation (Department of Economics, State University of New York, Stony Brook, NY).

White, B.B. (1978), "Empirical tests of the life-cycle hypothesis", American Economic Review 68: 547–560.

Wilhelm, M. (1991), "Bequest behavior and the effect of heirs' earnings: testing the altruistic model of bequests", Typescript (Department of Economics, Pennsylvania State University, University Park, PA).

Wolff, E.N. (1988), "Social security, pensions and the life cycle accumulation of wealth: some empirical tests", Annales d'Economie et de Statistique 9: 199–226.

Yaari, M.E. (1965), "Uncertain lifetime, life insurance and the theory of the consumer", Review of Economic Studies 32: 137–150.

Chapter 17

THE ECONOMICS OF POPULATION AGING

DAVID N. WEIL*

Brown University

Contents

1. Introduction   968
2. Population aging: facts and determinants   969
   2.1. Facts and forecasts on population aging   969
   2.2. Sources of aging: fertility and mortality   970
   2.3. Immigration   975
3. Aging, production, and consumption   977
   3.1. The effect of population aging on youth and old-age dependency   977
   3.2. Age structure, population growth, and dependency in stable populations   979
   3.3. Implications of changes in morbidity and mortality for support ratios   981
   3.4. Aging and sustainable consumption in a model with capital   983
   3.5. Aging and the labor market   989
4. Aging in a life-cycle model   994
   4.1. Demographic change in a two-period life-cycle model   995
   4.2. Aging and saving in partial equilibrium   996
   4.3. Aging and saving in general equilibrium   997
   4.4. Limitations of the life-cycle model   998
5. Social security and other government programs   1000
   5.1. Dependency ratios for government programs   1000
   5.2. Interaction of age structure, social security, and life-cycle saving   1001
   5.3. The response of social security to demographic change   1003
   5.4. Political economy of social security benefits and of increased aged population 1005
6. Within-family intergenerational relations and aging   1006
   6.1. Parent to child transfers   1007
   6.2. Child to parent transfers   1008
7. Conclusion   1009
References   1010

*I am grateful to David Cutler, Rachel Friedberg, Laurence Kotlikoff, and Louise Sheiner for comments, and to James Jones and Aditya Joshi for research assistance.

Handbook of Population and Family Economics. Edited by M.R. Rosenzweig and O. Stark
© *Elsevier Science B.V., 1997*

1. Introduction

Around the world, and especially in the industrialized countries, populations are aging. The median age of the population and the fraction of the population that is elderly are climbing well above the levels that have ever been witnessed. At the same time, the fraction of the population made up of children, and the rate at which the population is growing, are falling.

While population aging is not a new phenomenon, currently anticipated increases in the average age of the population are likely to have more radical effects on the economy than in the past. While past aging generally lowered the burden on society posed by dependent children and the elderly, the future aging will raise this burden. Furthermore, the aging currently in prospect will affect governments' role to a larger degree (and once again, in a more adverse fashion) than in the past. Finally, the dramatic shifts in fertility which took place after World War II have led to a rapid increase in the rate of population aging.

Predicting how population aging will affect the economy is inherently difficult.[1] Since even rapid aging is a slow process in comparison to the other experiments considered by macroeconomists (for example, the effect of monetary policy), it is almost impossible to disentangle empirically the effects of aging from the effects of other, contemporaneous changes. Thus, predicting the effects of aging must rely heavily on the application of "off the shelf" macroeconomic models. In this chapter I examine how changing the age structure of the population in these models affects such variables as consumption, wages, government spending, and saving.

The rest of this chapter is organized as follows. Section 2 presents the basic data on how the age structure of the population is evolving over time. It also explores the causes of the change, examining trends in fertility and mortality and the relative importance of these two factors in current aging. Finally, the section discusses the potential for immigration to affect the process of population aging.

Section 3 considers the effects of population aging on production and consumption in the economy as a whole. Most of the section focusses on how aging affects the overall burden of dependents (children and the elderly) who must be provided for by working-age adults. But the section abstracts from the question of how resources are transferred to these dependents. The section also considers how aging affects the labor market.

In abstracting from the details of how dependents are provided for, Section 3 misses many of the important effects of aging. In the real world it is not only important that dependents are cared for, but also how they are cared for. For elderly dependents, there are three sources of support: the use of resources acquired during working life, the state, and the family. For dependent children, only the latter two sources are

---

[1] Recent surveys of the subject include Bos and Weizsacker (1989), Habib (1990), OECD (1988), Schulz et al. (1991), United Nations (1985).

available. The analysis in Sections 4, 5, and 6 considers the effects of aging in light of the three sources of support just mentioned. The life-cycle model, discussed in Section 4, focuses on the ability of individuals to transfer resources from their working years to their old age via saving. The key effect of aging in a life-cycle framework is to lower the saving rate, by increasing the fraction of the population that is dissaving and decreasing the fraction that is saving. Section 5 takes up the role of government programs in transferring resources to dependents, particularly the elderly. The section examines how demographic change will alter the size of government transfers, and also how changes in these transfers will impact the rest of the economy. Section 6 looks at transfers within the family, and at how these flows will be affected by the process of aging.

Section 7 concludes by discussing the magnitude of the effects of aging, and how they compare to another slow, inexorable process affecting the macroeconomy: growth. At their most severe, the effects of population aging are roughly comparable to those of the post-1973 productivity slowdown. At the same time, however, aging will lead to changes in specific channels through which support flows to dependents. Less money will flow through families to children, but more will flow through the government to the elderly. These changes will be much larger than the change in the *net* burden of dependency.

2. Population aging: facts and determinants

2.1. Facts and forecasts on population aging

Table 1 shows the age structure of the population for the world as a whole, for the 24 countries of the OECD, and for the US.[2] Population aging is seen in both a reduction in the fraction of the population that is under 20, and in an increase in the fraction over 64. In the OECD, most of the decrease in the fraction that is young has already taken place, and the most dramatic change in the future will be in the fraction of the population that is elderly. In the less developed countries, the process of population aging is not as far along, and over the next several decades the largest change will be the reduction in the fraction of the population that is young.

In the US, population aging is not a new phenomenon, but it has recently increased its pace. Between 1870 and 1990, the median age of the US population rose from 20.2 to 33.1 (a rate of 1.1 years per decade). Over the period 1990–2025, the median age is

---

[2] Throughout this chapter I rely on demographic forecasts from official sources to illustrate the expected magnitude of population aging. Mankiw and Weil (1989) show how inaccurate these forecasts can be: The US Census Bureau's forecast of births for 1963, made in 1953, was 443 000 births (11%) short of the mark, while the forecast for 1974 made in 1964 was 1.83 million births (58%) too high. Similarly, Ahlburg and Vaupel (1990) argue that uncertainty about future population growth is far greater than suggested by Census Bureau projections.

Table 1
Age structure of the population

	1950	1990	2025
World			
0–19	44.1	41.7	32.8
20–64	50.8	52.1	57.5
65+	5.1	6.2	9.7
OECD			
0–19	35.0	27.2	24.8
20–64	56.7	59.9	56.6
65+	8.3	12.8	18.6
US			
0–19	33.9	28.9	26.8
20–64	57.9	58.9	56.0
65+	8.1	12.2	17.2

forecast to rise to 40.9 (a rate of 2.2 years per decade). Comparing past aging to projected future aging, much more of the action in the past was in the reduction in the number of young people rather than in the increase in the number of old people: The fraction of the population that is aged above 64 rose 9.6 percentage points, from 3.0% to 12.6%, over the 120-year period between 1870 and 1990, compared with a projected increase of 7.2 percentage points over the next 35 years. The fraction below 15 fell from 39.2% to 21.4% over the last 120 years, and is projected to fall to 17.9% over the next 35 years.[3]

2.2. Sources of aging: fertility and mortality

In an economy closed to migration (which is discussed in Section 2.3), population aging results from two sources: an increase in the age at which people die, and a decrease in the rate at which births take place. An increase in longevity raises the average age of the population by raising the number of years in which each individual is old relative to the number in which he is young. A decrease in fertility raises the average age of the population by changing the relative numbers of people born recently (the young) and people born further in the past (the old). A second effect of reduced fertility, of course, is to reduce the rate at which the population grows. Throughout the world, both decreased fertility and decreased mortality are contributing to the aging of

[3] Bogue (1985), United Nations (1991).

Table 2
Changes in fertility: 1965–2000[a]

	1990 population (millions)	1990 GNP/capita (dollars)	Total fertility rate		
			1965	1990	2000
Low income					
China and India	1983.2	360	6.3	3.1	2.5
Other low income	1075.1	320	6.4	5.2	4.6
Lower-middle income	629.1	1530	5.6	4.0	3.4
Upper-middle income	458.4	3410	5.1	3.4	2.7
High income	816.4	19590	2.8	1.7	1.8

[a]Figures are population-weighted averages.
Source: World Bank (1992).

populations. The next two sections look at the relevant data. Throughout this chapter, I take changes in vital rates as being exogenous. For a discussion of determinants of these rates, see Birdsall (1988) and Parts II and III of this *Handbook*.

2.2.1. Declining fertility

Table 2 shows the total fertility rate for the years 1965 and 1990, along with projections for 2000, for the major groups of countries as classified by the World Bank. The fertility rate is the number of children that would be born to a woman if she were to live to the end of her childbearing years and bear children at each age in accordance with the prevailing age-specific fertility rate. In the richest countries, the fertility rate is currently below the level required to sustain a constant population (roughly 2.1 children per woman).

Fig. 1 shows the fertility rate in the US for the years 1860 through 1989, and the Social Security Administration's three alternative forecasts through 2040.[4] The figure shows both the long-term decline of fertility and the large, temporary rebound – the Baby Boom – which took place in the years after World War II. The Baby Boom interrupted the process of fertility reduction, and led to the creation of a cohort larger than both those that preceded it and those that followed, in most other industrialized countries as well as the US.[5] The presence of the Baby Boom cohort complicates the process of aging, leading, for example, to a ratio of elderly people to the total population that will be temporarily higher than its long-run forecast level.

[4] Coale and Zelnik (1963) and Wade (1989). Data prior to 1926 are for whites only.
[5] See OECD (1988).

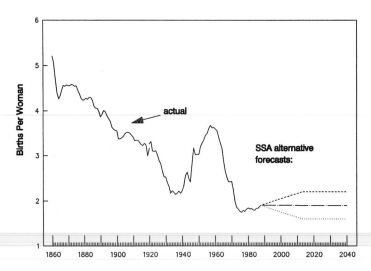

Fig. 1. Fertility rate: actual and forecast. Data prior to 1926 are for whites only.

2.2.2. Declining mortality

Table 3 shows the life expectancy of men and women in the US at different ages from 1900 projected through 2050. Among the points to note about the table are that increases in life expectancy at birth are increasingly the result of improvements in old-age life expectancy. For example, the 8.6 year improvement in men's life expectancy at birth that took place between 1930 and 1960 was accompanied by an increase of only 1.2 years in life expectancy at age 60, while the increase in life expectancy at birth of 5.7 years that took place between 1960 and 1990 was accompanied by an increase of 2.7 years in life expectancy at age 60. Declines in mortality have also been more dramatic for women than for men: the gap between women's and men's life expectancy at birth grew from 3.4 years to 7.6 years over the period 1930–1990, and the gap at age 60 grew from 1.3 to 5.2 years.

2.2.3. Fertility and mortality declines in stable populations

Insight into the sources of population aging can be gained by looking separately at the effects of changes in birth and death rates on a *stable population*. A stable population is one in which the age-specific rates of birth and death have been constant for sufficiently long that the age structure of the population – that is, the fraction of the popu-

Table 3
Changes in life expectancy by age in the US

	Year					
	1900	1930	1960	1990	2020	2050
Men						
Birth	46.6	58.0	66.6	72.3	74.4	75.8
Age 20	41.7	45.1	49.7	53.7	55.7	57.0
Age 40	27.5	28.8	31.3	35.3	37.1	38.5
Age 60	14.2	14.7	15.9	18.6	20.0	21.2
Age 80	5.0	5.4	6.1	7.5	8.4	9.2
Women						
Birth	49.1	61.4	73.2	79.9	82.1	83.8
Age 20	42.9	47.5	55.6	60.9	63.1	64.7
Age 40	28.7	31.0	36.6	41.6	43.7	45.3
Age 60	15.0	16.0	19.6	23.8	25.7	27.1
Age 80	5.3	5.8	7.0	9.9	11.3	12.4

Source: Faber (1982).

lation made up of people of each age – has stabilized.[6] Note that there is nothing inconsistent with a population growing (or shrinking, for that matter) and it being stable. Of course, birth and death rates have never been constant long enough for a stable population to be observed, but an examination of stable populations allows one to ask questions such as: "what if the birth rate fell while the death rate remained constant?" An examination of stable populations also makes it possible to gauge the relative importance of changes in birth and death rates in producing the actual changes in population age structure that are taking place.

Table 4 presents information about four stable populations, along with the US population in 1989 as a reference. The four stable populations are created by combining two birth profiles with two mortality profiles. The first birth profile used is that for the cohort of women born 1930–1934, which experienced the highest fertility of the cohorts that went through the Baby Boom, returning fertility to the level not experienced since the cohort born around 1875.[7] The second birth profile used is the cross-sectional pattern of birth rates for 1986, which, with slight alteration, is the one used in the Social Security Administration 1989 forecasts (Wade, 1989). The death rates are those for 1980 and 2030 (Faber, 1982). The standard assumption of 105 male births for every 100 female births is used in constructing the stable populations.

[6] See Keyfitz (1985: Chapter 4 for a discussion of stable population theory; Chapter 7 for an application to population aging).

[7] See Fig. 5.3 in Goldin (1990).

Table 4
Stable populations under alternative fertility and mortality[a]

Fertility:	1930–1934 cohort	1930–1934 cohort	1986	1986	Actual 1989
Mortality:	1980	2030	1980	2030	
Growth rate (%)	1.45	1.48	−0.50	−0.47	1.06
Fraction 0–19	0.384	0.374	0.228	0.214	0.288
Fraction 65+	0.098	0.118	0.208	0.249	0.125
Fraction 80+	0.023	0.036	0.060	0.094	0.027
Fraction 90+	0.004	0.009	0.012	0.028	0.004

[a]Actual figures for 1989 from US Bureau of Census (1991). Growth rate of population for 1989 is the growth from 1989 to 1990.

Using Table 4, one can gauge the relative importance of changes in births and changes in deaths by considering changing only one component at a time. Moving from the birth rate for the 1930–1934 cohort to the 1986 birth rate raises the fraction of the population that is aged 65 or over by 10.1 percentage points if death rates are held constant at their 1980 level, or by 13.1 percentage points if death rates are held constant at their 2030 level. By contrast, moving the death rate from its 1980 level to its 2030 level raises the fraction of the population aged 65 and over by 2.0 percentage points holding birth rates at the level of the 1930–1934 birth cohort, or 4.1 percentage points holding birth rates at their 1986 level. The total change in the fraction of the population 65 and over when both fertility and mortality decline, 15.1 percentage points, is the sum of these two effects along with a small interaction effect. Thus at least two-thirds of the increase in the fraction of the population over 65 is due to the change in birth rates. Similarly, at least 90% of the fall in the fraction 19 and under is due to the change in births.[8]

Although both fertility and mortality changes lead to population aging, they differ in how they affect aging as seen from the point of view of the individual. Changes in fertility do not affect the fraction of an individual's life that he or she can expect to spend in each age group, while changes in mortality have precisely such an effect. Lee (1994c) shows that for life expectancies at birth of between 35 and 70 years, an increase in life expectancy leads to a larger increase in the expected time spent in the 15–64 age group than in the time spent in the 65+ age group, although the proportional change in the number of years spent in the latter age group is far larger. Beyond

[8] Holding age-specific mortality rates constant, a reduction in fertility rates unambiguously leads to an aging of the population. A similar hypothesis – that holding constant fertility rates, a reduction in age-specific mortality also unambiguously leads to population aging – is not true. Lee (1991) shows that for populations with life expectancies below 65 or so, decreases in mortality lead to a reduction in the average age of the population – the mechanism being that reduced mortality raises the number of women who live to childbearing age, and thus raises the population growth rate.

a life expectancy of 70, increases in life expectancy raise the absolute number of years spent in the 65+ age group by more than the number of years spent in the 15–64 age group.

A final point to note about Table 4 is the relation between the current age structure and the stable populations. If one takes the first column as representing a starting point, and the fourth column as representing a destination, it is clear that the younger part of the age structure is much further along on its adjustment than is the older part. Roughly speaking, the transition from a young population to an old population is seen first in the younger part of the age distribution, and only later in the older part of the age distribution. This fact, which is crucial in understanding the dynamics of changes in dependency during the transition to an older population, is discussed further below (see Sections 3.1 and 3.4).

2.3. Immigration

The above analysis considered the determinants of population aging in a closed economy. In fact, immigration has played an important role in the evolution of the population in many countries. The annual flow of legal immigrants as a fraction of the current population in the US was 0.34% in 1993,[9] but historically it has ranged much higher. Over the period 1844–1910, annual immigration to the US averaged 0.79% of the population.[10] To the extent that population aging is viewed as an economic problem, changes in immigration policy hold the possibility of ameliorating its effects.

Fig. 2 graphs the age structure of the US population in 1987 along with the age structures of the net flows of legal and illegal immigrants assumed in the Social Security Administration's 1989 middle forecast. Both groups of immigrants are significantly younger than is the current US population, much less the population as it will exist in several decades.

In order to assess the potential effects of changes in immigration on the age structure of the population, Table 5 considers the experiment of changing the level of net migration as a fraction of the total US population, holding constant the age and sex composition of net migration. It is assumed that immigrants will have the same fertility and mortality profiles as natives.[11] The age and sex composition of immigrants and the ratio of legal to illegal immigrants are those underlying the Social Security Administration's forecasts.[12] Variations in the ratio of net migration to total population,

---

[9] US Immigration and Naturalization Service (1994). Estimates of the size of the illegal immigration differ greatly. See Warren and Passel (1987) and Borjas et al. (1991).

[10] US Bureau of the Census (1991).

[11] See Blau (1992).

[12] Wade (1989). The SSA assumes that the net flow of illegal immigrants will be one half the net flow of legal immigrants. The SSA forecasts assume a constant absolute level of immigration; in these projections I assume a constant ratio of immigrants to total population.

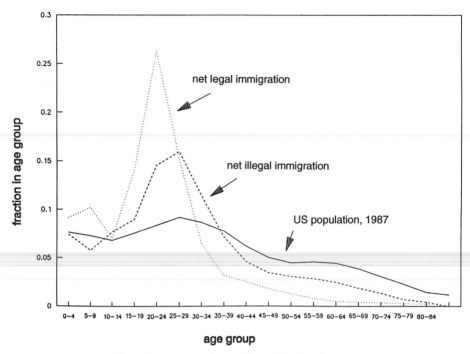

Fig. 2. Age structure of population and immigration flows.

ranging from zero to 1.0%, the level experienced during the peak decade of 1901–1910, are considered. It is assumed that the level of immigration relative to total population is constant at its new level starting in 1990. The table shows the total size of the population and its age structure under each scenario.

The table shows that increases in the flow of immigrants hold the potential to forestall population aging, but only at the cost of greatly increasing the size of the population. Raising the rate of immigration from 0.25% to 0.5% would raise the projected size of the population in 2040 by 18%, and lower the fraction of the population that is 65 and over from 19.1% to 17.7%. Raising the rate of immigration to 1.0% would lead to an age structure of the population only slightly older than the current one (15.3% aged 65 and older, compared to 12.5% in 1989), but to a population of 476 million by 2040. The last column of the table considers the experiment of holding the rate of immigration at 0.25% until 2019, then increasing it to 1.0% for the period 2020–2040. Such a policy might come about if the government increased the flow of immigrants in response to aging.[13] It leads to the same decrease in the fraction of the population

---

[13] Felderer (1994).

Table 5
Projected population under alternative rates of immigration[a]

Immigration rate (%)	0	0.25	0.5	0.75	1.0	0.25/1.0
Population in 2040: (millions)	249	294	346	406	476	353
% aged 0–19	22.7	23.3	23.8	24.4	24.8	24.6
% aged 65+	20.8	19.1	17.7	16.4	15.3	16.7

[a]This table shows the size and age structure of the population under alternative assumptions about the rate of immigration as a fraction of total population. The last column assumes an immigration rate of 0.25% from 1990 to 2019, and 1.0% from 2020 to 2040. All projections use mortality estimates from Faber (1982) and 1986 age specific fertility rates. Estimates of the age/sex composition of immigrants (both legal and illegal) come from Wade (1989).
Source: Author's calculations.

that is elderly with a smaller increase in total population than the policy of immediately increasing the flow of immigrants.

3. Aging, production, and consumption

This section considers the effects of population aging on the production and consumption in the economy. It considers the effect of aging in changing fraction of the population made up of non-productive dependents, but abstracts from the question of how resources are transferred to these dependents. The section highlights two important effects: first, the change in the dependency burdens of the young and the elderly contingent on population aging. Second, the economic effects of slower population growth, which is an integral part of population aging induced by lower birth rates.

3.1. The effect of population aging on youth and old-age dependency

The simplest measure of the economic impact of a dependent age group on society's resources is the *dependency ratio*, the number of people in a dependent age group divided by the working-age population. Fig. 3 graphs the youth and old-age dependency ratios for the US from 1950 to 1990, and the projected movements of the ratios through 2060. The aging of the population will have opposite effects on the burdens of youth and old-age dependency. The passage of the Baby Boom cohort appears as a bulge in youth dependency starting in 1960, and a bulge in old-age dependency starting in 2020.

Adding the youth and old-age dependency ratios together gives the total dependency ratio. Doing so is problematic, however, since there is no presumption that old people and children are dependent in the same way or to the same degree. Cutler et al. (1990) construct a measure of consumption "needs" that varies by age, adjusting for

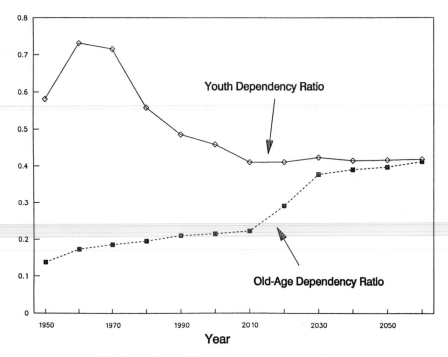

Fig. 3. Youth and old-age dependency ratios: 1950–2060.

the different levels of education spending, medical spending, and other consumption of children, the elderly, and working-age adults. Their summary measure weights people aged under 20 at 0.72 the consumption need of a working-age adult and people over 65 at 1.27 times the consumption need of a working age adult. Using these weights, one can construct a needs-adjusted dependency ratio.

Fig. 4 graphs the two measures of the dependency ratio for the period 1950–2060. The figure shows that, by either measure, the US is currently experiencing a transitory lull in the total burden of dependency: low population growth has reduced the burden of youth dependency, but has not yet increased the burden of old-age dependency.[14] When the consumption needs are not adjusted for age, the projected dependency ratio will rise by 8.0% of its 1990 value between 1990 and 2060. Using the adjusted measure of consumption needs, the ratio of dependents to working-age population rises by 13.0% of its 1990 level between 1990 and 2060. In both cases, almost all of the in-

---

[14] A similar pattern holds for the OECD taken as a whole, as well as for most OECD countries individually (OECD, 1988).

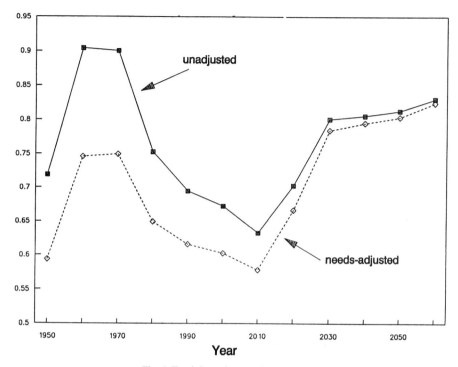

Fig. 4. Total dependency ratio: 1950–2060.

crease in dependency takes place between 2010 and 2030. Using the unadjusted measure of dependency, the long-run burden of dependency is lower than the burden faced when the Baby Boom generation was going through childhood. Adjusting for consumption needs reverses this conclusion, however.

3.2. *Age structure, population growth, and dependency in stable populations*

As discussed above, the primary force driving the population aging that is taking place today is reduced fertility. The effect of the reduced fertility, via the channel of slower population growth, on age structure, dependency, and consumption, can be analyzed using a simple model in which output is produced with only labor.[15] Total consumption at every point in time is equal to total output. Let $c(x)$ be consumption by people of age x, $y(x)$ be the output produced by people of age x, and $N(x)$ the number of peo-

[15] Lee (1980).

ple aged x. The economy's budget constraint is that total consumption be equal to total output:

$$\int_0^T N(x)c(x)\,dx = \int_0^T N(x)y(x)\,dx, \tag{1}$$

where T is the maximum age to which a person can live.

It is assumed that individuals have consumption needs that vary by age, where $\hat{c}(x)$ is the vector of consumption needs. Define the *support ratio* (α) as the ratio of the productive capacity of the economy to the consumption needs of the population:[16]

$$\alpha = \frac{\int_0^T N(x)y(x)\,dx}{\int_0^T N(x)\hat{c}(x)\,dx}, \tag{2}$$

Actual consumption of people at each age is assumed to be proportional to consumption needs. The support ratio then determines the level of consumption that is consistent with the aggregate budget constraint: $c(x) = \alpha\hat{c}(x)$. The larger is the part of the population that is in its productive years relative to the part of the population that has high consumption needs, the larger is the support ratio. The higher is the support ratio, in turn, the higher will be each individual's needs-adjusted consumption.

To analyze how the rate of population growth affects the support ratio, we consider the case of stable populations. Let $p(x)$ be the probability of living from birth to age x, and n the growth rate of the population. In a stable population, with the total population size normalized to one, the number of people at each age will be

$$N(x) = \frac{e^{-nx}p(x)}{\int_0^T e^{-nx}p(x)\,dx}. \tag{3}$$

Substituting this expression into the equation for the support ratio gives

$$\alpha = \frac{\int_0^T e^{-nx}p(x)y(x)\,dx}{\int_0^T e^{-nx}p(x)\hat{c}(x)\,dx}. \tag{4}$$

---

[16] Cutler et al. (1990). This same ratio, at the level of households, is examined by Chayanov (1966). In the case where all people have equal consumption needs, α is just the inverse of one plus the total dependency ratio.

We can now look at the effect of changing the growth rate of the population, n, on the support ratio in a stable population. Taking logs of both sides of Eq. (4) and differentiating:

$$\frac{d \ln(\alpha)}{dn} = \frac{-\int_0^T x\, e^{-nx} p(x)y(x)\, dx}{\int_0^T e^{-nx} p(x)y(x)\, dx} + \frac{\int_0^T x\, e^{-nx} p(x)\hat{c}(x)\, dx}{\int_0^T e^{-nx} p(x)\hat{c}(x)\, dx} = A_c - A_y, \tag{5}$$

where A_y is the average age (looking cross-sectionally at the population) at which production takes place, and A_c is the average age at which consumption takes place.[17] The change in the support ratio resulting from an increase in population growth (looking across stable populations) is proportional to the difference between the average age of consumption and the average age of production. If A_c is greater than A_y, then increasing population growth raises the support ratio and the level of needs-adjusted consumption, since it shifts the population toward younger ages. Assuming that $y(x)$ is more concentrated toward the center of life than is $c(x)$, the average age of production will be higher than the average age of consumption for rapidly growing populations, and a reduction in n will increase the support ratio. Similarly, A_y will be lower than A_c for populations with sufficiently small n. For the rate of population growth which maximizes the support ratio, it will be true that $A_y = A_c$.[18]

3.3. Implications of changes in morbidity and mortality for support ratios

In analyzing the effects of population aging on the burden of old-age dependency, Section 3.1 assumed an equal burden of dependency for all people over 65. However, aging due to either lower mortality or to lower fertility will affect the age distribution within the group traditionally treated as elderly. Moving between the first and second columns of Table 4, that is, holding fertility constant and reducing mortality, raises the fraction of the over-65 population that is over 80 from 23.7% to 29.0%. Moving between the first and third columns of the table, that is, holding mortality constant at its

---

[17] This is a special case of a more general result presented in Lee (1991): let $g(x)$ be the quantity of some characteristic exhibited by people of age x, A_g be population-weighted average age of characteristic g, A_p be the average age of the population, and G_p be the average amount of the characteristic in the population. Then looking across stable populations: $d \ln(G_p)/dn = A_p - A_g$.

[18] Lee (1994a–c) estimates that for the US, $A_c - A_y = 4$. Ermisch (1989a, b) reports similar estimates for Japan and the UK. Ermisch also reports that even with fertility rates as high as those of the baby boom and mortality rates as high as those of the UK in the late nineteenth century (but holding lifetime paths of consumption needs and productivity at their current levels), it would be the case that A_c exceeded A_y in a stable population. Willis (1982) models the relation between the average ages of producing and consuming, on the one hand, and the rate of fertility, on the other, as being simultaneously determined.

1986 level, and reducing fertility, raises the fraction of the over-65 population that is over 80 from 23.7% to 30.8%. Combining fertility and mortality reductions would raise the fraction of the elderly population that is aged 80 and over to 37.5%.

In cross-section, there is great variation in the health burden imposed by old people of different ages: of the US population aged 65–74 in 1985, 1.3% lived in nursing homes, compared to 5.9% of the population aged 75–84 and 23.0% of the population aged 85 and above.[19] Thus treating the population over 65 as a homogeneous group will clearly understate the increase in the health burden of aging. Such a problem can, of course, be addressed by subdividing the elderly population into more finely-delineated age groups.

A more subtle question is whether and how the age-specific needs of the elderly can be expected to change in the face of population aging. To the extent that population aging is due to reductions in fertility with constant mortality, the assumption of a constant age-specific dependency burden seems reasonable. To the extent that aging is due to reduced mortality, however, it is questionable. As the life expectancy of people at each age increases (that is, as the probability of dying at any given age falls), will the average health of people at each age also change, and in which direction?

There are potential effects that should both increase and decrease the age-specific rates of morbidity. To the extent that mortality improvements come about by saving the lives of people who remain disabled, we would expect to see a deterioration in age-specific health. Poterba and Summers (1987) calculate that 9.0% of the men and 16.9% of the women over 60 in 1980 would not have been alive if their cohort had experienced the mortality of cohorts born 30 years earlier. At higher ages, the fraction of the population made up of these "marginal survivors" is even higher: for example 15.1% of men and 35.2% of women over 80 in 1980 would not have been alive given the mortality experience of the cohort 30 years older. Marginal survivors may be in worse health than people who would have lived anyway either because they were more frail to begin with, or because the disease which would have killed them has left them disabled. In either case, lowering mortality will lead to a rise in age-specific disability rates. Poterba and Summers estimate that the presence of marginal survivors, as compared to the cohort born 30 years earlier, lowered the life expectancy of the pool of 70-year-olds by approximately one year in 1980.

On the other hand, to the extent that a reduction in life-ending disease is paralleled by a reduction in disabling disease, the health of people at each age could be expected to improve.[20] A simple example of this second effect is end-of-life medical expenditures, which make up a large part of health-care costs. Improvements in mortality lower the fraction of the population in any age group that are near the end of their lives, and thus lower age-specific rates of spending on end-of-life medical care.[21] The

---

[19] US Senate (1991). The total for all people above 64 was 5.0%.

[20] Fries (1980).

[21] Fuchs (1984).

belief that reduced mortality will be paired with improved age-specific health under-lies the legislated increase in the US Social Security program's normal retirement age (the age at which a retiree receives full benefits) from 65 to 67 over the period 2003–2025.

Which of these two effects predominates is an empirical question. Poterba and Summers find that past increases in the frailty of the pool of survivors at each age have approximately offset overall reductions in morbidity, leaving the age-specific health approximately unchanged. They write: "Reductions in mortality do not seem to be associated with reductions in morbidity at each age. There is little reason to think that the health status of the typical 65-year old twenty years from now will be better than it is now" (p. 51). Schneider and Guralnik (1987), reviewing a large number of empirical studies, reach a similar conclusion. Crimmins et al. (1989) find that the ef-fect of mortality improvements on disability is sensitive to the definition of disability used: looking at white women aged 65, for example, overall life expectancy increased by 1.7 years between 1970 and 1980; over the same period expected remaining life free from any disability increased by only 0.2 years, but expected life free from bed disability increased by 1.2 years.

3.4. Aging and sustainable consumption in a model with capital

An increase in the dependency ratio, holding constant both the amount of output pro-duced by each working-age adult and the fraction of that output that is consumed, clearly implies a reduction in the amount of consumption per person. Friedlander and Klinov-Malul (1980) and Cutler et al. (1990) point out that in the case of population aging due to a reduction in fertility, there is a second important effect on consumption: slower population growth reduces the fraction of output that must be devoted to pro-ducing new capital. For a country to retain a constant capital–labor ratio, some output must be diverted to investment in order to supply new workers with capital. Fewer new workers means lower required investment and more consumption.[22]

Consider an economy in which the consumption needs and labor supplies of indi-viduals vary by age. Specifically, let consumption needs of individuals aged x be given by $\hat{c}(x)$, as in Section 3.2, and assume that the population can be divided into dependents and workers, with the latter each supplying one unit of labor and the for-mer supplying zero. Let k be the level of capital per worker and $f(k)$ be the production

---

[22] An example of this effect is the decline in required housing investment, and, possibly, a decline in the price of housing, that should accompany a slowing of population growth. See Ermisch (1988) and Mankiw and Weil (1989).

function in per-worker terms. Analogously with Section 3.2, define α (the support ratio) as the ratio of workers (W) to the total consumption needs of the population:[23]

$$\alpha = \frac{W}{\int_0^T N(x)\hat{c}(x)\,dx}, \tag{6}$$

where $N(x)$ is the number of people aged x.

Define C as total consumption in the economy, and define c as needs-adjusted consumption per capita:

$$c = \frac{C}{\int_0^T N(x)\hat{c}(x)\,dx}. \tag{7}$$

Let δ be the rate of depreciation, and n the growth rate of the labor force (which, in a stable population, is the same as the rate of growth of the population).[24] The derivative of the per-worker capital stock with respect to time is given by

$$\frac{dk}{dt} = f(k) - (n+\delta)k - \frac{c}{\alpha}. \tag{8}$$

In steady state, capital per worker is constant. The steady-state locus of feasible combinations of needs-adjusted consumption per capita and capital per worker is given by

$$c = \alpha[f(k) - (n+\delta)k]. \tag{9}$$

A decrease in α (that is, an increase in the number of dependents relative to the number of workers) will reduce the level of consumption possible at any level of capital per worker. A reduction in n, the rate of labor force growth, will reduce the burden of providing capital to new workers, and will raise the consumption level consistent with any steady-state capital stock. Population aging associated with lower fertility will lower n and have an ambiguous effect on α, depending on the average ages of production and consumption.

[23] In the model of Section 3.2, where output was produced using labor alone, α was defined as the ratio of output to consumption needs. If each worker produces a single unit of output, the two definitions are the same.

[24] For convenience, I hold technology constant. Labor-augmenting technological progress could be incorporated by redefining k and c to be their levels in this model divided by the number of efficiency units per worker.

Table 6
Effect of demographic change on consumption in steady states[a]

n (%)	Fraction of population aged (%)		α	Effect of dependency (%)	Effect of labor force growth (%)	Total consumption in per capita change (%)
	0–19	64+				
(1)	(2)	(3)	(4)	(5)	(6)	(7)
−1.00	19.2	24.5	0.556	−3.5	2.6	−0.9
−0.75	21.0	22.6	0.563	−2.2	1.9	−0.3
−0.50	22.8	20.7	0.569	−1.2	1.3	0.1
−0.25	24.6	19.0	0.573	−0.5	0.6	0.2
0.00	26.5	17.5	0.576	0.0	0.0	0.0
0.25	28.6	15.8	0.577	0.2	−0.7	−0.5
0.50	30.5	14.4	0.577	0.2	−1.4	−1.1
0.75	32.6	13.1	0.576	0.0	−2.1	−2.1
1.00	34.6	11.8	0.573	−0.5	−2.7	−3.2
1.25	36.7	10.6	0.569	−1.3	−3.4	−4.6
1.50	38.8	9.6	0.563	−2.2	−4.0	−6.2
1.75	40.9	8.6	0.556	−3.4	−4.6	−8.0
2.00	42.9	7.7	0.549	−4.7	−5.2	−9.9

[a]This table shows the effect of population growth on dependency and sustainable consumption in stable populations. Each row presents calculations for a different population growth rate, which is given in column (1). Column (4) gives the support ratio, α: working-age population divided by total age-adjusted consumption needs. Column (5) shows the effect on consumption relative to the base case of zero population growth of the change in the support ratio. Column (6) shows the effect of labor force growth on consumption, again relative to the case of zero population growth. Column (7) shows the combined effects of the support ratio and the labor force growth effects.
Source: Author's calculations.

In a stable population, of course, the rate of labor force growth, n, and the support ratio, α, are related. Table 6 explores how changing growth affects needs-adjusted consumption per capita, both through the effect on the dependency ratio and through the change in labor force growth. Each row considers a different labor force growth rate, given in column (1). For each rate of labor force growth, the age distribution of the stable population (based on 1980 mortality rates) is calculated, and the fractions of the stable population that are under 20 and over 64 are presented in columns (2) and (3). Column (4) shows the support ratio, α, calculated using the weights for old age and youth consumption needs from Cutler et al. (1990). The fifth column of the table shows the effect on consumption relative to the base case of zero labor force growth, of the change in the support ratio. Considering dependency alone, the labor force growth rate consistent with maximum consumption would be between 0.25% and 0.5%. This is simply the optimal population growth rate from the model that consid-

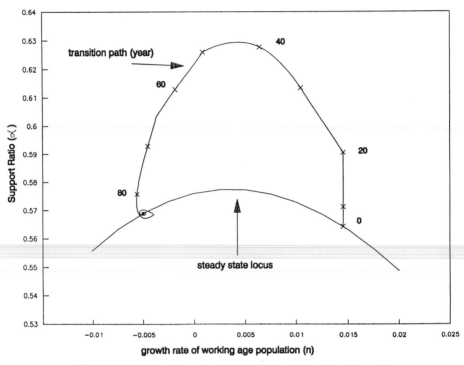

Fig. 5. Combinations of n and α in steady states and along transition path.

ered production without capital, presented in Section 3.2. The sixth column of the table shows the effect of labor force growth, via required investment, on consumption, again relative to the case of zero growth.[25] Lower labor force growth always leads to the investment effect on consumption being bigger. Column (7) of the table shows the combined effects of the support ratio and the labor force growth effects: the population growth rate that maximizes consumption is now *negative*: somewhere between −0.25% and −0.5%.

Table 6 says that in steady state needs-adjusted consumption would be approximately 6.1% lower in a country with a labor force growth rate of 1.5% than it would be in a country with a labor force growth rate of −0.5%. This is approximately the size of the change in population growth rates taking place in the US (as shown in Table 4). But in addition to the steady-state change, there are important effects that take place

---

[25] Following Cutler et al. (1990), the second-order term, representing the interaction of changes in both α and n, is assigned to n. Cutler et al. also show that in steady state the optimal level of capital per worker is invariant to the rate of population growth.

along the transition path from one level of population growth to another. Fig. 5 traces the combinations of the support ratio (α) and the growth rate of the working age population (n) along a transition path from high to low fertility. The figure is generated by holding mortality constant at its 1980 level throughout, and allowing age-specific fertility rates to linearly adjust over a 30-year period from their levels in the 1930–1934 cohort to their cross-sectional levels in 1986. The figure shows that along the transition path there is a far more dramatic change in the support ratio than one observes looking across steady states. This is because of the time lag between a decline in youth dependency and an increase in old-age dependency, both of which result from the fertility change.

Fig. 6 examines the level of consumption that could be sustained while maintaining a constant capital–labor ratio, for the same demographic transition examined in Fig. 5. The increase in consumption along the transition path is far larger than the difference between consumption in the two steady states. The fertility transition raises consumption first by reducing youth dependency, and then by lowering the rate of growth of the labor force. Consumption peaks 47 years after the beginning of the transition at a

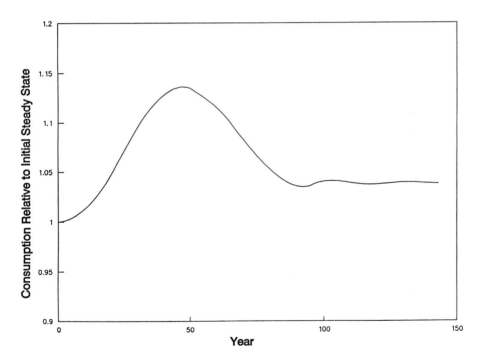

Fig. 6. Consumption during a demographic transition.

Table 7
Effect of projected demographic changes on steady-state consumption[a]

Year	n (%)	α	Effect of dependency (%)	Effect of labor force growth (%)	Total change in per capita consumption (%)
1960	0.79	0.573	−7.4	0.4	−7.1
1970	1.61	0.572	−7.7	−1.8	−9.5
1980	1.80	0.606	−2.0	−2.4	−4.5
1990	0.88	0.619	0.0	0.0	0.0
2000	0.89	0.622	0.8	0.0	0.8
2010	0.52	0.634	2.3	1.0	3.4
2020	−0.22	0.600	−3.1	2.9	−0.2
2030	−0.10	0.560	−9.5	2.4	−7.1
2040	0.15	0.557	−10.0	1.8	−8.3
2050	−0.12	0.554	−10.4	2.4	−8.0
2060	0.03	0.548	−11.5	2.0	−9.4

[a] n is the rate of growth of the working age population. α is the support ratio: working-age population divided by total age-adjusted consumption needs. The last three columns measure the effect of changes in the support ratio, changes in labor force growth, and the total effect of demographic change on the level of consumption that would keep the ratio of capital to efficiency unit of labor constant, given the values of α and n.

Source: Cutler et al. (1990: Table 3 and Data Appendix).

level 14% higher than its initial steady state. In the new steady state, consumption is only 4% higher than its initial level.[26]

The actual aging of the population taking place in the US is more complicated than the scenario in Figs. 5 and 6, since mortality is changing as well as fertility, and the Baby Boom interrupted a monotonic fertility decline. But the key effect – that the transition allows for a temporary boom in consumption – remains. Cutler et al. (1990) calculate the effect on per capita consumption (adjusted to reflect varying consumption needs by age) of projected population aging over the period 1960–2060. They calculate the difference between the level of consumption that could be sustained in each year, given that year's values for α and n, and the level that could be sustained in 1990, in both cases holding capital per worker at its 1990 level. Their results are presented in Table 7. As in Table 6, the difference between sustainable consumption in each year and sustainable consumption in 1990 is decomposed into two parts: one due

[26] Although the optimal level of capital per worker in steady state is not affected by the rate of population growth, the same is not true along the transition path; see Cutler et al. (1990) for a full treatment of the transitional dynamics. The deviation of the level of capital per worker along the transition path from its steady-state level is not large, however: over the period 1990–2060, they find that the optimal level of capital per worker deviates from its steady-state level by at most 5%.

to the effect of dependency, and the other to the effect of changes in the labor force growth. The effect of changes in dependency is to increase the sustainable level of consumption over the period 1970–2010. This period corresponds to the lull between the decrease in youth dependency and the increase in old-age dependency, both of which follow from the slowdown in fertility. The depressing effect of changes in the labor force growth on sustainable consumption in 1970 and 1980 corresponds to the rapid increase in the growth rate of the labor force (and the corresponding need to supply new workers with capital) due to the entry of the Baby Boom. The overall effect of demographic change is to increase sustainable consumption over the period 1970–2010, and to lower it over the period 2010–2060. Once again, the largest impact of aging comes over the period 2010–2030, when sustainable consumption falls by over 10%.

3.5. Aging and the labor market

Just as population aging means more old people as a fraction of the population, it also means more old workers as a fraction of the labor force. To the extent that old and young workers differ in the input that they supply, the wages that they receive, the jobs that they occupy, and in their propensity to be unemployed or to move, population aging can be expected to have effects on the labor market. These will be both composition effects due to changes in the relative weights of different age groups in the total labor force, as well as general equilibrium effects on age-specific wages, mobility, and employment status.

The most natural experiment with which to analyze the effects of demographic change on the labor market – the experience of the large Baby Boom cohort – is discussed in Chapter 2 of this *Handbook*. The more long-term effects of population aging are in some ways similar, and in others different, from those encountered by the Baby Boomers. The Baby Boom cohort brought about a large increase in the relative size of every age group that it entered. For example, the fraction of the labor force aged 20–34 moved from 31.5% to 40.1% over the period 1966–1976 (Freeman, 1979). The changes in the relative sizes of different age groups in the process of aging in the United States is of roughly similar size: comparing the high fertility–high mortality population to the low fertility–low mortality population in Table 4, the fraction of the population aged 20–64 that is aged 20–34 falls from 42.3% to 32.1%. Similarly, using Social Security Administration forecasts, the fraction of the population aged 20–64 that is aged 20–34 will fall from 42.8% to 34.5% over the period 1990–2000. On the other hand, two salient features of the Baby Boom experience are not present in the case of permanent population aging. First, members of the Baby Boom generation were always in a crowded group. By contrast, to the extent that some age groups could become relatively crowded in the process of population aging, individuals will only be in the crowded group for part of their lives. Second, the movement of the Baby Boom generation through the age structure has produced repeated changes in the age structure of the labor force, with consequent adjustment costs. By contrast, a permanent aging of the population will have no such adjustment costs in the long run.

3.5.1. Lifetime wage profiles

Over an individual's working life, his or her wage grows both because of changes in the average level of wages (due to capital deepening and technological progress) and because at each point in time there exists a cross-sectional age–earnings profile. One explanation for the existence and shape of the age–earnings profile is that younger and older workers provide different factors of production, and that these factors earn different wages. In particular, older workers possess higher levels of experience and skill, but lower levels of physical stamina. In such a case, demographic change, by changing the relative supplies of these factors, will lead to a change in the wage profile. Freeman (1979) finds that just such a model explains the changes in the relative wages of younger and older men over the period in which the Baby Boom cohort entered the labor force. Similarly, Welch (1979) estimates that a 10% increase in cohort size reduced wages to college graduates by 9% and to high school graduates by 4% upon entry into the labor force. On the other hand, Murphy et al. (1988) argue that over the course of a lifetime, the effects of generational crowding are relatively small: while members of large cohorts can suffer wages 10% below those of average-sized cohorts in the early years of their careers, such crowding effects diminish with experience, so that the present discounted value of lifetime wages for members of large cohorts is only 3% below that for average-sized cohorts.

The complementarity in production of workers of different ages implies that members of large birth cohorts, such as the Baby Boom, will be disadvantaged, since they will always be in the age group which is in large supply. In the case of a permanent aging of the population due to reduced fertility, however, the situation is more complicated. Population aging will raise the wages of the young relative to the old. But since every worker will be both young and old during his or her life, the welfare implications of such aging are not immediately clear. A simple model (Lam, 1989) can be used to demonstrate this point and to examine the welfare implications of changes in the growth rate of the population. Normalize the population to one, and let l_1 and l_2 ($= 1 - l_1$) be the numbers of young and old workers, respectively. Production is assumed to use only the two types of labor as inputs, $y = f(l_1, l_2)$, and to be constant returns to scale. Workers are paid their marginal products.

The present value of lifetime wages is

$$W = f_1 + \frac{f_2}{1+r}, \tag{10}$$

where the interest rate, r, is taken as exogenous. Differentiating Eq. (10) with respect to l_1 yields

$$\frac{dW}{dl_1} = f_{11} - f_{12} + \frac{f_{21} - f_{22}}{1 + r}. \tag{11}$$

Given constant returns to scale, factor payments exhaust output:

$$f(l_1, l_2) = l_1 f_1 + l_2 f_2. \tag{12}$$

Differentiating Eq. (12) with respect to l_1 and rearranging yields

$$f_{21} = -f_{11} \left(\frac{l_1}{l_2} \right). \tag{13}$$

Differentiating Eq. (12) with respect to l_2 yields a similar expression. Using these and the equality $f_{12} = f_{21}$, Eq. (11) can be re-written as

$$\frac{dW}{dl_1} = f_{11} \left(1 + \frac{l_1}{l_2} \right) \left(1 - \frac{l_1 / l_2}{1 + r} \right). \tag{14}$$

Finally, assuming that the population is growing at rate n, Eq. (14) can be re-written as

$$\frac{dW}{dn} = f_{11}(2 + n) \left(1 - \frac{1 + n}{1 - r} \right). \tag{15}$$

When $r = n$, changes in the rate of growth of population have no effect on the present value of lifetime wages. But this is a global *minimum*: workers are made better off the farther n is from r, no matter in which direction. The above result can be generalized to show that when productivity is growing at a rate of g per generation, the condition for the present value of wages being at their global minimum is $(1 + n)(1 + g) = (1 + r)$.

One can now analyze the welfare implications of reducing n. Lower labor force growth will raise the wages of young workers, and lower those of old workers. The effect on the present value of lifetime wages will depend on how the sum of the growth rate of the labor force and the growth rate of productivity compares to the relevant interest rate. If $(1 + n)(1 + g) > (1 + r)$, then reducing n will lower the present value of lifetime wages, while if $(1 + n)(1 + g) < (1 + r)$, then further reductions in n will raise the present value of wages. The latter condition probably holds true.[27]

[27] See Abel et al. (1989).

3.5.2. Deviations between wages and marginal products

The model presented above derives the age–wage profile as a result of differences in the marginal product of labor. A different approach is that of Lazear (1979), who argues that upwardly sloping wage profiles are part of a mechanism to prevent shirking by workers in the presence of imperfect monitoring. Workers post a "bond" (which is forfeit if they are fired) in the form of wages below their marginal products when young, and receive repayment in the form of wages above their marginal products when they are old. Among the virtues of the model is that it explains the desire of companies to apply mandatory retirement ages. Kotlikoff (1988a) finds strong evidence in favor of the Lazear model: wages start off below productivity, but rise above it as workers near retirement age.

The implications of population aging for a Lazear-type model of the age–wage profile depend on the manner in which firms finance deviations between wages and productivity (in a manner analogous to the funding of Social Security, discussed below). If this gap is financed on a "pay as you go" basis, then population aging will lead to a funding shortfall: the reduction in young workers' wages below marginal product will no longer cover the excess of older workers' wages above it. Thus population aging will have to lead to a reduction in the wages of one of the groups of workers. If, on the other hand, firms finance the deviation of wages from productivity on a "funded" basis – that is, if the firm actually puts aside the money to pay workers wages above their marginal products in their later years – then aging of the labor force will not necessarily affect the wage profile. (See Lazear (1990) for a more formal treatment of this problem.)

3.5.3. Unemployment, mobility, and labor force participation

A notable way in which young workers differ from older workers is that they have higher rates of unemployment. Holding these rates constant, demographic changes can have large effects on the average rate of unemployment. Flaim (1990) finds that shifts in the age structure of the labor force do a good job in explaining movements in unemployment over the period 1960–1990. It is not clear, however, whether these age-specific differences will be sustained in the face of future demographic shifts. To the extent that unemployment among the young is generated by last-in–first-out firing on the part of employers, demographic change will result in an increase in unemployment rates for older workers, leaving the natural rate of unemployment constant.

Related to the issue of unemployment is that of mobility. Young workers are more mobile than their older peers, partly because they have a longer period over which to recover the costs of moving, and also because they are less likely to have found a good match for their skills. Mobility of the young lends flexibility to the workforce in the face of sector- or location-specific shocks. An older workforce, if age-specific mobility rates do not change, will be less mobile, and more prone to long-term unemployment.

The aging of the population, in affecting the age–wage profile, may also affect the timing of the retirement decision. Secular declines in labor force participation of the elderly have been dramatic – see Lumsdaine and Wise (1994) for a discussion. But it is hard to make the case that these observed declines are attributable to population aging. For the reasons given in Section 3.5.1, increasing the fraction of the labor force that is old should lower the relative wages of the elderly, and this might be likely to lower their labor force participation. Working against this trend will be the desire of governments to postpone retirement as a way of balancing public pension systems.

3.5.4. Seniority and promotion

A final labor market effect of population aging is on the speed with which individuals progress up the seniority ladder (Keyfitz, 1973, 1985; Cantrell and Clark, 1982). If promotions are based on seniority, and if the fraction of the workforce at each given rank is fixed (for example, the number of generals relative to the size of the army), then slower population growth implies that the age at which people attain given rank rises.

Let k be the percentile rank in the seniority distribution at which one obtains a given promotion. This rank is taken as fixed. Then in a stable population, the age, x, at which one attains this rank satisfies the condition

$$k = \frac{\int_x^\gamma e^{-na} p(a)\, da}{\int_\beta^\gamma e^{-na} p(a)\, da}, \tag{16}$$

where β is the age of beginning work, $p(a)$ is the probability of being in the labor force at age a, γ is the latest age of retirement, and n is the rate of population growth.

Table 8 shows the age at which workers will attain different ranks in the labor force for the stable populations considered in Table 4 as well as for the 1989 actual population. The table assumes that people start working on their 20th birthday and retire on their 65th birthday. Comparing the high-fertility, high-mortality population (Column 2) to the low-fertility, low-mortality population (Column 5), the age at which one reaches halfway up the seniority ladder rises by five years in the older population.

Bos and Weizsacker (1989) suggest that as consequence of population aging there is a danger that young people will be frustrated and discouraged by their slow rate of promotion. An alternative to later promotion is, of course, no promotion at all. If an

Table 8
Age of attaining different levels of seniority[a]

Fertility:	Stable populations				Actual 1989 population
	1930–1934 cohort	1930–1934 cohort	1986	1986	
Mortality:	1980	2030	1980	2030	
(1)	(2)	(3)	(4)	(5)	(6)
10%	23.2	23.3	24.7	24.8	23.0
25%	28.4	28.5	31.6	31.8	27.7
50%	38.1	38.3	42.8	43.0	37.0
75%	49.7	50.0	53.7	54.0	50.5
90%	58.2	58.4	60.4	60.5	58.8
95%	61.4	61.6	62.6	62.7	61.7

[a]This table shows the age at which an individual will achieve a given rank (shown in column (1)) in the labor force, which is taken to be all individuals aged 20–64. Columns (2)–(5) show the age at which the rank is achieved for the four stable populations calculated in Table 4. Column (6) shows the age at which the rank is achieved for the 1989 US population.
Source: Author's calculations.

occupation has an "up or out" career track, in which people must be promoted to a certain grade by a certain age, and if the fraction of workers that can be in the higher grade is fixed, then a slower rate of population growth will mean that a smaller fraction of the eligible population will ever be promoted. Examples of such systems are the promotion of military officers and the tenuring of junior faculty.

4. Aging in a life-cycle model

This section examines the effects of aging in a life-cycle model. The life-cycle model is concerned with how the saving of individuals in order to smooth consumption over the course of their lives in the face of varying income leads to the accumulation of wealth at the individual level and of the capital stock at the national level. Individuals make saving and labor supply choices taking as exogenous aggregate conditions in the economy. Since the life-cycle model predicts that the elderly will be running down their assets, it implies that the aggregate saving rate will fall in response to population aging brought on by lower fertility.[28] The section begins by examining the simplest possible life-cycle model, with wage and interest rates taken as exogenous. It then

---

[28] As discussed in Section 2, reduced fertility is the primary driving force behind current population aging. For a discussion of the effects of reduced mortality on saving in the life-cycle model, see Kotlikoff (1981) and Skinner (1985).

expands the model to allow for general equilibrium effects of changes in the capital stock. The last part of this section examines alternative models of saving and how they behave in the face of demographic change.

4.1. Demographic change in a two-period life-cycle model

First, the effect of demographic change in a simple overlapping generations life-cycle model is considered (see Auerbach and Kotlikoff (1987) for a more extensive discussion).[29] Individuals are assumed to live for two periods, supplying labor only in the first period of life. They get utility only from consumption in the two periods:

$$U_t = U(C_{y,t}, C_{o,t+1}),$$ (17)

where $C_{y,t}$ is the consumption of people who are young in period t and $C_{o,t+1}$ is the consumption of the same people when they are old in period $t + 1$. Individuals take as exogenous their wage during the first period of life, W_t, and the interest rate on saving held between the first and second periods of life, r_{t+1}. Individuals face the lifetime budget constraint

$$C_{y,t} + \frac{C_{o,t+1}}{1+r_{t+1}} = W_t.$$ (18)

The saving of the young is $S_{y,t} = W_t - C_{y,t}$. The consumption of the old in period t is equal to their saving when young plus accumulated interest: $C_{o,t} = (1 + r_t)(W_{t-1} - C_{y,t-1})$. Given that they have earned interest of $r_t(W_{t-1} - C_{y,t-1})$ on the wealth that they put aside when young, the saving of the old in period t is $S_{o,t} = -W_{t-1} + C_{y,t-1}$. Consider first the case where W and r are constant, and thus optimal consumption of the young, C_y, is also constant. To incorporate population age structure into the model, let n be the rate of population growth. Thus the young generation is $(1 + n)$ times the size of the old generation. The aggregate saving rate is

$$s = \frac{n(W - C_y)}{(1+n)W - r(W - C_y)}.$$ (19)

Population aging brought on by a decline in fertility – that is, a decline in n – will lower the saving rate. Further, when n is zero, that is, when the old and young generations are the same size, the saving rate will be zero. Finally, under the assumption that

---

[29] By fixing the number of periods in life and the relative size of working life and retirement, this model constrains us to look only at the effects of fertility-induced demographic change.

W and r are constant, the saving rate in period t depends only on the ratio of old to young in that period.

The assumption of exogenous interest and wage rates is appropriate for a small open economy, but not otherwise. The partial equilibrium model presented here can be closed by assuming that the capital stock in each period is equal to the saving of the current elderly. Capital per worker is then given by $k_t = (W_{t-1} - C_{y,t-1})/(1 + n)$. The wage and interest rates are determined by a productive technology using capital and labor.

Allowing for general equilibrium effects, an assessment of the effect of population aging on the saving rate rapidly becomes analytically intractable. An increase in the ratio of old to young people will increase the amount of capital per worker, and thus raise the wage and lower the interest rate. In the special case where preferences are homothetic the saving rate of the young cohort, s_y, will be invariant to the interest rate. In this case, the general equilibrium effect of changes in population age structure on the saving rate in steady state will be the same as the partial equilibrium effect. If preferences are not homothetic, however, then there will be a secondary effect of changes in n on the saving rate of the young. For example, if the interest elasticity of saving is positive, then population aging will reduce the saving rate both by raising the fraction of the population that is old and by lowering the saving rate of the young. A second sort of complication in the general equilibrium model is that saving in period t depends on the interest rate (and thus the ratio of old to young) that will hold in period $t + 1$. Thus saving in each period depends on expectations of future population growth rates. Similarly, if one allows more than one period of working life, the saving decision made early in life depends on the expected path of lifetime wages. Finally, changes in the population age structure which change the steady-state level of capital per worker will lead to dynamic adjustments in the levels of capital, wages, and interest rates along the path to a final steady state.

To handle the complications which arise in the general equilibrium model, one must resort to simulations. This approach is discussed in Section 4.3. Another approach is to ignore the effects of changes in interest and wage rates, and use the observed cross-sectional saving profile in combination with expected changes in population age structure in order to forecast saving. Such an approach, which is discussed in Section 4.2, can be justified by the assumption of an open economy in which factor prices are set at world levels and are unaffected by domestic capital accumulation and population growth.

4.2. Aging and saving in partial equilibrium

Partial equilibrium analyses forecasting the effect of demographics on the saving rate have generally started with household data on saving rates and income levels by age. Saving is forecast by assuming that the age–wage and age–saving profiles will remain constant while the number of people in each age group varies. The forecast changes in saving from such exercises have been surprisingly small. Wachtel (1984), using saving rates from the 1962–1963 Surveys of Consumer Finances, projects a change in the saving rate between 1985 and 2020 of between −0.5 and 0.2 percentage points, depending on the source of saving data used. Auerbach and Kotlikoff (1990) forecast the effect of demographic change on the saving rate, having first allocated government consumption by age group. Depending on the base year they use, they forecast an increase in the US saving rate between the 1980s and the 2020s of between 2.3 and 2.8 percentage points. Bosworth et al. (1991) argue that demographic changes have not had significant effects on saving rates in the past. They decompose saving changes between 1963 and 1985 into changes in within-age-group saving and income on the one hand and changes in the fractions of the population made up of different age groups on the other. They find that changes in the latter factor had only trivial effects on the saving rate over the period they examine. They also report similar results for Canada and Japan.

A second set of studies has tried to forecast the effect of demographic change on saving using age–saving profiles derived by regressing national saving rates on the fractions of countries' populations in different age groups. The estimated saving coefficients for the elderly from such regressions are negative and large compared to those derived from household level data, and forecasts of the response of saving to changes in demographics are accordingly much more dramatic. Heller (1989), projecting the effect of demographic change on the US private saving rate over the period 1980–2025 reports estimated declines in saving ranging from 3.8 to 10.5 percentage points. Masson and Tryon (1990) report similar results. Weil (1994) suggests that the divergence between the micro- and macro-based forecasts of the effect of demographics on saving may be due wealth transfers between households. When the elderly transfer wealth to their children (through inter vivos transfers, intentional bequests, or accidental bequests), they reduce their children's need to save. Thus the presence of a larger elderly cohort may reduce national saving by reducing the saving rate of the young generation. This approach is discussed further in Section 6.1.

4.3. Aging and saving in general equilibrium

Auerbach and Kotlikoff (1987) present a somewhat realistic, but computationally very complex, simulation model with which one can examine the general equilibrium effects of demographic change. Individuals live for 75 periods, the first 20 as dependent children whose consumption is determined by their parents. The intertemporal utility function for individuals is defined over consumption, leisure, and the utility of dependent children. Labor supply is endogenous, determined by the wage and interest rates and by a lifetime productivity profile that declines in old age, leading to retirement and life-cycle saving. The wage rate and the interest rate are determined by the

Table 9
Behavior of endogenous variables during a baby bust transition

Year	Saving rate	Wage rate	Interest rate
0	7.6	1.00	9.9
1	6.1	1.00	9.9
5	6.6	1.00	10.0
10	7.4	1.00	10.0
20	7.9	1.02	7.4
50	3.0	1.10	7.3
70	0.0	1.11	7.1
110	−1.5	1.11	7.1
∞	0.0	1.11	7.1

Source: Auerbach and Kotlikoff (1987).

supplies of labor and capital, which is in turn composed of life-cycle savings. In each period, individuals make optimizing decisions given the entire future paths of the endogenous variables. The model is solved iteratively to find rational expectations paths of all of the dependent variables. There is no uncertainty.

Auerbach and Kotlikoff consider the effects of a fertility transition in which the birth rate moves from a level consistent with 3% annual population growth to a level consistent with zero population growth. The change in fertility is taken to be unexpected, but as soon as it has taken place the time paths for all variables are recalculated. After the initial shock there is again no uncertainty, and all variables follow the rational expectations paths.

Table 9 shows the paths of the key endogenous variables in the initial steady state (year zero), along the transition path, and in the final steady state. Comparing the initial and final steady states, the wage rate rises and the interest rate falls, reflecting the increase in the capital–labor ratio as the number of high capital retirees rises relative to the number of workers. The saving rate falls to zero in the new steady state, since there is no population growth (see Section 4.1). Interestingly, the time paths of the endogenous variables are not monotonic along the transition path. The saving rate falls in the initial years of the transition not because of an increase in the number of old people, but because working-age people expect a rising wage profile, and thus save less in order to smooth consumption. Twenty years after the reduction in fertility occurs, the saving rate is higher than in the initial steady state, but following this point it falls, as the ratio of retirees to workers rises.

4.4. Limitations of the life-cycle model

Although it provides a good benchmark from which to begin analysis of demographic change, there are a number of problems with the life-cycle model – both with its ability to fit the data and with the assumptions it uses.

One of the most salient empirical problems with the life-cycle model is the "failure" of the old to dissave to the extent predicted in the model. Explanations for this phenomenon are discussed in Chapter 16 of this *Handbook*. The low rates of dissaving by elderly households explain why partial equilibrium predictions of how changes in demographics will affect saving (that is, taking the observed age–saving profile as constant) lead to smaller predicted reductions in saving than do simulations such as those by Auerbach and Kotlikoff (1987) which impose life-cycle preferences on agents.

Comparing the life-cycle model's predictions about wealth holding to what is observed in the economy, two problems arise. First, simulating the model for reasonable sets of parameters, life-cycle saving does not produce a ratio of wealth to income as high as that observed in the economy (White, 1978). Second, observed saving does not accord well with the predictions of the life-cycle model: Carroll and Summers (1991) find that lifetime consumption patterns of individuals closely match lifetime income profiles, rather than being smoother than income, as the model predicts. A number of authors (Carroll and Summers, 1991; Deaton, 1991) have argued that observed saving of most households is far lower than would be implied by a life-cycle motive. Deaton proposes a buffer stock model of saving, in which households smooth consumption over a very short time horizon. Complicating this analysis, the economic environment in which most households in developed countries find themselves, most importantly the existence of Social Security and employer-mandated private pension schemes, means that it may not be optimal for these households to be doing any saving anyway. Whether these households would react to a change in their environment such as a reduction in future Social Security benefits due to changing demographics by raising saving, as predicted by the life-cycle model, or by keeping saving constant, as predicted by the buffer stock model, is hard to know.

The extreme skewness of the wealth distribution greatly complicates the analysis of how an aging population will affect capital accumulation. We know little about the saving motives of wealthy households – although we do know that their fertility experience has paralleled that of the population as a whole[30] – and so it is hard to know how their saving will be affected by demographic change.

Another line of criticism of the life-cycle model has been that the time horizon over which it assumes optimization – individuals' own lifetimes – is too short. This is a view associated with Barro's (1974) model of Ricardian equivalence, in which changes in the timing of tax collections that hold the present value of taxes constant do not affect consumption. If decision-makers are altruistic toward the members of generations that follow, then the impact of shocks that affect birth cohorts differentially will be smoothed away. In the extreme case, family dynasties can be treated as

---

[30] Russell (1982).

single individuals solving an infinite horizon optimization problem. This approach to the determination of optimal saving in the face of demographic change is explored by Cutler et al. (1990) and Auerbach et al. (1991). Proponents of intergenerational altruism point to the large size of bequest flows as evidence of the presence of a bequest motive. Section 6.1 of this chapter discusses how demographic change will affect the role of bequests in capital formation.

5. Social security and other government programs

5.1. Dependency ratios for government programs

Table 10 shows relative government social expenditures (including transfers) by age among the G-7 countries. Per capita expenditures on the elderly range between 3.5 and 5.7 times as high as expenditures on working-age adults. The US has the highest relative expenditures on the elderly because, unlike the other members of the group, it publicly funds health care only for the old. Expenditures on children range between

Table 10
The effect of demographic change on social expenditures[a]

| | Per capita social expenditures in 1980 relative to 15–64 age group | | Impact of projected demographic change on | | | |
| | | | Social expenditure (1980 = 100) | | Financing burden per head of 15–64 age group (1980 = 100) | |
	0–14	65+	2010	2040	2010	2040
Canada	1.4	3.7	141	187	109	145
France	1.9	5.1	116	128	104	132
West Germany	1.7	5.3	104	97	113	154
Italy	0.9	3.5	108	107	106	139
Japan	2.3	5.3	141	140	137	154
United Kingdom	1.9	4.0	101	110	96	111
United States	1.5	5.7	125	165	99	131

[a]The first two columns show 1980 government social expenditures per capita on the 0–14 and 65+ age groups relative to those on the 15–64 age group. Social expenditures are spending on health, education, unemployment compensation, family benefits, and old age, survivor, and disability pensions. The next two columns show the effect of projected demographic change on total social expenditure, holding social expenditure per capita constant within age groups. The final two columns show the effect of projected demographic change on total social expenditure divided by the population aged 15–64.
Source: OECD (1988).

0.9 and 2.3 times as high as expenditures on working-age adults. Comparing these expenditure weights to the overall consumption needs weights presented in Section 2 (0.72 for children and 1.27 for the elderly) it is clear why an increase in old-age dependency that is approximately equal to the decrease in youth dependency seems so much more problematic when one takes the perspective of the government than when one takes the perspective of society as a whole.

The second two columns of Table 10 show the effect of projected demographic change on total social expenditures, holding per capita social expenditures constant at their 1980 levels. The table shows, for example, that holding spending per member of each age group constant, total social expenditures would have to rise by 41% between 1980 and 2010 in rapidly-aging Japan. The final two columns of the table show the change in the financing burden of social expenditures per member of the 15–64 age group – that is, the size of total social expenditures divided by the size of the part of the population that pays for them. The increase in the projected financing burden can be read in either of two ways: if the real level of benefits remains constant, then the table gives the increase in social expenditures that each worker would have to fund. Under this interpretation, the effect of demographic change is not particularly threatening: in Japan, for example, total social expenditures per worker over the period 1980–2010 would only rise by 1.1% per year, well below the expected rate of income growth. An alternative interpretation of the table, however, is more alarming: if the level of social expenditures per capita grows at the same rate as output per working-age adult, then the last two columns of the table show the increase in the fraction of output that will have to be devoted to social expenditures. In Japan, the financing burden rises by 37% between 1980 and 2010. In the US, the financing burden per worker is unchanged between 1980 and 2010, but then rises by 32% between 2010 and 2040, as the Baby Boom generation retires.

5.2. Interaction of age structure, social security, and life-cycle saving

To the extent that individuals anticipate the amount of government transfers that they will receive, government policies can be expected to affect individual saving behavior. This perspective is applicable to any program of spending on the elderly. But because they are so large, and because they transfer resources in the form of cash rather than services, special attention has been focused on public pensions (in the US, Social Security).

The age structure of the population interacts with the Social Security system in several ways. Most importantly, the ratio of elderly to young people in the economy determines the tradeoff between the level of Social Security taxes paid by the young and the size of the benefits received by the old. In addition, the age structure of the population affects the way in which Social Security interacts with the saving rate. Increases in pay-as-you-go Social Security will reduce national saving by reducing the private saving of the young. The ratio of the elderly to the young determines the nature of this tradeoff.

These two effects are demonstrated in a simple overlapping generations model: Individuals live for two periods, working and paying Social Security taxes in the first period of their lives, receiving Social Security benefits in the second period. The level of pre-tax wages in the first period, W, and the real interest rate, r, are assumed to be constant. Let τ be the fraction of their income that the young pay in Social Security taxes and let the young generation be $(1 + n)$ times as large as the old generation. The Social Security replacement rate (the fraction of after-tax income that is returned in the form of benefits) is

$$R = \frac{(1+n)\tau}{1-\tau}. \tag{20}$$

Let utility from consumption be Cobb–Douglas:

$$U = C_y^\pi C_o^{1-\pi}. \tag{21}$$

The lifetime budget constraint is

$$C_y + \frac{C_o}{1+r} = W(1-\tau) + \frac{(1+n)\tau W}{1+r}. \tag{22}$$

Maximizing Eq. (21) subject to Eq. (22) gives optimal consumption in each period. Young people will consume a constant fraction π of their full lifetime income, that is, their after-tax income when young plus the discounted value of their future Social Security benefits:

$$C_y = \pi W\left(1 + \frac{n-r}{1+r}\tau\right). \tag{23}$$

Assuming that $r > n$ (see Abel et al., 1989), an increase in τ will lower first-period consumption and lifetime utility. The reason is that the rate of return that a person receives on money "invested" in the Social Security system, n, is less than the rate received if the person invested the money elsewhere.

The fraction of the (pre-tax) wages of the young that is saved is

$$s_y = (1-\tau) - \pi\left(1 + \frac{n-r}{1+r}\tau\right). \tag{24}$$

Fig. 7 graphs both the saving rate of the young generation and the Social Security replacement rate as functions of the Social Security tax rate (τ) and the population

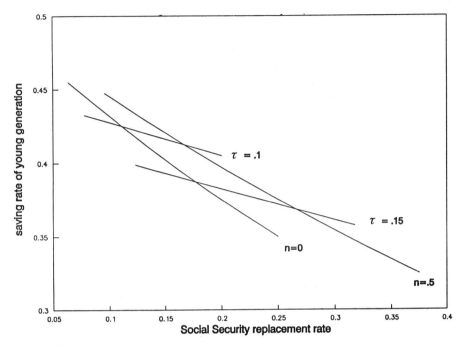

Fig. 7. Effects of tax and population growth rates on saving and Social Security replacement rates.

growth rate (n).[31] Holding the tax rate constant, a decrease in the population growth rate (which is consistent with population aging) reduces the replacement rate but raises the saving rate. The reason for this effect is that when population growth falls, the rate of return to Social Security contributions must also fall. Since this does not affect the rate of rate of return on marginal saving, there is a pure income effect, which lowers the consumption of the young. More generally, reducing n worsens the tradeoff between the saving rate of the young and the replacement rate: either the replacement rate or the saving rate (or both) must fall. The choice of the Social Security tax rate, τ, determines which of these will occur.

5.3. The response of social security to demographic change

In the face of population aging due to a fertility reduction, the response of the Social Security system can have large effects on shifting welfare between different birth co-

---

[31] The values of the other parameters used in creating the figure are $\pi = 0.5$ and $r = 1$.

horts.[32] Among the options facing Social Security planners are keeping the level of benefits to retirees constant (and allowing the tax rate on workers to adjust), keeping the tax rate on workers constant (and allowing the benefit levels to adjust), and building up a trust fund in order to smooth the paths of both benefits and taxes.[33]

Policy with regard to fertility transitions (as well as to the more complicated actual pattern of declining fertility interrupted by a Baby Boom) has implications for both the level of saving in the economy and for the differential impact on different birth cohorts. Current policy in the US calls for the accumulation of a trust fund which will peak at 30% of GNP in 2030 (Hambor, 1987). Such a policy, if carried out (and if not offset by similarly large deficits in the rest of the federal budget) would lead to the Baby Boom cohort funding part of its own Social Security benefits. Compared to the policy of keeping benefits constant and funding the system on a pay-as-you-go basis (with tax rates adjusting in response to changes in the dependency ratio), the trust fund policy raises the burden on the Baby Boom generation and lowers the burden on its children.

Boskin and Puffert (1988) look at the rate of return of the "investment" that workers make in Social Security, and how this return varies across birth cohorts in response to different Social Security financing policies. The analysis is partial equilibrium, holding constant the real interest rate, the path of real wages, and the labor force participation rate.[34] The first column of Table 11 shows the projected average real rates of return to members of different birth cohorts who survive to retirement age under the post-1983 Social Security rules. Early birth cohorts received extremely high rates of return, due mostly to the massive expansion of the Social Security system in the post-war period (and only slightly to demographic factors). Cohorts born after World War II will get a much lower return.[35]

The large trust fund that the Social Security system is projected to build up is widely viewed as a dangerously tempting target for politicians. The rest of Table 11 considers two scenarios in which the trust fund projected to be accumulated under the current law does not materialize. The second column, labelled "PAYG tax rates", con-

---

[32] For theoretical discussions of the welfare effects of Social Security in the face of shifting demographics and of optimal policy responses, see Blanchet and Kessler (1991), Boadway et al. (1991), and Peters (1991).

[33] Aaron et al. (1989).

[34] Since fluctuations in Social Security taxes and benefits produced by demographic changes will have large effects on saving rates and labor force participation, and these will in turn affect interest rates and wages, partial equilibrium analysis may be inappropriate. Auerbach and Kotlikoff (1987) use their general equilibrium model to simulate the welfare effects of different Social Security funding policies in the face of a demographic transition. Their results turn out to be qualitatively similar to those of Boskin and Puffert. See also Auerbach et al. (1989) and Jensen and Nielsen (1992).

[35] The rate of return to Social Security contributions is not, of course, a full measure of the financial effect of the program, since the size of contributions changes over time. Later cohorts, which earn low rates of return on their contributions, also make larger contributions as a fraction of wages.

Table 11
Rates of return to Social Security under alternative scenarios

Birth cohort	Base case	PAYG tax rates	PAYG benefits
Before 1912	11.61	11.61	11.62
1913–1922	5.74	5.74	5.94
1923–1932	3.72	3.73	4.16
1933–1942	2.75	2.84	3.18
1943–1952	1.96	2.17	1.96
1953–1962	2.31	2.56	1.89
1963–1972	2.18	2.37	1.56
1973–1982	2.22	2.26	1.54
1983–1992	2.28	2.09	1.54

Source: Boskin and Puffert (1988).

siders a scenario in which for each year after 1990, tax rates are set at exactly the level which covers that year's benefits. In this scenario, the tax rate falls below its currently legislated level until 2025 (it reaches its minimum rate in 2008). The third column, labelled "PAYG benefits", considers the scenario of holding Social Security *taxes* constant at their 1990 rates, and allowing benefits to adjust on a PAYG basis. In comparison to the base case, both of these scenarios favor the Baby Boom cohorts at the expense of those that follow them. Under PAYG benefits, the winners are those cohorts that have finished receiving their benefits by 2025 (that is, cohorts born 1923–1942). Under PAYG taxes, the winners are a younger group: those who retire before 2025. In this case the losers are those not shown in the table: the small cohorts born after 1992 who will have to bear higher tax rates. Hagemann and Nicoletti (1989) offer a similar analysis of the options for financing public pensions in the face of demographic transition for four OECD countries. Keyfitz (1988) also performs similar calculations, and explores the effects of deviations of fertility from its currently-projected path.

5.4. Political economy of social security benefits and of increased aged population

In a simple forward-looking model, as long as the interest rate is greater than the growth rate of output, Social Security reduces lifetime consumption. This can be seen in the model of Section 5.2, and in particular the lifetime budget constraint, Eq. (22). Why, then, do such programs exist? One explanation is that individuals are not sufficiently forward-looking to save for their own retirement, and so the government has to do it for them. But whatever the initial impetus for the creation of public pension systems, their structure and size is determined in a democratic system in which both contributors and beneficiaries have a voice.

Preston (1984) points out that there are three constituencies in favor of government aid to the elderly: the elderly themselves; working-age adults with elderly relatives, whose burden of family support would be lessened by government transfers to the elderly; and working-age adults who anticipate becoming elderly, and thus stand to benefit from government largesse to the elderly. In the case of support for the other demographic group to receive government support – children – there is only one constituency: working-age adults with children. The effect of population aging due to a reduction in fertility is to expand the first two constituencies supporting transfers to the elderly, while reductions in mortality expand the size of all three constituencies.

Auerbach and Kotlikoff (1992) argue that the political effects of a larger elderly population have already been seen: they attribute the increases in the size of Social Security benefits over the course of the 1970s to the increased share of the elderly in the population. They point out that the fraction of the voting-age population that is over 55 will rise from 28% in 1991 to 36% in 2010 and 42% in 2040. Thus, even as the burden of transfers to the elderly borne by the working-age population becomes more onerous, the likelihood that a majority of the electorate would favor reducing Social Security benefits will fall.

6. Within-family intergenerational relations and aging

Chapters 4 and 5 of this *Handbook* lay out the flows of resources between members of families in different generations, both within and between households.[36] The family is one of the two major institutions (the other being the government) that transfers resources to dependent members of society. Since population aging will affect the relative numbers of people on the different sides of these flows – the average number of children per parent, the average number of siblings per adult, the average number of living parents per adult – it should be expected to change the size of the flows. In the face of population aging generated by reduced fertility, for example, it is possible for the average size of intergenerational transfers given by parents to all of their children to be constant, or for the average size of intergenerational transfers received by each child to remain constant. But it is not possible for both these magnitudes to be constant. Where the change will come, in turn, depends on the model underlying the transfers. And changes in the size of transfers will in turn affect both the need for government intervention and the saving of individuals.

Intergenerational resource flows can take the form of direct transfers of money, the provisions of services, and shared living arrangements. Often, it may be hard to isolate a single direction of resource flow: Crimmins and Ingegneri (1990) find that in the

---

[36] See also Lee and Lapkoff (1988).

case of an elderly person co-residing with one of his or her children (the likelihood of which is a positive function of the number of children that the elderly person has), there are benefits which flow in both directions.

Intra-family transfers need not be altruistically motivated. Kotlikoff and Spivak (1981) model such relationships as annuity contracts undertaken by non-altruistic life-cycle agents. Resource flows between parents and children may be payments for services little different than what is observed in markets (Bernheim et al., 1985). Finally, flows such as bequests may be accidental.

6.1. Parent to child transfers

As discussed in Section 4.4, intergenerational transfers from parents to children – and in particular bequests – have played a central role in attempts to understand saving and capital accumulation. Whether or not bequests represent transfers by altruistic parents who get utility from their children's consumption is a central question in evaluating the Ricardian equivalence proposition of Barro (1974). The problems of the life-cycle model in explaining the size of the capital–output ratio have directed further attention to bequests. Kotlikoff and Summers (1981) find that only a small fraction of existing wealth can be attributed to the accumulated difference between the income and consumption of people currently alive – most of the capital stock is not life-cycle wealth, but accumulated bequest wealth.[37]

The effect of changes in the ratio of children to parents on the size of intergenerational transfers, and in particular on bequests, depends on the motivation which generates these bequests. This motivation has, in turn, been widely debated among macroeconomists. In the extreme case where bequests are completely accidental, reductions in fertility will dramatically raise the size of bequests per child by reducing the number of siblings among whom they are shared.[38] In many models of bequests, the increase in the total parental resources available per child will be divided up between larger bequests per child and larger non-bequest consumption by parents. This will be the case, for example, if parents get marginal utility from giving bequests that decreases in the size of bequests per child (Blinder, 1974).

Increases in the size of bequests received by children will in turn affect their saving and the economy's level of capital. The anticipation of future bequests may lower the saving of the young (Weil, 1994). Blinder suggests that bequests have a negative effect on the labor supply of the young.

In addition to potentially changing the size of bequests, population aging will change their timing. Since changes in mortality have not been accompanied by a delay

---

[37] See also Modigliani (1988), Kotlikoff (1988b), and Gale and Scholz (1994).

[38] Smith and Orcutt (1980).

in the average age at which children are born,[39] children will be receiving bequests ever later in life. Wolf (1988) in a simulation discussed further below, finds that a reduction in mortality leading to a 5% increase in life expectancy is accompanied by an increase from 32% to 44% in the fraction of the population aged 55–59 that has a living mother. Galor and Stark (1993) suggest that delaying the point in life at which a bequest is received will increase the propensity of children to invest in human capital.

6.2. Child to parent transfers

The effect of changes in the age structure of the population on child-to-parent transfers has generally been analyzed in terms of the prospective burden of government support for the elderly. Particularly in the case of support for the elderly, government transfers and private transfers may be substitutes. Although the role of family in providing support (and in particular income) for the elderly has greatly diminished, children still play a large role in support. Disabled elderly women aged 75–84, for example, receive 38% of their days of care from children, and only 15% from formal caregivers. (US Senate, 1991). In countries without well-developed social security systems, private transfers between households bulk much larger than in the US (Cox and Jimenez, 1990).

Cutler and Sheiner (1994) find that the number of children has a significant negative effect on the probability of being in a nursing home, controlling for health, age, marital status, and economic status. They find that having one fewer child raises the probability of being in a nursing home by more than having one additional limitation in an Activity of Daily Living.[40]

Wolf (1988) uses a micro-analytic simulation to explore the effects of population aging on individual family structures. He simulates family trees, which can then be sampled to show changes in the cross-sectional pattern of kinship. Wolf uses his simulation to examine stable populations. The base population is that of the Netherlands in 1970. He then simulates two variants: one with the total fertility rate reduced from 2.65 to 1.6 (the actual drop in fertility in the Netherlands between 1970 and 1980), and one with age-specific mortality rates reduced by 25% (in turn increasing life expectancy at birth by 5%).

Wolf shows that reducing either mortality or fertility raises the fraction of the elderly who do not have living children, although the fertility change has a much larger effect. Reduced mortality raises the fraction of the aged without working-age offspring from 4% to 5%, while reduced fertility raises the fraction to 17%. The fraction

---

[39] Glick (1977) reports that comparing 1905 to 1975, married women's median age at the birth of first children fell by 0.3 years, and the median age at the birth of last children fell by 3.3 years.

[40] These are indicators of the ability to undertake commonly-impaired functions, such as dressing, bathing, or eating.

of 75–79 year olds without living daughters rises from 27% to 42% when fertility is reduced.

At the same time that the availability of family members to supply support falls for the elderly, there will be an increase in the burden of old-age dependency as viewed from the perspective of working age adults. Reduced mortality will raise the fraction of working-age adults with living parents. Reduced fertility will raise the burden of caring for the elderly faced by working age adults by sharply reducing the average number of siblings with whom the burden can be shared. From both the elderly and the working age, then, there will be pressure to increase care for the elderly by the government.

7. Conclusion

One of the salient themes of this chapter is that the "costs" of population aging currently in prospect are to a large extent simply the passing of the transitory benefits of reduced fertility. Resources no longer needed in caring for dependent children and supplying new workers with capital are being transferred toward caring for dependent elderly. The costs of these two dependency burdens are roughly equal. But in the period in which the population age structure changed in response to the fertility decline, there was a window of roughly fifty years in which the overall burden of dependency on society was lower than it had been or would be again. Over the period 2010–2030, during which the negative effect of aging on consumption in the US will be growing most rapidly, the effect of aging will be to reduce needs-adjusted consumption by a total of approximately 10.5%, or 0.5% per year (see Table 7). Similarly, over the period 1970–1990, when the burden of caring for the young and supplying capital to new workers was falling, the effect of aging was to raise needs-adjusted consumption by 0.45% per year. It is precisely the fact that this window will be closing, and that the burden of caring for dependents will be rising in the near future, that has led to population aging being viewed as such a costly phenomenon. If one takes a longer view, and acknowledges the benefits that have been reaped from aging, the situation looks less alarming, or at least less unjust.

A natural yardstick against which to assess the effects of population aging on the standard of living is the process of long-term economic growth. Output per capita in the US grew at an average rate of 2.0% per year over the period 1948–1991. By this standard, the effects of aging on aggregate consumption – half a percent per year over the worst two decades – will be large, but not overwhelming. A second comparison is to the post-1973 productivity slowdown. The growth rate of output per capita in the US fell from 2.2% per year over the period 1948–1972 to 1.7% per year over the period 1973–1991. This is roughly the same magnitude as the projected effect of aging on consumption in the 2010–2030 period. But while the duration of aging's effects are limited, the duration of the productivity slowdown is unknown.

A second theme of this chapter is that although aging will not appreciably change the overall burden of transfers that society makes to dependents, it will greatly change the channels through which these transfers flow. Families, which make the largest fraction of transfers to children, will see the direct burden of such transfers eased. A larger fraction of transfers to dependents will end up flowing through the government – although, of course, the source of these transfers is still originally incomes of families.

Population aging has a larger effect on individual transfer schemes considered in isolation than on the net flow of transfers taken together. As shown in Section 3.2, the effect of a change in population growth on the quantity of a resource flow depends on the difference between the average age of the flow's recipients and the average age of its providers. In the case of the total resource flow to dependents, the average age at which resources are received and at which they are provided are not very different. This is a consequence of the dependent groups being found on both sides of the age continuum, while the group that provides net transfers is in the middle. But the same analysis can be applied to individual components of the resource flow – that which goes through the government and that which goes through the family. In this case, the average ages at which transfers are provided and received are quite different. In Western, industrialized countries, the burden of caring for children has remained in the family, while the burden of caring for the aged has been substantially shifted to the government. The average age of receiving benefits from one's family is substantially lower than the average age of providing benefits to other family members. Thus reductions in fertility ease the burden of direct transfers on families. In the case of government transfer schemes to dependents, which focus particularly on the elderly, the average age of providing is younger than the average age of receiving – and thus population aging enlarges the burden of such transfer schemes.

References

Aaron, H., B. Bosworth and G. Burtless (1989), Can America afford to grow old? Paying for social security (Brookings Institution, Washington, DC).

Abel, A., N.G. Mankiw, L. Summers and R. Zeckhauser (1989), "Assessing dynamic efficiency: theory and evidence", Review of Economic Studies 56: 1–20.

Ahlburg, D. and J. Vaupel (1990), "Alternative projections of the US population", Demography 27: 639–652.

Auerbach, A. and L. Kotlikoff (1987), Dynamic fiscal policy (Cambridge University Press, Cambridge).

Auerbach, A. and L. Kotlikoff (1990), "Demographics, fiscal policy, and US saving in the 1980's and beyond", in: L. Summers, ed., Tax policy and the economy 4 (MIT Press, Cambridge, MA).

Auerbach, A. and L. Kotlikoff (1992), "The impact of the demographic transition on capital formation", Scandinavian Journal of Economics 94: 281–295.

Auerbach, A., J. Cai and L. Kotlikoff (1991), "US demographics and saving: predictions of three saving models", Carnegie-Rochester Conference Series on Public Policy 34: 135–156.

Auerbach, A., L. Kotlikoff, R. Hagemann and G. Nicoletti (1989), "The economic dynamics of an ageing population: the case of four OECD countries", OECD Economic Studies 12: 97–130.

Barro, R. (1974), "Are government bonds net wealth?", Journal of Political Economy 82: 1095–1117.

Bernheim, B., A. Shleifer and L. Summers (1985), "The strategic bequest motive", Journal of Political Economy 93: 1045–1076.

Birdsall, N. (1988), "Economic approaches to population growth", in: H. Chenery and T.N. Srinivasan, eds., The handbook of development economics (North-Holland, Amsterdam).

Blanchet, D. and D. Kessler (1991), "Optimal pension funding with demographic instability and endogenous returns on investment", Journal of Population Economics 4: 137–154.

Blau, F. (1992), "The fertility of immigrant women" in: G. Borjas and R. Freeman, eds., Immigration and the work force (University of Chicago Press, Chicago, Chicago, IL).

Blinder, A. (1974), Toward an economic theory of income distribution (MIT Press, Cambridge, MA).

Boadway, R., M. Marchand and P. Pestieau (1991), "Pay-as-you-go social security in a changing environment", Journal of Population Economics 4: 257–280.

Bogue, D. (1985), The population of the United States: historical trends and future projections (The Free Press, New York).

Borjas, G., R. Freeman and K. Lang (1991), "Undocumented Mexican-born workers in the United States: how many, how permanent?", in: J. Abowd and R. Freeman, eds., Immigration, trade, and the labor market (University of Chicago Press, Chicago, IL).

Bos, D. and R. Weizsacker (1989), "Economic consequences of an aging population", European Economic Review 33: 345–354.

Boskin, M. and D. Puffert (1988), "The financial impact of social security by cohort under alternative financing assumptions", in: R. Ricardo-Campbell and E. Lazear, eds., Issues in contemporary retirement (Hoover Institution Press, Stanford, CA).

Bosworth, B., G. Burtless and J. Sablehaus (1991), "The decline in saving: evidence from household surveys", Brookings Papers on Economic Activity, 183–241.

Cantrell, R. and R. Clark (1982), "Individual mobility, population growth and labor force participation", Demography 19: 147–159.

Carroll, C. and L. Summers (1991), "Consumption growth parallels income growth: some new evidence", in: B. Bernheim and J. Shoven, eds., National saving and economic performance (University of Chicago Press, Chicago, IL).

Chayanov, A.V. (1966), The theory of peasant economy (D. Thorner et al., translators) (Richard Irwin, Homewood, IL) (originally 1925).

Coale, A. and M. Zelnik (1963), New estimates of fertility and population in the United States (Princeton University Press, Princeton, NJ).

Cox, D. and E. Jimenez (1990), "Achieving social objectives through private transfers: a review", World Bank Research Observer 5: 205–218.

Crimmins, E. and D. Ingegneri (1990), "Interaction and living arrangements of older parents and their children: past trends, present determinants, future implications", Research on Aging 12: 3–35.

Crimmins, E., Y. Saito and D. Ingegneri (1989), "Changes in life expectancy and disability-free life expectancy in the United States", Population and Development Review 15: 235–267.

Cutler, D. and L. Sheiner (1994), "Policy options for long-term care", in: D. Wise, ed., Studies in the economics of aging (University of Chicago Press, Chicago, IL).

Cutler, D., J. Poterba, L. Sheiner and L. Summers (1990), "An aging society: opportunity or challenge?", Brookings Papers on Economic Activity 1: 1–56.

Deaton, A. (1991), "Saving and liquidity constraints" Econometrica 59: 1221–1248.

Ermisch, J. (1988), "Demographic patterns and the housing market", in: R. Lee, W. Arthur and G. Rodgers, eds., Economics of changing age distributions in developed countries (Clarendon Press, Oxford).

Ermisch, J. (1989a), "Demographic change and intergenerational transfers in industrialized countries", in: P. Johnson, C. Conrad and D. Thomson, eds., Workers versus pensioners: intergenerational justice in an ageing world (Manchester University Press, Manchester).

Ermisch, J. (1989b), "Intergenerational transfers in industrialized countries: effects of age distribution and economic institutions", Journal of Population Economics 1: 269–284.

Faber, J. (1982), Life tables for the United States: 1900–2050, Actuarial study no. 87 (US Department of Health and Human Services, Social Security Administration, Washington, DC).

Felderer, B. (1994), "Can immigration policy help to stabilize social security systems?", in: H. Griesch, ed., Economic aspects of international migration (Springer-Verlag, Berlin).

Flaim, P. (1990), "Population changes, the baby boom, and the unemployment rate", Monthly Labor Review 113: 3–10.

Freeman, R. (1979), "The effect of demographic factors on age–earnings profiles", Journal of Human Resources 14: 289–318.

Friedlander, D. and R. Klinov-Malul (1980), "Aging of populations, dependency and economic burden in developed countries", Canadian Studies in Population 7: 49–55.

Fries, J. (1980), "Aging, natural death, and the compression of morbidity", New England Journal of Medicine 303: 130–135.

Fuchs, V. (1984), "'Though much is taken': reflections on aging, health, and medical care", Milbank Memorial Fund Quarterly 62: 143–166.

Gale, W. and J. Scholz (1994), "Intergenerational transfers and the accumulation of wealth", Journal of Economic Perspectives 8: 145–160.

Galor, O. and O. Stark (1993), "Life expectancy, human capital, and economic development", Mimeo. Working paper 93-17 (Brown University, Providence, RI).

Glick, P. (1977), "Updating the life cycle of the family", Journal of Marriage and the Family 39: 5–13.

Goldin, C. (1990), Understanding the gender gap: an economic history of American Women (Oxford University Press, Oxford).

Habib, J. (1990), "Population aging and the economy", in: R. Binstock and L. George, eds., Handbook of aging and the social sciences (Academic Press, New York).

Hagemann, R. and G. Nicoletti (1989), "Population ageing: economic effects and some policy implications for financing public pensions", OECD Economic Studies 12: 51–96.

Hambor, J. (1987), "Economic policy, intergenerational equity, and the social security trust fund buildup", Social Security Bulletin 50: 13–18.

Heller, P. (1989), "Aging, saving, and pensions in the group of seven countries: 1980–2025", Journal of Public Policy 9: 127–153.

Jensen, S. and S. Nielsen (1992), "Population aging, public pensions, and the macroeconomy", Mimeo. (Institute of Economics, Copenhagen Business School, Copenhagen).

Keyfitz, N. (1973), "Individual mobility in a stationary population" Population Studies 27: 335–352.

Keyfitz, N. (1985), Applied mathematical demography (Springer Verlag, Berlin).

Keyfitz, N. (1988), "Some demographic properties of transfer schemes: how to achieve equity between the generations", in: R. Lee, W. Arthur and G. Rodgers, eds., Economics of changing age distributions in developed countries (Oxford University Press, Oxford).

Kotlikoff, L. (1981), "Some economic implications of life-span extension", in: J. March and J. McGaugh, eds., Aging: biology and behavior (Academic Press, New York).

Kotlikoff, L. (1988a), "The relationship of productivity to age", in: R. Ricardo-Campbell and E. Lazear, eds., Issues in contemporary retirement (Hoover Institution Press, Stanford, CA).

Kotlikoff, L. (1988b), "Intergenerational transfers and savings", Journal of Economic Perspectives 2: 41–58.

Kotlikoff, L. and A. Spivak (1981), "The family as an incomplete annuities market", Journal of Political Economy 89: 372–391.

Kotlikoff, L. and L. Summers (1981), "The role of intergenerational transfers in aggregate capital accumulation", Journal of Political Economy 89: 706–732.

Lam, D. (1989), "Population growth, age structure, and age-specific productivity: does a uniform age distribution minimize lifetime wages?", Journal of Population Economics 2: 189–210.

Lazear, E. (1979), "Why is there mandatory retirement?", Journal of Political Economy 87: 1261–284.

Lazear, E. (1990), "Adjusting to an aging labor force", in: D. Wise, ed., Issues in the economics of aging (University of Chicago Press, Chicago, IL).

Lee, R. (1980), "Age structure, intergenerational transfers and economic growth: an overview", Revue Economique 31: 1129–1156.

Lee, R. (1991), "Population aging and its social and economic consequences", Mimeo. (University of California at Berkeley, Berkeley, CA) October.

Lee, R. (1994a), "Fertility, mortality and intergenerational transfers: comparisons across steady states" in: J. Ermisch and N. Ogawa, eds., The family, the market, and the state in ageing societies (Oxford University Press, Oxford).

Lee, R. (1994b), "Population age structure, intergenerational transfers, and wealth: a new approach with applications to the US", Journal of Human Resources, Fall.

Lee, R. (1994c), "The formal demography of population aging, transfers, and the economic life cycle" in: L. Martin and S. Preston, eds., Demography of aging (National Academy Press, Washington, DC).

Lee, R. and S. Lapkoff (1988), "Intergenerational flows of time and goods: consequences of slowing population growth", Journal of Political Economy 96: 618–651.

Lumsdaine, R. and D. Wise (1994), "Aging and labor force participation: a review of trends and explanations", in: Y. Noguchi and D. Wise, eds., Aging in the United States and Japan: economic trends (University of Chicago Press, Chicago, IL).

Mankiw, N.G. and D. Weil (1989), "The baby boom, the baby bust, and the housing market", Regional Science and Urban Economics 19: 235–258.

Masson, P. and R. Tryon (1990), "Macroeconomic effects of projected population aging in industrial countries", IMF Staff Papers 37: 453–485.

Modigliani, F. (1988), "The role of intergenerational transfers and life cycle savings in the accumulation of wealth", Journal of Economic Perspectives 2: 15–40.

Murphy, K., M. Plant and F. Welch (1988), "Cohort size and earnings in the United States", in: R. Lee, W. Arthur and G. Rodgers, eds., Economics of changing age distributions in developed countries (Clarendon Press, Oxford).

OECD (1988), Ageing populations: the social policy implications (OECD, Paris).

Peters, W. (1991), "Public pensions in transition: an optimal path", Journal of Population Economics 4: 155–175.

Poterba, J. and L. Summers (1987), "Public policy implications of declining old-age mortality", in: G. Burtless, ed., Work, health, and income among the elderly (The Brookings Institution, Washington, DC).

Preston, S. (1984), "Children and the elderly: divergent paths for America's dependents", Demography 21: 435–457.

Russell, L. (1982), The baby boom generation and the economy (The Brookings Institution, Washington, DC).

Schneider, E. and J. Gurlanik (1987), "The compression of morbidity: a dream which may come true, someday!", Gerontologica Perspecta 1: 8–14.

Schulz, J., A. Borowski and W. Crown (1991), Economics of population aging: the "graying" of Australia, Japan, and the United States (Auburn House, New York).

Skinner, J. (1985), "The effect of increased longevity on capital accumulation", American Economic Review 75: 1143–1150.

Smith, J. and G. Orcutt (1980), "The intergenerational transmission of wealth: does family size matter?", in: J. Smith, ed., Modelling the distribution and intergenerational transmission of wealth (University of Chicago Press, Chicago, IL).

United Nations Department of International Economic and Social Affairs (1985), The world aging situation: strategies and policies (United Nations, New York).

United Nations (1991), World population prospects 1990, Population studies no. 120 (Department of International Economic and Social Affairs, New York).

US Bureau of the Census (1991), Statistical abstract of the United States: 1991 (US Bureau of the Census, Washington, DC).

US Immigration and Naturalization Service (1994), Statistical yearbook of the immigration and naturalization service 1993 (Government Printing Office, Washington, DC).

US Senate Special Committee on Aging (1991), Aging America: trends and projections (Government Printing Office, Washington, DC).

Wachtel, P. (1984), "Household saving and demographic change, 1950–2050", in: J. Ehrenberg, ed., Research in population economics, Vol. 5 (JAI Press, Greenwich, CT).

Wade, A. (1989), Social security area projections 1989, Actuarial study no. 105 (US Department of Health and Human Services, Social Security Administration, Washington, DC).

Warren, R. and J. Passel (1987), "A count of the uncountable: estimates of undocumented aliens in the 1980 census", Demography 24: 375–393.

Weil, D. (1994), "The saving of the elderly in micro and macro data", Quarterly Journal of Economics 109: 55–81.

Welch, F. (1979), "Effect of cohort size on earnings: the baby boom babies' financial bust", Journal of Political Economy 87: 565–598.

White, B. (1978), "Empirical tests of the life cycle hypothesis", American Economic Review 68: 547–560.

Willis, R. (1982), "The direction of intergenerational transfers and demographic transition: the Caldwell hypothesis reexamined", Population and Development Review 8 (supplement): 207–234.

Wolf, D. (1988), "Kinship and family support in aging societies", in: Social and economic consequences of population aging (U.N. Department of International Economic and Social Affairs, New York).

World Bank (1992), World development report (Oxford University Press, Oxford).

Chapter 18

DEMOGRAPHIC VARIABLES AND INCOME INEQUALITY

DAVID LAM

University of Michigan

Contents

1. Introduction   1016
2. Age structure and income inequality   1017
    2.1. Decomposing the effects of age structure   1017
    2.2. Evidence on the effects of age structure on inequality   1022
    2.3. Direct effects of age structure on wages and inequality   1023
3. Marital sorting and inequality among married couples   1024
    3.1. Empirical evidence from the US   1027
    3.2. Empirical evidence from other countries   1029
    3.3. The role of assortative mating   1030
4. Household composition and income distribution   1031
5. Differential fertility, intergenerational mobility, and inequality   1035
    5.1. The mathematics of population growth and inequality   1036
    5.2. Differential fertility and intergenerational mobility   1038
    5.3. Welfare implications of endogenous fertility   1043
6. Effects of population growth on wages and inequality   1044
    6.1. Relative wages, factor shares, and income distribution   1044
    6.2. Empirical evidence on the effects of population growth on inequality   1046
7. Demographic change and trends in inequality in the US   1050
8. Summary and conclusions   1052
References   1054

Handbook of Population and Family Economics. Edited by M.R. Rosenzweig and O. Stark
© Elsevier Science B.V., 1997

1. Introduction

Demographic variables are frequently cited as important determinants of the distribution of income. The range of issues included in such discussions is broad and often imprecise. They range from issues that might be considered directly related to economic welfare, such as the tendency for increases in population size to lower wages and raise returns to land and capital, to issues that might be considered mostly empirical nuisances, such as the potential confusion in comparing income distributions of populations with different age structures.

Increased attention has been given to the effect of demographic variables on inequality as researchers have documented a substantial increase in recent decades in income inequality among both families and full-time males in the US and other high-income countries. Potential demographic explanations include effects of changing age structure, increases in female labor force participation, changing family structure, and changes in marital sorting.

Distributional issues have often been raised in the debate over the economic consequences of rapid population growth. A World Bank report in the 1970s concluded, "whereas some people regard the effect of reduced fertility on per capita income growth as ambiguous, there appears to be no explicit dissent from the view that lower fertility contributes to greater income equality" (World Bank, 1974: p. 35). The World Bank's 1984 report on population and development took a similar position, identifying undesirable consequences of population growth on both the inter-household distribution of income and on the intra-household distribution of economic well-being by age and sex.[1]

This paper surveys a variety of areas in which demographic variables may play an important role in the distribution of income.[2] The first issue considered is the relationship between age structure and inequality, analyzed in Section 2. In addition to its direct importance, the case of age structure is instructive because it demonstrates the need to carefully model the effects of compositional changes when working with measures of dispersion. While compositional effects on measures of dispersion are considerably more complex than compositional effects on means, they often lend themselves to useful analytical decompositions.

Many researchers argue that households, rather than individuals, should be used as the basis for analysis of the distribution of income. Using the household as the unit of analysis introduces a host of demographic issues relating to marriage, fertility, and household living arrangements. Section 3 focuses on the large literature that has analyzed the effects on the distribution of income among married couples of marital

---

[1] For a history of thought on the subject and further discussion see the previous surveys of the distributional effects of population growth by Sirageldin (1975), Boulier (1977), Potter (1979), Visaria (1979), Kuznets (1980), Rodgers (1978, 1983), and Lam (1986).

[2] See Lam (1986), Birdsall (1988), and Pestieau (1989) for previous reviews of related issues.

sorting and the joint labor supply behavior of husbands and wives. Section 4 extends the analysis beyond married couples to the household, analyzing issues related to the choice of recipient unit and the treatment of family size.

Another important topic with broad applications is the issue of changing population composition due to differential fertility, migration, and mortality by income classes. Section 5 analyzes the effects of differential fertility across income classes on the distribution of income. The analysis includes consideration of the role of intergenerational mobility across income classes.

Section 6 discusses the attention given to the effects of population growth on relative wages by the classical economists and considers theoretical issues in the link between changes in factor supplies and changes in the distribution of income. Empirical evidence on the link between population growth, wages, and inequality in historical and modern populations is briefly surveyed.

Section 7 discusses the substantial changes in wage inequality observed in the US in recent decades, and considers evidence on the role of demographic variables, especially age structure, in those changes. Most research suggests that changes in labor supply associated with the baby boom played a substantial role in some of the changes in relative wages observed in the 1970s and 1980s. The empirical evidence also demonstrates, however, that demographic variables are considerably less important than changes in the structure of labor demand. Section 8 concludes the paper.

2. Age structure and income inequality

One of the most important demographic variables differentiating populations across time and space is the age composition of the population. The percentage of the population under the age of 15, for example, ranged from 15% in Germany to over 50% in Kenya in recent estimates (World Bank, 1991).

To the extent that changes in age structure affect economic variables such as saving rates and the age profile of wages, it is natural to suspect that there will be effects on the observed distribution of income. Even if the direct economic effects of age structure are small, age structure may affect standard measures of income inequality for purely compositional reasons. We may want to consider, for example, whether a population in which workers are concentrated in young ages tends to have higher income inequality than a population in which workers are concentrated in older ages, as a result of purely compositional effects of age structure.

2.1. Decomposing the effects of age structure

As will be seen throughout this survey, analysis of income inequality frequently lends itself to decompositions of some overall measure of dispersion into contributions

coming from different sources of income or different groups in the population. Age groups are one natural variable to use for such decompositions. This section uses one standard measure of inequality that is easily decomposable, the variance of log income, combined with a stable population model, to demonstrate a number of theoretical points about the pure compositional effects on cross-sectional inequality of changes in age structure caused by changes in the population growth rate.

Treat age as a continuous variable, and represent the mean of log income at age a by $y(a)$, the variance of log income at age a by $v(a)$, and the proportion of the population aged a by $c(a)$. The total variance of log income, $V_T(y)$ has a simple additive decomposition into "between-group" and "within-group" components as

$$V_T(y) = \int_0^\omega c(a)[y(a) - \bar{y}]^2 \, da + \int_0^\omega c(a)v(a) \, da, \tag{1}$$

where ω is the oldest age in the population. We can think of $V_B(y) = \int_0^\omega c(a)[y(a) - \bar{y}]^2 \, da$ as the "between-group" component, and $V_W(y) = \int_0^\omega (a)v(a) \, da$ as the "within-group" component.

It is straightforward to imbed this decomposition into a stable population model and exploit the analytics developed in the mathematical demography literature. This will make it possible to consider how income inequality will be affected by changes in age structure associated with changes in the population growth rate. Consider a stable population with a continuous age distribution and a constant population growth rate. If age-specific fertility and mortality rates remain constant over time, then by well-known ergodicity properties the population will converge to a stable population with a constant proportional age distribution.[3] The number of births and the size of each age group will grow at some constant exponential growth rate g. Expressed in continuous time, the proportion of the population aged a, can be shown to be

$$c(a) = \frac{e^{-ga} p(a)}{\int_0^\omega e^{-ga} p(a) \, da}, \tag{2}$$

where $p(a)$ is the probability of survival to age a. Substituting into Eq. (1), the variance of log income in the population can be decomposed into "between-group" and "within-group" components as

$$V_T(y) = V_B(y) + V_W(y) = \frac{\int_0^\omega e^{-ga} p(a)[y(a) - \bar{y}]^2 \, da}{\int_0^\omega e^{-ga} p(a) \, da} + \frac{\int_0^\omega e^{-ga} p(a)v(a) \, da}{\int_0^\omega e^{-ga} p(a) \, da}. \tag{3}$$

---

[3] See Arthur (1981) for a proof of standard results. See Coale (1972) and Keyfitz (1977) for general treatments of stable population theory.

The comparative steady-state effect of a change in age structure can be seen by taking the derivative of $V_T(y)$ with respect to the population growth rate g. A change in g holding the $p(a)$ schedule constant implies an increase in fertility with mortality held constant, a change that will make the population younger by increasing the proportion of the population in all ages below the mean age. The result can be summarized as

$$\frac{d \ln V_t(y)}{dg} = \alpha(\bar{a} - \bar{a}_b) + (1 - \alpha)(\bar{a} - \bar{a}_w), \tag{4}$$

where $\alpha = V_B/V_T$ is the proportion of total variance that is attributable to between-group variance in Eq. (3), $\bar{a}$ is the mean age of the population, $\bar{a}_b$ is a weighted mean age of the population where each age is weighted by its contribution to between-group variance, and $\bar{a}_w$ is a weighted mean age of the population where each age is weighted by its contribution to within-group variance.[4] The result states that income inequality will increase when the population growth rate increases if the mean age of the population is greater than a weighted average of the "mean ages" of intra-cohort and inter-cohort variance. The intuition is straightforward. If both intra-cohort variance (due to high age-specific variance) and inter-cohort variance (due to age-specific mean incomes far from the population mean) are relatively concentrated in young ages, higher population growth will tend to increase inequality.

The weighted mean ages that determine the sign of the derivative of the variance of log income with respect to the population growth rate can in principle be estimated given an actual or hypothetical age structure and age profiles of income and income variance. Lam (1984) presents results based on profiles for the US and Brazil, with the estimated mean ages giving conflicting evidence regarding the age structure effects of population growth on inequality. When 15–19-year-olds are included in the US age profiles, the results indicate a disequalizing effect of a younger age structure. The Brazilian profiles, however, indicate an effect that is much smaller in magnitude and opposite in sign. A similar small but equalizing effect of a younger age structure is estimated for the US when the 15–19-year-old age group is omitted. These results do not take account of the potential effects of population growth on the age profiles of income and income inequality themselves, but assume constant age profiles and hence abstract to what might be thought of as the pure compositional effects. The direct effects of age structure on age-specific earnings and earnings inequality will be discussed in more detail below.

The between-group and within-group components of the effects of age structure on inequality are clarified by Figs. 1 and 2, which show mean earnings and the variance

---

[4] See Lam (1984) for details.

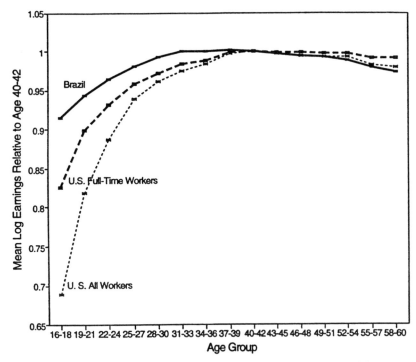

Fig. 1. Relative mean log earnings by age for males, Brazil and US, 1985.

in log earnings for male workers in Brazil and the US in 1985.[5] In both countries mean incomes have the characteristic life-cycle profile, although the overall variation in means is lower in Brazil, and the age–earnings profile peaks somewhat earlier in Brazil. The US age profile for the variance of the log of income, shown in Fig. 2, is an inverted U pattern that has also come to be viewed as a typical age profile of age-specific inequality, often linked to Mincer's (1974) hypothesis of an "overtaking point". At young ages some individuals trade off current earnings for schooling and training, creating relatively high intra-cohort inequality. As these better trained individuals reach the "overtaking" age at which their faster rising age income profiles cross the profiles of individuals with less training, there will be relatively low inequality. Beyond the overtaking age the income profiles for those with larger investments in human capital will rise above the profiles for less well trained individuals, causing a return to the high inequality of the youngest ages.

Age profiles such as that shown for the US, where the youngest age groups have low means and high variances, will tend to give the result that a younger age structure

---

[5] US data are based on the March 1985 Current Population Survey. Brazilian data are based on the 1985 PNAD, an annual household survey similar to the CPS. See Lam and Levison (1992) for details.

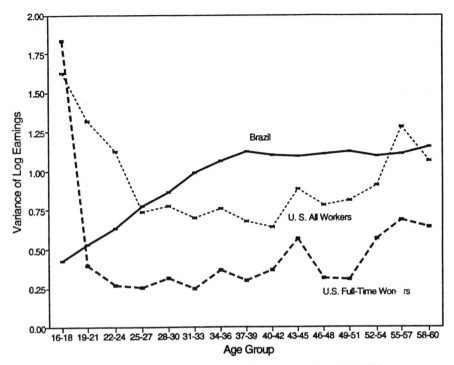

Fig. 2. Variance of log earnings by age for males, Brazil and US, 1985.

increases cross-sectional inequality, since both intra-cohort and inter-cohort inequality will tend to increase when the proportion of young people increases. The data for age-specific inequality in Brazil exhibit a different pattern, however. As seen in Fig. 2, the age profile for intra-cohort inequality has a shape similar to the age profile for mean earnings, with both having lower values at younger ages. This Brazilian profile implies that inter-cohort variance will tend to increase with a younger age structure, since the young have relatively low mean incomes. Intra-cohort variance, on the other hand, will tend to decrease with a younger age structure due to the low variance in the young ages. Profiles like Brazil's, then, produce offsetting effects. Using the analytical result in Eq. (4) above, the weighted mean ages of within-group and between-group inequality in Brazil imply that overall inequality is almost neutral with respect to age structure in Brazil.

Lam and Levison (1992) decompose the age profiles of log variance in Brazil and the US based on a standard human capital earnings equation, and analyze the consistency of both countries' profiles with Mincer's model. The cross-sectional age profile of inequality in Brazil is shown to differ so dramatically from the US pattern not because of differences in life-cycle investments in human capital, but because of strong cohort effects associated with increases in the mean and variance of schooling in

Brazil in recent decades (Lam and Levison, 1991). The interaction of these cohort patterns in the variance of schooling with the substantially higher returns to schooling in Brazil generate the shape of the age-specific inequality profile seen in Fig. 2.

2.2. Evidence on the effects of age structure on inequality

The pure compositional effects of age structure on cross-section measures of inequality have been noted by numerous researchers, and a wide variety of approaches have been taken to dealing with them. One approach that attracted a great deal of attention was that of Paglin (1975), who argued that trends in wage inequality in the US were distorted by the failure of researchers to control for the changing age composition of the population. Paglin argued that life-cycle income variation should not be included in measures of income inequality, and proposed an age-standardized Gini coefficient designed to remove the effects of life-cycle variation in income. Paglin's proposed age-standardized Gini coefficient launched a lively debate, and has been influential in subsequent research.[6] Criticisms of Paglin's measure included normative arguments about the extent to which variation in income across age groups should be considered in evaluating the degree of inequality in a population, and methodological arguments over Paglin's decomposition. The methodological debate was intensified by Paglin's choice of the Gini coefficient as the basis for his analysis. Unlike the log variance used in the analysis above, the Gini coefficient is not an additively decomposable measure of inequality (see Shorrocks, 1980; Mookherjee and Shorrocks, 1982), making it a dubious choice for the kind of decomposition Paglin proposed. The Gini coefficient cannot be cleanly separated into within-group and between-group components, inevitably producing "overlap" or interaction terms that complicate the accounting. The issue of whether age-adjusted inequality increased or decreased over the time analyzed by Paglin depends critically on how Paglin's overlap term is treated.[7] Morley (1981) applied a variant of Paglin's approach to identify the contribution of changes in age structure to the increase in inequality in Brazil between 1960 and 1970. Morley concluded that the compositional effect of a younger age structure was to increase inequality in Brazil, although the magnitude of the pure age structure effects between 1960 and 1970 was quite small.

Confusion over the compositional effect of age structure on inequality is easy to find in the empirical literature on population growth and inequality. Winegarden

[6] Five comments on Paglin's paper were published in the June 1977 *American Economic Review*, including Danziger et al. (1977), Johnson (1977), and Nelson (1977), along with a reply by Paglin.

[7] Formby et al. (1989) show, not surprisingly, that Paglin's decomposition is highly sensitive to the width of age intervals used to control for age variation. Since, according to Paglin, inequality *within* age groups is the component of inequality that has real welfare significance, the level of inequality can be substantially affected by the choice of, for example, five-year versus ten-year age groups.

(1978, 1980) asserts that the disequalizing effects of a younger age structure are one reason more rapid population growth may lead to higher inequality. Others, such as Repetto (1979) and Lindert (1978) have hypothesized that the effect goes in the opposite direction, with older age structures being associated with greater income inequality. Repetto, for example, argues that "lower fertility and mortality rates, by elongating the age pyramid and increasing the variation in age among earners, would tend to increase the current inequality in the distribution of earned income" (1979: p. 21). None of these studies provides either empirical evidence or theoretical analysis as a basis for their speculation about the effects of age structure on inequality. The confusion in this literature results from the fact that the "between group" component of the effects of a younger age structure on inequality will often move in the opposite direction of the "within group" component. Because the young have relatively low mean incomes, an increase in their share in the population will often increase the "between group" component of total inequality. On the other hand, if age-specific inequality in earnings tends to increase with age, then an increase in the proportion of young workers will have an equalizing effect by reducing the "within group" component of total inequality. As shown in the formal analysis above, the combined effect may go in either direction, and may differ across populations.

2.3. Direct effects of age structure on wages and inequality

The effects of changes in age structure on earnings inequality clearly go beyond the pure compositional effects discussed in the previous section, effects which can in general be dealt with in empirical research by various types of age standardization and decomposition. The formal analysis above assumes that the age profiles of income and income inequality do not themselves change as a result of changing age structure, a dubious assumption in the face of theoretical and empirical research on the effects of age structure fluctuations on wages. Empirical research on the effects of cohort size on wages has documented the sensitivity of age-specific wages to the relative sizes of age groups.[8] Although empirical research in this area has focused on the effects of short-term fluctuations in cohort size, the results can be interpreted as evidence that age-specific wages will be influenced by age structure in long-term demographic steady states as well. Even if all other features of two economies are similar, for example, workers in a rapidly growing population with a young age distribution can be expected to face a significantly different wage profile than workers in a population with a low growth rate and a relatively uniform age distribution. Lam (1989) analyzes the

---

[8] See, for example, Easterlin (1978), Welch (1979), Freeman (1979), Stapleton and Young (1984), Berger (1985, 1989), Murphy et al. (1988). It is beyond the scope of this paper to survey the extensive literature on the effects of cohort size and wages. Recent work analyzing the role of cohort-size effects in recent trends in inequality in the US will be surveyed below.

effects of changes in age structure on life-cycle wage profiles in stable populations, and demonstrates the surprising result that under constant-returns-to-scale technologies a uniform age distribution produces the *minimum* sum of lifetime wages of all possible age distributions.

In addition to the potentially depressing effect of cohort size on mean earnings, Dooley and Gottschalk (1984) hypothesized that age-specific inequality may increase when cohort size increases. They find supporting evidence in trends in age-specific inequality in the US in the 1970s. If, as the US evidence suggests, a younger age structure causes a decline in mean wages and an increase in wage inequality for younger workers, then there may be a greater tendency for population growth to increase wage inequality in the cross-section. As will be discussed in greater detail below, many researchers have tried to identify the extent to which the fluctuations in age structure caused by the baby boom have contributed to the substantial increase in wage inequality in the US in recent decades. Although most research suggests that shifts in the structure of labor demand are the dominant factor in the increase in wage dispersion in the US, labor supply effects associated with age structure fluctuations also emerge as playing a substantial role during the 1970s and 1980s.

3. Marital sorting and inequality among married couples

Many researchers argue that analysis of income inequality should be done at the level of families or households rather than individuals. Using households as the unit of analysis introduces a host of demographic issues relating to marriage, fertility, and household living arrangements. This section focuses on the large literature concerned with marital sorting, female labor supply, and income inequality among married couples. Most of this literature uses the term "family income" to refer to the aggregation of husband's and wife's income. The term "family income" has been used so pervasively in this literature that it will be used here as well, even though "household income" might be more appropriate. Even when the analysis moves beyond married couples to include other household members, the focus has generally been on the aggregation of income across members of the same residential household, rather than across different households linked by family relationships. While there are a host of interesting questions that could be raised about the distribution of income across non-co-resident family members, these issues are beyond the scope of this paper.[9] Section 4 will consider issues relating to the choice of recipient unit and the treatment of household size in analysis of the distribution of income across households.

An important link between demographic behavior and the distribution of income works through marriage markets and the correlation in income-related characteristics

---

[9] See Chapter 5 by Laitner in this volume for a discussion of one dimension of these issues, the intergenerational linkages between family members.

of husbands and wives. One of the many research issues associated with the rapid increases in women's labor force participation rates in both high-income and low-income countries in recent decades has been the effects of these increases on the distribution of family income. The issue is directly related to the nature of marital sorting with respect to wages (whether direct or indirect) and the cross-price relationship between one spouse's wage and the other spouse's labor supply. In his early work on labor market activity of married women, Mincer (1962) noted the empirical regularity of a negative relationship between husband's income and wife's labor supply. Mincer argued that this negative relationship will tend to have an equalizing effect on family income because the labor market earnings of married women will raise family income for families with low husband's income more than for families with high husband's income. Mincer (1974) found empirical support in 1960 census data, observing that inequality in family income (i.e., the sum of husband's income and wife's income) tended to be lower than inequality in husbands' income. He argued that "growth of the female labor force, while increasing the earnings inequality among all persons, has actually been a factor in the mild reduction of income inequality among families" (1974: p. 125).

A large literature has continued to analyze this issue in recent decades, a period characterized by rapid increases in female labor force participation and substantial changes in the distribution of both individual and family incomes.[10] Decompositions of family income inequality into components attributable to different family members have been a staple of this literature. Mincer (1974) provided one of the first examples, noting the simple decomposition of the variance of joint marital income as

$$\sigma_T^2 = \sigma_H^2 + \sigma_W^2 + 2\sigma_{HW},\tag{5}$$

where σ_T^2 is the variance of total family income, σ_H^2 is the variance of income earned by husbands, σ_W^2 is the variance of income earned by wives, and σ_{HW} is the covariance of husbands' and wives' income. Eq. (5) demonstrates the fundamental point that inequality in total family income depends on the inequality in each of the components and on the correlation between husbands' and wives' earnings.

It is instructive to convert Eq. (5) into the squared coefficient of variation, a standard measure of inequality that is independent of the mean:[11]

$$C_T^2 = C_H^2 \alpha_H^2 + C_W^2 \alpha_W^2 + 2\rho C_W C_H \alpha_H \alpha_W,\tag{6}$$

---

[10] See Michael (1985) and Cancian et al. (1992) for surveys of this literature.

[11] See Smith (1979), Lehrer and Nerlove (1981), Gronau (1982), and Schirm (1988) for similar decompositions and extensions.

where $C_i = \sigma_i/\mu_i$, μ_i is the mean income for source i, ρ is the correlation of husband's and wife's income, and $\alpha_i = \mu_i/\mu_T$. Not surprisingly, we see from Eq. (6) that a necessary condition for total family income to be less equal than husbands' income ($C_T > C_H$) is that wives' income is less equal than husbands' income ($C_W > C_H$). If this condition holds, then inequality in total family income will be an increasing function of the marital sorting correlation ρ. A common misconception, however, is that whenever $C_W > C_H$ and $\rho > 0$, then wives' income will tend to be disequalizing in the sense that $C_T > C_H$. To see that this is not the case, begin with the simple special case in which wives' incomes and husbands' incomes have identical distributions, i.e., $\mu_H = \mu_W$ and $C_H = C_W$. In this case

$$C_H^2 - C_T^2 = 0.5 C_H^2 (1 - \rho). \tag{7}$$

According to Eq. (7), inequality in total family income will always be lower than inequality in husband's income except when $\rho = 1$, in which case the two will be equal. Analysis of Eq. (6) also demonstrates that wives could have higher income inequality than husbands and ρ could be positive (both of which are typically true empirically) and it will still be the case that family income is more equally distributed than husband's income.

Many find this result counterintuitive, expecting that any degree of positive assortative mating on earnings would tend to cause the addition of wives' income to increase inequality whenever wives' inequality is greater than husbands' inequality. The logic of the result is straightforward, however, and applies to any measure of inequality. Barros (1990) provides an insightful general analysis using Lorenz curves. A simple example is to take two identical income distributions, which by definition have identical Lorenz curves, and generate a new distribution by combining a draw from the first with a draw from the second. If we combine the two with perfect rank-order sorting, i.e. match the ith ranked income in the first distribution with the ith ranked income in the second distribution, then the new distribution will have an identical Lorenz curve to the original and will therefore have identical inequality by any standard mean-adjusted inequality measure. Combining with perfect rank-order sorting is equivalent to simply doubling the incomes in the first distribution, an exercise that will not change the Lorenz curve or any mean-adjusted measure of inequality. If we do anything other than perfect rank-order sorting in combining the distributions, however, then the new Lorenz curve will lie above the original Lorenz curve, implying that the new distribution is more equal. The reason is that the pooling with anything less than perfect rank-order matching tends to equalize the distribution, an effect that is magnified as the correlation between the two draws decreases. This pooling effect exerts a powerful tendency for combined family income to be more equal than the income of either husbands or wives taken separately.

3.1. Empirical evidence from the US

A common empirical exercise in this literature is to compare income inequality for husbands with income inequality for families or couples. If an inequality index is higher for husbands' income than for couples' income then wives' income contribution to the family is interpreted as being equalizing. This exercise is potentially misleading, since it does not take account of the simultaneous determination of husbands' and wives' earnings in the family. It is nonetheless a simple empirical exercise that has been done for a variety of populations in different time periods and provides a useful reduced-form summary measure of the role of assortative mating and female labor supply in family income inequality. A number of researchers, including Smith (1979), Lehrer and Nerlove (1981, 1984), and Schirm (1988), have also attempted to estimate potential wages for husbands and wives, making it possible to hold labor supply constant across couples in estimating hypothetical distributions of family income.

Analyzing 1960 and 1970 US Census data, Smith (1979) found a pattern in data for family income inequality among whites that was similar to Mincer's earlier result – inequality in family income was lower than inequality in husbands' income for white families. An opposite result was found among blacks, however, with family income inequality being higher than husbands' income inequality. Smith's decompositions indicated that the different result for blacks resulted from the combination of a higher positive correlation between spouses' wage rates for blacks and a less negative relationship between husband's income and wife's labor supply for blacks.

Danziger (1980) found a similar discrepancy in the results for whites and non-whites in data from the US Current Population Survey. For whites the Gini coefficient for total family income was lower than the Gini coefficient for family income minus wives' earnings in both 1967 and 1974. The addition of wives' earnings lowered the Gini coefficient by 5–6%. For nonwhites, however, the Gini for total family income was about 1% higher than the Gini for total family income minus wives' earnings in both years.

Lehrer and Nerlove (1981, 1984) also found that wives' earnings were more equalizing for whites than for blacks. Accounting for variations over the life cycle Lehrer and Nerlove found that in the period between marriage and child-bearing the effect of wives' earnings was to increase family income inequality among black families.

More recent evidence indicates that the effect of wives' earnings is no longer disequalizing for blacks. Betson and van der Gaag (1984) analyzed CPS data from 1968 to 1980 and found that black wives had an increasingly equalizing effect on family income inequality over the period. Cancian et al. (1992) found that wives' earnings continue to have an equalizing effect for white families and now have an equalizing effect for nonwhite families as well. They conclude that the equalizing contribution of wives' earnings has increased for both groups over time.

Table 1 presents components of family income inequality for all families in the US

Table 1
Components of family income, US 1973–1987[a]

Year	μ_T	μ_H	μ_W	μ_W/μ_T	C_T	C_H	C_W	ρ	% change
1973	30049	25538	4510	0.150	0.608	0.672	1.538	−0.034	−10.41
1974	29402	24738	4664	0.159	0.610	0.676	1.495	−0.028	−10.81
1975	29159	24329	4829	0.166	0.629	0.701	1.484	−0.026	−11.55
1976	29945	24833	5112	0.171	0.619	0.687	1.469	−0.018	−11.10
1977	30421	25175	5246	0.172	0.609	0.675	1.434	−0.008	−10.81
1978	30428	24909	5520	0.181	0.595	0.659	1.391	−0.006	−10.91
1979	30061	24364	5696	0.189	0.584	0.646	1.345	0.006	−10.70
1980	29222	23379	5843	0.200	0.584	0.649	1.315	0.008	−11.16
1981	30086	23929	6157	0.205	0.628	0.710	1.306	0.014	−13.07
1982	30517	23985	6532	0.214	0.668	0.752	1.330	0.049	−12.48
1983	30841	23931	6910	0.224	0.672	0.749	1.314	0.080	−11.42
1984	32431	25132	7299	0.225	0.685	0.769	1.320	0.074	−12.21
1985	33734	25971	7763	0.230	0.675	0.753	1.301	0.087	−11.53
1986	34452	26217	8235	0.239	0.670	0.754	1.257	0.084	−12.57
1987	36145	27270	8875	0.246	0.664	0.743	1.235	0.102	−11.91

[a]Estimated from US Current Population Survey.

from 1973 to 1987 based on data from the Current Population Survey.[12] Fig. 3 shows the trends from 1973 to 1987 in income inequality among families, husbands, and wives, as measured by the coefficient of variation. Inequality among wives is significantly higher than income among husbands in all periods, although wives' inequality has declined as female participation rates have increased.[13] The typical result that family income inequality is lower than husbands' income inequality continues to be the case in these data.

One common empirical answer to the question of whether increases in female participation rates have tended to be equalizing or disequalizing for family income inequality is provided in the final column of Table 1, which shows the percentage difference between inequality in total family income and inequality in husbands' earnings. The negative numbers show that wives' earnings have had an equalizing effect on family income throughout the period. This effect has tended to increase over time, implying that the effect of wives' income has become more equalizing over time. This is somewhat surprising, since the table suggests two reasons why wives' contribution would have become less equalizing. First, as shown in the table, the correlation in husbands' and wives' income has increased substantially over this period, actually switching signs from negative to positive. Second, wives' income has become an in-

[12] Summary data for these estimates based on CPS tabulations were generously provided by Maria Cancian, who also provided useful discussions on the literature surveyed in this section.
[13] The calculations include wives with zero income, a major determinant of inequality among wives.

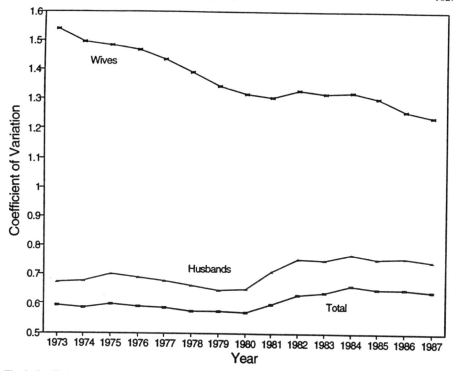

Fig. 3. Coefficient of variation of family income, husbands' income, and wives' income, US 1973–1987.

creasingly large component of total family income over this period, rising from 15% in 1973 to 25% in 1987. According to the decomposition in Eq. (6), this increase in and of itself should be disequalizing since inequality in wives' income is much higher than inequality in husbands' income. These two trends have obviously been offset by some other trend that has made wives' contribution more equalizing. That trend, easily seen in Fig. 3, is the substantial decline in the coefficient of variation in wives' incomes. In all of these trends the increasing labor force participation of women, and the resulting decrease in the proportion of women with zero income, play a critical role.

3.2. Empirical evidence from other countries

Similar exercises to those discussed above have been conducted for a number of other countries. Analyzing data for the United Kingdom, Layard and Zabalza (1979) estimated a coefficient of variation in family income similar to the coefficient of variation for husbands. For Israel, Gronau (1982) found an equalizing effect of wives' earnings similar to the effect for whites in the US. Schirm (1988) also found an equalizing effect of wives' earnings using data from Quebec. Blackburn and Bloom (1991) compare the US, Canada, and Australia and the changes in each country during the 1980s. Wives' income is equalizing in both the US and Canada, but is roughly neutral in Australia. Blackburn and Bloom also attempt to explain the increases over time in family income inequality in the three countries. In all three countries increases in inequality of husbands' earnings play the major role in explaining the increase in family income inequality. They find that an increase in the correlation of husbands' and wives' earnings is also an important factor in increased inequality, especially in the US and Canada.

In one of the few studies available from a developing country Barros and De Mendonça (1992) find that inequality in family income is very similar to inequality in husbands' income in Brazil. This relative neutrality of wives' income occurs in spite of the fact that wives' contribution to family income is not insignificant, averaging about 15% in 1985, and the fact that there is much higher inequality among women than men. Although there is a positive correlation in spouses' income, the correlation of 0.4 is low enough to produce a net effect of wives' income that is close to neutral.

3.3. The role of assortative mating

Becker's (1991) analysis of assortative mating in marriage markets and specialization in the family provides an important theoretical background for analyzing the relationship between marriage and family income inequality. One of the few explicit predictions Becker made about marital sorting was a prediction of negative assortative mating with respect to wages. This prediction followed logically from his assumption that the gains to marriage derived from comparative advantage and economic specialization within the family. As demonstrated by Lam (1988b) and Stapleton (1987), the prediction does not necessarily hold when gains to marriage result from joint consumption of household public goods. In that case it is possible for the gains from joint consumption to generate positive assortative mating on wages. Becker's prediction of negative assortative mating on wages has received little empirical support, although it is important to note that empirical tests are inevitably contaminated by the endogeneity of human capital investments and labor supply. Behrman et al. (1994), exploiting information on exogenous ability differences provided by comparing monozygotic and dizygotic twins, do find evidence of negative sorting of husbands and wives with respect to potential labor market earnings.

The model of assortative mating with household public goods presented in Lam (1988b) demonstrates that the magnitude and even the direction of assortative mating may differ across populations and over time. The degree of assortative mating depends on the magnitude of cross-wage effects on labor supply, the income elasticity of demand for household public goods (including, for example, children), and the total quantity of household public goods demanded. To the extent that any of these variables have changed in recent decades, they may have induced changes in the degree of assortative mating on wages. Recent trends in family income inequality are in fact suggestive that there has been an increase in the tendency toward positive assortative mating, an increase that may be economically important in its effects on the distribution of family income.

4. Household composition and income distribution

The previous section analyzed the distribution of income among married couples, focusing on issues of marital sorting and the labor supply of husbands and wives. Having moved beyond the individual in analyzing the distribution of income, it is difficult to stop with the married couple as the appropriate unit of aggregation. It is natural to consider questions about the distribution of income at the household level. This inevitably raises issues about the treatment of income earners other than the husband and wife and issues about appropriate adjustments for the number of adult and child consumers in the household. At this point it is more appropriate to refer to households rather than families, recognizing that researchers and data collectors have typically emphasized co-residency rather than kinship as the defining characteristic.

It is often argued that the household is more appropriate than the individual for analysis of income inequality because of the household's role as a primary consumption and resource allocation unit. The argument is influenced by the economics of household production and the internal resource allocation functions that households provide. The case for using the household as the unit of analysis would appear to be based on an interest in the distribution of consumption rather than the distribution of income per se. If households substantially redistribute resources across members, the distribution of individual income may provide an imperfect picture of the distribution of individual welfare. A measure of household income may be preferred, but this raises the issue of how to account for the composition of the household. If income is pooled within the household and all goods are private goods, then per capita household income may be a good measure of individual welfare. On the other hand, if there are large joint consumption economies within the household, individual welfare may be better indicated by the total income of the household in which an individual resides. The extent of internal redistribution within the household and the extent of joint consumption economies are fundamentally empirical questions, with good empirical evidence necessary to inform decisions about the theoretically appropriate unit of analysis. A review of the empirical evidence on joint consumption economies and the intra-household distribution of economic resources is beyond the scope of this paper, although both are clearly relevant to the issue of how household composition and family size affect the distribution of income. Without attempting to answer the question of what is the "right" unit of analysis for analyzing the distribution of income, this section reviews some of the issues related to the sensitivity of inequality measures to the treatment of household composition.

One straightforward question that often arises in the literature on income inequality among households is whether total household income or per capita household income is distributed more equally. Some analytical insights into this question are provided by a simple decomposition similar to that used by Schultz (1982). Writing the logarithm of per capita household income as $\ln y = \ln Y - \ln N$, where Y is total household income, N is household size, and $y = Y/N$, a decomposition of the variance of the log of y implies that

$$V(\ln y) - V(\ln Y) = V(\ln N)[1 - 2\varepsilon_{yn}], \tag{8}$$

where V denotes variance and ε_{yn} is the elasticity of household income with respect to household size implied by a regression of $\ln Y$ on $\ln N$.[14] Comparing inequality in per capita household income with inequality in total household income, we see from Eq. (8) that $V(\ln y) > V(\ln Y)$ if $\varepsilon_{yn} < 0.5$. If the elasticity of total household income with respect to household size is greater than 0.5, then per capita household income will be more equal than total household income, at least according to the log variance measure. Although from a behavioral standpoint it is probably more appropriate to think of household size as a function of income rather than the other way around, the result in Eq. (8) suggests that we may want to follow the lead of Kuznets (1976, 1978, 1981) in simply looking at the empirical relationship between household income and household size in order to the understand the relationship between these alternative measures of income inequality.

In a series of papers, Kuznets (1976, 1978, 1981) explored the relationship between household income and household size, and considered the implications for the distribution of household income. One of the consistent cross-national empirical regularities demonstrated by Kuznets is a tendency for household size to vary directly with total household income but inversely with per capita household income (i.e., total household income divided by the number of persons in the household). This relationship often causes the income rankings of particular households to change dramatically when the unit of analysis is changed from total household income to per capita household income and causes inequality comparisons across populations and over time to be highly sensitive to the choice of recipient unit.

It is interesting to consider whether Kuznets' stylized fact, namely that total household income tends to increase with household size, while per capita household income tends to *decrease* with household size, allows us to predict whether total household income will be more or less equal than per capita household income. Such a prediction has been suggested, without deriving formal analytical results, by Visaria (1979) and others. Eq. (8) provides a simple demonstration that the empirical regularity observed by Kuznets does not in and of itself determine whether total household income or per capita household income will be more unequal. Total household income will rise with

---

[14] That is, $\varepsilon_{yn} = C(\ln Y, \ln N)/V(\ln N)$, where C denotes covariance.

household size, while per capital household income falls with household size, as long as the elasticity of household income with respect to household size is greater than zero but less than one. According to Eq. (8), using the log variance measure of inequality, per capita household income will be more equal than total household income inequality when $\varepsilon_{yn} > 0.5$, but will be less equal when $\varepsilon_{yn} < 0.5$, both regimes being consistent with Kuznets' observed pattern.

Kuznets took the position that some kind of per capita or per consumer measure of household income was the theoretically appropriate measure for measuring the distribution of income. Numerous other researchers, including Danziger and Taussig (1979), Visaria (1979), and Datta and Meerman (1980), have shared the view that measures based on per capita household income are better indicators of the welfare of household members than are measures of total household income. Danziger and Taussig show that the changes over time in US income distributions depend critically on the choice of income unit. Gini coefficients indicate that US incomes became less equal between 1967 and 1976 based on a total household income criterion, but became more equal based on a per capita household income criterion. Danziger and Taussig also show that the relative position of particular groups can be highly sensitive to the unit of analysis, as demonstrated by the aged, 25% of whom fell within the lowest income decile in 1976 based on total household income, but only 6% of whom fell in that category based on per capita household income.

A number of studies have analyzed the effects of changing from total household income to per capita household income in developing countries. Visaria (1979), using data from Nepal, Sri Lanka, Taiwan, and India, finds that indices based on per capita income indicate significantly lower inequality than indices based on total household income. Visaria's interpretation of this result is that inequality measures based on total household income "overstate the degree of inequality because they overlook the fact that low total income is associated with a lower average household size" (1979: p. 293). As demonstrated above, however, the simple fact that smaller households have lower total household income is not sufficient to generate the result that per capita household income will be more equally distributed that total household income. As an indicator of the sensitivity of household rankings to the unit of analysis, Visaria finds that fewer than 20% of the households in Nepal, Sri Lanka, and the two Indian states he studies fall in the same decile when the unit of analysis is changed from total household to per capita household income.

Datta and Meerman (1980) find similar results for Malaysia. They point out that the choice of target groups to reduce poverty can be influenced by the unit of analysis. Their results indicate, for example, that female-headed families in Malaysia had significantly below-average incomes using total household income, but had mean incomes identical to male-headed households using per capita household income. Kusnic and DaVanzo (1982) compared four alternative units of analysis in their analysis of the Malaysian Family Life Survey – households using total household income; households using per adult household income; households using per capita household income; and individuals using per capita household income. The last two measures use the same income measure but in the first case use one observation per household and in the second case use one observation per individual. No clear ranking on inequality measures emerges from their comparisons. The Gini coefficient based on household market income is higher using per capita household income than using total household income. The share of income to the lowest quintile, however, is identical (2.3%) for both per capita household income and total household income.

As Kusnic and DaVanzo point out, the choice between total versus per capita household income as the appropriate unit of analysis depends in part on the presumed source of variations in household size. If fertility is viewed entirely as a choice variable, then from the parents' perspective there may be no welfare distinctions between a couple with $10 000 income and no children and a couple with $10 000 and four children. If, on the other hand, fertility is viewed as exogenous and outside the scope of choice, a per capita income measure may provide a more appropriate welfare comparison. A per capita measure may also be justified on the grounds that children should be given equal weight independent of their parents in welfare comparisons across households, or may be thought of as an indirect index of second generation inequality since per capita household income or wealth may be a rough proxy for per capita endowments to children.

The choice of recipient unit may play an important role in understanding the relationship between population growth and inequality, since changes in household composition over time are likely to lead to changes in the distribution of income. In their analysis of trends in income distribution in Taiwan, for example, Fei et al. (1979) point to a decline in both the mean and variance of family size between 1966 and 1972 and conclude that "changes in the size and composition of families must have contributed to the reduction of inequality" (1979: p. 256). They do not explain the mechanism for such an effect, however. They also point out that the direction of causality is unclear, since changes in household size were affected by changes in economic conditions, including improvements in the distribution of income.

Schultz (1982) provides the most detailed empirical evidence on the interactions of household composition, household income, and inequality. Schultz divides total household size into the numbers of adults and children, generating a decomposition with three variance and three covariance terms. These variances and covariances are then estimated using data from Colombia and rural India. Schultz finds that total household income is more equal than per capita household income in Colombia, while the opposite is the case in rural India. Schultz estimates an elasticity of family income with respect to the number of adults that is close to one for all age groups in Colombia, the result that would be expected if the propensity of adults to live together is uncorrelated with their potential income contributions to the household. Schultz estimates a lower elasticity in rural India, ranging from 0.44 to 0.59, implying that household income increases less than proportionately with increases in the number of adults. Schultz suggests this may be due to the absorption of poor widows and other disadvantaged adult members and concludes that "the distribution of families by number of adults contributes substantially to Indian family per capita income inequality, with the families having many adults being notably poorer in terms of per adult income" (1982: p. 46).

Turning to the contribution of fertility to inequality, Schultz concludes that the negative covariance of fertility and total household income tends to increase inequality in per capita household income in both India and Colombia, with a larger effect in Colombia. Schultz suggests that the greater income differentials in fertility in Colombia may result from Colombia being further advanced in its demographic transition, with the initial fertility reductions in the country occurring primarily among higher income families. Whether larger income differentials in fertility are an important explanation of the higher level of inequality in Colombia than in India cannot be determined from Schultz's evidence alone. The results do suggest an important and relatively unexplored mechanism for effects of changing fertility levels on inequality.

5. Differential fertility, intergenerational mobility, and inequality

The previous section pointed out that differentials in fertility across income classes may have implications for the distribution of household income, especially if some measure of per capita household income is used for the analysis. Empirically, it is clear that there can be substantial differences in both the level and trend of inequality depending on whether total household income of per capita household income is chosen as a metric, with the number of children playing a central role. In addition to this fundamental measurement issue, there is another sense in which income differentials in fertility have been linked to changes in the distribution of income. A common argument made to connect demographic change and income inequality is that differential fertility rates across income groups will lead to systematic changes in the distribution of income across generations. Ahluwalia (1976), for example, argued that "the most important link between population growth and income inequality is provided by the fact that different income groups grow at different rates, with the lower income groups typically experiencing a faster natural rate of increase" (1976: p. 26). Adelman and Morris (1973) made a similar argument in their analysis of cross-national differences in inequality. They write, "To the extent that poor households have more children than rich households, and to the extent that they contribute less to family income than they consume, higher rates of population growth would ... increase the skewness of the distribution of income" (1973: p. 5). Potter (1979) argues a similar point in his analysis of differential fertility and inequality in Latin America. Potter provides evidence from Colombia suggesting that the difference between the fertility of high-income and low-income groups increased as the overall level of fertility declined, and hypothesized that this increase in income differentials in fertility could lead to increased inequality in subsequent generations.

Even if we are willing to take fertility differentials across income groups as exogenous, the dynamics of differential fertility and the distribution of income are considerably more complex than these studies suggest. Given differential fertility across income groups, compositional effects will confound observed relationships between population growth and inequality. This section provides an analysis of the links between differential fertility across income classes and the distribution of income, including the role of intergenerational mobility across income classes.

5.1. The mathematics of population growth and inequality

In considering the effects on the distribution of income of differential fertility across income classes, it is instructive to begin by focusing on what might be considered the purely compositional effects. The mathematics of differential fertility and inequality are formally similar to the effects of transferring individuals across income classes. One well-known example from the economic development literature is the effect of rural–urban migration on aggregate income inequality. Swamy (1967), Robinson (1976), Fields (1979), and Stark and Yitzhaki (1982) have all shown analytically that the process of transferring individuals from a low-wage rural sector to a high-wage urban sector can generate nonmonotonic changes in inequality over time, with inequality first increasing and then later decreasing. As emphasized by Fields (1979) and Stark and Yitzhaki (1982), the welfare implications of this urbanization process may be much different than inequality measures suggest. The transfer of individuals into higher income classes is an unambiguous Pareto improvement, in spite of the increase in inequality which standard inequality measures will indicate during part of the transition. The confusing signals given by the inequality measures in such a case occur because the composition of income classes changes between two periods. Similar issues confound analysis of differential growth rates of income classes.

As discussed in Lam (1986), the compositional effects of changes in the size of income classes on measures of inequality can be seen by considering the effect of some arbitrary expansion of the population on the variance of the logarithm of income, a standard inequality measure. Consider an initial population of n persons with mean of log income μ_n and variance of log income σ_n^2 to which we add a new group of m persons with log mean μ_m and log variance σ_m^2. The log mean will rise or fall as the entering group's mean is above or below the mean of the original population, a simple compositional effect that depends only on the difference in the two groups' mean incomes. Denoting the combined log variance as σ_{n+m}^2, a standard decomposition of between-group and within-group variances implies that

$$\alpha_{n+m}^2 = \frac{nm}{(n+m)^2}(\mu_m - \mu_n)^2 + \frac{n}{n+m}\sigma_n^2 + \frac{m}{n+m}\sigma_m^2. \tag{9}$$

The new log variance is a simple function of the two population sizes, the two original log variances, and the difference between the two original log means. Eq. (9) demonstrates that inequality in the combined population could be greater than, less than, or equal to inequality in the original population, the direction of the change depending on all of the parameters. The role of the size of the entering group m is particularly noteworthy, and is summarized by the following:

$$\sigma^2_{n+m} \begin{Bmatrix} < \\ = \\ > \end{Bmatrix} \sigma^2_n \quad \text{as} \quad m \begin{Bmatrix} > \\ = \\ < \end{Bmatrix} \frac{n(\mu_m - \mu_n)^2}{\sigma^2_n - \sigma^2_m} - n. \tag{10}$$

An interesting implication of Eq. (9) is that whenever the entering group's log variance is smaller than the original log variance and the new group's log mean is more than one standard deviation from the original log mean, then there exists some number of new entrants that will leave the original log variance unchanged. We can also satisfy either of the inequalities in Eq. (10), either increasing or decreasing log variance as we change the size of the entering group. We thus see the more complex nature of compositional effects on measures of dispersion compared to compositional effects on means. While a group of low-income entrants will always decrease the mean income of a higher income population, the direction of the effect on the log variance cannot be predicted without knowing all of the parameters in Eq. (10).

Similar results can be derived for all additively decomposable measures of inequality. Just as different inequality measures have different degrees of sensitivity to transfers at a given point in the distribution,[15] different measures will be affected in different ways by a given change in population composition. Thus it is easy to generate examples in which an increase in the density of the population at a given point in the income distribution will cause one standard measure of inequality to increase, while another standard measure shows a decrease. In fact, simple expansions of the population of the type considered in Eq. (9) will in general imply intersecting Lorenz curves before and after the expansion.

The Lorenz curve, which expresses cumulative shares of income as a function of cumulative shares of the population, is a general foundation for inequality comparisons.[16] Several important points about the effects of differential fertility and other

---

[15] See, for example, Atkinson (1970) and Kakwani (1980).

[16] For an income distribution with probability density function $f(y)$, the horizontal axis for the Lorenz curve is the cumulative distribution function

$$F(\hat{y}) = \int_0^{\hat{y}} f(y)\, dy.$$

The vertical axis is the first moment distribution function

$$\Phi(\hat{y}) = (1/\mu)\int_0^{\hat{y}} y f(y)\, dy,$$

where μ is the mean of the distribution.

changes in population composition on inequality can be seen by identifying the conditions under which individuals can be added to a population so that the Lorenz curve for the combined population lies above the Lorenz curve for the original population. Since inequality comparisons are inherently ambiguous when Lorenz curves intersect, establishing the necessary and sufficient conditions for Lorenz dominance provides additional insights into the problems with inequality comparisons under differential fertility.

If we begin with a population with an income distribution described by the density function $f_1(y)$ to which we add a second population with income distribution $f_2(y)$, we can find the conditions under which the new combined distribution, $f_3(y)$, Lorenz dominates the original distribution. The conditions, derived in Lam (1986, 1988a) turn out to be surprisingly restrictive: if $y_1^{min} > 0$, where y_1^{min} is the income of the poorest individual included in the income distribution, then

$$\Phi_3(F) \ge \Phi_1(F) \quad \forall F \quad \text{iff} \quad \mu_2 = \mu_1 \text{ and } \Phi_2(F) \ge \Phi_1(F) \quad \forall F \tag{11}$$

where $\Phi(F)$ is the Lorenz curve and μ_i is the mean for distribution $f_i(y)$. Eq. (11) states that the combined population's income distribution will Lorenz dominate the original population's income distribution if and only if the entering population has the same mean as the original population and the income distribution of the entering population Lorenz dominates the original population's income distribution. One of the most surprising results in Eq. (11), and the result most important for inequality comparisons under differential fertility, is the necessary condition that the entering population have the same mean income as the original population. Since this equal means condition will rarely be satisfied in practice, the result implies that the second-period distribution will either be unambiguously less equal than the original distribution or that the Lorenz curves for the two periods will intersect.

5.2. Differential fertility and intergenerational mobility

It can be misleading to analyze the relationship between differential fertility and the distribution of income without accounting for intergenerational mobility across income classes. For a wide class of models the introduction of intergenerational mobility has the important effect of generating a steady-state distribution of income as long as children of all income classes have some positive probability of entering any other income class. Introducing even a small degree of mobility is an important modification, since it means that persistent higher fertility for the poor will not cause the population to converge to 100% poor.[17]

---

[17] See Preston's (1974) analysis of the interaction of occupational mobility and occupation differentials in fertility. See also Preston and Campbell (1993) and Lam (1993) on differential fertility and the distribution of IQ in the population.

Given the existence of a steady-state distribution of income, we may be interested in questions such as how the steady-state proportion of the population in the lowest income class will be affected by an increase in the fertility rate of the lowest income class, or how some measure of income distribution in the steady state will be affected by a change in the fertility rate of some particular income class. These and related questions have been analyzed by Lam (1986), Chu (1987), Dietzenbacher (1989), and Chu and Koo (1990).

The basic model used to analyze these issues is a model of differential fertility and intergenerational mobility based on a simple Markov process governing transitions across income classes. Assume a vector P_t denotes the size of n discrete income classes in period t. Class-specific fertility rates are described by a $n \times n$ diagonal matrix of net reproduction rates F and intergenerational mobility is described by a $n \times n$ matrix M, where element M_{ij} is the probability that a child of class j becomes a member of class i. Thinking of each period as a generation, the distribution of income in period t is

$$P_t = MFP_{t-1} \tag{12}$$

The properties of the system in Eq. (12) are determined by the product of the income class transition matrix and the fertility matrix, which produce a combined transition matrix $T^* = MF$. The process governed by T^* will converge to a stable proportional income distribution if T^* is an irreducible primitive matrix.[18]

Ignoring mortality and age structure, the effects of differential fertility on both steady states and transitions can be seen in the dynamics of period-to-period changes in the relative size of the poorest class. If the size of income class i at time t is $P_{i,t}$ and the proportion of the population in income class i at time t is $\pi_{i,t}$, then the proportion of the population in the poorest class, $i = 1$, at time t is

$$\pi_{1,t} = \frac{\sum_{i=1}^{n} P_{i,t-1} F_i M_{1i}}{\sum_{i=1}^{n} P_{i,t-1} F_i} . \tag{13}$$

Considering the effect of a change in F_1, the net reproduction rate of the poorest class,

---

[18] The proportions of the population in each income class will converge to constant proportions, with the absolute numbers growing at the same constant exponential rate. Irreducibility requires that transitions can occur between all states in the system. The stronger condition of primitivity requires that some power of T^* has only positive elements. If all fertility rates and transition probabilities are positive, then this condition is satisfied, since T^* consists entirely of positive elements. See Parlett (1970), Mode (1971), and Keyfitz (1977).

on the proportion in that class in the next period, the result in elasticity form reduces to

$$\frac{\partial \ln \pi_{1,t}}{\partial \ln F_1} = M_{11} - \sum_{i=2}^{n} \gamma_{i,t} M_{1i}, \tag{14}$$

where $\gamma_{i,t} = P_{i,t-1}F_i/\Sigma P_{i,t}$ is the proportion of the tth period population born to parents from the ith income class. The elasticity of the proportion of the population in the poorest class with respect to the reproduction rate of that class is equal to the difference between the probability that a child of poor parents remains poor and the weighted average of the probabilities that children of all other classes become poor, with weights equal to the proportion of the period t population born to parents of each class.

From Eq. (14) we see that if there exists any $M_{1i} > M_{11}$, implying that parents in at least one class are more likely to produce poor offspring than are the poor themselves, then there will exist some initial income distribution (implying a set of weights γ_i) for which an increase in the fertility of the poor will cause a *decrease* in the proportion poor in the second period. If $M_{1i} \leq M_{11}$ $\forall i$, then an increase in the fertility of the poor must lead to an increase in the proportion poor in the second period. Since the income distribution, and hence the weights γ_i, will change in the second period and in every other period during the transition to the steady state, Eq. (14) implies that the effect of higher fertility among the poor may be different in every period until the ergodic income distribution is achieved. As shown by Chu (1987), the logic that higher fertility for the poor will increase the proportion poor whenever $M_{1i} \leq M_{11}$ $\forall i$, does not necessarily extend beyond the one period case to the comparison of steady states. This is because the weights γ_i will be different in the second period and, in general, in all subsequent periods until the steady state is reached. Chu provides a simple 3×3 example in which the poorest class has the highest probability of producing poor children and yet an increase in fertility for the poor actually reduces the proportion poor in the steady state. Surprisingly, then, it is possible for higher fertility for the poor to *reduce* the proportion of the population that is poor, even when poor parents are more likely than any other class to produce poor children.

The sometimes surprising properties of intergenerational income distribution processes with differential fertility have been further clarified by Dietzenbacher (1989) and Chu and Koo (1990). Dietzenbacher (1989) provides an instructive proof that, without making any restrictions on the mobility matrix, it must be true that an increase in the fertility rate of the poorest income class will increase the percent born to parents from the poorest class in the steady state. As is clear from the results in Lam (1986) and Chu (1987), this does not imply that the percent actually belonging to the poorest income class must increase in the steady state, but only that the percent with parents from that class must increase. Dietzenbacher's results also imply upper and lower bounds on the proportion poor in the steady state.

Chu and Koo (1990) demonstrate that under a set of assumptions about the structure of both the mobility matrix M and the fertility matrix F it is possible to show that a reduction in the fertility of the poorest income class will always lead to an unambiguous improvement in the steady-state distribution of income. The critical assumptions are that

$$F_1 \geq F_2 \geq \cdots \geq F_n \tag{15}$$

and that

$$\frac{\sum_{i=1}^{I} M_{i1}}{\sum_{j=1}^{J} M_{j1}} \geq \frac{\sum_{i=1}^{I} M_{i2}}{\sum_{j=1}^{J} M_{j2}} \geq \cdots \geq \frac{\sum_{i=1}^{I} M_{in}}{\sum_{j=1}^{J} M_{jn}} \quad (1 \leq I \leq J \leq n). \tag{16}$$

The assumption about fertility in Eq. (16) implies that fertility is nonincreasing across income groups. The assumption in Eq. (16) imposes conditional stochastic monotonicity on the mobility matrix. As Chu and Koo point out, it implies in this case that if a poor child and rich child are both born into any bottom J income classes, the poor child is expected to be poorer than the rich child. Under these assumptions, Chu and Koo (1990) show that an increase in the fertility rate of the poorest class will cause an increase in the percent in the poorest class in the steady state. This result follows from Dietzenbacher's result, given the assumptions made by Chu and Koo about the mobility matrix. Since Dietzenbacher shows that the percent born to poor parents must increase, the restriction that children of poor parents will probabilistically have lower positions in the income distribution implies that the percent in the poorest class will increase. The results of Chu and Koo imply that a decrease in the fertility rate of the poorest income class will generate a steady-state distribution of income that has unambiguously higher social welfare by the criterion of first-order stochastic dominance. In addition to a higher mean income, all standard inequality measures will show improvements in the steady state. Chu and Koo conclude that this result strengthens the case for family planning programs targeted at the poor, since, under the assumptions of their model, decreases in the fertility of the poor will lead to improvements in the distribution of income in future generations. The appropriateness of such policy conclusions will be discussed below.

The basic model considered so far abstracts from age structure and mortality, assuming simple one period transitions from generation to generation. The model can be generalized to include two other important demographic components, age structure and mortality (which will vary by both age and income), by constructing a multidimensional transition process that corresponds to the multistate life table used by demographers. Just as standard life tables describe transition probabilities across age groups, multistate life tables describe simultaneous transitions across age groups and other states.[19] Lam (1986) presents a model of transitions across income classes and age groups, which in the most general form combines age-specific and income-specific mortality and age-specific economic mobility for m age groups and n income classes to produce a separate conditional probability $T_{i_k, j_{k+1}}$ for each transition from income class i at age k to income class j at age $k + 1$, and which allows each income group at each age to have a separate fertility rate $F_{i,k}$. The generalization of the ergodicity result for the process without age structure in Eq. (12) is that the more general multistate process with age structure will converge to a steady-state population with constant proportions in each of the $n \times m$ age–income groups if the product of the mobility matrix and the matrix of fertility and mortality rates is an irreducible primitive matrix. If at least one age group has a mobility matrix which allows transitions across all income classes, plausible restrictions on the fertility sub-matrices guarantee convergence. A sufficient (but not necessary) condition for convergence is that fertility rates are positive for all income classes in two adjacent age groups.

Given data on income- and age-specific fertility, mortality, and inter-class mobility, these results can be used to analyze the dynamics of income distribution and age structure from some initial conditions to the steady state. Lam (1986) uses data from Brazil to simulate the effects of alternative fertility levels across income quintiles on the steady-state income distribution and transitions to the steady state. Household survey data are used to estimate the mean income, log variance of income, and number of children for income quintiles of male household heads. Intergenerational transition rates across income quintiles are estimated based on estimates of occupational mobility in Brazil. These estimates are used to construct a multi-dimensional transition process with five income classes and four 15-year age groups. Given the estimated fertility, survival, and mobility matrices, the implied steady-state age–income distribution is generated by applying the multidimensional transition matrix to an initial age–income distribution. The steady-state distribution implied by actual fertility patterns is used as the initial distribution for two counterfactual simulations, a 100% increase in the fertility of the bottom quintile, and a reduction in the fertility of each quintile to the level of the top quintile. The log variance and coefficient of variation of income for each age group are derived from the age-specific density functions for each period.

The results of these simulations imply that a 100% increase in the fertility of the poor leads, not surprisingly, to an increase in the steady-state percent poor, while the elimination of fertility differentials leads to a decrease in the steady-state percent poor. The two inequality measures, however, move in opposite directions under both counterfactuals. When the fertility rate of the poorest quintile is doubled, the coefficient of variation rises to a new higher level in the steady state, consistent with the widespread

---

[19] See the contributions in Land and Rogers (1982) for both theoretical analysis and applications.

notion that higher fertility for the poor will increase income inequality. The results for the variance of log income give just the opposite conclusion, however. The log variance declines in every period to a new lower steady-state value in response to the 100% increase in the fertility of the poor. The fact that the coefficient of variation and the log variance move in opposite directions in response to an increase in the fertility of the poorest quintile points out the confusing signals given by inequality measures in the presence of income differentials in fertility. It is important to note that the counterfactuals assume there are no changes in the relative earnings of the poor relative to other classes. Changes in measured inequality occur only because of the changing population composition caused by the interaction of differential fertility and intergenerational mobility. If changes in relative earnings are introduced into the model, it is easy to generate cases in which there is an increase in measured inequality at the same time that the relative earnings of the poorest quintile are improving.

5.3. Welfare implications of endogenous fertility

It is clearly unrealistic to treat fertility differentials across income groups as exogenous. The previous set of models help clarify the dynamics of differential fertility and the distribution of income, but it would be dangerous to draw strong policy conclusions from the results. Chu and Koo (1990) conclude that their results showing that lower fertility for the poor would reduce steady-state income inequality "provide strong theoretical support in favor of family planning programs that encourage the poor in developing countries to reduce their reproductive rate". Their policy conclusion is dubious, even if one accepts the assumptions leading to their result. Such a conclusion implies that lower income classes would be better off if they reduced their reproduction rate. In the model of Chu and Koo (1990) there would appear to be no bound on the extent to which lower fertility by the poor would lower income inequality. Taking their policy argument to extremes, policy makers concerned with income inequality should try to reduce fertility among the poorest classes to zero and maximize fertility among the richest classes. But any existing group of low-income parents is unlikely to find it in its interest to reduce fertility below some finite level, even if the parents include all future generations in an optimization of dynastic utility. The policy problem is in some respects similar to the issue of migration and inequality discussed above. The choice by rural residents to move to the city in order to raise their wages may increase wage inequality, as shown by Robinson (1976), Fields (1979), and Stark and Yitzhaki (1982). It would be inappropriate to conclude from this result, however, that there should be policy interventions to limit rural–urban migration in order to reduce income inequality.

It is impossible to analyze the welfare implications of differential fertility across income groups without understanding the determinants of fertility. A number of models of overlapping generations with endogenous fertility have been used to analyze issues related to the distribution of income, including Chu (1990), Eckstein and Wolpin (1985), Becker and Barro (1988), and Raut (1991). An inverse relationship between quantity and quality of children (where quality typically refers to investments in human capital) is often generated endogenously in these models. In Raut (1991), for example, higher fertility for lower income parents is derived as the optimizing behavior in the face of incomplete capital markets. While it is possible to imagine policy interventions, such as improvements in capital markets, that would simultaneously raise the welfare of poor parents, lower their fertility, and improve the steady-state distribution of income, it does not follow in general from these models that any policy intervention that lowers the fertility of the poor will lead to an improvement in the steady-state distribution of income or in the welfare of poor parents. A tax on children, for example, might lower the fertility of the poor more than the fertility of the rich, and might or might not improve the distribution of income. Even if it did improve the steady-state distribution of income, however, it almost surely will make poor parents worse off in every generation, and would be a dubious policy conclusion to draw from the relationship between differential fertility and inequality.

6. Effects of population growth on wages and inequality

Concern with the distributional consequences of population growth goes back to the foundations of modern economics. Thomas Malthus, Adam Smith and David Ricardo were all concerned with the depressing effect of population growth on wages, focusing on diminishing returns to labor in the presence of fixed resources, notably land.[20] The concern of the classical economists with diminishing returns to labor in the presence of a fixed factor of production was updated to a concern about the capital-dilution effect of population growth with the development of neoclassical growth models based on capital accumulation, such as the well-known model of Solow (1956). Like classical economic models driven by diminishing returns to fixed factors, neoclassical economic growth models with exogenous population growth rates generated strong predictions about the negative effects of population growth on relative wages. These predictions are frequently cited in discussions of the relationship between population growth and the distribution of income.

6.1. Relative wages, factor shares, and income distribution

Economic theory and considerable empirical evidence suggest that population growth will tend to lower relative wages, ceteris paribus. The link from changes in relative wages to changes in standard measures of wage inequality is not always straightfor-

[20] See Wrigley (1988) for an interesting comparison of the views of Malthus, Smith, and Ricardo.

ward, however. The confusion in mapping from changes in relative wages to changes in measures of inequality results from the fact that the changes in population that are causing the decline in wages also enter directly into the calculation of inequality measures.

It is instructive to consider the case of functional shares, where the basic theoretical prediction regarding the effect of changes in the supply of one factor is well known. Consider a two-factor production function $Y = F(L, X)$, where L represents labor and X represents some other factor such as land or capital, and each factor is paid its marginal product $w = \partial F/\partial L$ and $r = \partial F/\partial X$. Denoting the ratio of labor's total income to the other factor's total income as $\pi_L = wL/rX$, the elasticity of this factor payment ratio with respect to the number of workers L will be

$$\varepsilon_{\pi_L, L} = \frac{\partial \ln \pi_L}{\partial \ln L} = 1 - 1/\sigma, \tag{17}$$

where $\sigma = \partial \ln(X/L)/\partial \ln(w/r)$ is the elasticity of substitution between X and labor. In other words, labor's share of total output will decrease when the number of workers increases if the elasticity of substitution between labor and the other factor is less than one. This result is little more than a mathematical identity and does not depend on any particular model of the economy as long as factor payments are equal to marginal products. It describes the effect of exogenous increases in population size on factor shares in a classical model with fixed land, and it also describes the effect of exogenous increases in the population growth rate on factor shares in different steady states in a neoclassical model of capital accumulation.

Given evidence that elasticities of substitution are not likely to be greater than one (see, for example, Morawetz, 1976), the result in Eq. (17) implies that higher rates of population growth will tend to reduce labor's share of total income. To the extent that labor's share of income is of interest as a measure of income distribution, this result may be of direct interest. The result is often also used as an intermediate step in linking predictions about factor payments to predictions about more conventional measures of income inequality related to population shares. The argument is often made, for example, that since wages are a larger share of income for low-income groups than for high-income groups, a decline in labor's share of income will imply a decline in the share of income going to the lowest income groups. The same argument is applied to the relative shares of wages and land rents or the relative shares of unskilled wages and skilled wages, each case assuming that the poorest groups in the population begin with relatively smaller endowments of productive assets (physical capital, land, and human capital) whose returns increase when the population growth rate increases.

It is not necessarily true, however, that a declining factor share to labor will imply a declining income share to the poor as long as the poor receive a higher proportion of their earnings as wages. As a simple example, consider a case in which there are L_p

poor workers who receive only wage income and L_r rich workers who receive both wage income and income from capital, all labor being homogeneous. Total income is divided as

$$\frac{wL_p}{Y} + \frac{wL_r}{Y} + \frac{rK}{Y} \equiv S_{Lp} + S_{Lr} + S_K = 1. \tag{18}$$

Suppose that the elasticity of substitution between labor and capital is unity, so that the share of total output paid out as wages, $S_{Lp} + S_{Lr}$, does not change and the share paid as rents on capital, S_K, does not change when the size of the labor force changes. Suppose that the number of poor workers increases and the number of rich workers remains constant. The share of total income paid as wages to the rich, S_{Lr} must decline, since the wage falls and total income increases. The share of income paid as capital, S_K, will stay constant by assumption, so the share of income to the rich, $S_r = S_{Lr} + S_K$ must decrease. The share of total income paid to poor workers, S_{Lp}, must increase. In other words, when the number of poor workers increases, the share of income paid to capital remains constant, the share paid as wages to the rich declines, and the share paid as wages to the poor increases. Even if the elasticity of substitution were less than one it is easy to see that it would be possible for the share of income paid to the poor to increase even though labor's total share declines, as long as the rich receive some labor income. Of course it will be little consolation to the poor that their collective share of total income has increased, since each poor person will be receiving a lower wage than before. Factor shares are simply a poor measure of relative welfare when the quantities of factors are changing as well as the factor payments.

One must use caution, then, in moving from factor payments to factor shares to individual shares in predicting the effects of population growth on the distribution of income. In general there will be no necessary relationship between the share of income paid as wages and the share of income going to some bottom percentile of the distribution, even in very simple models. Similarly, there will in general be no necessary relationship between changes in wages relative to rents and changes in standard measures of inequality. Whenever possible, then, it is useful to be able to look directly at both relative wages and summary inequality measures.

6.2. Empirical evidence on the effects of population growth on inequality

As pointed out above, one of the fundamental links between demographic variables and inequality is the connection between population size and wages that captured the attention of Malthus and the other classical economists. A large empirical literature has examined these links in historical populations, and it is beyond the scope of this paper to provide a survey of that literature. Lee (Chapter 19, this volume) provides an extensive review of the empirical evidence. Although poor data and identification problems complicate all of this research, there is considerable evidence supporting the classical economic model in pre-industrial Europe, with population growth exerting a negative effect on wages and a positive effect on returns to other factors such as capital and land.

While a large literature has examined the link between population growth and wages, empirical studies looking at the effects of population growth on standard measures of inequality are less common. One of the few sources of historical data on both factor payments and standard inequality measures is Williamson and Lindert's analysis of the history of inequality in the US (Lindert, 1978; Williamson and Lindert, 1980). Williamson and Lindert (1980) investigate the extent to which wage differentials between skilled and unskilled workers move in the same direction as summary inequality measures in their time series. For periods in which data on both wage differentials and summary inequality measures are available they find high correlations in the movements of the two series. In the period 1913–1934, for example, regressions of the annual share of income earned by the top 1% of the population on annual unemployment rates and the ratio of skilled wages to unskilled wages show that the "wage gap" has a statistically significant positive effect on the income share of the top 1% (Williamson and Lindert, 1980: pp. 80–82). The authors conclude that the series move enough in parallel to justify using wage ratios alone to infer movements in inequality measures during periods when the latter are unavailable.

Williamson and Lindert conclude from their analysis that population growth, whether from immigration or natural increase, had unequalizing effects on the income distribution in the US, with the wage depressing effect of increased labor supply playing a major role. Lindert writes in an earlier book, "No other potential influence on the distribution of income fits the long-run movements in inequality as well as the behavior of the labor supply" (1978: p. 257). Having documented the role of fertility as a major determinant of historical movements in US labor supply, Lindert concludes that the apparent disequalizing effects of increases in fertility are strong enough that "the case for collective policies to encourage birth restriction in countries with rapid population growth is strengthened" (1978: p. 259). This limited historical evidence from the US, then, appears to support the argument that higher rates of population growth cause declines in the wages of unskilled workers relative to skilled wages and returns to capital and land. These effects on relative wages appear in turn to lead to increased inequality in personal income by conventional measures.

A larger set of empirical studies has examined the link between population growth and the distribution of income in currently developing countries. This literature has been dominated by cross-national comparisons, with the typical study estimating cross-national regressions in which the dependent variable is some measure of inequality and the independent variables are a wide variety of country characteristics, including demographic measures. In one of the earliest of these studies, Adelman and

Morris (1973) included both fertility rates and the population growth rates as explanatory variables, and found positive effects of both variables on the level of inequality. They attributed this result to a tendency for high fertility rates in rural areas to generate a larger "reserve army" of urban unemployed (1973: p. 35) and to the fact that the poor have higher fertility than the rich. The population growth rate was also included as an explanatory variable in Ahluwalia's (1976) analysis of income distribution using data from 60 countries. Ahluwalia's single-equation cross-national regressions showed a significantly positive effect of the population growth rate on the income share of the top 20% and a significantly negative effect on the income shares of the middle 40%, the bottom 60%, and the bottom 40%. According to Ahluwalia's results, a one percentage point increase in the population growth rate would lead to a 1.2 percentage point decrease in the income share of the bottom 40% of the population. A similar cross-country regression analysis of income distribution data by Ram (1984) found a significant negative relationship between population growth and the income share of the bottom 40% and bottom 80% of the distribution, controlling for a variety of other variables such as mean and variance of schooling, income growth, and share in agriculture.

There are obvious concerns about the causal interpretation of these single-equation regressions of inequality measures on demographic rates, given the potential for causation in the other direction. A number of researchers argued that there would plausibly be a causal effect of income inequality on both fertility and mortality, including Kocher (1973), Rich (1973) and Repetto (1978, 1979). In order to account for effects in both directions, simultaneous equations models of fertility, mortality, and income distribution have been estimated by Repetto (1979), Winegarden (1978, 1980), Ogawa (1978) and Rodgers (1983).[21] Attempts to estimate simultaneous equations models suffer from the obvious difficulty of finding plausible instrumental variables to identify the effects of demographic variables on inequality. Ideally we would like to find variables that cause exogenous movements in demographic rates without otherwise being correlated with inequality. The identifying restrictions used in this empirical literature are far from ideal. Repetto (1979) uses variables such as literacy rates and newspaper circulation as instrumental variables for fertility, and uses nutritional measures (average caloric intake per capita) as instruments for mortality. To the extent that these variables are endogenous outcomes directly affected by the level of inequality, they will be poor instruments for identifying the causal effect of demographic rates on inequality. Rodgers (1983) attempts to use a recursive time structure to identify his model, using lagged population growth as a determinant of current inequality. To the extent that fixed country effects correlated with inequality and population growth are persistent over time, this is unlikely to be a convincing identifying restriction. Winegarden (1978) uses the urbanization rate and, more plausibly, legality of abortion as instruments for demographic rates.

---

[21] See Boulier (1982) for a critical review of this literature.

These studies give mixed results regarding the causal effects in both directions. Most authors have estimated a positive effect of inequality on fertility. These results are consistent with Repetto's hypothesis that because of a nonlinear relationship between income and fertility, a transfer of income from the rich to the poor decreases fertility at low incomes by a greater proportion than it increases fertility at high incomes. The major exception to this result is Winegarden (1980), who found insignificant or negative direct effects of inequality on fertility. There is greater unanimity in the estimated effects in the other direction, with all studies prior to Rodgers (1983) supporting the single-equation studies' conclusion that higher population growth causes greater inequality. Rodgers finds effects of population growth on inequality that are statistically insignificant.

It would be useful to supplement these cross-national comparisons of income distribution with the time-series experience of particular countries. Unfortunately there is limited time-series data available on income distribution in developing countries. The limited data that do exist have not been systematically analyzed from the standpoint of the possible influence of population growth or other demographic variables. The most extensive surveys of income distribution data have been done by Fields (1980, 1989, 1991), who has focused on the relationship between economic growth and changes in inequality. In Fields (1980) earlier survey he found no consistent pattern in the relationship between the rate of economic growth and changes in inequality in the 13 countries which had reliable measures for more than one point in time. His more recent survey, which has a considerably expanded set of countries and time periods, comes to similar conclusions. Examining 70 "spells" of economic growth in 22 countries, for example, Fields (1991) finds no systematic relationship between economic growth and changes in the distribution of income. There were 31 economic growth spells in which Gini coefficients increased, 35 spells in which Gini coefficients decreased, and four in which the Gini was unchanged.

Fields does not discuss the relationship between population growth rates or other demographic variables and changes in the distribution of income in the countries for which he has data on inequality for more than one point in time. Unlike the historical analysis for the US and pre-industrial Europe, in which data for hundreds of years make it possible to look at population growth over a number of periods that are each several decades in length, data on income distribution in developing countries consists in the best of circumstances of a small number of data points spread over 20–30 years. Although some changes in population growth rates for particular countries are observed over this period, they move collinearly with so many other social and economic changes that it would be difficult to identify the partial effect of demographic variables. In general the data are much too limited both within and across developing countries for the kind of careful multivariate analysis that would be necessary to identify a relationship between demographic variables and inequality measures based on time-series observations.

7. Demographic change and trends in inequality in the US

It is now well documented that there was a substantial increase in wage inequality in the US beginning around the late 1970s and continuing through the 1980s.[22] The basic patterns can be seen in Fig. 4, which presents Karoly's (1992) estimates of the variance in log wages for males and females. Most researchers looking for explanations of the recent increase in wage dispersion in the US have considered the potential role of age structure fluctuations caused by the entry of baby boom cohorts into the labor market in the 1970s. The effect of the baby boom on the supply of workers of particular ages has often been considered jointly with the changes in the educational composition of the labor force. In the treatments by Bound and Johnson (1992), Murphy and Welch (1992), and Katz and Murphy (1992), for example, the analysis focuses on labor market groups distinguished by gender, education, and experience. Shifts in labor supply are represented as changes in the relative size of these cells. The documented increase in the relative importance of young college-educated workers in the labor market in the 1970s is thus a combination of the baby-boom cohorts entering the labor market and the increased college attendance rates of the period.

Several common themes emerge from analyses of recent inequality in the US. The increase in the relative number of young college-educated workers in the 1970s appears to have been at least partly responsible for the increase in relative wages of older better educated workers. The decline in the relative supply of young workers in the 1980s, however, did not lead to an increase in their relative wages. Katz and Murphy provide a simple test of whether labor supply effects alone can explain changes in relative wages during the period 1963–1987. A vector of relative changes in labor supply and a vector of relative changes in wages are constructed, where a component of the vectors corresponds to one gender/schooling/experience group. If labor demand is stable, they argue, then the inner product of the vector of labor supply changes and the vector of wage changes will be negative. Using this test, changes in labor supply and relative wages are reasonably consistent with a stable demand explanation for the period 1965–1980. Wage changes in the 1980s are clearly not consistent with stable labor demand, however. Groups with the largest increases in labor supply in the 1980s tended to have the largest increases in relative wages. They find support for an explanation that combines a rapid increase in the demand for human capital, including education and experience, with changes in the supply of college graduates in different age groups.

Bound and Johnson (1992) come to similar conclusions, arguing that biased technological change was the major cause of the increased wage premium to workers with greater experience and education in the 1980s. They attribute a relatively small role to

---

[22] For a survey of the extensive literature on this topic see Levy and Murnane (1992). Bound and Johnson (1992), Katz and Murphy (1992), Murphy and Welch (1992), and Karoly (1992) analyze the dominant trends and possible explanations.

Fig. 4. Variance of log wages for men and women, US, 1963–1987.

demographic effects on the supply side for most of the observed changes in relative wages, although at least one observed change, the increase in relative wages of older compared to younger noncollege workers, is substantially influenced by changing age structure.

Burtless (1990) devotes considerable attention to the role of age structure in explaining trends in earnings inequality in the US. He calculates separate Gini coefficients by age group from 1967 to 1987 for both men and women, and calculates overall Gini coefficients by standardizing the age distribution to the distribution for 1967. Age-specific Ginis are thus allowed to change over time while the pure compositional effect of changing age structure is removed. Burtless finds that the simple compositional effect of the changes in age structure caused by the US baby boom do not play an important role in explaining increasing earnings inequality in the US in recent decades. He finds, in fact, that for both men and women the age-standardized Gini coefficients show greater increases in overall inequality than were actually observed. In other words, his results imply that age structure shifts during this period actually tended to offset the trend toward increasing inequality in the total population.

Moving beyond the purely compositional effects of age structure, Burtless (1990) uses the Theil inequality index, a measure with convenient decomposition properties, to decompose overall inequality into between-group and within-group components across age groups. His results indicate that the proportion of total male inequality attributable to between-group inequality remains quite stable over the period 1967 to 1987. In other words, the increase in inequality over the period in earnings inequality for men (an increase in the Theil index from 0.211 to 0.276) resulted from almost equal proportional increases in within-group and between-group inequality. For women the results are quite different, suggesting that the relative importance of within-group inequality declined over the period.

8. Summary and conclusions

It is hard to imagine a change in some fundamental demographic variable that will not potentially have an effect on the distribution of income across individuals or households. Changes in fertility, mortality, migration, marriage, household composition, and age structure will plausibly have a variety of effects on income inequality. Many of these are what might be considered pure compositional effects. A change in the age structure of the population, for example, will in general change the measure of income inequality in the population, even if there is no change within each age group in mean income or age-specific income inequality. Identifying compositional effects on measures of dispersion is more difficult than identifying compositional effects on means. This chapter has demonstrated that it is nonetheless possible in many cases to derive instructive analytics about these compositional effects. In a number of cases these analytical results clarify longstanding points of confusion in the empirical literature on demographic change and the distribution of income.

In the case of age structure, the combination of a simple decomposition into "within-group" and "between-group" inequality and the analytics of stable population theory produce a number of useful insights. The results demonstrate, for example, that the aging of a population can produce offsetting effects on the distribution of income. An increase in the proportion of young people tends to increase between-group inequality in most populations, since the mean income of young workers is well below the population mean. The effect of a younger population on within-group inequality is less clear, however, since young workers in some populations have relatively low within-group inequality. Age profiles from the US and Brazil give conflicting evidence on the net direction of these effects. Brazilian age profiles suggest that a shift toward a younger age structure would have a small equalizing effect on cross-sectional income distribution, while US profiles suggest that a younger population would have higher inequality. As suggested by research on the effects of cohort size on wages, there is good reason to believe that changes in age structure also have direct effects on income inequality that go beyond simple compositional effects. Evidence from recent trends in inequality in the US, for example, suggests that changes in the age composition of the labor force may have played a role in the decrease in wages of young college-educated workers compared to older college-educated workers in the 1970s.

The relationship between marriage patterns and the distribution of income has been considered in a large literature focusing on decompositions of inequality across married couples. Many researchers have decomposed family income inequality into components related to the inequality of husbands' income, inequality of wives' income, relative weights of each spouse's earnings in family income, and the correlation of spouses' incomes. A standard result in these models is that wives' earnings are "equalizing" in the sense that income inequality across married couples is lower than income inequality across husbands. This equalizing contribution of wives' earnings holds for a wide variety of countries, and appears to have been increasing over time in the US.

Extending the unit of analysis beyond married couples to a broader definition of the household, researchers have shown empirically that inequality comparisons across time and space can be highly sensitive to the treatment of household composition. Inequality across households in the US, for example, increases across some periods based on total household income, but decreases based on per capita household income. Researchers have also demonstrated that changes in the mean and variance of household composition over time can have substantial effects on the distribution of household income. The magnitude and even the direction of these effects are poorly understood, however, since they depend on the complex relationship between changes in the mean and variance of household size and changes in the covariances of household size and household income.

Differentials in fertility across income classes have frequently been identified as an important factor driving intergenerational transmission of inequality. The existence of income differentials in fertility may cause measured inequality to change over time simply because of changing proportions of the population in different income groups. Welfare interpretations of such changes are difficult, since children of the poor may be no worse off relative to higher income groups than their parents were, but measured inequality may increase or decrease as the proportion of the population which is poor increases. As shown above, the effect of higher fertility among the poor on standard inequality measures can be either positive or negative and may reverse direction if the differentials persist for long periods. In the presence of income differentials in fertility it is possible for the incomes of the poor to fall relative to higher income groups at the same time that standard indexes show decreasing inequality. Similarly, incomes of the poor may rise relative to higher income groups at the same time that standard indexes show rising inequality. These results demonstrate the importance of defining distributional criteria carefully and the need for caution in drawing inferences from cross-national or intertemporal differences in measured inequality.

Although there is a widespread view that higher rates of population growth have had negative distributional consequences in both pre-industrial populations and recently developing countries, the empirical evidence is quite limited, especially for developing countries. Empirical analysis of the link between population growth and inequality in modern populations has for the most part taken the form of cross-national regressions that include population growth as an independent variable explaining some summary inequality index. Although most of these cross-national studies have concluded that population growth increases inequality, they suffer from the standard limitations of attempts at inference from cross-national comparisons. The few attempts at making population growth endogenous in these models suffer from the absence of theoretical justifications for their identifying restrictions.

The observed increases in wage inequality in the US in recent decades provide an interesting case study for considering the role of demographic variables. The studies of increased wage dispersion in the US demonstrate quite convincingly that labor supply effects related to the baby boom, increased labor force participation of women, or population aging, are not the major factors behind the recent increase in wage inequality. Most studies do find significant effects of these demographic changes, but the effects are dominated by large shifts in labor demand. As shown in the discussion of inequality among married couples, analysis of family income inequality suggests that the increases in inequality of male earnings has been partially offset by changes related to marital sorting and labor supply of women. The contribution of wives' earnings to family income has become increasingly equalizing during recent decades, an effect that has partially mitigated the increased dispersion of wages among men.

References

Adelman, I. and C.T. Morris (1973), Economic growth and social equity in developing countries (Stanford University Press, Stanford, MA).

Ahluwalia, M.S. (1976), "Inequality, poverty and development", Journal of Development Economics 3: 307–342.

Arthur, W.B. (1981), "The ergodic theorems of demography: a simple proof", Demography 19: 439–445.

Atkinson, A.B. (1970), "On the measurement of inequality", Journal of Economic Theory 2: 244–263.

Barros, R.P. (1990), "Aggregating inequalities", Unpublished manuscript (Department of Economics, Yale University, New Haven, CT).

Barros, R.P. and S.P. De Mendonça (1992), "A research note on family and income distribution: the equalizing impact of married women's earnings in metropolitan Brazil", Sociological Inquiry 62: 208–219.

Becker, G.S. (1991), A treatise on the family, Enlarged edition (Harvard University Press, Cambridge, MA).

Becker, G.S. and R.J. Barro (1988), "A reformulation of the economic theory of fertility", Quarterly Journal of Economics 103: 1–25.

Behrman, J.R., M.R. Rosenzweig and P. Taubman (1994), "Endowments and the allocation of schooling in the family and in the marriage market: the twins experiment", Journal of Political Economy 102: 1131–1174.

Berger, M.C. (1985), "The effect of cohort size on earnings growth: a reexamination of the evidence", Journal of Political Economy 93: 561–573.

Berger, M.C. (1989), "Demographic cycles, cohort size and earnings", Demography 26: 311–321.

Betson, D. and J. Van der Gaag (1984), "Working married women and the distribution of income", Journal of Human Resources 19: 532–543.

Birdsall, N. (1988), "Economic approaches to population growth", in: H. Chenery and T.N. Srinivasan, eds., Handbook of development economics (North-Holland, New York) pp. 478–542.

Blackburn, M.L. and D.E. Bloom (1991), "The distribution of family income: measuring and explaining changes in the 1980s for Canada and the United States", Working paper no. 3659 (NBER, Cambridge, MA).

Boulier, B.L. (1977), "Population policy and income distribution", in: C.R. Frank and R.C. Webb, eds., Income distribution and growth in the less-developed countries (Brookings Institution, Washington, DC).

Boulier, B.L. (1982), "Income redistribution and fertility decline: a skeptical view", in: Y. Ben-Porath, ed., Income distribution and the family, Population and Development Review 8 (Supplement): 159–173.

Bound, J. and G. Johnson (1992), "Changes in the structure of wages during the 1980's: an evaluation of alternative explanations", American Economic Review 82: 371–392.

Burtless, G. (1990), "Earnings inequality over the business and demographic cycles", in: G. Burtless, ed., A future of lousy jobs? (Brookings Institution, Washington, DC) pp. 77–122.

Cancian, M., S. Danziger and P. Gottschalk (1992), "Working wives and the distribution of family income", in: S. Danziger and P. Gottschalk, eds., Uneven tides: rising inequality in America (Russell Sage Foundation, New York).

Chu, C.Y.C. (1987), "The dynamics of population growth, differential fertility and inequality: note", American Economic Review 77: 1054–1056.

Chu, C.Y.C. (1990), "An existence theorem on the stationary state of income distribution and population growth", International Economic Review 31: 171–185.

Chu, C.Y.C. and H. Koo (1990), "Intergenerational income-group mobility and differential fertility", American Economic Review 80: 1125–1138.

Coale, A.J. (1972), The growth and structure of human populations: a mathematical investigation (Princeton University Press, Princeton, NJ).

Danziger, S. (1980), "Do working wives increase family income inequality?", Journal of Human Resources 15: 444–451.

Danziger, S. and M.K. Taussig (1979), "The income unit and the anatomy of income distribution", Review of Income and Wealth 25: 365–375.

Danziger, S., R. Haveman and E. Smolensky (1977), "The measurement and trend of inequality: comment", American Economic Review 67: 505–512.

Datta, G. and M.K. Meerman (1980), "Household income or household income per capita in welfare comparisons", Review of Income and Wealth 26: 401–417.

Dietzenbacher, E. (1989), "The dynamics of population growth, differential fertility and inequality: comment", American Economic Review 79: 584–587.

Dooley, M. and P. Gottschalk (1982), "Does a younger male labor force mean greater earnings inequality?", Monthly Labor Review 105(11): 42–45.

Dooley, M.D. and P. Gottschalk (1984), "Earnings inequality among males in the United States: trends and the effect of labor force growth", Journal of Political Economy 92: 59–89.

Easterlin, R.A. (1978), "What will 1984 be like? Socioeconomic implications of recent twists in age structure", Demography 15: 397–432.

Easterlin, R.A., M.L. Wachter and S.M. Wachter (1978), "Demographic influences on economic stability: the United States experience", Population and Development Review 4: 1–23.

Eckstein, Z. and K. Wolpin (1985), "Endogenous fertility in an overlapping generations growth model", Journal of Public Economics 27: 93–106.

Fei, C.H., G. Ranis and S.W.Y. Kuo (1979), Growth with equity: the Taiwan case (Oxford University Press, New York).

Fields, G.S. (1979), "A welfare economic approach to growth and distribution in the dual economy", Quarterly Journal of Economics 93: 325–353.

Fields, G.S. (1980), Poverty, inequality and development (Cambridge University Press, Cambridge).

Fields, G.S. (1989), "Changes in poverty and inequality in developing countries", World Bank Research Observer 4: 167–185.

Fields, G.S. (1991), "Growth and income distribution", in: G. Psacharopoulos, ed., Essays on poverty, equity and growth (Pergamon Press, New York) pp. 1–52.

Formby, J.P., T.G. Seaks and W.J. Smith (1989), "On the measurement and trend of inequality: a reconsideration", American Economic Review 79: 256–264.

Freeman, R.B. (1979), "The effect of demographic factors on age–earnings profiles", Journal of Human Resources 14: 289–318.

Gronau, R. (1982), "Inequality of family income: do wives' earnings matter?", Population and Development Review 8 (Supplement): 119–136.

Johnson, W.R. (1977), "The measurement and trend of inequality: comment", American Economic Review 67: 502–504.

Kakwani, N.C. (1980), Income inequality and poverty: methods of estimation and policy applications (Oxford University Press, Oxford).

Karoly, L.A. (1992), "Changes in the distribution of individual earnings in the US: 1967–1986", Review of Economics and Statistics LXXIV: 107–115.

Katz, L.F. and K.M. Murphy (1992), "Changes in relative wages, 1963–1987: supply and demand factors", Quarterly Journal of Economics 107: 35–78.

Keyfitz, N. (1977), Applied mathematical demography (Wiley, New York).

Kocher, J. (1973), Rural development, income distribution and fertility decline (The Population Council, New York).

Kusnic, M. and J. DaVanzo (1980), Income inequality and the definition of income: the case of Malaysia (Rand Corporation, Santa Monica, CA).

Kusnic, M.W. and J. DaVanzo (1982), "Who are the poor in Malaysia? The sensitivity of poverty profiles to the definition of income", Population and Development Review 8 (Supplement): 17–34.

Kuznets, S. (1955), "Economic growth and income inequality", American Economic Review 45: 1–28.

Kuznets, S. (1976), "Demographic aspects of the size distribution of income", Economic Development and Cultural Change 25: 1–94.

Kuznets, S. (1978), "Size and age structure of family households: exploratory comparisons", Population and Development Review 4: 187–224.

Kuznets, S. (1980), "Recent population trends in less developed countries and implications for internal income inequality", in: R. Easterlin, ed., Population and economic change in developing countries, Report no. 30 (NBER, Cambridge, MA).

Kuznets, S. (1981), "Size of households and income disparities", in: J. Simon and P. Lindert, eds., Research in population economics (JAI Press, Greenwich, CT).

Lam, D. (1984), "The variance of population characteristics in stable populations, with applications to the distribution of income", Population Studies 38: 117–127.

Lam, D. (1986), "The dynamics of population growth, differential fertility and inequality", American Economic Review 76: 1103–1116.

Lam, D. (1987), "Distribution issues in the relationship between population growth and economic development", in: D.G. Johnson and R.D. Lee, eds., Population growth and economic development (University of Wisconsin Press, Madison, WI) pp. 589–627.

Lam, D. (1988a), "Lorenz curves, inequality and social welfare under changing population composition", Journal of Policy Modeling 10: 141–162.

Lam, D. (1988b), "Marriage markets and assortative mating with household public goods: theoretical results and empirical implications", Journal of Human Resources 23: 462–487.

Lam, D. (1989), "Population growth, age structure and age-specific productivity", Journal of Population Economics 2: 189–210.

Lam, D. (1993), Comment on Preston and Campbell, "Differential fertility and the distribution of traits: the case of IQ", American Journal of Sociology 98: 1033–1039.

Lam, D. and D. Levison (1991), "Declining inequality in schooling in Brazil and its effects on inequality in earnings", Journal of Development Economics 37: 199–225.

Lam, D. and D. Levison (1992), "Age, experience and schooling: decomposing earnings inequality in the United States and Brazil", Sociological Inquiry 62: 218–245.

Land, K. and A. Rogers (1982), Multidimensional mathematical demography (Academic Press, New York).

Layard, R. and A. Zabalza (1979), "Family income distribution: explanation and policy evaluation", Journal of Political Economy 87(5), part 2: S133–S162.

Lee, R.D. (1973), "Population in preindustrial England: an econometric analysis", Quarterly Journal of Economics 87: 581–607.

Lee, R.D. (1978), "Models of preindustrial population dynamics with application to England", in: C. Tilly, ed., Historical studies of changing fertility (Princeton University Press, Princeton, NJ).

Lee, R.D. (1980), "A historical perspective on economic aspects of the population explosion: the case of preindustrial England", in: R.A. Easterlin, ed., Population and economic change in developing countries, Report no. 30 (NBER, Chicago, IL).

Lee, R.D. (1987), "Population dynamics of humans and other animals", Demography 24: 443–465.

Lehrer, E. and M Nerlove (1981), "The impact of female work on family income distribution in the U.S.: black–white differentials", Review of Income and Wealth 27: 423–431.

Lehrer, E. and M. Nerlove (1984), "A life-cycle analysis of family income distribution", Economic Inquiry XXII: 360–374.

Levy, F. and R.J. Murnane (1992), "U.S. earnings and earnings inequality: a review of recent trends and proposed explanations", Journal of Economic Literature 30: 1333–1381.

Lindert, P. (1978), Fertility and scarcity in America (Princeton University Press, Princeton, NJ).

Lindert, P.H. (1985), "English population, wages and prices: 1541–1913", Journal of Interdisciplinary History 15: 609–634.

Michael, R.T. (1985), "Consequences of the rise in female labor force participation rates: questions and probes", Journal of Labor Economics 3(1), part 2: S117–S146.

Mincer, J. (1962), "Labor force participation of married women: a study of labor supply", in: National Bureau of Economic Research, Aspects of labor economics (Princeton University Press, Princeton, NJ) pp. 63–105.

Mincer, J. (1974), Schooling, experience and earnings (National Bureau of Economic Research, Columbia University Press, New York).

Mode, C.J. (1971), Multitype branching processes: theory and application (Elsevier, New York).

Mookherjee, D. and A. Shorrocks (1982), "A decomposition analysis of the trend in UK income inequality", The Economic Journal 92: 886–902.

Morawetz, D. (1976), "Elasticities of substitution in industry: what do we learn from econometric estimates?", World Development 4(1): 11–15.

Morley, S.A. (1981), "The effect of changes in the population on several measures of income distribution", American Economic Review 71: 285–294.

Morley, S.A. (1988), "Relative wages, labor force structure and the distribution of income in the short and long run", Economic Development and Cultural Change 36: 651–668.

Murphy, K.M. and F. Welch (1992), "The structure of wages", Quarterly Journal of Economics CVII: 285–326.

Murphy, K., M. Plant and F. Welch (1988), "Cohort size and earnings in the USA", in: R.D. Lee, W.B.

Arthur and G. Rodgers, eds., Economics of changing age distributions in developed countries (Clarendon Press, Oxford) pp. 39–58.

Nelson, E.R. (1977), "The measurement and trend of inequality: comment", American Economic Review 67: 497–501.

Ogawa, N. (1978), "Fertility control and income distribution in developing countries with national family planning programmes", Pakistan Development Review 17: 431–450.

Paglin, M. (1975), "The measurement and trend of inequality: a basic revision", American Economic Review 65: 598–609.

Parlett, B. (1970), "Ergodic properties of populations, I: the one sex model", Theoretical Population Biology 1: 191–207.

Pestieau, P. (1989), "The demographics of inequality", Journal of Population Economics 2: 3–24.

Potter, J. (1979), "Demographic factors and income distribution in Latin America", in: International Union for the Scientific Study of Population, Economic and demographic change: issues for the 1980s, Vol. 1 (IUSSP, Liege) pp. 321–336.

Preston, S.H. (1974), "Differential fertility, unwanted fertility and racial trends in occupational achievement", American Sociological Review 39: 492–506.

Preston, S.H. and C. Campbell (1993), "Differential fertility and the distribution of traits: the case of IQ", American Journal of Sociology 98.

Ram, R. (1984), "Population increase, economic growth, educational inequality and income distribution", Journal of Development Economics 14: 419–428.

Raut, L.K. (1991), "Capital accumulation, income distribution and endogenous fertility in an overlapping generations general equilibrium model", Journal of Development Economics 34: 123–150.

Repetto, R. (1978), "The interaction of fertility and the size distribution of income", Journal of Development Studies 14(3): 22–39.

Repetto, R. (1979), Economic equality and fertility in developing countries (Johns Hopkins University Press, Baltimore, MD).

Rich, W. (1973), Smaller families through social and economic progress (Overseas Development Council, Washington, DC).

Robinson, S. (1976), "A note on the U hypothesis relating income inequality and economic development", American Economic Review 66: 437–440.

Rodgers, G.B. (1978), "Demographic determinants of the distribution of income", World Development 6: 305–318.

Rodgers, G. (1983), "Population growth, inequality and poverty", International Labour Review 122: 443–460.

Schirm, A.L. (1988), "Marital sorting, wives' labor supply and family income inequality", Working paper (Population Studies Center, University of Michigan, Ann Arbor, MI).

Schultz, T.P. (1982), "Family composition and income inequality", Population and Development Review 8 (Supplement): 137–150.

Sirageldin, I.A. (1975), "The demographic aspects of income distribution", in: W.C. Robinson, ed., Population and development planning (The Population Council, New York).

Smith, J.P. (1979), "The distribution of family earnings", Journal of Political Economy 87(5), part 2: S163–S192.

Solow, R.M. (1956), "A contribution to the theory of economic growth", Quarterly Journal of Economics 70: 65–94.

Stapleton, D.C. (1987), "Implicit marriage markets" (Department of Economics, Dartmouth College, Hanover, NH).

Stapleton, D.C. and D.J. Young (1984), "The effects of demographic change on the distribution of wages, 1967–1990", Journal of Human Resources 19: 175–201.

Stark, O. and S. Yitzhaki (1982), "Migration, growth, distribution and welfare", Economics Letters 10: 243–249.

Swamy, S. (1967), "Structural changes and the distribution of income by size: the case of India", Review of Income and Wealth 13: 155–174.

Visaria, P. (1979), "Demographic factors and the distribution of income: some issues", in: Economic and Demographic Change: issues for the 1980s, Proceedings of the International Population Conference, 1978, Vol. 3 (IUSSP, Liege).

Welch, F. (1979), "Effects of cohort size on earnings: the baby boom babies' financial bust", Journal of Political Economy 87(5): S65–S97.

Williamson, J.G. and P.H. Lindert (1980), American inequality: a macroeconomic history (Academic Press, New York).

Winegarden, C.R. (1978), "A simultaneous-equations model of population growth and income distribution", Applied Economics 10: 319–330.

Winegarden, C.R (1980), "Socioeconomic equity and fertility in developing countries: a block-recursive model", De Economist 128: 530–557.

World Bank (1974), Population policies and economic development (Johns Hopkins University Press, Baltimore, MD).

World Bank (1991), World development report (Oxford University Press, New York).

Wrigley, E.A. (1988), "The limits to growth: Malthus and the classical economists", in: M.S. Teitelbaum and J.M. Winter, eds., Population and resources in western intellectual traditions, Population and Development Review 14 (Supplement): 30–48.

PART VI

AGGREGATE POPULATION CHANGE AND ECONOMIC GROWTH

Chapter 19

POPULATION DYNAMICS: EQUILIBRIUM, DISEQUILIBRIUM, AND CONSEQUENCES OF FLUCTUATIONS

RONALD D. LEE*

University of California, Berkeley

Contents

1. Introduction	1064
2. Population equilibrium	1064
2.1. Classical population theory	1064
2.2. Evidence for classical theory	1066
2.3. The behavior of the classical population system	1075
2.4. Modern theories of population equilibrium	1076
3. Population response to shocks	1078
3.1. Short-run shocks	1079
3.2. Long-run shocks	1086
4. The internal dynamics of population renewal: endogenous baby booms?	1089
4.1. Generational cycles	1090
4.2. Malthusian cycles	1092
5. Economic response to population fluctuations	1097
5.1. Consequences of fluctuating rates of population growth	1099
5.2. Compositional effects arising from age distribution fluctuations	1100
5.3. Behavioral effects of fluctuating age distributions	1105
6. Conclusions	1107
References	1109

*Helpful comments from Assaf Razin and an anonymous reviewer are gratefully acknowledged. Research for this paper was partially supported by a grant from NICHD, RO1-HD24982.

Handbook of Population and Family Economics. Edited by M.R. Rosenzweig and O. Stark
© *Elsevier Science B.V., 1997*

1. Introduction

This essay first discusses the possibility of long-run economic–demographic equilibrium, as viewed by Classical economists and historians, on the one hand, and by contemporary economists on the other. It examines empirical evidence bearing on the key relationships hypothesized to establish equilibrium – the preventive check, the positive check, and a depressing effect of population growth on real wages reflecting diminishing returns to labor. It then considers the nature of shocks to the equilibrium system, both short-run (such as weather, harvest, and epidemics) and longer run (such as changed disease environment, technological change, and trade), including historical examples from Europe. Next, it considers the possibility of Malthusian oscillations: in strongly equilibrating populations, might the lag between birth and labor force entry lead to long swings, limit cycles, or to chaotic population dynamics? Finally, it considers the economic consequences of demographic fluctuations for savings, consumer demand, labor supply and related variables.

2. Population equilibrium

2.1. Classical population theory

According to Classical economists, and early Neo-Classical economists as well, population size was determined by the demand for labor. In the long run, the supply of labor (and therefore population size) was believed to be infinitely elastic with respect to the real wage in the neighborhood of a socially defined "natural price of labor". This was the Law of Population which constantly operated behind the seemingly random variations in fertility and mortality induced by epidemic, famine, and war. Thus Malthus wrote:

> The actual progress of the population is, with very few exceptions, determined by the relative difficulty of procuring the means of subsistence, and not by the relative natural powers of increase...except in extreme cases, the actual progress of population is little affected by unhealthiness or healthiness. (1798/1970: p. 262.)

In this view, we conceive of population as expanding or contracting in long-run equilibrium with the demand for labor. If we seek to understand population dynamics, we must study fertility and mortality not independently, but as elements of a system which includes the size of the population in relation to the means of subsistence (demand for labor). In this system, we look for feedback between population levels and population change.

This Classical approach is quite remote from modern economic demographic theory of population change, which focuses on detailed analyses of each vital rate in isolation from population size. However, it is the way many anthropologists view prehistoric population dynamics, the way many social historians view historical population change, and the way biologists view animal populations. It lies behind the prescriptions of ecologists and environmentalists for contemporary population limitation. In this section, the Classical theory is discussed in more detail.

The relation of population size or labor supply to the demand for labor is well summarized by the marginal product of labor, or by the real wage. For this reason, interest has focused on the relation of the vital rates to the real wage or to income. Classical economists stressed what we would now call income effects on fertility, while largely neglecting the price effects which have dominated recent theory and analysis.[1] The effect of income on fertility, referred to by Malthus as the "preventive check", was believed to operate mainly through marriage. In Western Europe, with which these authors were largely concerned, it was customary that couples not marry until they had the wherewithal to establish an independent household and maintain a family. This required a period of training, saving, or simply waiting to inherit, and consequently marriage was late – a typical average age at first marriage for women was 25 years, and for men a few years more. When wages were high (or when mortality opened opportunities), the period could be shorter, and marriage earlier. Since there was apparently little conscious regulation of fertility within marriage until the later 19th century (Knodel, 1983), earlier marriage meant higher fertility and conversely. In principle, an income effect originating in marriage behavior could be reinforced by a corresponding effect within marriage – whether involuntary, and arising from stress, nutrition, or migration-induced separation of spouses, or voluntary, arising from prudence. Similarly, income was held to affect population growth through its effect on mortality, particularly infant and child mortality, an effect known as the "positive check". Evidence for these views will be considered later.

If higher incomes were thought to encourage population growth, population growth was in turn thought to depress incomes due to diminishing returns to labor in agriculture, about which more will be said below. Combining a positive relation of growth rates to income levels, and a negative relation of income to population size, evidently leads to an equilibrating system. The equilibrium income level in this system was viewed as a socially defined parameter, variously referred to as "subsistence", "conventional standard of living" or "standard of wretchedness", or "natural price of labor", below which laborers would not reproduce and above which they would. Thus Ricardo wrote:

> Labour, like all other things which are purchased and sold, and which may be increased or diminished in quantity, has its natural and its market price. The natural price of labour is that price which is necessary to enable the labourers, one with

---

[1] Of course, the main price effects in modern theory arise from variations in the wage, which influences the price of time; the difference is not so much in the choice of relevant variables as in their interpretation.

another, to subsist and perpetuate their race, without either increase or diminution. (1817/1971: p. 115.)

In a similar vein, Marshall wrote:

If conditions remain stationary sufficiently long, both machines and human beings would earn an amount corresponding to cost of production (including 'conventional necessaries'). (1920: p. 577.)

Similar ideas are expressed at least through the late 1950s (Taussig, 1939: p. 277; Harberger, 1958: pp. 109–110).

In such a system, population will grow until the wage is forced down to the socially defined natural wage. The equilibrium population size will depend both on the demand for labor, which determines how large a labor force yields a real wage equal to the natural wage, and in part by the natural wage itself, which could be high or low. Variations in the demand for labor would, in the long run, induce proportional variations in the size of the population, while the equilibrium wage would remain unchanged; this was the "Iron Law of Wages". Differences across nations in long-run living standards must be due to differences in the socially defined natural wage. Thus Malthus argued that the Chinese were poor because they were prepared to marry and reproduce even under miserable conditions.

Fig. 1 depicts a simple system of this sort. In the upper panel, fertility, b, and mortality, d, are both shown as functions of the real wage. Their point of intersection locates the real wage at which the population would just replace itself, "without either increase or diminution". The lower panel depicts the demand for labor schedule, and the population equilibrium occurs at the level corresponding to the equilibrium wage. It can readily be seen that the system has a stable equilibrium; that a shift in the demand for labor schedule induces a proportional shift in the equilibrium population, that an upward shift in the fertility curve leads to lower wages and a larger population or higher density (Malthus' interpretation of the Chinese case), while an upward shift in the mortality schedule would lead to higher wages and a smaller or less dense population. If the demand for labor were to rise at a constant rate, then a steady-state equilibrium would occur at the wage corresponding to the gap between b and d equal to that growth rate, rather than at the intersection of the curves.

2.2. Evidence for Classical theory

2.2.1. Economic consequences of population growth in Europe

In modern times, we are quite accustomed to the simultaneous occurrence of moderate or even rapid population growth and growth in per capita incomes at the national level; indeed this was the defining characteristic of modern economic growth accord-

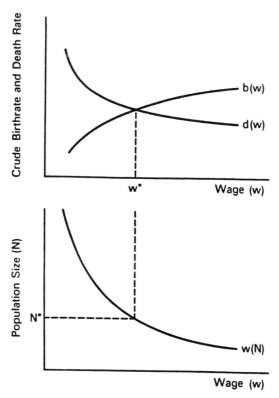

Fig. 1. Economic–demographic equilibrium in a simplified classical system.

ing to Kuznets (1966).[2] In Europe, this has been the case not only in the twentieth century, but in the nineteenth century as well (Bairoch, 1976). When we move back before 1800, however, the situation may have been quite different. It is generally believed that in preindustrial Europe, changes in population size or growth rate exerted a profound influence on many aspects of the economy (see Postan (1966) for the medieval period, and Phelps-Brown and Hopkins (1957), or Wrigley and Schofield (1981) for the later period, for example). This view was put strongly by Habakkuk:

> For those who care for the overmastering pattern, the elements are evidently there for a heroically simplified version of English history before the nineteenth century in which the long-term movements in prices, in income distribution, in investment, in real wages, and in migration are dominated by changes in the growth of population. (Habakkuk, 1965: p. 148.)

---

[2] This paragraph draws on Weir (1991).

Since there was a rough synchrony of long-term changes in population growth rates and in economic variables across much of Europe, the same argument may be extended to the Continent as well (Phelps-Brown and Hopkins, 1957). Interest in the evidence that long swings in population growth caused corresponding variations in the economy transcends concern with European economic history. The European experience may also inform us about the consequences of population change more generally (World Bank, 1984: p. 57; Lee, 1980), because changes in technology, trade and capital accumulation were less dramatic in preindustrial times than they are now, so the consequences of population change may emerge more clearly there than in the modern world.

The economic story might go something like this. When the amount of land potentially available for cultivation is relatively fixed, then when population grew, the application of increased supplies of labor led to diminishing returns to labor and increased returns to land: real wages (measured in agricultural goods) would fall, and real rents would rise. Since the main input to industrial production was labor, prices of industrial goods closely followed the real wage, falling as population grew. Thus population growth shifted the terms of trade between agriculture and industry in favor of agriculture. The aggregate demand for industrial goods could have either increased or decreased with population growth, depending on demand elasticities for consumption of industrial and agricultural goods, and on elasticities of output with respect to various inputs. To the extent that urban populations were sustained by industrial production, urbanization might have been either increased or decreased by population growth (see Kelley and Williamson, 1984; Lee, 1980). Gradual improvements in technology, agricultural and industrial capital, economic organization and trade would have raised the demand for labor, permitting the economy to sustain an increasing population under constant economic conditions; it was deviations of population from this expanding path that would cause the economic consequences just described. The rate at which population could grow along this hypothetical expansion path will be referred to as the "rate of absorption".

There is a growing literature which examines the economic demographic relations in preindustrial Europe in general, and particularly in preindustrial England. Data of varying quality on population size, nominal wages, prices and rents, extending in some cases back into the thirteenth century, provide the raw material for the analysis, sometimes supplemented by information on industrial prices and urbanization; Weir (1991) gives an excellent review of much of this literature. While the data themselves pose serious problems in many instances, the emphasis here will be on econometric problems, and particularly on the relation of population size to real wages.

Fig. 2 plots the log of a European real wage series along with the log of European population with a quadratic time trend removed, for 1200 to 1830. The figure clearly suggests an inverse association: a high level of (detrended) population in the early 13th century coincides with low real wages; the sharp population decline following the Black Death in 1348 and subsequent outbreaks of plague is accompanied by an

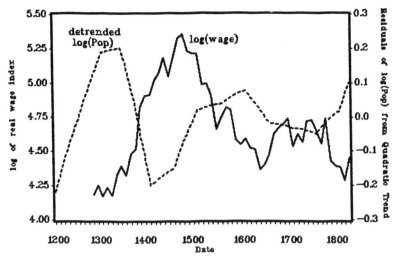

Fig. 2. Population and real wages in Europe, 1200 to 1830. Real wages and population size are based on data from England, France, Italy, Germany, Spain, Austria and Poland. Demographic data come from McEvedy and Jones (1978) modified after 1500 based on DeVries (1984), with details on the timing of turning points derived from country-specific sources. Wage data are for unskilled workers, deflated by grain prices. For English wages, the Phelps-Brown and Hopkins series as modified by Wrigley and Schofield (1981) was used, and as the longest series it served as the template in forming the European average. For some countries, multiple wage series were combined.

equally sharp increase in wages; population growth from the middle of the 15th century coincides with a long decline in real wages; population stagnation (a decline relative to quadratic trend) in the 17th century is followed eventually by an upturn in wages, after which both series are relatively stable during the 18th century.

The natural inclination is simply to regress the log of real wages, ln(W/Pr), on the log of population, ln(Pop), including a polynomial in time to allow for the rate of absorption:

$$\ln(W / Pr) = \delta + \beta \ln(Pop) + \rho t + \varepsilon,$$

where the time subscripts have been omitted. This kind of regression typically yields a highly significant negative estimate for β, consistent with the Classical hypothesis. However, there are several difficulties with this approach. First, according to Classical theory, the growth rate of population itself depended on the level of w, so population was an endogenous variable (see Lee, 1973, 1985), and estimates of β would be biased. Second, the disturbance term ε was highly autocorrelated. However, many procedures for reducing the autocorrelation, such as first- or second-differencing the time series, because they remove the longer run variance in the series and leave the shorter run variance, tend to worsen the simultaneity bias referred to in the first point above (Lee, 1993a). Third, as Lindert (1983, 1985) has pointed out, the surge of European population growth in the sixteenth century coincides closely with the surge in the general nominal price level, as does the attenuation of growth in the seventeenth century; the two series are highly positively correlated. If the price level is entered in the equation above, then the coefficient on population becomes insignificant (Lindert, 1983, 1985). Fourth, Bailey and Chambers (1993) assert that real wages and population are integrated to different degrees, and therefore cannot be analyzed in relation to one another. Fifth, some theory and some empirical work suggest that population growth drove technological progress (Boserup, 1981; Tsoulouhas, 1992), and if this were so, estimation would of course be complicated.

These problems have been approached in three ways: by widening the data base to include more European countries and deepening it to include earlier time periods (Lee, 1987; Weir, 1991), by imposing more theoretical structure on the empirical analysis (Lee, 1985, 1988), and by refining the econometric techniques (Bailey and Chambers, 1993).

Before turning to the empirical literature, it is necessary to consider the claim that the different degree of integration of wages and population precludes estimation of a relation between them. In my view, it does not. Malthusian theory itself implies that population should be integrated to a higher degree than wages. Over the long run, wages should fluctuate trendlessly around their equilibrium level, which is constant, while population should have a rising trend, tracking secular increase in the demand for labor; this is the Iron Law of Wages. What matters for wages is variation in the size of the population *relative to the demand for labor*, and these *relative* variations should themselves be statistically stationary, and integrated of the same order as wages. The key implication is that the unobserved demand for labor must be included on the right-hand side of the wage–population regression. In practice, this is accomplished in a variety of ways such as assuming that the demand for labor increases in proportion to a polynomial trend in time.

Weir (1991), in a very useful analysis, analyzes population, wage and price data for the UK and France from 1300 to 1800, and for the UK, France, Netherlands, Germany, Italy and Spain at 50-year intervals from 1500 to 1800. Analyzing the periods 1300–1500, and 1500–1800 separately, he finds a strong effect of population on real wages for both periods in France and England (Weir, 1991: p. 49), but this effect dwindles to insignificance when the price level is added to the regression. When Weir pools the data for six countries, and examines proportional changes over 50-year periods, he consistently finds a highly significant negative coefficient on population in the range −1.0 to −1.5 depending on variations in the specification, including country dummies, period dummies, and interactions of population's effect with time period. The rates of absorption were close to zero for all countries except the UK and the Netherlands, which had a rate of close to 0.3% per year: population growth at this rate would have left real wages constant. Because price inflation was a Europe-wide phenomenon, inclusion of period dummies effectively controls for it in this sample, and the population effect is not much changed. Because this analysis takes wage and population averages over six 50-year periods, the problem of autocorrelation in the year-to-year disturbances is largely eliminated. To the extent that technological progress benefited the six countries in the sample in similar ways, the inclusion of period dummies also alleviates the problem of population-induced technological change.

In response to Lindert's criticism (1983), Lee (1985) argued for imposing more theoretical structure on the analysis. Inflation might temporarily depress real wages, he suggested, but in the long run nominal wages should adjust so that the real wage equaled the marginal product of labor, independent of the level of prices. When the constraint is added that in the long run, price expectations must equal observed prices, Lee finds that while inflation does indeed depress real wages temporarily, the estimated effect of population size remains as strong as before. Using the same specification with decadal data, Lee (1987) found similar results for seven European countries, with all coefficients negative, and all but one highly significantly so. A regression for Europe as a whole yielded a highly significant elasticity of −1.6. Elsewhere, Lee (1988) also showed that even if population growth drives technological progress (endogenized with the rate of technological progress a linear function of the log of population size), this would have only a small effect on the estimated coefficient of log wages on log population, for fluctuations of up to several centuries length about underlying trends. That is, the major influence of endogenous technological progress is on the underlying trend, and not on the kinds of fluctuations manifested by the European data series. The conclusion was reached by calculating the gain and phase shift of the frequency domain transfer function linking wages and population when technological progress is endogenous.

A number of other approaches have also been employed. Lee (1973), using English data averaged over half century periods from 1250 to 1800, used TSLS with lagged values of death rates, wages and population as instruments − certainly not an ideal procedure. Stavins (1988) endogenized net migration, which certainly makes good sense in principle; however, the net migration data in the Wrigley–Schofield data set he uses are largely artifacts of the method used to reconstruct England's demographic history (see Lee, 1993b). Stavins also used the level of urbanization as a proxy for the level of technology, which leads to problems if population size itself affects urbanization as one would expect (Tsoulouhas, 1992; Lee, 1980). Tsoulouhas (1992) measured agricultural technological change by the numbers of first printings of books on agricultural techniques in each period, and urban technological change by industrial patents, with their cumulated sums measuring technological level. In his model, net migration, urbanization, and technological change are all endogenous, in addition to the usual variables. Unfortunately the analysis is marred by the omission of the technology measures in the wage equations, which in my view renders them uninterpretable. Lee and Anderson (1995) estimate a simple structural time-series model using Kalman filter techniques; technological level, an unobserved variable, is modeled as a random walk with drift, and the rate of drift is itself a random walk. Intercept terms in the fertility and mortality equations are also random walks. Identification is achieved through the explicitly modeled structure of disturbances: over shorter run fluctuations, causality runs from wage variations to the vital rates but only negligibly in the reverse direction, since the reverse causal path passes through population size, which averages out short-run variations in births and deaths. In this way, the effects of wage variations on the vital rates are estimated, which makes it possible to disentangle the effects of population size variation on wage rates from the longer run variations. This state space estimate of the wage-population elasticity is −1.0, agreeing closely with Weir's pooled cross-section time-series estimates.

Weir (1991) also presents a very useful analysis of additional predictions of the economic account given earlier, and spelled out formally in Lee (1980), pertaining to urbanization and income distribution. Lee's neoclassical model implied that population growth would lead to increased proportions of the population living in urban areas, given the very steeply diminishing returns to labor in agriculture implied by his estimated wage–population elasticity of −2.2. The more detailed neoclassical model simulated by Kelley and Williamson (1984) has a similar implication. In fact, however, Weir finds that population growth has little if any effect on proportions urban. This finding is consistent with Preston's (1979) extensive analysis of factors influencing urbanization in the contemporary world. In light of the earlier discussion, however, it appears that Lee's (1980) estimate of the elasticity was far too high, and that −1 would be closer to the truth. In this case, Lee's dual sector model would imply no effect of population growth on urbanization, consistent with Weir's finding.[3] Weir also examines the effect of population growth on the ratio of rents to real wages in the UK and France, and finds a large and highly significant elasticity of 2.5 to 3, consistent with theoretical predictions; however, when prices are added to the regressions, the coefficient on population vanishes for the UK.

Most analyses find the wage–population elasticity to be between −1 and −3, except when inclusion of prices reduces its value to near zero. These elasticities are puzzlingly large in absolute value. To a considerable degree, their size results from the practice of estimating relations between differenced data series; without differencing the estimates are generally around −1. These are still surprisingly high. If the elasticity of substitution of labor for land were 1, as assumed in a Cobb–Douglas production function, then the wage–population elasticity would be minus the share of labor in output, or perhaps about −0.5. The very large negative elasticities that are found seem to suggest a much lower elasticity of substitution, which does not seem plausible

---

[3] See Eq. A20 in Lee (1980) which sets out the relevant equation. Note that Weir's (1991) estimates of the wage–population elasticity, which lie between −1.0 and −1.5 for this sample, are also biased downwards (that is, towards larger negative values) by first-differencing of the series before estimation.

based on results found from more direct studies of agriculture in other settings. The estimated wage–population elasticity actually confounds a labor demand elasticity and a short-run labor supply elasticity; if the labor supply schedule were backward bending, then the wage–population elasticity would overestimate the absolute value of the demand for labor elasticity. It is also possible that a substantial portion of the wage was paid in kind, including the large mid-day meal, for example. If this part of the wage is constant, then the full burden of adjustment would fall on the monetized portion of the wage, which would then vary proportionately more than the total wage. In this case, the estimated wage–population elasticity would be biased upwards in absolute value.

Appraisals of the historical evidence will differ depending on the view taken of the possible role of price level and change. For those who agree that in the long run, the level of nominal wages must adjust to the level of prices, other things equal, and that the depressing effect of inflation on real wages must be transitory, the evidence is strong that long swings in population growth played a pivotal role in the preindustrial European economy.

2.2.2. Economic influences on vital rates: the preventive and positive checks

Most modern theoretical discussions of fertility treat children as a normal good, so that an increase in income is expected to raise the demand for children and hence fertility, other things equal. The difficulty is that other things do not remain equal: the demand for quality of child will also rise with income, increasing the price of children; the parents' value of time rises with increase in wages, which also raises the price of children; rising husband's income may increase the shadow price of time for women who do not work for a wage; and higher-income couples may have readier access to contraception. Consequently, in modern populations we are not surprised to observe a negative association of wages or incomes and fertility. Nonetheless, we might expect that in preindustrial economies where formal education was rare, and was not undertaken to raise productivity; where human capital was relatively unimportant as a form of wealth; and where women's labor was more compatible with child-rearing – that in such circumstances, a positive income elasticity for fertility would be more likely to be observed. And in practice, this is so. Even in contemporary Third World populations, it is not uncommon to observe positive income elasticities for fertility in the rural sector (Mueller and Short, 1983).

A very wide range of studies sheds light on the relation of fertility to income or wealth in predominantly agricultural populations. Fig. 3 summarizes the findings from over forty of these. Some examine long-run changes in fertility over time in preindustrial Europe. Some examine short-run responses of vital rates to fluctuations in grain prices or real wages (these will be discussed in detail later in this chapter). (For comparability, elasticities of fertility with respect to real wages have been converted to elasticities with respect to density using an estimated wage–population elasticity.)

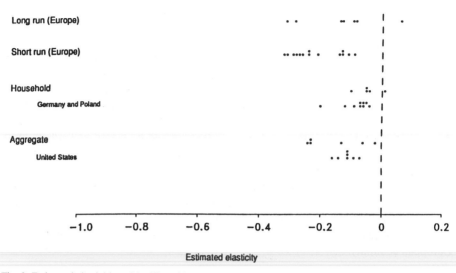

Fig. 3. Estimated elasticities of fertility with respect to population density for preindustrial Europe, North America, Asia, Africa and Latin America, based on various methods. Each line shows the distribution of the estimated elasticities for the populations and methods indicated by the line labels at the left side. The lines of points under "Household" and "Aggregate" with no geographic label are mostly from Third World populations in Asia, Africa and Latin America. Each point represents an estimated elasticity. For details on sources and methods, see Lee (1987).

Some examine the relation between fertility and size of land holding on the individual family level for farmers. Still others examine the relation between population density and fertility across areal units for agricultural populations (Stokes and Schutjer, 1985). As can be seen from Fig. 3, the estimates overwhelmingly indicate negative elasticities of fertility with respect to population size or density, or positive elasticities with respect to wealth or wages. The studies are based on contemporary data from Africa, Latin America, and Asia, and from historical Europe and historical North America; evidently the relation is very pervasive. Most elasticities fall between 0.0 and –0.3. Unfortunately, most studies do not distinguish between variations in marriage and variations in marital fertility.

The relation of mortality to economic conditions for preindustrial populations is less clear-cut. In part, this is because the frequency and severity of epidemics introduced more noise into the relationship, in part because higher incomes do not necessarily translate into improved nutrition (Behrman and Deolalikar, 1988). Nonetheless, studies of short-run fluctuations in mortality, to be reviewed later, do quite consistently show evidence for the positive check. Preston's (1980) cross-national analysis of low-income countries indicates an elasticity for life expectancy with respect to per capita income of –0.12 for both 1940 and 1970.

2.3. The behavior of the Classical population system

This review of the evidence for the elements of the Classical population theory is generally quite supportive. A strong but not overwhelming case can be made that preindustrial populations did tend to equilibrate through negative feedback as the Classical economists had suggested. This does not mean, however, that actual populations were typically to be found at or close to equilibrium. We can think of the Classical system as defining probability distributions for population size and wages, in which the tightness of the distribution about the mean or equilibrium values would depend in part on the strength of the shocks to which the system was subject, and in part on the strength of the equilibrating forces.

The most basic model has two equations, one for the log of wages as a linear function of the log of population size, the other for the population growth rate as a linear function of the log of wages. The real wage equation is as given earlier. Letting lower case letters stand for the deviations of the logs of the variables from the logs of their equilibrium values, and abstracting from the time-shift in the demand for labor, the equation becomes

$$w_t = -\beta p_t + \varepsilon_t.$$

The corresponding equation for the population growth rate, combining the positive and preventive checks and ignoring lagged effects greater than a year, is

$$p_t - p_{t-1} = \alpha w_{t-1} + v_{t-1}.$$

Lee (1993a) solves this model recursively to express population size and the wage level in year t as infinite weighted sums of the disturbances to the wage equation and the disturbances to the population growth rate equation:

$$p_t = \sum (1-\alpha\beta)^{i-1}(\alpha\varepsilon_{t-i} + v_{t-i}) \qquad \text{(sum is from 1 to infinity)},$$

$$w_t = \sum (1-\alpha\beta)^i\left[(\varepsilon_{t-i} - \varepsilon_{t-i-1}) - \beta v_{t-i-1}\right] \quad \text{(sum is from 0 to infinity)}.$$

These equations show clearly the important role of the strength of feedback, measured by $\alpha\beta$, for the behavior of the system. We can calculate that the half life of a disturbance ε or v is given by $H = -\ln(2)/\ln(1-\alpha\beta)$, which for typical empirical values of α and β of 0.01 and 1.0 would be 70 years. For example, if an epidemic or other transitory shock dropped population size to 10% below equilibrium, with other things equal it would take roughly 70 years before the population had recovered to 5% below equilibrium. Evidently, the equilibrating forces were very weak.

It is also relatively straightforward to calculate the variances and covariances of wages and population about their equilibria. If ε and ν were white noise, then given their estimated variances for preindustrial England, the standard deviation of population size about its equilibrium would be about 7%, and of real wages about their equilibrium, about 20%. The actual location of population size and real wages within their probability distributions would depend on the past history of shocks, the influence of which would decay as time passed.

The Classical system can usefully be viewed as a filter which amplifies or attenuates exogenous shocks to the demand for labor and to reproduction. In accordance with the Iron Law of Wages, long-term variance in the demand for labor (introduction of new crop varieties, for example) is completely filtered out for wages, while it is completely passed on to population size. Long-term shocks in the reproduction equation, such as a worsening of the disease environment which reduces population growth rates, are attenuated in their effects on population and wages (see Lee, 1993a); in this example, population would not decline indefinitely, but rather only until wages rose enough to induce an offsetting endogenous increase in the population growth rate. These results can be obtained formally, and in much more detail, by calculating the frequency domain transfer functions corresponding to the two equations (Lee, 1993a).

The expressions can also be used to calculate the bias of OLS estimates of β. If ε and ν have the same first-order autocorrelation ρ, for example, then the bias of OLS equals $\rho/3$ times β, or less than one-third of β.

2.4. Modern theories of population equilibrium

There are numerous models in which population growth is endogenous, and labor and capital are the only inputs to production; in such models, steady-state growth is a typical outcome. The models of Nelson (1956), Leibenstein (1954) and Solow (1956) are examples, although the first two of these also have stationary equilibria. There are also models with endogenous population growth in which a natural resource is an input to production, but is non-essential because capital is a close substitute. These models behave much like the growth models in which the only inputs are capital and labor. These models will not be discussed further since they are not in the spirit of Classical theory.

Classical population theory is distinguished by the presence of a natural resource in fixed supply which is essential for production. This feature, which was ignored by economists as irrelevant to modern growth a few decades ago, now has many advocates among biologists and to an increasing degree economists as well. Modern theories with a Classical flavor share this feature, and in addition elaborate on the basic fertility theory in one or more of several ways: fertility is modeled as an explicit choice, depending on income and on prices including the price of time; the fertility choice is influenced by altruistic feelings towards children; and overlapping generations are introduced; the decision to save and invest in human and physical capital is modeled explicitly.[4] A few examples will illustrate the contributions of the modern approach.

Locay (1987) draws insights from the New Home Economics theory of fertility (Willis, 1973) to enrich the Classical theory. He develops a theoretical and empirical analysis of the distribution of North American Indians in the pre-contact period. His central theoretical idea is that the time-cost of children varies across different production systems, for example hunting and gathering in contrast to sedentary agriculture. Because the nomadic life style of hunters and gatherers involves high costs of moving young children, the time-cost per child is high and can offset the income effect on fertility arising from a low-density, high-productivity situation. Therefore, under a hunting and gathering regime, population equilibrium may be sustained despite a high marginal product of labor. This runs counter to the simplest Malthusian prediction that population would grow under such circumstances. Under sedentary agriculture, children have a lower time-cost, so equilibrium is reached at higher density and lower marginal product of labor. Thus there may be multiple equilibria possible with different population densities and per capita incomes. Locay conducts an empirical analysis of North American Indian population distribution and density by production system; he argues that the results support his theory against naive Malthusian theory.

Other analyses examine the nature of equilibrium when fertility choice is explicitly modeled as described earlier. One question asked is whether the equilibrium per capita income corresponds to the biological subsistence level, or alternatively population increase is halted short of this point through the preventive check (fertility limitation). Pestieau (1989) analyzes a model with a fixed factor and in which parents get satisfaction from the number of children they bear, but may or may not have altruistic feelings towards children. He finds that if parents care only about the number of children but not their next-period consumption levels, then parental demand for children drives consumption to subsistence levels. However, if parents care about their children's consumption in the next period, whether or not they care about their children's utility, this need not occur. In general, the stronger the altruistic feelings towards children, the higher will be the long-run equilibrium level of per capita consumption. Eckstein et al. (1989), however, reach a different conclusion. They show that in their model, which also has a fixed essential factor and parental satisfaction from numbers of children, altruism is not necessary in order for equilibrium to occur short of subsistence.[5] According to Pestieau, the conclusion of Eckstein et al. is due to the fact that they include in their budget constraint a fixed cost per child. According to Eckstein et al., Pestieau reaches a different conclusion because he does not incorporate private ownership of the fixed factor in his analysis. Unfortunately it remains unclear under

---

[4] Models with endogenous technical progress are discussed elsewhere in this volume, and will not be covered here (see Nerlove and Raut, Chapter 20, this volume). Modern fertility theories have many other key assumptions, but the ones mentioned seem the most relevant for the behavior of interest here.

[5] They believe (1989: p. 115) that this result is inconsistent with Malthusian predictions, although it is not clear to me in what sense this is so.

what theoretical conditions the preventive check will halt population growth before the positive check is invoked.

Many people have suggested that because each child that survives to join the labor force will reduce the wages of all other workers, there is a negative externality to child bearing, and the equilibrium living standard towards which the system tends will be lower than the socially optimal one. Nerlove et al. (1987) address this deep and important issue. They show that with private ownership of land and altruism towards children, the decentralized fertility choices are both individually and socially optimal, in the sense that they maximize the utilities of the couples, including their concern for their own children's welfare. In other words, no externality arises in this case, and the path of the population towards equilibrium is Pareto optimal from the point of view of the current parental generation.[6]

Despite the theoretical appeal of many of these approaches, most theories of population equilibrium have a tough time when confronted with contemporary economic–demographic empirical relations. First, it is not clear that more rapid population growth leads to economic adversity as it apparently did in preindustrial times, although this situation may alter as populations move closer to environmental limits. Second, modern economic theories of fertility, with empirically estimated parameters, predict that economic growth should lead not to increased fertility, but rather to lower fertility (since the price effect of rising women's wages is found to dominate the income effect from general wage growth; see, for example, Butz and Ward, 1979). Therefore the basic mechanisms for bringing about equilibrium are either inoperative or behave perversely.

3. Population response to shocks

Having considered the idea that population size tends towards an equilibrium, or at least did under preindustrial conditions, we will now examine the various shocks which may displace population from its equilibrium. Since these shocks enter the system through the very mechanisms which maintain equilibrium – the responses of fertility and mortality to incomes, and the responsiveness of incomes to population size – their study should also shed light on these mechanisms themselves. Indeed, in the absence of shocks to the system, it would be difficult to estimate any relationships.

Here short-run shocks and long-run disturbances are considered separately. Under "short run" will be subsumed fluctuations in population flows – fertility, mortality and migration – which are short enough to have little effect on the stock of population, and therefore on the level of real wages or other macroeconomic variables. For these

---

[6] The Pareto optimality of fertility decisions can only be considered from the point of view of the current generation of parents, since the membership of every later generation is variable across fertility trajectories.

shorter fluctuations, we do not need to worry about economic feedback, in which changed population size or structure alters wages and therefore indirectly affects flows of births and deaths, and thereby population size. Likewise, we do not need to worry about demographic feedback, in which changed vital rates alter the future number of reproductive age adults, and thereby alter future births. Operationally, this will mean fluctuations of period up to ten years or so.[7] Long-term fluctuations, by contrast, are those long enough that population age distribution changes very slowly, so that simple population size is a useful measure. For these longer run fluctuations, the reciprocal causality of demographic and economic change is central. The middle range, in which population age distribution matters to the economic demographic dynamics, gives rise to a very different set of problems which will be considered later in this chapter.

3.1. Short-run shocks

Short-run fluctuations in demographic rates are an interesting and satisfying subject for statistical time-series analysis. Chronic underregistration of births and deaths has little effect on the results, and series of births and deaths, without denominators to form rates, suffice. Demographic time series are relatively long, sometimes hundreds of years. A typical time series contains dozens of fluctuations, and therefore there is little danger of confusing trend with fluctuation. Studies have found richly detailed patterns (to be reviewed below) which are robust and are found consistently across many different data sets (Galloway, 1988; Lee, 1990).

While there are obvious dangers in attempting to infer long-run relations of any sort from short-run responses, the appeal of short-run studies has proven difficult to resist, and they have been used to address many kinds of questions. Recent studies of Third World populations have sought to evaluate the demographic consequences of the structural adjustment policies of the International Monetary Fund and World Bank, particularly in relation to infant and child mortality (National Research Council, 1993; International Union for the Scientific Study of Population, 1992). Other studies have examined the relation of famine to mortality more generally in the Third World (Sen, 1981; Ravallion, 1987; McAlpin, 1983; Ashton et al., 1984). Studies of developed country populations have mainly sought answers to other questions: Do business cycles and unemployment cause loss of life (Brenner, 1983; Wagstaff, 1985; Stern, 1983)? Does the demand for children have a positive income elasticity (Becker, 1960)? Does the price effect of rising female wages dominate the income effect, and how are these altered by the level of female labor force participation (Butz and Ward, 1979)? By far the greatest number of studies are of historical populations, and these

---

[7] Viewing the accounting identities of population renewal as approximately linear filters for variations in the vital rates, and analyzing their squared gain by frequency, indicates that there is little problem with feedback for components of variance shorter than ten or 15 years (see Lee, 1981).

have mainly been used to shed light on the mechanisms through which long-run equilibrium may have been maintained: What was the role of famine-induced mortality in limiting populations in the past (Watkins and Menken, 1985; Malthus, 1798/1970; Lee, 1981)? What were the roles of nuptiality and marital fertility in the preventive check? How did the relative importance of the preventive and positive checks vary across countries or levels of economic development? (Weir, 1984; Galloway, 1988). Can studies of the demographic impact of weather be used to illuminate the consequences of global warming?

For studies of preindustrial populations, the main interest is in the effects of economic crises on the vital rates. There are many kinds of economic crisis. Most typically, in the economies of Third World and historical European populations, the crisis originates in a weather-induced harvest failure, in which there is simultaneously a reduction of agricultural output and an increase in agricultural prices. For landless laborers, this is an unmitigated disaster. Large landowners may be net beneficiaries, depending on the price elasticity of demand for food, and the degree of closure of the local food market. Small holders occupy an intermediate position. Nonagricultural laborers may be doubly hurt, because rural demand for their products may decline at the same time food prices rise (see Fogel, 1989). Sen (1981) and Ravallion (1987) have argued that sharp rises in food prices may sometimes occur despite normal harvests, arising from the inaccurate expectations of grain speculators, for example. Such crises should have slightly different effects. Political and military events may also cause crises, sometimes in combination with other factors, as in China's Great Leap Forward, or in Ethiopia and the Sudan in recent years. Fluctuations in terms of trade or in international demand for an export crop may likewise lead to a crisis (National Research Council, 1993).

If capital markets were perfect, then the demographic response to economic crisis would be muted, but would remain to some degree. It would remain in part because supply shocks in agricultural societies are spatially highly correlated. It would remain in part because relative prices as well as incomes vary in crises. For example, when food prices are high, people might consume less, and changed nutrition might then affect demographic outcomes (see Behrman and Deolalikar (1988) for the possibility that nutrition might improve when real incomes drop). Furthermore, involuntary unemployment and altered incentives to work would change time use and its costs; thus Butz and Ward (1979) argued that women with a labor force attachment would time their births for periods of slack demand for labor and high unemployment. The crisis may also lead to displacement of family members in search of work in distant places, which, on the one hand, may spread disease and affect their mortality risks, and on the other hand, may lead to sustained periods without coitus.

In reality, of course, capital markets and food storage technologies are very far from perfect. Laborers with patrons may be able to go into debt. More typically, those with assets in the form of land, livestock, or jewelry will sell them to raise money (Caldwell and Caldwell, 1987; and see Rosenzweig and Wolpin, 1993, for an analysis of the purchase and sale of bullocks to smooth across production shocks in India). Other household expenditures will be reduced to buy food, and there will be a shift within food expenditures to cheaper sources of energy (which will not necessarily be less nutritious; see Behrman and Deolalikar (1988)). Nutrition will likely suffer, reducing immune response; housing may be more crowded; sanitary conditions and health care may slip; and there may be greater exposure to pathogens. Because of these changes, morbidity and mortality will likely rise in time of economic crisis. However, this is less likely to happen when food takes a smaller share of the normal budget; when the diet initially includes more costly items such as meat for which cheaper substitutes can be found; and when the exposure to infectious disease is lower due to effective public health measures.

Births are likely to be voluntarily postponed in times of economic crisis because they require additional caloric intake by the mother and because they interfere with her ability to devote time to coping with the crisis – foraging, seeking work, taking on extra agricultural tasks while the husband temporarily migrates, and so on. Additionally, reduced nutrition, if severe, may reduce fecundity, although studies find this link to be tenuous (Bongaarts, 1980). Spousal separation may reduce sex; psychic stress may lead to amenorrhea or reduce coitus; and marriages may be postponed. If the crisis leads to greater morbidity, this will also lead to lower fertility for various reasons. All of these changes would tend to reduce births.

Data for studies of short-run fluctuations typically consist of time series of annual vital events or vital rates, and a food price or real wage series, or alternatively unemployment, per capita income, some index of exports or terms of trade, or some other indicator of economic activity. Naturally, studies of contemporary developed countries have more refined data available. Sometimes data on temperature or rainfall are used as well. The data are transformed in some manner to achieve stationary time series. Because the repercussions of an economic shock take a number of years to work their way through the demographic system, it is essential to allow for effects spread over time. The failure to do so is the major failing of the dozens of older studies which examined only bivariate correlations. To describe the lag pattern of response, many studies use standard distributed lag models or transfer function models. Recent studies have used newer statistical methods such as VAR, VARMA, and ARMX (Eckstein et al., 1985; Entorf and Zimmermann, 1990; Bengtsson and Brostrom, 1986; Hagnell, 1989), and state space models (Bailey and Chambers, 1993). For a detailed discussion of methods, see Lee (1993b).

Studies of preindustrial or Third World populations can be conveniently categorized by continent: Europe, Asia, Latin America and sub-Saharan Africa. Results for preindustrial Europe have been remarkably consistent across locations and time periods. This is most strikingly evident in the work of Galloway (1988, 1994), who analyzed dozens of data sets. Marital fertility is negatively related to grain prices (positively to real wages), with cumulative elasticities in the range −0.05 to −0.3. Mortality is positively related to prices (negatively to real wages), with cumulative elasticities in the range +0.05 to +0.6. Nuptiality is negatively related to prices, with cumulative elasticities in the range 0 to −0.3. Galloway (1988) has shown that cumulative elasticities, particularly for mortality, are generally higher in absolute value in poorer, more agricultural settings. A number of studies have also investigated the impact of temperature and rainfall on fertility and mortality net of price or wage effects. Unusually hot summers and unusually cold winters raise mortality and reduce births nine months later (Lee, 1981; Galloway, 1994); these are direct effects of weather on vital rates, and there surely are additional indirect effects operating through agricultural production. Such effects continue to operate in the US today.

There have also been a number of studies of Asian populations. Some of these focus on particular crises, such as famines in Bangladesh and China. In Bangladesh, in 1974–1975, rice prices rose briefly to two and half times their normal level, causing severe famine conditions. Langsten (1980) estimated a monthly distributed lag model, from 1966 to 1976. Despite the shortness of the series, his results are quite similar to those for preindustrial Europe. It is interesting that Langsten found far stronger results using prices than using agricultural production, consistent with Sen (1981) who showed that food production was slightly higher than normal during this famine. This provides encouraging support for the common practice of analyzing price data rather than quantity data.[8]

During the Great Leap Forward, China experienced a severe decline in grain production, causing a reduction by about 25% in food energy available per capita (see Ashton et al., 1984), and a number of demographers have documented the enormous loss of life (30 million excess deaths), and decline in fertility by nearly 50% (see Ashton et al., 1984). Estimated responses fit well with the general European pattern and with Bangladesh (Lee, 1990).

There have also been studies of longer series covering more typical periods for contemporary and historical Asian populations (Feeney and Hamano, 1988; Reher, 1989; Ortega-Osona, 1993). Interest in the consequences of structural adjustment policies in Latin America and sub-Saharan Africa has led to studies in these regions. The African study (National Research Council, 1993) pioneered in using individual level retrospective data from single surveys, together with a variety of macro-indicators, to estimate responses for seven countries.

The median values of the cumulative elasticities of fertility and mortality responses for these regions, with respect to a variety of economic variables, are given in Table 1. Although the distributions of values within each region can be fairly wide, particularly for mortality, the medians are in quite striking agreement despite the variety of economic indicators that have been used. Median elasticities for fertility range from +0.12 to +0.32, and for mortality from −0.15 to −0.30. Median elasticities for preindustrial

---

[8] Quantity data, indicating the size of the harvest, for example, have a number of difficulties, since they take no account of the possibilities of trade, nor of storage from earlier years by speculators, consumers, or public institutions.

Table 1
Cumulative elasticities of fertility and mortality with respect to real incomes: median values for sets of studies for four regions[a]

	Fertility	Mortality
Preindustrial Europe (14)	+0.12	−0.15
Asia (7)	+0.26	−0.19
Latin America (9)	+0.31	−0.20
Sub-Saharan Africa (7)	+0.32	−0.30

[a]The number of populations studied is given in parentheses. For Europe and Asia, most of the elasticities are for the negative of food prices. For Latin America and sub-Saharan Africa, most of the elasticities are with respect to per capita GNP. For Africa, retrospective individual demographic data are used; for other regions, aggregate rates are used.
Sources: For preindustrial Europe and Asia, see Lee (1990). For mortality in Latin America, see Palloni and Hill (1992); for fertility in Latin America, see Reher and Ortega-Osona (1992). For sub-Saharan Africa, see National Research Council (1993).

Europe are distinctly closer to zero than those for the other regions. Median fertility elasticities for Asia, Latin America and Africa are essentially equal, while for mortality, the African median elasticity is greater in absolute value than the others.

It is also interesting to examine the effect of an economic crisis on the timing of demographic events, which is obscured in the cumulative elasticities. In Galloway's (1988) analysis of European data, the similarity of the distributed lag patterns for the response of fertility is particularly striking across the fourteen populations; for mortality and nuptiality the agreement is less close.

Fig. 4 shows median values of the response elasticity by years since the economic variation for fertility (panel A) and mortality (panel B), for the four regions. Fig. 4A reveals the similarity in timing of response for fertility. In the year of a price variation there is little change in fertility, because of the nine month gestational period, plus a median waiting period of a few months before a planned conception occurs. There would also be a delay before reduced food intake led to a change in nutritional or health status. In the year after the economic variation, the brunt of the fertility reduction occurs, whether due to conscious birth limitation or bio-cultural response. In the following year (at lag 2) fewer women than usual are removed from risk of conception by pregnancy or lactational amenorrhea, so more than usual conceive leading to *more* births than usual. The next two years see a continuation of this oscillating pattern. The basic pattern is exactly what one would expect from biometric models such as those developed in Henry (1972) or Sheps and Menken (1973). Occasionally the major response occurs at lag 0, perhaps reflecting greater reliance on abortion.

Fig. 4B shows the lag patterns of response for mortality, which are evidently much less similar to one another. This dissimilarity between regions is consistent with the considerable dissimilarity which is also observed within regions. For Europe, high

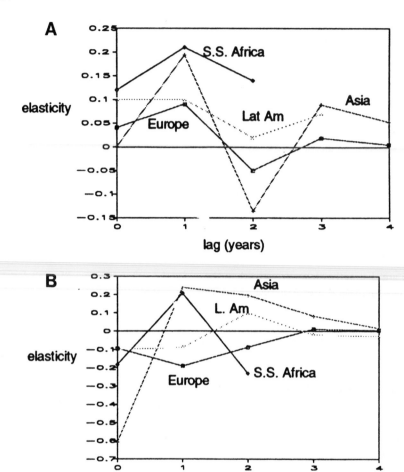

Fig. 4. The response of (A) fertility and (B) mortality to real income variation by lag for four regions: median elasticity for sets of studies. The points plotted at each lag for each region represent the median estimated elasticity for that lag for a collection of studies done on that region. The European studies are found in Galloway (1988). The sub-Saharan African studies are found in National Research Council (1993). The Asian studies are documented in Lee (1990). The Latin American studies for mortality are taken from Palloni and Hill (1992), and for fertility from Reher and Ortega-Osona (1992). Where necessary, the original estimates were converted to elasticities.

mortality continues for two years past the year in which the price variation occurs. This pattern suggests that famine weakens some people who never regain their strength, and later die from causes other than starvation. Caldwell and Caldwell (1987) report a similar phenomenon following an African famine. In the median

European pattern, there is very little rebound of mortality, yet many countries show a strong tendency for mortality to fall *below* its normal levels some time after the initial increase. The median Asian pattern is different: a strong and immediate initial response in the year of the shock, followed by several years of compensating rebound. Perhaps the really severe crises in the Asian data kill outright and leave fewer weakened survivors. The Latin American pattern is midway between the European and Asian. The African pattern is too fragile to interpret.

There is also a long tradition of analyses of the causes of short-run fluctuations in the fertility of developed nations in Europe and North America. Many older studies (Silver, 1965; Galbraith and Thomas, 1941; Kirk, 1960 for example) concluded that fertility was procyclical in Developed Countries (DCs) during the first half of the twentieth century. However, an influential study by Butz and Ward (1979) argued that as the participation of women in formal market employment increased, the opportunity cost of childbearing and rearing in periods of high demand for labor came to be more important, so that fertility became countercyclical. Methodological problems (serially correlated disturbances, inappropriate multiplicative specification) and data problems make interpretation difficult, and call the Butz–Ward empirical results into question[9] (McDonald, 1983; Macunovich, 1989).

On the side of mortality, the controversy is equally strong. One influential writer believes there are strong adverse health consequences of recessions in the US, and calculates a number of deaths associated with each notch in the unemployment rate (Brenner, 1983). But this work has been heavily criticized (Stern, 1983; Wagstaff, 1985) on methodological grounds.

In summary, the experience of European populations before the twentieth century is consistent with the experience of historical and contemporary Third World countries up to the present. The cumulative effect of a crisis on fertility is negative, and on mortality is positive. The timing of fertility's response is strikingly similar in all populations, while the timing of the response of mortality and nuptiality is more variable. Larger crises are generally followed more rapidly by a mortality increase and offsetting rebound than are smaller crises. Evidence from these studies suggests that demographic rates did respond in an equilibrating manner in historical populations and in contemporary LDCs. These studies also suggest that the structural adjustment policies of the 1980s probably did lead to higher mortality and lower fertility, to the extent that the policies were responsible for the economic reversals of this period. Nonetheless, demographic response to economic crisis is seldom a quantitatively important influence on population trends; even the massive Chinese famine of 1959–

---

[9] The original specification incorrectly used a multiplicative form for overall fertility in relation to that of women in and out of the labor force, when an additive specification was clearly called for. Furthermore, despite poor Durbin–Watson statistics, no effort was made to correct for autocorrelated disturbances. Efforts to replicate the results with a more statistically appropriate procedure have been unsuccessful. Finally, the lag patterns of response that were found are very suspicious. In any event, the Butz–Ward study was not strictly of short-run fluctuations, but sought to explain longer term fluctuations as well.

1961 represented loss of only a few years' natural increase (Caldwell and Caldwell, 1987; Watkins and Menken, 1985). For developed country populations in recent decades, there is considerable controversy about short-run variations in both fertility and mortality, and no clear and consistent conclusions can be drawn. The decreasing clarity of empirical results is probably due to the decreasing importance of agricultural production in national economies, the decreasing importance of food in household budgets, rising levels of per capita incomes, the growth of need-based government transfer programs, improved credit markets, and the greater incompatibility between modern employment and child care.

3.2. Long-run shocks

The previous section considered the origins of short-run variations in the vital rates, variations which tend to average out over the longer run, and which consequently have very little effect on the longer run movements of population size. Historical population size series from around the World over the past several thousand years, however, do exhibit irregularities in their growth rates which might be described as long fluctuations or waves of one to five centuries duration (McEvedy and Jones, 1978; Kates et al., 1985). The series do not show periodicities, but rather rough and variable waves on the underlying trends. A comparison of these fluctuations across different regions and nations suggests a striking synchronism, particularly for China and Europe. For example, the stagnation during the century before 1350, the decline in the century thereafter, the rapid growth during the sixteenth century, the stagnation of the seventeenth, and the acceleration of growth at the end of the eighteenth, all can be seen in many parts of the World.

What are we to make of these long fluctuations and their synchrony? Are they purely random in origin, are they due to epidemics, or to global climatic shifts, or are they perhaps an intrinsic feature of Malthusian population dynamics?

To begin with, it is important to realize how easily such fluctuations can arise through the cumulation of historical accidents. The logarithm of population size for some period can be expressed as the log of population size for some earlier period, plus the summation of the population growth rates for all intervening years:

$$n(t) \equiv \ln Pop(t+1) - \ln Pop(t),$$

$$\ln Pop(t) = \ln Pop(0) + \sum_{0}^{t-1} n(i).$$

If n were a random variable, with no serial correlation and uncorrelated with $\ln Pop$, then $\ln Pop$ would be a random walk process, with variance increasing with-

out limit as time passed: $\text{var}[\ln(Pop(t))] = t\,\text{var}(n)$. If population equilibrates, however, as our earlier review suggested was the case, then the growth rate will be negatively correlated with the size of the population, and the influence of each shock will slowly wear off. Let

$$n(t) = c - \gamma[\ln(Pop(t))] + \varepsilon(t),$$

where γ represents Malthusian feedback from population size to the rate of population growth, and $\varepsilon(t)$ is a shock at time t.[10] Then it follows that

$$\ln Pop(t) = \ln Pop(0) + \sum_{0}^{t-1}(1-\gamma)\varepsilon(i).$$

Estimates discussed earlier suggest that $\gamma \approx 0.01$, so that $1 - \gamma \approx 0.99$.[11] Stochastic simulations of this process over many centuries, either with or without homeostasis ($\gamma = 0.01$ or $\gamma = 0$), show that simulated population tends to move in long fluctuations not unlike those in the historical population size series, which will surprise no one who has seen realizations of random walk processes. The analysis can be refined by adding age structure, but this has little discernible effect on simulated outcomes (see Lee, 1987). It can be further refined by adding a realistic autocovariance structure to the disturbances, but this also has little effect. Could a simple summing of random disturbances account for the long swings in historical series that have so tantalized social historians?

As an explanation of the long swings, this story has two serious flaws: first, it cannot explain the global synchronism[12], and second, it cannot explain why the growth rate, $n(t)$, should itself exhibit long-run fluctuations which are uncorrelated with population size fluctuations, which it clearly does. The first difficulty is troublesome; the second is decisive. We must look elsewhere for an explanation.

One interesting possibility is that these long swings are really Malthusian oscillations, generated because there is a lag of 15 years or so between the response of fertility to labor market conditions, and entry of the new births into the labor force. This kind of hypothesis will be explored in a later section; for the present, suffice it to say that unless feedback were very much stronger than all estimates to date suggest, it is very unlikely that Malthusian oscillations would arise in preindustrial populations.

---

[10] The error structure is more complicated when shocks can enter either through the demand for labor equation or the reproduction equations.

[11] The calculation reported earlier of a half life of 70 years for a shock comes from: $0.99^{70} \approx 0.5$.

[12] Unless, of course, the disturbances were identical in all parts of the World, which would be very unlikely.

Having eliminated the possibility that these long fluctuations characteristic of historical populations are somehow generated internally by the process of reproduction and cumulation of shocks, we must now look for possible driving forces that could have imposed these fluctuations on the populations and economies of preindustrial Europe and much of the rest of the World. There appear to be two or three leading possibilities: global climatic variations, widespread exchanges of disease, and widespread diffusion of technological progress or exchange of plant varieties.

A number of scholars have considered the possibility that climatic variation may have driven population change (Utterstrom, 1965; Braudel, 1973; Parker, 1979; DeVries, 1981; Galloway, 1986). Galloway (1986: pp. 20–21), in a very interesting study, concludes by affirming the "striking synchrony in the long-term movements of temperature, agricultural yield, and population series across space (the middle latitudes) and time (before AD 1800). ...An important driving force behind long-term fluctuations in population may be long-term variations in climate and their effects on carrying capacity and vital rates". Increases in temperature could affect population growth directly, by reducing mortality or by increasing fertility; there is weak evidence from the study of short-run fluctuations to support such effects (Lee, 1981). It seems likely, however, that populations would successfully adapt to the small variations in mean temperature that the historical data suggest occurred, particularly in light of the enormous differences in temperature across areas inhabited by humans. Perhaps it is more likely that warmer temperatures indirectly affected population growth rates by raising agriculture productivity in areas in which cool weather was a limiting constraint. This was only so in certain regions, while in other parts of the world, hotter weather reduced output, and the availability of water was the limiting constraint.

For most parts of the World, historical data for fertility and mortality are unavailable before 1800 or so. For parts of Europe, we have scattered estimates of mortality going back in some cases to the fourteenth century and of marital fertility going back to the sixteenth century. These data suggest that marital fertility tended to remain quite steady from century to century, while levels of life expectancy showed more long-run variability, falling in the fourteenth century, rising in the fifteenth, stabilizing in the sixteenth, sagging somewhat in the seventeenth, and then beginning a slow secular increase towards the end of the eighteenth century. These variations do not correlate well with the level of wages, and were more likely due to independent changes in disease – in terms of the model of Fig. 1, they would represent long-term shifts in the $d(w)$ curve rather than movements along it. There are a number of possible explanations for such variations in mortality. Contacts with other populations, following voyages of exploration, for example, could have led to an exchange of diseases.[13] As time passed, selection and co-evolution reduced the impact of new diseases which would at

---

[13] Voyages of exploration could, of course, be viewed as endogenously driven by increasing population density.

first have been great (McNeill, 1976). Mutation might have led to new diseases, followed by the same process of accommodation. Climatic change may also have played a role (Helleiner, 1965).

A last possibility is that variations in the demand for labor, resulting either from invention and diffusion, or from exchanges of plant varieties following new contacts with other civilizations, induced corresponding variations in population size, as the Classical theory would predict. Such a role is sometimes assigned to the potato in Europe, which enabled far more people to be supported on a given amount of land than did grains.

It should be obvious that we have speculations but little firm knowledge on the source of long-term variations in population size and growth rate. Yet these variations appear to have had a profound effect on most aspects of economic life in preindustrial economies, so the question is an important one. Some of these hypotheses imply differing patterns of covariation across cycles. For example, if the demand for labor is the driving force, then population size should lag wages by a quarter cycle. If mortality is the driving force, then real wages should be negatively associated with population with no lag (Lee, 1985). Unfortunately, the length of series and the quality of the data have so far precluded definitive tests.

4. The internal dynamics of population renewal: endogenous baby booms?

To this point, we have viewed population only as an aggregate. Because we have largely restricted our attention either to short-run fluctuations or to long waves, the age distribution has not really mattered. However, if instead we consider demographic fluctuations of between, say, 20 and 100 years, there are interesting and distinctive dynamic possibilities arising from the interaction of the age structures of reproduction and of labor supply with the economy. Demographic fluctuations in this range can also have important effects on various aspects of the economy. These economic effects will be considered later. Here, the focus is on the origin of the fluctuations.

Fluctuations in numbers of births and deaths lead to fluctuations in the population age distribution in later periods. Such fluctuations may come about in three ways. In the first and simplest case, fluctuations are simply imposed on fertility or mortality by some external driving force, such as climate or the economy, and transmitted accordingly to the numbers of births and deaths and eventually the population age distribution. This is the case which we have just considered in the last section, for both short- and long-run fluctuations; this case is referred to as "imposed cycles". But it is also possible that the population renewal process itself creates damped waves about 30 years long in births, deaths and age distribution out of completely unstructured background disturbances. This is the second case, which is referred to here as "generational cycles". The third possibility is that "Malthusian cycles" occur, due to the lags between the response of fertility to current labor market conditions, and the time when the resulting births actually enter the labor force. In this case, labor supply may oscillate about its equilibrium growth path either in damped cycles, or possibly in self-exciting limit cycles or even chaotic variations. There are many examples of animal populations exhibiting Malthusian cycles of these kinds. For humans, the twentieth century baby booms in a number of countries, and particularly in the US, have been interpreted by Easterlin (1962, 1968, 1987) in this way.

4.1. Generational cycles

Generational cycles arise from the typically shaped age distribution of reproduction, and have nothing to do with the age structure of labor supply. They are therefore purely demographic in origin, rather than economic–demographic.

If any closed population is subject over a long period of time to unchanging age-specific fertility and mortality, then its proportional age distribution converges to a unique and unchanging shape, and thereafter every age group grows at exactly the same rate, which is also the rate of growth of the total population, and of births and deaths. This is referred to as the "stable" age distribution. A unique stable population age distribution is associated with each pair of age schedules of fertility and mortality. These points are established by the fundamental theorem of stable population theory (Coale, 1972; Keyfitz, 1977).

The age distribution of a population subject to specific vital rates is referred to as "distorted" if it differs from the stable age distribution associated with those rates. Most actual age distributions are quite distorted, resulting from past fluctuations or trends in fertility or mortality. In this case, the series of births to the population, under a regime of constant future vital rates, will tend to move in cycles about one generation long (25–33 years), which damp over time. This arises from the tendency of an above average number of reproductive age women to give birth to an above average number of girls, who in turn become an above average number of potential mothers. This pattern continues indefinitely, but the waves to which it gives rise diminish rapidly in amplitude.

More formally, let $B(t)$ be the number of births in year t, and let $\phi(a)$ be the product of the probability of surviving from birth to age a and of a surviving woman giving birth at age a. $\phi(a)$ is known as the "net maternity function", and the sum over a of $\phi(a)$ is known as the Net Reproduction Rate, or NRR. The net maternity function typically rises from zero at an age around 15 years to a peak in the twenties, and declines again to zero by age 50. From $\phi(a)$ and the stable age distribution it implies, we can calculate the mean age at child bearing in the stable population, μ, which is the common measure of generation length, and typically falls between 25 and 33 years.

The renewal process is written

$$B(t) = \sum_{15}^{49} \phi(a)B(t-a). \tag{1}$$

Such a process will settle down to a stable exponential growth path, if the characteristic roots of $\phi(a)$ lie within the unit circle. But as the B series converges to this growth path from an irregular past, it will fluctuate, and the fluctuations can be characterized by further examination of the characteristic roots of $\phi(a)$. There will generally be one real root, describing the steady-state growth rate (called the "intrinsic rate of growth"), and the others will come in pairs of complex conjugates. The pair with the largest modulus is the only one of substantive interest. It describes a damped oscillation with length roughly equal to the mean age of child bearing, μ (Coale, 1972; Keyfitz, 1977).

The scenario just described, in which a distorted age distribution is subsequently subject to unvarying age-specific fertility and mortality, is highly artificial. Actual vital rates are constantly perturbed by economic and other influences. However, the analysis can be generalized to cover the case of a population whose net maternity function is subject to constant stochastic disturbance of any autocovariance structure.

Consider a weakly homeostatic population, and define $b(t)$ to be the proportional deviation of $B(t)$ from the equilibrium number of births. In a stationary population such as one in equilibrium, the NRR must be unity. Suppose the NRR is varying stochastically about unity, and let $\varepsilon(t) = NRR(t) - 1$. Then to a linear approximation

$$b(t) = \sum \phi(a)b(t-a) + \varepsilon(t).$$

This is a stationary autoregressive process. ϕ can be viewed as a linear filter which transforms the input, ε, into the output, B (Lee, 1974). The effect of the filter can be determined by calculating its squared gain. The squared gain indicates by what factor the variance of the input is multiplied as it is passed on to the output at each frequency. Fig. 5 plots the squared gain for the US net maternity function, for which the mean age of childbearing, μ, was 27.5 years (see the line labeled $\beta = 0$). Inspection shows it amplifies variance at frequencies corresponding to wave lengths around μ, leaves variance unchanged at wave lengths shorter than this, reduces variance at wave lengths around 2μ, and increasingly amplifies variance at wave lengths longer than this. The squared gain reveals the manner in which the age structure of reproduction creates generational cycles out of white noise or other input.

According to this analysis, we would expect that birth series and population age distributions in perturbed environments would tend to exhibit fluctuations of around 25–33 years, and would rarely show fluctuations 50–70 years long. It is striking that the birth series of many preindustrial populations, at the parish level and at higher levels of aggregation, do indeed exhibit generation-length waves. Whether they are in fact generational waves, rather than imposed cycles coincidentally of this length, has not yet been established empirically. However, based on casual observation, the ampli-

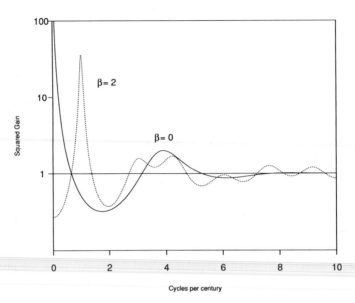

Fig. 5. Theoretical squared gain of population renewal with and without Malthusian feedback ($\beta = 2$ and $\beta = 0$). Based on average US net maternity function. For method of calculation, see text and Lee (1974).

tude of the waves is too great, and their damping is too slow, to be consistent with the generational mechanism just described.

Some economists have seen a major economic influence in such population waves, but that view now appears exaggerated. In actuality, waves generated in this way are generally quite mild. They have low amplitude, and they damp fairly rapidly following an identifiable disturbance.

4.2. Malthusian cycles

To Malthus (1798/1970) it seemed obvious that populations would perpetually oscillate irregularly about their equilibrium in long, slow swings, "as no reflecting man who considers the subject deeply can well doubt". This notion is now taken seriously as an interpretation of long swings in the fertility of many contemporary developed countries. The interest in dynamic economic–demographic models of population renewal, stressing fluctuations arising from the age structure of economic–demographic interactions, was prompted by the long "cycle" in US fertility, with a trough in the 1930s, peak in the late 1950s, and a trough in the 1970s. Easterlin (1962, 1968) suggested that these fertility fluctuations might reflect the economic conditions faced by young labor market entrants, conditions which in turn were worse for large cohorts, and better for smaller ones. This insight led him to forecast correctly the sharp decline in fertility which occurred in the 1960s, as larger cohorts aged into the labor market, and a flattening out of fertility in the late 1970s and early 1980s. He developed a detailed theory, buttressed by extensive empirical investigation, leading to a tentative prediction of self-generating economic–demographic cycles two generations long, as small birth cohorts had high fertility and gave birth to large cohorts, who in turn reared small cohorts, and so on. Such hypothetical cycles are known as "Easterlin cycles". This theory predicts an upturn in US fertility in the late 1980s, and a new baby boom in the 1990s and early 2000s (Easterlin, 1978; Lee, 1976), which have so far failed to materialize despite a slight rise in fertility in the late 1980s. Increased openness to immigration weakens this prediction, however. Easterlin (1968) argued that prior to the 1930s, immigration permitted the supply of labor to respond quickly and elastically to wage variations, forestalling a fertility response. After legal restrictions on immigration were introduced in the 1920s, greater disequilibria in the labor market developed and persisted, and the fertility response was brought into play. It is arguable that the recent growth in immigration, both legal and illegal, again forestalls the fertility response by depressing or preventing a rise in the earnings of younger workers – although whether immigration to the US has reduced earnings of natives is a subject of controversy.

A considerable empirical literature has since appeared on the subject. Aggregate level studies have provided considerable support for the Easterlin Hypothesis in the US and some other countries (Easterlin and Condran, 1976; Lee, 1976; O'Connell, 1978) although there are important exceptions (Wright, 1989), but given very little at the micro level (for example, Behrman and Taubman, 1989). One element of the theory is that the size of a birth cohort exerts a strong negative influence on its wages or unemployment rates. This idea, originating with Easterlin (1962), has received empirical support from many studies in the US, Israel, Japan, and elsewhere. That literature is reviewed elsewhere in the volume, and will not be covered here.

The account of the renewal process given earlier implicitly assumed that net maternity at time t, $\phi(a, t)$, was independent of the population age distribution at time t, or equivalently that it was independent of the preceding series of births. Easterlin's interpretation of Malthusian oscillations suggests, however, that this independence does not hold. In this case, the dynamics of renewal may be strikingly altered.

Suppose that the net maternity function depends on some set of economic variables, let us say wages for concreteness. Suppose that these in turn depend both on some set of economic variables, Z, which are independent of age distribution (such as technology and capital stock[14]), and on the current population age distribution (for example, the number of people of working age). If mortality is constant and the population closed to migration, as we here assume, then the current age distribution is

---

[14] Capital stock is more properly viewed as dependent on past age distribution fluctuations, but this turns out to make little difference to the dynamics.

completely determined by past births. We can then solve out the wage variable, by expressing it as a function of the vector of past births and Z. The renewal equation then becomes

$$B(t) = \sum \phi[\boldsymbol{B}(t), Z(t)]B(t-a),$$

where $\boldsymbol{B}(t)$ denotes the vector of past births (see Lee, 1974). This renewal process will have an exponential equilibrium growth path, $B(t) = B * \exp(nt)$, which satisfies the equation for all t. For simplicity, suppose that $Z(t)$ is such that $n = 0$, so that the equilibrium path is stationary. This also means that the equilibrium NRR = 1.

Once again, it is helpful to consider the process of proportional deviations about this equilibrium path, denoted $b(t)$. Let $\eta(a)$ be the elasticity of the NRR with respect to the size of age group a, or equivalently with respect to births a years previously, $B(t-a)$. These elasticities are derived from the expression for ϕ (see Lee, 1974). Then the renewal process for fluctuations about the equilibrium growth path of births is simply

$$b(t) = \sum [\phi(a) + \eta(a)]b(t-a) + \varepsilon(t),$$

where $\phi(a)$ is the net maternity function evaluated at equilibrium, and a stochastic disturbance, with the same interpretation as given earlier, has been added.

Evidently, the smaller the Malthusian effect of the current age distribution on fertility, $\eta(a)$, the more the population renewal process is dominated by $\phi(a)$ and therefore resembles purely demographic renewal. If $\eta(a)$ is substantial, however, it can dominate in shaping the dynamic behavior of births.

Exactly the same procedures can be used to study the dynamic behavior of birth fluctuations in this model as were used for the previous. The first step is to check the characteristic roots to assess stability. If the oscillations of the process tend to explode away from the equilibrium growth path, then a different kind of analysis, to be discussed below, is called for. If the roots indicate that oscillations are damped, then the analysis of dynamic behavior in the neighborhood of equilibrium will be informative.

We can now consider various specifications of the model which have been proposed in the literature. The first is the simplest Malthusian model, in which all age groups in the labor force are assumed to be perfect substitutes in production although differentially productive. The wage varies inversely with labor force size, and fertility at each age varies directly with the wage, and therefore inversely with the size of the potential labor force (Lee (1974); here and elsewhere, the $Z(t)$ variable expressing variables insensitive to age distribution will be ignored). In this case, $\eta(a) = -\beta k(a)$, where β is independent of age, and expresses the sensitivity of response of fertility at all ages to wages, and of wages to the potential labor force size. The $k(a)$ depend only on survival probabilities to age a, and the equilibrium labor supply of survivors to age a, and are therefore easily calculated. Depending on values of β, this model will generate cycles ranging from one generation for β near 0 (as in the purely demographic model) to a century or so for β near two. This can be seen in Fig. 5, which compares the squared gain for $\beta = 0$ to that for $\beta = 2$. Empirical estimates for the US in the twentieth century put β at around 7.5. For such high values, births explode away from equilibrium and this kind of analysis of the linearized model is inappropriate (for this reason, results for large β in Lee (1974), are incorrect; see Wachter and Lee (1989)). Wachter (1991) has shown that the simple Malthusian specification described above is incapable of generating a "cycle" like that in twentieth century US data, with a length of about 45 years.

Another specification makes the fertility of a birth cohort depend only on its own size (measured relative to a stable growth path), and be independent of all other age group sizes. This specification is closer to Easterlin's (1968) analysis of the baby boom and prediction of the baby bust in the US. The simplest form of this specification leads to

$$b(t) = (1-\alpha)\sum \phi(a)b(t-a) + \varepsilon(t),$$

where α is the elasticity of each age's fertility with respect to cohort size (in more flexible specification, these elasticities may vary by age) (Lee, 1974; Frauenthal, 1975; Frauenthal and Swick, 1983). For α less than one, there is still a generation long cycle, as in the pure demographic model. It diminishes in strength as α approaches unity, and vanishes altogether when α equals unity. For α greater than one but less than two, there is a damped two-generation cycle of 50–66 years. This happens because a large cohort size causes births per woman to drop so much that the large cohort gives birth to a number of births below the equilibrium number. When the resulting small birth cohort comes of age, it in turn has very high fertility per woman, and produces a number of births that is above equilibrium. In this way, fertility and births continue to oscillate about their equilibrium paths with a period of two generations, and potential labor force will do the same. When fertility responds even more sensitively to cohort size, with α greater than two, an explosive two-generation cycle occurs and the linearized model can no longer be used to analyze the dynamics.

Specifications reflecting other degrees of substitutability of age groups of labor could of course be analyzed. Easterlin himself typically has used a ratio of younger to older workers to drive fertility (this could be derived from a CES model with two age groups of labor as separate factors, for example). The general expression can be used to explore dynamics under a wider variety of specifications involving effects beyond those arising from the labor market. For example, the burden of supporting the elderly retired population might lead to a reduction in fertility; this would be expressed as a suitable negative $\eta(65+)$. If couples were led to desire larger families when they observed other couples' children, then $\eta(0-10)$ would be positive.

When the cyclic behavior near equilibrium is found to be explosive (characteristic roots of $(\eta(a) + \phi(a))$ outside the unit circle), then we need to consider behavior farther from equilibrium, at which point nonlinearities become important (unless, of course, the behavior is truly linear, in which case population extinction soon results). One possibility is that dynamic behavior becomes "chaotic", an endless series of non-repeating fluctuations. Such chaotic behavior would require response elasticities that are implausibly high for human populations, and perhaps for animal populations as well. It is more likely that limit cycles would occur, with amplitude and period determined not by the pattern of disturbances, but rather by the functional relations themselves. Such cycles are observed in animal populations in laboratories and occasionally in the wild; in human populations their occurrence is conjectural, with 20th Century US fertility as a possible example. Samuelson (1976) considered a particular three-age-group model leading to limit cycles, and Frauenthal and Swick (1983) studied limit cycles in the cohort model with applications to the US. However, the first general treatment using tools of modern mathematics is by Tuljapurkar (1986). Wachter (1993) has shown that in many cases, the period implied by the linearized model continues to hold for the locally explosive model when it gives rise to limit cycles.

One might reasonably wonder whether these models of Malthusian oscillations really have any application to actual human populations. Estimates of feedback strength were discussed earlier for preindustrial populations, and it was found that response elasticities were fairly low. The elasticity of the NRR with respect to population size was perhaps in the neighborhood of –0.3.[15] This is well below the level needed to generate interesting dynamics. The effect of such weak feedback on dynamics would be mainly to weaken the generational cycle. Lee (1987) compares long simulations of stochastically disturbed populations with feedback of this strength, and with no feedback at all, given identical series of stochastic shocks. The two simulated series are barely distinguishable for the first few hundred years.

Nonetheless, there are reasons to expect that the strength of feedback may have increased substantially in modern industrial populations. First, the average level of fertility is now only a third of what it was in preindustrial times. Given the same propensity to add or subtract a birth at the margin, in response to economic conditions, this decline in the mean would have meant a tripling of the response elasticity. Second, it is certainly arguable that fertility behavior has become much more subject to rational optimizing decision making. A strong case can be made that in preindustrial times, fertility within marriage was typically at "natural" levels, as determined by age at marriage, breast-feeding practices and other biological and cultural factors largely outside individual choice (Knodel, 1983). Third, the technology for controlling fertility has obviously made great gains, so that regulation has become much less costly in all respects. For these reasons, it may well be that response elasticities of fertility have increased dramatically; there is no direct evidence that this is so, however. The time

---

[15] Recall that I earlier suggested that: $n(t) = c - 0.01 \ln(Pop(t))$. The NRR is roughly equal to $\exp(\mu n(t))$. Taking μ equal to 30, we find that $(dNRR/dPop)(Pop/1) \approx -0.3$.

series of US fertility and population age distribution in the twentieth century do not offer enough variation either to derive solid estimates of response elasticities or to test for Malthusian oscillations. Nonetheless, if we fit models of the sort described above to these data we find an estimate of $\beta = 7.5$ for the labor force model, which is large enough to lead to limit cycles – but limit cycles whose period is too long to fit the observations. If we fit the cohort size model, we find $\alpha = 1$. At this magnitude, there are no interesting dynamics at all; even the generational cycle is obliterated. Again, this is not dynamically consistent with the behavior of the birth series in the US. It is interesting to note that some years ago, the US Census Bureau prepared a special supplementary population projection based on the cohort model; they also estimated $\alpha = 1$ (US Bureau of the Census, 1975).

Research on models of this sort continues. It may be that when they incorporate variations in the timing of cohort fertility as well as in the level of fertility, they will be better able to match the striking dynamics of the US, and the dynamics of a number of other developed nations such as Canada, Australia and New Zealand. For the present, these models of Malthusian oscillations, although elegant and intriguing, must be viewed as quite speculative in their application to any actual population. All versions of these models predict an upturn in US fertility in the late 1980s and following decades. In fact, US fertility did begin a steep rise from 1987–1990; however, it was interrupted by the recession, and has not resumed subsequently. If fertility rises strongly again, then interest in these models will no doubt do so as well.

It should be noted that there has also been some exploration of models in which population oscillations arise endogenously for other reasons. One striking example is the work of Usher (1989), who developed a model of the dynastic cycle, involving occupational switching among farmers, who grow food; bandits, who steal food; and rulers, who tax farmers and punish bandits. Society alternates between despotism, under which population grows, and anarchy, under which it declines. Population growth under despotism leads to diminishing returns in agriculture which impoverishes farmers, leading them to switch to banditry, and reducing the taxable surplus for rulers. Eventually population growth drives society to anarchy, but then population decline resurrects despotism, and the cycling continues. Chu and Lee (1994) developed an estimable model for this theory and estimated it using data covering 2000 years of Chinese history, finding support for Usher's theory.

5. Economic response to population fluctuations

There are interesting and important consequences of demographic fluctuations in industrial economies, whether or not these form part of an equilibrating system in the Classical sense. In this section the literature on these consequences is discussed.

The age distributions of closed populations are determined much more by past variations in fertility than in mortality, since deaths remove members at all ages, while births add members only at age 0. In preindustrial populations, fertility variations were typically milder than those in mortality, and consequently population age distributions, although jagged, were not marked by wide dents and bulges. In modern industrial populations, mortality variations are nearly nonexistent[16], while fertility time series are characterized by long and deep variations (perhaps for reasons discussed earlier) leading to highly distorted age pyramids. Similarly, Third World populations in which fertility has begun to fall have strongly distorted age distributions. Therefore the economic effects of fluctuating age distributions is a topic of considerable importance.

It is useful to think of population as a survival-weighted sum of past births, $Pop(t) = \Sigma s(a)B(t-a)$. The weights are the probabilities $s(a)$ of survival from birth to age a (here assumed fixed over time), and they act as a linear filter, transforming past births into population size. It is obvious that short fluctuations in births will be effectively filtered out in this summing process, and have very little effect on population size or growth rate.

Now consider the proportional population age distribution, given by $p(a, t) = s(a)B(t-a)/Pop(t)$. For age distributional economic impacts we will be interested in numbers of people in broad life-cycle stages such as childhood, old age, young adult and middle-aged adult, each covering about 20 years of age; these are 20-year sums over the proportions at single ages. Once again, fluctuations of less than 20 years duration will be largely filtered out, and so can be ignored for our purposes. Very long run fluctuations in births will have trend-like effects on the age distribution, and changes of this sort are considered elsewhere in this volume (see Chapter 17 on population aging, for example). So here we will be interested in fluctuations of intermediate length, between 15 and 75 years, like the US baby boom and bust. Note that the age distribution in any period is shaped by events a considerable distance in the past, and can safely be taken as a predetermined and exogenous causal influence on current economic variables. Therefore age distribution fluctuations, which can be quite dramatic, sometimes provide something like a natural experiment (Ben-Porath, 1988).

Consider the economic effect of a variation in population age distribution, for example on aggregate consumption in year t, $C(t)$. Suppose that consumption at each age depends on a vector of variables X, such as age-specific earnings or the interest rate. Total consumption can be written as the sum of these age-specific consumptions, $c(a, X(t))$, times the population at each age, $Pop(a, t)$. Suppressing time, we have

$$C = \sum_a c(a, X)Pop(a).$$

[16] Mortality trends downward, but in most cases does not fluctuate. Mortality associated with wars is an exception.

Now suppose that the population age distribution changes at age a by an amount $\delta\ dev(a)$, where δ indexes the amount of the shift, while $dev(a)$ indicates its distribution across ages. To see the effect of an age distribution perturbation of this sort, we differentiate C with respect to δ, and evaluate the derivative at $\delta = 0$. This gives

$$\left.\frac{dC}{d\delta}\right|_{\delta=0} = \sum c(a, X)\, dev(a) + \sum Pop(a) \frac{\partial c(a, X)}{\partial X} \frac{\partial X}{\partial \delta}.$$

The first term is the sum of the original age profile of consumption times the pattern of deviations in the population size at each age; this is known as the "composition effect". The second term is the sum of the initial population age distribution times the change in age-specific consumption rates due to changed population age distribution, as it affects age-specific earnings or the interest rate, for example. This is sometimes called a "rate effect".[17] The composition effect is straightforward to evaluate, and requires no theory or subtle estimation: all that is necessary is the average age-specific behavior profile, in this example, consumption by age. Demographers often estimate composition effects while ignoring behavioral effects, presumably because the calculation is so straightforward and concrete. Calculation of behavioral effects, by contrast, requires behavioral theory and corresponding econometrics. Even if correctly estimated, however, behavioral effects tell only half the story. Composition effects must be included as well to assess the total effect of population age distribution change. Economists sometimes make elaborate calculations of behavioral effects, while ignoring composition effects.[18]

An additional kind of effect arises when it is not a change in the population age distribution, but rather a change in the rate of growth of a population element, such as population size or the potential labor force, which affects economic variables, such as investment demand or wages.

It will be convenient to discuss the effects of demographic fluctuations categorized into rate of growth effects, age composition effects, and behavioral effects, following the decomposition just given.

5.1. Consequences of fluctuating rates of population growth

According to the familiar accelerator model of investment, investment demand is related not to the expected *level* of future demand for output, but rather to the expected

---

[17] To evaluate the effect of an actual age distribution change, one would multiply the sums on the right by the actual appropriate value of δ.

[18] For example, when studying the effect of a change in fertility on aggregate saving, economists may look only at the effect on the pattern of life-cycle saving, which is a rate effect, while ignoring the fact that a fertility change also changes the age distribution of adults in the population (Tobin (1967) and Mason (1987) consider both effects).

rate of change of future demand for output. A growing population leads to expectations of growing demand for output, other things equal, and therefore stimulates investment demand. This point was made by Keynes (1937), was reiterated by Hansen (1939) and has been reappraised by Neal (1978). Keynes and Hansen raised the specter of secular stagnation due to the hypothesized effect of slowing population growth on investment demand in Europe and the US, a concern that subsequent historical experience and recent scholarship reject. The theory may have greater validity when applied to fluctuations rather than secular change, however, as in the case of the Kuznets cycle.

There is an extensive literature on "long swings", also known as Kuznets cycles, with durations of 15–25 years. This literature focuses primarily on the nineteenth and early twentieth century, as patterns apparently changed markedly thereafter. One set of issues centers on the interrelations of the Atlantic economies, linked by trade, investment and migration, and including England, Sweden, Canada and the US, with Australia sometimes added (Easterlin, 1965; Kelley, 1965; Wilkinson, 1967; Thomas, 1973). Thomas proposed an intricate theory embracing many aspects of the economy of both England and the overseas countries. The central idea, however, is that a swing in the demand for labor in a country like the US would raise real wages and induce an inflow of migrants, both from the rural farm population in the US and from overseas. The migrants, finding employment, would then fuel and prolong the original boom by raising the demand for new housing and consumer durables, as well as consumption goods. The increased demand for capital goods in the US would be satisfied in part by exports from England, which would in turn be experiencing a slump in construction due to the outflow of young migrants to the US.

The basic argument, then, is that when a demographic response to high aggregate demand takes the form of migration, the demographic response will sustain the original impetus. In the 1920s, however, new legislation restricted immigration to the US, and the pool of rural population from which internal migrants to cities were drawn was greatly diminished. Thereafter, according to Easterlin (1968), the demographic response to the demand for labor began to operate through fertility, and the dynamics became quite different. For one thing, the effect on the labor supply was delayed by 15 or 20 years, and for another, new births did not have the same effect on aggregate demand as did new workers (I will later discuss the work of Mankiw and Weil (1989) which finds that population under age 20 has no effect at all on the demand for housing).

5.2. *Compositional effects arising from age distribution fluctuations*

Many theories predict, and abundant data confirm, that certain ages in the life cycle will be characterized by more or less saving, investment in education, marriage and household formation, labor force entry or retirement, housing demand, and so on. Aggregate or per capita measures of such variables are population-weighted sums of the age-specific behaviors of individuals or households, as expressed formally above. For this reason, we naturally expect such measures to be affected by variations in population age distributions. This kind of straightforward reasoning lies behind several analyses to be discussed in this section, by Fair and Dominguez (1991), Mankiw and Weil (1989), and Kelley (1972).

In the earlier formal expression of compositional effects, it was assumed that we knew the age schedule, $c(a, X_0)$, in advance. In practice, it may not be readily available. For example, where would one find the consumption demand of an 11-year-old child, $c(11)$? Or more specifically, the demand for housing services generated by an 11-year-old child? In the literature, there are two approaches to estimating the age-specific behaviors, when these cannot simply be looked up in a published table of data. One way is to regress the time series of a variable of interest, such as aggregate consumption expenditures, on measures of the population age distribution.[19] But we could not hope to identify fifty or a hundred separate effects, the $c(a)$, for single years of age, or even for 25-year age groups. One possibility is to use fewer and broader age groups – say children, working age population, and the elderly; for an example of this approach, see the later discussion of Leff (1969). Another possibility, illustrated by Fair and Dominguez (1991), is to constrain the coefficients – in the case of Fair and Dominguez to a quadratic shape which sums to zero, so that only two coefficients (β_0 and β_1 in the following equation) are used to summarize the effect of the age distribution. They estimate regressions like

$$c(t) = \gamma z(t) + \sum_{17}^{70+} \left(\beta_0 + \beta_1 a + \left(1 - \beta_0 - \beta_1 \right) a^2 \right) Pop(a,t) + \varepsilon_t,$$

where $c(t)$ is per capita consumption at time t, and $z(t)$ is a vector of all other relevant per capita influences on consumption, such as income, and $Pop(a, t)$ is the proportional age distribution.

Another way, illustrated by Mankiw and Weil (1989), is to proceed in two steps and thereby to impose more structure on the problem. In the first step, cross-sectional micro level data are used to establish the age pattern of behavior – in their case, the impact on the value of housing services consumed by a household of its members at each age. This age pattern is then used to compute a time series of weighted sums over the population age distribution for each period, which is interpreted as a shifter of the demand for housing. Suppose that net of other influences, the estimated effect of a household member of age a on the value of housing services demanded is $h(a)$. Then

---

[19] In principle, coefficients should reflect the total effect of changing age distributions, both compositional and behavioral; such regressions are usually interpreted as reflecting only the compositional effect, however.

given a series of changing population age distributions, $Pop(a, t)$, we can form an index $H(t)$ of demographic influences on the demand for housing in year t as

$$H(t) = \sum h(a)Pop(a,t).$$

$H(t)$ can then be included as a regressor in the second step regression, with either aggregate housing prices or the aggregate value of housing services consumed as the dependent variable.

In the first approach, one hopes to learn something about life-cycle behavior and also about the macroeconomic relevance of age distribution. In the second approach, the life-cycle behavior is studied separately and directly in the first step, using individual or household data, and then taken as given in the second step. One advantage of this latter approach is that it economizes on the macroeconomic time-series information by using richer micro level data to impose structure on the time-series analysis. With this approach, the single coefficient on $H(t)$ summarizes the demographic influence in the equation of ultimate interest.

The first approach has the advantage that the aggregate age distribution variations can safely be treated as exogenous. However, it is likely to encounter very serious difficulties in identifying the effects of these age distribution variations. When age distributions are changing, by suitable choice of weights one can construct a wide range of time paths for the weighted sums of the age distribution. There is no reason to believe that the estimated age weights (those implied by β_0 and β_1 in the example above) actually are picking up compositional effects rather than tracking the changing influence of important variables omitted from the vector Z. For this reason, values of β significantly different from zero do not really tell us anything about whether and how the population age distribution matters, nor need they trace changes in behavior over the life cycle, as intended in this specification. The second method, illustrated by Mankiw and Weil (1989) avoids this problem by imposing weights based on the relevant life-cycle behavior. Another advantage of the second approach is that no limits need be placed on the shapes of the estimated life-cycle profiles, whereas in the first approach they are constrained to a shape parameterized by two or three coefficients. Thus Mankiw and Weil found in the first step of their analysis that household members under age 20 have no effect on the value of housing demanded by the household. Older ages do, however, with a peak effect at 35 years, followed by a slow decline. The quadratic pattern assumed by Fair and Dominguez could not have matched this shape. A possible problem with this approach is that the variations in household age composition may not be exogenous – in part because living arrangements of some people may be based on the availability of space in the houses of relatives, and in part because fertility, marriage and divorce, which determine household composition, may reflect decisions that are taken jointly with decisions about asset accumulation and housing.

The second-stage analysis of Mankiw and Weil (1989) indicated that the demographic shift variable $H(t)$ constructed from this age profile had no effect on the total value of housing services, but that it did exert a strong effect on housing prices, with an elasticity of five. When combined with standard demographic forecasts, it predicted a strong decline in housing prices in the 1990s, as the baby boom moves out of the stage of household formation.

There are a number of age compositional effects bearing on the labor force. Unemployment rates are highly structured by age, and are of course particularly high for young members of the labor force. During the 1950s the small birth cohorts of the 1930s were joining the labor force, which therefore had relatively few young members, and consequently, for purely mechanical reasons, had a somewhat lower average unemployment rate than it would have otherwise had. During the 1970s, when the baby boom generations were entering the labor force, the opposite occurred, making average unemployment rates somewhat higher than they would have been. Easterlin et al. (1978) argued that this purely compositional effect interacted with fiscal policy to cause more rapid inflation in the 1970s. They argued that the government aimed for a target unemployment rate that it believed was consistent with non-accelerating inflation (NAI). If changing population age composition raises the NAI unemployment rate as in the 1970s, while the government, not realizing this, adopts fiscal policies designed to reduce unemployment to the target level, then inflation results.

Productivity of workers also varies with their ages, peaking in the late 1940s if cross-sectional wage data are a reliable guide. Periods, such as the 1970s, that have unusually high proportions of young workers will have lower average productivity, other things equal. Likewise, periods in which the proportion of young workers is increasing will also experience slower growth in average productivity. As with unemployment, the simple procedure of standardizing the measures on age distribution would make them more informative.

There may also be important age compositional effects on aggregate saving rates. Life-cycle saving theory suggests that workers save for retirement, and dissave when elderly. A common sense view, and some empirical evidence, also suggests that the presence of children in a household increases consumption pressures and consequently reduces its saving rate. From these ideas it follows that greater proportions of either children or elderly in a population should depress its savings rate, while greater proportions of those in the working ages should raise aggregate savings. In an influential article, Leff (1969) regressed aggregate savings rates on youth and elderly dependency ratios as well as on economic variables in an international cross section. His results appeared to confirm the hypothesized effects of age distribution on savings rates: for both the Third World and Developed Country subsamples, he found significant negative effects of both the youth dependency ratio and the elderly dependency ratio; for Developed Countries, the effects of a marginal child or marginal elder were approximately equal. However, Leff's analysis has been widely criticized (see Mason (1987) for a review of the controversy). First, the specification of the empirical model has been questioned; for example, the log of the growth rate of per capita income, which is not always defined, was a right-hand side variable. Second, some have argued that household saving, rather than total saving (which includes government and business saving), should be analyzed. Third, questions of simultaneity have been raised. A reestimation on data for the 1970s (Ram, 1982) does not support the original study. For a more tightly specified study with an empirical specification derived explicitly from the life-cycle savings model, see Mason (1987).

Kelley (1972: pp. 23–24) applied Leff's estimated weights to the changing age distribution of the US from 1870 to 1970, and found in his preferred calculation that age distribution changes would have tended to raise savings rates steadily from 1870 to 1940, but that thereafter they would reduce savings strongly and abruptly. He suggests that demographic aging may tend to reduce saving rates in the next century. This analysis is entirely compositional; the next section will consider behavioral changes as well.

Some authors have used similar methods to study the effects of changing population age distribution on the composition of consumption. Espenshade (1978), for example, analyzes variations in the composition of consumption according to the age composition of the household, using household level data. Then he applies the resulting age profiles to the actual and projected population age distribution changes in the US. He concludes that changing age distribution will have only a very minor effect on the kinds of goods and services consumed, across ten categories. The strategy employed in this analysis is quite similar to that of Mankiw and Weil (1989) as described earlier.

Age distribution changes pose vexing problems for pay-as-you-go pension systems. In a defined benefit system like that in the US, large generations will have lower pay roll taxes in their working years, because they can spread the pension costs of the retired population across greater numbers of workers. When they retire themselves, they will nonetheless receive an undiminished benefit. Thus larger generations will earn a higher implicit rate of return, and smaller generations a lower one. The situation is reversed in a defined contribution plan: a large generation pays at the same rate as a small one, but on retirement it has to share a fixed revenue among more retirees, and therefore receives a lower rate of return. Keyfitz (1988: p. 96) has calculated the implicit rate of return that different past and future birth cohorts in US will earn, based purely on demographic factors, and ignoring such economic influences as the rate of growth of productivity, changing labor force participation rates, and inflation. He finds that the late baby boom birth cohort of 1960–1965 would earn a rate of return of 1.05% per year; the baby bust cohort of 1980–1985, only 0.49%; and the projected birth cohorts of 2000–2005, 2020–2025, and 2040–2045, only –0.12, –0.22, and –0.21%.[20] This is a complicated kind of compositional analysis.

---

[20] Assuming that fertility continues in the future at its level for 1979.

5.3. Behavioral effects of fluctuating age distributions

The naive sort of compositional analysis just discussed is sometimes quite useful. Often, however, such analyses make demographic influences appear to be unrealistically powerful ex ante, when ex post their influence may turn out to have been quite minor. This can happen simply because other forces, not clearly related to demographic change, swamp the demographic influences. In this case it is necessary to broaden the analysis. However, it can also happen because the economic system and individual behavior adjust to the new demographic situation, perhaps in response to price changes, in such a way as to alter the age-specific rates which were assumed constant in the naive calculation. In this case we need to deepen the analysis of economic–demographic interactions. This section discusses this latter possibility in reference to Easterlin's (1968, 1978, 1987) work on the US baby boom and baby bust, and Tobin's (1967) analysis of demographic influences on savings and capital formation in the US.

If we were to apply a naive compositional approach to predict the number of births in the US each year since World War II, we would make very large and systematic errors. We would predict a trough in births when the small cohorts born in the depression entered reproductive ages (1950–1965), whereas in fact the baby boom occurred; and we would predict a peak in births when the large cohorts comprising the baby boom entered peak reproductive ages (1970–1990), whereas in fact the baby bust occurred. Easterlin's (1962, 1968, 1978, 1987) theory explains this apparent anomaly by suggesting that unusually small birth cohorts typically experience unusually high wages, low unemployment, and rapid promotion during their early years in the labor force (and conversely for large birth cohorts). This happens to a greater extent for young men than young women, because, Easterlin (1978) argues, younger male workers and older male workers are imperfect substitutes in production, while younger and older women are closer substitutes. In response to this favorable experience, members of these cohorts choose to marry at younger ages, to have higher fertility, and to have the wife work less in the market (a well-established pattern for wives with husbands earning higher incomes). Since younger women are supplying less labor to the market, while the demand for female labor continues to rise on trend, older women (who are close substitutes for younger women) are drawn into the labor market at accelerated rates. When a large generation comes of age, all these patterns are reversed: marriage is delayed, fertility is reduced, while young women's labor supply rises more rapidly and older women's less rapidly. If the response of fertility to birth cohort size is sufficiently strong, then the number of births can move inversely to the number of young women, as in fact has happened in the twentieth century US. Formal models containing such possibilities were discussed in an earlier section. Easterlin's comprehensive theory is consistent with many patterns and changes over the post World War II period, and Easterlin (1962, 1968) used his theory to predict successfully the subsequent delay of marriage, the baby bust, and the economic misfortunes of the baby boom generation. However, his use of informal statistical methods, and the central role accorded relative income effects in his theory to explain fertility, while largely ignoring the effect of female wage variations on the price of time, has led some economists to view the theory with skepticism. Empirical evidence was discussed earlier.

Easterlin suggests that cohort size has additional effects beyond those included in the core theory outlined above. For example, a large cohort will receive less investment in the human capital of each member, due both to dilution of parental resources including time inputs and to pressure on public educational resources. Symptoms include lower scores on the SAT (Standard Aptitude Test used for College admissions) for the baby boom generation (Easterlin, 1978, 1987). A larger cohort will also experience more psychological stress due to its economic difficulties, leading to higher suicide rates.

Tobin (1967) developed a rich analysis of the effects of changing demographic age composition on aggregate savings and capital accumulation, by refining the demographic aspect of the standard life-cycle saving theory. Unlike Easterlin, he took the changes in fertility and age distribution as exogenous. In his model, couples seek to maintain a steady level of consumption per equivalent adult consumer (EAC) over the life cycle. Variations in fertility (or survival) alter the numbers of family members present in the household at each age of the parents. Higher fertility does not mechanically reduce household saving due to "consumption pressure", as in the compositional analyses discussed above. Instead it causes a postponement of life-cycle saving to a later age of the parents, and because it reduces their individual levels of life-cycle consumption (since household resources must be shared more widely), it also reduces somewhat their need to save for old age. In other words, in Tobin's analysis, the age profile of saving and dissaving over the life cycle is itself endogenous, and varies in theoretically derived ways when fertility or survival varies. Then, in an additional step, the age distribution of households in the population is also derived from fertility and mortality as they determine the population age distribution, and the saving behavior generated by the life-cycle saving model is applied to the age distribution of households. At this point additional effects are generated: when fertility has been higher, the age distribution of households is younger, there are fewer elderly dissavers, and consequently aggregate savings rates are higher, other things equal. Thus compositional and behavioral effects are combined in a general equilibrium model, which Tobin (1967) used to simulate the effects of the changing US age distribution on aggregate savings rates and capital formation.

One might expect that the growing literature on real business cycles would provide some insights for the role of demographic change in causing macroeconomic fluctuations. In fact, judging by Stadler's (1994) survey, it is far from doing so. Exogenous shocks in the core model come from stochastic productivity growth, not population. The literature is criticized for relying on a representative agent formulation, and it appears that even the most ambitious efforts to introduce heterogeneous agents do so in only the most modest ways (Stadler, 1994), ruling out different behavior by age, for example. Since this literature focuses on business cycles, which are relatively short-run fluctuations, and since demographic variables such as age distributions change only slowly, it may make sense for the literature to ignore demographic change. If similar methods were brought to bear on longer fluctuations, say with periods above 15 or 20 years, there might be a payoff to incorporating population variation.

In recent work, Rios-Rull (1994) does just this. He employs the basic model from the real business cycle literature (see Stadler, 1994: pp. 1754–1755), but now a fully age distributed population is incorporated, while productivity growth occurs at a deterministic rate. Forward looking individuals seek to maximize utility over a life cycle limited by uncertain survival, by choosing paths of consumption, saving, labor and leisure, in light of their expectations about future wages, interest rates, and survival. The aggregation of these individual decisions determines savings, capital stock, labor supply, and therefore wages and interest rates. Stochastic shocks influence the evolution of fertility through a fitted AR(2) process, leading to uncertain age distributions. Examining the case of Spain, Rios-Rull (1994) concludes that if fertility remains low (the total fertility rate is currently 1.3 children per woman) rather than returning to replacement levels, the aging of the baby boom reduces savings nearly to zero. The general equilibrium setting contributes to this result by generating lower interest rates in response to a rising capital–labor ratio, which in turn discourage saving. The computational difficulties of solving such models require a number of simplifying assumptions, such as exogenous fertility and no economic role for children, and little if any role for government – this last a potentially serious problem in this context, given the important role of pay-as-you-go public sector pensions for life-cycle savings decisions, and their potential adverse effects on capital accumulation. This promising new direction revisits themes pioneered by Auerbach and Kotlikoff (1987) and Auerbach et al. (1989), who focused on demographic transitions to an older population rather than fluctuations, and who used a different methodology.

6. Conclusions

This chapter has considered a wide variety of topics, organized loosely around the theme of population equilibrium and disequilibrium, and the causes and consequences of both. The concept of population equilibrium is useful in the historical context for which it was originally developed by Malthus. Empirical work suggests that convergence towards equilibrium was very slow in preindustrial Europe and probably elsewhere as well. Nonetheless, the concept of equilibrium is important for understanding the broad sweep of history, and economic–demographic equilibration leads to statistical traps which are a danger even for the visual interpretation of simple plots of historical data series, since lead–lag relations are often misleading across long cycles. The concept of demographic equilibrium might appear to lack relevance for the contemporary world, but the increasing attention to environmental and natural resource constraints leads to renewed interest in the idea. Recent work has combined Malthusian production constraints arising from a fixed factor with modern fertility theories to consider the role of parental altruism towards children in avoiding an equilibrium at the subsistence level, and to consider possible externalities to childbearing.

Economic–demographic equilibrium requires that population growth encounter negative feedback of some kind, and in the Classical system, this took the form of diminishing returns to labor and capital in the presence of fixed amounts of land. The literature which attempts to estimate the effect of population size on incomes in Europe is controversial. Exploitation of new economic and demographic historical data for Europe and for other regions of the world may permit progress in this area, particularly with models that are tightly specified in relation to error structure and dynamic implications.

There is a substantial literature on the response of population to short-run variations in wages, prices, unemployment, and weather. The results for preindustrial populations, both historical and contemporary Third World, agree in finding a procyclical response for fertility and counter-cyclical response for mortality. For fertility, a robust pattern of lagged response is widely found; for mortality, the lag pattern of response is less uniform. Results for nuptiality are less solid, although a pro-cyclic response is often found. The next step in this literature is to develop models which incorporate unobserved health status variables, and which model storage and speculative behavior.

For developed countries in recent decades, findings are mixed and controversial. It is not clear why further work which focuses specifically on short-run variations is of particular interest. For agricultural societies, this kind of study is often possible even when data limitations preclude studies of longer term variations. Also, the effects of weather induced variations in agricultural productivity are a natural subject of study. For industrial populations neither of these conditions holds. Most of the literature examining time series of fertility and economic variables makes no distinction between short- and long-run variation, and this is probably the right direction for research to take.

The influence of long-term environmental variation on population movements is an important and promising area of historical research. The regional and global synchrony of demographic change in certain eras remains largely unexplained, undermining historical interpretations that are specific to particular areas. A clearer understanding of the influence of climatic variation and independent disease processes on population and the economy would help clarify these issues. The development and analysis of improved historical data series for world regions other than Europe could move research in this area forward; rich new climatological data sources for China are a case in point.

Given the substantial lags between birth and labor force entry, and birth and reproductive ages, we would expect that an equilibrating economic and demographic system might exhibit interesting dynamic behavior. The formal literature exploring the possibility of limit cycles for equilibrating populations is of exceptionally high technical quality, and has pushed out the frontier of applied mathematics in this area. Unfortunately the empirical support for the propositions on which this work is based is flimsy, and it may well be that limit cycles do not occur in human populations, given the necessary strength of feedback (analogous to the $\alpha\beta$ value discussed earlier in this chapter). Nonhuman populations are a more promising area for applications.

Fluctuations in the rate of population growth and in the population age distribution could potentially have large effects on the macroeconomy. All industrial populations exhibit major fluctuations of this sort, fluctuations which are largely exogenous in relation to current economic behavior. Their influence on economic phenomena such as savings, consumption, housing demand, education and markets for teachers, labor force participation, and productivity growth, forms a promising area for research. It is surprising, therefore, that such effects have not yet been much studied except in the context of the labor market (reviewed in a different chapter). One of the problems facing such research is the need to include a whole vector of population by age, a problem which forces the analyst to adopt one or another strategy for economizing on parameters and estimated coefficients, strategies which inevitably have major disadvantages as well as advantages. Another difficulty is that there are often both behavioral consequences of demographic change and compositional consequences. Demographers tend to ignore the behavioral consequences that are the main interest of economists; economists tend to ignore the compositional effects which are often strong. More recent efforts to take a dynamic general equilibrium approach are promising, but require substantively important sacrifices to attain a computable model.

References

Ashton, B., K. Hill, A. Piazza and R. Zeitz (1984), "Famine in China, 1958–61", Population and Development Review 10: 613–646.

Auerbach, A.J. and L.J. Kotlikoff (1987), Dynamic fiscal policy (Cambridge University Press, Cambridge).

Auerbach, A.J., L.J. Kotlikoff, R.P. Hagemann and G. Nicoletti (1989), "The economic dynamics of an ageing population: the case of four OECD countries", OECD Economic Studies 12: 97–130.

Bailey, R.E. and M.J. Chambers (1993), "Long-term demographic interactions in pre-census England", Unpublished manuscript (Department of Economics of the University of Essex, Colchester).

Bairoch, P. (1976), "Europe's gross national product: 1800–1975", Journal of European Economic History 273–340.

Becker, G.S. (1960), "An economic analysis of fertility", in: Universities–National Bureau of Economic Research, ed., Demographic and economic change in developed countries (Princeton University Press, Princeton, NJ) pp. 209–231.

Behrman, J. and A. Deolalikar (1988), "Health and nutrition", in: H.B. Chenery and T.N. Srinivasan, eds., Handbook of development economics (North-Holland, Amsterdam) pp. 425–468.

Behrman, J. and P. Taubman (1989), "A test of the Easterlin fertility model using income for two generations and a comparison with the Becker model", Demography 26: 117–124.

Bengtsson, T. and G. Brostrom (1986), "A comparison of different methods of analyzing cycles in population and economy", Paper presented at the Ninth International Economic History Conference, Bern, Switzerland.

Ben-Porath, Y. (1988), "Market, government, and Israel's muted baby boom", in: R. Lee, W. Arthur and G. Rodgers, eds., Economics of changing age distributions in developed countries (Oxford University Press, Oxford).

Bongaarts, J. (1980), "Does malnutrition affect fecundity? A summary of evidence", Science 208: 564–569.

Boserup, E. (1981), Population and technological change: a study of long-term trends (University of Chicago Press, Chicago, IL).

Braudel, F. (1973), Capitalism and material life 1400–1800 (Weindenfeld and Nicolson, London).

Brenner, M.H. (1983), "Mortality and economic instability: detailed analyses for Britain and comparative analyses for selected industrialized countries", International Journal of Health Services 13: 563–620.

Butz, W. and M. Ward (1979), "The emergence of U.S. countercyclical fertility", American Economic Review 69: 318–328.

Caldwell, J. and P. Caldwell (1987), "Famine in Africa", Presented at the IUSSP Seminar on Mortality and Society in Sub-Saharan Africa in IFORD, Yaounde.

Chu, C.Y.C. and R.D. Lee (1994), "Famine, revolt, and the dynastic cycle: population dynamics in historic China", Journal of Population Economics 7: 351–378.

Coale, A. (1972), The growth and structure of human populations: a mathematical investigation (Princeton University Press, Princeton, NJ).

DeVries, J. (1981), "Measuring the impact of climate on history: the search for appropriate methodologies", in: R.I. Rotberg and T.K. Rabb, eds., Climate and history (Princeton University Press, Princeton, NJ).

DeVries, J. (1984), European urbanization 1500–1800 (Harvard University Press, Cambridge, MA).

Easterlin, R.A. (1962), "The American baby boom in historical perspective", Occasional paper 79 (National Bureau of Economic Research, New York).

Easterlin, R.A. (1965), "Long swings in U.S. demographic and economic growth: some findings on the historical pattern", Demography 2: 490–507.

Easterlin, R.A. (1968), Population, labor force, and long swings in economic growth (National Bureau for Economic Research, New York).

Easterlin, R.A. (1978), "What will 1984 be like? The socioeconomic implications of recent twists in age structure", Demography 15: 397–432.

Easterlin, R.A. (1987), Birth and fortune: the impact of numbers on personal welfare, 2nd edn. (Basic Books, New York).

Easterlin, R.A. and G. Condran (1976), "A note on the recent fertility swing in Australia, Canada, England and Wales, and the United States", in: H. Richards, ed., Population, factor movements, and economic development: studies presented to Brinley Thomas (University of Wales Press, Cardiff).

Easterlin, R.A., M.L. Wachter and S.M. Wachter (1978), "Demographic influences on economic stability: the United States experience", Population and Development Review 4: 1–23.

Eckstein, Z., S. Stern and K.I. Wolpin (1989), "On the Malthusian hypothesis and the dynamics of population and income in an equilibrium growth model with endogenous fertility", in: K.F. Zimmerman, ed., Economic theory of optimal population (Springer-Verlag, Berlin) pp. 105–116.

Eckstein, Z., K. Wolpin and T.P. Schultz (1985), "Short-run fluctuations in fertility and mortality in preindustrial Sweden", European Economic Review 26: 295–317.

Entorf, H. and K.F. Zimmermann (1990), "Interrelationships between mortality and fertility in Germany: rural and urban Prussia and modern Germany", Genus 46: 133–146.

Espenshade, T. (1978), "How the trend towards a stationary population affects consumer demand", Population Studies 32: 147–158.

Fair, R.C. and K.M. Dominguez (1991), "Effects of the changing U.S. age distribution of macroeconomic equations", American Economic Review 81: 1276–1294.

Feeney, G. and K. Hamano (1988), "Rice price fluctuations and population change in late Tokugawa Japan", Working draft (East-West Population Institute, Honoloulu, HI).

Fogel, R.W. (1989), "Second thoughts on the European escape from hunger: famines, price elasticities, entitlements, chronic malnutrition, and mortality rates", Working paper no. 1 on historical factors in long-run economic growth (NBER, Cambridge, MA).

Frauenthal, J. (1975), "A dynamic model for human population growth", Theoretical Population Biology 8: 64–73.

Frauenthal, J. and K. Swick (1983), "Limit cycle oscillations of the human population", Demography 20: 285–298.

Galbraith, V.L. and D.S. Thomas (1941), "Birth rates and inter-war business cycles", Journal of the American Statistical Association 36: 465–476.

Galloway, P.R. (1986), "Long-term fluctuations in population and climate in the preindustrial era", Population and Development Review 12: 1–24.

Galloway, P.R. (1988), "Basic patterns in annual variations in fertility, nuptiality, mortality, and prices in pre-industrial Europe", Population Studies 42: 275–302.

Galloway, P. (1994), "Secular changes in the short term preventive, positive, and termperature checks to population growth in Europe, 1460–1909", Climatic Change 26: 3–63.

Habakkuk, H.J. (1965), "The economic history of modern Britain", in: D.V. Glass and D.E.C. Eversley, eds., Population in history (Aldine, Chicago, IL) pp. 147–158.

Hagnell, M. (1989), "A multivariate time series analysis of fertility, adult mortality, nuptiality and real wages in Sweden 1751–1850", Paper no. 8 (Department of Economic History, Research Group in Population Economics, Lund University, Lund).

Hansen, A.H. (1939), "Economic progress and declining population growth", American Economic Review 29: 1–15.

Harberger, A. (1958), "Variations on a theme by Malthus", in: R.G. Francis, ed., The population ahead (Minnesota University Press, Minneapolis, MN).

Helleiner, K.F. (1965), "The vital revolution reconsidered", in: D.V. Glass and D.E.C. Eversley, eds., Population in history (Aldine, Chicago, IL) pp. 79–86.

Henry, L. (1972), On the measurement of human fertility (translated and edited by M.C. Sheps and E. Lapierre-Adamcyk) (Elsevier, Amsterdam).

International Union for the Scientific Study of Population (1992), The demographic consequences of structural adjustment in Latin America (Bound papers for a conference of that title held in Belo Horizonte, Brazil, 1992).

Kates, R.W., J.H. Ausubel and M. Berberian (1985), Climate impact assessment: scope 27 (Wiley, New York).

Kelley, A. (1965), "International migration and economic growth: Australia, 1865–1935", Journal of Economic History 25: 333–354.

Kelley, A. (1972), "Demographic changes and American economic development: past, present and future", in: E.R. Morss and R.H. Reed, eds., Economic aspects of population change, Commission research reports, Vol. II (US Commission on Population Growth and the American Future, Government Printing Office, Washington, DC).

Kelley, A. and J.G. Williamson (1984), What drives Third World city growth? (Princeton University Press, Princeton, NJ).

Keyfitz, N. (1977), Applied mathematical demography (Wiley, New York).

Keyfitz, N. (1988), "Some demographic properties of transfer schemes: how to achieve equity between the generations", in: R.D. Lee, W.B. Arthur and G. Rodgers, eds., Economics of changing age distributions in developed countries (Oxford University Press, Oxford) pp. 92–105.

Keynes, J.M. (1937), "Some economic consequences of a declining population", Eugenics Review 29: 13–17.

Kirk, D. (1960), "The influence of business cycles on marriage and birth rates", in: Universities–NBER demographic and economic change in developed countries (Princeton University Press, Princeton, NJ) pp. 214–257.

Knodel, J. (1983), "Natural fertility: age patterns, levels, and trends", in: R. Bulatao and R. Lee, eds., Determinants of fertility in developing countries (Academic Press, New York) pp. 61–102.

Kuznets, S. (1966), Modern economic growth: rate, structure, and spread (Yale University Press, New Haven, CT).

Langsten, R.L. (1980), Causes of changes in vital rates: the case of Bangladesh, Unpublished dissertation (University of Michigan Department of Sociology, Ann Arbor, MI).

Lee, R.D. (1973), "Population in preindustrial England: an econometric analysis", Quarterly Journal of Economics 87: 581–607.

Lee, R.D. (1974), "The formal dynamics of controlled populations and the echo, the boom and the bust", Demography 11: 563–585.

Lee, R.D. (1976), "Demographic forecasting and the Easterlin hypothesis", Population and Development Review, Sep./Dec.: 459–468.

Lee, R.D. (1980), "A historical perspective on economic aspects of the population explosion: the case of preindustrial England", in: R.A. Easterlin, ed., Population and economic change in developing countries (University of Chicago Press, Chicago, IL) pp. 517–566.

Lee, R.D. (1981), "Short-term variation: vital rates, prices and weather", in: E.A. Wrigley and R.S. Schofield, eds., The population history of England 1541–1871: a reconstruction (Harvard University Press, Cambridge, MA) pp. 356–401.

Lee, R.D. (1985), "Population homeostasis and English demographic history", Journal of Interdisciplinary History XV: 635–660.

Lee, R.D. (1987), "Population dynamics of humans and other animals", Demography 24: 443–466.

Lee, R.D. (1988), "Induced population growth and induced technological progress: their interaction in the accelerating phase", Mathematical Population Studies 1: 265–288.

Lee, R.D. (1990), "The demographic response to economic crisis in historical and contemporary populations", Population Bulletin of the United Nations 29: 1–15.

Lee, R.D. (1993a), "Accidental and systematic change in population history: homeostasis in a stochastic setting", Explorations in Economic History 30: 1–30.

Lee, R.D. (1993b), "Inverse projection and demographic fluctuations: a critical assessment of new methods", in: D. Reher and R. Schofield, eds., Old and new methods in historical demography (Oxford University Press, Oxford) pp. 7–28.

Lee, R.D. and M. Anderson (1995), "Malthus in state space: reestimating macro economic–demographic relations in English history", Paper presented at the annual meetings of the Population Association of America, San Francisco, CA.

Leff, N. (1969), "Dependency rates and savings rates", American Economic Review 70: 886–895.

Leibenstein, H. (1954), A theory of economic demographic development (Princeton University Press, Princeton, NJ).

Lindert, P.H. (1983), "English living standards, population growth and Wrigley–Schofield", Explorations in Economic History 20: 131–155.

Lindert, P.H. (1985), "English population, wages and prices: 1541–1913", Journal of Interdisciplinary History 115: 609–634.

Locay, L. (1987), "Population equilibrium in primitive economies", Paper presented at the 1987 meetings of the Population Association of America, Chicago, IL.

Macunovich, D.J. (1989), "An evaluation of the Butz–Ward hypothesis of countercyclical fertility", Manuscript (Department of Economics, Williams College, Williamstown, MA).

Malthus, T.R. (1798/1970), in: A. Flew, ed., An essay on the principle of population (Penguin Books, Baltimore, MD).

Mankiw, N.G. and D.N. Weil (1989), "The baby boom, the baby bust, and the housing market", Regional Science and Urban Economics 19: 235–258.

Chapter 20

GROWTH MODELS WITH ENDOGENOUS POPULATION: A GENERAL FRAMEWORK

MARC NERLOVE

University of Maryland

LAKSHMI K. RAUT*

University of California

Contents

1. Introduction	1118
2. Models of economic growth with endogenous population	1124
2.1. Solow–Swan	1124
2.2. Niehans	1130
2.3. Malthus–Boserup	1132
2.4. Lucas and Romer: new directions in growth theory	1139
3. The microeconomics of endogenous population: fertility, mortality and investment in children	1141
3.1. Quality versus quantity: The Becker–Lewis model	1142
3.2. Parental altruism and investment in human capital	1147
3.3. Survival probability, fertility and investment in health care	1155
3.4. Transfers from children to parents and fertility: old-age security motive	1160
3.5. Two-sided altruism and transfers from children to parents	1168
4. Concluding remarks	1171
References	1172

*We are indebted to the editors of this volume and to T.N. Srinivasan for helpful comments.

Handbook of Population and Family Economics. Edited by M.R. Rosenzweig and O. Stark
© *Elsevier Science B.V., 1997*

1. Introduction

For most of human history, birth rates and death rates have fluctuated roughly in tandem so that population itself remained stable or grew only slowly. With the development of agriculture some 12 000 years ago, it is believed that both birth and death rates increased substantially, but that there was some acceleration in the rate of growth of population (Coale, 1974). A second major change occurred in Western Europe following what has been called "the second agricultural revolution" and preceding the Industrial Revolution (Bairoch, 1976). This was a remarkable fall in death rates followed only slowly by a fall in birth rates, so that population literally exploded. In the eighteenth and nineteenth centuries, the excess of population was relieved by the vast migrations of European population to the new lands of the Western Hemisphere and Oceania. It was against this backdrop that Malthus (1798, 1830) wrote.

Malthus' theory of population and growth is well-known: Passion between the sexes, unless checked by human misery, leads to a continual growth in population. Positive checks to population growth included "... war, disease, hunger, and whatever ... contributes to shorten the duration of human life". Preventative checks included abstinence from sexual relations, continence within marriage, and/or delay of marriage. But Malthus didn't think that even the preventative checks would operate to any great extent in the absence of the incentives forced on mankind by increasing misery. As long as living conditions did not deteriorate greatly, population would grow exponentially. Since, however, Malthus believed that food supplies and ultimately the means to human welfare more generally could only grow linearly, he predicted population growth with increasing immiserization until equilibrium was reached for a large population living under the most abysmal conditions.

That Malthus' dire prediction has not yet been realized is the result of many factors. First, in Western Europe and later in Eastern Europe, North America and Japan, as death rates, particularly infant and child mortality rates, fell, birth rates ultimately came down as well, although with a substantial lag. Second, agricultural productivity increased substantially and new lands were opened reducing population pressure in older settled areas and making more food and other resources available to support a growing world population. In the twentieth century, even as modern medical advance and public health investments have reduced death rates in other parts of the world, a similar pattern of falling birth rates, agricultural extension and intensification (recently through so-called "Green Revolution" technology), and general economic growth, has been followed in large parts of the world. (Africa is a notable exception.) The pattern of falling death rates followed after a lag by falling birth rates has been called the "demographic transition" (Beaver, 1975; Caldwell, 1982). But, to date, a rigorous theory about whether and how this demographic pattern might be linked to economic growth has proven elusive.

In this connection, it is important to make a distinction between endogenous population change and endogenous fertility. Models can be constructed in which there is a

relation between economic and other factors and the size of, composition of, and changes in population, but in which no decision-making mechanism is presupposed. Purely biological models of animal populations in which food supplies or predator population limit the size of the population in question are of this character. The Malthusian theory, discussed above, comes close to this paradigm.

On the other hand, recent developments in population and family economics suggest many causal paths between the economic environment and *human* family formation and fertility decisions as well as the possibility that mortality may be influenced by families' decisions on the investments in human capital, in the form of health and nutrition, they make in their children and fertility decisions. In particular, recent *economic* theories of fertility focus on explicit family decision-making models in which optimal fertility choices are made in a utility-maximizing framework. Fertility is, of course, only one component of population change. In a closed population without migration, demographic composition and mortality also play a role over which families have little control.

The problem of explaining the demographic transition in these terms is to show how family decisions with respect to fertility, investment in the human capital of their children and their bequests to them in other forms of capital, and other variables interact over time to determine the size of the population and the stocks of capital, both human and physical, and the well-being of successive generations, and then to deduce the demographic transition as a possible outcome of these interactions.

In the early 1970s when the outlines of the "new home economics" were just emerging, Nerlove (1974, pp. S215–S217) speculated on what such a model might look like:

Good nutrition and health care increase youngsters' chances of survival and may also affect their ability to absorb future investments in intellectual capital. To the extent that such investments increase the life span, particularly the span of years over which a person can be economically active, such an increase in quality will raise the return to investments in human capital which sons and daughters may later wish to make in themselves. To the extent that better health and nutrition result in a reduction in child mortality, they increase the satisfactions accruing to parents from other forms of investment which also raise child quality, for the returns to these investments may then be expected to be enjoyed over a longer period of time on average. Increases in longevity, particularly of an individual's economically productive years, increase the amount of human time available without increasing population; such an increase would tend by itself to lower the value of time per unit, but, as we know, most of the effects of better health care and nutrition occur in childhood and enhance the quality of a unit of time in later years more than increasing the number of children. On net balance, therefore, I would conjecture that better health and nutrition lower the costs of further investments in human capital relative to those in other forms of capital and increase the returns therefrom. ...

For reasons which I feel certain we do not fully understand, but which are due in part to the presence of children's utilities in the utility function of the family to which they belong, parents do desire to bequeath a stock of capital to their children. Since the stock of capital, material and intangible, human and nonhuman, is growing per capita in Western economies, one must assume that parents desire to pass along more than that which they received from their parents, or that institutions in the economy function in such a way as to induce this outcome. Irrespective of the motivation, however, the increasing value of human time must have an effect on the form in which this capital is passed on. As long as the rates of return to investments in human capital remain above, or fall more slowly than, the rates of return to investments in other forms of capital, parents will be induced to bequeath a greater part in the form of human capital. Thus the tendency toward increasing quality of children will be intensified by the bequest motive, despite the opposite tendency, resulting from the increasing cost of time, to invest in bequests which are less time-intensive. But as rates of return tend to equality over time – if they ever do – parents should tend to bequeath less in the form of human capital and more in the form of financial and physical capital. [In equilibrium, rates of return will be the same. If they differ, parents will invest in those assets yielding the highest rates of return.] Nonetheless, as long as investment in human capital occurs, the value of a unit of human time will continue to rise with increases in the stock of capital per capita, reinforcing the tendency to fewer children of ever-higher quality. Substitution will occur in favor of fewer children of higher quality and perhaps eventually against both quality and quantity of children in favor of commodities and knowledge. [There is considerable evidence that an increasing proportion of total capital formation in this century has occurred in the form of human capital (Schultz, 1961, 1971, 1973) which suggests] ... that we may be far from the point at which such substitution begins to take place against children, quality and quantity combined.

The outlines of a revised Malthusian model begin to emerge, albeit dimly, from the foregoing conjectures and speculations. In this model, the value of human time and changes in that value over time are pivotal, and the limitations imposed by natural resources are mitigated, if not eliminated, by technological progress and increases in the stock of knowledge and of capital, both human and nonhuman. The main link between household and economy is the value of human time; the increased value of human time results in fewer children per household, with each child embodying greater investments in human capital which in turn result in lower mortality and greater productivity of the economically active years. Such greater productivity in turn further raises both the value of a unit of time and income in the subsequent generation and enables persons of that generation to make efficient use of new knowledge and new physical capital. Eventually, rates of return to investments in physical capital, new knowledge, and human capital may begin to equalize, but as long as investment occurs which increases the amount of human capital per individual, the value of a unit of human time must continue to increase. It is not possible to say whether the diminishing ability of a human being to absorb such investment would eventually stabilize the number of children per household and at what level, given the satisfactions parents obtain from numbers of children as well as their quality. Nonetheless, over time the model does predict in rough qualitative fashion declining rates of population growth (perhaps eventually zero rates or even negative rates for a time) and declining rates of infant mortality. These are the main features of the demographic transition.

What may have happened sometime in the nineteenth and early twentieth centuries in the West was that a small exogenous shock which reduced infant and child mortality set off a cumulative process of investment in better health and nutrition and in public health leading to a surge in economic growth and population but eventually resulting in substitution of quality in the form of further human capital investments for numbers of children. And what may be happening in many places in the world today is the same cumulative process now set off by the import of modern medical knowledge and public health technology. But the occurrence of the demographic transition in these areas depends, if these conjectures are valid, on the existence of opportunities for, and absence of obstacles to, further investments in human capital.

The World Bank (1992: p. 26) projects that between now and 2160 the current world population of 5.5 billion will about double or more than quadruple depending on the rapidity of the demographic transition in those countries of the world which have not yet experienced it or where it is not fully complete. Understanding how and why the transition occurs is thus a matter of great importance if we, of the present generation, are to formulate appropriate economic and demographic policies, for such policies will determine whether world population stabilizes at moderate levels and a relatively high standard of living, or at high levels with a poor quality of life for the majority. This Chapter seeks to provide a framework for further analysis. Limitations of the present state of knowledge more than limitations of space preclude any definitive models which show the possibility of such transitions and reveal the circumstances under which they may occur.

The elements of a complete theory of the relation between population and economic growth along the lines envisaged would include a theory of family decisions with respect to fertility, investments in the human capital of their children, and bequests to them, in response to their expectations of future rates of return, income and prices, and embed these in a dynamic general equilibrium model, which would determine these rates as functions of state variables, such as population and the stocks of human and physical capital. Mortality, especially infant and child mortality, would not be wholly exogenous but would depend, in part, at least at very low levels of income, on the investments in the health and nutrition that parents were prepared to make in their children at the expense of their own consumption. We do not carry out this plan in this Chapter; a full development is left for others who may be so inspired, or for our own subsequent research. What we do attempt is to lay out a general framework into which the elements of such an economic theory of the demographic transition can be fit, to survey briefly recent related work in the "new home economics" and growth literatures, and assess the linkages among stocks, flows, and rates of return in this context.

We begin with a formal analysis of models of economic growth in which population is endogenous in the sense that its rate of change over time depends on per capita consumption or wages without explicit determination of fertility within a utility-maximizing model of family decision-making. We develop a general framework for the analysis of economic growth with endogenous population and three factors of production, physical capital, labor, and a third, unspecified factor Z. The factor may be a fixed or a renewable natural resource or a stock of knowledge, which contributes generally to the production of consumption goods and additional physical capital but which is not subject to control by individual economic agents.

We adopt a discrete time formulation in order to facilitate intergenerational analysis and the integration of models of endogenous fertility. We show that if production technology is homogeneous of degree one in the three factors and if the dynamic equation characterizing the law of motion of the third factor Z is also homogeneous of degree one in all three factors (i.e., if Z were truly variable), then the economic growth with endogenous population may be modeled as a dynamic planar (two-dimensional) system. The analysis of global and local properties of such a planar system may be carried out using methods developed in Nerlove (1993).

We begin with the Solow–Swan model (Solow, 1956; Swan, 1956), both of whom suggested (Solow: p. 91 and Swan: p. 339) that their model might be modified by introducing a simple form of endogenous population by assuming that the rate of growth of population depends on the real wage or per capita consumption. Growth with exogenously growing population is a very special case of the general two-dimensional system developed here. In fact, this case and the case in which the rate of growth depends on per capita consumption is obtained by eliminating the factor Z and thus reducing the system to one-dimensional dynamics. Niehans' (1963) model in which both savings and population are endogenously determined at the aggregate level in a neoclassical, constant-returns-to-scale context is a special case which is also one-dimensional. Finally, we provide a detailed analysis of the full model in which both population and savings are endogenous. We also consider a model in which there is a third factor of production, which is not under the direct control of economic agents but which nonetheless affects the output obtainable from capital and labor. This model is inspired by recent work of Lee (1986) in which he tries to encompass the theories of Malthus and Boserup in a single model. Our third factor may be environmental or other natural resources or a stock of technology and is unpriced. See, for example, Nerlove (1991) and Raut and Srinivasan (1993). The owners of capital are assumed to receive the surplus, so that total product can be exhausted despite the unpriced nature of the third factor. The full power of the planar (two-dimensional) framework is exploited in this context.

Recent work on endogenous growth focuses on human capital and its joint determination at the family level with fertility decisions and the effects of human capital investments on mortality. The important distinction between human capital and physical capital or natural resources or general knowledge is that human capital is fully embodied in the human agent and therefore affects production only through the individual and is extinguished with the death of the individual. This fact makes it possible to continue the analysis largely within a planar context within the general framework outlined here, although such considerations underscore the need for a deeper analysis of family decisions, the elements of which we next sketch.

We close Section 2 with a brief review of the new directions in growth theory initiated by Lucas (1988) and Romer (1986). This theory emphasizes increasing returns and the effects of a growing stock of knowledge. It is designed to eliminate exogenous technical change as the main source of growth and to explain the continuing divergence in rates of per capita income growth, in contrast to the prediction of neoclassical growth theory that growth rates should converge, and is of limited usefulness in answering the central question addressed here.

Next we recall the basic theory of household choice with respect to consumption, saving, fertility and investment in the health and future welfare of their offspring. Our discussion suggests how the development of Chapter 5, pp. 53–58, of Nerlove et al. (1987) may be extended to models of utility-maximizing behavior which encompass decisions not only on how many children to have but how much to invest in their future well-being and in physical or financial resources available to parents in future time periods and, subsequently, to their children. We are particularly concerned with the effects of infant and child mortality and the ability of parents to influence these risks by devoting additional resources to the care and nutrition of their children. The purpose of this discussion is to suggest what further research might be necessary to provide an underpinning for an economic theory of the demographic transition advanced above.

The chapter concludes with a brief review of the nature of the interactions between household decisions and the main stock and flow variables which characterize the evolution of the economy over time: household decisions with respect to fertility and the investments in human capital made in their children and bequests to them, on the one hand; and population, the stock of human capital embodied in that population, and the stock of physical capital, on the other. Given the rules of distribution and tax–subsidy policies, the latter, state, variables, determine, via production technology, per household incomes and the rates of return to human and physical capital; these, in turn, are the main variables to which households respond in addition to the rates of mortality, particularly infant and child mortality. At low levels of income and of human capital in the form of investments in health and nutrition, these rates themselves may be partly endogenous. We then turn to a discussion of the effects of motives for intergenerational transfers such as old-age security and bequests, and introduce two-sided altruism as way of endogenizing such transfers. The possibility of strategic behavior and its effects on capital accumulation and population growth is briefly touched upon (see Cigno, 1991, Chap. 9; Raut, 1993). In the model of Azariadis and Drazen (1993) such strategic considerations play a pivotal role in explaining overall population growth and its sectoral composition.

2. Models of economic growth with endogenous population

2.1. Solow–Swan

Consider first the standard Solow–Swan model with exogenous population growth in discrete time form: Let Y_t = output, K_t = capital stock, N_t = labor force assumed to be the same as population, S_t = savings, I_t = investment, s = the savings rate, δ = depreciation rate, $\bar{n}$ = the exogenous rate of growth of population and labor force. Production can be represented by a constant returns to scale function:

$$Y_t = F(K_t, N_t) \quad \text{or} \quad y_t = f(k_t), \tag{2.1}$$

where $y_t = Y_t/N_t$, $k_t = K_t/N_t$, and $f(k) = F(k, 1)$. Solow–Swan assume that savings equals gross investment and is a constant fraction s of output:

$$I_t = S_t = sY_t. \tag{2.2}$$

The change in the capital stock equals gross investment minus depreciation:

$$K_{t+1} = (1 - \delta)K_t + I_t = sF(K_t, N_t) + (1 - \delta)K_t. \tag{2.3}$$

Population grows exogenously at a rate $\bar{n}$:

$$N_{t+1} = (1 + \bar{n})N_t. \tag{2.4}$$

Thus

$$k_{t+1} = \frac{sf(k_t) + (1 - \delta)k_t}{1 + \bar{n}} = g(k_t), \quad k_0 \text{ given}. \tag{2.5}$$

The dynamics of the Solow–Swan model are entirely described by the path of k_t, the capital–labor ratio, since population grows exogenously, capital depreciates at a fixed rate, and gross investment is proportional to output.

The existence of stationary solutions to Eq. (2.5), i.e. k^* for which

$$k^* = g(k^*) \tag{2.6}$$

and the local stability of such solutions depend on the shape of the function g. The conditions which yield a nonnegative globally stable steady-state solution are the following:

$$g'(0) > 1,$$

$$g'(k) < 1, \quad \text{for some } k > 0,$$

and g is concave. These properties follow if the production function satisfies:

$$f(0) = 0,$$

$$f'(0) > \frac{\delta + \bar{n}}{s},$$

$$f'(k) < \frac{\delta + \bar{n}}{s}, \quad \text{for some } k > 0,$$

and f is concave. A stationary solution k^* is locally stable if $|g'(k^*)| < 1$. Clearly $k^* = 0$ is unstable. Under concavity of f, whenever Eq. (2.6) holds for some $k^* > 0$, then there can be no other $k^* > 0$ for which Eq. (2.6) holds and at that point $|g'(k^*)| < 1$, so the solution is necessarily unique.

In the model described above, substitute an equation determining the growth rate of population endogenously. Continue to assume that the savings rate is exogenously fixed. Suppose simply that the rate of growth of population depends on the level of per capita consumption:

$$\frac{N_{t+1}}{N_t} = 1 + n[(1-s)f(k_t)] = h(k_t), \quad h' > 0 \tag{2.7}$$

and $n(c_m) = 0$ for some level of per capita consumption, $c_m = f(k_m)$. Then, in place of Eq. (2.5), the function $g(k_t)$ is now defined as

$$k_{t+1} = \frac{sf(k_t) + (1-\delta)k_t}{h(k_t)} = g(k_t), \quad k_0 \text{ given}. \tag{2.8}$$

The capital–labor ratio continues to determine the dynamics of the economy, that is, the system remains univariate, but is now more complex since h in the denominator of g now depends on k_t.

In this case, however, concavity of f and conditions on s and δ no longer guarantee the existence of stationary points nor do they determine unambiguously the local stability or instability of such equilibria. However, considerable insight into the location and properties of nontrivial steady states can be obtained by comparing them with the steady states of the Solow–Swan model with *exogenous* population growth. Let $\bar{k}^*$ be the stationary point of the system (2.5). Then,

$$\bar{k}^* = \frac{sf(\bar{k}^*) + (1-\delta)\bar{k}^*}{1+\bar{n}}$$

or

$$\frac{\bar{n}+\delta}{s}\bar{k}^* = f(\bar{k}^*). \tag{2.9}$$

Provided the conditions on the production function previously specified are satisfied, $\bar{k}^* = 0$ is a stationary point and $f(k)$ intersects a straight line through the origin with slope at a point $(\bar{n}+\delta)/s$ at a point $\bar{k}^* > 0$ as well.

Let us use the same notation to denote $n(k) = n[(1-s)f(k)]$. When population is endogenous, from Eq. (2.8), we have

$$\left[\frac{n(k^*)+\delta}{s}\right]k^* = f(k^*), \tag{2.10}$$

where, k^* denotes the stationary solution of Eq. (2.8). Comparing Eqs. (2.9) and (2.10), we note that while the left-hand side of Eq. (2.9) which corresponds to Solow–Swan model with exogenous population growth is a linear function of k, in the case of endogenous population, Eq. (2.10), it is a nonlinear function $\rho(k)$ given by

$$\left[\frac{n(k)+\delta}{s}\right]k = \rho(k).$$

As before, a stationary point is characterized by $\rho(k^*) = f(k^*)$. The properties of $\rho(k)$ depend on the function $n(k)$. If $n(k)k \to 0$ as $k \to 0$, and therefore y and $(1-s)y \to 0$, $\rho(0) = 0$. Let us assume that $n(k)$ is increasing in k, positive for k greater than some small value and $n(k) > \bar{n}$ for some $k > 0$. Since

$$\rho'(k) = \frac{n(k)+\delta}{s} + \frac{n'(k)\cdot k}{s},$$

which must be greater than $(\bar{n}+\delta)/s$ as $n' > 0$, there exists a unique k_0 such that $n(k_0) = \bar{n}$. At this point $\rho(k)$ crosses the line

$$\left[\frac{\bar{n}+\delta}{s}\right]k$$

and, under the assumptions made, lies everywhere above it. If the form of $\rho(k)$ is such that $k_0 < \bar{k}^*$ then the stationary capital–labor ratio, k^*, of the Solow–Swan model with endogenous population is less than $\bar{k}^*$, the capital–labor ratio of the Solow–Swan model with exogenous population; otherwise, $k^* > \bar{k}^*$. The first case is shown in Fig. 1.

In general, however, $n(k)$ may be increasing for smaller values of k and eventually turn down and recross the line $\bar{n}$ with $n' < 0$. Then another equilibrium may occur at a capital–labor ratio greater than $\bar{k}^*$. Alternatively, $n(k)$ may fall after very low levels of the capital–labor ratio are reached and may never reach the level $\bar{n}$. In this case there may be no nontrivial stationary point or an equilibrium only at a very large value of the capital–labor ratio. It is clear that merely endogenizing population growth at the macro level does not shed light on the shape of $n(k)$ and thus on the nature of dynamics; a utility-maximizing model should be used to elucidate the nature of the function $n(k)$, as we attempt in Section 3.4.

Suppose we have found a nontrivial steady-state solution to the Solow–Swan model with endogenous population growth. What are its dynamic properties? Differentiating g with respect to k in Eq. (2.8) and utilizing Eq. (2.10), we have

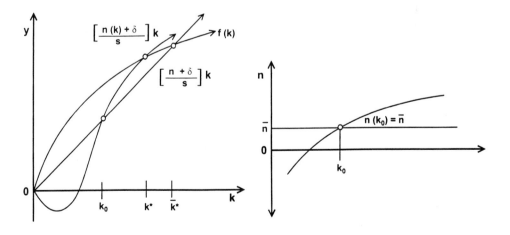

Fig. 1.

$$g'(k^*) = \frac{sf'(k^*) + (1-\delta) - k^*n'(k^*)}{1 + n(k^*)}. \tag{2.11}$$

This expression is greater than -1 if

$$f'(k^*) > \frac{-[1+n(k^*)] - (1-\delta) + k^*n'(k^*)}{s},$$

which is satisfied unless $n'(k^*)$ is very large and positive. Let us assume that $n(k)$ is such that the above is satisfied. For local stability analysis, it suffices to focus on whether $g'(k^*) \gtrless 1$. This will be the case according as

$$f'(k^*) \mathrel{\substack{> \\ <}} \frac{n(k^*) + \delta + k^*n'(k^*)}{s} = \rho'(k^*). \tag{2.12}$$

It follows that, if $\rho(k)$ crosses $f(k)$ from below in Fig. 1, the stationary point so determined is stable, and, if from above, the stationary point is unstable.

As shown in Fig. 1, $\rho(k)$ is essentially a transformation of $n(k)$, so everything depends on the behavior of this function which may be quite nonmonotonic in $(1-s)y$ and therefore in k. In contrast to the usual Solow–Swan model with exogenous population growth and the usual assumptions about the production function, endogenous population entails the possibility of multiple equilibria and instability of some of the equilibria. Another interesting point is that even if the rate of population growth at a stationary point is the same as the corresponding rate which would have led to that stationary value when population is assumed exogenous, i.e., even if $n(k^*) = \bar{n}$, it does not follow that the equilibrium is stable, in contrast to the Solow–Swan model with exogenous population. From Eq. (2.12), the condition is

$$f'(k^*) \mathrel{\substack{> \\ <}} \frac{\bar{n} + \delta}{s} + \frac{k^*n'(k^*)}{s},$$

so that even if the equilibrium would have been stable with exogenous population, i.e.,

$$f'(k^*) < \frac{\bar{n} + \delta}{s},$$

we may nonetheless have

$$f'(k^*) > \frac{\bar{n} + \delta}{s} + \frac{k^*n'(k^*)}{s}$$

if $n'(k^*) < 0$. In Section 3.4, however, we show that utility maximization implies $n'(k) > 0$ and thus demonstrate how a utility-maximizing model of endogenous fertility can clarify the dynamic properties of the growth model.

Example

To illustrate, suppose that population growth is simply equal to the ratio of actual consumption to some minimal, positive, level of consumption per capita, c_m:

$$h(k_t) = \frac{(1-s)f(k_t)}{c_m}. \tag{2.7'}$$

This formulation is more general than it may seem since it can be derived by appropriate choice of the units of output and consumption per capita from a linear approximation to the function $n(\ )$ in Eq. (2.7):

$$h(k) = 1 + \gamma[(1-s)f(k) - c_m].$$

If we choose $\gamma = 1/c_m$, then $h(k)$ is equal to $(1-s)f(k)/c_m$.
At a stationary point k^*, we can write

$$g'(k^*) = \frac{sf(k^*)+(1-\delta)}{h(k^*)} - e^*, \tag{2.11'}$$

where

$$e^* = \frac{h'(k^*)k^*}{h(k^*)}$$

is the elasticity of the rate of population growth factor at the stationary value of the capital–labor ratio; in this case

$$e^* = \frac{f'(k^*)}{f(k^*)}k^*$$

depends only on the production function. For a Cobb–Douglas production function,

$$f(k) = k^\sigma, \quad 0 < \sigma < 1, \tag{2.1'}$$

so that $e^* = \sigma$. In general, of course, e^* depends on the response of fertility and mortality to increases in the capital–labor ratio and, therefore, in income. In the case of a

Cobb–Douglas production function, $1 > e^* > 0$, but for more general models e^* may be negative.

The point $k = k^*$ is locally stable if $|g'| < 1$. From Eq. (11'), local stability implies

$$\frac{-(1-e^*)(1+n^*)-(1-\delta)}{s} < f'(k^*) < \frac{(1+e^*)(1+n^*)-(1-\delta)}{s},$$

where n^* is the rate of growth of population at that point. As we saw, it is not possible to say whether this condition is satisfied in general. However, for a Cobb–Douglas function, Eq. (1'), the problem is somewhat simpler, since $e^* = \sigma$ and $1 + n^* = (1 - s)y^*/c_m$, where y^* is per capita output at the stationary point. Then

$$g'(k^*) = \frac{s\sigma y^*/k^*+(1-\delta)}{(1-s)y^*/c_m} - \sigma \overset{<}{\underset{>}{=}} 1 \tag{2.11''}$$

according as

$$s\sigma + (1-\delta)\frac{k^*}{y^*} \overset{<}{\underset{>}{=}} (1+\sigma)(1-s)\frac{k^*}{c_m}.$$

Unless c_m is very large relative to k^*, this condition will generally be satisfied as $<$ for $0 < s, \sigma, \delta < 1$. Thus, there exists a locally stable unique nonzero steady state for the extended Solow–Swan model in this example.

2.2. Niehans

Niehans (1963) develops a model in which both savings and population growth vary endogenously. The basic structure of Niehans' model turns out to be very similar to the Solow–Swan model with endogenous population growth, so our analysis can be brief. Population and labor force are again equated, but now there exists a "capitalist" class, whose numbers do not matter, and who save according to the excess or shortfall of the return per unit of capital from some fixed rate. Population, on the other hand, grows or declines according to the excess or shortfall of the wage from some minimum. Let $w_t =$ per capita wage of labor and $r_t =$ return per unit of capital. Assuming the same constant-returns-to-scale production function as before, Eq. (2.1), and that capital and labor are each paid their marginal products,

$$r_t = f'(k_t) > 0, \tag{2.13}$$

$$w_t = f(k_t) - k_t f'(k_t) > 0. \tag{2.14}$$

Then, in place of Eqs. (2.2) and (2.4) we have

$$I_t = s(r_t)Y_t, \quad s' > 0, \quad s(0) = 0,$$ (2.15)

and

$$N_{t+1} = [1 + n(w_t)]N_t, \quad n' > 0,$$ (2.16)

and $n(w) < 0$ for w less than some minimum wage.

It is easy to see that the Niehans model is basically a minor modification of the Solow–Swan model in which the growth of the economy is entirely determined by the dynamics of the capital–labor ratio and population according to

$$\frac{N_{t+1}}{N_t} = h(k_t) = 1 + n[f(k_t) - k_t f'(k_t)] = 1 + n(k_t).$$ (2.16')

Substitution of Eqs. (2.13) and (2.15) in Eq. (2.3) yields

$$k_{t+1} = \frac{(1-\delta)k_t + s[f'(k_t)]f(k_t)}{1 + n(k_t)} = g(k_t).$$ (2.17)

Eqs. (2.16') and (2.17) are a model identical to Solow–Swan except that the savings rate now depends on the capital–labor ratio via the marginal product of capital. Once again, using the same notation $s(k) \equiv s(f'(k))$, all the conditions deduced above can be repeated with the following simple modification:

$$\rho(k) = \frac{n(k) + \delta}{s(k)}.$$

$\rho(k)$ is, however, now not a simple linear transformation of $n(k)$ as it was when only population was assumed to be endogenous and the savings rate exogenously determined. The following example shows that a nontrivial stationary point may not exist.

Example

Suppose

$$f(k) = k^\sigma, \quad 0 < \sigma < 1,$$

and the rate of population growth and of savings are proportional to some minimum wage, w_m, and minimum rate of return, r_m, respectively:

$$n(k_t) = \frac{f(k_t) - k_t f'(k_t)}{w_m},$$

$$s(k_t) = \frac{f'(k_t)}{r_m}.$$

Substitution then yields

$$\rho(k) = \left(\frac{(1-\sigma)y + \delta w_m}{\sigma y}\right)\left(\frac{k r_m}{w_m}\right),$$

where $y = f(k) = k^\sigma$. For k^* to be stationary, $\rho(k^*) = f(k^*)$ as before so

$$\frac{w_m}{r_m}\sigma(k^*)^{2\sigma-1} - (1-\sigma)(k^*)^\sigma = \delta w_m.$$

If $0 < \sigma \le 1/2$, the left-hand side of this expression is a decreasing function of k^*. Moreover, it is zero when $k^* = 0$. Therefore no nontrivial stationary point exists.

2.3. Malthus–Boserup

Models such as Solow–Swan or Niehans with endogenous population growth and a constant-returns-to-scale, two-factor production function yield univariate dynamics in the capital–labor ratio. The major difference is that the dynamic behavior becomes more complex with endogenous population growth since it no longer depends solely on concavity properties of the production function and the values of a few exogenously determined parameters. In this subsection, we develop a model based on a three-factor production function inspired by recent work of Lee (1986) on Malthus and Boserup. In our model, labor receives its marginal product but the rest, the "surplus", goes to capitalists who save all of it. Because a third factor of production, which may be the stock of knowledge or a fixed resource such as land or a renewable resource such as environmental quality, is involved, this model also encompasses non-constant returns to scale in the two-factor case with labor and capital. The model generally requires two dimensions to describe its dynamic behavior. It cannot be reduced to univariate dynamics but requires planar analysis, as discussed by Nerlove (1993).

Let Z be a variable which denotes the stock of technological knowledge, of environmental quality or other renewable resources, or of a fixed resource such as land or one which may be permanently depleted through use. In general, we will assume that Z varies over time. The case when Z is fixed is then an important special case, the one which Malthus presumably had in mind. Generally, however, Z may vary over time, reversibly or irreversibly, in response to levels or changes in the stock of physical capital or population. Boserup's arguments suggest a reversible process in response to population pressure.

To describe production, we replace Eq. (2.1) by

$$Y_t = F(K_t, N_t, Z_t),$$

which we assume to be constant returns to scale in all three factors. It will be convenient to express everything in per capita terms for which we use lower case letters. Thus

$$y_t = f(k_t, z_t) = F\left(\frac{K_t}{N_t}, 1, \frac{Z_t}{N_t}\right) \tag{2.18}$$

and $F_N = f - kf_k - zf_z$ is the marginal product of labor. Thus, the condition that labor is paid its marginal product becomes

$$w_t = f(k_t, z_t) - k_t f_k - z_t f_z.$$

Assume that labor saves nothing and that the growth of population (labor force) is determined by w_t, which is thus per capita consumption:

$$\frac{N_{t+1}}{N_t} = 1 + n[f(k_t, z_t) - k_t f_k(k_t, z_t) - z_t f_z(k_t, z_t)] = 1 + n(k_t, z_t). \tag{2.19}$$

If the entire surplus is saved and can be used only to augment the capital stock, Eq. (2.2) is replaced by

$$I_t = K_t F_K + Z_t F_Z$$
$$= Y_t - N_t w_t$$
$$= N_t(y_t - w_t).$$

Thus,

$$k_{t+1} = \frac{(1 - \delta)k_t + (y_t - w_t)}{1 + n(k_t, z_t)} = g(k_t, z_t). \tag{2.20}$$

The function g depends only on k_t and z_t since $y_t = f(k_t, z_t)$ and w_t is also a function of k_t and z_t.

We assume that the evolution of Z is governed by

$Z_{t+1} = H(K_t, N_t, Z_t),$

where H is homogeneous of degree 1 so that we can write

$$z_{t+1} = \frac{\psi(k_t, z_t)}{1 + n(k_t, z_t)} = h(k_t, z_t), \tag{2.21}$$

where $\Psi(k_t, z_t) = H(k_t, 1, z_t)$. The system (2.20) and (2.21) is a planar system in k_t and z_t, of the kind described in Nerlove (1993).

Eqs. (2.20) and (2.21) define two functions:

$$k^* = M(z^*), \quad z^* = N(k^*), \tag{2.22}$$

which may not be one-to-one or even continuous; that is, $M(\ )$ and/or $N(\ )$ may have several branches and one or more discontinuities. Nonetheless, if we plot these two functions in the k^*–z^* plane, points at which they cross are stationary points. Moreover, the derivatives of these functions may be obtained at any point of continuity along any branch by means of the implicit function theorem. Thus, along a branch

$$
\begin{aligned}
M' &= \frac{dk^*}{dz^*} = \frac{\varphi_z}{1 - \varphi_k} = \frac{(1+n^*)g_z + n_z k^*}{1 - [(1+n^*)g_k + n_k k^*]}, \\
N' &= \frac{dz^*}{dk^*} = \frac{\psi_k}{1 - \psi_z} = \frac{(1+n^*)h_k + n_k k^*}{1 - [(1+n^*)h_z + n_z k^*]}.
\end{aligned}
\tag{2.23}
$$

Under general circumstances $k^* = 0 = z^*$ is a stationary point. Thus at least one branch of $M(\ )$ and one of $N(\ )$ must begin at the origin.

Our interest is focused on the positive quadrant of the k^*–z^* plane since negative values make no economic sense. In Fig. 2 we have plotted the curves

$$z^* = M^{-1}(k^*), \quad z^* = N(k^*).$$

$M^{-1}(\ )$ is defined for the particular branch of $M(\ )$ starting at the origin; there may be other branches. Both curves start from $(0, 0)$ and are initially increasing (if not increasing there would be no nontrivial stationary point in the positive quadrant for this branch). The curve M_1^{-1} is plotted first increasing, then decreasing. When N_1 has a slope initially less than M_1^{-1} and the latter turns down, we find that a nontrivial stationary point (k_1^*, z_1^*) exists. When N_2 has a slope initially greater than M_1^{-1} and does not decrease, there is no nontrivial stationary point. When M_2^{-1} is not strictly concave, there may be several nontrivial stationary points with different local stability properties. And, of course, if N is not strictly increasing there may be a great many nontrivial equilibria. Furthermore, since several branches of both functions not starting at the

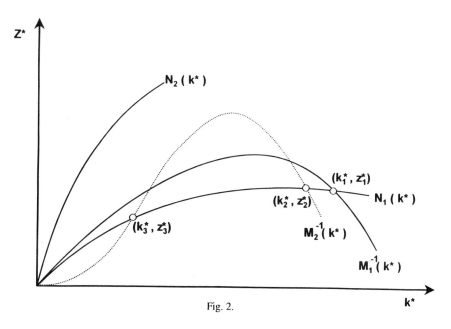

Fig. 2.

origin may exist, these too define stationary points where they intersect. The method discussed there may be used to analyze the dynamic properties of the system. The analysis is, however, complicated and does not, at this level of abstraction, lead to much insight.

The following extended example, however, is helpful in understanding the nature and existence of stationary points: Let the per capita surplus available for investment (and thus, by assumption, per capita investment itself) be

$$s_t = y_t - w_t = k_t f_k(k_t, z_t) + z_t f_z(k_t, z_t), \tag{2.24}$$

and denote functions or values evaluated at a nontrivial stationary point (k^*, z^*) by affixing an asterisk.

Example

Assume a Cobb–Douglas production function

$$y_t = k_t^\sigma z_t^\mu, \quad 0 < \sigma, \mu; \quad \sigma + \mu < 1, \tag{2.18'}$$

and a linear approximation to $n(w_t)$ which yields

$$1 + n(k_t, z_t) = \frac{N_{t+1}}{N_t} = \frac{w_t}{w_m}, \quad w_m > 0. \tag{2.19'}$$

Then Eq. (2.20) becomes

$$k_{t+1} = \frac{(1-\delta)k_t + s_t}{w_t / w_m}, \tag{2.20'}$$

where

$$s_t = (\sigma + \mu)y_t$$

and

$$w_t = y_t - s_t = (1 - \sigma - \mu)y_t.$$

Hence, the function M^{-1} introduced above is defined explicitly by

$$M^{-1}(k^*) = z^* = \left\{ \frac{(1-\delta)(k^*)^{1-\sigma}}{\left[\dfrac{1-(\sigma+\mu)}{w_m} \right] k^* - (\sigma + \mu)} \right\}^{1/\mu} \tag{2.25}$$

Suppose that $\psi(k_t, z_t)$ is also linear in logs:

$$z_{t+1} = k_t^\alpha z_t^\beta, \quad 0 < \beta < 1, \tag{2.21'}$$

but α may be negative. Then

$$N(z^*) = (k^*)^{\alpha/(1-\beta)}. \tag{2.26}$$

If $0 < \alpha < (1 - \beta)$, that is, if $\alpha + \beta < 1$, $N(z^*)$ in Eq. (2.24) is a concave function of z^*, since $0 < \beta < 1$ is assumed. This assumption might be violated if, for example, Z represented environmental quality, so that per capita environmental quality might be degraded at higher capital–labor ratios.

The shape of $M^{-1}(z^*)$ in Eq. (2.25) depends on the parameters and on their relationship to one another. When, for example, $1/\mu$ is an even number, $M^{-1}(k^*)$ increases from 0 to $+\infty$ as k^* goes from zero to $k_m = w_m(\sigma + \mu)/[1 - (\sigma + \mu)]$. For larger values of k^*, $M^{-1}(k^*)$ is a decreasing function of k^*, with

$$\frac{dz^*}{dk^*} = \frac{-z^*}{\mu} \cdot \frac{\dfrac{\sigma(1-\sigma-\mu)}{w_m}k^* + (\sigma+\mu)(1-\sigma)}{k^*\left[\dfrac{(1-\sigma-\mu)}{w_m}k^* - (\sigma+\mu)\right]} < 0 \quad \text{for } k^* > k_m.$$

Thus, for $k^* > k_m$, $\alpha, \beta > 0$ and $\alpha + \beta < 1$ and $\sigma, \mu > 0$ and $\sigma + \mu < 1$, there exists a unique nontrivial stationary point. Moreover, this point is a stable equilibrium. It is interesting to note that the location of this equilibrium depends on the value of the minimum wage, w_m. The values of k^* and z^* determine the rate of growth of population from Eq. (2.19'):

$$\frac{N_{t+1}}{N_t} = \frac{[1-(\sigma+\mu)](k^*)^{\sigma}(z^*)^{\mu}}{w_m}$$

$$= \frac{[1-(\sigma+\mu)](k^*)^{\sigma+(\alpha\mu/(1-\beta))}}{w_m}.$$

If

$$w_m = [1-(\sigma+\mu)](k^*)^{\sigma+(\alpha\mu/(1-\beta))},$$

population too will be stationary. If w_m exceeds this value, population will be declining (eventually to zero). If w_m is less, population will be increasing. In general, the smaller w_m, the higher the rate of population growth at a stationary point and the lower per capita consumption.

In this example

$$\xi_k = \frac{w_m}{1-(\sigma+\mu)}\left\{\frac{(1-\delta)(1-\sigma)}{y^*}\right\},$$

$$\xi_z = \frac{w_m}{1-(\sigma+\mu)}\left\{\frac{-\mu(1-\sigma)}{y^*}\right\},$$

$$\eta_k = \alpha,$$

$$\eta_z = \beta.$$

Thus

$$\operatorname{tr} J = \frac{(w_m/y^*)(1-\delta)(1-\sigma)}{1-(\sigma+\mu)} - \beta,$$

$$\det J = \frac{(w_m/y^*)(1-\delta)}{1-(\sigma+\mu)}(\alpha\mu + \beta(1-\sigma)).$$

That is

$$\det J = \left[\frac{\alpha\mu + \beta(1-\sigma)}{1-\sigma}\right] \text{tr } J + \beta\left[\frac{\alpha\mu + \beta(1-\sigma)}{1-\sigma}\right] = A \text{ tr } J + B. \tag{2.27}$$

Eq. (2.27) determines a straight line in the tr J–det J plane with slope

$$A = \frac{\alpha\mu}{1-\sigma} + \beta$$

and intercept

$$B = \frac{\alpha\beta\mu}{1-\sigma} + \beta^2.$$

Under plausible assumptions: $0 < \sigma < 1$, $0 < \mu < 1$, $\sigma + \mu < 1$, and $0 < \beta < 1$, but the sign of α is ambiguous.

Consider first the case in which $\alpha > 0$, that is increases in the capital–labor ratio favorably affect the stock of Z. Then A and B are clearly positive. For example, if $\sigma = 0.5$, $\mu = 0.25$, $\alpha = 0.25$, and $\beta = 0.5$, $A = 0.675$ and $B = 0.3125$.

If, on the other hand, $\alpha < 0$, so that an increase in the capital–labor ratio negatively impacts on the stock Z, then the signs of A and B are ambiguous. $A \gtrless 0$ according as $(\mu/(1-\sigma)) \lessgtr (-\beta/\alpha)$. For example, in the previous case suppose $\alpha = -0.25$, then $A = 0.375$ and $B = 0.1875$. But suppose that instead $\beta = 0.25$ and $\alpha = -0.75$, then $A = -0.125$ and $B = -0.03125$.

Plot the line det $J = A$ tr $J + B$ on a background similar to Fig. 1, Nerlove (1993), for positive A and B. The line clearly crosses regions of both stability and instability. Where on this line we are determines whether or not the equilibrium is stable. In the first numerical example

$$\text{tr } J = \frac{(w_m/y^*)(1-\delta)(1-\sigma)}{1-(\sigma+\mu)} - \beta$$

$$= 2\left(\frac{w_m}{y^*}\right)(1-\delta) - \frac{1}{2}.$$

It follows that the issue of stability or instability turns on the magnitude of $(w_m/y^*)(1-\delta)$ and since $(1-\delta)$ is likely to be close to one, on the ratio of the minimum wage to per capita output at the stationary point. Only if this is rather small, will the equilibrium be stable. In particular tr J must be less than $(1-B)/A$, which places a clear constraint on $(w_m/y^*)(1-\delta)$ given the values of α, β, σ and μ.

This extended example shows that the existence and nature of an equilibrium of the capital–labor and resource–labor ratios with endogenous population turn crucially on the minimum wage in relation to output or to the capital–labor ratio. If this is very large, the resulting equilibrium, although likely to exist, will generally be unstable.

2.4. Lucas and Romer: new directions in growth theory

Recent work extending Solow's and Swan's earlier contributions focuses on the implications of increasing returns and investment in human capital. Solow (1992) characterizes the neoclassical growth model, i.e. Solow–Swan and its derivatives, as follows: "The main implication of this model is that, no matter where it starts, it tends eventually to a steady state independent of the initial conditions (i.e. the initial stock of capital). In that steady state extensive quantities like aggregate output are growing at a rate equal to the sum of the rates of labor-force growth and labor-augmenting technological progress. Thus per capita output, capital and consumption all grow at the same rate as technology is improving. …the asymptotic growth rate for the model economy depends only on *the exogenously given rates of technological progress and population growth* [italics supplied]". Modifying the basic Solow–Swan model so as to allow for endogenous population growth and/or endogenous saving does allow for a somewhat richer set of conclusions; in particular the possibility that multiple stationary equilibria exist allows each economy to arrive at a point depending on the initial capital stock and population. It remains true, however, that per capita growth in output, consumption and capital stock can only occur asymptotically at the same rate as technical progress.

Romer (1986, 1990) and Lucas (1988) argue that this conclusion does not accord with even the most basic facts: new technology is widely accessible everywhere with little lag. Thus, even though the actual levels of capital stock, consumption and output per capita may differ depending on initial conditions, *rates of growth* should tend to equality everywhere. If there were only one unique stationary equilibrium, the model predicts that poor countries should grow faster than rich countries but that all should eventually grow at the same rate. Although the facts are in some dispute (see Baily and Schultze, 1990; Mankiw et al., 1992), there is some evidence that it is primarily the poorest countries that continue to fall behind those that entered the modern industrial age by mid-twentieth century, which is clearly at variance with the implication of neoclassical growth theory without endogenous population growth. Rather, however, than seek an explanation in terms of one of several stable equilibria in a model with endogenous fertility and/or mortality, both Lucas and Romer, as well as other contributors who have followed their lead, seek an explanation in terms of endogenous technical change and thus to endogenize the per capita growth rate.

One way to endogenize growth is to augment the neoclassical model so that investment in knowledge, and thus technical change, is economically motivated. Boserup's approach, discussed in the preceding section, represents a variant of this, although without additional assumptions, cannot explain growing per capita consumption or divergencies among countries. The assumption of increasing returns may also provide an avenue, as Young (1928) recognized long ago, although, as Solow (1992) notes increasing returns by itself is not sufficient to achieve endogenous growth. What Lucas does, in addition, is to identify technical progress with the accumulation of "human" capital, but as a stock of knowledge which survives the bearer rather than as a stock of skills which must be embodied in a particular human agent and which disappears when that agent dies. Both Lucas and Romer model production technology so that individual firms see constant returns to scale in the inputs they control but, because of favorable spillovers, there are increasing returns in the aggregate. This is in sharp contrast to the way in which Nerlove (1974) treated human capital in his explanation of the demographic transition; there the central feature of human capital was precisely that it died with the bearer so that an exogenous fall in death rates, particularly infant and child mortality, greatly enhanced the returns to parental investment in the human capital of their children, one form of which were in the form of better health and nutrition, further increasing the probability of survival. Additionally, Lucas assumes that aggregate production technology can be represented as $F(K, HL)$, where K is the stock of physical capital, L is employment (proportional to population), and H is the accumulated stock of "human" capital or of knowledge per capita. That aggregate output depends only on the total stock of "human" capital or knowledge and not on how it is embodied is an extremely strong assumption and one which we would regard as unrealistic: Are ten workmen who can read, for example, always worth one hundred who cannot no matter what the size of the labor force?

Increasing returns are fundamental to the arguments of both Romer and Lucas but in different ways: Romer assumes that the creation of new "knowledge" by one firm has positive external effect on the production possibilities of other firms so that the production of the consumption good as a function of stock of knowledge exhibits increasing returns. Lucas, on the other hand, assumes that individuals acquire productivity enhancing skills by investing time in learning; accumulation of skills by one individual not only enhances his productivity, it also enhances the productivity of all workers through its positive spill-over effect on the average skill level of the whole labor force; "human" capital or the stock of individual skills is produced from accumulated average level of skills and foregone labor time with increasing returns (constant returns to each factor individually) (see Raut and Srinivasan (1993) for an extensive survey of these models).

It should be noted that the spill-over effects of the average stock of human capital per worker in the Lucas model and of knowledge in the Romer model are exter-

nalities unperceived (and hence not internalized) by individual agents. However, for the economy *as a whole* they generate increasing scale economies even though the perceived production function of each agent exhibits constant returns to scale. Thus by introducing nonconvexities through the device of a Marshallian externality Lucas and Romer are able to work with intertemporal competitive (albeit a socially nonoptimal) equilibrium. Both in effect make assumptions that ensure that the marginal product of physical capital is bounded away from zero, and, as such, it is not surprising that in both models sustained growth in *income* per *worker* is possible. Thus Lucas and Romer avoid facing the problem that research and development (R&D) which leads to technical progress, is naturally associated with imperfectly competitive markets. (Raut and Srinivasan, 1993: p. 8.)

Under either set of assumptions, it is possible to show that steady-state growth rates depend on preferences and on policies affecting private incentives or disincentives to invest in either form of capital. So, while these models are ad hoc, the purpose of explaining why steady-state growth rates do not converge is accomplished. Because of Lucas' treatment of "human" capital as a stock of general knowledge, which lives on after its initial embodiment in an individual human being, and Romer's treatment of a general stock of knowledge, however, their models are of little use in accounting for the demographic transition. What is required for that is a deeper understanding of the incentives of parents to invest in the individual-specific human capital of their children. Growth in general knowledge and endogenous technical change are undoubtedly important to the understanding of the process of economic growth more generally, but families' decisions with respect to the numbers of children they have and those that affect their survival are crucial to understanding how economic growth and demographic change are related.

3. The microeconomics of endogenous population: fertility, mortality and investment in children

In this section, we explore a number of recent models of family decision-making relevant to the relation between demographic change and economic growth. We begin with a discussion of the fundamental trade-off between the quality and the quantity of children. We continue with a survey of models which emphasize parental altruism as the motivation for parental concern with both numbers and quality of children. Next, we turn to nonaltruistic motives for having surviving children such as parental security in old age and discuss models in which parents may invest in their children so as to enhance the chances for their survival or to improve their future productivity. Finally, we return to a discussion of two-sided altruism (parents for children and children for parents) as a basis for parents' transfers to children and children's subsequent transfers to parents.

3.1. Quality versus quantity: the Becker–Lewis model[1]

The trade-offs between quantity and quality of children and between quantity of children and income, explored in this section, were advanced by Becker and Lewis (1973). If parents care about the numbers and welfare of their children and, at least partly, control these variables so as to maximize their own utility, certain nonlinearities and nonconvexities are introduced in the budget constraint which they face, and certain characteristics of the utility function which they maximize are modified in contrast to the constraint and maximand encountered in the traditional theory of consumer choice. The seminal paper of Becker and Lewis (1973) shows how these modifications may affect the relation between income and desired fertility even when children are a normal good.

Consider a pair of parents as an individual decision-maker who consumes units of a single composite consumption good (c). The parents also extract utility from the number of their children (n) and the quality, or well-being (b), of each one of them. This quality is measured by the units of the single composite good spent on these children (e.g., on their education, health, etc.). For the sake of simplicity, we treat n as a continuous variable. We come back to the importance of the discrete variability of n below. In addition, we assume that all children are identical and that the parents treat them symmetrically, so we use the symbol b for the quality of every child.

The parents have a direct utility function,

$$u^*(c, b, n), \tag{3.1}$$

where $u_i^* > 0$, $i = 1,2,3$. This means that the parents extract positive utility from all three variables, c, b, and n. The parents choose both b and n in addition to c. Note that we implicitly assume that parents correctly anticipate that each of their children will be identical and all will be born at the beginning of the decision period. Let the parents' income, in terms of the single composite good, be I. They spend c on themselves and a total of bn on their children. We also allow for a pecuniary benefit from each child, denoted by a and measured in terms of the single composite good. Parents correctly anticipate this benefit, which could be a child allowance paid by the government, a wage earned by the child and contributed to the household income, etc. The benefit could also be negative if there is a tax on children. Thus, the parents' budget constraint is

$$c + bn \leq I + an. \tag{3.2}$$

The term bn makes the budget constraint nonlinear. Furthermore, the budget set $\{(c, b, n) \mid c + bn < I + an\}$, describing the parents' feasible bundles of c, b, and n, is

---

[1]This section draws on the earlier exposition of Nerlove et al. (1987: Ch. 5).

not convex. Notice, however, that the utility function, Eq. (3.1), can still have all the properties conventionally assumed, such as increasing monotonicity and quasi-concavity.

The analysis and results of traditional theory hold for a linear budget constraint but with some modification can be applied to this case. The basic idea is that, since, as long as the Marshallian and Hicksian demand functions are well defined and differentiable, standard results follow. The analysis is carried out in Nerlove et al. (1987: Ch. 5) by simply redefining the choice variables of the consumer unit so as to obtain a linear budget constraint at the expense of losing the conventional properties of the utility function. Then, the conventional results apply with respect to the newly defined variables.

Specifically, defining by q the total expenditure on children (i.e., $q = bn$) and letting

$$u(c, q, n) = u^*(c, q/n, n),\tag{3.3}$$

the parents' optimization problem is to choose c, q, and n so as to maximize Eq. (3.3) subject to the following linear budget constraint:

$$c + q \leq I + an.\tag{3.4}$$

Observe that while u^* is monotonically increasing in its third argument, n (i.e., $u_3^* > 0$), it follows from Eq. (3.3) that u need not increase in n because of the term q/n in u^*:

$$u_3 = u_3^* - \frac{qu_2^*}{n^2}.$$

Furthermore, the number of children in the budget constraint, Eq. (3.4), appears in the same way as the labor supply appears in a conventional model, i.e., it adds to income rather than to expenditures (assuming $a > 0$). Thus, at the parents' optimum, the marginal utility of n (namely, u_3) must be negative. With this linear budget constraint, all the conventional results of traditional theory hold with respect to the variables c, q, and n.

If the economy, in the context of which the representative household makes its fertility decisions, is growing, the typical family's income will be growing. In the Becker–Lewis model, it is possible that fertility is reduced even though children are a normal consumption good. To see this, consider first the consumer optimization problem in terms of the original utility function, u^*, and the nonlinear budget constraint Eq. (3.2):

$$\max_{c,b,n} u^*(c,b,n), \quad \text{such that } c + bn \leq I.\tag{3.5}$$

(To simplify the analysis and make it comparable to that of Becker and Lewis, we let $a = 0$. $a \neq 0$ will play a further role in multiperiod models in which transfers from children to parents also occur.) One can see that the quality of children (b) is the "price" of the quantity of children (n) and vice versa. Thus, some of the parents' choice variables also act as prices, and the usual conditions on the utility function that guarantee the normality of a certain good do not apply. New conditions must be derived.

The optimal c, b, and n in the problem, Eq. (3.5), all depend on income I. Denote the optimal c, b, and n by $C(I)$, $B(I)$, and $N(I)$, respectively; we are interested here in the sign of the elasticity of N with respect to I. As we noted, this is not the standard question as to whether a certain good is a normal good, and one cannot use the standard conditions for normality. Therefore, we form a hypothetical problem that is a standard consumer optimization problem; we explain below how it is related to our true problem, Eq. (3.5).

Consider the following problem:

$$\max_{c,b,n} u^*(c,b,n), \quad \text{such that } c + p_b b + p_n n \leq I + M, \tag{3.6}$$

where $p_b > 0$, $p_n > 0$, and M are parameters. One can interpret p_b and p_n as the "prices" of quality and quantity of children, respectively; M is interpreted as a lump-sum transfer. Now Eq. (3.6) is a standard consumer optimization problem, and one denotes the optimal bundle of c, b, and n by $\overline{C}(p_b, p_n, I + M)$, $\overline{B}(p_b, p_n, I + M)$, and $\overline{N}(p_b, p_n, I + M)$, respectively. The latter functions are conventional Marshallian demand functions and, in particular, we assume that they exhibit normality:

$$\overline{C}_3, \overline{B}_3, \overline{N}_3 > 0.$$

Comparing Eq. (3.5) with Eq. (3.6), it is straightforward to establish the relationship between (C, B, N) and $(\overline{C}, \overline{B}, \overline{N})$. Evaluated at $p_b = N(I)$, $p_n = B(I)$ and $M = N(I)B(I)$, the bundle $(\overline{C}, \overline{B}, \overline{N})$ is equal to (C, B, N):

$$\overline{C}(N(I), B(I), I + N(I)B(I)) = C(I),$$

$$\overline{B}(N(I), B(I), I + N(I)B(I)) = B(I), \tag{3.7}$$

$$\overline{N}(N(I), B(I), I + N(I)B(I)) = N(I).$$

Differentiating totally the last two relationships with respect to I:

$$(\overline{B}_1 + B\overline{B}_3)\frac{dN}{dI} + (\overline{B}_2 + N\overline{B}_3 - 1)\frac{dB}{dI} = -\overline{B}_3,$$

$$(\overline{N}_1 + B\overline{N}_3 - 1)\frac{dN}{dI} + (\overline{N}_2 + N\overline{N}_3)\frac{dB}{dI} = -\overline{N}_3.$$

(3.8)

Employing the Hicks–Slutsky equations corresponding to the hypothetical problem, Eq. (3.6), one sees that $\overline{B}_3 + B\overline{B}_3$ is the Hicks–Slutsky substitution effect of the "price" of the quality of children on the quantity of children demanded. Denote this effect by $\overline{S}_{bb}$. Also, $\overline{B}_2 + N\overline{B}_3$ is the Hicks–Slutsky substitution effect of the "price" of the quantity of children on the quality of children demanded: denote it by $\overline{S}_{bn}$. Similarly, $\overline{N}_1 + b\overline{N}_3 = \overline{S}_{nb}$, and $\overline{N}_2 + N\overline{N}_3 = \overline{S}_{nn}$. By the symmetry of the Hicks–Slutsky effects, $\overline{S}_{bn} = \overline{S}_{nb}$. Substituting these relationships into Eq. (3.8) and solving for dN/dI:

$$\frac{dN}{dI} = \frac{\overline{N}_3(1 - \overline{S}_{nb}) + \overline{B}_3\overline{S}_{nn}}{(1 - \overline{S}_{nb})^2 - \overline{S}_{bb}\overline{S}_{nn}}.$$

(3.9)

In elasticity terms, Eq. (3.9) becomes

$$\eta_{nI} = k\frac{\overline{\eta}_{nI}(1 - \overline{\varepsilon}_{nb}) + \overline{\eta}_{bI}\overline{\varepsilon}_{nn}}{(1 - \overline{\varepsilon}_{nb})^2 - \overline{\varepsilon}_{bb}\overline{\varepsilon}_{nn}},$$

(3.10)

similarly,

$$\eta_{bI} = k\frac{\overline{\eta}_{bI}(I - \overline{\varepsilon}_{nb}) + \overline{\eta}_{nI}\overline{\varepsilon}_{bb}}{(1 - \overline{\varepsilon}_{nb})^2 - \overline{\varepsilon}_{bb}\overline{\varepsilon}_{nn}},$$

(3.11)

where

$$\eta_{nI} = \frac{dN}{dI}\frac{I}{N}, \qquad \text{income elasticity of } N(I),$$

$$\overline{\eta}_{nI} = \overline{N}_3\frac{\overline{I + NB}}{\overline{N}}, \qquad \text{income elasticity of } \overline{N}(\ ) \text{ (assumed positive)},$$

$$\overline{\eta}_{bI} = \overline{B}_3\frac{\overline{I + NB}}{\overline{B}}, \qquad \text{income elasticity of } \overline{B}(\ ) \text{ (assumed positive)},$$

$$k = \frac{I}{\overline{I + NB}} < 1,$$

$$\bar{\varepsilon}_{nn} \equiv \frac{\bar{S}_{nn}P_n}{\bar{N}} = \frac{\bar{S}_{nn}\bar{B}}{\bar{N}}, \qquad \text{own-substitution elasticity of } \bar{N}(\ ),$$

$$\bar{\varepsilon}_{bb} \equiv \frac{\bar{S}_{bb}P_b}{\bar{B}} = \frac{\bar{S}_{bb}\bar{N}}{\bar{B}}, \qquad \text{own-substitution elasticity of } \bar{B}(\ ),$$

$$\bar{\varepsilon}_{nb} \equiv \frac{\bar{S}_{nb}P_b}{\bar{N}} = \bar{S}_{nb}, \qquad \text{cross-substitution elasticity.}$$

Thus, one can see from Eq. (3.10) that, if there is a unitary substitution elasticity between the quantity and quality of children (i.e., $\bar{\varepsilon}_{nb} = 1$), then $\eta_{nl} = -(k/\bar{\varepsilon}_{bb})\eta_{bl} > 0$, by the negativity of own-substitution elasticity, $\bar{\varepsilon}_{bb}$, and the normality of $b(\bar{\eta}_{bl} > 0)$. In this case an increase in income increases fertility (and, as can be seen from Eq. (3.11), child quality as well).

Now assume that the substitution elasticity between the quantity and quality of children is larger than 1 (i.e., $\bar{\varepsilon}_{nb} > 1$). Also assume that total expenditure on children increases with income (i.e., $N(I)B(I)$ increases in I). This means that at least one of the components of this expenditure, $N(I)$ or $B(I)$, must be increasing in income. Suppose then that $\eta_{bl} > 0$. Since it is assumed that $\bar{\varepsilon}_{nb} > 1$, it follows that the numerator on the right-hand side of Eq. (3.11) is negative. Hence the denominator must also be negative. But it then follows from Eq. (3.10) that η_{nl} is positive. Thus, under the assumption that total expenditure on children increases in income, a high degree of substitutability between child quality and quantity (i.e., $\bar{\varepsilon}_{nb} > 1$) implies that income has a positive effect on both the quantity and the quality of children (i.e., both η_{nl} and η_{bl} are positive).

However, as this quantity–quality problem is not a standard consumer choice problem, one can extract from Eq. (3.10) many cases in which income has a negative effect on fertility (i.e., $\eta_{nl} < 0$). If the substitution elasticity between the quantity and quality is smaller than one ($\bar{\varepsilon}_{nb} < 1$), there are two possibilities.

One possibility is that the denominator of Eq. (3.10) or Eq. (3.11) is positive. This occurs when the own-substitution elasticities ($\bar{\varepsilon}_{bb}$ and $\bar{\varepsilon}_{nm}$) are relatively low. In this case one can see from Eq. (3.10) that if the income elasticity of quality in the hypothetical problem, Eq. (3.6) (namely, η_{bl}) is substantially higher than the income elasticity of quantity in the same problem (namely, η_{nl}), then child quantity falls with income ($\eta_{nl} < 0$) while child quality rises ($\eta_{bl} > 0$).

The other possibility is that the denominator of Eq. (3.10) or Eq. (3.11) is negative. This occurs when the own-substitution elasticities ($\bar{\varepsilon}_{bb}$ and $\bar{\varepsilon}_{nm}$) are relatively high. In this case, if $\bar{\eta}_{bl}$ is substantially lower than $\bar{\eta}_{nl}$, then, again, $\eta_{nl} < 0$ and $\eta_{nl} > 0$.

Introducing the quantity and "quality" of children in parents' utility function introduces a nonlinearity and nonconvexity in the budget constraint. However, a reformulation in which the budget constraint is linear but the utility function is no longer monotonically increasing and strictly quasi-concave permits us to apply the conventional theory of consumer choice to derive the result that, even if the income elasticities of demand for both quantity and quality of children are positive, the observed (uncompensated) elasticity of fertility (numbers of children) with respect to income may be negative. Whether or not this occurs depends in part on the elasticity of substitution between quantity and quality of children in parents' utility function.

3.2. Parental altruism and investment in human capital

In a series of papers, Becker (1988), Becker and Barro (1988), Barro and Becker (1989), and Becker et al. (1990, extended in Tamura, 1992), seek to establish a connection among fertility, bequests which may be in the form of human capital formation, parental altruism and economic growth. In their basic model, parents choose both the number of children and the capital, both human and physical, bequeathed to each child. One possible interpretation of the "quality" variable in the Becker–Lewis formulation, presented in Section 3.1, is as the investment or bequest in the form of human capital to the child. Parents' choices are driven by the trade-off between the altruism which they feel towards their children and the satisfactions which they derive from their own consumption and from having children. More formally, parents choose the optimal values of their own consumption, the number of children and the capital transferred to each child, taking into account the costs of rearing children and the dependence of their own utility on the utility of their children. This analysis thus represents an extension of the Becker–Lewis model of the trade-off between quality and quantity of children. The difference between the model discussed here and the earlier model is that the "quality" of children is now given an explicit interpretation in terms of bequests to children in the form of human and/or physical capital, and an explicit rationale for the inclusion of such a "quality" measure in parental utility functions is given in terms of the "love" which parents feel towards their children, i.e., the degree to which children's utilities enter parents' utilities and trade-off with parents' own consumption and desires for children.

In this formulation there is no explicit recognition of the reasons why even basically altruistic parents might want surviving children. Although many would not regard such an omission as a serious shortcoming (need we offer any reason for the enjoyment of a symphony?), even in economically developed societies parents derive obvious benefits from surviving children in old age, and concern with old age security is an even more important consideration in poor countries with limited means for parents to transfer consumption from productive and healthy years to years of decline. In the next section of this part, we consider a model in which parents have children and invest in them both because they "love" them and because they expect benefits from their children in old age. This formulation raises an extremely difficult issue as to why parents might expect their children to contribute to parents' welfare at the expense of their own consumption and contribution to their own children's welfare. The answer is presumably "reverse altruism", that concern of children for their parents' welfare. But, as we shall see, certain asymmetries, across generations backwards versus forwards, complicate the analysis, as well as divergencies among individual endowments which may result when survival is stochastic.

The aim of the Barro and Becker (1989), analysis is to describe the way in which the economy and population evolve through time in consequence of the endogeneity of fertility *and* capital formation. Becker (1988), for example, is quite explicit about this aim, in describing research designed to model economies which have both low-welfare equilibria with high fertility or population and low levels of capital and those with low fertility and high levels of capital and/or economic growth. Extension of microeconomic models of fertility and human and physical capital formation in this direction requires, however, certain general equilibrium considerations.

Suppose that parents care about the number of their children and their children's welfare or utility. Employing the notation of the model presented above but adding the generational subscript t, we now have first-generation utility

$$u_t = u(c_t, n_t, u_{t+1}).$$ \hfill (3.12)

If parents and children do not differ each from the other and from one another,

$$u_{t+1} = u(c_{t+1}, n_{t+1}, u_{t+2})$$

and so on. Moreover, each child receives the same bequest from her parent. (Suppose one-parent families.) Imagine this bequest, b_t, to be in the form of physical capital and to act simply as an addition to the endowment of each child, i.e., each individual in the next generation. Thus the problem of each parent is to maximize u_t in Eq. (3.1) subject to the budget constraint

$$c_t + (b_t + a)n_t \leq I_t + b_{t-1},$$ \hfill (3.13)

where a denotes additional exogenous costs (or benefits) of rearing a child. This is an extremely difficult problem and not one which, as far as we know, is capable of any general solution. However, Becker and Barro (1988) (see also Nerlove et al., 1987: p. 78; Barro, 1974; Razin and Ben Zion, 1975) assume a particular form of additively separable utility:

$$u_t = v(c_t, n_t) + \beta(n_t) n_t \hat{u}_{t+1}.$$ \hfill (3.14)

$\beta(n_t)$ measures the degree of altruism per child which Becker and Barro (B-B) assume to be decreasing with n, $\beta' \leq 0$. We have put a hat over the utility of the next generation to indicate that it is the parent's "estimate" of each child's utility. B-B assume perfect foresight and replace $\hat{u}_{t+1}$ with u_{t+1}, but this is quite a leap, although, of course, if one does take perfect foresight seriously, it is a natural starting point. Somewhat different and not uninteresting conclusions emerge if $\hat{u}_{t+1}$ is some function of the *parent's* choices of b_t and n_t. In this case, $\hat{u}_{t+1}$ is the maximum taken over c_{t+1}, b_{t+1} and n_{t+1}, given I_t, b_t and the expectation (or estimate) of per child endowment, $\hat{I}_{t+1}$, but it is not necessarily the same as u_{t+1}.

3.2.1. A nonrecursive formulation with altruism and bequests

Let us define $f_t(b_t, \hat{I}_{t+1}) = \hat{u}_{t+1}$ to be the parent's expectations of her child's future welfare. Then the parent's problem is

$$\max_{c,n,b}\{v_t(c_t,n_t) + \beta(n_t)n_t f_t(b_t, \hat{I}_{t+1})\},$$

such that $c_t + (b_t + a)n_t \leq I_t + b_{t-1}$, $\qquad\qquad\qquad\qquad\qquad (3.15)$

where I_t, $\hat{I}_{t+1}$ and b_{t-1} are given. Neglecting the integer restriction on n_t and assuming an interior solution, the first-order conditions are

$$v_1 = \lambda,$$
$$v_2 + \beta(n_t)[1 - \varepsilon_\beta]f(b_t, \hat{I}_{t+1}) = \lambda[b_t + a], \qquad\qquad\qquad (3.16)$$
$$\beta(n_t)n_t f'(b_t, \hat{I}_{t+1}) = \lambda n_t,$$

where $\varepsilon_\beta = -n\beta'/\beta$ the elasticity of the degree of altruism with respect to the number of children. These conditions have the following interpretation: λ is the marginal utility of the parent's consumption. The elasticity ε_β is defined as positive since $\beta' \leq 0$ is assumed. If $\beta' = 0$, $\varepsilon_\beta = 0$ and β is a constant, equivalent in the B-B formulation to the usual form in which the future is discounted. If $\varepsilon_\beta < 1$, there is a positive benefit from having an additional child in addition to the direct marginal utility v_2 which results from the altruistic impact of the child's welfare. These benefits, in turn, are set equal to the marginal costs of the child valued in terms of the parent's own consumption, $\lambda[b_t + a]$. These costs are not parameters of the problem because they depend on the parent's choice of bequest, through λ, and on the choice of her own consumption level, as well. Finally, cancelling n_t from both sides of the last equation, the marginal benefit of increasing the bequest, which is solely altruistic, is equated to the marginal utility of consumption. If $u_t = u[c_t, n_t, b_t] = v_t(c_t, n_t) + \beta n_t f(b_t, \hat{I}_{t+1})$ is assumed to be a concave function of the three arguments, the conditions Eq. (16) are necessary and sufficient for an interior maximum. The problem is identical to the one which we analyzed above with $z_t = b_t + a$ and I replaced by $I_t + b_{t-1}$.

While, for the reasons adduced above, increases in exogenous endowment or previous parent's bequest need not increase fertility n_t, other effects may be less ambiguous: an increase in the exogenous cost of a child unambiguously increases the cost of having an additional child and therefore results in substitution of bequests and own consumption for child numbers, i.e., a reduction in fertility. What about the effect of an exogenous increase in the degree of altruism? Let β be constant. An increase in β, holding bequests, child numbers and the parent's expectations constant, unambiguously increases the parent's utility. While such an increase in altruism may increase both child numbers or bequests at the expense of the parent's own consumption, fertility may not increase for the same reason that an increase in the exogenous endowment of the parent need not increase fertility even if both child numbers and their welfare are normal goods.

Note that parental bequests act only through parent's altruism and their effects on parent's expectations of the welfare of her offspring. Eliminate altruism, and bequests are eliminated. Assuming minimal effects on parental expectations of her ability to influence the welfare of her children, standard theory applies with respect to the effects of changes in child-rearing costs and in exogenous parental endowment. But, even in this case, it is interesting to note that parents will unambiguously have more children than if there were no altruism (because of the additional utility generated by the term $\beta n f(\hat{I}_{t+1})$ in the utility function) despite the fact that they leave no bequests.

3.2.2. A recursive formulation with altruism and bequests

The formulation of the preceding subsection does not lend itself to the analysis of growth paths of population and bequests because parents' behavior depends on their expectations of the future welfare of their children, which only partly depend on the bequest left to each. Change parental expectations and you change everything. In a deterministic world, rational expectations and perfect foresight coincide. If in addition, children have the same utility functions, then under the separability assumption of the previous section, the recursive utility function (3.12) yields the following *dynastic utility function* of the parent in period 0:

$$\sum_{t=0}^{\infty}\left[\prod_{\tau=0}^{t}\gamma(n_{t-1})\right]v(c_t,n_t) \quad \text{where } \gamma(n_t)=\beta(n_t)n_t \text{ and } \gamma(n_{-1})\equiv 1, \tag{3.17}$$

where the constraint set involves equality. In order for the infinite sum in Eq. (3.17) to converge, it suffices that $v(.)$ is bounded and

$$0 < \beta(n_t)n_t < 1 \tag{3.18}$$

for the sequence in question. Clearly this will not be the case for all sequences. If we further assume that the children have the same exogenous endowments (independent of parental bequests) as their parents do, the counterpart of the maximization problem of the previous section becomes

$$\max_{\{c_t,n_t\}_{t=0}^{\infty}} \sum_{t=0}^{\infty}\left[\prod_{\tau=0}^{t}\gamma(n_t)\right]v(c_t,n_t),$$

such that $c_t + (b_{t+1} + a)n_t = I + b_t, \quad t \geq 0.$ (3.19)

We have replaced the inequality in the constraint of problem (3.15) by equality, since it will never be optimal to leave anything over if children and their welfare and consumption are all desirable.

Under certain conditions, the problem in Eq. (3.19) can be solved using dynamic programming techniques. For all $t \geq 0$, let $u^*(b_t)$ be the value function of generation t for given level of bequest, b_t, that a parent of generation t received from his/her parents. Then the Bellman equation or functional equation of the problem in Eq. (3.19) is

$$u^*(b_t) = \max_{c,n,b_{t+1}}\{v(c_t,n_t) + \beta(n_t)n_t u^*(b_{t+1})\},$$

such that $c_t + (b_{t+1} + a)n_t = I + b_t.$ (3.20)

The problem is then to solve for a differentiable concave value function $u^*(.)$ that satisfies Eq. (3.20). Given this value function, from the first-order conditions of problem (3.20) one obtains the optimal solution for n_t and b_{t+1} (and hence c_t) as a function of b_t:

$$b_{t+1} = g(b_t), \quad n_t = h(b_t).$$ (3.21)

Usually, one starts with the formulation in Eq. (3.17) and derives Eq. (3.20), and characterizes the solutions (see Stokey et al. (1989: pp. 66–102) for an exposition of this technique). A serious problem in our context of endogenous fertility is that even when we assume that the utility function $v(c_t, n_t)$ and the degree of altruism $\beta(n_t)n_t$ are all concave, the value function defined in Eq. (3.20) is not concave. Assuming Eq. (3.22) below, Benhabib and Nishimura (1989) within the above framework, and Nishimura and Raut (1993) in a somewhat more general framework, characterize the local dynamics of the optimal solution of Eq. (3.20) around a convex neighborhood of a steady state in which the optimal value function u^* is differentiable and concave.

B-B (1988, 1989), Becker et al. (1990), and Tamura (1992), for example, all restrict that part of the additively separable utility function of the parent referring to the parent's *own* utility from consumption and children, to depend on the parent's consumption alone, that is

$$v_n = 0. \tag{3.22}$$

Even then the analysis is too difficult to be carried out explicitly.

Two further restrictions introduced in B-B (1988) are:

(a) Constant elasticity altruism:

$$\beta(n_t) = \beta_0 n_t^{-\beta_1}.$$

(b) Constant elasticity utility of own consumption:

$$v(c_t) = c_t^{\sigma}, \quad 0 < \sigma < 1.$$

Two extensions to the formulation above designed to make the micro model adaptable to an equilibrium growth framework are:

(c) Replace I by w_t, a variable adult wage rate.

(d) Replace b_t by $(1 + r_t)k_{t-1}$, where k_t is the per capita stock of physical capital bequeathed to each child and r_t is the rate of return to physical capital.

The parent's budget constraint in Eq. (3.19) then becomes

$$c_t + (k_t + a)n_t = w_t + (1 + r_t)k_{t-1} \tag{3.23}$$

and his/her problem to maximize the so-called *dynastic utility* function:

$$u_0(c_0, n_0, c_1, n_1, \ldots) = \sum_{t=0}^{\infty} \left[\prod_{\tau=0}^{t} \gamma(n_{\tau-1}) \right] c_t^{\sigma}, \tag{3.24}$$

subject to constraint (3.23). The variables controlled by the parent are his/her own consumption, c_t, the number of children he/she has, n_t, and his/her bequest per child of physical capital, k_t. Variables exogenous to the parent's decision are the adult wage, w_t, his/her parent's bequest, k_{t-1}, and the rate of return on physical capital, r_t. The cost of rearing a child, a, and the elasticities $-\beta_1$ and σ, and the coefficient β_0 are also parameters of the parent's problem.

One of the underlying assumptions in these models is that the parent perfectly foresees the paths of future w_t and r_t (and, of course, his/her children as parents do so too). We leave it to the reader to judge how realistic such a perfect foresight assumption is, but it is essential to the development which follows.

For the existence of a solution with a positive number of children, the condition

$$\sigma < 1 - \beta_1 \qquad (3.25)$$

is necessary, which can be seen as follows. Let

$$N_i = \prod_{t=0}^{i-1} n_t$$

be the number of descendants in the ith generation of an individual alive now. $C_i = N_i c_i =$ total consumption in the ith generation. Then, since

$$u_0 = c_0^\sigma + \beta_0 n_0 n_0^{-\beta_1} c_1^\sigma + \beta_0^2 (n_0 n_1)(n_0 n_1)^{-\beta_1} c_2^\sigma + \cdots$$
$$= c_0^\sigma + \beta_0 N_1^{1-\beta} c_1^\sigma + \beta_0^2 N_2^{1-\beta} c_2^\sigma + \cdots$$
$$= c_0^\sigma + \beta_0 N_1^{1-\beta_1-\sigma} (N_1 c_1)^\sigma + \cdots,$$

it follows that

$$\frac{\partial u_0}{\partial N_i} = (1 - \beta_1 - \sigma) \frac{\beta_0^i N_i^{1-\beta_1-\sigma} (N_i c_i)^\sigma}{N_i}.$$

Hence, Eq. (3.25) is a condition that $\partial u_0 / \partial N_i > 0$, a condition which must hold near the maximizing values of n_1 and k_1 if parents are to produce children at all.

Neglecting integer restrictions, as we have throughout this section, B-B obtain the first-order conditions by setting the derivatives of the Lagrangian

$$u_0^* \equiv \sum_{i=0}^{\infty} \{c_i^\sigma \beta_0^i N_i^{1-\beta_1} - \lambda_i [c_i + (k_i + a) n_i - w_i - (1 + r_i) k_{i-1}]\} \qquad (3.26)$$

equal to zero:

$$\frac{\partial u_0^*}{\partial c_j} = \frac{\sigma V_j}{c_j} - \lambda_j = 0,$$

$$\frac{\partial u_0^*}{\partial n_j} = \sum_{i=j+1}^{\infty} \frac{(1-\beta_1) V_i}{N_i} \frac{\partial N_i}{\partial n_j} - \lambda_j (k_j + a),$$

$$= \frac{1}{n_j} \sum_{i-j+1}^{\infty} (1 - \beta_1) V_i - \lambda_j (k_j + a) = 0,$$

$$\frac{\partial u_0^*}{\partial k_j} = -\lambda_j n_j + \lambda_{j+1}(1 + r_{j+1}) = 0, \quad j = 1, 2, \ldots, \qquad (3.27)$$

where $V_j = \beta_0^j N_j^{1-\beta_1} c_j^\sigma$. There is also a "dynastic" budget constraint based on the fact that the individual budget constraints must hold each period:

$$k_0 + \sum_{i=0}^{\infty} \frac{N_i w_i}{\prod_{j=0}^{i}(1+r_j)} = \sum_{i=0}^{\infty} \frac{[N_i c_i + N_{i+1} a]}{\prod_{j=0}^{i}(1+r_j)}. \tag{3.28}$$

Taking ratios of successive equations in Eq. (3.27) yields three intertemporal "arbitrage" conditions:

$$\frac{\lambda_{j+1}}{\lambda_j} = \frac{n_j}{1+r_{j+1}}$$

$$= \frac{V_{j+1}}{V_j} \frac{c_j}{c_{j+1}}$$

$$= \frac{n_j(k_j + a) \sum_{i=j+2}^{\infty} V_i}{n_{j+1}(k_{j+1} + a) \sum_{i=j+1}^{\infty} V_i}. \tag{3.29}$$

Since

$$\frac{V_{j+1}}{V_j} = \beta_0 n_j^{1-\beta_1} \left(\frac{c_{j+1}}{c_j}\right)^\sigma,$$

these equations can be rewritten in terms of the "discounted" value of the ratios of consumption in successive periods and the ratio of total costs (bequests plus rearing cost) of children:

$$\frac{\lambda_{j+1}}{\lambda_j} = \frac{n_j}{1+r_{j+1}} = \beta_0 n_j^{1-\beta_1} \left[\frac{c_{j+1}}{c_j}\right]^{\sigma-1}. \tag{3.30}$$

The ratio of the birthrate to returns to physical capital $(1 + r_{j+1})$ provides the key intertemporal link between the trade-off between the total costs of having children in different generations and per capita consumption of parents in each generation. Given an initial bequest endowment in the first generation, Eqs. (3.29) or (3.30) determine the law of motion of birthrates and bequests, and, since the constraint (3.20) holds

in each period, of consumption per capita, as functions of rearing costs, wage rates and returns to capital. Coupled with an economy-wide production function which would determine wage rates and returns to capital as functions of total population and total capital stock, the B-B model provides a complete endogenous explanation with only initial wealth, k_0, and rearing costs, a, as exogenous. Indeed, such an explanation is B-B's aim in B-B (1989). We note here some of the implications of changes in wages, rates of return to capital, rearing costs and altruism on the behavior of fertility, bequests and consumption. Some of these implications are sensitive to the functional form of the utility function and the way in which altruism enters.

1. Consumption per capita, c_j, rises across generations only if the rearing cost a rises, and does not depend on β_0, the degree of altruism (time preferences), on fertility, nor on the return to capital, r_j (interest rates).
2. Changes in the returns to capital affect mainly fertility, n_j. This variable increases with the interest rate and with the degree of pure altruism.
3. Changes in initial wealth, k_0, do not affect future consumption per person if child rearing costs do not change. Greater wealth affects initial consumption of the "dynasty" head but also results in increased fertility which offsets this effect for future generations. Nor are future bequests per child affected by changes in initial wealth.
4. A tax on children in the jth generation, compensated by an increase in initial wealth, increases consumption and reduces fertility only in the jth generation (if the return to capital is unaffected). Even a permanent compensated tax on children reduces fertility only in the generation enacted, but, of course, total population in successive generations is lower as a result even though its rate of growth is unchanged.
5. Constancy of w, r, and a over time and the particular form of the altruism function and utility function ensure that a unique steady state of fertility, consumption and bequests, *across* generations, exists and is globally stable. Such a state is reached in one generation starting from any initial position. Note, however, that such a steady state is not a steady state of the economy in general equilibrium.

The model in B-B (1988) is the basis for the discussion in B-B (1989), but in Becker et al. (1990) it is modified so that the stock of a parent's human capital affects the time costs of rearing children and market wages. In turn, stocks of human capital affect the relative desirability of investing in the human capital of one's children and bequests in the form of physical capital. The 1990 model is primarily directed to an economy-wide explanation of fertility and per capita consumption and relies heavily on the assumption that increases in the total stock of human capital in the economy lead to increased rather than decreased returns.

3.3. Survival probability, fertility and investment in health care

In the Becker–Lewis model, parents value the number of their offspring and their

"quality" as measured by the bequests parents leave their children, but there is no hint in the formulation about why parents might be concerned with the number of children they have. Willis (1980) suggests that a major motive for having children in less developed economies may be to provide for old-age security (see also Nerlove et al., 1987: Ch. 9). In this subsection we explore the model of Sah (1991) and its extension by Dalko (1992), in which fertility choices result from a dependence of parents' utility on the number of *surviving children*, because, for example, the consumption of parents when they are old depends on the number of their offspring who are around to support them. Why this should be so, and explicitly what the trade-off between present consumption and future consumption (number of surviving children) is, is not considered until the following subsection. The focus of Sah's model is on the discrete nature of both births and surviving children and on the stochastic nature of the latter. Dalko focuses on the way in which parents can influence survival probabilities by investments in their children.

3.3.1. The basic model

Let n be the number of children born in an individual family (a choice variable) and N be the number who survive to adulthood. N is a random variable which is assumed to follow a binomial distribution for given n and survival probability s, which we assume to be known to the family and exogenous to its choice. The ex ante costs of a birth, $C(n)$, are assumed to be nondecreasing and a concave function of n. Ex post costs and benefits are summarized in the parents' utility function, $u(N)$, which is a concave function of N, first increasing and then decreasing, and assumed to account for the costs of raising surviving children and the effect of increased numbers on parents' current consumption. Parents, who are not altruistic in the sense of caring about their children's future welfare, are assumed to maximize the expected utility of births, given the survival probability s:

$$\max_{n} U(n,s) = \sum_{N=0}^{n} b(N,n,s)u(N), \tag{3.31}$$

where

$$b(N,n,s) = \binom{n}{N} s^{N}(1-s)^{n-N}$$

is the probability that exactly N children survive from n births.

$U(n, s)$ is a discrete function of the discrete variable n and a continuous function of the continuous variable s. The binomial density is "bell-shaped" although discrete, and its values are approximated by the ordinates of a normal density with the same mean,

ns, and variance, $ns(1 - s)$. The expectation of $u(N)$ is obtained from the binomial distribution conditional on n, the number of births, so it has both a larger mean and a larger variance for a higher n, given the survival probability, s. Since $u(N)$ is "parabolic" in shape, the effect of convoluting it with $b(N, n, s)$ is to "flatten" it out and, as long as $u(N)$ remains positive, to move more mass into the upper tail: thus, if $u(N)$ is rising, $U(n, s)$ will also be rising but at a lower rate. For given n, the mean of the binomial increases but the variance rises or falls according as $s \leq 1/2$ or $s \geq 1/2$; thus, for $s \geq 1/2$ more weight is given to values of $u(N)$ above and near to the previous mean, $U(n, s)$.

One further rather drastic simplification of the Sah model is that the number of births is determined once and for all at the beginning of the decision period and not sequentially. Sequential determination makes quite a difference, as Wolpin (1984) shows.

While it is natural to focus on infant and child mortality as Sah's model does, in the real world maternal mortality, particularly in child birth (or in abortion-averted births), is extremely important. To the extent that $C(n)$ reflects these factors, ex ante costs are a much more integral part of the analysis than may appear.

If $U(n, s)$ and $C(n)$ were continuous functions of n, the optimum number of births would be obtained by equating the marginal utility of an additional birth, U_n, to its marginal cost, C_n. Conditions for the existence of a positive optimum number of births are apparent in this case: U_n is falling, eventually becoming negative after $U(n, s)$ reaches its maximum, so as long as C_n is nondecreasing and does not exceed U_n at $n = 0$, a positive optimum exists. If we had been dealing with continuous functions of a continuous variable, we would simply differentiate this optimum with respect to s in order to discover the effects of increasing survival probability on the number of births. Unfortunately nothing so simple is possible in this case.

Provided there is a maximum number of children attainable, it is possible to formulate a discrete analog to the usual first-order conditions which determine the optimal number of births, $\hat{n}$, as a *discontinuous* function of the survival probability s. Sah (1991) proves the following propositions about this function:

Proposition 1: $\hat{n} = n(s)$ *is either unique or there are at most two neighboring values for the same value of s.*

Proposition 2: $\partial n(s)/\partial s \leq 0$.

He proves additionally that parents' utility is nondecreasing in s, that is parents are no worse off and possibly better off if infant and child mortality declines:

Proposition 3: $\partial U(\hat{n}, s)/\partial s \geq 0$.

While Proposition 3 is not astonishing, its implication for Proposition 2 is a little surprising. Although a fall in infant and child mortality makes parents better off and, therefore, if children are a normal good, might be expected to increase the demand for surviving children and thus to offset partially the negative effects on births of greater survival probabilities, it does not do so in this case as long as the number of births is near the optimum simply on account of the way in which s enters the binomial coefficients in Eq. (3.1). The result has nothing to do with the shape of the ex post utility function. Consequently, if the independence of surviving births were not assumed or if ex ante costs were not assumed to be separable, this rather strong conclusion would not necessarily be obtained.

3.3.2. Implications for population growth

Notwithstanding the qualifications which must be attached to Sah's Proposition 2 that increasing survival probabilities result in a fall in the optimal number of births, there is considerable empirical evidence to support such a relationship (see Freedman, 1975; Preston, 1978; Schultz, 1981). But to say that *fertility* falls with increasing survival probability is not the same as the proposition that the *rate of growth* of population declines with falling infant and child mortality. Indeed, in general, it does not do so at all levels of survival probability, as shown in Nerlove (1991).

In one of the models developed there, it is assumed that survival probability is the only exogenous factor influencing parental decisions with respect to fertility, and it is also assumed that, together with its effects on mortality, it is the only exogenous factor influencing the rate of growth of population. Of course, survival probability may be influenced in part by family decisions or by macroeconomic conditions influencing the availability of food or other environmental factors. Abstracting from such complications, let births per family be a decreasing function of s, the survival probability. If all families were identical one-parent households with exactly the same perceptions of survival probability, then aggregate behavior would also be discrete. On the other hand, if family preferences differ and/or perceptions of survival probabilities, then under appropriate assumptions we can treat the aggregate function as continuous and differentiable. Let the total number of parents in the population in period t be N_t. If births per parent in the tth generation are n_t, then

$$\frac{N_{t+1}}{N_t} = sn_t \tag{3.32}$$

in the aggregate, provided N_t is large. Suppressing the subscript t, let

$$\rho(s) = sn(s) \tag{3.33}$$

be the rate of growth of the aggregate population. Then

$$\rho' = n\left(1 + s\frac{n'}{n}\right).$$ \hfill (3.34)

Although $n' < 0$, $0 \leq \rho' \leq 0$ according as the elasticity of births with respect to survival probability is less than, or greater than one in absolute value. In terms of the preceding analysis, whether this is the case depends on factors affecting the shape of the ex post utility function beyond concavity or lack of it with respect to the number of surviving children. It is argued in Nerlove (1991), however, that even if the elasticity of births is greater than one in absolute value in relatively favorable regimes of infant and child mortality, it must nonetheless approach zero as survival probabilities decline to very low levels simply because of the biological maximum to the number of children a women can have. We might also suppose that ex ante costs of child bearing would also increase in regimes of high mortality. Thus, at very low levels of survival probability, the rate of growth of population will generally *increase* as a result of falling infant and child mortality even though the number of births per parent declines. When survival probabilities become high, the fall in the optimal number of births as infant and child mortality declines further will more than offset the larger numbers of such births which survive.

3.3.3. Investment in health care and survival probability

Without altruism, the only incentive parents have to invest in their children is to increase their own consumption in old age. More surviving children will augment parents' consumption but so will an increase in the endowment each surviving child is able to attain. The preceding analysis can be extended simply by dividing $c_{0,t}$ into two parts:

$$c_{0,t} = h_t + k_t,$$ \hfill (3.35)

where h = health care investment and k = investment in other forms of children's human capital. Ex ante costs of births and survival probability become functions of h and e_{t+1} becomes a function of k. Because

$$c_2 = \mu N e_{t+1}(k),$$

we see there are two ways to influence expected old-age utility, through increasing the expected number of survivors and by increasing the endowment of each. The division of c_0 into two parts thus requires obvious modifications in the first-order conditions, breaking them into two and replacing $c_{0,t}$ by $h_t + k_t$ in the constraint. In general, after allowing for the marginal effect, e_{t+1}, on a surviving child's endowment, the conditions require simultaneous equality *at the margin* of the expected old-age utility of an increase per birth in health care, affecting survival, and the other investment, affecting a surviving child's endowment, with the marginal disutility of the necessary decrease in parents' consumption as young adults. These marginal utility rates of return to the two forms of investment depend on the responsiveness of the survival probability, on the one hand, and the child's endowment, on the other, to the two different forms of investment. Both affect young–adult consumption, but health care expenditures may have a partially offsetting effect by reducing ex ante birth costs.

In other respects the analysis closely parallels that given in the preceding subsection. The possibility of influencing child survival and the earnings capacity of one's offspring means that increases in parents' endowments or those of their children, which make parents better off, may lead to decreases in fertility because such improvements in parents' welfare lead them to spend more on their children, which, in turn, increases the probability that their children will survive. Similarly, a small exogenous upward shift in the survival function may lead to either higher or lower rates of population growth.

3.4. Transfers from children to parents and fertility: old-age security motive

So far we have considered models in which motivation for children, and bequest in the form of health, nutrition and education and physical capital are assumed to be either parental concern for their children's welfare or for the number of surviving children. We have examined the effects of survival probabilities, child rearing cost and other factors on the growth rates of population and income. Some of the studies along these lines also examine the interaction between household decisions and the aggregate economy. In this section, we survey a similar literature that developed almost independently of the above. In this literature, the decisions regarding children, and investment in their skill, health and nutrition are motivated by the amount of transfers that parents can obtain from such investments in their old-age. It is apparent that such decisions will depend on the mechanism by which intergenerational transfers are made and that these decisions are affected by the existence of publicly provided transfer mechanisms such as pay-as-you-go social security program, or subsidies to children's education, health and nutrition. We begin with a summary of a few models of endogenous fertility and growth in which the transfer mechanism from children to parents is assumed to be determined by social norms; we point out what bearing these optimizing models have on the nature of dynamics of the models we discussed in Section 1; we then discuss how these models could be more appropriately integrated with the previous models of this section by introducing two-sided altruism and discuss the associated technical difficulties.

3.4.1. The old-age pension motive for children

When the capital markets are missing or imperfect, parents may treat their children analogously to capital goods, i.e., as a vehicle for transferring consumption from present to future. Although many authors have pointed out this possibility, and Leibenstein (1957, 1974) attempted partial microeconomic analysis of fertility demand, Neher (1971) was the first to model formally the old-age security hypothesis and study its consequences on aggregate population and income growth. We consider a simplified version of Neher's model.

3.4.1.1. Ethics of equal sharing within household

Neher (1971) considers an agrarian economy of overlapping generations, all living in an extended family and having a certain plot of land. Let L_t denote the number of adults in the family in period t. Adult members of the family work on the family land and produce food C_t that is shared equally among all members. Assume that food cannot be stored. The food production in period t ($t \geq 0$) is given by

$$C_t = F(L_t).$$

$F(.)$ is assumed to exhibit first increasing and then decreasing marginal product of labor. Let n_t be the number of children that an adult of period t decides to have. All adults are assumed identical. Those living in period t are denoted by the superscript t. With this convention, we denote the parent's consumption in youth in period $t - 1$ by c_{t-1}^t, the parent's consumption in adulthood in period t by c_t^t and the parent's old-age consumption in period $t + 1$ by c_{t+1}^t The equal sharing rule means that for given L_{t-1}, L_t and n_{t+1}, the constraints, Eq. (3.36) and Eq. (3.37) below, hold. Thus the problem of the adult head of family of period t is to

$$\max U(c_t^t, c_{t+1}^t) = \alpha u(c_t^t) + \beta u(c_{t+1}^t), \tag{3.36}$$

subject to

$$c_t^t = \frac{F(L_t)}{L_t(1+n_t) + qL_{t-1}},$$
$$c_{t+1}^t = \frac{F(L_t n_t p)}{L_t n_t p(1+n_{t+1}) + qL_t}, \tag{3.37}$$

where p is the survival probability of children to adulthood, and q is the survival probability from adulthood to old-age. In the above utility function, β may be regarded as discount factor adjusted for the probability of old-age survival. Assuming that $\lim_{c \to 0} u'(c) = \infty$, then clearly $n_t > 0$ for all $t \geq 0$. Thus the first-order condition for the above problem after simplification becomes

$$\frac{\alpha u'(c_t^t)c_t^t L_t}{L_t(1+n_t)+qL_{t-1}} = \frac{\beta u'(c_{t+1}^t)[F'(L_t n_t p)]pL_t}{pL_t n_t(1+n_{t+1})+qL_t}.$$ (3.38)

Notice that it is not possible to derive the dynamics of this economy from Eq. (3.38), since for all $t \geq 0$, the equation can determine only n_t for given n_{t+1}, and there is no other equation that can determine n_{t+1}. Neher restricts his analysis to steady state. A *steady state* of an economy is a situation when all per capita variables are constant over time. Let N_t be the total population in period t. It is apparent that in a steady state

$$L_t = L^* \text{ and } c_t^t = c_{t+1}^t = c^* \text{ and } \frac{L_t}{N_t} = \frac{p}{1+p+pq}$$

for all $t \geq 0$. The steady-state consumption is thus given by

$$c^* = \frac{F(L^*)}{N^*} = \frac{F(L^*)L^*}{L^* N^*} = \frac{F(L^*)}{L^*} \frac{p}{1+p+pq}.$$ (3.39)

Let us denote a steady-state competitive equilibrium solution with a tilde. It can be shown that the steady-state equilibrium is given by

$$F'(\tilde{L}^*) = \frac{(\alpha+\beta p)\tilde{c}^*}{\beta p}.$$ (3.40)

The size of the adult population $\hat{L}^*$ that yields the maximum possible consumption in the steady state is said to be *golden rule of fertility*. From Eq. (3.39) it follows that $\hat{c}^*$ is maximized when average product is maximized. Let us denote the golden rule consumption as $\hat{c}^*$. Given the nature of production function, average product is maximized when the average product is equal to the marginal product of labor. Thus golden rule $\hat{L}^*$ satisfies

$$F'(L^*) = \frac{F(L^*)}{L^*} = \frac{1+p+pq}{p}.$$ (3.41)

It is easy to note that the golden rule of fertility and the competitive equilibrium level of fertility in the steady state are both given by $\hat{n}^* = \tilde{n}^* = 1/p$. Thus higher infant mortality leads to higher fertility in the steady-state in this model.

Let us adopt the golden rule as our optimality criterion as did Neher. Comparing Eqs. (3.40) and (3.41), it is obvious that the steady-state competitive equilibrium results in:

$$\begin{bmatrix} \text{over} \\ \text{optimal} \\ \text{under} \end{bmatrix} \text{population according as } \frac{\alpha + \beta p}{\beta p} \begin{bmatrix} < \\ = \\ > \end{bmatrix} \frac{1 + p + pq}{p}. \qquad (3.42)$$

Since the agents cannot fully internalize the consequences of their decisions, their decisions are not socially optimal. Let us take an extreme case by assuming that the agents do not discount their future utilities, i.e., $\alpha = \beta = 1$; then from Eq. (3.41) it is clear that competitive equilibrium always results in overpopulation. The same result is true when agents discount future utilities very little, i.e., for β close to one and $\alpha = 1$. In fact, given mortality rates, there exists $\beta_* < 1$ such that the competitive equilibrium will result in overpopulation for all $\beta_* < \beta \leq 1$.

Equal-sharing ethics implicitly assumes that all household members live in a commune and do not try to break out of the sharing principle. If we further assume that an agent can inherit a share of the family land only if he or she stays in the household, and that there are no other assets that can transfer consumption from working age to old-age, it is reasonable to assume the equal sharing principle. However, if there are other assets such as physical capital, gold or paper money, then some agents may be better off by breaking out of the joint family transfer arrangements and instead of depending on their children for an old-age pension, they might prefer to accumulate other assets for old-age support.

We do observe that household members leave their families and move to cities for better opportunities and yet send remittances to their old parents. Even if they stay in the rural areas, we observe that joint family structure often breaks down and new atomistic household units are formed, and yet children continue to transfer income to their old parents. Some of these limitations, which Neher (1971) also pointed out, have been rectified in recent growth models based on old-age security hypothesis. For instance, Willis (1981) replaces the equal sharing assumption in Neher's framework with the assumption that adult children transfer a fixed amount of income to their old parents. This is more realistic and does not presume that parents live with their children to get this old-age support. However, the determination of the amount of transfer remains unspecified. Willis does not have capital accumulation in his model. Raut (1985, 1991, 1992a) and Bental (1989) allow accumulation of physical assets. While Bental assumes perfect capital markets, Raut assumes imperfection in the capital markets and studies the effect of making capital markets perfect and also examines the long-run effects on population growth, capital accumulation and income distribution of various policies (Raut 1991, 1992a). In the next subsection, we review a framework with imperfect capital markets and study the dynamic consequences of old-age security motives for children and then study the effects of various macro-economic policies.

3.4.1.2. Imperfect capital markets and old-age security hypothesis
Consider a model of overlapping generations in which a member of each genera-

tion lives for three periods, the first of which is spent as a child in the parents' household. The second period is spent as a young person working, having and raising children, as well as accumulating capital. The third and last period of life is spent as an old person in retirement living off support received from each of one's offspring and from the sale of accumulated capital. All members of each generation are identical in their preferences defined over their consumption in their working and retired periods. Thus, in this model the only reason that an individual would want to have a child is the old-age support that the child will provide during the parent's retired years.

Assume that technology is characterized by a constant-returns-to-scale production function $Y_t = Z_t F(K_t, L_t)$ which uses capital K_t and labor L_t to produce output Y_t in period t, $t \geq 0$, Z_t is the level of Hicks-neutral total factor productivity in period t. For the moment we assume that $Z_t = 1$ for all $t \geq 0$. We adopt the convention that the producer borrows from the households K_t amount of the $(t-1)$th period aggregate good and promises to pay $(1 + r_t)K_t$ amount of the tth period aggregate good. Each adult of period t supplies one unit of labor. We also assume for simplicity that capital depreciates in one generation. Denote the average product of labor by $f(k) \equiv F(k, 1)$. Assume perfect competition in all markets. Profit maximization by producers yields

$$w_{t+1} = f(k_{t+1}) - k_{t+1} f'(k_{t+1}), \tag{3.43}$$

$$1 + r_{t+1} = f'(k_{t+1}). \tag{3.44}$$

Formally, a typical individual of the generation which is young in period t has n_t children, consumes c_t^t and c_{t+1}^t in periods t and $t + 1$, and saves s_t in period t. The parent supplies one unit of labor for wage employment. The individual income from wage labor while young in period t is w_t and that is the only income in that period. A proportion a_t of this wage income is given to parents as old-age support. We assume for now that a_t is exogenously given. Later we consider mechanisms determining a_t. While old in period $t + 1$, the parent sells accumulated saving to firms and receives from each of the parent's offspring the proportion a_{t+1} of his/her wage income. The parent enjoys a utility $U(c_t^t, c_{t+1}^t)$ from consumption. Thus the parent's choice problem can be stated as

$$\max_{s_t, n_t > 0} U(c_t^t, c_{t+1}^t) \tag{3.45}$$

subject to

$$c_t^t + \theta_t n_t + s_t = (1 - a_t)w_t,$$
$$c_{t+1}^t = (1 + r_{t+1})s_t + a_{t+1}w_{t+1}n_t, \tag{3.46}$$

where θ_t is the output cost of rearing a child while young, $1 + r_{t+1}$ is the rate of interest between period t and $t + 1$ and w_t is the competitive wage rate in period t.

Note that, in equilibrium, the private rates of returns from investing in children and physical capital must be equal in order to rule out arbitrage, which implies that

$$\frac{a_{t+1}w_{t+1}}{\theta_t} = 1 + r_{t+1}. \tag{3.47}$$

Substituting Eqs. (3.43) and (3.44) in Eq. (3.47), we obtain an implicit relation among k_{t+1}, θ_t and a_{t+1}. It can be shown that under standard neoclassical assumptions on the production function, we can solve this implicit function uniquely to obtain $k_{t+1} = \Psi(\theta_t/a_{t+1})$. Since it is assumed that capital depreciates fully in one generation, $k_{t+1} = s_t/n_t$ and the budget constraints Eq. (3.43) and Eq. (3.44) become respectively

$$c_t^t = (1 - a_t)w_t - S_t \tag{3.43'}$$

and

$$c_{t+1}^t = (1 + r_{t+1})S_t, \tag{3.44'}$$

where $S_t = [\theta_t + \Psi(\theta_t/a_t)]n_t$. S_t may be thought of as total savings. Denote the solution of this utility maximization problem by $S_t = H(w_t, 1 + r_{t+1})$. We can now express the solutions for n_t and s_t as

$$n_t = \frac{H(w_t, 1 + r_{t+1})}{\theta_t + \Psi(\theta_t/a_t)} \quad \text{and} \quad s_t = \frac{H(w_t, 1 + r_{t+1})}{\Psi(\theta_t/a_t)\,[\theta_t + \Psi(\theta_t/a_t)]}. \tag{3.48}$$

Child rearing involves parents' time which we specify by assuming that $\theta_t = \theta + \eta w_t$ where $\eta > 0$ is the fraction of parents' time spent in rearing each child. We simplify by assuming that $a_t = a$ for all generations. From Eq. (3.47), we have

$$\frac{w(k_{t+1})}{f'(k_{t+1})} = \frac{\theta + \eta w(k_t)}{a}, \tag{3.49}$$

where $w(k) \equiv f(k) - kf'(k)$. Under the assumption that $f(k)$ is strictly concave and satisfies the Inada condition, it can be shown that the left-hand side of Eq. (3.49) is a strictly increasing function of k_{t+1} which goes to zero when k_{t+1} tends to zero and goes to infinity as k_{t+1} tends to infinity. Hence for given k_t there exists a unique k_{t+1}, which leads to a first-order nonlinear difference equation

$$k_{t+1} = \Phi(k_t). \tag{3.50}$$

Eq. (3.50) determines the dynamics of the economy, for once we know the series k_t, we know the series r_t and w_t from Eqs. (3.43) and (3.44) and the series n_t and s_t from Eq. (3.48). Since this is a first-order difference equation, using well-known techniques (Devaney, 1989), the global dynamics of this system may be analyzed. Applying the implicit function theorem to Eq. (3.49), it can be easily shown that

$$\frac{dk_{t+1}}{dk_t} = \frac{\eta k_t f''(k_t)[f'(k_{t+1})]^2}{af(k_{t+1})f''(k_{t+1})} > 0.$$

Thus a positive shock in the capital–labor ratio and hence in the per capita income in period t will have positive effects on the capital–labor ratios and per capita incomes in all future periods. Furthermore, a higher child rearing cost, θ_t, in period t or a lower transfer from children, a_t, results in a higher capital–labor ratio and thus per capita income in the next period.

In general we do not know how k_t, s_t and n_t behave over time. It is, however, interesting to note that if $\eta = 0$ we can see immediately from the above that k_t will jump to steady state in period $t = 1$. The dynamic properties of these variables, assuming Cobb–Douglas utility and production function, are considered in the following example.

Example

Assume that utility and production functions are of Cobb–Douglas form:

$$U(c_t^t, c_{t+1}^t) = \alpha \log c_t^t + (1-\alpha)\log c_{t+1}^t, \quad 0 < \alpha < 1,$$

$$f(k) = k^\sigma, \quad 0 < \sigma < 1.$$

Eq. (3.49) simplifies to

$$k_{t+1} = \frac{\sigma\theta}{a(1-\sigma)} + \frac{\sigma\eta}{a}k_t^\sigma. \tag{3.51}$$

From the above it easily follows that $\Phi(k_t)$ is an increasing concave function and for large k_t, $\Phi(k_t) < k_t$. Thus the capital–labor ratio will behave exactly as in the Solow–Swan growth model: there exists a unique globally stable steady-state capital–labor ratio, $k^* > 0$. Moreover, it can be easily shown that

$$\frac{\partial k^*}{\partial \theta} > 0, \quad \frac{\partial k^*}{\partial a} > 0,$$

and that

$$n_t = \left[\frac{(1-a)(1-\alpha)(1-\sigma)a}{a(1-\sigma)+\sigma}\right]\left[\frac{w(k_t)}{\theta + \eta w(k_t)}\right]. \tag{3.52}$$

Since $s_t = \Phi(k_t)n_t$ note that once the dynamic path for k_t is known, we can determine the dynamic paths of n_t and s_t. Moreover, it can be easily shown that $dn_t/dk_t > 0$. It follows that if $k_0 < k^*$, then both k_t, n_t, and s_t will be growing over time and in the long-run they converge to their respective steady-state values.

In Eq. (2.7) of the Solow–Swan model and Eq. (2.16′) of Niehans' model the specifications of the $n(k)$ function were arbitrary and did not help us very much in simplifying the dynamics of the underlying economies. The form in Eq. (3.52) is, however, the result of optimizing individual behavior in the aggregate economy and this form of $n(k)$ leads to simpler dynamics of the underlying economy.

Raut (1985, 1991) uses a more general formulation of the above basic framework in which parents simultaneously choose savings in physical capital, number of children, and investment in their skills. In this model, investment in human capital of children is motivated by old-age transfers as contrasted with the altruistic motives for such investments which we considered earlier. Under certain assumptions it is shown that in general equilibrium the low-skill parents tend to have larger number of low-skill children and no savings in physical capital. Lower-skilled workers earn lower wages in general equilibrium. At the aggregate level this provides different explanation for the commonly observed negative relationship between quality and number of children and that between income and number of children of households.

One of the implications of the old-age security hypothesis is that when a publicly funded pay-as-you-go social security program is introduced in an economy with imperfect capital markets, fertility will decline. Nerlove et al. (1987: Ch. 9), on the other hand, show in a two-period model of old-age security without a capital market that, if parents care about the welfare of their children, then introduction of capital markets may increase the general equilibrium fertility rate due to an income effect strong enough to outweigh the substitution effect.

There have been a number of empirical attempts to examine the effect of introducing publicly provided social security on fertility levels. Although many of these studies suffer from lack of appropriate data to test such an hypothesis, general consensus is there are negative effects on fertility (for a summary, see Nugent (1985), Raut (1991)). The literature on the US and other developed countries focuses mainly on the effect of social security on savings and ambiguous effects have been found. Very little empirical evidence is available on the joint effect of social security on fertility and savings, and on the welfare of different generations. The above framework and its extension have been used to study the long-run effects on income distribution, population and income growth rates of various income redistribution policies such as lump-sum tax transfers, subsidies to human capital of children of unskilled parents, introduction of a pay-as-you-go social security program, and making the capital markets more perfect; see Raut (1991).

The main policy conclusions which emerge from the aforementioned studies are that the dynamic effects of introducing a pay-as-you-go social security program, within the framework described, are that both fertility and saving will decline in the short run and long run, and furthermore, if the percentage of voluntary old-age transfers, *a*, is smaller than a threshold level, then introduction of such a social security program is welfare-enhancing for all agents in the present and all future generations. Similar conclusions are reached by Bental (1989) and, in a framework with parental altruism, by Nishimura and Raut (1992). Furthermore, income transfers to reduce intra-generational income inequality cause higher income gaps for the children in subsequent generations; if such a redistributive scheme persists over time, then the economy will end up with higher population growth, and a lower rate of capital accumulation in the long run. On the other hand, subsidies to the unskilled parents for the purpose of investing in their children's skills, or introduction of a social security program will lead to slower population growth, lesser income inequality and a higher rate of capital accumulation and intergenerational social mobility.

In the Malthus–Boserup model of Section 2, we introduced a third factor of production, technological knowledge, together with labor and capital. Because our specifications were at the aggregate level, we could not reduce below two the dimension of the underlying dynamic system of the economy. Optimizing models can sometimes simplify the study of dynamics by reducing the model to a lower dimension. Raut and Srinivasan (1994) use the basic framework of this section and assume that as a result of conglomeration and congestion effects of population density on productivity level, population size affects Z_t; however, this effect is treated as Marshallian externality by the individual optimizing agents. They find that the cost of child rearing, θ_t, and the nature of dependence of Z_t on L_t, determine the dynamics of the competitive equilibrium path. For instance, when the child rearing cost is constant, i.e., $\eta = 0$, or when cost involves only the time cost, i.e., $\theta = 0$, the dynamics of the economy reduce to one dimension. The nonlinear dynamics of the model nonetheless generate a plethora of outcomes (depending on the functional forms, parameters and initial conditions); these include not only the neoclassical steady state with exponential growth of population with constant per capita income and consumption, but also growth paths which do not converge to a steady state and are even chaotic. Exponential, and even superexponential growth of per capita output are possible in some cases.

3.5. Two-sided altruism and transfers from children to parents

So far we have assumed that the inter vivos transfers from children to parents are exogenously given or that children simply "tithe" for reasons of custom to support their aged parents. Recently attempts have been made to motivate transfers from children to parents as utility maximizing behavior and how it interacts with fertility and savings decisions (see Srinivasan, 1988; Cigno, 1991; Nishimura and Zhang, 1992; Raut, 1992b). In the basic overlapping-generations framework of this section, Nishimura and Zhang and Srinivasan assume that agents care not only for their own life-cycle consumption but also for their parents' old-age consumption. It is argued in Raut

(1992b) that while this framework provides a motivation for children to transfer part of their incomes to their parents as old-age support, the theory of fertility choice based on such utility functions is incomplete since parents will have no motive to have children, if for example there is a social security program which transfers the amount that the children were voluntarily transferring to their parents.

In contrast to Becker and Barro and Becker et al., discussed above, assume that all transfers from parents to children are inter vivos transfers in the first period of life designed to augment the child's consumption in youth. We begin with a simpler model where all transfers from adults to their aged parents are also inter vivos, solely for the purpose of augmenting the old people's consumption. We allow savings for retirement during productive years. All children born are assumed to survive. We also assume, more restrictively, that the young adult applies the same utility function to the consumption of his/her offspring, his/her aged parent and himself/herself. That is, we assume that there is no difference in the utility of consumption when young or old. Then, if $u(c)$, $u' > 0$, $u'' < 0$, is the utility attached to consumption at level c by anyone in any period of life, the aggregate utility of an individual of generation t is

$$V_t = \delta(n_{t-1})u(c_t^{t-1}) + \alpha u(c_t^t) + \beta u(c_{t+1}^t) + \gamma(n_t)u(c_{t+1}^{t+1}). \tag{3.53}$$

An adult of period t earns wage income w_t in the labor market and *expects* to receive a bequest $b_t \geq 0$ from his/her parents. These two sources of income constitute his/her budget during adulthood. Rearing cost per child in period t is $\theta_t > 0$ units of the period t good. Given his/her adulthood budget, he/she decides the amount of savings $s_t \geq 0$, the number of children $n_t \geq 0$, the fraction of income to be transferred to his/her old parents $a_t \geq 0$; in the next period, he/she retires and expects to receive $a_{t+1}n_t w_{t+1}$ amount of gifts from his/her children, earns $(1 + r_{t+1})s_t$ as return from his/her physical assets, and decides the amount of bequest $b_{t+1} \geq 0$ to leave for each of his/her children. Moreover, agent t's tth period decisions, (a_t, n_t, s_t), overlap with his/her parent's bequest decision, b_t; similarly, his/her bequest decision, b_{t+1}, overlaps with the children's gift decisions, a_{t+1}. The effects of agent t's action, $\alpha^t = (a_t, n_t, s_t, b_{t+1})$ on the levels of his/her own life-cycle consumption and the levels of consumption of his/her parents and children in the periods that overlap with his/her life cycle, depend on his/her parent's action, α^{t-1}, and his/her children's action, α^{t+1}, as follows:

$$c_t^t + s_t + \theta_t n_t = (1 - a_t)w_t + b_t, \tag{3.54}$$

$$c_{t+1}^t + n_t b_{t+1} = (1 + r_{t+1})s_t + a_{t+1}w_{t+1}n_t, \tag{3.55}$$

$$c_t^{t-1} = (1 + r_t)s_{t-1} - n_{t-1}b_t + a_t w_t n_{t-1}, \tag{3.56}$$

$$c_{t+1}^{t+1} = (1 - a_{t+1})w_{t+1} + b_{t+1} - s_{t+1} - \theta_{t+1}n_{t+1} \quad \text{and} \quad c_t^t, c_{t+1}^t > 0. \tag{3.57}$$

Most authors use open-loop Nash equilibrium to characterize equilibrium choices in the above framework (see Fudenberg and Tirole (1991) for all the game theoretic concepts used in this section). Note that there may exist various types of Nash equilibria. In one type, intergenerational transfers may be from children to parents in all periods; refer to such an equilibrium as "gift" equilibrium. In another type, the transfers may be from parents to children in all periods; refer to such an equilibrium as a "bequest" equilibrium. There may be other types of equilibria in which transfers are from children to parents in one period and from parents to children in other periods. As has been pointed out in Raut (1992b), the set of Nash equilibria is in general indeterminate for a given economy; however, steady-state equilibria are always determinate, although they may be multiple.

There are examples of economies in which there exist only two equilibria, one with zero savings and the other with positive savings. At both equilibria, the transfers are from children to parents. Furthermore, the equilibrium with positive savings is characterized by lower levels of fertility, transfers from children and welfare levels than the equilibrium with a zero savings rate.

Since there are multiple Nash equilibria, agents have no clue a priori which of the two equilibria will materialize; this brings a difficult problem of coordinating agents' expectations and thus renders a serious weakness of rational expectations to explain observed behavior.

Open-loop Nash equilibria have serious deficiencies in characterizing adequately the incentives of, and describing the behavior of, economic agents. More specifically, an open-loop Nash equilibrium assumes that each agent takes the actions of other agents as given. At such an equilibrium there may be scope for agents to manipulate their children's behavior to extract more transfers from them. For instance, since parents make their consumption and fertility decisions prior to their children's, parents may find it strategically advantageous to consume more when adult and save little so that they can extract maximum transfers from their children. In addition, the Nash equilibrium concept does not deal with agents' behavior out of equilibrium. Raut (1992b) argues that a sequential game framework and the use of subgame perfection are most appropriate in this context because subgame-perfect equilibrium takes into account behavior or reactions of agents out of equilibrium. Azariadis and Drazen (1993) suggest an alternative nonsequential bargaining framework.

The framework presented here is useful in explaining why transfers from children to parents are observed in many economies, and why the amount of transfers declines with the introduction of public-transfer policies; why a pay-as-you-go social security program exists, and whether it is possible for the current living generations to legislate a pay-as-you-go social security benefit scheme for the current and all future generations such that the policy is time-consistent, i.e., the future generations will have no incentives to amend it; and whether such programs lead to Pareto optimality. This framework is also useful for investigation of the strategic aspects of bequests in the form of health, nutrition and education as well as physical capital; if followed through, the resulting theory could be integrated into a general equilibrium framework to examine what effects there may be on the pattern of the demographic transition, and economic growth.

4. Concluding remarks

Our aim in developing growth models with endogenous population is principally to explain why, as income grows, both birth and death rates fall, and stocks of both human and physical capital per capita increase over time. If multiple stationary paths exist, under what conditions does the economy approach one with a low rate of population growth, and high levels of capital per capita and well-being, and under what the opposite? At present, the state of our knowledge is far from complete.

Review of existing neoclassical growth models with endogenous, but unspecified, population growth, suggests a wide variety of possibilities: multiple equilibria, some of which may be stable and others unstable, characterized by large populations with low per capita incomes or by small populations with high per capita income. Without knowing how population change is related to the stocks of capital, the level of population and other state variables of the economy, however, there is little to distinguish which path may be followed. In a market economy, parents choose freely how many children to have, how much to invest in them in the form of health, nutrition and education, and how much to bequeath to them in the form of claims to physical capital. Rates of return to different forms of investment, taxes and subsidies, and incomes all constrain parents' choices which are made in order to maximize their utilities which depend on their preferences for children and consumption in various periods of life and on their concern for the future well-being of their offspring. The problem is thus to relate the relevant rates of return to family decisions, on the one hand, and to the stocks and other state variables of the economy, on the other. Thus, the interaction of household and economy, acting through rates of return and constrained by production technology and by taxes and subsidies, determines which path the economic-demographic system will follow.

Our survey of recent developments in the literature of the "new home economics" reveals various bits and pieces of the complete model we seek. Becker and Lewis have shown us how the quality and quantity of children interact to allow the possibility of a negative income elasticity for child numbers even though children, in a more general sense, are a normal good. Such an outcome, however, depends on the elasticity of substitution between numbers and quality in parents' preferences being sufficiently high. The plausibility or implausibility of this being the case depends on how quality is interpreted and on a more precise specification of why children are valued by parents.

In attempting to account for a large and increasing proportion of bequests in the form of human capital as well as declining fertility over time, Becker and Barro and co-workers focus on parental altruism. Their analysis falls short, however, in failing to account for how parental expectations about, and perceptions of, their children's future welfare are determined. Their assumption of perfect foresight is implausible for an economy out of equilibrium. And, in order to resolve the question of what path the economy will follow and to which of several possible equilibria from any given initial conditions, it is necessary to characterize out-of-equilibrium behavior.

Next, we turn to recent work of Neher, Willis, and Sah, extended by Dalko, which deals with parents' motivations for having surviving children. The principal conclusion of this analysis is to demonstrate under what conditions improvements in survival probability will result in lower fertility and how parents might trade off investments to enhance survival probabilities of children for numbers. The possibility that a small exogenous change in child and infant mortality might set off a cumulative process of declining mortality and fertility is revealed.

Finally, recent work of Raut and others dealing with the old-age security motive for having children is discussed. The focus in this work is to examine what effects the public policies such as introduction of social security, improvement of capital markets, subsidization of poor's education and lump-sum tax transfers from rich to the poor have on population growth, income inequality and income growth both in the short run and long run. While endogenous determination of transfers from children to parents and from parents to children by introducing two-sided altruism within a sequential framework with subgame perfection as an equilibrium concept is useful for analyzing the incentives that agents face while deciding the number of children and the amount of transfers to children and parents, for analyzing the way in which capital markets and the social provision of old-age security interact with fertility decisions, and also for analyzing out-of-equilibrium behavior, the exercise is often technically insurmountable. Further research along these lines is needed.

In general, accumulating stocks of human and physical capital and of population might be expected ceteris paribus to reduce the respective rates of return, as well as to equalize them, and thus to reduce incentives to invest in these forms of capital, to have children, and to slow the rates of growth of per capita incomes. We do not, at this stage, know whether initial conditions matter, to what extent different societies would be driven to a common or to different equilibria, or whether stable equilibria are likely to be characterized by high levels of well-being and low rates of population growth or the opposite. Answers to these questions remain to be discovered in future research by us or by our readers.

References

Azariadis, C. and A. Drazen (1993), "Endogenous fertility in models of growth", Revista de Análisis Económico 8: 131–144.

Baily, M. and C. Schultze (1990), "The productivity of capital in a period of slower growth", Brookings Papers on Economic Activity (Microeconomics), pp. 369–406.

Bairoch, P. (1976), "Agriculture and the industrial revolution, 1700–1914", in: C.M. Cipolla, ed., The Fontana economic history of Europe, Vol. III (The Harvester Press, London) pp. 452–506.

Barro, R.J. (1974), "Are government bonds net wealth?", Journal of Political Economy 82: 1095–1117.

Barro, R.J. and G.S. Becker (1989), "Fertility choice in a model of economic growth", Econometrica 57: 481–501.

Beaver, S.E. (1975), Demographic transition theory reinterpreted: an application to recent natality trends in Latin America (Lexington Books, Lexington, MA).

Becker, G.S. (1988), "Family economics and macro behavior", American Economic Review 78: 1–13.

Becker, G.S. and R.J. Barro (1988), "A reformulation of the economic theory of fertility", Quarterly Journal of Economics 103: 1–25.

Becker, G.S. and H.G. Lewis (1973), "On the interaction between the quantity and quality of children", Journal of Political Economy 81: 279–288.

Becker, G.S., K.M. Murphy and R. Tamura (1990), "Human capital, fertility and economic growth", Journal of Political Economy 98: S12–S37.

Benhabib, J. and K. Nishimura (1989), "Endogenous fluctuations in the Barro–Becker theory of fertility", in: A. Wenig and K.F. Zimmermann, eds., Demographic change and economic development (Springer-Verlag, Berlin).

Bental, B. (1989), "The old age security hypothesis and optimal population growth", Journal of Population Economics 1: 285–301.

Caldwell, J.C. (1982), Theory of fertility decline (Academic Press, New York).

Cigno, A. (1991), Economics of the family (Clarendon Press, Oxford).

Coale, A.J. (1974), "The history of the human population", Scientific American, Reprinted in: The human population, a Scientific American Book (W.H. Freeman, San Francisco, CA) pp. 12–25.

Dálkó, V. (1992), "Endogenous fertility and human capital investment", Unpublished Ph.D. dissertation (Department of Economics, University of Pennsylvania, Philadelphia, PA).

Devaney, R.L. (1989), An introduction to chaotic dynamical systems, 2nd edn. (Addison-Wesley, Reading, MA).

Freedman, R. (1975) The sociology of human fertility (Irvington Publishers, New York).

Fudenberg, D. and J. Tirole (1991), Game theory (The MIT Press, Cambridge, MA).

Kreps, D.M. (1990), Game theory and economic modelling (Clarendon Press, Oxford).

Lee, R.D. (1986), "Malthus and Boserup: a dynamic synthesis", in: D. Coleman and R. Schofield, eds., The state of population theory: forward from Malthus (Basil Blackwell, Oxford) pp. 96–130.

Leibenstein, H. (1957) Economic backwardness and economic growth (Wiley, New York).

Leibenstein, H. (1974), "An interpretation of the economic theory of fertility: promising path or blind alley?", Journal of Economic Literature 12: 457–479.

Lucas, R.E., Jr. (1988), "On the mechanics of economic development", Journal of Monetary Economics 22: 3–42.

Malthus, T.R. (1798), An essay on the principle of population (J. Johnson, London).

Malthus, T.R. (1830), A summary view of the principle of population (John Murray, London).

Mankiw, N.G., D. Romer and D.N. Weil (1992), "A contribution to the empirics of economic growth", Quarterly Journal of Economics 107: 407–437.

Neher, P. (1971), "Peasants, procreation and pensions", American Economic Review 61: 380–389.

Nerlove, M. (1974), "Household and economy: toward a new theory of population and economic growth", Journal of Political Economy 82: S200–S218.

Nerlove, M. (1991), "Population and the environment: a parable of firewood and other tales", American Journal of Agricultural Economics 73: 1334–1357.

Nerlove, M. (1993), "Procreation, fishing and hunting: problems in the economics of renewable resources and dynamic planar systems", American Journal of Agricultural Economics 75: 59–71.

Nerlove, M., A. Razin and E. Sadka (1987), Household and economy: welfare economics of endogenous fertility (Academic Press, New York).

Niehans, J. (1963), "Economic growth with two endogenous factors", Quarterly Journal of Economics 77: 349–371.

Nishimura K. and L.K. Raut (1992), "Family expansion and capital accumulation of a dynasty", Discussion paper no. 92-40 (University of California-San Diego, San Diego, CA), October.

Nishimura K. and J. Zhang (1992), "Pay-as-you-go public pensions with endogenous fertility", Journal of Public Economics 48: 239–258.

Nugent, J.B. (1985), "The old-age security motive for fertility", Population and Development Review 11: 75–97.

Preston, S.H. (1978), The effects of infant and child mortality on fertility (Academic Press, New York).

Raut, L.K. (1985), "Three essays on intertemporal economic development: essay II", Unpublished Ph.D. dissertation (Yale University, New Haven, CT).

Raut, L.K. (1991), "Capital accumulation, income distribution and endogenous fertility in an overlapping generations general equilibrium model", Journal of Development Economics 34: 123–150.

Raut, L.K. (1992a), "Effects of social security on fertility and savings: an overlapping generations model", Indian Economic Review 27: 25–43.

Raut, L.K. (1992b), "Subgame perfect manipulation of children by overlapping generations of agents with two-sided altruism and endogenous fertility", Discussion paper no. 92-54 (University of California-San Diego, San Diego, CA), December.

Raut, L.K. and T.N. Srinivasan (1993), "Theories of long-run growth: old and new", in: K. Basu, M. Majumdar and T. Mitra, eds., Capital, investment and development (Basil Blackwell, New York).

Raut, L.K. and T.N. Srinivasan (1994), "Dynamics of endogenous growth", Economic Theory 4: 777–790.

Razin, A. and U. Ben Zion (1975), "An intergenerational model of population growth", American Economic Review 69: 923–933.

Romer, P. (1986), "Increasing returns and long run growth", Journal of Political Economy 94: 1002–1037.

Romer, P. (1990), "Endogenous technical change", Journal of Political Economy 98: 71–102.

Sah, R.K. (1991), "The effects of child mortality changes on fertility choice and parental welfare", Journal of Political Economy 99: 582–606.

Schultz, T.W. (1961), "Education and economic growth", in: N.B. Henry, ed., Social forces influencing American education (University of Chicago Press, Chicago, IL).

Schultz, T.W. (1971), Investment in human capital (Free Press, New York).

Schultz, T.W. (1973), "Explanation and interpretations of the increasing value of human time", Woody Thompson Lecture (Midwest Economics Association, Chicago, Chicago, IL).

Schultz, T.P. (1981), Economics of population (Addison-Wesley, Reading, MA).

Solow, R.M. (1956), "A contribution to the theory of economic growth", Quarterly Journal of Economics 70: 65–94.

Solow, R.M. (1992), "New directions in growth theory", Unpublished manuscript.

Srinivasan, T.N. (1988), "Fertility and old-age security in an overlapping generations model", Journal of Quantitative Economics 4: 11–17.

Stokey, N.L., R.E. Lucas, Jr. and E.C. Prescott (1989), Recursive methods in economic dynamics (Harvard University Press, Cambridge, MA).

Swan, T.W. (1956), "Economic growth and capital accumulation", Economic Record 32: 324–361.

Tamura, R. (1992), "Fertility, human capital and the wealth of families", Unpublished working paper (Department of Economics, University of Iowa, Iowa City, IA).

Willis, R.J. (1980), "The old-age security hypothesis and population growth", in: T. Burch, ed., Demographic behavior: interdisciplinary perspectives on decision making (Westview Press, Boulder, CO).

Wolpin, K.I. (1984), "An estimable dynamic stochastic model of fertility and child mortality", Journal of Political Economy 92: 852–874.

World Bank (1992), Development and the environment, World development report 1992 (Oxford University Press, New York).

Young, A.A. (1928), "Increasing returns and economic progress", Economic Journal 38: 527–542.

Chapter 21

LONG-TERM CONSEQUENCES OF POPULATION GROWTH: TECHNOLOGICAL CHANGE, NATURAL RESOURCES, AND THE ENVIRONMENT

JAMES A. ROBINSON

University of Southern California

T.N. SRINIVASAN*

Yale University

Contents

1. Introduction	1177
1.1. Population past and population present: a review	1183
1.2. Growth, development, demography and resources: a perspective	1187
1.3. Our approach	1197
1.4. Overview of the paper	1200
2. Long-run development with exogenous population and exogenous technical change	1202
2.1. Neoclassical growth: infinitely-lived agents	1202
2.2. Neoclassical growth with finite lifetimes	1220
2.3. Neoclassical growth with resources	1228
3. Endogenizing population and technical change	1245
3.1. Models of endogenous fertility and mortality with exogenous technical change	1246
3.2. Natural resources in economies with endogenous population	1250
3.3. Theories of endogenous technical change	1253
3.4. Population and endogenous growth	1260
3.5. Resources and endogenous growth	1269
3.6. Endogenous population and growth in the presence of natural resources	1271

*The research for this paper was conducted while James Robinson was a member of the Department of Economics at the University of Melbourne and visiting the University of the Andes in Bogota, Colombia, and the University of Pennsylvania. He would like to thank the respective faculties for their generosity and warm hospitality. We would also like to thank, without implicating, Anita Chaudhuri and Stephen Morris for general discussions and Andy Abel, David Alden and Andy Foster for their expert advice on the altruism, environmental and demographic literatures respectively.

Handbook of Population and Family Economics. Edited by M.R. Rosenzweig and O. Stark
© Elsevier Science B.V., 1997

4. Assessment 1272
   4.1. Sustainable development 1272
   4.2. Discounting 1275
   4.3. Uncertainty 1278
   4.4. International issues 1279
5. Conclusions 1279
References 1283

1. Introduction

This chapter surveys the long-term implications of population growth and its interaction with technological change, resources utilization and the environment. We ask: what are the key determinants of the processes of population growth and technical change and how do they interact with each other? Under what conditions can the people of the world enjoy rising living standards, and if they do, does population have to stabilize for this to be feasible? How do the answers to these questions depend on the relationship between human progress and the natural environment? Will growth be limited by lack of resources or negative environmental repercussions? Will the development of the world economy necessarily mean the despoiling of the environment?

This is a wide brief and we make it manageable by concentrating on what we see as the core analytical issues and using these to provide a framework with which to assess the empirical literature. While formulating a satisfactory overarching framework is virtually impossible, we think the evidence and the theory provides certain strong intuitions about the right way to see the issues and, in particular, to evaluate their welfare and policy implications. One of our main purposes is to elucidate these central issues and intuitions.

The questions which we address are arguably the earliest to be carefully studied in economics, yet they remain amongst the most controversial. Since ancient times social thinkers have speculated about the tensions between the size and growth of populations and the resources available for them. Such speculation has usually led to dire predictions most famously associated with the name of Thomas Malthus. While we touch on the classic "Malthusian debate", since this critically involves the nature of the relationship between technical progress and population change, the main concerns of the chapter are the issues raised by "neo-Malthusians" – those concerned with the fragility of the environment, the impact of economic and population growth on the "natural capital stock" and the "sustainability" of development.

The economic history of the nineteenth and twentieth centuries has not been kind to Malthus in his prediction that the finiteness of resources and basic procreation behavior would trap society into a situation of economic stagnation. The result of this was a serious neglect of any such issues in the formal theory of growth which developed in the 1950s and 1960s. The 1970s changed this. In this decade much attention was focused on resource extraction and exploitation. This literature concentrated on the extent to which the finiteness of certain natural resources (oil, minerals, etc.) could place a bound on per capita income. The results were encouraging: under certain, arguably reasonable, assumptions about technical change and production technology (which we discuss in Section 2.3.2) society could substitute man-made for natural capital in such a way as to allow for a sustained growth in living standards. The dire predictions of Forrester (1971) and Meadows (1974), which received so much public attention, were relatively mechanistic extrapolations which ignored exactly the issues, which seemed of central importance to economists (see the discussion of Solow

(1974b) or Koopmans (1979), or from another (but equally balanced) perspective, Demeny (1988)). The experience of adjustment to higher fuel prices, for example, the increased efforts to develop alternative energy sources, seemed to largely vindicate the economists views. Apocalyptic pronouncements, such as the forecast of Ehrlich (1970) that 65 million Americans would die of starvation in the 1980s, were made to appear foolish. As Michaels (1993) points out, "in fact 60 million Americans dieted during the period".

Since the 1970s, however, the argument has shifted to a form which is not so easy to dismiss as that pertaining to finite resources. The more recent concerns focus not on whether or not the economy can find a suitable substitute energy source for coal, for example, but rather on the far more ambitious and elusive question of how economic processes and human activities are embedded in the global environment and the implications which population and income growth and economic activity have for this relationship.

Economy–environment interactions go in both ways and are subtle, pervasive, and mostly suppressed in economic analysis. The recent literature has brought these issues to the surface and into sharper focus. Their empirical implications and importance are, however, highly contentious. We suggest a way of integrating these issues with standard models of economic growth. While such a formalization is severely limited (due to a very inadequate understanding of the nature and dynamics of environmental processes), it is exceedingly helpful in elucidating the crux of the interaction between environmental phenomena, demographic processes and the nature of technical change. As Partha Dasgupta (1993c) puts it, "modern economic analysis has for some while provided us with a language in which to discuss the private and social management of environmental resources. In some cases the prescriptions are sharp and precise; in others they are outlines, but only because of the deep uncertainties we face about the nature of ecological processes and about our own values, and not because we do not have a precise language in which to think through them". This framework has the additional advantage of bringing the tools of welfare economics to bear on the issues.

The interaction between the environment and the economy is obviously multifaceted. One cannot, for example, hope to capture the ramifications of the exploitation of local commons and the economic impact of climate change in a single model. We deal with this by using different models, each tailored to address an issue, or issues, which we feel to be central. Far from being a limitation of our approach, this is an advantage. In particular, we argue that the environmental problems, and their interaction with population growth, faced by developing economies are often qualitatively different from those facing developed economies. Many key environmental issues for the poor nations of the world, such as lack of potable water, inadequate sanitation, and air pollution due to the use of biomass fuels, are best solved by economic development. In these cases there is no trade-off between environment and growth. This is important since environmental improvement is often regarded as a luxury which poor nations cannot afford. We argue, along with the World Bank (1992), that there are strong

complementarities between policies to improve the environment, influence population growth and promote development in general. We also echo their conclusion that, in terms of orders of magnitude for human welfare, these problems are the most serious environmental problems facing the world.

We also argue that there is a more fundamental sense in which development and efficient utilization of the environment are complementary. This stems from the fact that both a major cause and symptom of underdevelopment is dysfunctional social and political institutions (as we argue in Section 3.3, this is one lesson of the recent revival of growth theory). Development necessitates institutional innovation and transition in order to stimulate capital accumulation and technological change, and institutions which impede these key aspects of development are highly unlikely to be able to implement efficient ownership structures or desirable policies with respect to resource use or the environment.

The situation is different in developed economies. While problems of local commons and inadequate property rights are also important, the main environmental problems are pollution, toxic waste disposal and worries about the global commons. While there are still local issues, such as for example, protection of natural habitats, these seem minor in comparison to those faced by developing countries. This seems to be the key reason why global environmental problems loom so large in the debate in developed economies. This is ironic since, if anything, poor countries face larger risks and will certainly find it more difficult to adjust to the economic impact of climate change. It is not that global problems do not affect poor countries, but rather that other problems are more tangible and pressing.

While we make this the main focus, this is a fledgling field with tremendous controversy amongst experts over the pertinent facts. Both the effects of economic growth and population growth on the natural capital stock are in dispute, as is the reverse relationship. Indeed, the perspective we adopt is that the main issues are empirical. In our theoretical treatment we stress that the evolution of population, technology and resource usage are all the jointly endogenous outcome of the decisions of agents in the economy. Much of the literature ignores one or other facets of this joint relationship. The literature is full of misleading and erroneous causal associations between population growth, income growth, and resource use.

Consider, as an example, the over use of local common resources in the presence of rapid population growth. It is tempting to attribute causality from population pressure to resource over-use, and indeed this may be read from a regression equation. We argue that both phenomena (rapid population growth and environmental degradation) are two consequences of poverty and underdevelopment and related institutional and policy failures. Both are a result of the actions of poor people attempting to cope with the situation in which they find themselves. The most plausible explanations for rapid population growth in developing economies link this to poverty, high infant mortality, and inadequate institutions (lack of insurance and saving possibilities, markets, and social infrastructure) and thus to the very roots of underdevelopment itself. Birdsall and Griffin (1988) stress that because of their joint endogeneity, while it is always possible to find counterexamples to the relationship between poverty and fertility, nevertheless, "certain household characteristics that seem everywhere to be associated with poverty – low educational achievement, poor health, and lack of access to education and health services – are also generally associated with high fertility". Moreover, poverty causes large family size which is itself a cause of future poverty – large families allocate less resources per child and this leads to the perpetuation (intergenerational transmission) of poverty. For example, educational expenditure per-child is consistently found to be smaller in large families (Birdsall and Griffin, 1988).

The inefficient over use of common resources is closely linked to these phenomena. As the World Bank (1992) put it, "the poor are both the victims and agents of environmental damage". Poverty, low life expectancy, and highly imperfect capital markets lead to shortening fallow periods, which leads to soil erosion and a deteriorating resource base. It is poverty which generates this preoccupation with day-to-day survival. Such behavior is exacerbated by inadequate institutions (such as ill-defined property rights) and inappropriate policies and incentives.

Also jointly endogenous in any convincing account of development are government policymaking and social institutions. Indeed, inappropriate government policies and institutions are frequently to blame for environmental stress. A recurrent theme throughout the paper, for example, is the need to clarify and enforce property rights. While communities have developed institutions to ensure the efficient allocation of common resources (Ostrom (1990) provides insightful examples), it is these very institutional structures that are often disrupted in the process of development. Salient examples of policies affecting the environment are subsidies in Brazil to ranching which has caused a large amount of deforestation (see Binswanger, 1989 or Feder, 1977, 1979), and migration incentives in Indonesia (for example, Barbier et al., 1989). Repetto (1988) lists other related examples. The subsidization of fuel inputs in Eastern European countries before the fall of communism led to the adoption of fuel intensive technologies which tended to produce high levels of pollution. Agricultural policies which depress the prices for farmers undermine profitability and reduce the adoption of more efficient and durable farming practices. The World Bank (1992) estimated that in a sample of five African countries logging fees represented only 33% of the costs of replanting. Similarly, charges for irrigation are far below efficient levels. Apart from these, there is a sad litany of major development projects which had severe, and largely uncontemplated, environmental impacts.

We draw from this a relatively optimistic conclusion that tackling the central problems of underdevelopment is likely to be effective in solving both environmental problems and in initiating the demographic transition. What is critically important is that the problems are correctly identified and addressed. In the above examples it is underdevelopment, both in terms of low per capita income and in terms of social and political infrastructure (for example, the lack of representative, open and democratic political institutions) which is the heart of the problem.

It is also apparent, however, that to the extent that markets are incomplete and institutional responses inadequate or inappropriate the scope for potential Pareto improvements is large and no trade-offs have to be faced until all inefficiencies are eliminated. It is in an economy with complete and perfect competitive markets where equilibrium allocations are efficient (or in situations where some concept of constrained efficiency is appropriate) that real trade-offs occur. In such a world, society may have to choose between consumption of physical commodities and environmental resources, or between consumption per capita and aggregate population. We do little more than raise such issues. They clearly present all the well-known intractable normative questions of ordinal welfare economics. Our view is that there is much to be done before economists have to face these issues and that the real job is to find ways of implementing potential welfare improvements. This requires a careful study of the type of potential inefficiencies surrounding both the processes of population growth, technical change and that of resource utilization.

We adopt a remorselessly choice theoretic approach throughout the chapter and it is clear that this may have disadvantages. Indeed, as T.W. Schultz (1974) has remarked in a similar context, "I anticipate that many sensitive, thoughtful people will be offended by these studies (which) may seem far beyond the realm of the economic calculus". Especially with respect to the modeling of choices about fertility and family, the nature and specification of both the constraint set and the objective function are difficult. Many factors seem pertinent to the conditioning of fertility choices, some of which are: the availability of contraception, social norms and marriage patterns, the division of labor between males and females. Similarly, specification of the objective function seems equally fraught with complexity: do parents care about the welfare of their children, or how this welfare is generated, do they desire children for themselves or for what they can get out of them? The vexed nature of preferences becomes even more problematic at the level of social choices about population.

From the long-run perspective of human evolution, however, adopting the choice theoretic approach seems by far the most promising methodological approach. In prehistory hominid groups experienced moderate fertility. Both modern hunter-gatherers and our closest kin in the animal world, the sub-human primates, exhibit low fertility, certainly far below the physiological possible maximum (see Davis (1989) for an interesting perspective). One might ask: why? A plausible explanation is that, given the rudimentary nature of their ability to provide food for themselves, they deliberately controlled population to find some equilibrium with resources. This changed around 10 000 B.C. when humans began to settle and develop agricultural societies. Both situations have plausible economic explanations. The settling of previous itinerant populations, the domestication of animals and systematic cultivation of crops, created an enormous expansion of output. At the same time the division of labor changed. This is not to deny the existence of exogenous forces on population, for instance the development and diffusion of diseases or parasites (though the evolution of these themselves is clearly not exogenous to the organization of human society, McNeill

(1976)), but it suggests that the best method to understand the implications is through the lens of choice theory, at least if we take an eclectic enough position about the relationship between individual motivations and the interaction between individual and social constraints. The evidence also suggests that the crucial determinant of actual fertility is "desired" fertility (Pritchett, 1994) so that choices matter.

We see this approach as being complementary to others. Demographic processes are modeled in evolutionary biology. While the objective functions and constraints may be unusual for economists (such as stress on "reproductive success", "fitness", and "adaptive traits"), the conceptual framework is often surprisingly similar (see Cronk, 1991). As in the economics literature, there is no automatic stress on optimality. Previously adaptive behavior may persist even after it no longer confers any advantages (such as a preference in humans for sweet foods which previously helped to select nonpoisonous food), just as social behavior may persist due to norms and conventions long after it has become dysfunctional or redundant.

The derivation of behavior from individual preferences also allows us to treat welfare issues explicitly. One of our major conclusions concerning population growth is that we need to better understand the nature of inter-familial and inter-generational preferences. In lieu of such knowledge, the voluminous philosophical literature on optimal population growth, for example, is largely sterile.

In the next two sections we provide an overview of some of the facts about population growth, development and resources. It is difficult to come away from these with a firm understanding of these processes. The relationship between demographic phenomena and the economy is highly complex and does not yield to simple generalizations (see Caldwell, 1990; Birdsall and Griffin, 1988), and that between the economy and environmental features perhaps even more uncertain. For instance, Slade (1987) concludes her wide ranging survey by stating, "it should be abundantly clear that all attempts here to draw conclusions about the effects of resource scarcity on the growth of population and economic well-being at the macro level failed". We stress that little can be concluded from the aggregate evidence about the relationship between population and economic development or about the more complex relationship between these variables and resource exploitation and the environment. This is in line with the theory, which we discuss in Section 3.4, which suggests that the relationship is ambiguous and contingent on the exact structure of society and the responses and behavior that population growth or development induces.

As a salient example of this, consider the relationship between the level of per capita income and population growth. Birdsall (1989) concludes that "the exceptions suggest the importance of factors other than average income which affect demographic variables – factors that operate at the individual and family level: education, availability and distribution of health services, women's status, access to family planning, prevailing religious views, a country's population policy, and so on". These same complexities have foiled the attempt to construct "threshold" levels of economic and social indices which might signal the onset of demographic transition (see Caldwell, 1990;

Coale and Watkins, 1986). Similarly, while there are many examples of variegated and even seemingly alarming environmental problems, the evidence does not allow one to conclude that there is in any sense a crisis, or that, as we argued above, properly interpreted, development and growth have deleterious effects on the environment. The evolution of population, the environment, per capita income, and resource extraction are inexorably intertwined with the whole process of economic, political and social change which we call development, and this process does not yield to simple monocausal explanations or sweeping generalizations.

The introduction concludes by outlining our approach in more detail and then providing an overview of the paper.

1.1. Population past and population present: a review

Before commencing on the analytical heart of the paper, it is important to have some feel of the historical processes at work and the evidence. We first describe the facts about the evolution of population and its main determinants. We then focus on a key issue for this paper, the econometric evidence concerning the aggregate relationship between population growth and the level of per capita income. In Section 3.4 we turn in detail to more disaggregated studies.

In synthesizing the literature, we are fortunate in being able to call on authoritative summaries due to Cassen (1976), McNicholl (1984), World Bank (1984), National Research Council (1986), Kelley (1988), Birdsall (1988, 1989), Srinivasan (1988, 1992), Caldwell (1990), and Jha et al. (1994). In this section we wish to give a sense of what is known. While what is known is far less than one would wish, this section will orientate our discussion in the rest of the paper. The literature is full of shrill and vitriolic rhetoric and Cassandra-like warnings of impending doom, one of the more scholarly sources being the work of Keyfitz (1991a,b). Our reading of the evidence supports the more agnostic view prevalent in the recent scholarly literature on population growth (good examples being Kelley (1988, 1991)). We also try to persuade the reader that this seems the best approach to thinking about natural resources. Kelley (1988) suggests that the agnostic view has four essential aspects: "First, population growth may have positive as well as negative aspects, second, both direct and indirect linkages are important in connecting population and economic growth, third, several problems typically attributed to population are due largely to other causes, and finally, the role of population is sometimes to exacerbate other problems and to reveal their symptoms sooner and/or more dramatically".

At first glance the size of the issue is enormous. It took millions of years for the population of the planet to reach one billion, 120 years to add a further billion, 35 years for the next, 15 years for the next, and another 13 years until the five billion mark was reached. Current estimates (World Bank, 1992) predict that world population will level off at around 12.5 billion in about 2150. Different scenarios give stationary populations between 10.1 and 23 billion. Although these forecasts are debatable, given the uncertainties surrounding base-line population estimates as well as those of fertility and mortality rates in many developing countries, nobody disagrees that there will be considerable increases in population, even if all societies were to reach replacement fertility today. This latter phenomena has been called "population momentum" by Keyfitz (1982), who calculated that a developing country with a representative age structure could still expect population to grow by about one third after replacement fertility was attained. The World Bank has predicted that most developing countries would reach replacement fertility between 2005 and 2025 (though for some countries in the Middle East and Africa it is later). This is based on most countries already having experienced significant fertility declines (though this is not true of all countries, Nigeria for instance). As Sen (1993) points out, the number of people added to world population between 1980 and 1990 (923 million) is approximately the same as the population of the entire world at the time of Malthus.

The historical evidence is in fact relatively supportive of Malthus's hypothesis for the period before 1800. The evidence presented in Lindert (1985) and Weir (1989) (see also World Bank, 1984) suggests that Malthus was basing his theory on sound evidence. The prediction that living standards would grind along at subsistence levels seems born out. Life expectancy was probably about the same in 1600 as it had been 2000 years before (World Bank, 1984). Population growth was positively related to wage increases and seems to have led to a consequent reduction in wages and fertility – the classic Malthusian cycle. This changed some time in the late 18th century (as Keynes put it, "the Malthusian devil was chained"). The industrial revolution heralded a period with both rising population and rising per capita income.

While in seventeenth century Britain fertility rose and mortality fell, fertility was much lower than that of contemporary developing economies, and mortality much higher. In Western Europe, marriage rates were low and those who married, married late. The mean rate of marriage in the seventeenth and eighteenth centuries in Belgium, France, England, Sweden and Germany was 25. In 1871, 50% of women aged 25–29 in Ireland were unmarried, while in England the figure was still a high 36%. The main reason for this appears to be that to marry young, people had to set up a separate household and this required resources. The greater relative poverty in Ireland explains the difference with England. The crude birth rates of European countries when their demographic transition took off were far lower than those of currently developing economies. Similarly, mortality was much higher. From this it follows that population growth rates were in aggregate very modest compared to those currently or recently experienced. In England, population growth peaked at 1.6% in the 1820s, and in France it never exceeded 1% in the nineteenth century. The demographic transition has now evolved so far that several countries have dropped below replacement fertility levels which itself has caused concern (Keyfitz, 1986).

The picture in the contemporary developing countries is different. Starting after the first World War mortality began to decline. The main cause seems to be the large improvements in medical science and practice (one famous example being the effect of the control of malaria on mortality in Sri Lanka). These mortality declines took place at much lower levels of income than those in western countries. For example, in 1982 life expectancy in India was 55, while its per capita income was below US$300 (in 1982 prices). In 1900, life expectancy in England, the United States and Sweden was below 50, and yet their average income was over US$1000 (in 1982 prices, see World Bank, 1984). It is also worth noting that the literacy rate of India was below 40% in 1982, while in these European countries it was over 80% in 1900. They were also (or maybe as a result) not immediately followed by significant falls in fertility. While these have now taken place, the rates of population growth experienced since World War II are unprecedented historically. For developing countries as a whole population growth rates rose from 2% in 1950 to 2.4% in 1965, mostly as a result of the falling death rates. Since then, rates of fertility have fallen faster than mortality, and current growth rates are, on average, over 2%, with considerable regional variation. In Africa, for example, the rate is 3% (the United Nations forecasts that the proportion of world population in Africa, which was 11% in 1980, will increase to 26% by 2100). Moreover, the declines in fertility rates have been much faster than those experienced by the developed countries. The average decline is dominated by that in China (which accounts for one third of all people in developing countries), although the East Asian countries have also experienced fast falls in fertility. However, there has hardly been any fall in fertility in Sub-Saharan Africa.

In an interesting comparison between European fertility declines during the period 1882–1900 and those of Taiwan and Thailand (which began in 1963 and 1970 respectively), Knodel and van der Walle found large differences. European economies began their transition to low fertility with a fertility rate which was two thirds of the Asian level and much higher infant mortality (between 150 and 200 first year deaths per 1000 live births as opposed to figures of 49 and 77 in Taiwan and Thailand respectively; see World Bank (1984)).

The empirical evidence overwhelmingly suggests that fertility and mortality are negatively related to per capita income, though, as mentioned above, this is not uniformly the case. For instance, there are many counter-examples to the claim that fertility will only fall when per capita income increases. Lutz (1990) provides an examination of one such case – Mauritius – of particular interest since the fertility rate declined spectacularly by 50% in less than a decade. Other famous examples are the states of Kerala and Tamil Nadu in India (see Sen, 1993) and Sri Lanka, all of which are close to achieving replacement rates of fertility. This demonstrates that a whole vector of variables, not closely correlated with per capita GDP, affect both fertility and mortality.

These facts describe the contours of the "demographic transition" both historically, as it happened in the developed countries, and as it is currently occurring in developing countries. There is a strong sense here that, while the details matter, on balance fertility, mortality and the rate of population growth, all fall as economies develop and per capita income rises. This is due, not just to some simple relationship between income level and fertility and mortality, but also to the social and economic changes that accompany and are an intrinsic part of this process of development. Innovations and changes in institutions can disrupt simple correlations between variables.

The empirical consensus is that, despite many assertions to the contrary, there is no robust relationship between the rate of population growth and economic growth. This has been confirmed by a large number of works beginning with Kuznets (1966) and Easterlin (1967). Kelley (1988) provides an authoritative survey of this literature. He notes that "while several models predict a negative net impact of population growth on economic development, it is intriguing that the empirical evidence documenting this outcome is weak or nonexistent". More recent work, with better data and more sophisticated econometric techniques, has found a small negative relationship.

Important recent examples are Bloom and Freeman (1988), Brander and Dowrick (1994) and Kelley and Schmidt (1994). These studies are sophisticated in trying to recognize the joint endogeneity (for example, by using instrumental variable techniques for estimation) of the series under consideration and in controlling for other factors in attempting to statistically isolate the relationship. They also broaden the scope of earlier work by assessing the influence of not just population growth, but also possible separate effects of fertility and mortality. Changes in these, while both sources of changes in population growth, might plausibly affect economic growth in differing ways. Indeed, Bloom and Freeman find that the breakdown of a rate of population growth into fertility and mortality is important. A particular growth rate of population has a smaller effect on income growth if it results from low fertility and low mortality. Using the Heston–Summers data set, Brander and Dowrick (1994) do find a negative relationship between population growth rates and birth rates and economic growth. However, the coefficients in their regression equations are typically insignificant statistically. The results are stronger for developed than for less developed countries, and stronger for recent rather than earlier years. They also find that investment is negatively, and significantly related to birth rates. Population growth tends to be unrelated to income and investment which is why Brander and Dowrick concentrate on birth rates. It is not clear, however, how robust these results are.

An important recent study by Kelley and Schmidt (1994) also finds evidence of a negative relationship between the rates of population and per capita income growth for the 1980s, while confirming the insignificance of the relationship for the 1960s and 1970s. They find, in contradistinction to Brander and Dowrick, that this effect is much more pronounced for developing countries and in fact is sometimes positive for developed countries. When they disaggregate this effect, Kelley and Schmidt find that it is accounted for by the emergence in the 1980s of a negative effect from the number of births (net of infant deaths) on income growth. This paper is also interesting because it provides the first corroborating evidence supporting the results of Simon (1986) who has found a statistically significant positive effect of population density on income growth. They also find a pure size effect emerges in the 1980s. They further find that population growth exerts a negative effect on the saving rate.

The problem with interpreting all of this evidence is that, even if a robust negative relationship between population growth and income growth should emerge, we need to understand whether this is really causal or just a joint facet of the dynamics of technological change and demographic transition. As Cassen (1976) puts it, "in general a large amount of specification is needed to yield a prediction about the sign of the simple correlation between the growth of population and that of total of per capita income. Those found in practice are of negligible interest. And they are quite immaterial to the question of whether, in the given circumstances of a particular country, per capita income would grow more or less rapidly were population growing more slowly". He goes on to conclude that "the one thing we can infer from these correlations is that whatever the influence of population on economic growth, it is relatively small in comparison to other influences".

1.2. Growth, development, demography and resources: a perspective

Having considered the salient demographic evidence, we now proceed to assess the environmental evidence. Where possible we integrate this with demographic trends (as some empirical work has explicitly attempted to do). We wish to concentrate on environmental and renewable resources since these are the resources which seem most critical to human welfare. A large theoretical literature (which we review in Section 2.3.2) has examined the interconnections between exhaustible resources and growth. A number of empirical investigations have been conducted to try and estimate to what extent, if any, the world is running out of these resources, or the sense in which they might become a constraint on human activities. That this empirical literature exists is a testament to the fact that exhaustible resources differ from other environmental resources in that they tend to be owned and allocated on the basis of well defined property rights and, moreover, traded in markets at prices which we can observe. Contrast this to the problem of generating data on whether or not natural habitats are becoming more scarce.

1.2.1. Exhaustible resources

The consensus is that there is in fact little evidence that any serious scarcity is developing. Nordhaus (1994b) has estimated that real oil prices in 1986 were at the same level as in 1900. In Meadows et al. (1972), world supplies of lead in 1970 were put at 91 million metric tons. Beckerman (1993) reports that world consumption of lead between 1970 and 1989 was 98.5 tons, and yet in 1989 world reserves were estimated to be 125 million tons. There are many such examples. Simon (1981) also argues that there has been a decline in the real cost of resources and uses this as evidence that worries about shortages or increased scarcities are unfounded. One would expect that, if the world were suffering a resource crisis, relative prices would be rising. MacKellar and Vining (1987) in their comprehensive review found that no simple general answers were possible to questions such as: "Are natural resources becoming more scarce? Are conservation and population control policies called for?".

The evidence suggests that as long as resources are priced, so that prices can reflect scarcity and give incentives for substitution and conservation, then there seems to be little prospect that resources will constrain living standards. Exhaustible resources must eventually disappear, though there is of course the possibility of recycling to extend their life. Chandler (1984) estimates, for example, that the world steel industry uses scrap metal for 45% of its input requirements. Despite exhaustibility, it does seem possible to be optimistic, though, about the effect of pricing on the discovery of new resources and substitutes. For example, when Zaire, producer of about half of the world's production of cobalt, restricted supply by 30%, prices rose from $11 per kilo to $35. This led to an extensive introduction of substitutes and US demand fell by 50% (Goeller and Zucker, 1984). National Academy of Sciences (1986) list many other examples.

It is sensible to attempt to measure scarcity of these resources by looking at their long-term price movements (Barnett and Morse (1963) is a classic example). Although the evidence is mixed on balance, there seems to be no evidence of increasing scarcity. Thus far, depletion has been successfully met by new supplies being discovered (or becoming economical) or substitutes being developed (Slade, 1982, 1987). While the reliance of the world on petroleum is important, MacKellar and Vining (1987) point out that the potential supply from nonconventional sources (such as oil shale) is vast.

1.2.2. Renewable resources

On the topic of this section there are many preconceptions. Two types of problems are commonly raised when discussing the interaction of population growth, development in general and environmental resources in a wide sense.

Firstly, that growth can only be sustained by using up resources and despoiling the environment beyond its ability to regenerate, and, secondly, as per capita income increases, the flows of wastes and pollutants increase as well, and the earth "sinks" and the natural ability of the environment to regenerate and absorb waste, will become overburdened.

There are two facets to these arguments. Firstly, a positive claim that the environment puts an upper bound on feasible per capita output and, worse, if damaged irreparably, may lead to the planet becoming uninhabitable. Second, that even if growth in per capita income is feasible, it cannot lead to increased human welfare if the environment is destroyed in the process.

Many caveats apply to these simple propositions. Development involves not just increases in total and per capita output, the composition is also important. For example, later stages of development are characterized by the increasing importance of service industries which are much less resource intensive. Price incentives also stimulate the adoption of new "clean" technologies. The evidence we report below substantiates this intuition. As societies develop, the relative valuation of produced goods and the amenity services of environmental resources changes in ways which are conducive to conservation (this is a possible foundation for the environmental "Kuznets curve" which we discuss below). Moreover, the arguments implicitly assume an enormous myopia in human decision-making and disregard for the welfare of future generations which needs theoretical clarification and empirical substantiation.

We also argue that this common perception about growth and the environment is altered by widening what one means by the environment. Serageldin (1993) estimates that one billion people do not have access to clean water, 1.7 billion do not have access to sanitation, and 2–3 million children die annually because of diseases associated with this lack of water and sanitation. The World Bank (1992) estimates that 300 million to 700 million women and children suffer from severe indoor air pollution from cooking fires; lack of sanitation is the major contributor to 900 million cases of diarrheal diseases each year which cause the death of three million children; and two million of these could be prevented if adequate sanitation and clean water were available. Lack of sanitation has direct as well as indirect economic costs. For example, the World Bank (1992) also calculated that about 1% of the GDP of Jakarta in Indonesia was spent simply on boiling water. Another striking example is that in the first ten weeks of a recent cholera epidemic in Peru, losses in agricultural exports and revenues from tourism were more than three times the amount the whole country invested on improving sanitation and water supply facilities in the whole of the 1980s (World Bank, 1992). Certainly these numbers are subject to wide margins of error and biases, however, they do give an indication of the order of magnitude of the problem.

Economic growth has a big impact in reducing these environmental problems. The World Resources Institute (1990) estimates that, in 1985, while on average only 39% of people in the poorest quintile of countries had access to safe drinking water, on average 87% of people in the richest quintile had such access. Similar findings apply to sanitation.

Despite examples of this type, there seems to be a strong presumption that growth is inconsistent with environmental preservation. We argue that resource use is a natural part of a dynamic path. LDCs have much larger ratios of environmental resources to either physical and human capital, and it seems sensible that they would wish to exploit the former to obtain both of the latter. What is more crucial is the extent to which this use is efficient. This rests not on the growth rate per se, but rather on the economic, social, and political institutions of society. Even without growth in per capita income, resource usage may easily be disastrous without the correct set of institutions and incentives.

It is also thought that population growth has large adverse impacts on environmental resources. The World Bank (1992) concluded: "Population growth increases the demand for goods and services, and, if practices remain unchanged, implies increased environmental damage. Population growth also increases the need for employment and livelihoods, which – especially in crowded rural areas – exerts additional direct pressure on natural resources. More people also produce more wastes, threatening local health conditions and implying additional stress on the earth's assimilative capacity".

We would like to know what the evidence is on these issues. The great difficulty in compiling this section is the tremendous variety of environmental phenomena. To make the discussion more manageable, we introduce the standard distinction between local and global environmental phenomena. This is not simply for convenience, but also because the distinction turns out to have important implications for policy. Local environmental problems seem far more amenable to policy solutions such as defining property rights. Global problems seem to require much more direct intervention, and possibly more problematical, international cooperation. A recurrent theme is the problem of valuing such resources. While some are relatively tangible and yield to analysis, others, such as "biodiversity", are less so. Nevertheless there are good examples suggesting even this is important. For example, several US pharmaceutical companies have recently signed agreements with the government of Costa Rica to exploit forests for medical products. A Costa Rican research institute is prospecting for indigenous plants and organisms which may be useful to Merck and Company. Merck is supporting the project financially with payments going to sustain natural habitats (New York Times (1992), as quoted in Chichilnisky (1993b)). At the same time, however, the government of Panama are allowing the construction of the Pan American highway to proceed through the Darien Gap to link Colombia to Central America. The experience of Brazil, for example, suggests that this could have a disastrous effect on the remaining forests.

Having made this distinction and discussed the evidence about resource use, we then assess what role population plays in all this.

Local environmental phenomena. As Dasgupta and Mäler (1995) stress, in 1988 about 65% of the people in countries which fit the World Bank's definition of low-income lived in rural environments. This figure is only 6% for industrialized economies. The livelihood and well-being of these people is directly linked to the environmental resource base (for example, Jodha (1986) estimated that 15–25% of poor family income in seven states of India came directly from common property resources). As they put it, "the dependence of poor countries on their natural resources, such as soil and its cover, water (lakes and acquifers), forests, animals, and fisheries should be self-evident". The critical resources are renewable ones. These include land, forests, fish and bird populations, even animal species.

It is easy to find what appear to be startling data about the deterioration of local environmental resources in developing economies and close correlations with demographic trends. For instance, the population of Nepal has increased from 8 millions in 1950 to 17 millions in 1980, while at the same time the area of land forested has fallen by two-thirds (Myers, 1986). Though one should treat these numbers with circumspection (it is problematic to define unambiguously "forested land"), this gives a classic example of the types of interrelationships which have received attention. How should one interpret this? It is good to recall that startling figures for deforestation could be produced for currently developed countries. In Britain, for instance, it was the Tudor ship-building industry and the use of charcoal for fuel which caused this, both of which yielded to technical change. Nobody suggests that the process of deforestation was inimical to the economic or social development of Britain.

Even without directly considering population, there are many disturbing estimates of environmental degradation worldwide. Mabbut (1984) estimates that 40% of productive drylands are under the threat of desertification. It has been estimated that 200 million people in Africa are suffering from acute problems of water shortage (see Dasgupta and Mäler, 1995). It is perhaps interesting to recall that North Africa, now mostly desert, was the "bread basket" of the Roman Empire. Barbier et al. (1989) study many other such examples. Salinization of irrigated land is a serious problem in many areas of the world. The vanishing of the Peruvian anchovies in 1972 has been blamed on overfishing (Clark, 1978). It has also been estimated that Asia lost tropical forests at an annual rate of 1.2% between 1980 and 1990 as compared to 1% in Africa and Latin America, and that an extraordinary 80% of Africa's pasture and range areas are exhibiting signs of damage (World Bank, 1992). At this level these examples tell us little which is critical in determining whether resources are used well or not. For instance, it is quite possible that an efficient extraction policy can run a fish stock to zero (Dasgupta and Heal, 1979). It is difficult to know about the efficiency of particular outcomes without a detailed knowledge of the costs and benefits.

Consider the issue of deforestation. Shifting cultivation accounts for about 45% of all forest clearing according to Postel (1984). Postel also estimates that 75% of all wood gathered from forests in developing countries is used for fuel – even though wood is an inefficient source of fuel. This suggests that poverty is the root cause of deforestation. At higher income levels individuals shift to kerosene or gas and also adopt more capital-intensive and sedentary agricultural techniques than "slash and burn". In Gambia and Central Tanzania, firewood has become so scarce that the average household requires 250–300 worker-days to meet its needs (National Research Council, 1986). This represents an extraordinary relative price for fuel. However, this case, while startling, seems atypical. In general, the critical problem with deforestation is the common resource nature of forests in many poor economies, and it is the abundance of forest resources which leads to their common access. Sedjo and Clawson (1984) convincingly argue that this issue is the key one in determining the efficiency with which forest resources are utilized. As their value rises, the incentives to define property rights and utilize the resources more efficiently increase (as in Demsetz, 1967). This is one interpretation (though not an uncontested one) for the motivation behind the enclosure movement in pre-industrial Britain, for example (see Polyani, 1944).

These problems do not loom so large in developed nations where local commons barely exist anymore and forests have been felled (except insofar as they suffer from the atmospheric effects generated by deforestation). What is difficult to extract from this data is the extent to which these patterns of resource extraction and depletion represent a socially inefficient path of development. Even if they do, as is perhaps plausible, the important issue is what types of policies does this suggest and what are the main causal factors.

Global environmental problems. (a) Global warming. Perhaps the best example of a global environmental issue is global warming. Greenhouse gases warm the Earth by reducing the radiation of heat into space and thus increase the net inflow of radiative energy. The most important of these gases is water vapor which is largely unaffected by human activity (Schmalensee, 1993). These gases are vital in sustaining life on Earth and the relative temperatures of the Earth, Mars and Venus can be largely explained by differing concentrations of greenhouse gases (Manne and Richels, 1992). The concentration of another important greenhouse gas, CO_2, has increased by 27% since the beginning of the Industrial Revolution and is rising at 0.5% a year. Although natural sources of emissions are ten times more important than human emissions, this build up, found by examining ice core samples which give relatively reliable data (see Houghton et al., 1990), is generally attributed to human activities. These activities are primarily burning fossil fuels (which accounts for 85% of the total) and from changes in land use (mostly deforestation), which accounts or about 12%. While the US has contributed about 20% of recent emissions of CO_2, most forecasts suggest that the majority of future emissions will emanate from outside the OECD (primarily India and China). For example, Manne and Richels (1992) report that industrialized countries accounted for 64% of total carbon emissions in 1990, but that this figure will fall to 30% in 2100. Other greenhouse gases have also accumulated. The concentration of methane is increasing by 0.7% per annum, and that of nitrous oxide 0.25% per annum. Again this is generally attributed to human activity. The main effect of this build up of gases is to increase the amount of solar radiation trapped by the atmosphere and thus increase the average surface temperature of the Earth. Climate models predict that a doubling of the atmospheric concentration of CO_2 will raise the average surface temperature by 1.7–5°C. The Intergovernmental Panel on Climate Change (IPCC) predicted that unchanged emissions would cause the Earth's surface temperature to rise by 3–6°C by 2100 (relative to 1900). As Nordhaus (1993b) points out, "these projections are worrisome because climate appears to be heading out of the historical range of temperatures witnessed during the span of human civilizations".

The dynamics of the climate and atmosphere are highly complex and poorly understood (Broome (1992), Cline (1992) and National Academy of Sciences (1992) provide accessible discussions). Both the sources and sinks of greenhouse gases are not completely understood. Of especial importance are feedback effects (such as the ability of oceans to absorb both gases and heat) which cause the time lags between gas build-up and temperature rises to be "long and variable". The scientific consensus is that some global warming must take place if there are not drastic cuts in gas emissions, but there is a large amount of uncertainty about the time horizon over which this will take place and the extent of the increase.

From an economic viewpoint, this aspect of uncertainty is the simplest part of the analysis. Even more uncertainty surrounds the likely economic impact of such climate change (see Nordhaus, 1993b). A clear implication seems to be that agricultural production will relocate, with the "wheat belts" of North America and Asia moving further north. Global warming may have strong distributional implications for countries and this may be important in terms of negotiating international agreements. However, as Nordhaus (1993a) reminds us, there have been many famous and misdirected attempts to provide a climatic theory of economic history. Human beings have shown a remarkable ability to adapt to inhospitable climatic conditions, and there seems to be no real evidence that global warming will have disastrous aggregate effects. Anderson (1981) has argued that historically, long-run climate changes have been offset by economic adjustments. Nordhaus (1991) notes that only a very small portion of US GDP is sensitive to the climate. The one exception to this is possible flooding of low-lying coastal areas and the complete submersion of some islands barely above sea level. This may be a real problem for countries such as Bangladesh, the Netherlands and Maldives. Estimates of the increase in sea levels due to warming range from 0.6 to 4.0 meters (Hekstra, 1989). Problems will be greater in developing countries where there is much more reliance on agriculture and natural resources which may be temperature sensitive (such as the ecosystems of various types of forest). Another important issue is whether international trade will be able to help countries adapt to the possible adjustment problems (Reilly and Hohmann, 1993).

Nordhaus (1991), Cline (1992) and Frankhauser (1993) have all estimated the economic impact for the USA, in terms of current real GNP, of climate change. The estimates are losses of 1.1% of GNP for a 2.5°C warming (Cline), 1% of GNP for a 3°C warming (Nordhaus and Frankhauser). Nordhaus (1994a), using a survey of experts, arrived at an estimated loss of 1.8% of world output resulting from a 3°C rise in temperature. Several authors (in particular Nordhaus (1991) and Jorgenson and Wilcoxen (1991), see also the useful surveys of Ayres and Walter (1991), and Clarke et al. (1993)) have also conducted sophisticated intertemporal cost–benefit analyses of controlling greenhouse gas emissions (by the use of carbon taxes). These studies suggest that while the optimal policy involves positive tax rates, it does not demand strong measures (this should be evident from the rather modest estimates of the damages).

Manne and Richels (1992) show that the present value of costs of controlling carbon emissions depends very sensitively on forecasts about technological change in energy supply and conservation. Applying large taxes on current emissions is wasteful if carbon emissions would in any case be stabilized by technical change. They concentrate on computing the costs of carbon emissions under different scenarios about the availability of new technology and alternative fuel sources. They estimate that stabilizing emissions at 1990 levels until the year 2000 and then initiating a 20% cut would cost 1–2% of GDP per annum for OECD countries. For the US this is 2.5%. Even this policy still implies that carbon concentration doubles relative to the beginning of the Industrial Revolution by 2100. To stabilize the concentration of CO_2 at 1990 levels would entail a 70% cut in current emissions. This doubles the losses for the OECD economies. Manne and Richels stress the huge potential payoff to research which increases our knowledge about the nature and effects of climate change. They also show that great care is required in designing effective policies. For example, carbon taxes may well have perverse effects since they will encourage a switch to "cleaner" fuels such as oil and gas and nuclear energy, but the world stocks of these are much smaller than those of coal, and nuclear power has the potential to be environmentally disastrous.

(b) Pollution and the environmental Kuznets Curve. There has also been much recent interest in comparing the incidence of various forms of pollution to the level of economic development. The World Bank (1992) publicized the notion of the "environmental Kuznets curve" where pollutants were often in low levels of concentration for low-income countries, increased for middle-income countries, and then fell again with higher incomes. The idea of an environmental Kuznets curve has been carefully examined by Grossman (1993) and Grossman and Krueger (1994). Their results show that not all measures of environmental quality are affected in the same way by economic growth. Concentration of lead and cadmium in river basins and concentration of coarse suspended particles in urban air improve monotonically with per capita income (other results are ambiguous, Grossman and Krueger find that the concentration of mercury, arsenic and nickel first increases, then decreases, and then increases again once per capita income rises above $13 000). Other pollutants have the inverted U shape – sulfur dioxide (generated during the burning of fossil fuels), fecal coliform (bacteria found in human and animal feces that indicate the presence of pathogens), the oxygen regime of rivers (level of dissolved oxygen which is important for the health of local ecosystems), nitrate concentrations (mostly reflecting agricultural runoff), and other types of "suspended particulate matter". Turning points are very different for different pollutants. Some pollutants show no sign of improving – estimated emissions of carbon dioxide and nitrous oxides have continued to rise with income.

Grossman (1993) argues that the strongest link between pollution and income is via induced policy response, and may be due to income effects on consumer preferences. The evidence supports the "policy response" hypothesis. US public and private expenditures on pollution control and abatement represent 2% of GNP (OECD, 1990). These expenditures rose by 3.2% a year on average between 1972 and 1987, compared to the average growth rate of GNP of 2.6%. The situation is the same in other OECD countries (see Beckerman, 1993). Other explanations are related to the changing structure of production as economies develop, in particular the movement toward service industries, and income effects from higher per capita income on the demand for the amenity services of the environment.

Important factors conditioning effective policy are, according to Grossman (1993), "salience of environmental damage, the cost of avoiding such damage, and the degree to which the harm inflicted by the pollution coincides in its geographic and temporal extent with the political jurisdiction of the bodies empowered to establish property rights and enforce regulations".

1.2.3. The role of population

There is clear evidence of environmental degradation in many developing countries. Is there also evidence that this is directly exacerbated by population growth? It is difficult here to identify the role of population growth separately from the role of per capita income, though one can imagine that there are separate effects. For example, if an increase in population growth led to a fall in per capita income (as suggested by simple interpretations of the recent econometric evidence of Bloom and Freeman (1988) and Brander and Dowrick (1994)), then this would give a way of identifying these separate effects.

There has been some interesting formal econometric work on the interrelationships between population growth and the environment, though it is based on very noisy data. Allen and Barnes (1985) found that higher population growth rates were associated with higher rates of deforestation throughout the world. Their results imply that a reduction of one percent in the rate of population growth will cause a reduction in annual rates of deforestation of between 0.33 and 0.5 of one percent. Jha et al. (1994) use data from the Food and Agriculture Organization to estimate the relationship between the annual rate of deforestation 1975–1986 and population growth rates. They find a significant positive relationship, though smaller than Allen and Barnes. Of course such correlations do not uncover causal relationships and so the counterfactual calculations must be treated with caution. Deforestation has also been found to directly contribute to global warming. There are two effects at work linking deforestation to global warming. First, the deforestation itself generates greater emissions, and, second, the destruction of forests reduces the ability of the atmosphere to regenerate. Bongaarts (1992) estimated that population growth will account for 35% of projected global increase in CO_2 emissions between 1985 and 2050. Cross-country regressions of CO_2 emissions from land use changes, particularly deforestation, against population growth rates also show a strong positive relationship. Jha et al. (1994) estimate that a one percentage point reduction in population growth rates is associated with a 0.32 percentage reduction in CO_2 emissions from land use changes.

The FAO (1993) assumes that the ratio of forest land to total land area is a logistic function of population density. They then use this relationship to forecast deforestation rates. They assume that population growth causes deforestation, but other factors (stage of development, technology etc.) which they do not control for must be important in this relationship. Cropper and Griffiths (1994) recently find an environmental Kuznets curve for deforestation in non-OECD countries. The curve is significantly affected by population density which shifts the relationship upwards. Their results imply that both population density and population growth have a positive effect on deforestation holding per capita income constant.

Though there does seem tentative evidence that population growth has an adverse effect on deforestation and greenhouse gas build-up, this work is very partial. There are severe conceptual and econometric problems to be resolved before using these results to motivate policy proposals. We therefore hesitate to draw the conclusion that population policy can be motivated on these grounds. Birdsall (1992) argues that the effect of feasible reductions in population growth rates (based on World Bank scenarios) on emissions of greenhouse gases and global warming are small. She estimates that such reductions might reduce fossil fuel emissions by 10% by 2050. These are small relative to projections that emissions will triple over this period. She does, however, make an interesting calculation which is, although the total impact may be relatively small, population policy may actually be a cost effective way of reducing emissions relative to direct taxes on carbon emissions. We would argue, however, that given the uncertainties surrounding such calculations, thinking of population policy in this way is probably a conceptual error.

As Jha et al. (1994) put it, slowing "population growth by itself is unlikely to halt or even slow the rate of environmental degradation and depletion of forest, marine, and water resources. Other policies that limit access to common property resources, manage rural–urban migration, regulate greenhouse gas emissions, and eradicate poverty will be needed... However, rapid population growth will certainly make it more difficult for countries to improve the environment with a given set of policies and interventions".

There is less clear evidence of environmental stress in developed economies. There seems to be little direct connection between population growth and environmental issues in developed economies since individual choice sets are not connected to them as intimately as in poor countries.

We can conclude this section in no better way than quoting at length one of the central conclusions from the 1992 World Development Report. "The reason some resources – water, forests, and clean air – are under siege while others – metals, minerals, and energy – are not, is that the scarcity of the latter is reflected in market prices and so the forces of substitution, technical progress, and structural change are strong. The first group is characterized by open access, meaning that there are no incentives to use them sparingly. Policies and institutions are therefore necessary to force decision-makers to take account of the social value of these resources in their actions. This is not easy. The evidence suggests, however, that when environmental policies are publicly supported and firmly enforced, the positive forces of substitution, technical progress, and structural change can be just as powerful. This explains why the environmental debate has rightly shifted away from concern with the *physical limits* of growth, toward concern about incentives for *human behavior* and policies that can overcome *market and policy failures*".

1.3. Our approach

To what extent is it possible to draw definitive conclusions from the empirical work as it stands? While there is clearly much uncertainty surrounding the qualitative and quantitative properties of the dynamics under consideration, there are certain conclusions that one can reach. Firstly, there is no evidence of adverse effects of population growth on economic growth. This suggests that in formulating models we want to allow either for a neutral effect, or for offsetting positive and negative effects. Secondly, models of development need to incorporate the elements of the demographic transition. Thirdly, the evidence suggests that market mechanisms have been remarkably effective in allocating finite resources which are priced in markets, however, we need to be open minded about the nature and efficiency of the evolution of environmental resources. Finally, in studying the interactions between population growth, resources and environment, we need to be scrupulously careful to isolate the causal relationships otherwise we cannot say anything interesting about welfare or policy.

Unfortunately, for a large class of phenomena, the theory orders what we would like to know, not what we conclusively do know. We try and understand the joint phenomena both positively and normatively via the tools of intertemporal welfare economics. This bears fruit in analyzing issues pertaining both to population and the environment. For example, while it is often said that population growth reduces income growth, and this proposition is true in some simple growth models, this in itself says nothing about the desirability or otherwise of this result. If population growth is the conscious outcome of individual decisions, then it is possible that individuals will willingly make these types of trade-offs (see Lee (1990) for an example). One position is that if this is a Pareto optimal situation, then there is little to be said (see Ng (1986) for a strong affirmation of this view). The same goes for environmental "degradation" and resource use. On the other hand, one might view this as evidence that Pareto optimality is a woefully blunt tool in this context. As is well-known, in standard welfare economics the fact that an allocation of resources is Pareto efficient is only a necessary condition for it to be socially optimal. Such models assume that the population, constant or changing, is exogenous, so that there is a fixed pool of people the welfare of whom can be compared under different allocations. When population is endogenous, it becomes moot as to whether or not Pareto optimality, as conventionally defined, is even necessary for social optimality.

Now consider the environment. Perhaps the clearest distinction between economists and environmentalists is that economists can conceive of a dynamic path which runs a renewable resource to zero as being optimal. This position is typically regarded as preposterous by environmentalists. Along an optimal transition path it seems highly likely that resources will be run down and exploited. The perspective of welfare economics suggests that concentrating on the preservation of environmental resources directly is confusing ends with means (see Solow (1992, 1993); Dasgupta (1993c) and Dasgupta and Mäler (1995) all make similar points). What we are interested in is welfare and not the preservation of any particular environmental asset per se. Preservation becomes vital when the asset is essential to production or human welfare. This attitude conditions our approach to the topic of "sustainable development" in Section 4.1.

What we attempt to do is to think about the type of joint dynamic behavior of population, resource usage and technical change that we would expect to see along an equilibrium growth path. We do this in different models, not only because a general model is of too high a dimension to handle, and also because, as we have already argued, neither population growth nor resource usage really lend themselves to a general model. We are still too uncertain about critical features of these phenomena. We then repeatedly ask several key questions. Firstly, what are the asymptotic implications of this path for population and resources? Secondly, how does this behavior relate to the empirical evidence. Thirdly, can per capita income grow unboundedly or will it be constrained by lack of natural resources or similar Malthusian phenomena? Finally, is this path inefficient, and, if so, what are the fundamental sources of these inefficiencies?

In the course of the analysis, we do not devote much space to the pros and cons of various intertemporal welfare functions. Both the population and environmental literatures are plagued by this. In discussing dynamic paths, we deliberately do not commit ourselves to any particular social valuation function without seeing what is implied. In this we follow Koopmans (1967) who puts the issue in the following way, "ignoring realities in adopting "principles" may lead one to search for a nonexistent optimum, or to adopt an optimum that is open to unanticipated objections". This approach has recently been stressed by Dasgupta and Mäler (1995). To our mind the best way to proceed is to examine the equilibrium allocations corresponding to different sets of assumptions and see if these coincide with our ethical notions. An implication of our perspective is that we will be critical of the rather arid theoretical literature on optimal population growth with exogenous fertility. As we shall see, there are some classic examples of social welfare functions which generate intuitively ludicrous results. Much of the hand wringing about the form of society's objective function vanishes once fertility is made endogenous, and, in any case, as we have stated, we do not feel that a priori arguments about intertemporal welfare functions are convincing.

This topic also raises the interesting issue of how to construct aggregate measures of welfare which encompass environmental changes. It is in this context that the idea of Net National Product has been constructed taking into account the value of environmental and resource degradation. The effects of this can be large. For example, Repetto et al. (1989) estimated that, once environmental degradation was taken into account, the growth rate of Indonesia over the period 1971–1984 was 4% rather than the 7% based on standard national accounting techniques. Mäler (1991) and Dasgupta and Mäler (1990) have shown how intertemporal welfare economics and shadow pricing provides the conceptual framework for this analysis. While we do not attempt such derivations here, it should be clear that our analysis of the issues is very much in the same spirit.

This approach unifies our attitudes to population, technological change and environmental resource use and helps identify their potential welfare implications which might justify policy intervention. In the end this is what the topic is about. The debate about both population growth and the environment and the interaction between them focuses on the necessity of policies to stem population growth and the desirability of controls on environmental degradation. Consider initially population growth. While there are certain situations, for example, the dynastic economy we study in Section 2.1, where the rate of population growth which is chosen by private agents is the first-best one (identical to the one which would be chosen by a social planner), this turns out to be a far from general proposition. The assumptions necessary to induce dynastic preferences are restrictive (such as fully operational gift and bequest motives), and moreover they seem to rule out some of the key phenomena which are thought to be of importance in the determination of population growth in poor countries. It is quite plausible then that the rate of population growth may not be first-best. It is still possible, however, that it may be Pareto efficient (bearing in mind the problematical nature of this concept with endogenous population), but welfare economics gives us a set of tools to understand situations in which it may not be. For example, as we discuss in Section 3.4.2, either externalities or noncooperative behavior within the household can lead to rates of fertility and population growth which are inefficient under reasonable interpretations of the Pareto criterion.

Consider now the welfare issues surrounding technological change. In Section 3.3, we put into perspective recent developments in this area. Much of the work (following Romer (1986) and Lucas (1988)) has stressed external effects stemming from the public good and nonrivalrous nature of abstract "knowledge", "ideas", "technology" or "human capital". Such a perspective generates the strong implication that in laissez faire equilibrium innovation and investment will be socially inefficient (although, as we shall see, the empirical strength of these phenomena is hotly debated). The framework tells us what can go wrong and what can be done about this.

The same set of tools provide the best approach to the environment. Environmental resources provide one of the best examples of externalities since they are typically not traded in markets (the atmosphere being a good example). It is this which generates the presumption that they may be inefficiently exploited or utilized. Thinking of the environment in this way allows us to separate the issue of the efficiency of environmental preservation from the other central issues of this paper, such as whether or not there is a population problem, or whether or not development must lead to the inefficient destruction of the environment, which are so confusingly conflated with it in much of the literature.

In the present paper, we restrict our scope to outlining the conceptual issues and do not deal with detailed policy proposals. Designing policies requires a much more detailed specification of the structure of economies than is tractable for conceptual analysis. In practice one must deal with the complex interaction of numerous market failures and second-best problems. Bovenberg and van der Ploeg (1993a–d) provide an interesting first-step in modeling some of these issues in the context of environmental policy. Similar issues arise with population policy. One must design policies affecting the costs and benefits of fertility, which seems to be more amenable to such policy than mortality. We also warn that without an understanding of the dynamics of population growth, simple policies may have unanticipated side effects. Another strong argument for such incentive policies is that the most important candidates for such policy (for example, subsidization of human capital accumulation, building health and social infrastructure) seem to have strong rationales on other grounds and so there are strong complementarities, as we argue below, between population and other policy. Again this must be done in a general equilibrium context where other deviations from the first-best allocation of resources need to be taken into account. We do not undertake any analysis of this sort here (see Chomitz and Birdsall (1991) for a good discussion of the issues).

1.4. Overview of the paper

To keep the discussion relatively self-contained, we proceed in the next several sections with a development of a sequence of canonical models. These provide the framework to begin systematic study of the joint dynamics of growth, population and resource use. The models are often not very instructive in this regard. For example, the basic neoclassical model, due to Solow (1956) and Swan (1956), regards population growth and technical progress as exogenous and ignores environmental and resource issues altogether. These models are instructive, however, in building our intuition regarding the forces at work in the growth process and in understanding why the treatment of population and technology in these models is so unsatisfactory.

Our approach is primarily analytical and, in order to help the reader in understanding the motivation for a particular model or piece of analysis, we provide summaries of the "plot" at appropriate places, reminding the reader what we have established thus far and where the argument is headed.

Having developed the basic growth model, we investigate the positive and normative aspects of population policy. We raise the issue of the optimal rate of population growth by first thinking about the issue of the optimal size of population in a static model. Extending this to determine the optimal level of population at each point in time then generates naturally an optimal rate of population growth. We concentrate on the implications of various technological assumptions (such as the degree of returns to scale) and the form of the social objective function. We argue that the underlying inter-generational linkages between agents are crucial for the foundations of any particular objective function and hence the nature of desirable policy.

We then introduce both exhaustible and renewable resources into the analysis. We consider the nature of intertemporal equilibrium and again the positive and normative issues surrounding the dynamic path. We then re-examine the positive and normative issues of population growth. The analysis is very tentative, especially with respect to renewable resources. We emphasize that there is high uncertainty about the nature of the dynamics, involving nonlinearities, threshold effects, and irreversibilities, which are extremely difficult to model satisfactorily. There are also important complementarities between different resources. For example, forests control water run-off and flooding which stabilizes topsoil elsewhere. One cannot hope to capture these rich interactions with the type of aggregate model we study, but one can hope to direct attention to what is crucial and what we need to know.

In Section 3, we move to endogenize population and technical change. Both of these steps represent fundamental improvements on the basic neoclassical model, although they clearly complicate the models considerably. In Section 3.1, we present a condensed discussion of the issues involved in endogenizing fertility, mortality (though we only touch on this topic), and thus the rate of population growth. Our treatment is conditioned by the in-depth treatment of the issues elsewhere in the Handbook (see the chapter by Nerlove and Raut). Our aim is rather to apply versions of these models to the issues at hand. We begin in Section 3.2 by introducing endogenous population growth into models where resources are explicitly accounted for. Such a model no longer allows simple causal statements about the effects of population growth to be made. Section 3.2.1 examines a simple model of the joint dynamics of population and environmental resources. In Sections 3.2.2 and 3.2.3, we discuss models emphasizing the complementarities between population dynamics and resource use. These are both models of "no trade-off" situations where addressing the real problems, in 3.2.2 a classic "local commons" problem, and in 3.2.3 a public goods problem, solves not only the resource problem but also the population problem. In Section 3.3, we review recent theories of endogenous technical change. In Section 3.4, we discuss the considerable literature which models the interrelationships between population and economic growth, in particular different causal channels through which population growth influences development. Section 3.5 then discusses the implications of recent theories of technical change in economies with exhaustible and renewable resources. In Section 3.5, we present the most general discussion, assessing the implications of the joint endogeneity of population and technical change in the presence of natural and environmental resources.

In Section 4, we then provide an assessment of several contentious topics in the literature and in particular use the models of the paper to discuss the issues of discounting and sustainable development. We briefly discuss the importance of uncertainty and the implications of introducing international issues. Section 5 then offers our conclusions.

2. Long-run development with exogenous population and exogenous technical change

We begin our formal treatment of the issues addressed in this chapter with very simple familiar economies and propositions. Section 2.1 develops classical positive and normative results from growth theory when both population growth and technological change are exogenous, with infinitely-lived agents, a single produced good (i.e. a one-sector economy), and with no natural resources. Section 2.1.1 introduces the main normative and positive issues. In Section 2.1.2, we broach the question of optimal population for the first time, introducing the issues in a simple static setting and using it to clarify the key issues. We then extend the ideas (in Section 2.1.3) to examine the existence and characteristics of the optimal rate of growth of population in the growth model of Section 2.1.1. Section 2.2 extends the results from Section 2.1 to overlapping generations models where individuals live for only a finite number of periods. In Section 2.2.1, we analyze positive and normative issues in a version of the celebrated model due to Diamond (1965a). Section 2.2 derives the optimal rate of population growth in the overlapping generations model. Section 2.2.3 then discusses relationships between generations and their implications for the issues analyzed earlier.

In Section 2.3, we introduce renewable and exhaustible resources. In Section 2.3.1, we add exhaustible resources to the inputs of the production function of the basic neoclassical growth model of Section 2.1.1. Historically, the effects of the existence of exhaustible resources was the first to receive careful theoretical attention. Our central concerns are the conditions under which it is possible to maintain sustained growth by substituting out of the exhaustible resource into produced capital, and the impact of exogenous technological growth, and to re-assess the positive effects of exogenous population growth. We also return to the issue of optimal population growth in these models with results closely related to those of Section 2.1.2 and 2.1.3. Finite lives are treated in Section 2.3.3, and then in Section 2.3.4 we develop a more general model in which both exhaustible and renewable resources enter into production. Our model is general enough to encompass the issue of the effects of pollution on the growth path amongst other resource issues. We concentrate on renewable resource issues since these seem to be the most interesting and least understood area. We also allow for "amenity" affects of the resource to affect utility directly. Again we concentrate on the conditions necessary to ensure sustained growth in per capita income and the steady states that could plausibly arise.

2.1. Neoclassical growth: infinitely-lived agents

To fix ideas, we start with the one-good, discrete time, neoclassical growth model with infinitely-lived agents (henceforth, ILA), exogenous technical change, and exogenous population. With interaction between technical change and population absent,

their rates of change can be exogenously varied to analyze the positive comparative dynamic effects on steady-state income, etc. It seems natural to just consider physical capital in this section and leave human capital until we consider endogenous growth models in Section 3. Throughout the chapter we discuss models with a single produced good, where, in particular, the capital and the consumption good are not distinguished. A possible justification of this would be to place the discussion in the context of a small open economy where relative prices of goods are fixed by the world market. This allows aggregation of heterogeneous goods (by the Hicks theorem). However, for the purposes of the chapter it is easier to stick to a closed economy setting (for example, we want to determine the interest rate endogenously), and so we just make this an assumption.

2.1.1. Basic dynastic economy

In this section, we exposit the simplest model of economic growth based squarely on the accumulation of physical capital relative to labor and the consequent increase in the capital–labor ratio. Imagine a poor country with a low stock of capital relative to labor so that the marginal productivity of capital is high. In a perfectly competitive equilibrium this is equal to the interest rate which represents the return to saving. Thus the low capital stock generates a high incentive for individuals to save (as long as income effects are not strong) and this leads to a rapid growth of the capital stock. As the capital stock grows relative to labor its marginal product falls. As a consequence, the interest rate falls and thus the incentive to save. Eventually, under the standard assumptions, the marginal product falls so low that the return to future saving is exactly balanced by the costs and the growth of the capital–labor ratio stops. Such a situation is called a steady-state equilibrium. With exogenous technical progress of a labor augmenting type, the above story is still true except that the relevant variable which accumulates over time is "capital per effective worker" since workers are getting exogenously more productive. This is an unsatisfactory treatment of technological change. The treatment of population is equally unsatisfactory since it grows exogenously at a constant rate. In a steady state the endogenous variables are adapted to the exogenously growing rates of technology and population.

The demographic structure of the model conceives of the population as belonging to an altruistically linked dynasty with perfect foresight about the values of all relevant future variables and an infinite time horizon. This has the strong normative implication that allocations which arise in intertemporal competitive equilibria are Pareto optimal and, since all individuals are altruistically linked, the objective function of the dynasty is the only reasonable welfare function for society (since it is the same as the dynasty). It seems intuitively unreasonable to posit the existence of a social planner who weights the welfare of individuals differently from the dynasty.

Consider the representative agent neoclassical growth model. Time is discrete. There are two goods, a single produced good which can be consumed or used as

capital, and labor. We consider a real economy where the produced good is the numeraire with price normalized to unity in each period (hence we choose a different numeraire at each date as opposed to simply using the produced good at date one as the numeraire for all time). We assume that investment is irreversible and, once the consumption good is converted into capital, it cannot be consumed. The economy is inhabited by a single dynasty with an initial population of unity. All members of the dynasty born at any date live forever. There are two main assumptions about the demographic environment in this economy. The one we follow is to assume that the size of the dynasty grows at the constant exogenous rate of $(1 + n)$, so that the size of the dynasty at date t is $L_t = (1 + n)^t$ (since $L_0 = 1$). In this model each agent reproduces by parthenogenesis (marriage is abstracted from and leads to severe complications, see Bernheim and Bagwell (1988), Cigno (1991), Laitner (1991)) and has n children at the end of each period. The alternative is to assume that each "dynasty" is rather a single infinitely-lived individual and population growth occurs through the addition of new individuals. This model has implications closely related to the overlapping generations model (see Weil, 1989).

We assume that each agent has preferences defined over infinite sequences of consumption:

$$\{\hat{c}_t(i)\}_{t=\tau}^{\infty},$$

where $\hat{c}_t(i)$ represents the consumption of agent i in period t, born in period τ, and that these can be represented by a time separable utility function with constant exponential discounting,

$$V(i) = \sum_{t=\tau}^{\infty} \beta^{t-\tau} U(\hat{c}_t(i)). \tag{2.1}$$

$\beta \in (0, 1]$ is interpreted as the rate of subjective time preference. We assume that U is strictly increasing, strictly concave, and twice continuously differentiable, with $U: \mathfrak{R}_+ \to \mathfrak{R}$, and $U' > 0$, $U'' < 0$. Note that this implies that $V: \mathfrak{R}_+^{\infty} \to \mathfrak{R}$, so that the commodity space is infinite dimensional (as in Bewley, 1972). Each member of the dynasty is endowed with one unit of labor time in each period. We assume that the instantaneous utility function is identical for each agent in every period of life. The dynasty also holds a stock of capital in each period, denoted K_t. Since decision-making is at the level of the dynasty, we do not specifically keep track of intra-dynasty holdings of capital or other assets.

The dynasty treats all individuals alive at any date equally so $\hat{c}_t(i) = C_t/L_t$, where C_t is total consumption and L_t the number of people alive. Since we want to consider environments with technical progress, we need to define variables in such a way as to be constant in steady state. Per capita consumption will not be constant, but

$c_t(i) = C_t/A_tL_t$ (consumption per "effective person") will be. It is important to keep this in mind since below we write the budget constraint in terms of c_t, but Eq. (2.1) is in terms of $\hat{c}_t$.

There is a single competitive "representative firm" in the economy. The firm rents capital and labor on competitive factor markets, taking prices as given, to maximize profits. Given the nature of the technology, there are no intertemporal aspects to the firm's problem. Maximizing the present discounted value of profits (which will be unambiguously the firm's objective since we will specify a market structure which is isomorphic to complete markets) reduces to maximizing profits period by period. The firm's technology is represented by a production function, $Y_t = F(K_t, A_tL_t)$, which we assume to be concave, strictly increasing and twice continuously differentiable, where $F: \Re_+^2 \to \Re_+$. Let F_i represent the partial derivative of F with respect to variable $i = K,L$, and F_{ij} the partial derivative of F_i with respect to variable $j = K,L$. Then we assume that $F_K > 0$, $F_L > 0$, $F_{KK} < 0$, $F_{LL} < 0$, so that marginal products are positive but strictly diminishing. A_t represents the level of labor augmenting technology in period t, and K_t, L_t the stocks of capital and labor hired by a firm. There is no distinction between total population and the size of the labor force. Since we wish to examine steady states, the assumption of Harrod neutral (i.e. labor augmenting) technical change is necessary (Phelps, 1962). We assume that F is homogeneous of degree one so that by Euler's theorem we can re-write the production function in terms of per capita quantities. Denoting $y_t = Y_t/A_tL_t$, $k_t = K_t/A_tL_t$, as the output–labor and capital–labor ratios (where labor means "effective labor") the production function can be written, $y_t = f(k_t)$. It is immediate that f is strictly concave, strictly increasing and twice continuously differentiable, with $f: \Re_+ \to \Re$, and $f' > 0$, $f'' < 0$ (where f' and f'' are the first and second partial derivatives respectively of f with respect to k_t). Denote the competitive wage per effective unit of labor, and the rental rate for capital in terms of the numeraire as w_t, r_t, respectively. The level of technology increases exogenously over time at rate $(1 + g)$, so that $A_{t+1} = (1 + g)A_t$.

The equilibrium concept we use is a standard competitive one with sequentially complete markets and perfect foresight. This is equivalent to a model with complete markets where all trading is undertaken in the initial period. Since the economy is deterministic, and individuals have perfect foresight about all future prices, the single asset available in each period is sufficient to span the state space (the model is a degenerate multi-period version of Arrow's (1963–1964) model (see also Radner, 1972) and is thus equivalent – in terms of allocations – to a complete markets Arrow–Debreu economy).

At the start of each period a competitive capital and labor market opens. The dynasty rents its labor services and capital to firms who minimize unit costs of production. This generates factor demands per unit of output. Minimum cost is equal to the price of output which is equal to unity by the choice of numeraire. The assumption of inelastically supplied and fully utilized supplies of capital and labor then determines the scale of output. From unit cost equals price (equals unity) and cost minimization

we have, $A_t L_t [w_t + r_t k_t] = 1$, $A_t L_t f(k_t) = 1$, and $f'(k_t) = r_t$. Both labor and capital are supplied inelastically and market equilibrium requires, $L_t^d = L_t$, and $K_t^d = K_t$.

Each dynasty maximizes utility subject to the sequential budget constraint,

$$K_{t+1} + C_t \leq w_t A_t L_t + r_t K_t + (1-\delta) K_t, \tag{2.2}$$

where for simplicity, we have assumed that capital depreciates at the constant rate of $\delta \in (0, 1)$ per period. Since utilities are strictly increasing, Eq. (2.2) holds with equality. We ignore the issue of the irreversibility since we shall not consider situations where the dynasty desires negative net investment and so it is impossible to distinguish between the cases of irreversible investment and of potentially reversible investment. We now re-write Eq. (2.2) in per effective person terms:

$$\frac{K_{t+1}}{A_{t+1} L_{t+1}} \frac{A_{t+1} L_{t+1}}{A_t L_t} + \frac{C_t}{A_t L_t} = \frac{w_t A_t L_t}{A_t L_t} + \frac{r_t K_t}{A_t L_t} + (1-\delta) \frac{K_t}{A_t L_t} \tag{2.3}$$

or

$$k_{t+1}(1+g)(1+n) = w_t + r_t k_t - c_t + (1-\delta) k_t. \tag{2.4}$$

Euler's theorem for linearly homogeneous functions implies that Eq. (2.4) can be simplified by noticing that $f(k_t) = w_t + f'(k_t) k_t = w_t + r_t k_t$. Intuitively, since the dynasty owns all the factors of production, the whole of output must be distributed to it in various forms. Hence in effective per capita terms,

$$k_{t+1}(1+n)(1+g) = f(k_t) - c_t + (1-\delta) k_t. \tag{2.5}$$

The dynasty is composed of individuals maximizing $V(i)$ defined in Eq. (2.1). We assume that the dynasty itself maximizes the per capita welfare of a particular member alive at each date ignoring the number of its members alive at any date. Hence the objective function for the dynasty is

$$\sum_{t=0}^{\infty} \beta^t U(c_t A_t)$$

starting from $t = 0$. This might not be thought the most natural specification. Unfortunately the objective function of the dynasty is not usually derived from an explicit aggregation in the infinitely-lived agent setting, and in order to keep our analysis close to that of the literature, we similarly finesse this issue at this stage. Note that, in particular, this form of the objective function is only sensitive to the per capita welfare of

descendants and not the number of descendants as such. It also discounts the welfare of future generations at the same rate that each individual discounts his/her own lifetime consumption. However, a dynasty which takes into account the number of descendants could be viewed as maximizing the objective function,

$$\sum_{t=0}^{\infty} \beta^t (1+n)^t U(c_t A_t) \equiv \sum_{t=0}^{\infty} \tilde{\beta}^t U(c_t A_t),$$

where $\tilde{\beta} = \beta(1+n)$, and, as long as $0 < \tilde{\beta} < 1$, the formal analysis would be the same. We return to this issue in Section 2.2.3. In Section 3.1, we develop a model due to Becker and Barro (1986, 1988, 1989) where the dynastic utility function is derived from an explicit aggregation across altruistically linked generations. At this point it becomes clearer exactly what sort of assumptions are needed to generate the welfare function of the sort we adopt here.

Since labor and capital are supplied inelastically, the only decision is the consumption–saving choice. The Lagrangean for this problem is referred to as Problem 1:

$$\Lambda = \sum_{t=0}^{\infty} \beta^t U(c_t A_t) + \sum_{t=0}^{\infty} \lambda_t \{ w_t + r_t k_t - c_t + (1-\delta)k_t - (1+g)(1+n)k_{t+1} \}.$$

Note that $c_t A_t \equiv \hat{c}_t$. Problem 1 ignores the side constraints that $c_t \geq 0$, $k_t \geq 0$. We also assume that the problem is well defined in the sense that the objective function converges (we try to keep the discussion nontechnical in the chapter to the extent that we do not explicitly set out assumptions guaranteeing that the problems we analyze are mathematically well defined in all cases). Intuitively for this to be the case, the discount rate must be sufficiently high compared to the rate of technological progress. The initial condition on the capital–effective labor ratio is $k_0 = K_0/A_0 L_0 = K_0/A_0$. The standard necessary conditions for this problem are Eq. (2.5) and the following conditions, Eqs. (2.6) and (2.7):

$$\beta^t A_t U'(c_t A_t) = \lambda_t, \tag{2.6}$$

$$\lambda_t = \lambda_{t+1} \left(\frac{1 + r_{t+1} - \delta}{(1+n)(1+g)} \right), \tag{2.7}$$

and the transversality condition, Eq. (2.8):

$$\lim_{t \to \infty} \{ \lambda_t k_t \} = 0. \tag{2.8}$$

Leading Eq. (2.6) and using it in conjunction with Eq. (2.6) to substitute into Eq. (2.7) gives the standard form of the Euler equation:

$$U'(c_t A_t) = \left(\frac{1 + r_{t+1} - \delta}{1 + n}\right) \beta U'(c_{t+1} A_{t+1}). \tag{2.9}$$

Using the condition for factor market equilibrium, we derive

$$U'(c_t A_t) = \left(\frac{1 + f'(k_{t+1}) - \delta}{1 + n}\right) \beta U'(c_{t+1} A_{t+1}). \tag{2.10}$$

A perfect foresight competitive equilibrium of the economy is a set of sequences for the endogenous variables,

$$\{c_t\}_{t=0}^{\infty}, \quad \{k_t\}_{t=0}^{\infty}, \quad \{w_t\}_{t=0}^{\infty}, \quad \{r_t\}_{t=0}^{\infty},$$

such that at these prices, the dynastic objective function is maximized subject to Eq. (2.5) at the specified quantities, firm profit is maximized at these quantities, and all markets clear.

The aggregate dynamics of the economy are described by the two difference equations, Eqs. (2.5) and (2.10), in k_t and c_t. Given two boundary conditions, the initial capital–effective labor ratio, k_0, and the transversality condition for the dynasty, Eqs. (2.5) and (2.10) determine the evolution of all the endogenous variables of the economy. Consider the steady state (or balanced growth path) for this economy where all per effective capita variables are constant, per capita variables grow at the constant rate of g, and level variables grow at the constant rate of $n + g$ (approximately). Note that this implies $k_{t+1} - k_t = 0$. Thus in steady state

$$k^*(n + g + ng + \delta) = f(k^*) - c^*, \tag{2.11}$$

$$\frac{U'(c^* A_t)}{U'(c^* A_{t+1})} = \frac{\beta(1 + f'(k^*) - \delta)}{1 + n}. \tag{2.12}$$

For a steady state the marginal rate of substitution on the left-hand side of Eq. (2.12) must be a constant. Note that the right-hand side is independent of time. This implies, given $A_t = (1 + g)^t A_0$, with $g \neq 0$, that the elasticity of marginal utility is constant or that the utility function is of the form $\gamma c^{\eta} + \omega$.

Consider initially the case of logarithmic utility, $U(\hat{c}_t) = \log \hat{c}_t$. Eq. (2.12) now reduces to an intuitive form. The left-hand side of Eq. (2.12) now is $(1 + g)$. Notice that defining $\beta = 1/(1 + \rho)$, and then multiplying both sides of Eq. (2.12) by $(1 + \rho)$ and $(1 + n)$, the left-hand side of Eq. (2.12) is $(1 + n)(1 + g)(1 + \rho)$, which reduces to

$1 + n + \rho + g$ if we neglect all the product terms, since n, g, ρ are assumed to be small. Under this assumption, Eq. (2.12) can be written as

$$f'(k^*) = \rho + \delta + n + g. \tag{2.13}$$

Eq. (2.13) represents the steady-state capital stock in this economy. The left-hand side represents the marginal benefit to the dynasty of increasing the capital–effective labor ratio. The right-hand side is the marginal cost. Note that this is not the original Golden Rule proposed by Phelps (1966) (though it is often referred to as such). Phelps derived the Golden Rule by choosing the capital–labor ratio which maximized steady-state consumption per capita. In the current model, Eq. (2.13) includes a preference parameter which implies that, due to impatience (or imperfect altruism), the economy will not accumulate as much capital as would maximize steady-state consumption. Note that setting $k^* = \hat{k}$ where $f'(\hat{k}) = (1 + n)(1 + g) - (1 - \delta)$ maximizes steady-state consumption. Since U must be of constant elasticity for a steady state to exist, we consider the constant elasticity of marginal utility (or of intertemporal substitution) utility function

$$U(\hat{c}_t) = \frac{(\hat{c}_t)^{1-\sigma}}{1-\sigma}$$

(more generally the steady-state capital–effective labor ratio also depends on the preference parameter σ (which is simply the inverse of the elasticity of intertemporal substitution)). Now from Eq. (2.12), it follows that

$$f'(k^*) = (1+\rho)(1+n)(1+g)^{\sigma} - (1-\delta)$$

and so

$$f'(\hat{k}) - f'(k^*) = (1+n)(1+g)[1 - (1+g)^{\sigma-1}(1+\rho)].$$

Thus with $(1 + n) > 0$, $g > 0$, $\rho \geq 0$, then if $\sigma > 1$, $f'(\hat{k}) - f'(k^*) < 0$ so that $\hat{k} > k^*$. With logarithmic utility $\sigma = 1$, $k^* \to \hat{k}$ as $\rho \to 0$. With $\sigma \in (0, 1)$, $(1+\rho)(1+g)^{\sigma-1} \geq 1$ implies $k^* < \hat{k}$. If in this case, $(1+\rho)(1+g)^{\sigma-1} < 1$, then $g > \rho$, in which case the objective function does not converge and an optimal path does not exist. Then, regardless of parameters, if the optimal path exists and converges to a steady state, we have that $k^* < \hat{k}$.

We can now investigate the effects of an increase in the population growth rate on the steady state. Now

$$c^* = f(k^*) - k^*[(1+n)(1+g) - (1-\delta)]$$

so that

$$\frac{dc*}{dn}=[f'(k*)-\{(1+n)(1+g)-(1-\delta)\}]\frac{dk*}{dn}=[f'(k*)-f'(\hat{k})]\frac{dk*}{dn}$$

Since

$$f''(k*)\frac{dk*}{dn}=(1+\rho)(1+g)^{\sigma}$$

by concavity we have $dk*/dn < 0$. Hence as long as $k* < \hat{k}$, we have $dc*/dn < 0$.

It is straightforward to derive the sufficient conditions that guarantee the existence of a unique $k*$ satisfying Eq. (2.13). All one requires is that for low capital–labor ratios the marginal product is relatively large. Then by concavity the left-hand side of Eq. (2.13) is monotonically decreasing in $k*$ and, if it falls to the constant $\rho + \delta + n + g$, then a steady state exists. The conventional (though strong) sufficient conditions for this are the Inada conditions (e.g. $\lim_{k\to 0}f'(k) = +\infty$ and $\lim_{k\to\infty}f'(k) = 0$). Under these it is clear that such a steady state exists and that it is unique since $f''(k) < 0$.

The costate equation, Eq. (2.7), can be used to give a more intuitive content to the transversality condition Eq. (2.8). Eq. (2.7) is a difference equation in λ_t, solving this forward (and for simplicity letting $(1 + g)(1 + n) = 1 + n + g$) gives

$$\lambda_t = \lambda_0 \prod_{s=1}^{t}\left(\frac{1+n+g}{1+r_s-\delta}\right). \tag{2.14}$$

Now substitute Eq. (2.14) into the transversality condition Eq. (2.8),

$$\lim_{t\to\infty}\left\{k_t\lambda_0\prod_{s=1}^{t}\left(\frac{1+n+g}{1+r_s-\delta}\right)\right\}=0. \tag{2.15}$$

Eq. (2.15) represents a necessary condition for optimality. For the limit to go to zero, it must be the case that the product goes to zero (note that $\lambda_0 > 0$) which will be true if $n + g < r_s - \delta$. This says that the (geometric) average net interest rate must be greater than the sum of the rate of population growth and the rate of technical progress. Notice that this condition is satisfied in a steady state (this follows from Eq. (2.13)).

The welfare implications of steady-state allocations in this model are well known. Consider a social planner maximizing a social welfare function, W. Since the economy consists of a single unified decision-making entity, the standard assumption is that the social planner respects the preferences of this dynasty. It should be clear that it is a restrictive assumption. For instance, as we mentioned, a utility function such as the one maximized by the dynasty is not immediately derived from aggregating the preferences of successive altruistically linked generations. In particular, one must rule out specifications of preferences which induce time-inconsistencies. As Bernheim (1989) has argued, this is not obviously reasonable. Firstly, it is not derived from any deep axiomatic basis, and secondly, it rules out within-dynasty conflicts which seem to be important phenomena in reality. When it is derived from such an aggregation process, then ρ reflects not simply impatience but also the degree of altruism between generations. Does a planner have to respect this?

The planner chooses resource allocations directly, and suppose he or she solves the following optimization problem (ignoring nonnegativity), Problem 2:

$$\max_{\{c_t\}_{t=0}^{\infty} \{k_t\}_{t=0}^{\infty}} \sum_{t=0}^{\infty} \beta^t U(c_t A_t)$$

subject to the resource constraint

$$k_{t+1}(1+n)(1+g) = f(k_t) - c_t + (1-\delta)k_t .$$

As we have mentioned, the model is isomorphic to a convex, complete markets, Arrow–Debreu economy. It follows that competitive equilibria are Pareto optimal in the sense that the consumption of any individual living at any date t cannot be increased relative to its value in a competitive equilibrium without reducing the consumption of some individual living at some date, again relative to its value at the same competitive equilibrium. Since Problem 2 is a concave problem, there is in fact a unique such optimal allocation. Thus, associating the preferences of the dynasty with the social welfare function has a strong implication. The standard argument to show this in the present context is to directly compare the necessary conditions for Problems 1 and 2.

The messages of the neoclassical growth model for the present chapter are simple. Population growth is bad for development, since it induces capital widening at the expense of capital deepening. Along the transition path to the steady state, an increase in the population growth rate reduces the growth rate in per capita income, and in the steady state it reduces the capital–effective labor ratio and hence per capita income. What about resources? The model assumes constant returns to scale to the accumulation of capital and labor, and hence the scale of the economy is not constrained by the presence of any resource constraints. Many have argued that the model flagrantly assumes away resource issues. We return to this.

2.1.2. Optimal population: issues and static analysis

We first consider static models. In optimizing population size two factors are critical, the form of the objective function and the nature of returns to labor in the production technology. An immediate problem is that maximization of per capita utility in conjunction with diminishing marginal productivity of labor implies a zero optimal population size. The most obvious solution to this "problem" is to change the objective function to give explicit value to the number of people. With diminishing marginal productivity, this induces a trade-off between per capita consumption and the number of people enjoying any level of consumption. This can lead to an interior solution for the optimal level of population. The other solution to this problem is to relax the assumption of a monotonically diminishing marginal product of labor. This solution is less attractive, since in its usual form it involves a nonconvex technology.

The literature has concentrated on the "Genesis" problem. This, in the spirit of Rawls, considers the optimal population from behind the "veil of ignorance". In the Genesis problem, a social welfare function is posited, and the whole path of population is solved for. Such problems do not lead to fruitful analysis or much empirical content. In particular, they frequently invoke notions of "potential people" who weigh off the benefits from living against the costs of doing so. The more interesting agenda is to examine "actual" problems in situations where parents explicitly choose the number of their children and the resources to be allocated to them. The questions of optimal population can then be examined using standard tools of welfare economics, although it should be noted that the Pareto criterion is not well adapted to compare allocations when there are different numbers of people alive. In this case, the family utility functions have embedded within them exactly the issues which the philosophers have agonized over. With this framework, we argue that the crucial empirical issue is the nature of intergenerational preferences.

The standard models treat population growth and technical progress as given. In his original work, Solow (1956) suggested that one might endogenize the rate of population growth by making it a function of the capital–labor ratio (see Nerlove and Raut's chapter where they analyze various early models of this type). Another literature (the modern formal analysis which started with Dasgupta (1969)), continued to treat $(1 + n)$ as exogenous to private agents but subject to the control of the government (or planner). This literature attempts to discover the welfare effects of various population growth rates on the agents of a neoclassical growth model and to broach the issue of the "optimal" population. We now examine these issues. Before doing so, we need to clarify whether we are considering optimal population growth or optimal population size. Static analyses do not allow a meaningful discussion of this, so consider a dynamic model. Assume, as we shall, that a steady-state equilibrium exists. When population is exogenously controlled by a central planner or when we are examining normative issues in an economy where the population growth rate is endogenous, there will be some constant growth rate of population in this steady state. If this growth rate is zero, then it makes sense to talk of the optimal size of the population. In this case the optimal growth rate of population is zero. On the other hand, if this rate is positive (or for that matter negative), it only makes sense to talk of the optimal growth rate of population. There is no optimal size.

To see what are the important forces at work, we first consider the question of the optimal population in a static model. This clarifies the nature of the mapping from welfare functions to optimal allocations. It also shows the importance of various assumptions about returns to scale. This approach to the problem is associated with the founders of the modern literature: Cannan, Wicksell and Robbins (see Dalton, 1928; Gottlieb, 1945). Having clarified this, we move to a more satisfactory dynamic treatment. This is obviously required for our study, since many of the supposed effects of increased population which we shall consider later are concerned with dynamical phenomena such as capital accumulation, innovation, division of labor, and learning of various forms. The static analysis typically suppresses all of this by assuming that the available technology is independent of the level of population.

Assume that there are initially no people in existence but that the total number of people, *L*, has to be chosen in the "original position" to maximize some social welfare criterion (this is what Dasgupta (1987) calls the "Genesis problem"). As we shall see, while this perspective immensely simplifies the issues (for example, even if we can convincingly formulate and characterize a concept of optimal population, we may never be able to converge to it from an arbitrary starting population), it is probably a bad place to start philosophically. The use of this original position perspective (Rawls, 1971) also involves some implicit account of the utility of a "potential person" (Ng (1986) suggests the alternative term "prospective individuals") who may be brought into existence, but in fact ends up not being so. This is because the kernel of "Genesis problems" is the trade-off between the absolute size of the population and the average level of welfare of those alive. This trade-off is evaluated using different social welfare functions and different technological assumptions. The optimal population is found at the point where the value society attaches to creating another person is matched by the loss in value experienced by the reduced consumption and therefore utility that existing individuals have to incur to allow the new person to live.

A logically consistent approach to determining optimal population size can be derived from the contractual approach to social welfare. This would be to start with the complete pool of potential people and determine optimal population size by maximizing their expected utility. In this set-up, the population in equilibrium will represent the probability of being brought into existence (on the assumption that a random selection is made from the pool of potential people). This also forces us to make an assumption about the utility of not being born. While these contractual theories, following Harsanyi (1955), Vickrey (1960) and Rawls (1971) have been influential we do not consider this is a fruitful approach to thinking about optimal population. Rawls himself was worried about whether his theory applied to intergenerational issues, and its application to population policy is more troublesome still. It is not clear that the notion of a social contract between potential people is very useful, and in fact Rawls' construction with a variable population is confusing, since it is unclear exactly who is doing the choosing (there are clear logical problems in thinking of the original position as concerning only actual people, see Pasek (1993)). Dasgupta (1987) argues in this vein that we should resist thinking of the original position as a "congress of souls". Nozick (1974) comments, "Utilitarianism is notoriously inept with decisions where the number of persons is at issue".

There is a technology for converting labor into a produced good which can be consumed. This is represented by a twice continuously differentiable, strictly increasing, and strictly concave production function, $F: \Re_+ \to \Re_+$, where $Y = F(L)$. This implies that the derivatives of the function have the following signs: $F' > 0$, $F'' < 0$. Each individual is identical and is endowed with a continuously differentiable, strictly increasing and strictly concave utility function defined over consumption, $U: \Re_+ \to \Re$. We assume that the utility function is twice continuously differentiable with derivatives $U' > 0$, $U'' < 0$. The utility of consumption, c, is denoted $u(c)$.

The social planner wishes to choose L to maximize the welfare of society (in fact the early writers on the subject chose consumption or output per capita as the objective function rather than working with a utility function as we shall). We start with the reasonable criterion that society wishes to maximize utility of consumption per capita (under the assumption that output is divided equally amongst all individuals in existence). This is referred to as "average utilitarianism". In this case, the optimal level of population, L^*, solves the problem, $\max_L U(C/L)$ subject to $C = F(L)$ and $L \geq 0$. Substituting the first constraint into the objective function and letting λ be the Lagrange multiplier on the nonnegativity constraint, the first-order condition for this problem is

$$U'\left(\frac{F(L)}{L}\right)\left[\frac{F'(L)L - F(L)}{L^2}\right] + \lambda = 0. \tag{2.16}$$

An interior solution implies $LF' = F$. But by diminishing marginal productivity $F/L > F'$ for all L. This immediately implies that $\lambda > 0$ and the optimum is $L^* = 0$! It is apparent that this result depends on diminishing returns to labor. Because of diminishing marginal productivity extra people always produce less than they consume (since output is distributed evenly), per capita output must fall when population expands. If $F'' = 0$ then L^* is indeterminate, and if $F'' > 0$ then $L^* = \infty$. Pitchford (1974b) deals with these cases by assuming that F is first convex and then concave (the standard Marshallian assumption) which generates a unique interior optimal population. This is the assumption appealed to by the early writers to make population size determinate. These ideas extend to a model with a fixed factor. Assume that the technology is now $Y = F(L, T)$, where T is a fixed factor such as "land" or some sort of natural resource. In this case, diminishing marginal productivity of labor implies $L^* = 0$ (the argument is identical to that embodied in Eq. (2.16)).

A more utilitarian version of this formulation has been strongly advocated by Meade (1955) (building on the earlier work of Sidgwick (1907)). Indeed Sidgwick (1907) explicitly argued that "if the additional population enjoys on the whole positive happiness, we ought to weigh the amount of happiness gained by the extra number against the amount lost by the remainder". In this, known as the "total" or "Classical" utilitarian model, the maximand is $LU(F(L)/L)$, with first-order condition, where $\hat{c} = F(L)/L$,

$$U(\hat{c}) + U'(\hat{c})\left[\frac{F'(L)L - F(L)}{L}\right] + \lambda = 0. \tag{2.17}$$

It is clear that Eq. (2.17) may admit a positive solution for population in the case where the production function exhibits diminishing marginal productivity of labor (since $F'L - F < 0$ by concavity). Meade's argument for this formulation (versions of Eq. (2.17) are often referred to as the Meade–Sidgwick rule) centers on incorporating some notion that society may care about the size of the population directly and not just the effect it has on per capita consumption. Pitchford (1974b) considers other variants and extensions to multiple commodities. There are also other variants such as the "critical level utilitarianism" formulated by Blackorby and Donaldson (1984) (and recently defended by them in Blackorby et al. (1993)).

The intuition behind Eq. (2.17) is immediate. It balances the social costs and benefits of bringing another person into existence. The first term is the gain in social welfare from the utility of the new person. The second term is the loss in social welfare due to diminishing marginal productivity dragging down the average consumption level.

It seems plausible that individuals care not just about per capita consumption but also about total population so that the above welfare functions might be thought of as special cases of a more general form such as $U(C/L, L)$. A main argument against this formulation is that it may lead to very large numbers of people all enjoying very low levels of consumption. This result has become known as the "repugnant conclusion" (see Dasgupta, 1987; Parfit, 1984).

The repugnant conclusion raises nicely the difficult issue of the extent to which the welfare of existing individuals is to be traded off against the welfare and existence of potential individuals. On one level, this is a philosophical problem with no definitive solution. Broome, in a series of thoughtful papers (e.g., Broome, 1992, 1993a,b), has argued strongly against the importance of this trade-off. Broome's view is that unborn individuals have no rights on society which can force them to be brought into existence at the expense of the welfare of existing individuals. This perspective suggests that attempting to consider the welfare of "potential" people is otiose.

Average utilitarianism has also been extensively criticized. Broome (1993a) argues that adding a person with utility above average is justified under this criterion, whether or not the welfare of existing individuals is improved by the addition of this person. Narveson (1978) asks, should one refrain from having a child simply because it is known that it will enjoy below average welfare? Should one feel morally obliged to have a child if it is known that it's welfare will be above average? Sumner (1978) argues against average utilitarianism on the grounds that it discriminates in favor of existing individuals. On the other hand, Sikora (1978) has asserted that "it is *prima facie* wrong to prevent the existence of anyone with reasonable prospects for happiness". But how is such a dictum to be implemented in population policy?

One influential view, called the "person affecting view" is that "duties must always be duties to someone or other; if no person is affected by an action, then that action (or inaction) cannot be a violation or fulfillment of a duty" (Narveson, 1978). In this view it cannot be the case that we owe anything to future generations, since "if there is no subject of obligation, then there is no obligation". Of course we can leave assets to posterity, but this is not a debt we "owe". As Parfit (1983) points out, if this view is accepted, and if different policies lead to differing sets of future people becoming actual, then as long as these lives are not miserable, which policy we choose is not morally constrained by consideration for future people. However, Parfit (1983) argues that "it is bad if those who live are worse off than those who might have lived". This approach stresses that what matters is not identities (i.e. the fact that in different histories different potential people become actual) but rather the number of living happy people.

In the next section, we study "Genesis problems" in dynamic models. However, in the rest of the paper, we concentrate exclusively on actual problems. At any moment society is made up of a set of individuals with preferences over their own welfare and the welfare of their descendants and ancestors (and maybe over their friends or even enemies!). Intertemporal optimization of individual agents will generate a path for the evolution of population. The number of children an individual parent will have is determined by the costs and benefits facing the parent. To the extent these differ from the social costs and benefits, or to the extent that society weights the welfare of children differently from parents, there will be normative implications. From this perspective, the repugnant conclusion is an artifact of not formulating the problem of optimal population in terms of an explicit model of intergenerational preferences, constraints and set of social institutions where the rate of population growth is endogenous. In particular, when parents care about the welfare of their children, and this is part of the choice problem along with fertility, it seems unlikely that the repugnant conclusion could arise. It seems improbable that parents would want to bring impoverished children into the world. Of course, the fact that parents care about bringing happy people into the world is not the only motive for fertility. But whatever the case may be, the relevant questions can only be sensibly posed in an explicit model of population growth.

Of course, the moral obligations of parents to children and vice versa may not be adequately captured by such a specification. How much parents care about the welfare of children may not be the same as how much they should care. Unfortunately, while we can examine the positive and normative questions in models where preferences are given (determining how much parents do care and what will be equilibrium fertility and population growth), it is much harder to develop a convincing theory which deals with how much they should care which is separate from this, except to the extent that their behavior generates externalities, is noncooperative, or induces obvious deviations from efficient behavior. We should perhaps pause to consider the ramifications of this, since in this case, Pareto optimal population growth can imply that it is efficient for parents to bring children into the world when they are treated like slaves. We stress again that this issue can only be resolved by empirical work on the nature of preferences and intra-family relationships.

Unlike philosophers, economists have more generally given up the attempt to propose first-best efficient allocations based on interpersonal comparisons of utility. Perhaps it is not surprising that this should also be the case with regard to population growth.

2.1.3. Optimal population: dynamic analysis

We now consider the implications of average and total utilitarianism for the optimal rate of population growth in a dynamic context where agents live forever. We again derive analogues of the Meade–Sidgwick rule. However, as in the static case, maximizing average utility leads to implausible results (at least with standard technological assumptions). It implies that starting from any level of population, it is optimal to reduce population as quickly as possible, and it also implies, if the initial level of population can be controlled, that it be set to zero. The problem with this model is that while there are costs to having a positive rate of population growth (or larger size of population), there are no benefits. More plausible results emerge under the total utility version. In this case, there is a trade-off between the welfare of existing agents and the social value of creating more people. When the production function exhibits constant returns to scale, there is no optimum level of population but an optimum rate of growth of population. When the production function exhibits decreasing returns, the optimum involves a constant level of population. Hence, if diminishing returns are caused by fixed factors, such as resources, this implies that optimal population growth comes to a halt.

Now return to the dynastic growth model. Instead of treating the rate of population growth as fixed, assume that whilst still exogenous to choices by private individuals, it can be varied by the social planner to maximize welfare. What rate of population growth would maximize the welfare function of the social planner? Notice that in the context of the dynastic model, the answer to this question simultaneously reveals the rate of population growth the dynasty would itself choose. Index the rate of population growth by time, n_t. This rate must be nonnegative, so add to Problem 2 the side constraint that $n_t \geq 0$, this adds the term $\sum_{t=0}^{\infty} \mu_t n_t$ to the Lagrangean.

We assume that the rate of population growth is costlessly controllable by the social planner. Pitchford (1974b) proposes various models where the costs of altering population are explicitly modeled. However, this is an exercise which seems more interesting in a model where population growth is modeled from the choice theoretic perspective. This gives us a sound basis to assess the welfare implications of population growth, and moreover, it provides an explicit microeconomic foundation for policy. The necessary conditions are now Eqs. (2.5)–(2.8), the complementary slackness conditions and $\mu_t n_t = 0$, along with the following:

$$-\lambda_t (1+g)k_{t+1} + \mu_t = 0. \tag{2.18}$$

Eq. (2.18) shows immediately that no positive rate of population growth can be optimal. If $n_t > 0$ then $\mu_t = 0$ and Eq. (2.18) cannot be satisfied unless $\lambda_t = 0$. But $\lambda_t > 0$ as long as marginal utility is positive (see Eq. (2.6)). Hence $n_t = 0$, $\mu_t > 0$. The fact that the shadow price on the nonnegativity constraint is positive indicates that the value of Problem 2 could be increased by making n_t negative! Starting from any initial level of population, L_0, Eq. (2.18) then suggests that the optimal plan is to set $n_t = 0$ and accumulate capital until the steady state is reached. The intuition for these results seems to have been very influential on early work by authors attempting to assess the benefits of population control in developing economies (see for example, Coale and Hoover, 1958; Enke, 1971). Can we then determine what the optimal level of population might be? Consider the problem of choosing the level of population instead of the growth rate. The solution to this is to set $L_t = 0$. The intuition for this is identical to the static model with the average utilitarian welfare function (see Lane, 1977).

The implications of the model are not very plausible. One does not have to go as far as Julian Simon to disagree with the proposition that the optimal level of population is zero. This result seems to suggest, in the spirit of Koopmans' desiderata, that the model is badly formulated. There are two possibilities. The first is that the model fails to incorporate important relationships between population and productivity. We investigate this idea extensively in Section 3.3. The second, which we explore first, is that the objective function does not correctly capture the effects of population on social welfare.

In his seminal work on optimal population growth Dasgupta (1969) (see also Dasgupta, 1974) used not the average utilitarian but rather the Meade–Sidgwick total utilitarian formulation,

$$\sum_{t=0}^{\infty} \beta^t L_t U(\hat{c}_t). \tag{2.19}$$

Notice again that Eq. (2.19) is not the result of any obvious aggregation over individuals since future utilities are again being discounted from the point of view of the initial individual. The importance of Eq. (2.19) is, as we shall see later, that it can be derived from an aggregation over individual altruistically linked generations who choose the number of children to have endogenously (Becker and Barro, 1986, 1988, 1989). As we shall also see, the allocations which the Becker–Barro model generates are closely related to those which maximize the utilitarian objective function Eq. (2.19).

This formulation has a nice property, as the following example (due to Arrow and Kurz, 1970; Lane, 1977) makes clear. Imagine a country split into two islands, one with population L_1 and one with L_2, where $L_1 > L_2$. The social planner has a fixed endowment of goods, C, to distribute between the two islands where all individuals have identical utility functions and all individuals within an island will get equal treatment. The social budget constraint is $C = L_1 c_1 + L_2 c_2$, where c_1, c_2 are the per capita consumption (not in effective units) of individuals on the two islands respectively. Assume that the planner allocates the resources to maximize $U(c_1) + U(c_2)$. The first-order condition for this problem is $U'(c_1)L_2 = U'(c_2)L_1$. Since $L_1 > L_2$, $U'(c_1) > U'(c_2)$, and hence by concavity, $c_2 > c_1$. Now consider the welfare function $L_1 U(c_1) + L_2 U(c_2)$. The first-order condition now implies $c_1 = c_2$. We see that the average utilitarian framework discriminates against people on the first island, simply because they are more populous. In an intertemporal framework with positive population growth, future generations are similarly discriminated against. This seems a strong argument in favor of the specification in Eq. (2.19).

The natural approach to Eq. (2.19) is to assume that this is now the welfare function of the dynasty. How does this change our previous analysis? Consider Problem 1 with the objective function replaced by Eq. (2.19). Call this Problem 3. Note that we continue to assume that the production function exhibits constant returns to scale. To see the implications of the reformulation for the existence of an optimal rate of population growth, Eq. (2.19) can be re-written

$$U(\hat{c}_0) + \sum_{t=1}^{\infty}\left(\prod_{s=1}^{t}(1+n_s)\right)\beta^t U(\hat{c}_t).$$

More explicitly, this sum is

$$U(\hat{c}_0) + (1+n_1)\beta U(\hat{c}_1) + (1+n_1)(1+n_2)\beta^2 U(\hat{c}_2) + \cdots.$$

If the production function exhibits constant returns to scale then this problem can be solved for an optimal constant steady-state equilibrium rate of population growth. The first-order conditions for this problem are:

$$\prod_{s=1}^{t}(1+n_s)A_t \beta^t U'(c_t A_t) = \lambda_t, \tag{2.20}$$

$$\frac{1}{1+n_t}\sum_{\tau=t}^{\infty}\prod_{s=1}^{\tau}(1+n_s)\beta^\tau U(c_t A_t) - \lambda_t(1+g)k_{t+1} + \mu_t = 0. \tag{2.21}$$

If there is an interior solution then $\mu_t = 0$, and these equations can be combined to generate simultaneously a version of the Meade–Sidgwick rule as well as the standard Keynes–Ramsey rule (the consumption Euler equation). The intuition behind Eq. (2.21) is as follows. The sum represents the discounted total change in social welfare caused by a slight increase in the rate of population growth in period t. Such an increase means that the level of population will be higher in all future periods, and given the way that Eq. (2.21) is constructed, this has to be taken into account in calculating the change in social welfare. The second term in Eq. (2.21) is the marginal social cost of increasing the rate of population growth. In this neoclassical environment, increasing n_t reduces the capital–labor ratio, and this change is evaluated at the marginal utility of consumption. This term, therefore, captures the adverse effect of an increase in population growth on per capita utility. Hence Eq. (2.21) is the dynamic extension of Eq. (2.17).

If the production function exhibits decreasing returns to scale, then we instead determine a constant optimal level of population and a constant capital stock in a steady state. Consider maximizing Eq. (2.19) subject to the constraints $K_{t+1} = F(K_t, L_t) - c_t L_t + (1 - \delta)K_t$ (with multiplier λ_t) and $L_t \geq 0$ (with multiplier μ_t), where we set $g = 0$. The first-order conditions with respect to c_t and L_t are:

$$\beta^t U'(c_t) = \lambda_t, \quad \beta^t U(c_t) = \lambda_t [F_L - c_t].$$

From these two equations, along with the costate equation and the capital accumulation equation, we can determine the stationary values of K, L, λ and c. Note that the Meade–Sidgwick rule follows immediately from the above two conditions.

Having obtained this characterization of the optimal steady-state growth rate of population, there are many other questions we could examine, for example, what dynamic paths converge to this steady state. Along an optimal path from an initial population and capital stock, is n equal to its optimal level from the start and does the economy accumulate to the steady state with this constant rate of population growth? This question was raised by Dasgupta (1969). Consider starting from a low level of capital. Dasgupta shows that in the case when the production function exhibits decreasing returns to scale, the optimal approach to the stationary state involves monotonically increasing both the capital stock and the level of population over time until they reach their constant stationary levels. Intuitively, even though population is costlessly controllable, it is not optimal to set it immediately to its stationary level, because this would imply a very low per capita consumption (given the low capital stock).

2.2. Neoclassical growth with finite lifetimes

In Section 2.1, we stressed that certain strong implications of the model depended on the assumed demographic structure. We now develop the main alternative to the dynastic framework, the overlapping generations model. We focus on the simplest interesting case, where generations of two-period-lived individuals overlap forever, and where initially there are no intergenerational links. While the equation governing the dynamics of the model closely resembles that in Section 2.1.1, the current model allows, even when contingent markets are complete, intertemporally inefficient equilibria to exist. This was first discovered by Allais (1947) and independently by Samuelson (1958) and is due to the existence of equilibrium price systems which imply that the aggregate wealth of the economy is infinite. This implies that the first welfare theorem does not hold. Intertemporal transfer schemes can improve welfare above the decentralized equilibrium. The reason that such allocations cannot arise in the model of Section 2.1.1 is that the transversality condition rules them out. If aggregate wealth were unbounded, individual budget sets would not be well defined, and the dynastic problem would not have a solution. Therefore, inefficient allocations are ruled out by the necessary conditions for optimality. But with overlapping generations, although each generation has a well defined decision problem, the social allocation can imply infinite wealth (see Geanakoplos, 1987; Geanakoplos and Polemarchakis, 1992).

In this sub-section, we extend the analysis to simple discrete time overlapping generations models (henceforth, OLG). An alternative (which we do not pursue) would be to adopt the continuous time OLG framework due originally to Blanchard (1985). We do this initially by ignoring intergenerational links. The model follows closely the seminal work of Diamond (1965a) (who built on the work of Samuelson and Allais). Nowhere, however, is the consideration of intergenerational linkages more important than in the study of population growth. We, therefore, extend the model in later sections to consider the various forms this can take. This issue is also treated in depth by Nerlove and Raut in their chapter, and we make our exposition complementary with theirs. Results here turn critically on the exact form which relations take. We offer a discussion of altruism and bequests.

2.2.1. Overlapping generations and neoclassical growth without intergenerational links

As in the previous section, we assume that there is a single produced good (designated as numeraire) which can be consumed or used as capital and that investment is irreversible. Time is discrete. Each agent lives for two periods. In each period $t = 0,1,2, \ldots$, a generation of L_t identical individuals is born. Generation t is "young" in period t, "old" in period $t + 1$, and dead thereafter. Each agent has preferences defined over consumption when young, denoted C_t^t, and old, C_{t+1}^t (note that superscripts refer to generations and subscripts to periods) represented by the separable utility function, $U(C_t^t) + \beta U(C_{t+1}^t)$. We assume that the instantaneous utility function has the same properties as that in the previous sub-section and that $\beta \in (0, 1]$. Each individual is endowed with one unit of time in youth and none in old age. The structure of the model is standard: when young agents supply their unit of time to a competitive labor market. All the capital stock is owned by old agents at the start of any period who rent it to firms in a competitive capital market. Old agents consume their rental income (their marginal propensity to consume is unity), and for simplicity we assume that there is 100% depreciation. Young agents make a consumption/saving decision out of their wage income. The structure of firms is identical to that of the previous subsection. For simplicity, we assume a single price-taking, competitive, representative firm with the same technology. As in Section 2.1.1, there are no intrinsic intertemporal considerations, and the firm hires capital and labor in each period so as to minimize the costs of production. A representative young agent chooses saving, S_t, to solve the following Problem 4:

$$S_t(r_{t+1}, w_t, \beta) = \arg \max_{S_t} \{ U(w_t - S_t) + \beta U[(1 + r_{t+1})S_t] \} .$$

The solution to the problem is a saving function, $S_t(r_{t+1}, w_t, \beta)$, where $S : \Re_+ \times \Re_+ \times [0, 1] \to \Re_+$ (note that since the characteristics of agents are stationary over time, the function will be stationary, and so we drop the subscript on S_t from now on) implicitly defined by the first-order condition

$$U'(w_t - S_t) = (1 + r_{t+1})\beta U'[(1 + r_{t+1})S_t]. \tag{2.22}$$

The aggregate stock of capital is just the new saving, hence, $K_{t+1} = L_t S_t$. In per capita terms, using profit maximization by firms and factor market clearing we can write this as

$$k_{t+1}(1+n)(1+g) = S(f'(k_{t+1}), f(k_t) - k_t f'(k_t), \beta) . \tag{2.23}$$

Eq. (2.23) implicitly defines a difference equation in the capital–effective labor ratio. We denote this $k_{t+1} = \chi(k_t)$, where $\chi : \Re_+ \to \Re_+$. The dynamical system for the OLG model is thus one-dimensional. The behavior of this dynamical system has been intensively studied (see Azariadis, 1993).

We now consider the welfare properties of the above equilibrium allocation (Azariadis (1993) gives an extensive treatment). Capital–effective labor ratios which satisfy the model do not have to be efficient. There is also now a real problem of how to aggregate preferences. The usual approach is to adopt a Bergson–Samuelson type of social welfare function which is a weighted sum of welfares of all present and future individuals in the economy. It should immediately be apparent that difficulties arise as to the weighting of potential people. For the moment we take the rate of population growth as fixed, and so this gives a well defined set of individuals (present and future).

We assume that the economy begins at time zero and the social planner attaches a weight θ_{-1} to the welfare of the initial old person ($L_{-1} = 1$). The planner treats all agents within a particular generation equally and also discounts the welfare of future generations at a constant rate $\gamma \in (0, 1)$. The welfare function is

$$W = \theta_{-1}U(C_0^{-1}) + \sum_{t=0}^{\infty} \gamma^t L_t (U(C_t^t) + \beta U(C_{t+1}^t)). \tag{2.24}$$

Using the equal treatment embodied in Eq. (2.24) allows the aggregate feasibility constraint to be written

$$K_{t+1} + L_t C_t^t + L_{t-1}C_t^{t-1} = F(K_t, A_t L_t). \tag{2.25}$$

To derive the constraint in per capita effective terms, divide Eq. (2.25) by $A_t L_t$ which gives

$$k_{t+1}(1+n)(1+g) + c_t^t + \frac{c_t^{t-1}}{(1+n)(1+g)} = f(k_t). \tag{2.26}$$

The form of social welfare function embodied in Eq. (2.24) is not that typically used in the literature, however. It is more usual (e.g. Blanchard and Fischer, 1989) to specify Eq. (2.24) in per capita terms, so, letting

$$\hat{c}_t^t = C_t^t/L_t \quad \text{and} \quad \hat{c}_{t+1}^t = C_{t+1}^t/L_{t+1}$$

be per capita consumption when young and old, respectively, Eq. (2.24) is written (allowing for technological change)

$$W = \theta_{-1}U(c_0^{-1}A_0) + \sum_{t=0}^{\infty} \gamma^t (U(c_t^t A_t) + \beta U(c_{t+1}^t A_{t+1})). \tag{2.27}$$

Of course Eq. (2.27) brings the social welfare function as close as possible to the one we have initially used in examining the dynastic framework.

Problem 5 is to maximize Eq. (2.27) subject to Eq. (2.26). This problem has the Lagrangean

$$L = \theta_{-1}U(c_0^{-1}A_0) + \sum_{t=0}^{\infty} \gamma^t (U(c_t^t A_t) + \beta U(c_{t+1}^t A_{t+1}))$$
$$+ \sum_{t=0}^{\infty} \lambda_t \left\{ f(k_t) - c_t^t - \frac{c_t^{t-1}}{(1+g)(1+n)} - (1+g)(1+n)k_{t+1} \right\}.$$

The necessary conditions for this problem are:

$$\theta_{-1} A_0 U'(c_0^{-1} A_0) = \frac{\lambda_0}{(1+g)(1+n)},$$

(2.28)

$$\gamma' A_t U'(c_t^t A_t) = \lambda_t,$$

(2.29)

$$\gamma' A_{t+1} \beta U'(c_{t+1}^t A_{t+1}) = \frac{\lambda_{t+1}}{(1+g)(1+n)},$$

(2.30)

$$\lambda_t (1+g)(1+n) = \lambda_{t+1}(1+f'k_{t+1})).$$

(2.31)

Combining Eqs. (2.29), (2.30) and (2.31) gives the standard condition for optimality within each individual's lifetime

$$U'(c_t^t A_t) = \left(\frac{1+f'(k_{t+1})}{1+n} \right) \beta U'(c_{t+1}^t A_{t+1}).$$

(2.32)

Leading Eq. (2.32) by one period and combining it with Eq. (2.33) gives the condition showing the relationship between generations in the planning problem:

$$\beta U'(c_{t+1}^t A_{t+1}) = \frac{\gamma U'(c_{t+1}^{t+1} A_{t+1})}{(1+g)(1+n)}.$$

(2.33)

Here the welfare of future generations is "discounted" due to greater numbers, positive technological progress, and the fact that future welfare is weighted less in the specification of Eq. (2.27). Consider now steady-state allocations where

$$c_t^t = c_{t+1}^{t+1}, \quad c_{t+1}^t = c_{t+2}^{t+1}.$$

Leading Eq. (2.29) and using this and Eq. (2.29) to substitute into Eq. (2.31) gives

$$U'(c_t^t A_t) = \left(\frac{1+f'(k)}{1+n} \right) \gamma U'(c_{t+1}^{t+1} A_{t+1}).$$

(2.34)

Now let $\gamma = 1/(1+\tau)$, and consider the special case where the utility function is logarithmic. In this case Eq. (2.34) immediately gives the condition (neglecting terms involving products of τ, g and n)

$$f'(k) = \tau + g + n.$$

(2.35)

Notice that in Eq. (2.35) the steady-state capital effective labor ratio depends on the social rate of discount τ. The larger is τ the smaller is γ and the higher is the weight of present generations relative to future generations. From Eq. (2.35), this implies that a smaller capital–effective labor ratio is accumulated in steady state.

2.2.2. Optimal population with finite lives

We now consider the notion of optimal population growth in the OLG context. This was first explored by Samuelson (1975). Samuelson's intuition was that the OLG structure was different from the standard neoclassical growth model and this might allow for a positive optimum rate of population growth. Recall that for a positive optimal rate of population growth to exist, it must be the case that there are benefits to having a rate of population growth larger than zero. These do not arise under standard technological assumptions without adopting an objective function which explicitly gives weight to larger numbers of people. However, unlike in previous models, in OLG models there is a new feature emerging from the constraint (2.26). Increasing the rate of population growth has the standard social cost of capital "dilution" through the first term on the left-hand side of Eq. (2.26). There is now another term in Eq. (2.26), however. This is the ratio $c_t^{t-1}/(1+n)(1+g)$. An increase in n, since it increases the ratio of young workers to old dependents, decreases the dependency ratio, and this reduces the burden of feeding c_t^{t-1} to the old on the social planner.

Samuelson examined stationary allocations in the case with zero technological progress and chose $n \geq 0$ to maximize stationary welfare subject to Eq. (2.26). Samuelson's objective function was $U(c_t^t A_t, c_{t+1}^t A_{t+1})$ (nonseparable), but this does not alter the characterization of the optimum.

Now consider Problem 5 again. If the population growth rate is chosen by the social planner in Problem 5, then this delivers the following condition:

$$(1+g)^2 k^* = c_t^{t-1}(1+n)^{-2}. \tag{2.36}$$

The interpretation of Eq. (2.36), sketched above, seems plausible. However, as Deardorff (1976) was quick to point out (and Samuelson (1976) to acknowledge), the second-order condition shows that Eq. (2.36) actually characterizes a minimum in the Cobb–Douglas example used by Samuelson. However, this just demonstrated, unsurprisingly, that restrictions on utility and production functions are required to establish the existence of a stationary optimum with $n > 0$ (this should have been evident from the earlier literature (see Lane, 1977)). Michel and Pestieau (1993) have recently established conditions under which Eq. (2.36) characterizes an interior solution (see also Jaeger, 1989).

The question of optimum population size in an OLG model with a Meade–Sidgwick objective function has been examined by Gigliotti (1983). He assumed that the social planner discounted generations at the same rate that individuals discounted utility between periods and used the following objective function:

$$\sum_{t=0}^{\infty} \gamma^t (L_t U(c_t^t) + L_{t-1} U(c_t^{t-1})),$$

which is of course Eq. (2.27) when $\gamma = \beta$. The results of this model are very similar to those of Dasgupta (1969). Apart from inessential details, we again derive a version of the Meade–Sidgwick rule.

2.2.3. Intergenerational linkages

In this section, we consider the complex issue of the connection between generations. (Stark (1984) presents a useful conceptual discussion of this topic.) The OLG models developed in the previous sections assumed that there were neither interconnections between the preferences of distinct generations, nor did people belong to integrated family decision-making units. In two seminal papers, Barro (1974) and Becker (1974) argued that in fact one should extend individual preference relations to encompass some notion of the welfare of their descendants. The natural extension of this argument is that preferences might also encompass the welfare of predecessors. The theoretical importance of this innovation is that, to the extent that intergenerational linkages are operational, a sequence of overlapping generations generate equilibria which are identical to that produced by the dynastic model. Whether or not this occurs depends on how the intergenerational preferences are specified.

There are three basic models which consider how parents care about their children. Firstly, the "joy of giving model" where parents get utility directly from giving gifts to their children. Second is the model where parents care about the consumption levels of their children. This model is referred to as "paternalistic altruism". Finally, there is the model where the parent derives utility directly from the utility of the offspring. This latter is typically referred to simply as the "altruism model". These models are incomplete to the extent that it seems natural, having taken this step, to consider the utility that children might experience from the utility of their parents. Transfers from children to parents are referred to as "gifts" to distinguish them from "bequests". Again, these models could have children deriving utility from the giving itself, from the consumption of parents, or from the utility of parents. What is crucial in making a sequence of generations perform like a dynasty is that parents care about the utility of children and simultaneously children care about the utility of parents (the so-called "two sided altruism model"). It is only when utility is derived from utility itself that a recursive dynastic utility function is generated by overlapping generations. For example, parents care about the utility of their children, who in turn care about the utility of their children, and so indirectly parents care for the utility of their grandchildren (allowing directly for this effect does not change the situation substantively). While dynastic utility functions can be generated by one sided altruism (we will examine an important example of this later when we discuss the model of Becker and Barro (1988, 1989)), in general one sided altruism is not sufficient to rule out dynamically inefficient paths or guarantee Ricardian equivalence (and in this sense make equilibria generated by a sequence of generations identical to that of the infinitely lived agent model), although it is sufficient in some examples (see Stark, 1995). This was originally pointed out by Weil (1987). Weil noted that, in the standard example of dynamically inefficient equilibria, Pareto improvements involve transferring resources from children to parents. A bequest motive cannot generate such a transfer in the case where there is a nonnegativity constraint on bequests. What is required is gifts from child to parent and hence two sided altruism. In fact, it is not even sufficient to have two sided altruism, since it is necessary for altruism to be strong enough (otherwise individuals can be at a zero gift or bequest corner solution). These issues are discussed in Abel (1987), Kimball (1987) and Stark (1995).

Models which assume paternalistic altruism are analytically the hardest, because they embed incentives for strategic behavior. For example, consider a parent who inherits a bequest and must decide how much to consume and bequeath herself. If the utility of the parent depends on the consumption of the offspring, then the optimal bequest will depend on the amount of savings of the child. If the child can commit itself to saving a lot for its own children, then this may induce the parent to make larger transfers. Such behavior would of course be rational for the child, if it has preferences of the same form as the parent. These problems cannot be resolved by allowing children to value the consumption of their parents, since this induces new strategic phenomena. For example, parents may now save little in order to credibly induce children to make transfers to them. These models have to be solved using game theoretic tools (see for example, Leininger, 1986; Bernheim and Ray, 1987; Bernheim, 1989) and the type of issues discussed above have been analyzed in Bernheim and Stark (1988).

These extensions to preferences are not necessary for the purposes of examining the endogenous choice of fertility. In many developing countries, children perform productive tasks for the family and thus generate a return to their parents. The demand for children can be modeled not just as a matter of parental utility of children or child's welfare but because of the income stream children generate for the family (see our discussion in Section 3.1). These models typically assume that parents can enforce these income streams. Bernheim et al. (1985) show how bequests can be used as a "carrot" to enforce such income flows. Children provide services for parents in nonaltruistic models because they will receive a bequest. Here then bequests are driven by a pure exchange process. These models implicitly assume some sort of family structure which is missing from our exposition of the OLG model above.

Interestingly, there seems to be no model in the literature where siblings care for each other, apart from the analysis in Stark (1995), who shows how such considerations may be crucial in spreading cooperative behavior between generations in a model where children mimic parental behavior. This might be important, given the evidence that the amount of resources that a family devotes to each child decreases in the number of children parents have. The first child, once born, might have an incentive to oppose further births. There also seem to be many issues in altruistic relations not captured by existing theories. For example, while parents may care for children's welfare, they tend to have specific ideas about what constitutes a "good" or "fruitful" life. Pollak (1988) observes that parents treat differently a request for financial help from their children depending on what the money is to be spent on (a sportscar or a college education). He uses this to argue that it cannot be simply the utility of the children which is valued, unless a richer model is added (perhaps children's preferences are dynamically inconsistent).

2.3. Neoclassical growth with resources

Although historically the study of growth was closely connected to resources and particularly the issue of whether or not finiteness of natural resource stocks put bounds on the feasible paths an economy might follow, these issues were to a large extent ignored in the theoretical flowering of growth in the 1950s and 1960s. The discussion in the nineteenth century was initially focused on land as a fixed resource, but later in the century other exhaustible resources began to loom large. A famous example is Jevons's (1865) forecast that the British economy may be constrained by the running down of its coal stocks. Barbier (1989) contains a nice discussion of early views on the topic. The fact that such Cassandras seemed to have been refuted probably led to the neglect of these issues. The events of the 1970s resuscitated interest in resource constraints.

In this section, in the context of exogenous technical change and population growth, we introduce resources (both exhaustible and renewable). The distinction between the OLG and the ILA frameworks is important here because of the possibilities of intergenerational externalities without compensating altruism (individuals may deplete natural resources or despoil the environment and do not take into account the effects on the next generation (this phenomena has been explored by John et al. (1995)). This problem is particularly pressing for unowned and unpriced resources, since even if there is no altruism towards future generations, present generations may be induced to exploit resources efficiently, if they have the option of selling undepleted resources to future generations (though we shall see that this in itself does not ensure dynamic efficiency).

We start by introducing an exhaustible resource into the technology and review the well-known results due to Dasgupta and Heal, Koopmans, Stiglitz, and Solow. These clarified the extent to which finite resources could constrain growth. Many of the tools and intuitions developed in this literature proved to be useful later. In particular, the literature concentrated on the "essentiality" or "necessity" of resources to production and the extent to which resource depletion would constrain growth. This clearly depends on the extent to which capital accumulation and technical change are able to compensate for falling stocks of resources. This stimulated a number of authors, notably Dasgupta et al. (1976), Davidson (1978) and Kamien and Schwartz (1978), to endogenize technical change.

We synthesize the results in the literature by modeling the interaction between population growth and resource depletion. We then discuss the wider context of economy–environmental interrelationships. This leads us to move the emphasis away from exhaustible to renewable resources and their implications for growth. We develop a prototype growth model capturing what we see as being the most important interactions and extend it to the important case where utility depends not simply on consumption but also environmental "amenity" services.

2.3.1. Neoclassical growth with exhaustible resources: infinitely lived agents

In this section, we add exhaustible resources to capital and labor as inputs in the production function of a neoclassical growth model. Although resources eventually are completely used up, the economy may be able to exhibit sustained growth in per capita consumption, as long as resources are not "too important" (in a sense we make precise) in the production of output. Even without technical progress, capital accumulation can offset the depletion of the resource. Technical progress makes it more likely that consumption can be sustained. Exogenous population growth makes it harder to sustain growth in per capita consumption. Whatever happens to the resource stock or per capita consumption, the dynamic path of the economy is optimal in a dynastic setting. Optimal population growth introduces issues identical to those in Section 2.1.3. With finite lives, we may have inefficient underexploitation of the resource.

In this section, we review the literature on exhaustible resources developed in the 1970s before moving to the more interesting issue of renewable resources. Treating a resource as exhaustible implicitly assumes that there are no substitutes for the resource and that the ability to recycle the resource is limited. These are quite restrictive assumptions. The major contributions to this literature include Anderson (1972), Vousden (1973) and Mäler (1974), and in particular, Koopmans (1973), Dasgupta and Heal (1974), Solow (1974a), and Stiglitz (1974a,b). The literature is authoritatively surveyed in Dasgupta and Heal (1979). The surveys by Kamien and Schwartz (1982), and Withagen (1991) are also useful.

Consider the ILA model of Section 2.1 with the posited dynastic utility function. The production technology of the economy is now represented by the linear homogeneous function, $Y_t = F(K_t, A_t L_t, D_t)$, with $F: \Re_+^3 \to \Re_+$. D_t is the amount of the resource used in a period, and R_t is the stock of the resource at any date. We assume that the production function is twice continuously differentiable and concave with (using the previous notation for partial derivatives), $F_K > 0$, $F_{KK} < 0$, $F_L > 0$, $F_{LL} < 0$, $F_D > 0$, $F_{DD} < 0$. Notice that the assumptions mean that the economy does not exhibit constant returns with respect to the accumulation of capital and labor alone. The case which has received most attention is when F is of the constant elasticity of substitution form,

$$Y_t = [\alpha_1 (K_t)^v + \alpha_2 (A_t L_t)^v + \alpha_3 (D_t)^v]^{1/v},$$

where

$$\sum_{i=1}^{3} \alpha_i = 1 \quad \text{and} \quad -\infty \le v \le 1.$$

When $v = 0$ this reduces to the Cobb–Douglas function, where $Y_t = K_t^{\alpha_1}(A_t L_t)^{\alpha_2} D_t^{\alpha_3}$. The elasticity of substitution, which we denote by s (where $s = 1/(1-v)$), turns out to be critical in determining the extent to which it is possible for society to substitute out of finite resources and into other factors of production in order to sustain growth. First we give some important definitions (which stem from Dasgupta and Heal (1979)).

Definition 1: The resource is *necessary* if $D_t = 0$ implies $Y_t = 0$.

Definition 2: The resource is *essential* if the only sustainable rate of per capita consumption for the economy is zero.

If $s > 1$ then no input is necessary in the production process and the resource is both unnecessary and inessential (as we shall see this condition, and others, have been rediscovered in the endogenous growth literature). In this case it is possible for the economy to substitute out of the resource. If $s < 1$ then substitution possibilities are restricted. Each input is necessary for production and the resource is essential.

The stock of the resource again evolves according to $R_{t+1} = 1 = R_t - D_t$. There are no extraction costs. Assume that the dynasty owns the resource and that the price of a unit of the resource is q_t (notice that since we are assuming zero extraction costs the price of a unit of the stock of the resource in the ground is equal to the price of a unit of the flow). As in the previous section there is a competitive market where firms buy the resource in each period to maximize profits. Now the dynasty has the nontrivial problem of deciding on the dynamic supply of the resource.

The firm chooses K_t^d, L_t^d, D_t^d in each period to minimize costs. Homogeneity of the production function implies, $y_t = f(k_t, d_t)$, where $d_t = D_t/A_t L_t$ is the resource extracted per effective unit of labor. As in previous sections we model the firm in a way as to let the dynasty make all the dynamic decisions. Similar results would follow from allowing the firm to own the resource and repatriate profits to the dynasty (what is important for the present characterization is not who owns the resource but rather that someone does – it is important to stress that this is not in general true, a vital point to which we return later). Note that in the present case Euler's theorem states, $F = F_K K_t + F_L A_t L_t + F_D D_t$.

The dynasty now faces the following constraints. The first is the period-by-period budget constraint, the second limits the flows of the resource over time to the total available stock.

$$K_{t+1} - (1-\delta)K_t + C_t = w_t A_t L_t + r_t K_t + q_t D_t,$$ (2.37)

$$\sum_{t=0}^{\infty} D_t \le R_0.$$ (2.38)

We abstract from the further constraint that investment is irreversible, i.e., $C_t \le w_t A_t L_t + r_t K_t + q_t D_t$, since this is slack along paths with positive net investment. Dividing the above constraints by $A_t L_t$ and denoting $R_t / A_t L_t$ by Δ_t, we can write them in per effective person terms as

$$(1+g)(1+n)k_{t+1} = w_t + r_t k_t + q_t d_t - c_t + (1-\delta)k_t,$$ (2.39)

$$\sum_{t=0}^{\infty} (1+g)^t (1+n)^t d_t \le \Delta_0.$$ (2.40)

Note that the stock constraint for the resource is

$$\frac{R_0}{A_0 L_0} \ge \frac{D_0}{A_0 L_0} + \frac{D_1}{A_1 L_1} \frac{A_1 L_1}{A_0 L_0} + \cdots.$$

Now form the Lagrangean for the dynastic optimization problem. Call this Problem 6.

$$L = \sum_{t=0}^{\infty} \beta^t U(c_t A_t) + \sum_{t=0}^{\infty} \lambda_t \{w_t + r_t k_t + q_t d_t - c_t + (1-\delta)k_t - (1+g)(1+n)k_{t+1}\}$$
$$+ \omega \left\{ \Delta_0 - \sum_{t=0}^{\infty} (1+g)^t (1+n)^t d_t \right\}.$$

The necessary conditions are:

$$\beta^t A_t U'(c_t A_t) = \lambda_t,$$ (2.41)

$$\lambda_t q_t - \omega(1+g)^t (1+n)^t = 0,$$ (2.42)

$$-\lambda_t (1+g)(1+n) + \lambda_{t+1}(1+r_{t+1} - \delta) = 0.$$ (2.43)

Using Eqs. (2.41) and (2.42) and the fact that in a competitive equilibrium the price, q_t, is equal to the marginal product of the resource, denoted f_d, implies

$$\beta^t A_t U'(A_t c_t) f_d = \omega (1+g)^t (1+n)^t.$$ (2.44)

The left-hand side of Eq. (2.44) is the marginal benefit of using up an extra unit of the resource per effective labor unit at date t discounted back to time zero. The right-hand side is the marginal cost of using up this increment of resource at date t, i.e. the present value of the resource ω, times the unit resource increment per effective unit of labor, times the number of effective labor units at date t.

We can derive another fundamental result by leading Eq. (2.42) and eliminating ω:

$$\lambda_{t+1} q_{t+1} = (1+g)(1+n) \lambda_t q_t.$$ (2.45)

Now use Eq. (2.43) to substitute λ_{t+1} out of Eq. (2.45); this gives

$$0 = \lambda_t \left[\frac{q_{t+1}}{1 + r_{t+1} - \delta} - q_t \right].$$ (2.46)

Hence the term in brackets in Eq. (2.46) must be zero, rearranging this formula gives

$$\frac{q_{t+1} - q_t}{q_t} = r_{t+1} - \delta.$$ (2.47)

This result, first derived by Hotelling (1931) and hence called the Hotelling rule, says that the price of the resource rises over time at the net interest rate. The intuition for this is immediate: by arbitrage, the return to holding the resource in the ground must be equal to the return to holding capital.

We now consider the social planning problem for this economy, denoted Problem 7. Since the resource is privately owned and markets are complete, intuition suggests that the allocations characterized above are efficient. This intuition is correct. However, we are also interested in determining whether the presence of an exhaustible resource alters the characterization of optimal population policy. Problem 7 is almost identical to Problem 6, except that the budget constraint is removed and replaced by the social feasibility constraint. This constraint is written

$$k_{t+1}(1+g)(1+n) = f(k_t, d_t) - c_t + (1-\delta) k_t.$$ (2.48)

Note, $f_k > 0$, $f_{kk} < 0$, $f_d > 0$, $f_{dd} < 0$. The intensive form of the production function, f, inherits the properties of F in the natural way. The necessary conditions for Problem 7 are now Eqs. (2.48) and (2.41) and the following two conditions:

$$\lambda_t f_d(k_t, d_t) - \omega(1+g)^t (1+n)^t = 0,$$
(2.49)

$$\lambda_t (1+g)(1+n) - \lambda_{t+1}[1 + f_k(k_{t+1}, d_{t+1}) - \delta] = 0.$$
(2.50)

The Hotelling rule now becomes

$$\frac{f_d(k_{t+1}, d_{t+1}) - f_d(k_t, d_t)}{f_d(k_t, d_t)} = f_k(k_{t+1}, d_{t+1}) - \delta.$$
(2.51)

An optimal plan must satisfy the further necessary (transversality) condition for optimality that the resource be completely exhausted asymptotically.

From the above models, we can deduce the behavior of both the decentralized and the "planned" economy over time and in steady state. We first discuss the main results that one can derive from this framework. As in the literature we state these results in terms of the definitions of "necessity" and "essentiality". Notice that these definitions concern feasibility and not optimality. For example, it might be possible to sustain a positive level of consumption eternally, but yet this might not be the optimal thing to do.

Firstly, if $g + n = 0$ then in the Cobb–Douglas case the necessary conditions for the resource not being essential are a zero depreciation rate ($\delta = 0$) and a greater share of capital than the resource in output, $\alpha_1 > \alpha_3$. These conditions are also sufficient. To see why this is so, we show by construction, the existence of an infinite horizon extraction path with constant per capita consumption if and only if this inequality holds. Consider a dynamic path where output and consumption are constant over time. Consider, for simplicity the case where population is normalized to unity, in this case we have that $K_{t+1} - K_t = \kappa > 0$. From this it follows that

$$\frac{Y_{t+1}}{Y_t} = \frac{K_{t+1}^{\alpha_1} D_{t+1}^{\alpha_3}}{K_t^{\alpha_1} D_t^{\alpha_3}}.$$
(2.52)

Using the fact that $Y_{t+1} = Y_t$, Eq. (2.52) is a difference equation determining the extraction path for the resource in this case. This is

$$D_{t+1} = D_t (x_t)^{-\alpha_1/\alpha_3},$$

where $x_t = [t\kappa + K_0]/[(t+1)\kappa + K_0]$. Note that $x_t < 1$. The key issue now becomes the feasibility of this path. It is feasible if the sum $\sum_{t=0}^{\infty} D_t$ converges to less than or equal to R_0. This will be the case, if and only if $\alpha_1 > \alpha_3$. The sustainable level of consumption is then deduced from the initial size of the stock, since this will determine D_0 and hence output. In this case, even with zero technological change the economy can

maintain sustained consumption. Over time the input of the resource must fall, however, if $\alpha_1 > \alpha_3$ this can be offset by capital accumulation. If the inequality is not satisfied, then consumption must decline to zero asymptotically. This result was first derived by Solow (1974a). The fact that zero depreciation is required is a special feature of the type of depreciation we have assumed and is not general (Dasgupta and Heal, 1979: Chapter 7).

If $g + n > 0$ then a necessary condition (still in the Cobb–Douglas case) for the resource to be inessential is $g > n\alpha_3$. Again, this turns out to be sufficient (see Stiglitz, 1974a: Proposition 4). The ratio g/α_3 can be interpreted as the rate of resource augmenting technical change. This last condition has immediate implications for population growth. The higher is the rate of population growth, the harder it is for this situation to be satisfied. The basic intuition for this is identical to the standard neoclassical model. Higher population growth implies higher capital deepening, and this makes it harder for the economy to generate sustained consumption. For the resource not to be essential, it must not be "too important" for production. Notice that this inequality can never be satisfied if population growth is positive and there is zero technical progress. On the other hand, if population is constant, then the resource is always inessential if there is positive technical change.

These results tell us something about the feasibility of certain paths, but they are uninformative about what society actually wants to do. Whether or not it is optimal for the dynasty or society to have continued consumption growth depends on whether the return to accumulating is high enough. This depends, when $g = 0$, on whether the asymptotic marginal productivity of capital is greater than or less than the sum of the social rate of discount and the population growth rate (Dasgupta and Heal (1974: Proposition 8) for the case where $n = 0$). This condition has been extensively studied in the recent literature on endogenous growth (see Section 3.3). Notice that in the Cobb–Douglas case the asymptotic marginal product of capital is zero so that even if $\alpha_1 > \alpha_3$ so that sustained growth is feasible, it is not optimal.

Alternatively, Stiglitz (1974a) showed in the case where $g > 0$ that if the rate of technological progress is larger than the rate of discount then the optimal path is characterized by increasing consumption. If the rate of technical progress is sufficiently high, then sustained growth of consumption is feasible independently of the elasticity of substitution. As many authors have pointed out (e.g. Kolstad and Krautkraemer, 1993) for capital–resource substitution to generate continual consumption increases, it is necessary that the average and marginal productivity of the resource goes to infinity. It is not clear that this assumption is realistic empirically, or even consistent with basic physical principles.

Dasgupta and Heal (1979) give a sharp characterization of the optimal program when population is constant, technical change is zero and the production function is Cobb–Douglas (see Ingham and Simmons (1975) for growing population). If there is zero discounting, then per capita consumption rises monotonically over time. In this case, the economy accumulates a large capital stock and more than compensates for

the declining resource. If, on the other hand, there is positive discounting, then consumption asymptotes to zero. It does so monotonically if discounting is high, but if the discount rate is low the path of consumption per capita first rises and then falls towards zero.

Are the types of restrictions on parametric production functions discussed above at all realistic? Slade (1987) provides a useful discussion of the empirical status of these conditions. There seems to be no consensus about even the sign, let alone the magnitude, of the elasticity of substitution between capital and resources. There are difficult aggregation problems and estimates run from −3.2 (Berndt and Wood, 1975) to 1.43 (Pindyck, 1979). Berndt and Wood also find that, for US data, the shares of capital and resources (for which they use energy) in output are almost identical. There is evidence of resource saving technical progress, but this tends to be different in different sectors of the economy. Some technical progress is resource saving, and some is resource using (e.g. Jorgenson and Fraumeni, 1981). This makes it difficult to say much at an aggregate level.

2.3.2. *Optimal population*

The implications for the optimal path of population in the models of Section 2.3.1 differ little from the basic neoclassical models of Section 2.1. We observe here that the assumption of exponential population growth is certainly odd. As Dasgupta and Heal (1979) put it, "our concern is in the main part with the implications of a finite earth for the growth possibilities open to an economy. In this context the assumption of an exponentially rising population size is an absurdity, if only for reasons of space". Now increases in population have both capital and resource diluting costs and, with an average utilitarian formulation of the social objective function, no benefits. With a total utilitarian maximand, the issues are again identical. The most complete treatment of this problem appears in Dasgupta and Mitra (1982) (see also Lane, 1977). Dasgupta and Mitra show that the optimum path for population is characterized by the Keynes–Ramsey rule, the Meade–Sidgwick rule, the Hotelling rule, and transversality conditions for the capital and resource stocks. As in Dasgupta (1969), they show that there is no optimal program, if utilities are not discounted. They then show that, if future utilities are discounted, the optimal path for population implies that the population converges to zero. Intuitively, this follows from the results discussed above. With discounting, consumption goes to zero in this case, and when population becomes controllable the optimum reduces the population as consumption falls. The introduction of exhaustible resources, therefore increases the costs of population size in the social welfare function. This result extends that of Koopmans (1973) to a model where capital accumulation can potentially substitute for the depleted resource. While it is feasible to have equilibria with a constant population experiencing positive consumption for ever, such paths are not optimal.

2.3.3. Finite lives

The majority of the resource literature has been in the (implicit) context of dynastic models. We wish to make one point about finite lives. The main difference here is the possibility that the resource will not be extracted efficiently in a competitive equilibrium. OLG models with resources can generate the same type of dynamic inefficiency which can occur in simple OLG models of capital accumulation. The intuition for this is the same. Dynamic paths can be inefficient because the economy as a whole does not satisfy the transversality condition. Similarly, with resources, a dynamic path which satisfies the Keynes–Ramsey rule and the Hotelling rule may imply asymptotically inefficient underuse of the resource (the resource is "overaccumulated"). This result is proved formally in Homburg (1992).

2.3.4. Renewable resources

We now propose a simple formal framework for thinking about renewable resources. To keep the analysis tractable, we ignore exhaustible resources in this section. Renewable resources come in many forms from land, forests, acquifers, and complete local ecosystems, to global resources such as the climate and atmosphere. These clearly have widely differing implications concerning the extent to which one might be able to define property rights over them. The ownership structure is of course vital for our formalization and the welfare properties of decentralized equilibria.

Renewable resources are hard to include formally into growth models in convincing ways. The dynamics of environmental resources, for example, seem to be nonlinear, and we have little information which allows us to model them simply in aggregate models. We sketch the issues involved. One can write down optimal growth models which have steady-state growth paths where resources are conserved over time and per capita income grows due to capital accumulation and/or technical change. The real issue with environmental and renewable resources is the decentralization of such a path. Resources, particularly global ones, do not lend themselves to well-defined property rights. For local renewable resources, we also caution that the standard property rights solution must be applied with care. In this case, one cannot expect the laissez faire extraction path to mimic the optimal path, and one can construct models in which equilibria imply inefficient extraction and ultimate exhaustion of a renewable resource. The effects of population growth are closely related to those in previous models, a higher rate of population growth tends to reduce both physical capital per person and the level of the environmental stock per person, both along a transition path and in a steady-state equilibrium. Optimal population raises the previous issues and is again characterized by the Meade–Sidgwick rule, if society cares about the number of people alive rather than just per capita welfare.

Many aspects of economy–environmental interaction have received partial treatment. For example, the question of the effect of pollution on the economy over time has received treatment under a variety of various assumptions. The first model of this type was suggested by Keeler et al. (1971), and developed by Brock (1977) and Gruver (1976). Mäler's (1974) book also develops models which encompass this issue.

In the 1980s, however, the scope of these models has been widened. Pezzey (1989) provides an excellent overview of the "capital theoretic" approach to economy–environment interaction. Barbier (1989) develops a similar model, see also Mäler (1991). We begin by assuming that the aggregate production function of the economy for the produced good depends not only on produced capital and effective labor, but also on both the stock of a renewable resource, denoted E_t (the "environment"), and the flow of this resource over a period, S_t. The formalization does not distinguish between the quantity and quality of environmental resources (for example, pollution/waste reduces the stock but clearly in some cases pollution may affect the quality rather than the quantity or vice versa). A good example is soil degradation (Dasgupta (1982) discusses many of the issues in modeling natural resources). In general, it would be desirable to distinguish between a fall in soil nutrients and humus on the one hand, and erosion of the soil altogether (by wind or water). To highlight the special nature of renewable resources we think of the stock as being a public nonrivalrous good. The flows, since we shall treat them as inputs into production processes are private goods. Now

$$Y_t = F(K_t^c, A_t L_t^c, S_t, E_t) \tag{2.53}$$

where $F: \Re_+^4 \to \Re_+$. We assume that F is concave and twice continuously differentiable with partial derivatives, $F_S > 0$, $F_{SS} < 0$, $F_E > 0$, $F_{EE} < 0$. K_t^c and L_t^c denote the amount of capital and labor, respectively, allocated to the production of the consumption good. Allowing for both flow and stock effects encompasses all of the models in the literature (which typically concentrate on one or the other). For example, a forest can be harvested, and this harvest (timber) is a flow which increases production. However, the stock also matters. The total size of the forest affects greenhouse gas accumulation and maybe soil erosion and affects species diversity. Thus, one wants to allow for both effects in general.

The resource has a natural rate of recovery but is degraded as the result of production (we can think of this as "pollution" or the general result of waste products being deposited in the environment). We denote the quantity of capital allocated to abatement (or regeneration) activities (which we describe shortly) K_t^e, where $K_t^c + K_t^e = K_t$. We can also think of this as any activity which improves the quality of environmental resources. With L_t^c being the amount of labor devoted to current production, $L_t - L_t^c = L_t^e$ is devoted to abatement or environmental improvement. Denote the level of abatement activities by B_t. The resource stock evolves in the following way:

$$E_{t+1} = H(E_t, S_t, Y_t, B_t) \tag{2.54}$$

where $H: \Re_+^4 \to \Re_+$, concave and twice continuously differentiable. Here we might assume the following signs for the partial derivatives: $H_E > 0$, $H_{EE} < 0$, $H_S < 0$, $H_Y < 0$, $H_{YY} > 0$, $H_B > 0$, $H_{BB} < 0$. The specification of Eq. (2.54) simplifies, since it does not allow for a separate stock of pollution (as in Kamien and Schwartz (1982), for example). Instead we concentrate on the "net environmental quality", inclusive of pollution activities. Notice that we have also ruled out a direct negative effect of population on the evolution of the environment. If we were assuming that the economy was also constrained by exhaustible resources, then we would also be simplifying by assuming that the dynamics of environmental quality are not directly dependent on the extraction path of depletion of the exhaustible resource (though, there would be an indirect effect which works through the output of the consumption good and waste/pollution degrading the environment). To simplify the analysis, we make use of various plausible restrictions of Eq. (2.54) below. Abatement activities may take capital and labor resources so that there is an allocational problem in the economy. In any period, the total labor force (population) must be allocated between producing current output and abatement. The technology for abatement is denoted $B_t = G(K_t^e, L_t^e)$, where $G: \Re_+^2 \to \Re_+$. For simplicity, we assume that neither the stock of environment nor the exhaustible resource directly affect the abatement technology. We assume that this function is twice continuously differentiable and concave and has the following signs for the partial derivatives with respect to capital and labor inputs: $G_K > 0$, $G_{KK} < 0$, $G_L > 0$, $G_{LL} < 0$.

It is also important to consider the possibility that the state of the environment can directly affect welfare. To take this possibility into account, we respecify the objective function of the dynasty to be

$$\sum_{t=0}^{\infty} \beta^t U\left[\frac{C_t}{L_t}, E_t\right]. \tag{2.55}$$

We assume that the utility function, $U: \Re_+^2 \to \Re$, is again twice continuously differentiable, strictly increasing and strictly concave, with the following signs for the partial derivatives: $U_C > 0$, $U_{CC} < 0$, $U_E > 0$, $U_{EE} < 0$. It is also intuitive to assume that $U_{CE} \geq 0$. We exclude flow effects from utility since most of the plausible examples of amenity effects concern stocks rather than flows. We make no attempt here to discuss the conceptual problems involved in measuring these amenity services (which is clearly important for cost–benefit analysis), however, there is a lot of serious work on this. For example, Graves (1991) discusses fascinating attempts to value long-range visibility in the western USA which is considered to be important for viewing the scenery.

The most critical assumptions concern the structure of property rights in the economy. In particular: is the environment "owned" by anybody? Who, if anybody, is responsible for waste activities, and thus who would be the likely demander of abatement services? The most straightforward assumption is that there is a price for abatement services, m_t, and that these firms hire capital and labor from the dynasty in order to provide abatement services which are demanded by goods producing firms. To understand the nature of this problem, however, we concentrate on the characterization of optimal allocations. We then use this to discuss the welfare implications of alternative institutional arrangements and consequent distributions of property rights and the types of issues that surround the desirability of laissez faire paths.

The issue of property rights is of course critical in understanding the differences between the type of exhaustible resources we examined in the previous section and the renewable resources of this section. The type of environmental resources captured by our variable E_t tend to be goods over which it is logically and logistically very difficult to define property rights. There is a clear presumption that such resources will be inefficiently exploited in equilibrium. It is much easier to define property rights over a coal or oil deposit. This does not imply that the intertemporal extraction path will be efficient since, as is well known, such efficiency requires a complete set of contingent Arrow–Debreu markets. However, such resources do not generate the type of external effects which typically are associated with E_t, so potentially inefficiency seems to be of a differing order of magnitude.

Externalities and incomplete markets are intimately linked. The existence of widespread environmental externalities can be seen as stemming from the inability to define property rights which would allow the commodity to be traded (Mäler (1985a) provides a rigorous treatment of environmental resources from the perspective of Lindahl equilibrium and the Coase theorem). The role of institutions is especially important here. In the next section, we examine a typical local commons problem which arises in many situations in developing economies. An immediate response to this would be to think that the problem can be resolved by properly defining property rights. While we agree with this statement in general, one has to be very careful with the way such a scheme is implemented. Systems of property rights have important implications for income distribution. This point, stressed by Starrett (1972), has recently been raised in the context of developing nations by Dasgupta and Mäler (1995) and Van Arkadie (1989). As Van Arkadie puts it, "Thus while there has been a widespread presumption that a movement toward securely held registered title is economically desirable, recognition of the problems involved has been slower to emerge. For example, conferring land tenure rights on sedentary agriculturalists (already apparent occupants) may disrupt a system of pastoral seminomadism, based on rights of passage and of dry season grazing, which represented a sophisticated response to a particular ecological problem. Likewise, the allocation of land rights to an individual may misinterpret and disrupt arrangements within the family (displacing the rights of women, for example)". Many societies, while lacking the type of extensive formal system of property rights which characterizes much of the developed world, may nevertheless have developed highly sophisticated institutional solutions to allocational problems (see the discussions in Dasgupta (1993a) and Ostrom (1990)). Without an understanding of these, simple policy prescriptions are flawed. This perhaps explains some of the evidence that the types of productivity gains that we might expect to arise from defining private property rights do not always seem to occur (e.g., Migot-Adholla et al., 1991). One reason for this may be a connection between distribution and efficiency. Such a connection is common in models of incomplete contracts and markets and situations where there is asymmetric information. For example, in a general equilibrium model with incomplete markets, Roemer (1993) has studied the connection between distribution and efficiency in the context of pollution and other "public bads".

Simple "opening markets" solutions have other potential caveats. Starrett (1972) also pointed out that such situations naturally give rise to nonconvexities in production sets so that an equilibrium may not exist. In fact, there are robust situations where, while an equilibrium with markets does not exist, government designed tax equilibria may exist (see Dasgupta and Heal, 1979: Chapter 3).

We take the objective function of the social planner to be our amended dynastic welfare function, Eq. (2.55), and we start by ignoring the amenity value. We also make some restrictions on Eqs. (2.54) and (2.53). We assume that output of the consumption good does not directly affect the evolution of the environment and that abatement or regeneration expenditures can be captured by allocating capital to the task. This implies that Eq. (2.54) is now

$$E_{t+1} = H(E_t, K_t^e) - S_t.$$

We additionally assume that H is homogeneous of degree one. We also assume that there are no stock effects in the production function for the produced good and initially ignore technical progress. What now are the social feasibility constraints? The first is for the consumption–capital good, Eq. (2.56) below, and the second for the stock of environmental quality, Eq. (2.57). We write these in per capita effective form. To do this, we make several more simplifications. We assume that labor is only used to produce the consumption good,

$$k_{t+1}(1+n) - (1-\delta)k_t + c_t = f(k_t^c, s_t), \tag{2.56}$$

$$e_{t+1}(1+n) = h(e_t, k_t^e) - s_t. \tag{2.57}$$

This problem is obviously very complicated to analyze, so we begin by considering a much simplified version. We assume that population is constant (normalized to one), and for convenience we drop it from the production function. Output is produced using capital and a flow of resources, and resources regenerate in a way which is a strictly concave function of the current stock. We also start by ignoring amenity effects. Thus we have the constraints

$$K_{t+1} = F(K_t, S_t) - C_t + (1-\delta)K_t,$$ (2.58)

$$E_{t+1} = H(E_t) - S_t.$$ (2.59)

We assume that in this form H is still twice continuously differentiable, strictly increasing and strictly concave with derivatives, $H' > 0$, $H'' < 0$. To simplify the analysis, we take a recursive point of view (see Stokey et al., 1989) and formulate the Bellman equation for the social planner. Denote the value function for the planner $V(K_t, E_t)$. This function satisfies

$$V(K_t, E_t) = \max_{K_{t+1}, E_{t+1}} \{U(F(K_t, H(E_t) - E_{t+1}) + (1-\delta)K_t - K_{t+1}) + \beta V(K_{t+1}, E_{t+1})\}.$$

The necessary conditions are

$$U'(C_t)F_S = \beta V_E(K_{t+1}, E_{t+1}),$$ (2.60)

$$U'(C_t) = \beta V_K(K_{t+1}, E_{t+1}),$$ (2.61)

and the envelope conditions

$$V_K(K_t, E_t) = U'(C_t)[F_K + 1 - \delta],$$ (2.62)

$$V_E(K_t, E_t) = U'(C_t)F_S H'.$$ (2.63)

From these we derive the arbitrage relationship

$$H'(E_t)\frac{F_S(K_t, H(E_t) - E_{t+1})}{F_S(K_{t-1}, H(E_{t-1}) - E_t)} = F_K(K_t, H(E_t) - E_{t+1}) + 1 - \delta.$$ (2.64)

Since society can save for the future either by producing more of the consumption good today and storing it or by reducing the current exploitation of the environment so that the environment is more bountiful in the future, Eq. (2.64) says that at an interior optimum the marginal return to these two methods of saving must be equal.

A steady-state equilibrium in this economy will involve a set of constants E, K and C which satisfy the equations, $\delta K = F(K, H(E) - E) - C$, $F_K(K, H(E) - E) = \rho + \delta$, and the steady-state version of Eq. (2.64), $H'(E) = F_K(K, H(E) - E) + 1 - \delta$ (in a steady state $V(K_t, E_t) = V(K_{t+1}, E_{t+1})$, and these equations characterizing the steady state follow immediately from Eqs. (2.60)–(2.63)). Notice that these last two equations imply that $H'(E) = 1 + \rho$. Now standard (Inada type) assumptions on the renewal function guarantee the existence of an interior steady-state equilibrium. Denote this $E(\rho)$ where $E' < 0$ by the concavity of H. The equilibrium capital stock, denoted $K(\rho, \delta)$ satisfies $F_K(K, H(E(\rho)) - E(\rho)) = \rho + \delta$. Notice that across steady-state equilibria, as ρ changes, we have

$$\frac{dE}{dK} = \frac{F_{KK}}{H'' - F_{KS}(H'-1)} > 0. \tag{2.65}$$

Both the numerator and the denominator are negative. The sign of the denominator follows from the fact that H is concave, $H' > 1$, and since F is linear homogeneous and satisfies diminishing marginal productivity, $F_{KS} > 0$.

The two first-order conditions, Eqs. (2.60) and (2.61), implicitly define the policy functions $K_{t+1} = \Gamma(K_t, E_t)$ and $E_{t+1} = \Omega(K_t, E_t)$ and a two-dimensional dynamic system. Unfortunately, it is impossible to say much about the global or local behavior of these equations without putting a lot of special structure on the problem. There has been some work on the conditions under which models of this type may exhibit local saddlepoint behavior in the case where the environmental stock is interpreted as pollution. On this see Brock (1977), Becker (1982), van der Ploeg and Withagen (1991) and Tahvonen and Kuuluvainen (1991, 1993). Here one must remember that in reality we know very little about the form of the function H. In some cases, this may have discontinuities, in the sense that once the stock falls below a certain level, it cannot recover naturally. Clearly, aggregate dynamics are going to depend a lot on the form of this function, and so it would be surprising, if we could say anything very general.

If the economy converges to the above steady state, then it experiences a constant capital stock, constant environmental quality and constant per capita income.

To introduce population growth, we return to the assumption that $H(E_t) = H(E_t, K_t^e)$ where H is a linear homogeneous function. Population now grows at rate n. This implies that the environment can regenerate either because the stock is higher or because capital is allocated to regeneration activities. In this case, the constraints can be written in per capita terms as in Eqs. (2.56) and (2.57) above. Now we can solve the problem by directly substituting these constraints into the objective function

$$\sum_{t=0}^{\infty} \beta^t U(f(k_t - k_t^e, h(e_t, k_t^e) - e_{t+1}(1+n)) + (1-\delta)k_t - k_{t+1}(1+n)).$$

The necessary conditions are:

$$f_k(k_t - k_t^e, s_t) = f_s(k_t - k_t^e, s_t)h_k(e_t, k_t^e), \tag{2.66}$$

$$U'(c_t)(1+n) = \beta U'(c_{t+1})[f_k(k_{t+1} - k_{t+1}^e, s_{t+1}) + 1 - \delta], \tag{2.67}$$

$$U'(c_t)f_s(k_t - k_t^e, s_t)(1+n) =$$
$$\beta U'(c_{t+1})f_s(k_{t+1} - k_{t+1}^e, s_{t+1})h_e(e_{t+1}, k_{t+1}^e). \tag{2.68}$$

The analogue of Eq. (2.65) is

$$h_e(e_t, k_t^e)\frac{f_s(k_t - k_t^e, s_t)}{f_s(k_{t-1} - k_{t-1}^e, s_{t-1})} = f_k(k_t - k_t^e, s_t) + 1 - \delta. \tag{2.69}$$

A steady-state equilibrium for this economy is a set of constants, k, k^e, c and e which satisfy the following equations: first, a standard condition for the marginal product of capital, $f_k(k^c, e) = \delta + \rho + n$, next the steady-state version of Eq. (2.69), $h_e(e, k^e) = f_k(k - k^e, h(e, k^e) - e(1+n)) + 1 - \delta$. From these two equations, it follows that $h_e(e, k^e) = 1 + \rho + n$. There is also the steady-state form of the feasibility constraint, $k(n + \delta) = f(k - k^e, h(e, k^e) - e(1+n)) - c$. The final equation is the condition that the capital stock be allocated efficiently. This equation follows from Eq. (2.66):

$$f_k(k - k^e, h(e, k^e) - e(1+n)) = f_s(k - k^e, h(e, k^e) - e(1+n))h_k(e, k^e).$$

Notice that we are here making use of the approximations discussed in Section 2.1.

To see the effects in this type of model of allowing for the amenity value of the environment, let the momentary utility function take the separable form $U(c_t) + W(e_t)$, where U and W are both continuously differentiable, strictly increasing and strictly concave. In letting utility depend on the per capita resource stock in this way we are using the property that the resource is a pure public good. In this case, if the total stock is E_t, then this is also the stock per capita. In this case Eq. (2.68) has an extra term $\beta W'(e_{t+1})$ on the right-hand side. The effects of this is seen by re-deriving Eq. (2.69). In steady state, this now becomes $U'[f_k + 1 - \delta] = U'h_e + W'$. The equilibrium arbitrage relationship between capital and resource is altered because the resource has intrinsic value. In equilibrium, since $W' > 0$ we will have $f_k + 1 - \delta > h_e$. Now in the previous model, this would have unambiguously implied that the resource stock would have been higher in steady state. This is not necessarily the case here since the allocation of capital has to be determined endogenously. It could be the case that general equilibrium effects reduce the resource, though this seems a pathological case.

Now consider the effect of varying the rate of population growth. In a steady-state equilibrium, a higher rate of population growth increases the marginal products of both the resource and the capital stock. It seems plausible, modulo general equilibrium effects, that an increase in n would reduce the steady-state stocks of both capital and the resource. Hence, an increase in the rate of population growth has "capital widening effects" not just with respect to physical capital, but also with respect to natural capital. A higher rate of population growth, therefore, tends to lead to a lower quality of environment in steady state.

It is important to consider the nature of this equilibrium. With population growing exogenously at rate n, the equilibrium implies that the environmental stock is constant. This stems from the public goods assumption. However, a constant k^e implies that K^e is growing at the rate of population growth. In this equilibrium, as the economy accumulates capital, more of it is allocated to maintaining the resource stock so that a larger flow can be extracted from it to produce the consumption good. One could develop this model by adding exogenous technical progress. A major problem, however, in constructing steady-state equilibria is the behavior of the stock of natural capital. Does it make sense that the level of the environment can increase forever? The addition of technical change can allow the existence of growth paths along which per capita income grows and the quality of the environment continually improves. Even though increased per capita income may imply a higher degeneration of the environment, the stock is increased by allocating a larger and larger amount of resources (physical capital and in a more general model labor) to abatement and maintenance (such a model is constructed in van Marrewijk et al. (1993)). While constructing such a model is feasible, the extent to which it represents a realistic dynamic is not clear. A vital topic for future research is to understand more about the function H and attempt to develop better measures of renewable resources, which allow more convincing modeling.

Notice that Eq. (2.65) does not embody cross-sectional properties that are easily associated with the environmental Kuznets curve (i.e., that there is a nonmonotonic relationship between per capita income and capital–labor ratios and the quality of the environment). For example, think of countries as having converged to their steady states and as being distinguished by each having a different value for ρ. Eq. (2.65) shows that "impatient" countries with a low capital–labor ratio and low per capita income also have a low environmental quality. Similarly, "patient" countries have high steady-state stocks of both types of capital. In this model, Kuznets curve type behavior must be generated by the dynamics of the transition path. On the other hand, as the discussion on the previous page makes clear, once capital allocation between sectors is introduced, there is no logical reason why physical and environmental capital should move together, though perhaps this is the most plausible case in models, like the one considered, where environmental resources are used in producing the consumption good.

The types of necessary conditions studied above, taking into account not just the positive gain in future utility which comes from expanded technological possibilities, but also incorporating the negative side effect of increased environmental degradation, have recently been explored by Weitzman (1993a). He uses this to stress the fundamental point, that in the presence of environmental effects, the social rate of return to a project will typically be less than the private rate of return.

We now return to finite lives and optimal population. Finite lives have the usual implications. As in simpler models (without resources), it is possible to have paths where there is over-accumulation of resources, if there is not sufficient altruism between generations. The extra feature here, mentioned at the beginning of Section 2.3, is that when considering problems of decentralizing optimal allocations we have an inter-generational externality as well as an intra-generational externality (on which see John et al., 1995). Optimal population issues are standard. With no direct social benefit from the numbers of people, adding in renewable resources alters nothing. The optimal rate of population growth is negative. Adopting an objective function, such as Eq. (2.19), generates a version of the Meade–Sidgwick rule and generally an interior optimal rate of population growth under constant returns to scale.

3. Endogenizing population and technical change

In this section, we bring the analysis of the previous sections into closer contact with the data, and moreover make it more useful for normative and policy purposes. In particular, we bring fertility and mortality within the scope of behavior (Section 3.1), and develop their implications for the exploitation of resources (Section 3.2). This is an important step. The first two sections consider models either with no technical progress or with a constant exogenous rate of technical progress and concentrate on the types of conditions necessary to generate a "demographic transition". Imagine a world with no technical progress and resources. If population growth is exogenous and positive, such an economy is doomed if resources are nonrenewable (Section 2.3.1), if resources are renewable then there may be steady states where consumption per capita stabilizes at a positive level (Section 2.3.4). Endogenizing population forces us to specify the reasons that parents have children. If altruism is a plausible one of these then we might expect the prospect of bringing impoverished children into the world (something which happens on the transition to "doomsday") to put a break on fertility. Even without altruism, this may occur if children are normal goods so that as income falls fertility falls along with consumption. Our concern in this paper is to articulate the nature of the relationships between population, resources and development. Endogenizing fertility in plausible ways suggests that population growth may well adapt both to development (the "demographic" transition) but also to resource constraints and the onset of the doomsday. We aim to clarify these issues.

Section 3.2 moves away from the general development to stress situations in which there is no trade-off between protecting the environment and population growth. Section 3.3 introduces the central issues involved in the endogenization of technical progress. We then (in Section 3.4) examine the interaction between population growth and endogenous technical change. This area has deep roots both in economic history (exemplified by the work of Boserup, Habakkuk and McNeill) and also in the more recent formal literature (e.g. the existence of "scale effects" in endogenous growth models). Allowing for the joint endogeneity of technical progress and technical change can radically alter the tenor of the results of the previous sections. We examine mechanisms through which population growth in itself may foster increased technical change, and through which technical change influences individual decisions on fertility and mortality. We bring together some of the threads of the discussion in the final two sections to understand the feasibility of growth when the use of natural resources in a dynamic economy and the interactions between resource usage and demographic behavior are explicitly taken into account.

3.1. Models of endogenous fertility and mortality with exogenous technical change

In this sub-section, we build on the analysis of Section 2.2 by endogenizing fertility and mortality. Much of the impetus for this work stems from the research of Gary Becker, in particular his (1960) article and more recent book (1981) (although Leibenstein (1957) also made an important early contribution). Becker has not only extended decision theory to examine fertility and other aspects of family behavior, but has also examined, and has indeed stressed, the aggregate implications of these models (which is primarily our concern). The main aggregate implication of interest to our concerns is how fertility responds to development and the conditions under which a demographic transition will take place. This has motivated much of the literature.

Although population growth is simultaneously determined by fertility and mortality, the largest part of the literature focuses on endogenizing fertility rather than mortality since the latter has seemed more sensibly treated as exogenous. However, this consensus seems to be changing. The evidence in fact suggests that the stylized facts about trends in mortality in relation to modern industrial growth and the demographic transition are just as systematic and startling as those about fertility (Mokyr, 1993). As such, there seems little rationale for not endogenizing mortality (see Ray and Streufert, 1993). To keep the analysis within bounds, we do not treat these issues formally.

It is traditional, therefore, to start by endogenizing fertility. A good discussion of many of the different models in the literature is contained in the books by Nerlove et al. (1987) and Razin and Sadka (1995). There are two basic types of models: Altruistic models assume that the main reason for having children stems from some form of interdependence between the preferences of adults and children. If parents care about the utility of children, for example, then children must exist for children to experience utility. Parents then transfer resources to them to influence their utility. Such transfers go under the rubric of affecting "child quality" (the notions of child "quality" and "quantity" go back to Darwin (1871)). This can imply either transfers of a consumption good or subsidies aimed at human capital accumulation. This type of model, studied by Becker and Lewis (1973), is used by Razin and Sadka (1995) to study how increases in parental income (perhaps as part of the process of economic development) affects the choice between the quantity and quality of children. Nonaltruistic models assume people have children either because they like having children, or because of the resources they can extract from them, or the beneficial exchanges they can make with them. Stark (1995) shows that people may also want to have grandchildren in models where children learn how to behave by watching their parents. Grandparents want their children to look after them, but they will only do so if forced to do so by having to show a good example to their children (so they in turn will be looked after in old age).

Models where adults get utility from having children assume that the number of children is an argument in the utility function, and that it is a choice variable (we will henceforth treat the number of children as a continuous variable; not necessarily an innocuous assumption (Sah, 1991)).

Parents may be able to make exchanges with children which they cannot make with nonfamily members because the ties of kinship can be important in enforcing incomplete contracts. We partition these latter models into two; the "old-age security motive" and the "children as producer or capital goods" models. The first model develops the idea that capital and insurance markets are typically incomplete in underdeveloped countries, and having children is often the only way of providing for old-age needs. Cassen (1976) remarks, "it seems likely that high fertility is a characteristic of societies in which the family is the only source of social and economic security" (see Nugent, 1985). Important formalizations of this idea are due to Neher (1971) and Willis (1980) (see Razin and Sadka (1995: Chapter 4) and Nerlove and Raut in this Handbook). The "children as producer goods" model is based on the fact that, in poor economies, much production goes on within the household unit or family farm. Children play important roles in production and are needed to produce for the family.

All of these models can be used to explain the demographic transition. In models where parents are altruistic towards children, the opportunity cost of time devoted to child raising rises with development (since real wages rise), and this tends to reduce fertility. On the other hand, higher income may increase fertility if children are normal goods. These models tend to argue that development raises the return to child quality relative to quantity, and thus leads to substitution away from high fertility. In terms of old-age security models, the use of children as financial insurance rests on the unavailability of alternative assets. As the economy develops, these become available and, as Neher (1971) puts it, "the good asset (bonds) drives out the bad asset (children)" (though the introduction of new assets can also have positive income effects). Finally, models which stress the productive role of child labor in home production can also address the demographic transition. Azariadis and Drazen (1993) develop a model where children work on the family farm and bargain with their parents over the output. They then show how urbanization increases the outside option of the children and lowers the return to parents from having children (see also David and Sundstrom, 1988). There is debate as to the plausibility of this model. While Caldwell (1990) has calculated that the net wealth flows from children to adults can become positive by the middle of adolescence, Cassen (1976) argues that the evidence is not conclusive on whether or not having a child is really a good investment. In fact, Fogel and Engerman (1971) calculated that a slave raised from infancy brought a positive return to his owners after 27 years. Moreover, Stark (1991) has argued that the opening up of the formal economy may in fact generate an increased demand for children, since we do in fact observe remittances from children, and formal wages are both higher than and imperfectly correlated with agricultural productivity.

In developed economies, it is typical to think of the main motivation for childbearing as being altruistic in nature, and it is assumed that parents care directly for the utility of their children. However, even here it seems plausible that parents derive direct utility from having children. In developing economies, however, it is widely agreed that this misses some of the key motives for childbearing we have mentioned. In reality, all of these motives must be present. People in developing countries do not care less for their children than people in developed countries, it is just that the institutions and constraints in which they operate are different so that we suppress other motives when modeling what we perceive to be the critical aspects of behavior. A complicating feature is that, in reality, preferences are endogenous. For example, co-operative models of the family are often motivated by intra-family altruism, but such altruism must develop after marriage, and, thus, preferences in this literature are implicitly endogenous.

There are then a plethora of different assumptions about the motivations behind fertility. This is problematic since different models have different implications for social welfare and, in particular, whether or not there is a "population problem". In one extreme case, imagine that adults care about the utility of their parents and the utility of their children in a way which is sufficient to generate the dynastic utility function. In this case, population growth may be first-best efficient since the dynasty (society) solves the same optimization problem that a social planner would solve. Once we deviate from this case, however, the situation becomes considerably more complex. Consider a model where children were brought into the world just to work on the family farm and where parents do not care about their welfare. In this case, the rate of population growth might still be Pareto optimal, it might not be possible to reduce the number of children without harming the welfare of parents, but if society weighted the welfare of children explicitly, the rate of population growth might well be socially inefficient.

Inefficiency may also stem from more direct external effects; for example, rapid population growth rates may directly crowd the environment or per capita levels of natural resources, or it may congest infrastructure and public goods (though here the effects are ambiguous since new people add both to government expenditures and revenues). There is also the nature of decision-making within the family to consider. Even though such interaction is intrinsically noncompetitive, the models in the literature assume that the family acts as a unified decision-making unit. This seems a very strong assumption and has been criticized on empirical grounds by Alderman et al. (1995). It has typically been assumed that a corollary of the "unified household" axiom is that outcomes of family decision-making would be efficient, in particular, given the ability of family members to negotiate with each other. This assumption has recently been challenged in an important paper by Udry (1994), and if his view is correct, then noncooperative behavior within the household may be a potential source of inefficiency in fertility decisions. For example, if husbands and wives bargain noncooperatively, over the number of children to conceive, or if fertility is determined cooperatively, but other aspects of household decision-making are noncooperative (for example, the allocation of time to existing children), then the equilibrium fertility rate will not be efficient and, in general, will be too high (see Baland and Robinson, 1996a,b). Social norms of various sorts may also generate inefficient population growth if they become dysfunctional. Dasgupta (1993a,b) stresses that social norms may have a self-fulfilling character leading to multiple equilibria. A nice example of this is provided in Crook (1978). Individuals' preferences may be a function of family size relative to the average since this determines a family's influence in local political and social institutions (for example, the village council). It is clear that there may be many Nash equilibria in a game where individuals choose family size to maximize relative family sizes. There also seems to be strong evidence that some poor people lack information and knowledge about family planning. This is witnessed by the continual finding that there is an unmet demand for fertility limitation (see, for example, Birdsall, 1988).

We now consider the one-sided altruistic (parents care for children but not vice versa) model of Becker and Barro (1986, 1988, 1989) (these papers build on the work initiated by the seminal paper of Razin and Ben Zion (1975)). This model is a nonoverlapping generations model where each person lives only for one period and cares about his/her own level of consumption, the number of children that he has and the welfare of each child. This model generates a dynastic utility function of the form of Eq. (2.22) where the discount factor is explicitly related to the degree of intergenerational altruism. Our treatment is concise since this model is treated in great detail in Nerlove and Raut (1994). The utility function of a representative generation is

$$U_t = v(c_t) + a(n_t)n_t U_{t+1},$$ (3.1)

where $a(n_t)$ is the "altruism function". This takes the form $a(n_t) = \alpha(n_t)^{-\varepsilon}$ where $\alpha, \varepsilon \in (0, 1)$. Here, the utility of a parent depends on own consumption and both the number and utility of children, with the latter two terms being weighted by the degree of altruism. Recursive substitutions yield

$$U_0 = \sum_{t=0}^{\infty} \alpha^t (N_t)^{1-\varepsilon} v(c_t),$$ (3.2)

where

$$N_t = \prod_{s=0}^{t-1} n_s.$$

If the altruism function is linear in n_t (i.e. $\varepsilon = 0$), this objective function collapses to Eq. (2.22), the total utilitarian maximand where $\beta = \alpha$. Note that Eq. (2.1) can also be derived in this framework by assuming that a parent cares not about the total utility of his/her offspring, but rather about the average level of welfare. Eq. (3.2) is maximized subject to a sequence of budget constraints of the form

$$w_t + (1 + r_t)k_t = c_t + n_t(\vartheta + k_{t+1}). \tag{3.3}$$

In Eq. (3.3), the parent inherits an amount of capital, k_t, earns wage income from a unit of time inelastically supplied and allocates this between own consumption, bequest per child, k_{t+1}, and child rearing costs per child, $\vartheta > 0$. This problem has the first-order conditions

$$v'(c_t)(n_t)^\varepsilon = \alpha(1 + r_{t+1})v'(c_{t+1}), \tag{3.4}$$

$$v(c_t)[1 - \varepsilon - \sigma(c_t)] = v'(c_t)[\vartheta(1 + r_t) - w_t]. \tag{3.5}$$

Becker and Barro primarily study the steady-state equilibria of this economy under the assumption that the production function exhibits constant returns to scale (particularly in their 1989 paper). In this case, the dynasty chooses a constant steady-state rate of population growth. It is immediate from the above necessary conditions, however, that the fertility rate at any date is positively related to the interest rate and the degree of altruism. The unsurprising feature of Eq. (3.5) is that it is a version of the Meade–Sidgwick rule.

From this point on in the paper, we abandon making causal statements about how population growth affects development and resource utilization, but rather concentrate on the properties of their joint dynamic behavior.

3.2. Natural resources in economies with endogenous population

How does the endogenization of fertility affect the dynamic paths of resource extraction and exploitation that we have studied? Start by considering the Barro–Becker model of the previous section with diminishing returns to scale. In this case, the steady state is characterized by a zero rate of population growth. A similar result is deduced by Eckstein et al. (1988) in a nonaltruistic model where the only motivation for having children is that parents get utility from having children. They show that, with an essential resource present, there are diminishing returns to capital and labor combined, so that when population grows exogenously, per capita consumption must converge to zero. However, once fertility is endogenized, the economy converges to an equilibrium with constant population, and constant and positive per capita income. Their results essentially replicate, in a decentralized economy, the results of Dasgupta (1969) (discussed in Section 2.1.3) that when there are decreasing returns to scale, there is a finite optimal population. Eckstein et al. (1988) assume that the production function is a linear homogeneous function of capital, labor and the fixed resource (land). In a steady-state equilibrium, the ratio of land to labor must be a constant. Since the stock of land is a constant, population must be constant in such a steady state. The economy converges to this equilibrium because fertility and consumption move together. As adults get poorer, they reduce their fertility (children being normal goods) and eventually converge to a situation with constant fertility and consumption.

The situation is little different when an exhaustible resource is a necessary input in the production function. Under certain specifications of intergenerational preferences, population growth converges to zero (recall that without exogenous technical progress, such a model cannot sustain a positive consumption level with positive population growth). The key parameters determining steady-state equilibria are those describing altruism, the impatience of agents, the costs of rearing children, the amount of net resource flows between children and adults, and, in the OLG framework, the social welfare weights assigned to different generations. Parameter changes which lead to an increase in steady-state population typically reduce the steady-state resource stock (though this is not necessarily the case as we saw in Section 2.3). With renewable resources, one can define steady-state equilibria with positive population growth, constant per capita consumption, and a constant stock of environmental resources.

What about capital accumulation? In models where population is endogenous, higher rates of population growth will typically be associated with lower per capita income and lower rates of accumulation of capital per worker. For example, economies with higher degrees of altruism towards children would tend to have a lower capital–labor ratio in steady state. As we make clear in Section 3.3, however, the types of parameters which are exogenous in these models, and thus determine the steady-state values of endogenous variables, do not make for a convincing theory of development. It seems to us highly unlikely that strong altruism, for example, is a significant cause of either the lack of development or the high rate of population growth that we observe in many developing economies. Both are a joint product of other factors hampering development.

The only existing formal work on the interaction between renewable resources and fertility that we are aware of is due to Nerlove (1991, 1993) and Nerlove and Meyer (1993). These papers stress that population growth and resource extraction can be locked into a vicious circle in the context of a local commons phenomena (this interrelationship has also been stressed by Dasgupta (1993)). Higher population growth leads to more resource depletion which reduces the marginal productivity of the resource. In order to offset this, families have more children, further depleting the resource, and so on. Models of this sort, with severe externalities, often possess multiple Pareto ranked equilibria, some with high fertility and a low resource stock, and others with low fertility and a high resource stock. Such models allow for a potential role for policy to coordinate individual behavior on the desirable equilibria. We now discuss two examples of how, when population is endogenous, there are examples where good policy would help resolve both environmental and population "problems". The first of these is a model of multiple equilibria closely related to the above discussion.

3.2.1. Local environmental-demographic complementarities

Our example is based on degradation of the rangeland of Botswana and is designed to illustrate what the World Bank (1992) calls "no trade-off" situations which contradict the widespread belief that preserving the environment implies sacrificing consumption or welfare. In Botswana, the primary form of livelihood is cattle ranching. The rangeland is common land. While cattle fulfill social roles (in terms of status), they are also the primary intertemporal store of value in the society. There is evidence (Barbier et al., 1989; Dasgupta and Mäler, 1994) that this interrelationship can have perverse effects. In particular, the evidence suggests the presence of self-fulfilling expectational effects. The quality of the range affects the productivity of cattle. Since each herder perceives himself or herself to be too small to affect the quality of the range, he or she makes decisions about how many cattle to hold treating the quality of the range as given. However, in equilibrium, the quality of the range is a function of the joint decisions of herders since the more cattle that the range has to support the lower its quality, and the less productive is each cow. Children are the primary method of looking after cattle, and, thus, children can be thought of as a producer good which is complementary to cattle. This induces an interesting dynamic interaction between population growth and environmental degradation.

In Robinson and Srinivasan (1995a), we model this phenomena by building a simple overlapping generations general equilibrium model. We show that the economy has Pareto ranked multiple equilibria each of which may be supported by self-fulfilling sets of beliefs. Herders at any date must decide how many cattle to breed in a period (given their inherited stock), and how many children to have to look after the cows. They do this in the light of the expected quality of the rangeland. The evidence suggests that there is a strong dominance of the income effect of changes in the quality of rangeland over the substitution effect. Consider that herders imagine that the quality of the rangeland will deteriorate in the next period (perhaps a drought is anticipated – beliefs can also be conditioned on "sunspots"). If the income effect dominates the substitution effect they respond to this by increasing their herd of cattle and having more children. The increased stock of cows which these conjectures induce has the effect, in equilibrium, of leading to the degradation of the range which confirms the beliefs. Thus, one may have Pareto ranked equilibria with inefficient equilibria characterized by low environmental quality and high population growth, and efficient equilibria having high environmental quality and low population growth.

What is the source of inefficiency in this model? The clear problem is the "commons" nature of the environment. The rangeland is being overused because individual herders impose costs on others by increasing their herds which they do not take into account. This problem is intertwined with the fact that cattle are the only medium of saving, and so is exacerbated by the rudimentary nature of the financial infrastructure in the economy. One solution to this problem is to introduce an alternative store of value. Another is to internalize the "commons problem" by defining property rights over the rangeland (modulo the problems we discussed in Section 2.3.4).

The multiple equilibria in the above model give a nice example of "no trade-off" situations. If policy measures can change the nature of the equilibrium set and lead to the coordination of the economy on the Pareto preferred equilibria, then the rate of population growth will fall and the quality of the environment will improve.

3.2.2. Infrastructure, health, mortality and fertility

We now describe informally a simple theoretical model which stresses other types of complementarities which emerge between environmental issues and population growth rates which lead to "no trade-off" situations (the analysis is presented formally in Robinson and Srinivasan, 1995b). The aim of this model is to describe a key class of situations where policies to deal with inefficiencies will promote both an improved environment and the demographic transition.

In many less developed economies, there is a presumption that there is underinvestment in public goods and vital infrastructure. Socially efficient investment in infrastructure (such as the provision of potable water, refuse collection and sewerage) increases the health of individuals and is a form of investment in human capital. This makes individuals more productive (since productivity depends on their health as in the nutrition model of efficiency wages (see Dasgupta, 1993a)). If individuals wish to have children because of the "old age security" motive, the number of children that parents wish to have would depend on infant mortality (as in Sah (1991) or Ehrlich and Lieu (1991, 1993)). An improvement in infrastructure reduces child mortality implying that parents need to have less children to guarantee a surviving child to care for them in old age. Note that the improvement in the health of parents may also increase the opportunity cost of rearing children since market wages may increase. Both of these effects tend to reduce fertility (there is an effect which works in the opposite direction, which is that if parents are healthier, this increases the chance they will survive to old age and hence increases the expected return to having children). We show that increasing infrastructure expenditures raises welfare and reduces infant and adult mortality and parental fertility. Here, policies to improve the environment are complementary to the goals of reducing fertility and mortality.

3.3. Theories of endogenous technical change

In this section, we introduce the central issues surrounding the endogenization of technical progress. This literature has been extensively surveyed in Grossman and Helpman (1989) and Barro and Sala-i-Martin (1995). Other valuable surveys are Romer (1989), Raut and Srinivasan (1993), Hammond and Rodriguez-Clare (1993), and Schmitz (1993).

We start with an observation due to Solow (1956) (and recently rediscovered by Jones and Manuelli (1990)). Remove the exogenous technical progress from the basic growth model of Section 2.1.1 (set $g = 0$, $A_t = 1$). In this case, the economy converges to a steady state with a constant capital–labor ratio. Level variables grow at the rate n. Why does this occur? The key reason is indefinitely diminishing marginal productivity of capital. Along a transition path to the steady state, capital accumulates relative to labor. As the capital-labor ratio rises, the marginal product falls. In essence the marginal product is the return to saving. Consider the consumption Euler equation. If the economy is to grow over time, then it must be the case that the dynasty wishes the path of consumption per capita is upward sloping, $c_{t+1} > c_t$. This implies $U'(c_{t+1}) < U'(c_t)$. For this to be desirable it must be the case that

$$\frac{\beta[1 + f'(k_{t+1}) - \delta]}{1 + n} > 1. \tag{3.6}$$

The left-hand side of this inequality is monotonically decreasing in k_{t+1}. For small capital–labor ratios, the Inada condition implies that this inequality will be satisfied. However, the second Inada condition (used to guarantee the existence of a steady state) implies that, at some point, $\beta(1 + f'(k_{t+1}) - \delta) = 1 + n$. At this point, the return to accumulation has fallen so low that the dynasty desires $U'(c_{t+1}) = U'(c_t)$, and hence $c_{t+1} = c_t$, and the economy stops growing. In order to guarantee sustained growth in such an economy, all that is necessary is to put a sufficiently large lower bound under the marginal product of capital. In this case inequality (3.6) will always be satisfied. There are various technologies which will do this, in one the aggregate production function has the form $F(K_t, L_t) = AK_t + BL_t + K_t^\alpha L_t^{1-\alpha}$. In this case, the marginal product of capital goes to A as the capital–labor ratio goes to infinity, and if A is sufficiently large, then inequality (3.6) is satisfied. Alternatively, a CES production function with an elasticity of substitution greater than one will suffice (as Solow (1956) noted in his original paper).

From this perspective, it is easy to understand the results in the literature. The different mechanisms which authors have proposed to generate endogenous growth are just different methods for stopping diminishing marginal productivity bringing accumulation to a halt. Consider the seminal paper by Romer (1986). Consider the production function of a particular firm j, $Y_t(j) = A_t(j)F(K_t(j), L_t(j))$, where $A_t(j)$ represents the "state of technology" at date t. Romer argued that new technology of "knowledge" was generated by the process of aggregate capital accumulation itself and that this process was external to the firm (in the spirit of a "Marshallian externality"). If technology evolves as a function of aggregate investment, then the level of technology at any time is a function of past cumulative investment, or in the absence of discounting the aggregate capital stock. Assume that there are a continuum of identical firms distributed uniformly on the unit interval with a representative firm being indexed, $j \in [0, 1]$. Hence, $A_t(j) = A(K_t, j)$, where $K_t = \int_0^1 K_t(j) \, \mathrm{d}j$. The ideas underlying this model are closely related to Nicholas Kaldor's notion of a "technical progress function", recently revived by Scott (1989). Romer also appealed to the idea of learning-by-doing, put in a growth theory context by Arrow (1962).

How might this model generate sustained growth? As a firm builds capital, it expands its own production possibilities, but inadvertently it also generates new knowledge and ideas, and, thus, shifts out the production possibility frontier for all firms. One sees immediately that, if this effect is sufficiently strong, the effect of diminishing marginal productivity for an individual firm, holding A_t constant, can be just offset by the resulting increase in technology caused by the actions of all firms. To see what "sufficiently strong" means consider the Cobb–Douglas case where, $A(K_t, j) = K_t^\phi$, and $Y_t(j) = K_t^\phi K_t^\alpha(j) L_t^{1-\alpha}(j)$. Each firm treats K_t^ϕ parametrically. The private marginal product of capital is, therefore, $\alpha K_t^\phi K_t^{\alpha-1}(j) L_t^{1-\alpha}(j)$. Now integrate over the set of firms (recalling that they are all identical) to get the aggregate

$$\int_0^1 \alpha K_t^\phi K_t^{\alpha-1}(j) L_t^{1-\alpha}(j) \, \mathrm{d}j = \alpha K_t^{\phi+\alpha-1} L_t^{1-\alpha}.$$

If Eq. (3.6) holds, then the capital–labor ratio will be increasing over time. Note that $f' = \alpha k_t^{\phi+\alpha-1} L_t^\phi$. Under what conditions would the marginal product of capital be bounded away from zero as the capital–labor ratio increased? Clearly as long as $\phi + \alpha - 1 \geq 0$. In the case where $\phi + \alpha = 1$ then the marginal product of capital is a constant equal to $\alpha L_t^{1-\alpha}$, and it becomes easy to state a condition such that inequality (3.6) will hold for all time.

To see the implications of this technology for the growth rate of the economy over time, we need to embed it in a general equilibrium model. For simplicity, we remain in the single firm framework. Assume that preferences are represented by the constant elasticity of intertemporal substitution utility function, $U(c_t) = c_t^{1-\sigma}/(1 - \sigma)$. Following standard methods, we can derive the Euler equation for the dynasty:

$$c_t^{-\sigma} = \beta \left[\frac{1 + r_{t+1} - \delta}{1 + n} \right] c_{t+1}^{-\sigma}. \tag{3.7}$$

With a competitive capital market, the interest rate will be equal to the marginal product of capital, hence

$$r_{t+1} = \alpha K_{t+1}^\phi K_{t+1}^{\alpha-1} L_{t+1}^{1-\alpha}.$$

The production function in per capita terms is

$$y_t = K_t^\phi k_t^\alpha,$$

and hence,

$$r_{t+1} = \alpha K_{t+1}^\phi k_{t+1}^{\alpha-1} = \alpha L_{t+1}^\phi k_{t+1}^{\phi+\alpha-1}.$$

Substituting into the Euler equation and re-arranging,

$$\frac{c_{t+1}}{c_t} = \left[\frac{\beta(1+\alpha L_{t+1}^\phi k_{t+1}^{\phi+\alpha-1}-\delta)}{1+n}\right]^{1/\sigma}. \qquad (3.8)$$

Romer (1986) considers $n=0$ and $\phi+\alpha=1$. In this case, the right-hand side is a constant.

Notice however that if $\phi+\alpha>1$, then the economy exhibits increasing growth rates over time. The fact that the condition for a balanced growth path is balanced on a "knife-edge" has received criticism. While it is true that the condition for steady-state growth is not generic in the parameter space (formally, fix the Cobb–Douglas technology for the economy, then the set of economies which exhibit steady-state constant growth is a closed set of Lebesgue measure zero), the same could be said of constant returns to scale. However, an intuitively plausible "replication" argument can be offered in its favor. There seems to be no replication argument in favor of constant marginal productivity of capital. More generally, one might see this as a problem stemming from the restrictive nature of steady-state analysis. While focusing on steady states is attractive analytically, it is not clear that it is very useful as a description of actual growth experiences. Historically, growth has been rather spasmodic and cyclical (see Mokyr (1990) or Jones (1989) for many examples). Romer himself argues that the idea of increasing growth rates over time may not be so unreasonable as it sounds. He argues that the growth rate of the "leading nation" has historically been increasing (from the Netherlands to Britain, to the United States, to Japan, to Korea and Taiwan, and now perhaps to China)

Eq. (3.8) reveals something interesting about population growth. It shows immediately that the growth rate over time is an increasing function of the constant population under the conditions assumed by Romer. This has been called a "scale effect" in the literature. Such a state of affairs is not necessary however. In fact, examining Eq. (3.8) reveals that the presence of positive population growth rates now allows the condition for endogenous growth to be satisfied even in the case where $\phi+\alpha<1$. The scale effect can be removed by simply defining the external effect to be in terms of the aggregate capital–labor ratio instead of the capital stock. The question is: which specification seems more in the spirit of the motivation for the specification? To see how this works, simply re-write the production function as $Y_t = k_t^\phi K_t^\alpha L_t^{1-\alpha}$ and re-work the calculations.

These results show that in a one-sector economy, what is required for endogenous growth is constant returns to capital alone, or more generally, to a factor which can be accumulated. In Romer's model, it is external increasing returns to scale which generates the sustained growth. The above discussion suggests that this is not necessary since there are other ways of putting a bound under the marginal product of capital. Unfortunately, these other methods have drawbacks in a one-sector model. Firstly, as observed by Raut and Srinivasan (1993), the technology must be such that output can be produced without any factors other than capital. Second, as pointed out by Jones and Manuelli (1992) and Boldrin (1992), such a technology is not sufficient to generate growth in standard two-period OLG models where capital accumulation is generated only by saving from wage income. In the one-sector case, in order to get away from these implications, one is forced to assume that there are increasing returns to scale.

The external increasing returns also generates inefficient growth paths. Since individuals do not take into account the effect of capital accumulation on the level of technology, the private return to investment is less than the social return, and growth and accumulation is inefficiently low in the decentralized economy. In contrast, if the growth is generated by constant returns to scale but with a lower bound on the marginal productivity of capital, then, in the decentralized economy, the growth path is efficient. The empirical relevance of external economies is hotly disputed. Recently, at industry level, Caballero and Lyons (1993) have found evidence supporting the existence of external economies. Interestingly, Backus et al. (1992) also find some evidence in favor of pure scale effects across countries.

A primary attraction of external increasing returns is that it allows a competitive equilibrium to exist. There is an issue of substance here. An obvious approach to generating sustained growth would be to introduce a technology for improving A_t. We could think of firms in the economy dedicated to developing new technology and selling this to firms producing consumption goods. Unfortunately, with competitive factor markets and constant returns to capital and labor alone, there cannot be any revenues left over to pay for technology. This suggests that a more plausible aggregate production function would be $Y_t = F(K_t, L_t, A_t)$ with constant returns to all three factors together. Romer has argued strongly for such a specification. An alternative to external increasing returns would simply be to set the increasing returns be internal to the firm but introduce imperfect competition. The study of dynamic general equilibrium models of imperfect competition is far more complex technically.

We are sympathetic to the arguments of Grossman and Helpman (1994) and Solow (1994) that putting a bound under the marginal product of capital, while it "works" in a formal sense, does not seem to capture the essence of the growth process. The one-sector growth model has always been regarded as a "parable", in that it is clear that growth does not occur simply as the result of accumulating more and more of a homogeneous capital good. Historically growth has been connected to the introduction of entirely new goods and production techniques, and the continual improvement of existing ones. Recent research has provided a more promising line of research with tractable models which treat these features (albeit in a very rudimentary way). Romer (1987, 1990), Aghion and Howitt (1992) and Grossman and Helpman (1989) show how growth can be sustained by either the continual improvement in the quality of existing goods or the expansion of the set of available goods (either consumption or intermediate goods). In these models, growth is sustained because, plausibly, there are no diminishing returns to improving goods or introducing new goods.

There are various other models which achieve endogenous growth in a similar way. For example, Barro (1990) generates an aggregate technology which is linear in the capital stock by introducing public capital into the technology. Another approach is that of Lucas (1988). Lucas essentially reinterpreted the labor augmenting technical change as human capital. The aggregate production function is $Y_t = F(K_t, H_t L_t)$. L_t is now "raw workers" and H_t is the stock of human capital possessed by each individual. Lucas presented two models of human capital accumulation. The first was one of learning-by-doing where human capital accumulates passively as a linear function of current employment:

$$H_{t+1} = [\delta_H + \iota L_t] H_t .$$ (3.9)

In the second model, a separate sector for the accumulation of human capital (following Uzawa, 1965) is introduced. In each period, workers are allocated between producing for current consumption and producing more human capital. This is thus a two-sector model. Consider the learning-by-doing model. It is easy to see that the formulation of learning embodied in Eq. (3.9) will generate a scale effect in exactly the same way as the Romer model (again this can be removed by specifying things in per capita terms).

Assume that population is constant, and, for convenience, set $L_t = L$. The aggregate technology is $Y_t = F(K_t, H_t L)$, by homogeneity of degree one, we can write this as $y_t = f(k_t)$, where $y_t = Y_t / H_t L$, $k_t = K_t / H_t L$. In either of these human capital models, the key to the generation of growth is that there is no diminishing marginal productivity to the accumulation of human capital. This process can therefore drive increases in per capita income forever.

The recent literature has provided us with simple analytical methods to verify the conditions under which an economy will exhibit sustained growth. However, it is not clear that in themselves they add much to our understanding of the process of development. In reality, much of this process stems not simply from factor accumulation (which in the broad sense is at the heart of this literature), but from changes and innovations in political and social institutions which govern and condition the process of factor accumulation (see Rosenberg and Birdzell (1986) for an emphasis on institutional innovation and change). For example, North (1981) stresses that the key to whether or not a society grows or stagnates is in understanding the incentives of agents and rulers to create property rights and, in general, implement efficient policies. This view rejects the notion that cross-country experiences can be explained on the basis of different rates of time preference or the elasticity of intertemporal substitution, or, for that matter, simply on the basis of differences in technology. While it is true that the difference in per capita income between the US and Haiti can be described in terms of different technology or human capital, this does not explain why these differences are what they are. Such examples suggest that, in order to explain the distinction between a "miracle" and a "disaster", we need a much more ambitious political economy framework with a much broader scope than any present in existing growth models.

This message in fact emerges from the empirical work on growth (see particularly the discussion in Barro and Sala-i-Martin (1995) and Sala-i-Martin (1994)), though when considering this literature one must be very careful making causal inferences since there are severe identification and simultaneity problems. How does the growth model explain cross-country growth differences? If all countries have the same parameters, then they all converge to the same steady-state growth path and eventually have identical growth rates (so called "absolute convergence"). In this model, countries which have a lower level of per capita income must have a higher growth rate if there is any aspect of diminishing marginal productivity. This implication is false empirically. If, more realistically, we assume that countries have different parameters, then there is no unambiguous connection between the level of per capita income and its growth rates. The models imply that countries converge to different steady states determined by their different parameters ("conditional convergence"). Therefore, differences between countries are explained by these parameters. These are typically parameters describing preferences (such as impatience and the willingness of individuals to substitute consumption intertemporally), technology and government policy (such as taxes and expenditure). It seems improbable that a convincing theory of comparative development could be constructed on differences in preference parameters (unless one had some way of endogenizing these). What about technology? While it is clear that Zaire, for example, has a worse technology than the United States, to use this as an explanation for why their growth experiences have been different, does not advance us above simply assuming that growth rates are exogenous. To build a convincing theory here, we need a model of the incentives to adopt and transfer technology, and this has not been provided by the literature thus far. Most attention then has concentrated on the latter set of parameters, those describing government policy parameters, augmented by other variables describing social and political institutions. The implication of this is "bad growth" is caused by "bad policy" (high taxation of capital income for example) and "bad" institutions (such as ill-defined property rights or ineffective procedures for enforcing contracts). But in reality, policy variables and institutions are not exogenous. To argue that policy is at fault forces us to articulate a model where both political decision-making and the incentives to create institutions are endogenized. In short, we need a theory of bad policy and bad institutions. This, the growth literature has not provided, though it has been implicitly discussed in the more policy orientated literature on development (see Srinivasan, 1985; Findlay, 1990; Krueger, 1993).

Mokyr (1990) has described one fully fledged political economy model of growth and stagnation. His theory rests on the idea that in a world where compensating transfers cannot be made, innovations and new technologies take rents away from agents with sunk investments (exactly this phenomena occurs in the model of Aghion and Howitt (1992) for example). Technical progress in reality is rarely Pareto improving and has large effects on the distribution of income and of political power in society (witness the nineteenth century battle over the repeal of the Corn Laws in England). Agents with vested interests in the status quo have an incentive to suppress innovations through political mechanisms. Mokyr argues that the key to growth is in setting up institutions which allow innovators to succeed and prosper. One interpretation of Mokyr's ideas have been formalized in an interesting paper by Krusell and Rios-Rull (1992). Other recent research by Acemoglu (1994) and Tornell (1993) have begun to think about private incentives to create socially efficient institutions. This is an area where the returns to future research seem particularly large.

3.4. Population and endogenous growth

We now consider the effects of population size and growth on economies with endogenous technology. We also discuss normative issues in this section and we review the arguments that population growth may be beneficial rather than inimical to economic growth. These arguments are important because many of them allow population growth in itself to generate technical progress. The basic neoclassical models assume that population growth is bad because it increases the burden of raising the capital–labor ratio. In considering optimal population, this effect can be offset by giving value to people as such. This represents one approach. Another is to question the technological assumptions underpinning the neoclassical model. In particular, many scholars have argued that population growth is a key part of social and technological progress, and that these effects are completely missing from the basic neoclassical model. It seems important to take this seriously given the empirical evidence discussed in Section 1. There we noted the overwhelming failure to find negative effects of population growth on economic growth. This suggests that there may well be positive effects to balance the negative effects of the neoclassical model.

3.4.1. Population and economic development: the pros and cons

As we have mentioned, the relationship and causal interactions between population growth and development have given rise to much speculation. The Malthusian view is well known. This relates to a pre-industrial society where technology is fixed or exogenously changing and population growth is determined by a series of positive or preventative checks (or as Heckscher (1949) referred to the former, times when "nature audited her accounts with a red pencil"). There is much evidence that both checks were at work historically (Habakkuk, 1971). Population growth was limited by delayed marriage and rudimentary contraceptive techniques, and mortality was a severe disciplining force. These forces established an equilibrium for many centuries. For instance, it has been estimated (see Habakkuk, 1971) that the population of the Mediterranean countries and France was about the same in 1700 as it had been in the first century AD. This homeostatic equilibrium was changed during the eighteenth century (from about the 1740s onward). There seem to have been two main factors. The first (recently stressed by Razzell (1993)) was a fall in mortality due to improvements in domestic hygiene and improved medical practices (such as the widespread vaccination against smallpox (Razzell, 1978). Why did not population growth equilibrate to this situation through reduced fertility? The answer seems to be that the process of industrialization was causing structural changes in the fertility process. The movement from the countryside to the towns broke up social norms of delayed marriages. Industrialization also allowed children to be sources of income earlier and allowed women to work and earn income (thus also accelerating marriage). This latter phenomena is interesting since the European historical evidence suggests that marriage was often delayed until a high enough standard of living could be guaranteed. On the other hand, employment opportunities for women raise the opportunity cost of having children for women and thus reduce births. While it is necessary to have income to raise children, it also takes time. However, the evidence seems consistent with both views since it suggests that opportunities for employment in cottage and domestic industries were more favorable to fertility than factory work (Tucker, 1963).

The main question raised by Habakkuk is the relationship between the growth in population and the beginnings of the industrial revolution. While the Malthusian channels are well known, Habakkuk concentrates on five channels through which population may stimulate growth. Firstly, there may be pure economies of scale to a large population due to the division of labor and the creation of social overhead capital. Second, inspired by Lewis (1954), a large population may keep the wage rate low and thus encourage investment by capitalists. While this might be bad for per capita incomes initially, it may allow the economy to develop over a threshold from which sustained growth would be feasible. Thirdly, the pressure of population on finite natural resources may stimulate investment and induce capital substitution which induce a cumulative process of industrialization. Fourthly, population growth may have beneficial effects on effective demand, particularly by stimulating urbanization, and lastly, population pressures may induce people to work hard. As Habakkuk puts it, "I am not arguing that the effects of population growth were simple or straightforward or that they were invariably favorable. But I find it difficult to interpret the eighteenth century without supposing that, on balance, population increase was a stimulus to the development of the economy. Thus population growth and economic growth continuously interacted and this interaction is perhaps the principal reason why the population increase was sustained". (Habakkuk, 1971: p. 48.)

Habakkuk's theme finds many echoes in the literature. North and Thomas (1972) argued that population growth was a stimulant to industrialization. Their thesis is the broad one that population growth, by changing the factor price ratio, induced the institutional changes which led to the industrial revolution (expansion of trade, property rights). The notion that population fluctuations are a cause of institutional change is widespread. It occurs in Lal's (1988) theory that the Indian caste system was a response to labor shortage, and also in many accounts of the adoption of the "hacienda system" in Latin America following the precipitous drop in the native population due to imported diseases (Halperin, 1993). Echoing this, Hayami and Kikuchi (1982) state: "the basic force inducing agrarian change in Asia is the rise in the return to land resulting from strong population pressure". While the positive effects of these pressures have been stressed particularly by Boserup, there seems to be no presumption that in fact such institutional innovations will be conducive to economic growth.

The anti-Malthusian camp suggests that diminishing returns do not set in. There are various reasons for this. An early one emerged in the heyday of the Keynesian revolution. Hansen (1939), echoing earlier work, hypothesized that slow or stagnant population growth had a bad effect on demand and the economy. Hicks (1939) suggested "one cannot repress the thought that perhaps the whole Industrial Revolution of the last two hundred years has been nothing but a vast secular boom, largely induced by the unparalleled rise in population". Both Kuznets (1966) and Hirschman (1958) argued that population growth could stimulate growth through scale effects and innovation.

Another central reason stems from the observation that "the division of labor is limited by the size of the market". Larger populations may expand the size of the market and thus allow more productive techniques to be adopted through a finer division of labor. This may not hold useful policy advice for developing economies, however. As the World Bank (1984) points out, countries like Singapore and Hong Kong have successfully reaped the division of labor by exploiting international trade, thus giving their industries access to a much larger set of potential customers than domestic residents. Another argument is that larger populations have more geniuses, and that, presumably, there are increasing returns to geniuses (this argument is presented in Simon (1981) and has been recently formalized by Kremer (1993)). Another stems from the adage that "necessity is the mother of invention". In a series of works, Boserup (1965, 1981) has argued that population growth, by putting pressure on land, resources and wages, induces innovation. Her ideas have found support in several pieces of careful empirical work (see for example, Hayami and Ruttan, 1987; Pingali and Binswanger, 1987). While this is undoubtedly the best documented positive effect of population growth, it is not without prominent counterexamples. Birdsall (1989) cogently argues that the history of Bangladesh, for example, cannot be understood in this way. The National Research Council (1986) argue that the evidence suggests that the rate of return to agricultural innovation is already high and does not need to be stimulated by population growth. On the other hand, Kelley (1988) argues that the population density may have been important in inducing the adoption of "green revolution" technologies in Asia. The anthropologist Geertz (1963) argued that population pressure was closely linked to the extension of irrigated rice agriculture in Java. On balance, Kelley (1988) concludes, "A critical component in untangling the relationships between technology and demographic change is the impact of population pressures on institutions (land tenure arrangements, government policies, and the like), especially because the new technologies flourish mainly where institutional conditions are favorable. Regrettably, no generalization is possible here." Srinivasan (1987) reaches a similar assessment.

One problem with this argument is that there is not a clear theoretical model of how population density induces innovation (see Darity (1980), Pryor and Maurer (1982), Robinson and Schutjer (1984) and Lee (1986, 1988) for attempts at (in our view, not wholly satisfactory) formalization). If innovation is profitable why does it not occur at low population densities? It could be that a high population density allows for greater social learning, a phenomena which it has recently been argued was important in the adoption of "green revolution" technologies. Hence there is a positive externality to population density which reduces the adoption cost of new technology. Yet much of the literature has stressed that population growth stimulates institutional change though the precise mechanism is unclear. Preston (1984) has argued that population growth could be good for development because development necessitates change which is often opposed by people with sunk investments or vested interests in the existing institutional or economic structure. This argument is of course reminiscent of that of Mokyr (1990) discussed in Section 3.

Simon, perhaps the most vociferous advocate of the positive effects of population, has explored various causal channels in a series of works (see Simon, 1977, 1981, 1986). He has stressed the ideas that there may be increasing returns to scale and that a larger population may allow for a greater division of labor and specialization in society. While he has developed simple models of this, traditional aggregative models of homogeneous capital accumulation and labor force growth with a neoclassical technology are not a good representation of the process of transformation and change which we call development. Economies of scale at this level do not seem the key issue. Simon and his co-authors (reported in Simon, 1986) have found evidence supporting the idea that population density has a positive effect on growth (see also our discussion of Kelley and Schmidt (1994) in Section 1). Supportive of this is the finding of James (1987) that, in a cross-section of 45 developing countries, the rate of growth of labor productivity in agriculture between 1960 and 1970 was positively related to population density, whereas that in manufacturing was not. However, Evenson's (1984) evidence does not support this.

On the negative side, apart from capital deepening issues enshrined in the neoclassical growth model, there is the problem of the crowding and overuse of public services and fixed costs. Rapid population growth often leads social services such as schools to become overstretched. As the World Bank (1984) puts it, "in the short run, ideas may be lost and Einsteins go undiscovered if many children receive little schooling".

Population growth has also been much discussed in relation to income distribution. Population growth may raise the share of capital relative to wages. The empirical effect of population on income distribution has been estimated to be significant and negative. Ahluwalia (1976) finds a positive relationship between the rate of population growth and the income share of the richest quintile, while the evidence summarized in McNicholl (1984) and Jha et al. (1984) suggests that "the negative effect of population growth on the income shares of the poorest 30 or 40 percent of households is usually pronounced". Given the serious problems with data on income distribution these results have to be treated with extreme caution. Lam (1987), for example, examines the causal channels from population growth to income distribution and concludes that there is little evidence supporting any of them. Of course, even if population growth did induce greater inequality, this is not necessarily bad for growth. Some authors in the dual economy tradition (who typically adopt a "Classical" savings hypothesis) see a rise in inequality as necessary for capital accumulation. For example, Kelley and Williamson (1974) found that considerably higher rates of population growth would have made little difference to Japan's development. This is due to the classical saving hypothesis offsetting capital shallowing effects. On the other hand, more recent evidence (Alesina and Rodrik, 1995; Persson and Tabellini, 1994) suggests that income inequality may be harmful for growth.

Increases in population which reduce the wage rate may also affect the direction of technical change. David (1975), for example, argued that relative scarcity of labor in the US in the nineteenth century affected the nature of technology that it was profitable to adopt and the path of technical progress ever since.

Population growth caused by poverty also tends to transmit poverty between generations. If richer people in society start to have fewer children and, thus, each child will be wealthier on average, this may have the effect of widening the distribution of income. In fact, this suggests that endogenous population growth and intergenerational wealth transmission effects may in themselves provide an explanation for the Kuznets inverted U hypothesis of income distribution.

Population growth has also been related to saving (see Hammer, 1985). Faster population growth rates give a higher dependency ratio (this is the opposite of the Samuelson (1975) model discussed in Section 2.2.2, where a greater number of children helps in making transfers to the old since children are not dependent), and this can reduce saving since more resources are channeled to rearing children. On the other hand, poor people save little, and most saving in underdeveloped economies is by relatively rich people. In fact one aspect of the problem of rapid population growth

is often thought to be the lack of saving media. Mason (1987) found that the net effect of population growth on saving was positive when per capita income growth was zero and negative when it was 4%. Kelley (1988) concludes, "the hypothesis of an adverse impact of age dependency on saving rates has not been generally supported in empirical studies", and McNicholl (1984) states, "what then can be said about the net savings or investment impact of rapid population growth? The answer appears to be very little". We note also that, in terms of the process of growth and development, recent research has downplayed the role of aggregate saving. The efficiency with which it is allocated seems to be at least, if not more, important.

One serious issue is timing. Rapid population growth may have long-run benefits (in Simon (1981), it takes 80 years in his simulation model for population to have a positive effect), but it certainly has short-run problems. We have not discussed urbanization in this paper, but this is closely related to population growth and causes large problems of adjustment in the development process.

3.4.2. Population and social welfare: the pros and cons

We have treated the normative issues of population level and growth in both intuitive and formal ways. The message of the neoclassical model is simple. Population growth is bad for per capita income, but can be socially optimal if society places weight on the number of people existing. Over time, as capital accumulates, it can be optimal to bring more people into society and optimal population growth is positive. The arguments of the last section suggest that population growth may have a positive effect on growth. Introducing these effects implies that population growth is all benefits and no costs! There is, however, a large literature that suggests that the adverse effects of population growth are not simply in reducing the capital–labor ratio. We now consider these. Taken seriously, they add extra costs to balance the extra benefits. Willis (1987), Lee (1990) and Lee and Miller (1991) are excellent sources for this as are the surveys by Kelley (1988), Birdsall (1989) and McNicholl (1984).

There have been many claims that population growth is detrimental for social welfare (if not directly for economic growth) because population growth induces externalities. Perhaps the most famous example of this is the idea that when individual parents decide on the number of children to have, they take the future wage rate that their child will earn as given (this may be important because it determines the child's standard of living which the parent cares about, or because it determines the ability of the child to make transfers to parents later in life). However, if all parents have more children, this will increase the labor supply and push down the wage. As Willis (1987) shows, this is a pecuniary externality and as such does not represent a true market failure.

Another important problem is the potential crowding of public goods which may be subject to congestion. Schultz (1987) shows that, although school enrollment rates are not affected by population growth, the quality of education is reduced. National Re-

search Council (1986) finds that resources per child within the family and in educational system fall with population growth. One might, however, regard the latter phenomena as a policy failure.

Another possibly adverse effect of rapid population growth stems from human capital externalities. These have been stressed in the recent theoretical growth literature (see Lucas, 1988, 1990; Shleifer, 1990). This literature argues that individual productivity may depend not just on the amount of human capital possessed by the individual, but also on the average level of human capital of co-workers, or some other reference group. If it is the case that what matters is average human capital and, as is the case empirically, resources given to an individual child are negatively related to family size, and this results in lower human capital in a wide sense (especially lower health and educational attainment (see Jha et al., 1994), then parents may not be taking into account the true social benefits and costs of having children. Human capital externalities suggests that the rate of population growth will be too high relative to the efficient rate and, moreover, that this will have an adverse effect on the growth rate of the economy.

As mentioned in Section 3.1, Baland and Robinson (1996a,b) also show that if the family behaves noncooperatively, then fertility will also be inefficient, and the presumption is that it will be too high.

One the other hand, Nerlove et al. (1987) show that a larger population implies that the cost of public goods per capita falls, and they argue that this is a positive externality. There is also the possibility that population growth may lead to crowding of resources in fixed supply. For example, the amenity value of resources may be reduced by crowding, or population pressures may disrupt the regeneration of environmental resources.

In the most careful and comprehensive empirical investigation of this issue, Lee and Miller (1991) identify possible population externalities as coming from a variety of sources, "dilution of the per capita value of collective wealth, dilution of costs of collective projects with public good aspects, incentive reductions due to proportional tax rates and the effects of the age distribution on the tax rate necessary to support public sector activities such as health, education, pensions, social infrastructure and other service". They find little empirical evidence that any of these are significant for developing nations.

In sum, what is surprising is that there are really remarkably few conceptually sound and empirically relevant externalities stemming from population growth.

3.4.3. A model of endogenous fertility and endogenous technical change

The first integration of endogenous fertility and endogenous growth is due to Becker et al. (1990). They take the Becker–Barro dynastic model and replace physical capital with human capital which is passed between generations. Since human capital accu-

mulates in a way which does not involve diminishing marginal productivity (as in Lucas, 1988), this induces a simple model of endogenous, unbounded growth.

A main motivation for a model of this type is to study the demographic transition. As we discussed in Section 3.1, a central achievement of choice theoretic fertility models has been to provide a simple framework for this. However, these models have been unsatisfactory in that they have treated the process of growth as exogenous to the fertility and mortality transitions (Ehrlich and Lui, 1990, 1994) study how mortality can interact with fertility in a model where infant and adult mortality (treated as exogenous) affect the incentives to have children). Indeed the analysis of Becker et al. (1990) shows that this feature can be significant. This paper also links with an older theoretical tradition which had considered how the dynamics of endogenous population and income growth could lead to multiple equilibria and "development traps" (see Nelson, 1956; Leibenstein, 1957). The ideas behind the model are simple. Becker et al. take the dynastic model of one-period lived agents and let parents allocate their time between producing a consumption good and teaching children. Children are born with some endowment of human capital and parental teaching adds to this. In the simplest version of the model, the consumption good is produced using just human capital (though the authors also extend the results to show that they extend to physical capital accumulation modeled in the same way as in Becker and Barro (1989)). The key assumption is that there are increasing returns to human capital accumulation. Hence when the stock of human capital is low, the return to accumulating more is low. This means that an economy with an initial low stock of human capital may not find it worthwhile accumulating more and gets stuck in a low level equilibrium with a stagnant level of human capital and therefore per capita output. This has the implication that the population growth rate will be high since the opportunity cost of having children is small. If on the other hand, the economy starts with a high enough initial stock of human capital, it can converge to an equilibrium with a higher level of human capital and low birth rates. Becker et al. (1990) argue that to understand the demographic transition, we need to understand how society moves from one equilibrium to another.

In a sense, this model incorporates both the demographic transition and a type of doomsday. This is because both steady-state equilibria are stable. If the initial stock of human capital is low, the economy converges to the equilibria with high fertility and stagnant growth. On the other hand, the assumptions about the technology of production ignore any resource constraint issues. In the low level equilibrium, there is nothing preventing population growth continuing forever.

3.4.4. Simple analytical mechanisms

We now discuss two simple analytical models where the rate of population growth can be important in driving technological progress and yet be consistent with a steady-state equilibria (unlike the scale effects studied in Section 3.3). One approach to for-

malizing existing notions about the relationship between population growth and technical change is to develop an alternative model of learning-by-doing. In Section 3.3, the rate of human capital accumulation depends on current employment, hence the level of human capital at any date is a function of cumulative past employment (Becker et al. (1990) assume that the rate of human capital accumulation depends only on the allocation of time of parents between teaching children and producing consumption so there is no scale effect in the model). An alternative specification for this learning technology is to relate the growth of human capital between two periods to the growth of employment between those periods:

$$\frac{H_{t+1}}{H_t} = \varphi \left(\frac{L_{t+1}}{L_t} \right). \tag{3.10}$$

In Eq. (3.10), we assume that φ is continuously differentiable with derivatives, $\varphi' > 0$, $\varphi'' \leq 0$, and $\varphi(1) = 1$.

To see the implications of such a model, consider an overlapping generations model with logarithmic utility, $\log C_t^1 + \beta \log C_{t+1}^1$. The aggregate technology takes physical capital, human capital and "raw labor" and transforms it into a single produced good (which is the same good as physical capital). The production function is $Y_t = F(K_t, H_t L_t) = K_t^\alpha (H_t L_t)^{1-\alpha}$. Individual agents supply one unit of labor to a competitive labor market when young and, due to logarithmic utility, save a constant proportion of this income which becomes the physical capital stock at the next date. For simplicity we assume that capital can be "eaten" after production. The dynamics of the economy are governed by Eq. (3.10) and the equation,

$$K_{t+1} = \theta L_t w_t = \theta(1-\alpha)L_t H_t K_t^\alpha (H_t L_t)^{-\alpha}$$

(where $\theta = \beta/(1+\beta)$). Assume that Eq. (3.10) is linear so that the equation for the accumulation of human capital is, $H_{t+1}/H_t = \sigma(L_{t+1}/L_t)$, where $\sigma > 0$ is a constant (this allows us to describe the dynamics as an autonomous difference equation). For simplicity, set $\sigma = 1$. In effective per capita terms (where $k_t = K_t/H_t L_t$),

$$k_{t+1}(1+n)^2 = \theta(1-\alpha)k_t^\alpha. \tag{3.11}$$

This model converges to a steady state with interior capital–effective labor ratio of

$$k = \left(\frac{(1+n)^2}{\theta(1-\alpha)} \right)^{1/(\alpha-1)}.$$

At such a steady state $K_t/H_t L_t$ is equal to a constant. This implies that $g_K = g_H + g_L = 2(1+n)$. Output per capita, $y_t = Y_t/L_t$, is

$$y_t = K_t^\alpha H_t^{1-\alpha} L_t^{-\alpha}.$$

The growth rate of output per capita is, thus,

$$g_y = \alpha g_K + (1-\alpha)g_H - \alpha g_L = \alpha 2(1+n) + (1-\alpha)(1+n) - \alpha(1+n) = 1+n.$$

Thus, in steady state, the economy exhibits a constant rate of growth in per capita income. This rate of growth is increasing in the rate of population growth since this directly feeds through into the way that human capital is accumulated in the economy.

This model can be seen in another light as one without human capital accumulation but where there are increasing returns to scale. Instead of the technology proposed by Romer (1986) consider Raut and Srinivasan (1994). Motivated by the work of Simon and others, Raut and Srinivasan consider the case where the external economies stem not from capital accumulation but rather from population expansion. They develop an aggregate technology of the following form: $Y_t = A(L_t)F(K_t, L_t)$, where $A(L_t)$ formalizes the notion that the level of technology depends on the level of population and employment. This model is interesting since fertility is also endogenous. In their paper, Raut and Srinivasan examine a logistic specification for this function and analyze the type of dynamics that the economy may exhibit. They show the existence of multiple steady-state equilibria (which should not be surprising given the external effects) with constant levels of population and constant per capita income. However, the model may also (depending on the exact nature of the external effects) exhibit sustained growth in population and per capita income or even chaotic dynamics, depending on the form the externality takes.

3.5. Resources and endogenous growth

We now discuss models of natural resources with endogenous technology, but assuming that population is exogenous. This is a field which has received very little attention with, to our knowledge, only the work of John and Peccenino (1994), van Marrewijk et al. (1993), Smulders (1995), and Bovenberg and Smulders (1995) in existence. None of these papers concentrate on the central interaction between population growth and technical change.

A convenient place to start our discussion is Rebelo (1991). From the above analysis, it should be clear that the formal requirement to generate endogenous growth in a one-sector model is the presence of a bound under the marginal product of capital. To stay with a convex technology in a one-sector model we need to assume that any finite resource is not necessary in the sense of Section 2.3.1 This is not an attractive assumption. In the one-sector framework, to adopt a technology which does not have this implication, one is forced to move to a model with increasing returns to scale essentially because the capital and the consumption good are the same good. However, it is important to realize that one does not need constant returns to scale in the production of the consumption good even if all factors can be accumulated. What Rebelo showed was that once one moved beyond the one-sector set-up, all that was required for endogenous growth in consumption per capita (assuming that there is only one consumption good) was that there be some sector of the economy producing an input used to produce the consumption good in which it was not necessary to use resources. This result shows the sense in which convexity of the technology and endogenous growth are consistent with the use of resources. To the extent that one does not believe that there exists any such sector, then some form of increasing returns seems necessary to generate sustained growth.

This result really just extends those discussed in Section 2.3. In those models, we assumed the existence of exogenous technical progress, but many of the above models, such as the learning-by-doing model, have a similar analytical structure. Endogenous growth will be consistent with the finiteness of nonrenewable resources if there is sufficient scope for substitution of man-made, for natural capital, and it will occur in equilibrium (or in an optimal program) if the return to accumulating capital or technology remains high as the stock rises (marginal productivity does not diminish to zero). With respect to renewable resources, similar considerations apply. One can construct steady-state equilibria where human and physical capital accumulate, per capita income rises, and resource stocks are constant because, as the economy grows, even if rising income levels use or pollute resources, it is possible to allocate more resources to sustaining the environment (or perhaps because technological change reduces the reliance on or utilization of resources). For example, the dynastic (or social planning) model we developed in Section 2.3.4 can easily be extended to allow for a steady state of this form by allowing the production function for the consumption good to include a factor of production that can be accumulated linearly (for example, the human capital in Lucas (1988)). If the production function is a linear homogeneous function of physical capital, human capital and the resource flow, and human capital accumulates according to Eq. (3.9) (normalized to remove the scale effect), then we can describe a balanced growth path similar to that in Section 2.3.4 with the exception that per capita income now rises for ever. The difficulty is not in describing such a model, but knowing whether it is realistic empirically. The effects of exogenous population growth on such a model are as in Section 2.3.4.

In an interesting paper, John and Peccenino (1994) build a simple OLG model of the interaction between capital accumulation and environmental degradation. In their model, consumption degrades the environment and the level of the environment affects utility and not production possibilities. Individuals allocate their resources between accumulating capital and maintaining the environment. The model is simple enough to explicitly analyze the dynamics which they show may produce transition paths which resemble the environmental Kuznets curve.

3.6. Endogenous population and growth in the presence of natural resources

In this chapter, we have used the capital theoretic approach of growth theory to discuss what one might call the "dynamics of nations". We have also cautioned that specific predictions about policies or interpretations of empirical relationships between endogenous variables are fraught with difficulties. Consider as an example the relationship between the demographic transition and "convergence" (as described in Section 3.3). If the absolute convergence hypothesis were true, then richer countries have lower growth rates of per capita income. If the population growth rate falls as the level of income rises, then countries with fast growth rates in per capita incomes will also have fast rates of population growth. This prediction is the opposite of the one which takes population growth as exogenous and relates it to per capita income growth. If, on the other hand, the conditional convergence hypothesis is correct, there is no general relationship between population growth rates and the growth rates of per capita income, although if there is some absolute level of income which must be attained for the demographic transition to occur (a debatable notion), one can imagine situations where a country could converge to a steady state without the transition to low population growth having occurred.

It is impossible here to write down a model which is tractable enough to treat simultaneously the dynamics of technical change, capital accumulation (in a broad sense), population growth and resource depletion. Indeed, to our knowledge, no such model has been analyzed. However, we now try to draw the general implications of the models we have discussed.

On the normative side, one central implication is that, in lieu of specific market failures or absences, the laissez-faire equilibrium is likely to be Pareto optimal. Policy concerning intertemporal resource usage, capital accumulation or population must then be based on issues of intergenerational equity on which economists do not have unambiguous things to say. With respect to deviations from this position, there is a presumption that natural resources, particularly global ones such as the climate, will not be utilized efficiently. One cannot be confident, therefore, that the actual dynamics of the economy will represent an optimal path.

On the positive side, there are some robust lessons about the characteristics of steady-state equilibria. In equilibrium, different types of capital, be they physical, human or natural, will be accumulated or maintained up until the point where the marginal benefits of having more capital balance the marginal costs. One salient distinction between the different types of capital is that plausible initial conditions for most societies suggest that they will be well endowed with natural capital and lack physical and human capital and technology. In this situation, the marginal benefit to having more physical and human capital may be very high, whereas the marginal product of natural capital (and thus the marginal benefit) could be expected to be low. Along a transition path to a steady state, we would therefore expect to see natural resource stocks fall and physical and human capital accumulate, though this will of course be tempered to the extent that societies place intrinsic valuation on natural capital or resources. Given what theoretical and empirical knowledge we have, it seems plausible that such a steady state can be consistent with growing per capita income and the preservation of environmental resources.

At low levels of income, a variety of models also predict that parents will rationally decide to have large families. The human capital of poor countries tends to be in "quantity" rather than "quality". As income rises, however, a large body of evidence supports the notion of a demographic transition. The process and structural transformation of development changes the costs and benefits to parents of family size in such a way as to favor smaller families. Similarly, mortality falls in the face of rising per capita incomes.

This sketch of development is subject to many caveats. We have seen examples of where forms of increasing returns or externalities can lead to multiple equilibria. Here, there is not a unique attracting steady state to which economies converge, and where along a dynamic path economies allocate resources in a socially rational way to trade-off accumulating more of one capital stock against another. In such a model, maintaining a larger stock of natural capital in equilibrium seems to imply having lower stocks of other assets and probably lower per capita consumption. However, in models of multiple equilibria, countries may become stuck in a "development trap" with low income and high population growth (as in Becker et al., 1990). The interaction of poverty and missing institutions and markets may similarly result in inefficient over-exploitation of natural capital in such a trap. Here there are potentially enormous welfare gains to be made if society can coordinate on preferred outcomes and these outcomes can feature not only a lower rate of population growth but also an improved environment or larger natural capital stock.

As we made clear in Section 3.3, we also have severe reservations about the extent to which growth models, as presently constituted, provide a "theory of development".

Note also that, as the evidence of the environmental Kuznets curve suggests, convergence need not be monotone. Preferences need not be homothetic and at higher levels of per capita income, relative tastes may well change in favor of consuming the amenity services of natural capital.

4. Assessment

We collect here some comments, framed by the discussion of this paper, on some related and important topics which up until now we have not explicitly addressed.

4.1. Sustainable development

It is appropriate, given the wide currency attached to the phrase in the context of the issues studied in our survey, that we address the issue of "sustainable development" (our thoughts here echo those recently expressed by Hammond (1993), Nordhaus (1994b), Parikh (1991) and Dasgupta and Mäler (1995)). In our opinion, to the extent that it is coherent, the concept of sustainable development fits rather nicely into Koopman's (1967) conceptual framework. The roots of this literature lie with Georgescu-Roegen's (1971) claim that economic growth was inconsistent with the second law of thermodynamics. The main interesting implication of the second law is that the quantity of usefully concentrated energy and matter in an isolated system must decline. The earth is not, however, an isolated system since it receives solar energy. The question becomes an empirical one about the uses to which solar energy can be put, and the extent to which wastes can be re-cycled, and the material and energy content of goods reduced by technical progress. Some regard the end result as inevitable stagnation (e.g. Daly, 1991). But as Pezzey (1992) puts it, "on their own, thermodynamic laws tell us frustratingly little about sustainability (they do not tell us) how long material stocks will last, how much solar energy can be usefully captured by humans, what stock of material goods can be maintained in circulation, or what values these goods will have". As we have discussed, even if resources are essential for production, consumption can be sustained indefinitely if some form of resource economizing technical change is sufficiently high. Of course, this implies that there is no minimum physical resource content per unit of output value, and this may be regarded as implausible (Pezzey, 1992). For the path to be actually sustainable in the sense that consumption is maintained, discounting must be small in relation to the rate of technical progress.

Pezzey (1989) lists 19 different definitions of what sustainability might be about, and as Toman et al. (1993) put it, "there is not a "textbook" definition of sustainability that commands widespread agreement". However, they go on to add, "it is clear that the central issue is concern for the well-being of future generations in the face of growing pressure on the natural environment to provide a range of valued services (extractable materials, waste absorption, ecological system resilience, aesthetics)". Solow (1993) accepts that sustainable development is about obligations to future generations, but adds that "you can't be morally obliged to do something which is not feasible". He suggests the definition that sustainability is "an obligation to conduct ourselves so that we leave to the future the option or capacity to be as well off as we are". "You have to take into account in thinking about sustainability, the resources that we use up and the resources that we leave behind, but also the sort of environment we leave behind including the built environment, including productive capacity (plant and equipment) and including technical knowledge. What we are obliged to leave behind is a generalized capacity to create well-being, not any particular thing or any particular natural resource".

There seem to be two key issues in sustainability. First, it is about the ability of the economy to generate growth paths which sustain welfare in some sense, and, at the same time, do not decimate the environment. Second, it is about the intertemporal distribution of welfare. Writers in the sustainability literature see preservation of environmental resources as intimately connected to human welfare and worry that present generations are over-utilizing such resources to the detriment of future generations. When considering the nature of intergenerational welfare, it is worthwhile pondering the experience of the last two hundred years in the developed countries. Solow (1993) argues that our ancestors were probably excessively generous in providing for future generations given the extraordinary increase in living standards that has occurred.

In practice, most authors (see Pezzey, 1989; Toman et al., 1993) argue that the sustainability of an intertemporal program is best assessed in practice by examining whether or not per capita utility falls over time. If it does not, then the program is sustainable. This approach frees the concept from demanding preservation of any particular resource or environmental asset except in the case where it is uniquely irreplaceable or essential to production (the idea that natural capital stocks should be preserved results implicitly from a very strong assumption about substitutability).

What might determine sustainability? First consider the issue of feasibility. Consider a simple model of an exhaustible resource which can be consumed or left in the ground to be consumed in the future (Heal (1993) for a nice exposition). The objective function is the discounted sum of utilities,

$$\sum_{t=0}^{\infty} \beta^t U(c_t),$$

and the constraints are

$$S_T = S_0 - \sum_{t=0}^{T} c_t, \quad S_{t+1} - S_t = c_t.$$

In such a model, all consumption paths inevitably converge to zero. Krautkraemer (1985) shows that allowing amenity services to enter the utility function from the stock of the resource can imply that it is not optimal to exhaust the resource. Whether or not the resource is depleted depends in a natural way on boundary conditions on the marginal utility of consumption (Vousden (1973) provided an early discussion), and also on how productive the resource is. If sustainability means that a positive level of consumption is maintained forever or that utility is nondecreasing, then it is clear that no paths can be sustainable.

What about the more general models which allow for substitution and technical change? Consider the steady-state equilibria of the first model we developed in Section 2.3.4. If $H'(0) < 1 + \rho$, then the steady-state equilibria implies that the environmental resource will be exhausted in the optimal program. Could such an equilibrium represent part of a sustainable development program? It would seem not. Moumouras

(1991, 1993) offers a discussion of sustainability in these terms. But how should we respond to this? In the dynastic model, this is not at all clear. ρ represents here the altruism of the dynasty, or some mixture of altruism and time preference. The question becomes whether or not society discounts the welfare of future individuals at a lower rate than that implied by a laissez-faire equilibrium. If it does (as in the example we discuss in the next section), then the fact that the path implied by a particular discount rate implied the exhaustion of certain renewable resources might lead us to revise our welfare weights.

This type of reasoning suggests that sustainability is a criterion which can be applied to rule out the sort of accumulation paths which we described at the end of Section 2.3.2, and which Dasgupta and Heal (1979: p. 257) describe as "intertemporally efficient but perfectly ghastly". This seems best understood as a question of intergenerational distribution.

From this point of view, sustainability may appear as an extra welfare criterion in assessing development programs. Having derived the implications of a particular welfare function, we ask ourselves if this represents an acceptable path for the economy to develop along. In making this assessment we might want to ask does utility decline over time. If it does, then we may want to rethink the nature of our objective function.

Here, "sustainability" appears as a sort of litmus test that an allocation must pass to be ethically acceptable. This seems a useful device (and is in what we take to be the spirit of Dorfman (1993)). As we have explained, in our opinion, it is impossible to sustain an interesting abstract discussion of optimal growth paths without taking a particular criterion and putting it to work to see its implications in action. In a similar spirit, Dasgupta and Mäler (1990) argue that the time path of future changes in natural resource stocks have to be deduced "from considerations of population change, intergenerational well-being, technological possibilities, environmental regeneration rates, and the existing resource base. The answer cannot be pulled out of a hat". In assessing the implications of an optimality criterion, we need some desiderata which determine whether the solution we compute is acceptable, which we can then use to re-assess our objective function. Sustainability seems to have a potentially useful role here.

4.2. Discounting

The theoretical example discussed in the last section exhibits the crucial role of discounting in a simple way. Imagine now a reformulation of that model in terms of an OLG economy where the social welfare function was as in Eq. (2.27). The condition which guarantees the existence of a positive stock of environmental assets in equilibrium would become $H'(0) > 1 + \tau$. It is important to be clear about what one means by discounting. In project appraisal, cost and benefit streams are discounted to the present because of the supposition that the value of costs and benefits varies depending on the time at which they accrue. Why is this? There are basically three aspects. One is that "waiting" is productive. The opportunity cost of investing in a project is what one loses by not adopting another project. Since capital investment is productive, "waiting" increases output over time. The second consideration is individual impatience. This is encapsulated in our parameter $\beta = 1/(1 + \rho)$. The third consideration is the intertemporal distribution of income which appears as the parameter τ. This is the weight in a social welfare function which shows the relative weights of the welfare of different generations in total social welfare. The form this weighting takes is due to wishing to avoid problems of intertemporal inconsistency in the optimal allocation (Strotz, 1956). In the overlapping generations model without full altruism, there is a role for such a weighting between generations. The social optimum is relative to this set of weights, and given these, the planner can implement the social optimum through intergenerational transfers (i.e. a tax–transfer policy which determines the accumulation of capital). This logic is nothing other than the Second Fundamental Theorem of Welfare Economics in the overlapping generations model (see Bewley (1981) for a definitive treatment). While this should be clear, it has been re-discovered in a number of papers in the resource economics literature (e.g. Howarth and Norgaard, 1993).

The causality runs from society's preferences over intertemporal income distribution, to appropriate policy that implements this distribution, hence to the capital stock (widely conceived to encompass human capital, technology etc.), and thus to the marginal product of capital, viz. the interest rate. Hence, according to welfare economics, the weighting of current versus future generations in a sense determines the interest rate. It is the welfare weights which are the exogenous variables.

Discounting has often been connected to the sustainability debate. To see why, if given a choice of τ, we find that utility declines over time we might want to revise our value for this weight. What if $H'(0) < 1 + \tau$, but per capita utility was increasing? This suggests that declining utility per se is not all that sustainability is about. It also seems to be about the intrinsic value of natural and environmental resources. Hence the specification of the utility function is critical, and, in particular, the behavior of utility if resources go to zero. Common and Perrings (1992) provide a useful comparison of the distinctions between environmentalists and economists thinking on these issues. The main problem seems to be that, as yet, the languages are not commensurate enough for a productive dialogue to emerge.

The philosophical arguments about discounting, starting with Ramsey (1928), all without exception attack the moral justification for a positive rate of social time preference and proceed from this to state that costs and benefits should not be discounted since this discriminates against future generations (Parfit (1984) and Broome (1992) are eloquent statements of these positions). As Partridge (1981) puts it, "the concept of discounting the future is a point of fundamental contention between economists and moral philosophers. To economists the concept is virtually axiomatic and thus beyond dispute. To many philosophers, the notion is, at best, arbitrary and unproved and, at worst, absurd." The issue of a positive social rate of time preference is seen to be one of intergenerational equity. If one takes the dynastic model seriously, then this argument is redundant. The discount rate represents the intertemporal opportunity cost of resources, and this is determined by the degree of altruism of the dynasty. Even if this rate of "time preference" were zero, it may still be correct to discount because the productivity of capital implies that future individuals will be better off than we will be.

Discounting clearly has a big impact on resource models. Consider the example from Heal (1993) discussed in the last section. If $\beta \in (0, 1)$, then the results are as described above. However, if $\beta = 1$ then the model becomes the "cake eating" economy of Gale (1967) and the problem has no solution. Again, the results described at the end of Section 2.3.2 show that discounting makes the difference between consumption converging to zero and consumption monotonically increasing.

There are various other justifications for discounting in the literature. Dasgupta and Heal (1979) show that, if there is a probability that the world will end at any time and that this is governed by a Poisson process, then discounting can be justified by an "original position" type of argument (individuals put less weight on being born into a future that may cease to exist). Heal (1993) shows that introducing other sorts of uncertainty into the problem (such as about the existence of a backstop, or the date at which a substitute will become available) technology also induces discounting like phenomena. Koopmans (1972) and Diamond (1965b) have also provided an axiomatic basis for discounting.

There is also the problem that, while it is commonly assumed that reducing the discount rate would help preserve the environment since environmental benefits are seen as long lived, this is clearly not always so. Many authors have noted (e.g. Krautkraemer, 1988) that reducing the discount rate would also stimulate capital investment and, if this investment was resource intensive, then the net result might be a deterioration in the environment. It is easy to see how this sort of thing might happen in the context of steady-state equilibria of the model we developed in Section 2.4. There we noted that general equilibrium effects stemming from the allocation of capital between the production of the consumption good and the preservation of the environment could easily lead to perverse comparative steady-state results.

The perspective of the dynastic model is different from this since it then becomes problematical as to how the preferences of society can differ from those of the dynasty. In this case, it is rather the impatience of the dynasty which determines the characteristics of the growth path. If this implies that the resource stock is driven to zero, what do we conclude (recall that we are considering a world here with no externalities, market failures etc.)? In our view, this issue is not crucially damning to sustainability. The dynastic model is highly restrictive and perhaps not the most useful way of considering the issues.

It is well known that undiscounted problems raise difficult conceptual and mathematical issues. A conceptual problem is that no finite sequence of costs and benefits matters. A mathematical one concerns the convergence of the objective function. The obvious response to this difficulty is to use some partial ordering over paths such as the "overtaking criterion". Another response in this situation might be to forego the benefits of a fully computed optimum, and again resort to the methodology we propose. In this case again, sustainability may have a role: as a guide as to what policies are admissible when we cannot compute a full optimum over all feasible paths. However, in its present state of articulation, the concept of sustainability is clearly of only limited practical use.

4.3. Uncertainty

Thus far, and in the rest of the paper, we abstract from uncertainty in our analysis. This is a severe restriction. An important ingredient in environmental issues is uncertainty surrounding the form of environmental dynamics and the possible existence of threshold effects which have serious implications for economic activity and social welfare. Another source of uncertainty is about the value of many environmental assets. Environmentalists argue that biodiversity and the existence of species have potential value which we cannot assess (perhaps in the form of new drugs etc.). Weitzman (1993b) develops an interesting attempt to put a metric on "diversity". Uncertainty is important in these matters since much environmental change is irreversible. The important early work of Arrow and Fisher (1974) and Henry (1974) showed that, in such a situation, there was an imputed "option value" on the non-use of resources. With irreversibility and uncertainty, it is prudent to "wait and see what happens". Beltratti et al. (1992) show that if there is a possibility that future preferences will change in the direction of a greater value for the environment, then this leads to the optimal plan preserving a larger amount now than without such uncertainty.

Heal (1984, 1990, 1991) develops a model where the climate affects production possibilities and takes on one of two states ("good" and "bad"). The climate starts in the good state and may make a transition to the bad state (which is absorbing) as a function of the cumulative extraction of a resource ("fossil fuels"). Such a possibility leads to reduced resource extraction. The rate of extraction depends in intuitive ways on risk aversion and the properties of the function governing the transition probability. These papers also provide an interesting discussion on the approaches we could take to climate change (see also Chichilnisky and Heal, 1993). This is an obvious idea to provide insurance and is feasible as long as there is some global variation in the effects (agricultural production is relocated rather than devastated globally) at least as long as such contracts could be enforced. Heal argues however that, given the uncertainty, such attempts at insurance may have the adverse effect of reducing attempts to mitigate climate change (the standard moral hazard problem with insurance contracts).

4.4. International issues

International issues are critical in thinking about the global environment since possibly the most intractable problems relate to externalities across countries (international law being a notoriously unreliable enforcement mechanism). Mäler (1990) provides a discussion of many of the issues. Here the question of distributional issues between countries is of utmost importance. Reducing global environmental degradation requires a large amount of coordination between nations and agreements on how much each country may contribute to degradation. For example, imagine that it was agreed that it would be desirable to halt global warming. Even if a good estimate of the output by which greenhouse gas emission would have to be reduced to stabilize global warming could be made, it would then have to be decided exactly how this reduction was to de distributed across countries. If this reduction is a cost, then it is not clear that countries who already dominate greenhouse gas emission should automatically be given future rights to dominate such emission (purely on the basis that they managed to industrialize first).

There are other interesting international issues connected to environmental resources. Chichilnisky (1993a,b) has shown that, in a world where less-developed economies are relatively better endowed with natural resources, standard Heckscher–Ohlin considerations suggest that they specialize in the export of commodities which use environmental resources intensively. There are no implications concerning efficiency about this. However, she argues that it is plausible that resources are less well managed and, in particular, property rights are less well defined in underdeveloped nations. This then leads to trade and international specialization based purely on the imperfections of property rights in underdeveloped nations. Even two nations which have identical fundamental specifications of endowments, technology and preferences (and therefore identical autarkic price vectors) can specialize and trade on the basis of differing property rights. While the failure to properly define property rights is the key source of inefficiency, trade may exacerbate the tendency for underdeveloped economies to over-exploit their natural resources.

5. Conclusions

We now recapitulate on our fundamental themes. The interaction between economic growth, population dynamics and resource use is complex and the jointly endogenous outcome of the whole process of evolution and development of the economic and social system. As such, correlations do not imply causation. Unfortunately our empirical knowledge is very poor. Little is understood about the dynamics of growth or demography and even less about the relationships governing environmental resources. A key implication then is that we must bear in mind our uncertainty about how the economy will evolve. The most plausible view is that while population growth may impede development, it does so by exacerbating more fundamental unsolved issues. These revolve around the causes of underdevelopment and poverty themselves. One of the key things that population growth can directly exacerbate is inefficient exploitation of resources. It is clear that in reality markets are incomplete, and there may be many deviations from the conditions ensuring a first-best allocation of resources, especially in an intertemporal context under uncertainty. This may generate a role for population policy as a second-best instrument. However, as in all second-best situations, it is hard to say anything general here without detailed empirical knowledge. While these basic theoretical considerations suggest that the economy is unlikely to achieve the first-best intertemporal allocation of resources, the pertinent question is what set of feasible policies and institutions are likely to increase welfare.

Both the World Bank's influential World Development Report of 1984 and the 1986 report of the National Academy of Sciences Working Group on Population Growth and Economic Development conclude that, on balance, lower population growth rates would be beneficial for underdeveloped economies, and we accept this finding. Weir (1989) notes that "population has gone from being overlooked to the single dynamic element in European history" and this approach has been pushed in the influential work of North and Thomas (1972) and McNeil (1990). While it may be true that population growth has some positive effects, it is hard to imagine that population growth in itself has much to offer the developing nations in the solution to their economic and social problems. The real issues seem to lie in the adoption of technology and institutional changes which seem unlikely to be able to benefit from crude scale economies or the like. Birdsall (1989) argues that "mainstream debate now centers on the quantitative importance of rapid population growth – whether its negative effects are minimal, and in any event so interlinked with more central problems such as poor macroeconomic policies, weak political and social institutions and so on, as to hardly merit direct attention; or greater than minimal, and in effect contributory to other problems".

It also seems likely that, while in the long run, population size and growth may not be a key issue in the process of development, it may be an important issue in the short run. This is so since most of the costs are in short run while the benefits are enjoyed over longer time scales. As such, population policy may be useful in allowing any benefits to accrue. In practice, what matters is not just the total integral of the costs and benefits. The intertemporal distribution may be important from the point of view of social and political possibilities.

An important empirical issue we have concentrated on is the nature of intergenerational preferences. Even if there are no externalities to population growth (positive or negative), the rate of population growth might well not be socially optimal. Outside the dynastic context, it seems reasonable to posit a social welfare function encapsulating the preferences for society over the distribution of intergenerational welfare. Such a social welfare function would induce a particular rate of population growth. It seems improbable that this would be identical to the rate of population growth under

laissez faire. On the other hand, if preferences were such that the dynastic model were the correct benchmark, then it is not clear how society could care about the intertemporal distribution of welfare in a different way than the dynasty. Of course, with heterogeneity, society would care about the distribution of welfare across dynasties, and this would have implications for population growth (unless of course one took the ideas in Bernheim and Bagwell (1988) seriously that marriage means that all individuals are linked altruistically together in one big "family"). The crucial issue is not the presence or absence of altruism, since even in lieu of altruism, the rate of population growth may well be Pareto optimal. What is key is whether or not altruism is sufficient to induce dynastic preferences, and whether or not one can then argue that society should weigh different generations differently from this. Note that the dynamic consistency of these preferences is also important. If the dynastic preferences are dynamically inconsistent, then future rates of population growth will not be the same ones that would be chosen by the current cohort of the dynasty.

Unfortunately, the nature of altruistic preferences has received little attention empirically. As Altonji et al. (1992) put it, "in recent years the infinite-horizon altruism model has played an important role in theoretical analysis and policy debate. This is surprising given the lack of direct empirical support for the model." Altonji et al. (1992) test, and strongly reject, the implication of the altruism model that the distribution of consumption is independent of the distribution of resources (see also the findings of Goldin and Parsons (1989)). Given our present knowledge, it seems unlikely that we could formulate an operationally convincing population or resource policy on basis of our evidence about these. This makes the case for concentrating, in terms of policy, on issues that we have more chance of conclusively analyzing and quantifying, in particular the issues we have repeatedly stressed of externalities and property rights.

While we understand these issues much better, they are also complex since we have come to realize that the relationship between property rights and incentives is less obvious than was perhaps once thought. It is ironic that the fundamental work of Coase (1960), in a sense, belittles the importance of property rights for incentives. In the Coasian world of zero transactions costs, efficiency is guaranteed as long as property rights are well defined. Who actually possesses the rights only matters for the distribution of income. Recent advances in economic theory stress that the assumption of zero transactions costs is very strong, and outside of this theoretical ideal, it can matter a great deal for efficiency who actually owns the rights. For example, Hart and Moore (1990) argue that the ownership structure of firms is an efficient response to the inability of individuals to write complete contracts. This is an example of the more general recognition of the inseparability of efficiency and distribution. This implies that how property rights are allocated is very important.

The theoretical literature on fertility and population growth also needs to be extended to allow for more disaggregated models of household decision-making and for a better integration with the social environment. A key feature determining the health

of a society seems to be the social institutions it creates to aid the intergenerational transmission of culture, norms and human capital in a wide sense (see Coleman, 1988). In most existing societies, this institution is primarily the family (though aided by formal educational institutions). The evidence suggests that when the family breaks down or becomes "dysfunctional", then this can have severe implications for society. As yet, we hardly have a good language for discussing these issues. There seem to be many social phenomena concerning the family and fertility which are outside of the scope of existing models. As an extreme example, consider the discussion by Levi-Strauss (1957) of the relationship between the social structure of the Nambikwara tribe in central Brazil and their fertility rate. According to Levi-Strauss, the tribe became so obsessed by issues of relative social status that they practiced complete infanticide because of the destabilizing effects children born to different clans might have on the social equilibrium. To allow the tribe to persist, they instead kidnapped babies from other tribes.

What then of the population and environmental problems? We agree with Cassen (1976) that "the study of the factors which influence fertility decline suggest that it is socio-economic progress in general that brings about the demographic transition. If this is correct, the resolution of population problems may well lie in fundamental changes in society, removing the obstacles to what we nowadays name by the word development – the provision of a decent life not for some but for all". Our view is that to the extent that there are population and environmental problems, these will be best resolved by the process of development itself. To succeed, this process requires institutional, political and structural changes in society which are undoubtedly difficult to achieve. Most environmental disasters are due to the same types of problems which themselves impede development – inefficient policies, the failure to enforce property rights or inefficient structures of incentives. It is the interaction of population growth with these that causes it to have its worst effects.

In understanding why inefficient institutional structures and policies persist in equilibrium, we need theoretical advances well beyond those embodied in the current growth models. In this vein, Bardhan (1995) concludes his survey on the recent growth literature by stating, "notwithstanding popular impression to the contrary, the advances made so far in the new literature on growth theory have barely scratched the surface. The new emphasis on fixed costs and nonconvexities in the process of introducing new goods and technologies is important. But these fixed costs actually go much beyond the ordinary set-up costs in starting new activities: particularly in a developing country they encompass massive costs of collective action in building new economic institutions and political coalitions and in breaking the deadlock of incumbent interests threatened by new technologies. While the new interest in model-building will be helpful in sharpening our analytical tools and in critically examining our implicit assumptions, let us hope that it will not divert our attention from the organizational–institutional issues and distributive conflicts in the development process which are less amenable to neat formalization." Perhaps in thinking about these topics

we also need to bear in mind the maxim of the great social anthropologist Levi-Strauss who cautioned that "to say that society works is a truism, but to say that all parts of society work is an absurdity" (Levi-Strauss, 1963).

References

Abel, A.B. (1987), "Operative gift and bequest motives", American Economic Review 77: 1037–1047.

Acemoglu, D. (1994), "Reward structures and the allocation of talent", European Economic Review 39: 17–33.

Aghion, P. and P.W. Howitt (1992), "A model of growth through creative destruction", Econometrica 60: 323–351.

Alderman, H., P.-A. Chiappori, L. Haddad, J. Hoddinott and R. Kanbur (1995), "Unitary versus collective models of the household: is it time to shift the burden of proof?", The World Bank Research Observer 10: 1–19.

Alesina, A. and D. Rodrik (1995), "Distributive politics and economic growth", Quarterly Journal of Economics 109: 465–490.

Alhuwalia, M.S. (1976), "Inequality, poverty and development", Journal of Development Economics 6: 307–342.

Allais, M. (1947), Economie et interet (Imprimerie Nationale, Paris).

Allen, J.C. and D.F. Barnes (1985), "The causes of deforestation in developing countries", Annals of the Association of American Geographers 75: 163–184.

Altonji, J.G., F. Hayashi and L.J. Kotlikoff (1992), "Is the extended family altruistically linked? Direct tests using micro data", American Economic Review 82: 1177–1198.

Anderson, J.L. (1981), "Climatic change in European economic history", Research in Economic History 6: 1–34.

Anderson, K.P. (1972), "Optimal growth when the stock of resources is finite and depletable", Journal of Economic Theory 4: 256–267.

Arrow, K.J. (1962), "Economic implications of learning-by-doing", Review of Economic Studies 29: 155–173.

Arrow, K.J. (1963–64), "The role of securities in the optimal allocation of risk bearing", Review of Economic Studies 31: 91–96.

Arrow, K.J. and A.C. Fisher (1974), "Environmental preservation, uncertainty and irreversibility", Quarterly Journal of Economics 88: 312–319.

Arrow, K.J. and M. Kurz (1970), Public investment, the rate of return and optimal fiscal policy (Johns Hopkins University Press, Baltimore, MD).

Asheim, G.B. (1994), "Sustainability: ethical foundations and economic properties", World Bank policy research working paper 1302 (World Bank, Washington, DC).

Ayres, R.U. and J. Walter (1991), "The greenhouse effect: damages, costs and abatement", Environmental and Resource Economics 1: 237–270.

Azariadis, C. (1993), Intertemporal macroeconomics (Basil Blackwell, Oxford).

Azariadis, C. and A.M. Drazen (1993), "Endogenous fertility in models of growth" (University of Maryland, College Park, MD).

Backus, D.K., P.J. Kehoe and T.J. Kehoe (1992), "In search of scale effects in trade and growth", Journal of Economic Theory 58: 377–409.

Baland, J.-M. and J.A. Robinson (1996a), "Non-cooperative family behavior and the population problem", Unpublished working paper (Department of Economics, University of Southern California, Los Angeles, CA).

Baland, J.-M. and J.A. Robinson (1996b), "How many rotten kids?", Unpublished working paper (Department of Economics, University of Southern California, Los Angeles, CA).

Barbier, E.B. (1989), Economics, natural resource scarcity and development (Earthscan Publications Limited, London).

Barbier, E.B. and A. Markandya (1990), "The conditions for achieving environmentally sustainable development", European Economic Review 34: 659–669.

Barbier, E.B., A. Markandya and D.W. Pearce (1989), Sustainable development: economics and environment in the Third World (Earthscan Publications Limited, London).

Bardhan, P. (1995), "The contribution of endogenous growth theory to the analysis of development problems", in: J. Behrman and T.N. Srinivasan, eds., Handbook of development economics, Vol. III (North-Holland, Amsterdam).

Barnett, H.J. and C. Morse (1963), Scarcity and growth (Johns Hopkins University Press, Baltimore, MD).

Barro, R.J. (1974), "Are government bonds net wealth?", Journal of Political Economy 82: 1095–1118.

Barro, R.J. (1990), "Government spending in a simple model of endogenous growth", Journal of Political Economy 98: S103–S125.

Barro, R.J. and X. Sala-i-Martin (1995), Economic growth (McGraw Hill, New York).

Becker, G.S. (1960), "An economic analysis of fertility", in: A.J. Coale, ed., Demographic and economic change in developed countries (Princeton University Press, Princeton, NJ).

Becker, G.S. (1974), "A theory of social interactions", Journal of Political Economy 55: 1126–1150.

Becker, G.S. (1981), A treatise on the family (Harvard University Press, Cambridge, MA)

Becker, G.S. and R.J. Barro (1986), "Altruism and the economic theory of fertility", in: K. Davis, M.S. Bernstam and R. Ricardo-Campbell, eds., Below replacement fertility in industrial societies (Oxford University Press, New York).

Becker, G.S. and R.J. Barro (1988), "A reformulation of the economic theory of fertility", Quarterly Journal of Economics 106: 467–484.

Becker, G.S. and R.J. Barro (1989), "Fertility choice in a model of economic growth", Econometrica 57: 407–444.

Becker, G.S. and R.G. Lewis (1973), "On the interaction between quantity and quality of children", Journal of Political Economy 81: S279–S288.

Becker, G.S., K.J. Murphy and R. Tamura (1990), "Human capital, fertility and economic growth", Journal of Political Economy 98: S12–S37.

Becker, R.A. (1982), "Intergenerational equity: the capital–environment trade-off", Journal of Environmental Economics and Management 9: 165–185.

Beckerman, W. (1993), "The environmental limits to growth: a fresh look", in: H. Giersch, ed., Economic progress and environmental concerns (Springer-Verlag, Berlin).

Beltratti, A., G. Chichilnisky and G.M. Heal (1992), "Option and non-use value of environmental assets", Discussion paper series no. 620 (Department of Economics, Columbia University, New York).

Beltratti, A., G. Chichilnisky and G.M. Heal (1993), "Sustainable growth and the green golden rule", Working paper no. 4430 (NBER, Cambridge, MA).

Berndt, E.R. and D.O. Wood (1975), "Technology, prices and the derived demand for energy", Review of Economics and Statistics 57: 259–268.

Bernheim, B.D. (1987), "Ricardian equivalence: an evaluation of theory and evidence", in: S. Fischer, ed., NBER macroeconomics annual (MIT Press, Cambridge, MA).

Bernheim, B.D. (1989), "Intergenerational altruism, dynastic equilibria and social welfare", Review of Economic Studies 56: 199–228.

Bernheim, B.D. and K. Bagwell (1988), "Is everything neutral?", Journal of Political Economy 96: 308–338.

Bernheim, B.D. and D. Ray (1987), "Economic growth with intergenerational altruism", Review of Economic Studies 54: 227–243.

Bernheim, B.D. and O. Stark (1988), "Altruism within the family reconsidered", American Economic Review 78: 1034–1045.

Bernheim, B.D., A. Shleifer and L.S. Summers (1985), "The strategic bequest motive", Journal of Political Economy 93: 1045–1076.

Bewley, T.F. (1972), "The existence of equilibria in economies with infinitely many commodities", Journal of Economic Theory 4: 514–540.

Bewley, T.F. (1981), "On the indeterminacy of interest rates", Working paper no. 491 (Department of Economics, Northwestern University, Evanston, IL).

Binswanger, H. (1989), "Brazilian policies that encourage deforestation of the Amazon", Environmental discussion paper no. 16 (World Bank, Washington, DC).

Birdsall, N. (1988), "Economic approaches to population growth and development", in: H.B. Chenery and T.N. Srinivasan, eds., Handbook of development economics (North-Holland, Amsterdam).

Birdsall, N. (1989), "Economic analysis of rapid population growth", World Bank Research Observer 4: 23–50.

Birdsall, N. (1992), "Another look at population and global warming", Policy research working paper no. 1020 (World Bank, Washington, DC).

Birdsall, N. and C. Griffin (1988), "Fertility and poverty in developing countries", Journal of Policy Modeling 10: 29–55.

Birdsall, N. and C. Griffin (1993), "Population growth, externalities and poverty", Policy research working paper no. 1158 (World Bank, Washington, DC).

Blackorby, C. and D. Donaldson (1984), "Criteria for evaluating population change", Journal of Public Economics 25: 13–33.

Blackorby, C., D. Donaldson and W. Bossert (1993), "Intertemporal population ethics: a welfarist approach", Discussion paper no: 93-13 (Department of Economics, University of British Columbia, Vancouver, BC).

Blanchard, O.J. (1985), "Debt, deficits and finite horizons", Journal of Political Economy 93: 223–247.

Blanchard, O.J. and S. Fischer (1989), Lectures on macroeconomics (MIT Press, Cambridge, MA).

Bloom, D.E. and R.B. Freeman (1988), "Economic development and the timing and components of population growth", Journal of Policy Modeling 10: 57–81.

Boldrin, M. (1992), "Dynamic externalities, multiple equilibria and growth", Journal of Economic Theory 58: 198–218.

Bongaarts, J. (1992), "Population growth and global warming", Population and Development Review 18: 299–319.

Boserup, E. (1965), The conditions of agricultural progress (Allen and Unwin, London).

Boserup, E. (1981), Population and technological change: a study of long-term trends (Chicago University Press, Chicago, IL).

Bovenberg, A.L. and S. Smulders (1995), "Environmental quality and pollution-augmenting technological progress in a two-sector endogenous growth model", Journal of Public Economics 57: 369–391.

Bovenberg, A.L. and F. van der Ploeg (1993a), "Does a tougher environmental policy raise unemployment? Optimal taxation, public goods and environmental policy with rationing of labour supply", Discussion paper no. 869 (C.E.P.R., London).

Bovenberg, A.L. and F. van der Ploeg (1993b), "Environmental policy, public finance and the labour market in a second-best world", Journal of Public Economics, in press.

Bovenberg, A.L. and F. van der Ploeg (1993c), "Green policies in a small open economy", Discussion paper no. 785 (C.E.P.R., London).

Bovenberg, A.L. and F. van der Ploeg (1993d), "Direct crowding out, optimal taxation and pollution abatement", Economics Letters 43: 83–93.

Brander, J.A. and S. Dowrick (1994), "The role of fertility and population in economic growth: empirical results from aggregate cross-national data", Journal of Population Economics 7: 1–25.

Brock, W.A. (1977), "A polluted golden age", in: V.K. Smith, ed., Economics of natural and environmental resources (Gordon and Breach, New York).

Broome, J. (1992), Counting the cost of global warming (White Horse Press, London).

Broome, J. (1993a), "The value of living", Récherches Economiques de Louvain 58: 125–142.

Broome, J. (1993b), "Discounting the future", Discussion paper no. 93/343 (University of Bristol, Bristol).

Caballero, R.J. and R.K. Lyons (1993), "External effects in U.S. procyclical productivity", Journal of Monetary Economics 29: 209–225.

Cain, M. (1983), "Fertility as an adjustment to risk", Population and Development Review 9: 688–702.

Caldwell, J.C. (1990), "The soft underbelly of development: demographic transition in conditions of limited economic change", in: Proceedings of the World Bank Annual Conference on Development Economics (World Bank, Washington, DC).

Cannan, E. (1888), Elementary political economy (MacMillan, London).

Cassen, R.H. (1976), "Population and development: a survey", World Development 4: 785–830.

Chandler, W. (1984), "Recycling materials", in: L.R. Brown, ed., The state of the world (W.W. Norton and Co., New York).

Chichilnisky, G. (1993a), "Global environment and north–south trade", First Boston working paper series FB-93-16 (Graduate School of Business, Columbia University, New York).

Chichilnisky, G. (1993b), "North–south trade and the dynamics of renewable resources", Discussion paper series no. 644 (Department of Economics, Columbia University, New York).

Chichilnisky, G. and G.M. Heal (1993), "Global environmental risks", Journal of Economic Perspectives 7: 65–86.

Chomitz, K.M. and N. Birdsall (1991), "Incentives for small families: concepts and issues", in: Proceedings of the World Bank Annual Conference on Development Economics (World Bank, Washington, DC).

Cigno, A. (1988), "Macroeconomic consequences of the 'new home economics'", in: R.D. Lee, W.B. Arthur and G. Rodgers, eds., Economics of changing age distributions in developed countries (Clarendon Press, Oxford).

Cigno, A. (1991), Economics of the family (Clarendon Press, Oxford).

Cigno, A. (1993), "Intergenerational transfers without altruism", European Journal of Political Economy 9: 505–518.

Clark, C. (1978), Mathematical bioeconomics: the optimal management of renewable resources (Wiley, New York).

Clarke, R., G. Boero and L.A. Walters (1993), "Controlling greenhouse gases: a survey of global macroeconomic studies", Discussion paper no. 93-18 (Department of Economics, University of Birmingham, Birmingham).

Cline, W.R. (1992), The economics of global warming (Institute for International Economics, Washington, DC).

Coale, A.J. and E.M. Hoover (1958), Population growth and economic development in low-income countries (Princeton University Press, Princeton, NJ).

Coale, A.J. and S.C. Watkins (1986), The decline of fertility in Europe (Princeton University Press, Princeton, NJ).

Coase, R.H. (1960), "The problem of social cost", Journal of Law and Economics 3: 1–44.

Coleman, J.S. (1988), "Social capital in the creation of human capital", American Journal of Sociology 94: S95–S120.

Common, M. and C. Perrings (1992), "Towards an ecological economics of sustainability", Ecological Economics 6: 7–34.

Cronk, L. (1991), "Human behavioral ecology", American Review of Anthropology 20: 25–53.

Crook, N.R. (1978), "On social norms and fertility declines", in: G. Hawthorn, ed., Population and development (Frank Cass, London).

Cropper, M. and C. Griffiths (1994), "The interaction of population growth and environmental quality", American Economic Review 84: 250–254.

Dalton, H. (1928), "The theory of population", Economica 22: 28–50.

Daly, H. (1991), Steady-state economics, 2nd edn. (Island Press, Washington, DC).

D'Arge, R.C. and K.C. Kogiku (1973), "Economic growth and the environment", Review of Economic Studies 40: 61–77.

Darity, W.A. Jr. (1980), "The Boserup theory of agricultural growth: a model for anthropological economics", Journal of Development Economics 7: 137–157.

Darwin, C. (1871), The descent of man and selection in relation to sex (John Murray, London).

Dasgupta, P. (1969), "On the concept of optimum population", Review of Economic Studies 36: 295–318.

Dasgupta, P. (1974), "On optimum population size", in: A. Mitra, ed., Economic theory and planning (Oxford University Press, Oxford).

Dasgupta, P. (1982), The control of resources (Basil Blackwell, Oxford).

Dasgupta, P. (1987), "The ethical foundations of population policy", in: D.G. Johnson and R.D. Lee, eds., Population growth and economic development: issues and evidence (University of Wisconsin Press, Madison, WI).

Dasgupta, P. (1993a), An inquiry into well-being and destitution (Oxford University Press, Oxford).

Dasgupta, P. (1993b), "The population problem", Paper prepared for the Population Summit of the World's Scientific Academies, New Delhi.

Dasgupta, P. (1993c), "Optimal vs sustainable growth", Paper prepared for the World Bank Conference – Valuing the Environment.

Dasgupta, P. and G.M. Heal (1974), "The optimal depletion of exhaustible resources", Review of Economic Studies, Symposium on Natural Resources, 3–28.

Dasgupta, P. and G.M. Heal (1979), Economic theory and exhaustible resources (Cambridge University Press, Cambridge).

Dasgupta, P. and K.-G. Mäler (1990), "The environment and emerging development issues", in: Proceedings of the World Bank Annual Conference on Development Economics (World Bank, Washington, DC).

Dasgupta, P. and K.-G. Mäler (1995), "Poverty, institutions and the environmental resource base", in: J.R. Behrman and T.N. Srinivasan, eds., Handbook of development economics, Vol. III (North-Holland, Amsterdam).

Dasgupta, S. and T. Mitra (1982), "On some problems in the formulation of optimal population policies when resources are depletable", in: W. Eichhorn et al., eds., Economic theory of natural resources (Physica-Verlag, Wurzburg).

Dasgupta, P., G.M. Heal and M. Majumdar (1976), "Resource depletion and research and development", in: M. Intriligator, ed., Frontiers of quantitative economics, Vol. IIIB (North-Holland, Amsterdam).

David, P.A. (1975), Technical choice, innovation and economic growth (Cambridge University Press, Cambridge).

David, P.A. and W. Sundstrom (1988), "Old-age security motives, labor markets and farm family fertility in antebellum America", Explorations in Economic History 25: 164–197.

Davidson, R. (1978), "Optimal depletion of an exhaustible resource with research and development towards an alternative technology", Review of Economic Studies 45: 355–367.

Davis, K. (1989), "Low fertility in evolutionary perspective", in: K. Davis and M.S. Bernstam, eds., Resources, environment and population (Oxford University Press, New York).

Deardorff, A.V. (1976), "The growth rate of population: a comment", International Economic Review 17: 510–515.

Demeny, P. (1988), "Population and the limits to growth", in: M.S. Teitelbaum and J.M. Winder, eds., Population and resources in western intellectual traditions (Cambridge University Press, Cambridge).

Demsetz, H. (1967), "Toward a theory of property rights", American Economic Review 57: 347–359.

Diamond, P.A. (1965a), "Government debt in a neoclassical growth model", American Economic Review 55: 1126–1150.

Diamond, P.A. (1965b), "The evaluation of infinite utility streams", Econometrica 33: 170–177.

Dorfman, R. (1993), "On sustainable development", Working paper no. 1627 (Harvard Institute of Economic Research, Cambridge, MA).

Dornbusch, R. and J.M. Poterba (1991), Global warming: economic policy responses (MIT Press, Cambridge, MA).

Easterlin, R.A. (1967), "Effects of population growth on the economic development of developing countries", in: J.D. Durand, ed., World population, Special issue, Annals of the American Academy of Political and Social Sciences 369: 98–108.

Easterlin, R.A. (1978), "The economics and sociology of fertility: a synthesis", in: C. Tilly, ed., Historical studies of changing fertility (Princeton University Press, Princeton, NJ).

Easterlin, R.A., R.A. Pollak and M.L. Wachter (1980), "Toward a more general model of fertility determination: endogenous preferences and natural fertility", in: R.A. Easterlin, ed., Population and economic change in less developed countries (University of Chicago Press, Chicago, IL).

Eckstein, Z. and K.I. Wolpin (1985), "Endogenous fertility and optimal population size", Journal of Public Economics 27: 93–106.

Eckstein, Z., K.I. Wolpin and S. Stern (1988), "Fertility choice, land and the Malthusian hypothesis", International Economic Review 29: 353–361.

Ehrlich, I. and F.T. Lui (1991), "Intergenerational trade, longevity and economic growth", Journal of Political Economy 99: 1029–1059.

Ehrlich, I. and F.T. Lui (1993), "Social insurance, family insurance and economic growth", Unpublished working paper (S.U.N.Y. Buffalo, Buffalo, NY).

Ehrlich, P.R. (1970), "Looking backward from 2000 A.D.", The Progressive 34: 23–25.

Enke, S. (1971), "Economic consequences of rapid population growth", Economic Journal 81: 800–811.

Evenson, R.E. (1984), "Benefits and obstacles in developing appropriate agricultural technology", in: C.K. Eicher and J. Staatz, eds., Agricultural development in the Third World (Johns Hopkins University Press, Baltimore, MD).

Feder, E. (1977), "Agribusiness and the elimination of Latin America's rural proletariat", World Development, 5.

Feder, E. (1979), "Agricultural resources in underdeveloped countries", Economic and Political Weekly 14: 1345–1366.

Findlay, R. (1990), "The new political economy: its explanatory power for LDC's", Economics and Politics 2: 193–221.

Fogel, R.W. and S. Engerman (1974), Time on the cross (W.W. Norton & Co., New York).

Food and Agriculture Organization (1993), "Forest resources assessment 1990: tropical countries", Forestry paper no. 112 (FAO, Rome).

Forrester, J.W. (1971), World dynamics (Wright Allen Press, New York).

Frankhauser, S. (1993), "The economic costs of global warming: some monetary estimates", in: Y. Kaya, N. Nakicenovic, W.D. Nordhaus and F.L. Toth, eds., Costs, impacts and benefits of CO_2 mitigation (International Institute of Applied Systems Analysis, Laxenburg, Austria).

Friedman, D. (1981), "What does optimal population mean?", in: J.L. Simon and P.H. Linhart, eds., Research in population economics, Vol. 3 (JAI Press, Greenwich, CT).

Gale, D. (1967), "Optimal development in a multi-sector economy", Review of Economic Studies 34: 1–18.

Geanakoplos, J.D. (1987), "The overlapping generations model of general equilibrium", in: J. Eatwell, M. Milgate and P.G. Newman, eds., The new Palgrave dictionary of economics (Macmillan, London).

Geanakoplos, J.D. and H.M. Polemarchakis (1992), "The overlapping generations model", in: H. Sonnenschein and A. Mas-Colell, eds., Handbook of mathematical economics, Vol. IV (North-Holland, Amsterdam).

Geertz, C. (1963), Agricultural innovation in Indonesia (University of California Press, Berkeley, CA).

Georgescu-Roegen, N. (1971), The entropy law and the economic process (Harvard University Press, Cambridge, MA).

Gigliotti, G. (1983), "Total utility, overlapping generations and optimal population", Review of Economic Studies 50: 71–86.

Glover, D. and J.L. Simon (1975), "The effects of population density on infrastructure: the case of road building", Economic Development and Cultural Change 23: 453–468.

Goeller, H.E. and A. Zucker (1984), "Infinite resources: the ultimate strategy", Science 223: 456–462.

Goldin, C and D.O. Parsons (1989), "Parental altruism and self-interest: child labor among late nineteenth century American families", Economic Inquiry 27: 637–660.

Gottlieb, M. (1945), "The theory of optimum population for a closed economy", Journal of Political Economy 53: 289–316.

Graves, P.E. (1991), "Aesthetics", in: J. Barden and C.D. Kolstad, eds., Measuring the demand for environmental quality (North-Holland, Amsterdam).

Grossman, G.M. (1993), "Pollution and growth: what do we know?", Discussion paper no. 848 (C.E.P.R., London).

Grossman, G.M. and E. Helpman (1989), Innovation and growth in the global economy (MIT Press, Cambridge, MA).

Grossman, G.M. and E. Helpman (1994), "Endogenous innovation in the theory of growth", Journal of Economic Perspectives 8: 23–44.

Grossman, G.M. and A.B. Krueger (1994), "Economic growth and the environment", Working paper 4634 (NBER, Cambridge, MA).

Gruver, G. (1976), "Optimal investment in pollution control capital in a neoclassical growth context", Journal of Environmental Economics and Management 3: 165–177.

Habakkuk, H.J. (1971), Population growth and economic development since 1750 (Leicester University Press, Leicester).

Halperin, T.D. (1993), The contemporary history of Latin America (University of California Press, Berkeley, CA).

Hammer, J.S. (1985), "Population growth and savings in the LDC's: a survey article", World Development 14: 579–591.

Hammond, P.J. (1993), "Is there anything new in the concept of sustainable development?", in: L. Campiglio, L. Pineschi, D. Siniscalco and T. Treves, eds., The environment after Rio (Graham and Trotman, London).

Hammond, P.J. and A. Rodriguez-Clare (1993), "On endogenizing long-run growth", Scandinavian Journal of Economics 95: 391–425.

Hansen, A.H. (1939), "Economic progress and declining population growth", American Economic Review 29: 1–15.

Harsanyi, J.C. (1955), "Cardinal welfare, individualistic ethics and interpersonal comparisons of utility", Journal of Political Economy 63: 309–321.

Hart, O.D. and J. Moore (1990), "Property rights and the theory of the firm", Journal of Political Economy 98: 1119–1158.

Hayami, Y. and M. Kikuchi (1982), Asian village economy at the crossroads: an economic approach to institutional change (Johns Hopkins University Press, Baltimore, MD).

Hayami, Y. and V.W. Ruttan (1987), "Population growth and agricultural productivity", in: D.G. Johnson and R.D. Lee, eds., Population growth and economic development: issues and evidence (University of Wisconsin Press, Madison, WI).

Heal, G.M. (1984), 'Interaction between economy and climate: a framework for policy design under uncertainty", in: V.K. Smith and A.D. White, eds., Advances in applied microeconomics (JAI Press, Greenwich, CT).

Heal, G.M. (1985), "Depletion and discounting: a classical issue in the economics of exhaustible resources", American Mathematical Society, Proceedings of Symposia in Applied Mathematics 32: 33–43.

Heal, G.M. (1990), "Economy and climate: a preliminary framework for microeconomic analysis", in: R.E. Just and N. Bockstael, eds., Commodity and resource policies in agricultural systems (Springer-Verlag, Berlin).

Heal, G.M. (1991), "Risk management and global change", First Boston working paper series no. 91-20 (Graduate School of Business, Columbia University, New York).

Heal, G.M. (1993), "The optimal use of exhaustible resources", in: A.V. Kneese and J.L. Sweeney, eds., Handbook of natural resource and energy economics, Vol. III (North-Holland, Amsterdam).

Heckscher, E.F. (1949), "Swedish population trends before the Industrial Revolution", Economic History Review, Series 2, 2: 266–277.

Hekstra, G.P. (1989), "Sea-level rise: regional consequences and responses", in: N.J. Rosenberg, W.E. Easterking, III, P.R. Crosson and J. Darmstader, eds., Greenhouse warming: abatement and adaption (Resources for the Future, Washington, DC).

Henry, C. (1974), "Option values in the economics of irreplaceable assets", Review of Economic Studies, 89–104.

Hicks, J.R. (1939), Value and capital (Clarendon Press, Oxford).

Hirschman, A.O. (1958), The strategy of economic development (Yale University Press, New Haven, CT).

Homburg, S. (1992), Efficient economic growth (Springer-Verlag, Berlin).

Hotelling, H. (1931), "The economics of exhaustible resources", Journal of Political Economy 39: 137–175.

Houghton, J.T., G.J. Jenkins and J.J. Ephraums (1990), Climate change - the IPCC scientific assessment (Cambridge University Press, Cambridge).

Howarth, R.B. and R.B. Norgaard (1993), "Intergenerational transfers and the social discount rate", Environmental and Resource Economics 3: 337–358.

Ingham, A. and P. Simmons (1975), "Natural resources and growing population", Review of Economic Studies 17: 191–206.

Jaeger, K. (1989), "The serendipity theorem reconsidered: the three generations case without inheritance", in: K.F. Zimmerman, ed., Economic theory of optimal population (Springer-Verlag, Berlin).

James, J. (1987), "Population and technical change in the manufacturing sector of developing countries", in: D.G. Johnson and R.D. Lee, eds., Population growth and economic development (University of Wisconsin Press, Madison, WI).

Jevons, W.S. (1865), The coal question: an inquiry concerning the progress of the nation and the probable exhaustion of our coal mines (Augustus M. Kelley, New York).

Jha, S.C., A.B. Deolalikar and E.M. Pernia (1994), "Population growth and economic development revisited with reference to Asia", Asian Development Review.

Jodha, N.S. (1986), "Common property resources and the rural poor", Economic and Political Weekly, 21.

John, A.A. and R. Pecchenino (1994), "Growth and the environment: an overlapping generations model of external increasing returns and environmental externalities", Economic Journal 104: 1393–1410.

John, A.A., R. Pecchenino, D. Schimmelpfennig and S. Schreft (1995), "Short-lived agents and long-lived environment", The Journal of Public Economics, in press.

Jones, E.L. (1989), Growth recurring (Oxford University Press, New York).

Jones, L.E. and R. Manuelli (1990), "A convex model of equilibrium growth", Journal of Political Economy 98: 1008–1038.

Jones, L.E. and R. Manuelli (1992), "Finite lifetimes and growth", Journal of Economic Theory 58: 171–197.

Jorgenson, D.W. and B.M. Fraumeni (1981), "Substitution and technical change in production", in: E.R. Berndt and B. Field, eds., Measuring and modeling natural resource substitution (MIT Press, Cambridge, MA).

Jorgenson, D.W. and P.J. Wilcoxen (1991), "Reducing U.S. carbon dioxide emissions: the cost of different goals", in: J.R. Moroney, ed., Energy, growth and the environment (JAI Press, Greenwich, CT).

Kamien, M.I. and N.L. Schwartz (1978), "Optimal exhaustible resource depletion with endogenous technical change", Review of Economic Studies 45: 179–196.

Kamien, M.I. and N.L. Schwartz (1982), "The role of common property resources in optimal planning models with exhaustible resources", in: V.K. Smith and J.V. Krutilla, eds., Explorations in natural resource economics (Johns Hopkins University Press, Baltimore, MD).

Keeler, E., M. Spence and R.J. Zeckhauser (1971), "The optimal control of pollution", Journal of Economic Theory 4: 19–34.

Kelley, A.C. (1988), "Economic consequences of population change in the third world", Journal of Economic Literature 26: 1685–1728.

Kelley, A.C. (1991), "Revisionism revisited: an essay on the population debate in historical perspective" (Department of Economics, Duke University, Durham, NC).

Kelley, A.C. and R.M. Schmidt (1992), "Is a negative population and economic growth correlation emerging? If so, so what?" (Department of Economics, Duke University, Durham, NC).

Kelley, A.C. and R.M. Schmidt (1994), "Population and income change", Discussion paper no. 249 (World Bank, Washington, DC).

Kelley, A.C. and J.G. Williamson (1974), Lessons from Japanese development: an analytical economic history (University of Chicago Press, Chicago, IL).

Keyfitz, N. (1982), Population change and social policy (Abt Books, Cambridge, MA).

Keyfitz, N. (1986), "The family that does not reproduce itself", in: K. Davis, M.S. Bernstam and R. Ricardo-Campbell, eds., Below replacement fertility in industrial societies (Oxford University Press, New York).

Keyfitz, N. (1991a), "Population and development within the ecosphere: one view of the literature", Population Index 57: 5–22.

Keyfitz, N. (1991b), "Population growth can prevent the development that would slow population growth", in: J.T. Mathews, ed., Preserving the global environment (W.W. Norton, New York).

Kimball, M.S. (1987), "Making sense of two-sided altruism", Journal of Monetary Economics 20: 301–326.

Kneese, A.V. and W.D. Schultze (1985), "Ethics and environmental economics", in: A.V. Kneese and J.L. Sweeney, eds., Handbook of natural resource and energy economics (North-Holland, Amsterdam).

Kolstad, C.D. and J.A. Krautkraemer (1993), "Natural resource use and the environment", in: A.V. Kneese and J.L. Sweeney, eds., Handbook of natural resource and energy economics, Vol. III (North-Holland, Amsterdam).

Koopmans, T.C. (1967), "Objectives, constraints and outcomes in optimal growth models", Econometrica 35: 1–15.

Koopmans, T.C. (1972), "Representation of preference orderings over time", in: M. McGuire and R. Radner, eds., Decision and organization (North-Holland, Amsterdam).

Koopmans, T.C. (1973), "Some observations on "optimal" economic growth and exhaustible resources", in: H.C. Bos, H. Linnemann and P. De Wolff, eds., Economic structure and development (North-Holland, Amsterdam).

Koopmans, T.C. (1979), "Economics amongst the sciences", American Economic Review 69: 1–13.

Krautkraemer, J. (1985), "Optimal growth, resource amenities and the preservation of natural environments", Review of Economic Studies 52: 153–170.

Krautkraemer, J. (1988), "The rate of discount and the preservation of natural environments", Natural Resource Modeling 2: 421–437.

Kremer, M. (1993), "Population growth and technological change: one million B.C. to 1990", Quarterly Journal of Economics 108: 681–716.

Krueger, A. (1993), The political economy of policy reform in developing countries (MIT Press, Cambridge, MA).

Krusell, P. and J.-V. Rios-Rull (1992), "Vested interests in a positive theory of growth and stagnation", Unpublished working paper (University of Pennsylvania, Philadelphia, PA).

Kuznets, S. (1966), Modern economic growth: rate structure and spread (Yale University Press, New Haven, CT).

Kuznets, S. (1967), "Population and economic growth", Proceedings of the American Philosophical Society 111: 170–193.

Laitner, J. (1991), "Modeling marital connections among family lines", Journal of Political Economy 99: 1123–1141.

Lal, D. (1988), Cultural stability and economic stagnation (Oxford University Press, Oxford).

Lam, D. (1987), "Distribution issues in the relationship between population growth and economic development", in: D.G. Johnson and R.B. Lee, eds., Population growth and economic development (University of Wisconsin Press, Madison, WI).

Lane, J. (1975), "A synthesis of the Ramsey–Meade problem when population is endogenous" Review of Economic Studies 42: 57–66.

Lane, J. (1977), On optimal population paths (Springer-Verlag, Berlin).

Lee, R.D. (1986), "Malthus and Boserup: a dynamic synthesis", in: D. Coleman and R. Schofield, eds., The state of population theory (Basil Blackwell, Oxford).

Lee, R.D. (1988), "Induced population growth and induced technical progress: their interaction in the accelerating phase", Mathematical Population Studies 13: 265–288.

Lee, R.D. (1990), "Population policy and externalities to childbearing", in: S.H. Preston, ed., World population: approaching the year 2000, Special issue, Annals of the American Academy of Political and Social Sciences 510: 145–154.

Lee, R.D. and T. Miller (1991), "Population growth, externalities to childbearing and fertility policy in developing economies", in: World Bank Annual Conference on Development Economics, Washington, DC.

Leibenstein, H. (1957), Economic backwardness and economic growth (Wiley, New York).

Leininger, W. (1986), "On the existence of perfect equilibria in a model of growth with altruism between generations", Review of Economic Studies 53: 349–367.

Levin, J. (1993), "An analytical framework for environmental issues", WP/93/53 (International Monetary Fund, Fiscal Affairs Department, Washington, DC).

Levi-Strauss, C. (1955), Tristes tropiques (Penguin Books, New York).

Levi-Strauss, C. (1963), "History and anthropology", Structural anthropology, Chapter 1 (Penguin Books, New York).

Lewis, A. (1954), "Economic development with unlimited supplies of labour", Manchester School 22: 139–191.

Lindert, P.H. (1985), "English population, wages and prices: 1541–1913", Journal of Interdisciplinary History 115: 609–634.

Low, B.S., A.L. Clarke and K.A. Lockridge (1992), "Toward an ecological demography", Population and Development Review 18: 1–31.

Lucas, Jr., R.E. (1988), "The mechanics of economic development", Journal of Monetary Economics 22: 3–42.

Lucas, Jr., R.E. (1990), "Why doesn't capital flow from rich countries to poor countries?", American Economic Review 80: 92–96.

Lutz, W. (1990), "Population and sustainable development: a case study of Mauritius", Population Network Newsletter 18: 1–5.

Mabbut, J. (1984), "A new global assessment of the status and trends of desertification", Environmental Conservation 11: 103–113.

MacKellar, F.L. and D.F. Vining, Jr. (1987), "Natural resource scarcity: a global survey", in: D.G. Johnson and R.D. Lee, eds., Population growth and economic development (University of Wisconsin Press, Madison, WI).

Mäler, K.-G. (1974), Environmental economics: a theoretical inquiry (Johns Hopkins University Press, Baltimore, MD).

Mäler, K.-G. (1985), "Welfare economics and the environment", in: A.V. Kneese and J.L. Sweeney, eds., Handbook of natural resource and energy economics (North-Holland, Amsterdam).

Mäler, K.-G. (1990), "International environmental problems", Oxford Review of Economic Policy 6: 80–108.

Mäler, K.-G. (1991), "National accounts and environmental resources", Environmental and Resource Economics 1: 1–15.

Manne, A.S. and R.G. Richels (1992), Buying greenhouse insurance: the economic costs of carbon dioxide emission limits (MIT Press, Cambridge, MA).

Mason, A. (1987), "Population and savings", in: D.G. Johnson and R.B. Lee, eds., Population growth and economic development (University of Wisconsin Press, Madison, WI).

McNeill, W.H. (1976), Plagues and peoples (Anchor Press, Garden City, NY).

McNeill, W.H. (1990), Population and politics (University of Virginia Press, Charlottesville, VA).

McNicholl, G. (1984), "Consequences of rapid population growth: an overview and assessment", Population and Development Review 10: 177–240.

McNicholl, G. (1987), "Agrarian and industrial futures: comments on the preceding chapters", in: T.J. Espenshade and G.J. Stolnitz, eds., Technological prospects and population trends (Westview Press, Boulder, CO).

Meade, J.E. (1955), Trade and welfare (Oxford University Press, Oxford).

Meadows, D.H., D.L. Meadows, J. Randers and W.W. Behrens, III (1972), The limits to growth (Earth Island Press, London).

Michaels, P. (1993), "Global warming: failed forecasts and politicized science", Policy study no. 117 (Center for the Study of American Business, Washington University, St. Louis, MO).

Michel, P. and P. Pestieau (1993), "Population growth and optimality", Journal of Population Economics 6: 353–362.

Migot-Adholla, S., P. Hazell, B. Blarel and F. Place (1991), "Indigenous land rights systems in sub-Saharan Africa: a constraint on productivity?", The World Bank Economic Review 5: 155–175.

Mink, S.D. (1993), "Poverty, population and the environment", Discussion paper no. 189 (World Bank, Washington, DC).

Mokyr, J. (1990), The lever of riches (Oxford University Press, Oxford).

Mokyr, J. (1993), "Mortality, technology and economic growth, 1750–1914", Unpublished working paper (Department of Economics, Northwestern University, Evanston, IL).

Mourmouras, A. (1991), "Competitive equilibria and sustained growth in a life-cycle model with natural resources", Scandinavian Journal of Economics 93: 585–591.

Mourmouras, A. (1993), "Renewable resources, the environment and intergenerational equity in overlapping generations models", Journal of Public Economics 51: 249–268.

Myers, N. (1986), "Environmental repercussions of deforestation in the Himalayas", Journal of World Forest Resource Management 2: 63–72.

Narveson, J. (1978), "Future people and us", in: R.I. Sikora and B. Barry, eds., Obligations to future generations (Temple University Press, Philadelphia, PA).

National Academy of Sciences (1992), Carbon dioxide and climate: a scientific assessment (National Academy Press, Washington, DC).

National Research Council (1986), Population growth and economic development: policy questions (National Academy Press, Washington, DC).

Neher, P.A. (1971), "Peasants, procreation and pensions", American Economic Review 61: 380–389.

Nelson, R.R. (1956), "A theory of the low-level equilibrium trap in underdeveloped economies", American Economic Review 46: 894–908.

Nerlove, M. (1991), "Population and environment", American Journal of Agricultural Economics 73: 1334–1347.

Nerlove, M. (1993), "Procreation, fishing and hunting: renewable resources and the dynamics of planar systems", American Journal of Agricultural Economics 75: 59–71.

Nerlove, M. and A. Meyer (1993), "Endogenous fertility and the environment: a parable of firewood", in: P. Dasgupta and K.-G. Maler, eds., The environment and emerging development issues (Clarendon Press, Oxford).

Nerlove, M. and L.K. Raut (1994), "Endogenous population in models of economic growth", in: M.R. Rosenzweig and O. Stark, eds., Handbook of population and family economics (North-Holland, Amsterdam) this volume.

Nerlove, M., A. Razin and E. Sadka (1987), Household and economy: welfare economics of endogenous fertility (Academic Press, New York).

New York Times (1992), Science Times, January 28th.

Ng, Y-K. (1986), "The welfare economics of population control", Population and Development Review 12: 247–266.

Nordhaus, W.D. (1991), "To slow or not to slow: the economics of the greenhouse effect", Economic Journal 101: 920–937.

Nordhaus, W.D. (1993a), "Climate and economic development: climate past and climate change future" in: L.S. Summers, ed., Proceedings of the World Bank Annual Conference on Development Economics (World Bank, Washington, DC).

Nordhaus, W.D. (1993b), "Reflections on the economics of climate change", Journal of Economic Perspectives 7: 11–26.

Nordhaus, W.D. (1994a), Managing the global commons: the economics of climate change (MIT Press, Cambridge, MA) in press.

Nordhaus, W.D. (1994b), "Reflections on the concept of sustainable economic growth", in: L.L. Pasinetti and R.M. Solow, eds., Economic growth and the structure of long-run development (St. Martins Press, London).

North, D.C. (1981), Structure and change in economic history (W.W. Norton and Co., New York).

North, D.C. and R.H. Thomas (1972), The rise of the western world (Cambridge University Press, Cambridge).

Nozick, R. (1974), Anarchy, state and utopia (Basic Books, New York).

Nugent, J.B. (1985), "The old-age security motive for fertility", Population and Development Review 11: 75–97.

OECD (1990), Pollution abatement and control expenditures in OECD member countries (OECD, Paris).

Organski, M.F.K., J. Kugler, J.T. Johnson and Y. Cohen (1984), Birth, deaths and taxes: the demographic and political transitions (University of Chicago Press, Chicago, IL).

Ostrom, E. (1990), Governing the commons: the evolution of institutions for collective action (Cambridge University Press, Cambridge).

Page, T. (1988), "Intergenerational equity and the social rate of discount", in: V.K. Smith, ed., Environmental resources and applied welfare economics (Resources for the Future, Washington, DC).

Parfit, D. (1983), "Energy policy and the further future: the identity problem", in: D. MacLean and P.G. Brown, eds., Energy and the future (NJ).

Parfit, D. (1984), Reasons and persons (Oxford University Press, Oxford).

Parikh, K. (1991), "An operational definition of sustainable development", Revised version of the C.N. Vakil Memorial Lecture to the Indian Economic Association, Indira Gandhi Institute for Research on Development Economics.

Partridge, E. (1981), Responsibility to future generations (Prometheus Books, New York).

Pasek, J. (1992), "Obligations to future generations: a philosophical note", World Development 20: 513–521.

Pasek, J. (1993), "Philosophical aspects of intergenerational justice", in: H. Giersch, ed., Economic progress and environmental concerns (Springer-Verlag, Berlin).

Persson, T. and G. Tabellini (1994), "Is inequality harmful to growth?", American Economic Review 84: 600–621.

Pezzey, J. (1989), "Economic analysis of sustainable growth and sustainable development", Working paper no. 15 (Environmental Department, World Bank, Washington, DC).

Pezzey, J. (1992), "Sustainability: an interdisciplinary guide", Environmental Values 1: 321–362.

Phelps, E.S. (1962), "The new view of investment: a neoclassical analysis", Quarterly Journal of Economics 76: 548–567.

Phelps, E.S. (1966), Golden rules of economic growth (W.W. Norton & Co., New York).

Phelps, E.S. (1968), "Population increase", Canadian Journal of Economics 1: 497–518.

Pindyck, R.S. (1979), "Interfuel substitution and the industrial demand for energy", Review of Economics and Statistics 61: 169–179.

Pingali, P.L. and H.P. Binswanger (1987), "Population density and agricultural intensification: a study of the evolution of technologies in tropical agriculture", in: D.G. Johnson and R.B. Lee, eds., Population growth and economic development (University of Wisconsin Press, Madison, WI).

Pitchford, J.D. (1974a), The economics of population: an introduction (Australian National University Press, Canberra).

Pitchford, J.D. (1974b), Population in economic growth (North-Holland, Amsterdam).

Pollak, R.A. (1985), "A transactions cost approach to families and households", Journal of Economic Literature 23: 581–608.

Pollak, R.A. (1988), "Tied transfers and paternalistic preferences", American Economic Review 78: 240–244.

Pollak, R.A. and S.C. Watkins (1993), "Cultural and economic approaches to fertility", Population and Development Review 19: 467–498.

Polyani, K. (1944), The great transformation (Beacon Press, Boston, MA).

Postel, S. (1984), "Protecting forests", in: L.R. Brown et al., eds., State of the world (W.W. Norton & Co., New York).

Poterba, J.M. (1993), "Global warming policy: a public finance perspective", Journal of Economic Perspectives 7: 47–63.

Preston, S.H. (1984), "Children and the elderly", Demography 21: 435–457.

Pritchett, L.H. (1994), "Desired fertility and the impact of population policies", Population and Development Review 20: 1–55.

Pryor, F.L. and S.B. Maurer (1982), "On induced economic change in precapitalist societies", Journal of Development Economics 10: 325–353.

Radner, R. (1972), "Existence of equilibrium of plans, prices and price expectations in a sequence of markets", Econometrica 40: 289–303.

Ramsey, F.P. (1928), "A mathematical theory of saving", Economic Journal 38: 543–559.

Raut, L.K. and T.N. Srinivasan (1992), "Theories of economic growth old and new", Discussion paper 92-37 (Department of Economics, University of California at San Diego, San Diego, CA).

Raut, L.K. and T.N. Srinivasan (1994), "The dynamics of endogenous growth", Economic Theory 4: 777–790.

Ray, D. (1987), "Non-paternalistic intergenerational altruism", Journal of Economic Theory 41: 112–132.

Ray, D. and P.A. Streufert (1993), "Dynamic equilibria with unemployment due to undernourishment", Economic Theory 3: 61–86.

Razin, A. and U. Ben-Zion (1975), "An intergenerational model of population growth", American Economic Review 65: 923–933.

Razin, A. and E. Sadka (1995), Population economics (MIT Press, Cambridge, MA).

Razzell, P.E. (1978), The conquest of smallpox (Firle, UK).

Razzell, P.E. (1993), "The growth of population in eighteenth century England: a critical reappraisal", Journal of Economic History 53: 743–771.

Rebelo, S. (1991), "Long-run policy analysis and long-run growth", Journal of Political Economy 99: 500–521.

Reilly, J. and N. Hohmann (1993), "Climate change and agriculture: the role of international trade", American Economic Review 83: 306–312.

Repetto, R. (1987), "Population, resources, environment: an uncertain future", Population Bulletin 42: 2.

Repetto, R. (1988), "Economic policy reform for natural resource conservation", Discussion paper no. 7 (Environmental Department, World Bank, Washington, DC).

Repetto, R., W. Magrath, M. Wells, C. Beer and F. Rossini (1989), Wasting assets: natural resources in the national income accounts (World Resources Institute, Washington, DC).

Ridker, R. (1972), "Resource and environmental growth consequences of population growth in the US: a summary", in: R. Ridker, ed., Commission on population growth and the American future, Research reports, Vol. III, Population, resources and the environment (Government Printing Office, Washington, DC).

Robinson, J.A. and T.N. Srinivasan (1995a), "Local environmental-demographic complementarities", Unpublished working paper (Economic Growth Center, Yale University, New Haven, CT).

Robinson, J.A. and T.N. Srinivasan (1995b), "Environmental quality, infrastructure, health and fertility: complementarities in the process of economic development", Unpublished working paper (Economic Growth Center, Yale University, New Haven, CT).

Robinson, W. and W. Schutjer (1984), "Agricultural development and demographic change: a generalization of the Boserup model", Economic Development and Cultural Change 32: 355–366.

Roemer, J.E. (1993), "Would economic democracy decrease the amount of public bads?", Scandinavian Journal of Economics 95: 227–238.

Romer, P.M. (1986), "Increasing returns and long-run growth", Journal of Political Economy 94: 1002–1038.

Romer, P.M. (1987), "Growth based on increasing returns due to specialization", American Economic Review 77: 56–62.

Romer, P.M. (1989), "Capital accumulation in the theory of long-run growth", in: R.J. Barro, ed., Modern business cycle theory (Harvard University Press, Cambridge, MA).

Romer, P.M. (1990), "Endogenous technical change", Journal of Political Economy 98: S71–S103.

Rosenberg, N. and L.E. Birdzell (1986), How the west got rich (Basic Books, New York).

Sah, R.K. (1991), "The effects of child mortality changes on fertility choice and parental welfare", Journal of Political Economy 99: 582–606.

Sala-i-Martin, X. (1994), "Cross-sectional regressions and the empirics of economic growth", European Economic Review 38: 739–747.

Samuelson, P.A. (1958), "An exact consumption loan model with or without the social contrivance of money", Journal of Political Economy 66: 467–482.

Samuelson, P.A. (1975), "The optimum growth rate for population", International Economic Review 16: 531–538.

Samuelson, P.A. (1976), "The optimal growth rate of population: agreement and evaluations", International Economic Review 17: 516–525.

Schmalensee, R. (1993), "Symposium on global climate change", Journal of Economic Perspectives 7: 3–10.

Schmitz, Jr., J.A. (1993), "Recent progress on the 'problem of economic development'", Federal Reserve Bank of Minneapolis Quarterly Review, Spring: 17–35.

Schultz, T.P. (1987), "School expenditures and enrollments, 1960–1980: the effects of incomes, prices and population growth", in: D.G. Johnson and R.D. Lee, eds., Population growth and economic development (University of Wisconsin Press, Madison, WI).

Schultz, T.W. (1974), "The high value of human time: population equilibrium", Journal of Political Economy 82: S2–S10.

Scott, M.F.G. (1989), A new view of economic growth (Oxford University Press, Oxford).

Sedjo, R.A. and M.C. Clawson (1984), "Global forests", in: J.L. Simon and H. Kahn, eds., The resourceful earth: a response to global 2000 (Basil Blackwell, New York).

Sen, A. (1993), "Population and reasoned agency: food, fertility and economic development", Paper presented at the "Population-Environment-Development Seminars" at the Royal Swedish Academy of Sciences and the Beijer Institute.

Serageldin, I. (1993), "Making development sustainable", Finance and Development, Dec.

Shleifer, A. (1990), "Externalities and economic growth: lessons from recent work", Unpublished paper (GSB, University of Chicago, Chicago, IL).

Sidgwick, H. (1907), Methods of ethics, 7th edn. (Macmillan, London).

Sikora, R.I. (1978), "Is it wrong to prevent the existence of future generations?", in: R.I. Sikora and B. Barry, eds., Obligations to future generations (Temple University Press, Philadelphia, PA).

Simon, J.L. (1977), The economics of population growth (Princeton University Press, Princeton, NJ).

Simon, J.L. (1981), The ultimate resource (Martin Robertson, Oxford).

Simon, J.L. (1986), Theory of population and economic growth (Basil Blackwell, Oxford).

Slade, M.E. (1982), "Trends in natural resource prices: an analysis of the time domain", Journal of Environmental Economics and Management 9: 122–137.

Slade, M.E. (1987), "Natural resources, population growth and economic well-being", in: D.G. Johnson and R.D. Lee, eds., Population growth and economic development (University of Wisconsin Press, Madison, WI).

Smulders, S. (1995), "Environmental policy and sustainable economic growth", De Economist 143: 163–195.

Solow, R.M. (1956), "A contribution to the theory of economic growth", Quarterly Journal of Economics 70: 65–94.

Solow, R.M. (1974a), "Intergenerational equity and exhaustible resources", Review of Economic Studies, Symposium on Natural Resources, 29–46.

Solow, R.M. (1974b), "The economics of resources and the resources of economics", American Economic Review 64: 1–14.

Solow, R.M. (1992), "An almost practical step towards sustainability", Resources for the Future 40th Anniversary Lecture.

Solow, R.M. (1993), "Sustainability: an economists perspective", in: R. Dorfman and N. Dorfman, eds., Selected readings in environmental economics (Norton, New York).

Solow, R.M. (1994), "Perspectives on growth theory", Journal of Economic Perspectives 8: 45–54.

Solow, R.M. and F.Y. Wan (1976), "Extraction costs in the theory of exhaustible resources", Bell Journal of Economics 7: 359–370.

Srinivasan, T.N. (1985), "Neoclassical political economy, the state and economic development", Asian Development Review 3.

Srinivasan, T.N. (1987), "Population and food", in: D.G. Johnson and R.B. Lee, eds., Population growth and economic development (University of Wisconsin Press, Madison, WI).

Srinivasan, T.N. (1988), "Population growth and economic development", Journal of Policy Modeling 10: 7–28.

Stark, O. (1984), "Bargaining, altruism and demographic phenomena", Population and Development Review 10: 679–692.

Stark, O. (1991), The migration of labor (Basil Blackwell, Oxford).

Stark, O. (1993), "On population externalities and the social rate of discount", Technical report no. 54 (Stanford Institute for Theoretical Economics, Stanford, CA).

Stark, O. (1995), Altruism and beyond (Cambridge University Press, Cambridge).

Starrett, D. (1972), "Fundamental non-convexities in the theory of externalities", Journal of Economic Theory 4: 180–199.

Stewart, F. and E. Ghani (1991), "How significant are externalities for economic development", World Development 19: 569–594.

Stiglitz, J.E. (1974a), "Growth with exhaustible natural resources: efficient and optimal growth paths", Review of Economic Studies, Symposium on Natural Resources, 123–138.

Stiglitz, J.E. (1974b), "Growth with exhaustible natural resources: the competitive economy", Review of Economic Studies, Symposium on Natural Resources, 139–152.

Stokey, N.L., R.E. Lucas, Jr. and E.C. Prescott (1989), Recursive methods in economic dynamics (Harvard University Press, Cambridge, MA).

Strotz, R.M. (1955–56), "Myopia and inconsistency in dynamic utility maximization", Review of Economic Studies 23: 165–180.

Sumner, L.W. (1978), "Classical utilitarianism and population optimum", in: R.I. Sikora and B. Barry, eds., Obligations to future generations (Temple University Press, Philadelphia, PA).

Swan, T.W. (1956), "Economic growth and capital accumulation", Economic Record 32: 334–361.

Tahvonen, O. and J. Kuuluvainen (1991), "Optimal growth with stock pollution", in: F. Dietz, F. van der Ploeg and J. van der Straaten, eds., Environmental policy and the economy (Elsevier, Amsterdam).

Tahvonen, O. and J. Kuuluvainen (1993), "Economic growth, pollution and renewable resources", Journal of Environmental Economics and Management 24: 101–118.

Talbot, L.M. (1986), "Demographic factors in resource depletion and environmental degradation in East African rangeland", Population and Development Review 12: 441–451.

Toman, M., J. Pezzey and J. Krautkraemer (1993), "Economic theory and 'sustainability'", Discussion papers in economics no. 93-15 (University College, London).

Tornell, A. (1993), "Economic growth and decline with endogenous property rights", Working paper no. 4354 (NBER, Cambrdige, MA).

Tucker, G.S.L. (1963), "English pre-industrial population trends", Economic History Review 16: 205–218.

Udry, C. (1994), "Gender, agricultural production and the theory of the household", Unpublished paper (Department of Economics, Northwestern University, Evanston, IL).

Uzawa, H. (1965), "Optimum technical change in an aggregative model of economic growth", International Economic Review 6: 18–31.

Van Arkadie, B. (1989), "The role of institutions in economic development", in: Proceedings of the World Bank Annual Conference on Development Economics.

van der Ploeg, F. and C. Withagen (1991), "Pollution control and the Ramsey problem", Environmental and Resource Economics 1: 215–236.

van Marrewijk, C., F. van der Ploeg and J. Verbeek (1993), "Is growth bad for the environment? Pollution, abatement and endogenous growth", Policy research working paper no. 1151 (World Bank, Washington, DC).

Vickrey, W.S. (1960), "Utility, strategy and social decision rules", Quarterly Journal of Economics 74: 507–535.

Vousden, N. (1973), "Basic theoretical issues in resource depletion", Journal of Economic Theory 6: 126–143.

Weil, P. (1987), "Love thy children: reflections on the Ricardian debt neutrality theorem", Journal of Monetary Economics 19: 377–391.

Weil, P. (1989), "Overlapping families of infinitely lived agents", Journal of Public Economics 38: 183–198.

Weir, D. (1989), "An historical perspective on the economic consequences of rapid population growth", Discussion paper no. 600 (Economic Growth Center, Yale University, New Haven, CT).

Weitzman, M.L. (1993a), "On the environmental discount rate", Working paper no. 1625 (Harvard Institute of Economic Research, Cambridge, MA).

Weitzman, M.L. (1993b), "On diversity", Quarterly Journal of Economics 107: 363–406.

Willis, R.J. (1980), "The old-age security hypothesis and population growth", in: T. Burch, ed., Demographic behavior: interdisciplinary perspectives on decision making (Westview Press, Boulder, CO).

Willis, R.J. (1981), "The direction of intergenerational transfers and demographic transition: the Caldwell hypothesis re-examined", in: Y. Ben-Porath, ed., Income distribution and the family.

Willis, R.J. (1987), "Externalities and population", in: D.G. Johnson and R.D. Lee, eds., Population growth and economic development (University of Wisconsin Press, Madison, WI).

Withagen, C. (1991), "Topics in resource economics", in: F. van der Ploeg, ed., Lectures in quantitative economics (Academic Press, New York).

World Bank (1984), World development report (Oxford University Press, New York).

World Bank (1992), World development report (Oxford University Press, New York).

World Resources Institute (1990), World resources 1990–1991 (World Resources Institute, Washington, DC).

Zhang, J. and K. Nishimura (1993), "The old-age security hypothesis revisited", Journal of Development Economics 41: 191–202.

INDEX TO VOLUMES 1A AND 1B

Aaron, H., 574
Abel, A., 198, 217, 940, 1002, 1227
abortions, 290
Abowd, J.M., 801
accidental bequests in intergenerational links, 196, 200
Acemoglu, D., 1260
Activity of Daily Living, 1008
Adelman, I., 773–774, 1035, 1045
adult-good method, estimating cost of children, 248–249
AFDC transfers and fertility, 305–308
Africa
    economic crises on vital rates, 1080, 1082–1084
    life expectancy and infant mortality, 563
    urban growth, 725–726
age
    cohorts
        infant mortality by, 570
        life expectancy by, 564
        size and earnings, 1023–1024
    of immigrants, 802–803
    and internal migration, 655–656
    and marriage, 53–57
        classical population theory, 53–54
        transferable utility, 55–56
        two-sex mating theories, 54–55
        women and older men, 56–57
    and urban migration, 730–731
age distributions
    economic effects of, 1097–1099
    fluctuations in, 1100–1104
    and life expectancy, 562
age selectivity of migration, 687
age structure, 14–15
    and income inequality, 1017–1024, 1051
        effects of, decomposing, 1017–1022
        evidence of, 1022–1023
        and wages, 1023–1024
    and population aging, 979–981
    and stable populations, 974, 975
Aghion, P., 1258, 1260
aging
    and disability in elderly, 609–611
    economics of, 13, 891–966
        future research, 960–962

status of elderly, 948–960
    consumption-based measures, 954–956
    income, variation in, 950
    income-based measures, 948–954
    and need, 949
    resources, distribution of, 956–958
    see also population aging
retirement *see* retirement
see also elderly
Agricultural Revolution, second, 1118
agriculture
    harvest failure on vital rates, 1080
    production technology and fertility, 378
    productivity and internal migration, 759–760
Aharoni, Y., 767
Ahlburg, D.A., 472
Ahluwalia, M.S., 729, 1035, 1048, 1264
Ahmad, A., 165
Ahn, N., 387
AIDS, 583
Ainsworth, M., 381
Aitchison, J., 450
Aiyagari, S.R., 200
Akerlof, G., 308
Akerman, A., 586
Akin, J., 571
Albright, R., 623
alcohol consumption
    and life expectancy, 566
    and mortality risk, 583, 590
Alderman, H., 175, 580–581, 1248
Alesina, A., 1264
Alessie, R., 256
aliens, undocumented, in international migration, 812–814
Allais, M., 1221
Allen, D., 113
Allen, J.C., 1195
Allen, R.C., 449, 465
Almost Ideal demand system and costs of children, 255–256
Alter, G., 572, 614
Altig, D., 227
Altonji, J., 820, 825–826, 1281
Altonji, J.F., 98, 199, 210–211
altruism

and bequest motive for saving in retirement, 943–945
conscious choice of, 73–74
in developed countries, 1248
and endogenous fertility, 1246–1247
intergenerational and interhousehold links, 189–212
  economic linkages, 199–206
  egoistic model, 198, 209
  general equilibrium, 217–222
  and human capital, 222–227
  interfamily transfers, 206–211
  life-cycle model, 192–193
  and marriage, 202
  simple model, 191–196
  transfers, 196–199
  two-sided, 212–217
and international migration, 806
in models of intrahousehold allocations, 128, 132–133
one-sided, and fertility, 1249–1250
parental, and economic growth in endogenous population change, 1141
  nonrecursive formulation, 1149–1150
  recursive formulation, 1150–1155
paternalistic in intergenerational linkages, 1126, 1227
role of in family, 91–94, 116
two-sided, 64–65
  and economic growth, 1141, 1168–1171
  and intergenerational linkages, 1226
amenities and decision to migrate, 679, 680, 689–690
Anderson, J.L., 1193
Anderson, J.P., 607
Anderson, K., 593–594, 607
Anderson, K.H., 382, 916
Anderson, K.P., 1229
Anderson, M., 1071
Andres, R., 471–472
Andrews, E.A., 902, 953
Andrews, G., 601
Angst, J., 364
Anker, R., 381, 383
annuities and intergenerational links, 196–197
  protection, 231
Antel, J.J., 696
Appleby, A.B., 439, 449
Archibald, G.C., 60, 69
Arnold, F., 387
Arrow, K.J., 1205, 1219, 1255, 1278
Ashby, H.T., 435

Ashenfelter, O., 359, 585
Ashton, B., 387, 1079, 1082
Asia
  economic crises on vital rates, 1080, 1082–1084
  immigrants to USA, 834
  life expectancy and infant mortality, 563
  urban growth, 725–726
assortative mating
  and altruism, 204–205
  and income inequality, 1026, 1030–1031
Atkinson, A.B., 198
Atkinson, E., 619
Attanasio, O.P., 578
Auerbach, A., 219, 575, 946, 997–1000, 1006, 1107
Australia
  immigrants
    assimilation of, 835
    education, 803
    flow of, 802, 809
  life expectancy and infant mortality, 563
  residential mobility, 653
Austria: residential mobility, 653
Avery, R.B., 196, 220
Axelrod, R., 49
Ayres, R.U., 1193
Azariadis, C., 1124, 1170, 1222, 1247

Ba Loc, P., 565
baby boom, 7, 55
  USA, 278–279
    and age distributions fluctuations, 1105–1106
    and dependency ratio, 977
    Easterlin cycles in, 1092–1093, 1095
    and fertility, 971
    and internal migration, 657
Backus, D.K., 1257
Bagnoli, M., 56, 108
Bagwell, K., 64, 66, 202, 204, 1204, 1281
Bahrin, T.S., 779
Bailey, R.E., 1070, 1081
Bailit, H., 575
Baily, M., 1139
Bairoch, P., 1067, 1118
Baker, M., 836
Baland, J.-M., 1249, 1266
Banerjee, B., 735–737, 742, 744, 747, 753, 759, 774
Bangladesh: food shortages, 1082
Banister, J., 387

Barbier, E.B., 1180, 1191, 1237, 1252
Bardhan, P., 1282
Bardsley, P., 253
bargaining
    and altruism in marriage, 91, 93, 95
    and search model, 106, 107
Barker, D.J.P., 471–472
Barnes, D.F., 1195
Barnes, D.G., 468
Barnett, H.J., 1188
Barnum, H.N., 742, 755
Barro, R., 923, 999, 1044
    on demand for children, 377–378, 396
    on endogenous population, 1147–1148, 1155, 1169, 1171
    on the family, 60, 63–64, 127, 146
    on household linkages, 200, 202, 220
    on population growth, 1207, 1218, 1226–1227, 1249–1250, 1254, 1258–1259, 1266–1267
Barros, R.P., 1026, 1030
Bartel, A., 576, 577, 704–705, 804–805
Barten, A.P., 252, 255–256
Barten-type scaling in costs of children, 252–253, 257
Bartik, T.J., 648, 711
Bartlett, W., 768
basal matabolic rate (BMR), 446–447, 453, 468
Basu, A.P., 616
Baumol, W.J., 867
Bazzoli, G., 607
Beaver, S.E., 1118
Becker, C.M., 782
Becker, G.
    on ageing, 943
    on costs of children, 243, 248
    on demand for children, 355, 358, 359–360, 363–364, 372, 377–378, 380
    on endogenous population, 1142–1144, 1147–1148, 1151, 1155, 1169, 1171
    on fertility economics, 276, 293–299, 305, 342
    on income inequality, 1030, 1044
    on intergenerational and interhousehold links, 190, 191, 193, 201, 221, 232
    on internal migration, 669, 739, 746, 773
    on intrahousehold distribution, 128, 130–133, 135–137, 143–146, 151, 167, 177
    on marriage and divorce, 82, 84, 91, 102, 109, 112–113, 120
    on mortality, 489, 577, 590
    on population growth, 1207, 1218, 1226–

1227, 1242, 1246, 1249–1250, 1266–1268, 1272
    on theories of family, 22, 24, 30, 35–37, 57–58, 60, 67
Becker–Lewis model of economic growth, 1142–1147
Beckerman, W., 1187, 1194
Beckmann, M., 46–47
Beckwith, J., 584
Beebe, G., 599
beggars, 469
Beggs, J., 815
behavioural technology and fertility, 524, 527
Behrman, J.R., 4, 545, 1030
    on demand for children, 364, 372, 381
    on intrahousehold distribution, 125–187
    on migration, 751, 784
    on mortality and morbidity, 568, 571, 576, 580–581, 584–585, 617
    on population dynamics, 1074, 1080–1081, 1093
Belgium: residential mobility, 653
Bellman, R., 625–626
Beltratti, A., 1278
Ben-Porath, Y., 88, 828, 1098
    on demand for children, 356, 361, 370, 372, 384, 386–387
    on mortality and health, 489–492, 517
Ben Zion, U., 378, 1148, 1249
benefit–cost analysis in benevolent families, 69–71
Benefo, K., 381–382, 385
benevolence within families, 59–60
    evolutionary models of, 71–73
Bengtsson, T., 445, 1081
Benhabib, J., 1151
Benham, L., 87, 577, 593
Benjamin, D., 836
Bennett, J., 763–764
Bental, B., 1163, 1168
bequests
    economic growth in endogenous population change
        nonrecursive formulation, 1149–1150
        recursive formulation, 1150–1155
    in endogenous population change, 1119
    in intergenerational linkages, 1126
    in intergenerational links, 190, 204–205, 206, 207, 222
        accidental, 196, 200
    motive for saving in retirement, 939–947
    sibling differences, 168–170

and utility interdependence, 63
Berelson, B., 402–403, 405
Berger, M., 594
Berglas, E., 868
Bergstrom, T.C., 3–4, 234
    on intrahousehold distribution, 146
    on marriage and divorce, 93, 98, 108
    on theories of family, 21–79
Beringhaus, S., 749
Berkovec, J., 625, 911–912
Bernard, R.-J., 449, 451
Berndt, E.R., 1235
Bernert, E.H., 662
Bernheim, B.D., 92, 146
    on aging, 936, 944–945, 1007
    on the family, 60, 64, 66, 73
    on intergenerational and interhousehold links,
        197–230 passim
    on mortality and morbidity, 594
    on population growth, 1204, 1211, 1227,
        1281
Berry, A., 739
Berry, R.A., 770
Betson, D., 1027
Bewley, T.F., 1204, 1276
Bhagwati, J.N., 763, 866, 871
Billewicz, W.Z., 455
Billings, P., 584
Binmore, K.G., 43–44, 52
Binswanger, H., 1180, 1262
Birch, S., 601
Birdsall, N., 784, 971
    on demand for children, 364, 384
    on population growth, 1179–1280 passim
Birdzell, L.E., 1258
birth control in low income countries, 376–377
birth weight and infant mortality, 523, 546–550
births
    economic crises on, 1080–1081
    first
        mother's age at in USA, 281–283
        optimal timing, 317–319
        probabilities, 283
    interval between in household production
        functions, 374
    in low income countries
        regional trends, 351–355
        spacing, 373–376
    order of
        birth ratios by, China and Korea, 388
        health and nutrition variations, 164–166
        and infant mortality, 544

unequal concern in intrahousehold allo-
        cations, 163–164
    probabilities
        first birth, 283
        and infant mortality, 500, 503, 514
        ratios, China and Korea, 388
        second, timing, 284
        spacing of
            and infant mortality, 509, 544
            optimal, 319–321
        third, timing, 285
Bishop, J., 154, 161
Black, D., 329–330
Blackburn, M., 109
Blackburn, M.L., 1029–1030
Blackorby, C., 62–63, 251, 1215
Blake, J., 143, 363
Blanchard, O.J., 214, 220, 1221
Blank, R., 332
Blau, D.M., 737–738, 842–844
Blayo, Y., 445
Blejer, M.I., 749
Blinder, A.B., 198, 217
Blinder, A.S., 907, 916, 924, 1007
Bliss, C.J., 758
Blokland, J., 246, 265
Blomquist, G.C., 676, 732, 768
Bloom, D., 837
Bloom, D.E., 1029–1030, 1186, 1195
Blum, J., 451
Blundell, R.W., 256
Bodie, Z., 578
Bodmer, W.F., 160, 458
body mass indices and malnutrition, 452–460
body size variations and mortality, 460–466
Boertlein, C.G., 648, 652–654
Boldrin, M., 1257
Bongaarts, J., 372, 402–403, 1081, 1195
Borenstein, S., 86
Borjas, G.J., 881
    on internal migration, 695, 699, 701
    on international migration, 805–842 passim
Bös, D., 562, 993
Boserup, E.
    on demand for children, 378, 390
    on endogenous population, 1132–1139
    on population growth, 1070, 1245, 1262
Boskin, M.J., 902, 912–914, 1004
Bosworth, B., 997
Botswana
    cattle and environment, 1252–1253
    intergenerational economic links, 232

migration in, 750–751
Boulier, B.L., 359
Bouls, H., 580
Bound, J., 577, 607, 611, 1050
Bourgeois-Pichat, J., 437
Bourguignon, F., 172, 176–178
Bovenberg, A.L., 1200, 1269
Bradshaw, B.S., 571
Bradshaw, J., 245–246
Brainerd, C.P., 662
Brander, J.A., 1186, 1195
Bratsberg, B., 816
Braudel, F., 1088
Brazil
    age structure, 1019–1021, 1022
    fertility, 1042
    husband's income, 1030
breastfeeding, 509–510, 523, 526, 529, 535–540
Brenner, M., 563
Brenner, M.H., 1079, 1085
bride prices, 58, 101, 109
Brien, M., 109
Brock, W.A., 1237, 1242
Bronars, S., 807, 811
Broome, J., 1192, 1215
Brostrom, G., 1081
Brown, J.A.C., 450
Brown, L.A., 754
Brown, M., 24, 32, 37–38, 42, 44, 95, 172–173
Browning, M., 39–40, 42, 98–99, 244
Brownlee, J., 436
Bruce, N., 36, 146, 214–215
Brumberg, R., 192, 373
Bryant, W.K., 361
Buchanan, J., 36, 215
budget constraints
    and fertility, 313–314, 489
    time, in household economic models, 356
budget set nonlinearities in retirement models,
        906–907
    and social security, 913
Buehler, J.W., 546
buffer stock model of savings, 999
Buhmann, B., 262
Bulatao, R.A., 377
Bumpass, L., 120
Burkhauser, R.V., 577, 607, 917
Burnett, J., 451
Burney, M., 565
Burtless, G.
    on aging, 902, 912, 915–916
    on income inequality, 1051–1052

on mortality and morbidity, 581, 587, 594,
        607, 621
business cycles
    and age distributions, 1106–1107
    and migration, 687–688
Busschbach, J., 607
Butcher, K., 826
Butler, J., 577, 607, 623
Butz, W.P., 372, 537, 1078–1080, 1085
Byne, W., 584

Caballero, R.J., 1257
Caces, F., 724, 744
Cain, G., 113
Cain, M., 247, 388
Caldwell, J.C., 354, 414
    on population dynamics, 1080, 1084, 1086
    on population growth, 1118, 1182–1183,
        1247
Caldwell, P., 354, 414, 1080, 1084, 1086
Calhoun, C.A., 247–248
Califano, J., 575
California: infant mortality rates, 487
caloric consumption and mortality, 447, 461
    England & France, 449–452
calorie availability and fertility, 401
Calvo, G.A., 764–765
Campbell, D., 27
Campbell, J.Y., 223
Canada
    immigrants to
        assimilation of, 835
        education of, 803
        flow of, 802
        language proficiency of, 837–8
        skill levels of, 810, 812
        to USA, 834
    immigration, regulation of, 809–810
    internal migration in, 655, 673, 687, 699,
        701
        distance elasticities, 667
        trends, 657
    life expectancy and infant mortality, 563
    residential mobility, 653–654
    social expenditure by age, 1000
Cancian, M., 1027
Cannan, E., 1213
capital
    and internal migration in developing coun-
        tries, 746–748
        financing migration, 746–747
        tied rents, 747–748

and labor mobility in international trade, 865–867
capital accumulation
  and endogenous fertility, 1267
  and endogenous population change, 1251
  and endogenous technical change, 1254–1255
  and social welfare, 1265–1266
capital–labor ratio
  in dynastic economy, 1203–1204
  and endogenous technical change, 1254–1256
  and population growth, 1212
  and social welfare, 1265–1266
capital markets
  and fertility, 313–314
  imperfect and child to parent transfers, 1163–1168
  and marriage, 85
  and old age pension motives, 1161
  and timing of first births, 317–318
Card, D., 820, 825–826
Carlin, P., 109, 119
Carmichael, H.L., 49
Carr-Saunders, A.M., 437
Carroll, C.D., 196, 207, 220, 999
Case, R.A.M., 435
Cassen, R.H., 1183, 1187, 1247, 1282
Casterline, J.B., 413
Castro, L.J., 731
Cavalli-Sforza, L.L., 160, 458
chain migration, international, 807, 811
Chaloupka, F.J., 590
Chamberlain, G., 614
Chambers, M.J., 1070, 1081
Chamla, M.Cl., 459
Chan, P., 780
Chandler, W., 1188
Chapman, B., 815
Charney, A.H., 711
Chartres, J.A., 465
Chernichovsky, D., 381
Chiappori, P.-A., 33–34, 42, 99, 172, 175–178, 356, 359
Chichilnisky, G., 1190, 1278–1279
child allowance, 1142
child health services and fertility, 390
child mortality *see* infant and child mortality
child quality
  in low income countries, 363–365
  in quality–quantity model of economics of fertility, 296–298
  returns to schooling in intrahousehold allocation, 142–144

child quantity in low income countries, 363–365
child support among unwed parents, 58
child-to-parent transfers
  as old-age security motive, 1141, 1160–1168
    ethics of equal sharing, 1161–1163
    imperfect capital markets, 1163–1168
    inter vivos, 1168
    old age pension motives, 1161–1168
    two-sided altruism, 1168–1171
  within-family intergenerational relations, 1007–1008
childbearing
  marital and nonmarital in USA, 283–287
  trends in, 286
  out-of-wedlock, 305–308
childlessness in USA, 280–281
children
  in consensus parental preference models
    active children, 144–146
    equal concern for, 130, 133, 139–142
    passive children, 129–144
      returns to schooling, 142–144
      separable earnings-transfers (SET) model, 137–142
      wealth model, 130–137
    unequal concern for, 163–164
  and control of fertility, 312–313
  cost of, 5–6, 241–273
    adult-good method, 248–249
    assumptions and definitions, 244–245
    cost functions, 250–251
      and demand system, 255, 258
      critique (Pollak and Wales), 258–260
    Engel method, 249–250
    equivalence scales, 250–255
    estimates, 245–248
    Leyden approach, 260–263
    neo-classical demand systems, 250–255
      implementing, 255–258
    normative budgets, 245–246
    and revenues earned, 243
    subjective scales, 260–263
  demand for
    in low income countries *see* low income countries
    and time allocation, 298–305
  and divorce, 111, 113–116, 119
  mature, altruism towards, 190–194
  maximum a woman can have, and survival probability, 1159
  as normal consumption good, 1143
  opportunity value of time of, 383

as reasons for marriage, 82, 83
services
    output of, 300–304
    production of, 310–311
stock of and fertility, 508, 521
taxation on, 1142
time–cost of and fertility, 1077
well-being, and household public goods, 40–42
China
  birth ratios by birth order, 388
  food shortages on vital rates, 1082
  life expectancy and economic development, 565
  migration in, 755–756
Chirikos, T., 611
Chiswick, B.R., 806, 811, 828, 833, 836, 838–840
Chiswick, C.U., 737
choice theory, 1181–1182
Chollet, D., 902
Chomitz, K.M., 1200
Choudhury, S.A., 696, 700
Christensen, L.R., 255–256
Christenson, B., 583
Chu, C.Y.C., 1039–1041, 1043–1044, 1097
Chuma, H., 577, 593
Cigno, A., 82, 363, 1124, 1168, 1204
circular migration in developing countries, 729–730
Clark, C., 622, 1191
Clark, D.E., 680
Clark, R.L., 902–903
Clarke, R., 1193
class and migration, 684
Clawson, M.C., 1191
Cleland, J., 376, 387
Clement, D.G., 575
climate
  and global warming, 1192–1194
  and migration, 678–679
  shocks on vital rates
    long-run, 1088
    short-run, 1081, 1082
Cline, W.R., 1192–1193
Coale, A.J., 1090–1091, 1118, 1183, 1218
  on demand for children, 361, 376, 379, 387
Coase, R.H., 1281
Cochrane, S.H., 381
Cohen, L., 119
Cole, G.D.H., 451
Cole, W.E., 736

Coleman, J., 32
Coleman, J.S., 697
Colfer, C., 753
collective bargaining in labor markets in developing countries, 764–765
collective goods, sharing in marriage, 82, 86–87
college education, equal access to, 149–151
Collier, P., 739
Colombia
  income inequality in, 1034–1035
  migration in, 755
commitment in marriage, 49–50
Common, M., 1276
communal land and fertility, 390
Communism, collapse of, 853
comparative advantage in marriage, 84, 117
competing risk models of mortality in adults and elderly, 616–617
competitive equilibrium in households
  efficiency of with nonbenevolence, 67–68
  Pareto optimality of, 66–68
    sustainability of, 68–71
Comstock, G.W., 547
conception probabilities and infant mortality, 510–511
condoms, 287, 288–289
Condran, G., 1093
Connell, J., 723, 746–747, 754, 757, 774, 782
consensus parental preference models *see under* intrahousehold allocations
consumer behaviour, 3, 62–63
consumption
  and age distributions fluctuations, 1104
  consumer behaviour, 3
  following retirement, 919–948
    bequest motive for saving, 939–947
    change, 940
    by couples, 927–931
    life-cycle model, 923–931
      consumption data, 938–939
      wealth data, 931–935
    by singles, 924–927
    summary, 947–948
    wealth change, 935–938
  in intergenerational links
    possibilities, 228–229
    smoothing, 199–200, 203
  and migration, 671–672
  and population aging, 977–994
    age structure and population growth, 979–981
    and labor market, 989–994

lifetime wage profiles, 990–991
 seniority promotion, 993–994
 unemployment and labor force participation, 992–993
 wages and marginal products, 991
 morbidity and mortality, 981–983
 steady state, 985, 986
 sustainable in model with capital, 983–
  989
 youth and old-age dependency, 977–979
contraception
 and economics of fertility, 321
  in USA, 287–291
 in low income countries
  price of, 407–408
  unpredictable failures of, 364
contraceptive pill, 287, 288–289
Cooper, R., 568
cooperation in family decision-making, 95
cooperative Nash bargaining in decision-making
 in the family, 37–39
coordination of activities in marriage
 investment, 82
 work, 83
Corden, W.M., 761
Corder, L., 609
Corman, H., 552, 571
Corner, L., 750
Cornes, R., 27, 29, 34, 40
Cosgrove, J.C., 680
Costa, D.L., 471
couple-specific traits in household demand systems, low income countries, 358
Courant, P., 86
Courchene, T.J., 667, 673, 687
Cox, D., 73, 696, 944, 1008
 on demand for children, 373, 377, 389
 in household linkages, 191, 199, 201, 207–
  209, 224, 229–230, 234
 on mortality and mortbidity, 615–617
Crafts, N.F.R., 469
Cramer, J.C., 486
Crawford, V., 48, 902
credit markets
 and fertility in low income countries, 377,
  379
 imperfect market and marriage, 82, 85–86
 in transactions cost approach to intergenerational links, 230–233
Creedy, J., 682
Crimmins, E., 610, 983, 1006
Crimmins, E.M., 372, 377

Cronk, L., 1182
Crook, N.R., 1249
Cropper, M., 1196
cross-price effects of children in low income
 countries, 390–393
crowding effect of fertility, 384
Cuba: migration to USA, 571, 826–827
Cummins, G., 452
Curtain, R.L., 750
custody of children in divorce, 111, 114, 115,
 118
Cutler, D., 574, 977, 983, 985, 988, 1000

Dalko, V., 1156, 1172
Dalton, H., 1213
Daly, H., 1273
Damon, A., 458
Daniel, K., 85
Danziger, S., 1027, 1033
Darby, M.R., 923
Dardanoni, V., 594
Darity, W.A. Jr, 1263
Darwin, C., 1246
Das, S.P., 768
Dasgupta, P., 54, 759
 on population growth, 1178–1277 *passim*
Datta, G., 1033
DaVanzo, J., 368, 387
 on income inequality, 1033–1034
 on internal migration, 665, 684–686, 689,
  699, 705–706
David, M., 207–208, 924
David, P.A., 806, 1247, 1264
Davidson, R., 1229
Davidson, S., 447
Davies, J.B., 197–198, 449
Davies, J.B., 387
Davis, K., 1181
Davis, S., 833
Davis, S.J., 227, 864
Dawkins, R., 72
Day, K.M., 682, 692, 708
Day, R.H., 769
De Mendonça, S.P., 1029
De Montricher, G., 617
de Zarate, A.U., 710
Deardorff, A.V., 1225
deaths
 causes of, 603
  London, 439
 as exhaustive state, 597–598
 neonatal, and fertility, 523–524

regional trends in low income countries, 351–355

Deaton, A., 23, 165, 200, 248–250, 253, 255–256, 999

Devaney, R.L., 1166

DeBakey, M., 599

decision-making in the family, 31–44, 1119
  modes of, 94–96
    common objectives, 94–95
    cooperation, 95
    noncooperation, 95–96
  pluralistic, 37–44
    children's well-being, 40–42
    cooperative Nash bargaining, 37–39
    noncooperative bargaining, 42–44
    and Pareto efficiency, 40–42
    private-goods consumption, 39–40, 42
    proportional sharing rules, 37
  theory of, 1121
  unitary theories of, 32–37
    with household social welfare function, 34–35
    with Rotten Kid Theorem, 35–37
    with transferable utility, 33–34

deforestation, 1191, 1195

DeFreitas, G., 828

Del Bene, L., 601

Demange, G., 48

Demeny, P., 1178

demographic cost indices and costs of children, 251–255

demographic scaling effects on demand systems, 254

Demographic Transition, 8, 1118, 1180, 1185–1186, 1245, 1247
  and infant mortality, 484–485

demographic translation effects on demand systems, 254

demonstration effect in intergenerational links, 233–234

Dempster, A., 617

Demsetz, H., 1191

Denison, E.F., 396

Denmark: height of men, 459

Denslow, D.A., 667

Deolalikar, A.B., 164, 576, 580, 1074, 1080–1081

dependency
  and population aging, 977–979
  ratios, and population aging, 977, 983
    social security and government programs, 1000–1001

desertification, 1191

DeStefano, F., 568, 584

DeSweemer, C., 523

DeTray, D.N., 381

DeVany, A., 390

developed countries
  altruism in, 1248
  economics of fertility
    empirical implications, 322–342
      life-cycle models, econometrics of, 335–342
        applications, 335–336
        estimating structural models, 339–342
        hazard models, 336–339
      price and income effects, 322–333
        fixed-effects, 330–333
        instrumental variables, 328–330
        social experiments, 327–328
      and twins, 333–335
    life-cycle models of *see under* life-cycle models
    static models, 292–308
      marriage and out-of-wedlock child-bearing, 305–308
      quality–quantity model, 294–298
      time allocation and demand for children, 298–305
  environmental concerns, 1179
  fertility, economics of, 6–7, 275–347
  migration in *see under* internal migration; international migration
  short-run population fluctuations, 1085

developing countries/economies
  environmental degradation in, 1179, 1189–1192, 1195
  fertility, declining, 1184
  income inequality in, 1047–1048
  income pooling, 174–176
  infant mortality differentials, 148–149
  intrahousehold distributions in, 154–157
  migration in *see under* internal migration; international migration
  public institutions and environment, 1179
    and endogenous technical change, 1259–1260
  SET model estimates with unequal concern, 163–164
  see also low income countries

DeVries, J., 1088

Diamond, P., 105, 108, 593

Diamond, P.A., 219, 935, 1202, 1221, 1277
diaphragm (birth control), 288–289
Diaz-Briquets, S., 571, 722
Dickens, W.T., 766
Dicks-Mireaux, L., 933
diet and malnutrition, 446
dietary energy, 461
Dietzenbacher, E., 1039–1041
Diewert, E., 42
Diggle, P., 618–619
disability
    classification, 606
    and mortality, 609–610
    and population aging, 983
Disability-adjusted life years (DALYs), 562, 607
discounting in environmental issues, 1275–1278
disease
    chronic, 472
    and mortality, decline in, 437–438
displaced persons and migration in developing
    countries, 755–756
distance and internal migration, 660, 666–668
distance elasticity of migration, 667
division of labor
    in marriage, 82, 84, 102
    and population growth, 1261–1262, 1263
divorce
    custody of children in, 111, 114, 115, 118
    defensive investments, 117–119
    determinants of, 110–113
    economic consequences, 110–119
    and household allocation in marriage, 49–50
        as threat in bargaining, 39, 50–51
    insurance motives in, 116
    in noncooperative bargaining theory, 44
    rule, 118
    transfers, 113–116
Doll, R., 584, 612
Dominquez, K.M., 1101–1102
Donaldson, C., 604, 607
Donaldson, D., 60, 69, 251, 1215
Dooley, M., 1024
Dorfman, R., 1275
Dorn, H.F., 437, 584–585, 612, 617
Douglas, P., 808
Dowrick, S., 1186, 1195
dowry, 101, 109
Doyle, J.J., 683
Drazen, A., 221, 224, 227, 761, 1124, 1170, 1247
Drewe, P., 711
Drummond, J.C., 451
Dublin, L.I., 247, 434–435, 437

Duleep, H.O., 583, 599, 836
Dumond, D., 376
Duncan, G., 113
Duncan, O.D., 356
Dupâquier, J., 442, 445
Duraisamy, P., 391
Durch, J.S., 616
Dyer, C., 449
dynastic population cycles, 1097
dynastic utility function of parents, 1150

earnings
    and age structure, 1023
    capacity
        and divorce, 110, 112–113
        and marriage, 85–86, 102, 109
    and immigration, 828–829, 838
    in life-cycle hypothesis of consumption,
        923
    and life insurance, 946, 947
    and migration, 691–692
        differentials, 739–742
        model of, 688–689
        of wives, 705
    sibling differences, 167–172
Easterlin, R.A., 120, 551, 662, 1186
    on demand for children, 372, 377
    on population dynamics, 1090, 1092–1093,
        1095, 1100, 1103, 1105–1106
Easterlin cycles in population, 1092–1093
Eaton, P.J., 667
Eberstein, I.W., 524
Eberts, R.W., 679
Eckstein, Z., 445, 513, 625, 1044
    on demand for children, 374, 378
    on household linkages, 198, 217
    on population dynamics and growth, 1077,
        1081, 1250–1251
econometrics of international migration, 807–
    808, 821–827
economic crises on vital rates, 1080
economic growth and development
    in aging population, 1009
    demography and resources, 1187–1197
        exhaustible resources, 1187–1188
        population, role of, 1195–1197
        renewable resources, 1188–1195
            global problems, 1192–1195
            local phenomena, 1190–1192
    in endogenous population change, 15–16,
        1117–1174
        Becker–Lewis model, 1142–1147

human capital investment, 1147–1155
Lucas–Romer model, 1139–1141
Malthus–Boserup model, 1132–1139, 1168
Niehans model, 1130–1132
old age pension motives, 1161–1168
  ethics of equal sharing, 1161–1163
  imperfect capital markets, 1163–1168
old age security motives, 1141, 1160–1168
parental altruism, 1147–1155
  nonrecursive formulation, 1149–1150
  recursive formulation, 1150–1155
Solow–Swan model, 1124–1130
survival probability, 1155–1160
  basic model, 1156–1158
  investment in health care, 1159–1160
  and population growth, 1158–1159
two-sided altruism, 1168–1171
long-run, 1202–1245
in finite lifetimes, 1220–1228
  intergenerational links, 1226–1228
  optimal population, 1225–1226
  overlapping generations, 1221–1225
infinitely-lived agents, 1220–1228
  basic dynastic economies, 1203–1211
  optimal population
    dynamic analysis, 1217–1220
    static analysis, 1211–1217
with resources, 1228–1245
  exhaustible resources, 1229–1235
  finite lives, 1236
  international issues, 1245
  optimal population, 1235
  renewable resources, 1236–1244
mortality and morbidity and, 563–565
and population growth, 1186–1187
sustainable, 1272–1275
economic incentives to migrate, 805–807
economic linkages in intergenerational links, 199–206
economies of scale and population growth, 1263
education and schooling
college, equal access to, 149–151
and divorce, 113
and fertility, 381
of immigrants, 803
and infant mortality, 529
and internal migration, 655–656, 705
  in developing countries, 784–785
investment in, 86, 102
and marriage, gains from, 85–86

and models of intrahousehold distribution
  allocation, 158–162
  returns to and child quality, 142–144
  sibship similarity, 149–151
services and fertility, 390
and wage increases, USA, 1050
efficiency
of competitive equilibrium in households, 67–68
of intrahousehold allocations, 127, 131, 176–179
of marriage, 87, 89, 93, 97, 99
  and cooperation, 95
  and divorce, 114, 115
  ex ante, 115–116
  ex post, 115–116
efficiency wage models and internal migration, 765–766
egoistic model in intergenerational links, 198, 209
Ehrlich, I., 577, 593
Ehrlich, P.R., 1178, 1253, 1267
Eichenbaum, M., 587
elderly
economic status of, 948–960
  consumption-based measures, 954–956
  income, variation in, 950
  income-based measures, 948–954
  and need, 949
  resources, distribution of, 956–958
health demand models, one-period, 577–587
mortality and morbidity in, 562–575
  and economic development, 563–565
  and gender, 565–567
  and infant mortality, 569–571
  and migration, 571–572
  and nutrition, 572–573
  public policy on, 573–575
  and race, 565, 568–569
Eldridge, H.T., 662
Ellwood, D.T., 582, 600, 610, 902
employment
industrial, and migration in developing countries, 738–739
and internal migration, 681–688
  national, 687–688
  opportunities, 671, 680
  personal, 683–687
  regional, 681–683
endogenous fertility, 243–244
endowments in intrahousehold allocation, 174, 179–180

reinforcement versus compensation, 127,
 131–132, 142, 151–162
  schooling allocation, 158–162
  SET model estimates, 152–154
  in subsistence economy, 154–157
 in single period perference models, 146–162
 in wealth model, 129–137
energy requirements, mortality and malnutrition,
 445–449
Engel, E., 247–249
Engel method, estimating cost of children, 249–
 250
Engerman, S.L., 242, 448, 1247
Enke, S., 1218
Entorf, H., 1081
environment
 degradation of and population growth, 1189–
  1190, 1195–1197
 local, 1190–1192
 and economy, interactions, 1178–1179
 effects of fertility on, 377
 externalities in, 1239
 and resource use, 1187–1197
  exhaustible resources, 1187–1188
  population, role of, 1195–1197
  renewable resources, 1188–1195
   global problems, 1192–1195
   local phenomena, 1190–1192
Equivalence Scale Exactness property in demographic cost indices, 251
equivalence scales in cost of children, 250–255
 overview, 265–269
 Yugoslav scales, 264–265
Ericksen, E., 599
Ermisch, J., 119
Ernst, C., 364
Espenshade, T., 120, 247–248, 374, 1104
Eswaran, M., 758
Ethier, W., 814
ethnicity
 and life expectancy (USA), 563, 565
 and migration (USA), 571–572
Europe
 consequences of classical population theory,
  1066–1073
 famines, 466–468
 life expectancy and infant mortality, 563
 male heights, 459
 migration to (post-war), 853
 pre-industrial population size
  and economy, 1067–1068, 1070–1071
  and growth, 1184

Evans, A.W., 677
Evans, W., 594
Evenson, R., 326, 362, 365–366, 381, 383, 1263
evolutionary models of benevolence within
 families, 71–73
exhaustible resources
 in long-run development, 1229–1235
 and population growth, 1187–1188
exogenous shocks in household production functions, 371
extended families, 83

Faber, J., 973
factor content in international trade models, 859–
 860
factor prices in international trade models, 857–
 859
Fair, R.C., 1101–1102
Falaris, E., 698, 741–742, 771
falling in love, 73
Fallon, P.R., 736
family equivalence index, 251
family/families, 3–5
 decision-making in *see* decision-making in
  the family
 economic problems, solving, 89–99
  altruism, 91–94
  decision-making modes, 94–96
   common objectives, 94–95
   cooperation, 95
   noncooperation, 95–96
  modes of behaviour, testing, 96–99
  transferable utility, 89–91
 extensive forms, 356
 future of, 119–120
 intrahousehold distribution *see* intrahousehold distribution
 migration
  emigration, decision to, 806–807
   family unification, 810–811
  internal
   decision to, 702–707
   strategies in developing countries,
    749–753
 size, 6–7
  USA, 278–280
 theories of, 3–4, 21–79
  decision making, 31–44
  household technology, 22–31
  interdependent preferences, 59–74
  marriage and household membership, 45–
   59

family planning, 244
    and fertility, 390, 413, 551–552
    inter-country comparisons, 402–407
    in low income countries, 376–377
family utility function, 32–33
    and costs of children, 249
    and price of children, 292–293
famines
    mortality and nutrition
        European famines, 466–468
        secular decline in, 440–445
    on vital rates, 1082
Fan, Y.-K., 748
fecundity
    in household demand systems, low income
        countries, 358
    and infant mortality, 512–513, 520
Feder, E., 1180
Feeney, G., 1082
Fei, C.H., 1034
Feinstein, J.F., 576
Feldman, J.J., 580
Feldstein, M., 202
Fenn, P., 610
Ferraro, K., 601
fertility, 5–8, 175
    and age distributions fluctuations, 1105
    cumulative, recent and desired, world's re-
        gions, 382
    declining, world, 1184–1185
    declining and population aging, 971–972,
        972–975
    demand for children in low income
        countries
        and child mortality, 398
        contraception, price of, 407–408
        family planning, 402–407
        findings, 397–402
        inter-country comparisons, 393–417
        macroeconomics of, 377–380
            credit, security and savings, 379
            mobility and marriage, 379–380
            overlapping generations, 378–379
        and mortality, 368–370
        production-demand model, 361–363
        time-series changes, 408–413
    differential, and income inequality, 1035–
        1044
        in developing countries, 1047–1048
        intergenerational, and differential fertility,
            1038–1043

population growth, mathematics of,
        1036–1038
    welfare implications of, 1043–1044
economic crises on, 1081, 1082–1083
economics of, 6–7, 275–347
    life-cycle models, econometrics of, 335–
        342
        applications, 335–336
        estimating structural models, 339–342
        hazard models, 336–339
    life-cycle models of, 308–321
        and contraception, 321
        econometric approach to, 335–342
        features of, 308–317
            child services, output of, 300–304
            child services, production, 310–
               311
            control of fertility, 312–313
            household budget constraint, 313–
               314
            human capital investment, 315
            intertemporal optimization prob-
               lem, 315–317
            maternal time constraints, 312
            preference structures, 310–311
        first birth, optimal timing, 317–319
        spacing of births, optimal, 319–321
    marriage and out-of-wedlock childbear-
        ing, 305–308
    price and income effects, 322–333
        fixed-effects, 330–333
        instrumental variables, 328–330
        social experiments, 327–328
    quality–quantity model, 294–298
    static models, 292–308
    time allocation and demand for children,
        298–305
    and twins, 333–335
    in USA *see under* United States
in endogenous population change, 1118
    basic model, 1156–1158
    investment in health care, 1159–1160
    and population growth, 1158–1159
and generational population cycles, 1090–
    1091
Great Britain, pre-industrial, 1184
and income per capita, 1185
and infant and child mortality *see under* in-
    fant mortality
motivations behind, 1248–1249
period measures, world's regions, 355

technical change and population growth,
     1246–1250
     endogenous, 1266–1267
     and infrastructure, 1253
     transfers and international migration, 842–
        844
     on wages, 1073–1074
        and population size, 1064–1066
Fields, G.S., 607
     on aging, 903, 905, 912
     on income inequality, 1036, 1043, 1049
     on migration, 682–684, 734, 736–737
Filer, R., 826
Findlay, R., 761, 1260
Findley, S.E., 754, 778, 782, 784
Fingerhut, L., 574
first births
     mother's age at in USA, 281–283
     optimal timing, 317–319
     probabilities, 283
First Welfare Theorem, 66–68
Fischbein, S., 586
Fischer, S., 214, 220
Fisher, A.C., 1278
Fisher, R., 585
Flaim, P., 992
Flik, R.J., 262–263
Flinn, M.W., 437, 441–442, 445
Floderus, B., 585
Floud, R., 459, 463
Flug, K., 808
Fogel, R.W., 8, 399, 1080, 1247
     on cost of children, 242, 248
     on mortality
        and morbidity, 573
        and nutrition, 433–481
Folbre, N., 148
food
     costs, and costs of children, 245–246, 249
     supply, historical, 461–463
Food and Agricultural Organization (FAO), 156,
     157
Ford, E., 568, 584
Forrester, J.W., 1177
Forsdahl, A., 472
Foster, A., 577, 580, 591, 613
Foster, A.D., 413, 417
Foster, E., 767
frailty endowment and infant mortality, 512–513,
     523, 525, 527, 533
     and breastfeeding, 537
     determinants of, 544

France
     calorie consumption, 449–452
     height of men, 459
     immigrants, stock of, 802
     mortality, decline in, 440, 445
     residential mobility, 653
     social expenditure by age, 1000
Frankhauser, S., 1193
Frauenthal, J., 1095–1096
Fraumeni, D.M., 1235
Freedman, R., 405, 1158
Freeman, R., 801, 989–990, 1186, 1195
Freudenberger, H., 452
Fridlizius, G., 439, 572
Friedberg, R., 832
Friedlander, D., 983
Friedman, B.M., 197, 231, 924
Friedrich, K., 657
Fries, J., 573
Frijhoff, W., 451
Fuchs, V., 680, 916
     on mortality and morbidity, 561, 573, 574,
        582–583, 588
Fudenberg, D., 1170
fuel costs, developing countries, 1191
full-time work in retirement models, 901, 907–
     910
Fuller, T.D., 745
Funkhouser, E., 806

Gafni, A., 601
Galbraith, V.L., 1085
Gale, D., 45–47, 48, 61, 103–104, 1277
Gale–Shapley model of stable marriage assign-
     ment, 45–46
     and marriage market, 103–104
Gallaway, L.E., 667, 682, 696
Galloway, P.R., 445, 1079–1083, 1088
Galor, O., 224, 378, 749, 1008
Garcia-Ferrer, A., 773
Gaskins, R., 617
Gatica, J., 766
Geanakoplos, J.D., 1221
Geertz, C., 1263
gender
     health and nutrition variations, 164–166
     inequality in time allocation, 166–167
     and infant and child mortality, 544
     and infant mortality, India, 148–149
     life expectancy by, 567
     mortality and morbidity and, 565–567

parents' preferences in low income countries, 386–388
    unequal concern in intrahousehold alloca-
      tions, 163–164
    see also women
generational cycles and population renewal, 1090–1092
genes and benevolence within families, 72
Genesis problem in optimal populations, 1212, 1213
genetic factors as health risk, 583–586
George, H., 870–871
Georgescu-Roegen, N., 1273
Germany
    emigration, decline of, 852
    immigrants, stock of, 802
    immigrants to USA, 834
    internal migration in, 657
    social expenditure by age, 1000
Geronimus, A.T., 542–543, 549
Gertler, P., 356, 413, 417
Geweke, J., 621, 623–624
Ghosh, J.K., 616
G.I. Bill, 150–151
Gibson, J.R., 437
gifts
    and commitment in marriage, 49–50
    in intergenerational linkages, 1126
    intervivo, in intergenerational links, 190, 206, 207, 222
Gigliotti, G., 1225
Gillaspy, R.T., 389
Gille, H., 434, 436, 437
Glass, D.V., 436
Glazer, N., 836
global warming, 1192–1194, 1195
Godfrey, K.M., 472
Goedhart, Th., 262
Goeller, H.E., 1188
Goldberg, I., 749
Goldblatt, P.O., 581–582
Goldin, C., 108, 1281
Goldman, N., 613
Goldscheider, F., 120
Gonner, E.C.K., 436
Gönül, F., 594
Good, J., 617
Goodman, J.L., 743
Goodman, L., 582
Goodrich, C., 661–662
goods mobility in international trade, 856–864
    complementarity, 861–864

substitution, 857–861
Goody, J., 58, 356
Gordon, I., 687
Gordon, R., 907, 916
Gorman, W.M., 28–29, 33, 249
Gorman polar form of transferable utility, 28–29
Gorman specification on demand systems, 254
Gormley, P.J., 667
Goss, E.P., 687
Gottlieb, M., 1213
Gottschalk, P., 1024
Gottschang, T.R., 755
Gotz, G.A., 625
Goubert, P., 440, 451
Gourieroux, C., 618
Gove, W., 582
government
    and internal migration in developing coun-
      tries, 760–764
      taxation, 763–764
      wage subsidies, 762–763
    and mortality, 573–575
Grad, S., 925
grandchildren, 1226, 1247
Grant, E.K., 701
Grantham, G.W., 449, 465
Gratton, R., 618–619
Graves, P.E., 665, 668, 676–677, 680, 704–705, 1238
Great Britain
    calorie consumption, 449–452
    height of men, 459
    immigrants, stock of, 802
    internal migration, 685
    life expectancy and mortality, 574
    migration to USA, 834
    mortality, decline in, 435–436, 442–443, 445
    pre-industrial fertility, 1184
    residential mobility, 653–654
    social expenditure by age, 1000
    technical change and population size, 1071
Green Revolution, 1118, 1263
Greenwood, M.J., 10, 647–720, 742, 773, 800, 807
Grenier, G., 837
Griffin, C., 1180, 1182
Griffith, G.T., 436–437
Griffiths, C., 1196
Griliches, Z., 154, 161, 391
Grilo, C., 583
Groenenveld, L., 113

Gronau, R., 85, 248–249, 694, 1029
Gross Domestic Product in international trade, 854–855
Gross National Product
  and infant mortality, 570
  and life expectancy, 566
Grossbard, A., 109
Grossbard-Schechtman, A., 82, 109, 119
Grossman, G.M., 866, 1194–1195, 1254, 1257–1258
Grossman, J., 820, 822
Grossman, M., 525, 552
  on mortality and morbidity, 561–597 *passim*
Grossman model of health demand, 589–590
Grundy, E., 710
Gruver, G., 1237
Guralnik, J., 983
Gustman, A., 581, 903, 907, 912, 915–916

Habakkuk, H.J., 1067, 1245, 1261–1262
Haddad, L., 39–42, 580
Hagemann, R., 1005
Hagenaars, A.J.M., 260–261
Hagnell, M., 1081
Hahn, J., 574
Hajivassiliou, V., 621, 623
Haldane, J.B.S., 71
Hall, R.E., 223
Halperin, T.D., 1262
Hamano, K., 1082
Hamermesh, D.S., 593, 818–819, 823
Hamilton, B., 873
Hamilton, W.D., 71–72
Hamilton's rule of altruism, 71
Hammer, D., 1264583
Hammer, J.S., 1264
Hammond, P.J., 1254, 1273
Han, A., 617
Hance, W.A., 774
Hansen, A.H., 1100, 1262
Hansen, L.P., 596
Hansen, N., 781
Happel, S., 311, 318–319
Harberger, A., 1066
Harbison, S.F., 754
Harkman, A., 685, 687
Harris, J.E., 525, 541–542, 607
Harris, J.R., 733, 743, 760, 767
Harsanyi, J.C., 1213
Hart, O.D., 1281
Hartung, J., 57
harvest failure

and famine, 441–442
on vital rates, 1080
Haurin, D.R. and R.J., 687
Hauser, P., 568, 579, 580–581, 598, 612
Hausman, J.
  on demand for children, 391, 399, 401, 407, 409, 412
  on mortality and morbidity, 593, 606, 617
Hausman, J.A., 912, 914, 935
Haveman, R., 611, 623
Hayami, Y., 729, 1262
Hayward, M.D., 581–582
hazard rate of birth, 375
Heady, C.J., 767
Heal, G.M., 1191, 1228–1229, 1234–1235, 1240, 1274–1275, 1277–1278
health
  of children, 166–167
  economic models of, 576–598
    demand, one-period models, 577–587
      dynamic models, 587–596
      equations for, 586–587
      Grossman model, 589–590
      life expectancy, 593
      rational addictions, 590–591
      uncertainty, 593–596
      wage endogeneity, 591–592
    as exhaustive state, 597–598
    risk factors, 579–586
      genetic factors, 583–586
      human capital, 579–580
      lifestyle, 583–586
      marital status, 582–583
      nutrition, 580–581
      occupation, 581–582
  in endogenous population change, 1121
  intrahousehold distributions in subsistence economies, 154–157
  and labor productivity, 468–470
  measurement, in elderly, 601–611
    aging and disability, 609–611
    quality of life, 601–604
    self-assessed health, 604–609
  variations in subsistence economies, 164–166
health care, investment in, 1159–1160
health insurance and retirement, 895
Health Maintenance Organizations (HMOs, USA), 574
Heckman, J.J., 694, 699, 808
  on demand for children, 359, 367, 374–375
  on fertility, 319–321, 338–339
  on infant and child mortality, 507, 511, 519

on mortality and morbidity, 579, 612, 614–617, 621
Heckscher, E.F., 1261
Heckscher–Ohlin–Samuelson model of international trade, 857, 859–860
height and nutrition, 453–455, 459
Hekstra, G.P., 1193
Helleiner, K.F., 441, 1089
Heller, P., 997
Heller, P.S., 762
Helpman, E., 1254, 1257–1258
Hémardinquer, J.-J., 449
Henderson, A.M., 248
Henderson, J.V., 777, 780, 784
Henry, C., 1278
Henry, L., 436, 437, 1083
Hermalin, A., 551
Herzog, H.W. Jr., 683–687, 691, 706, 708
Heston, A., 866
heterosis (hybrid vigor), 458
Heywood, P.F., 452, 573
Hicks, J.R., 28, 670, 805, 1203, 1262
Hicks composite commodity theorem, 28
Hicks–Slutsky equations and substitution effect, 1145
Hicksian demand functions, 1143
Higgs, R., 439
Hill, A., 584, 612
Himmelfarb, G., 469
Hirschman, A.O., 1262
Hirshleifer, J., 146
hoarding of births and child mortality, 384, 486, 492, 495–497
Hoddinott, J., 39–42, 373
Hoehn, J.P., 676
Hoffman, S., 113
Hohm, C.F., 388
Hohmann, N., 1193
Holden, K., 610
Holderness, B.A., 449, 465
Homan, M.E., 243
Homberg, S., 1236
homotheticity in demographic cost indices, 251
Honoré, B.E., 614, 617
Hoover, E.M., 379, 1218
Hopkins, S.V., 1067–1068
Hori, H., 65
Horney, M., 98
    on demand for children, 356, 360, 380
    on the family, 24, 32, 37–38, 42, 44
    on intrahousehold distribution, 172–173, 177
Horton, S., 165, 455–456

Hosek, J.R., 689, 699, 705
Hoselitz, B.F., 738
Hoskins, W.G., 441, 466–467
Hotelling, H., 1232, 1235
Hotz, V.J., 6, 15, 374, 587, 595, 625
    on economics of fertility, 275–347
Hougaard, P., 586
Houghton, J.T., 1192
household budget constraints and fertility, 313–314
household demand functions/systems, 250–255
    and costs of children, 248–249
    couple-specific traits in low income countries, 358
    critique (Pollak and Wales), 258–260
    household-produced commodities in, 360
    implementing, 255–258
    in low income countries, 356, 357–360
household models of demand for children, low income countries, 355–377
    birth control and family planning, 376–377
    birth spacing, 373–376
    demands for children, 365–368
    elasticity of demand, 361
    fertility, production-demand model, 361–363
    fertility and mortality, 368–370
    general demand framework, 357–360
    production functions, 370–372
    quantity and quality of children, 363–365
    time-series changes, 372–373
household production functions, 22–23
    and cost of children, 243
    and infant mortality, 532, 533, 534, 542
    in low income countries, 358–359, 370–372
    and marriage, gains from, 83–85
household technology, 22–31
    production functions, 22–23
    public goods, 23–24
    transferable utility, 27–31
        and mate selection, 30–31
        with private goods, 28–29
        with public goods, 29–30
    utility possibility frontiers, 24–27
        with public goods, 25–27
households, 3–5
    economics of, 2
    and income inequality, 1024
        assortative mating, 1030–1031
        composition of, 1031–1035
    private goods in
        pluralistic, decision-making in, 39–40, 42
        transferable utility, 28–29

public goods in, 23–24
social welfare functions, 34–35
Houthakker, H.S., 251–252, 254, 294, 364
Howarth, R.B., 1276
Howitt, P.W., 1258, 1260
Hoynes, H.W., 578
Hrubec, Z., 585
Hubbard, R.G., 201, 220, 223
Hufton, O.H., 451
Hughes, G.A., 685
Hugo, G.J., 754, 782
Huh, K., 617, 621, 624
human capital
    and endogenous technical change, 1258
    health risk factors, 579–580
    investment in
        endogenous population change, 1119,
            1123
            economic growth in, 1147–1155
            by immigrants, 828, 833
        and intergenerational links, 222–227
        and internal migration, 669–671, 690
            in developing countries, 730
        in intrahousehold allocations, 127, 129–
            132, 136–137, 140–142
        in marriage, 84, 85, 88, 117
        maternal, 315
    in poor countries, 1272
    wage function and demand for children, 367
Hungary: height of men, 459
Hunt, G.L., 657, 677, 679–680
Hunt, J., 827
Hurd, M.D., 13, 169
    on aging, economics of, 891–966
    on household linkages, 198, 209–211
    on mortality and mortbidity, 578, 593, 625

Ichimura, H., 623
Idler, E., 601, 604
imitation and altruism, 73–74
immigrants/immigration
    age of, 802–803
    assimilation of, 827–840
        estimates of, 833–837
        language proficiency, 837–840
    education of, 803
    fertility of, 842–844
    industrial concentration of, 820
    lower earnings of, 828–829
    and population aging, 975–977
    skill levels of, 810, 812, 815
    to USA, origins of, 834

and wage levels, 817–821, 825
wage rises over time, 833–834
welfare participation of, 840–842
see also migration
imperfect capital markets and child to parent
    transfers, 1163–1168
imprinting and altruism, 73–74
income
    distribution
        in developing countries, 769–775
        and discounting, 1276
        in international trade and migration, 880–
            884
        and population growth, 1264
    of elderly, comparisons, 959
    and family size, 1272
    family's in household economic models, 362,
        383
    full, in household production functions, 358–
        359
    and migration, 671–672, 679
        movers and stayers, 769–774
        rural sector inequality, 774–775
        streams, and migration, 730–731
    and mortality in elderly, 578
    and population size, 1065, 1070
income-distance trade-off and migration, 672–
    673
income effects of parental fertility choices, 322–
    333
Income Evaluation Question on household wel-
    fare, 260–261
income inequality, 14, 1015–1059
    age structure and, 1017–1024
        effects of, decomposing, 1017–1022
        evidence of, 1022–1023
        and wages, 1023–1024
    and differential fertility, 1035–1044
        intergenerational, and differential fertility,
            1038–1043
        population growth, mathematics of,
            1036–1038
        welfare implications of, 1043–1044
    and household composition, 1031–1035
    and marital sorting, 1024–1031
        assortative mating, 1030–1031
        other countries, 1029–1030
        in USA, 1027–1029
    population growth and wages, 1044–1049
        empirical evidence, 1046–1049
        relative wages, 1044–1046
    in USA, 1049–1052

income pooling
    and intrahousehold allocations, 174–176
    in marriage, 95, 98, 110
Independent of Base property in demographic
    cost indices, 251
India
    demand for children, 365
    income inequality in, 1034–1035
    intergenerational economic links, 232
    internal migration in, 747, 753, 759
    rural–urban migration, 728
    urban job search in, 735–736, 737
industrial concentration of immigrants, 820
industrial employment and migration in devel-
    oping countries, 738–739
industrial location and internal migration in de-
    veloping countries, 780–782
Industrial Revolution, 452, 1118
    and population growth, 1261–1262
inequality in rural sector, developing countries,
    774–775
infant and child mortality, 8–9, 483–557
    determinants of, 523–553
        biological, 543–545
        and birthweight, 546–550
        and breastfeeding, 535–540
        framework of, 523–535
        maternal age at birth, 542–543
        non-biological, 545
        and prenatal care, 540–542
        public policy interventions, 550–553
    differentials, developing economies, 148–149
    and fertility, 488–522
        estimation, 498–499
        general model for, 511–513
        impact of risk on, 520–522
            non-structural estimation, 521–522
            structural estimation, 520–521
        mortality–fertility links, 509–511
        population-invariant mortality risk, 499–
            506
        population-variant mortality risk, 506–
            509
            observable heterogeneity, 506–507
            unobservable heterogeneity, 507–509
        replacement effects, 514–520
            approximate decision rules, 519–520
            birth and death history data, 514–517
            total births and deaths, 517–519
        sequential decision-making, 491–498
        static lifetime formulations, 488–491
    and life expectancy, 563

mortality and morbidity and, 569–571
    period measures, world's regions, 355
infectious diseases, 437–438
information and migration
    costs, 666
    networks, 743–746
infrastructure investment and internal migration
    in developing countries, 782–784
Ingegneri, D., 1006
Ingham, A., 1234
inheritances, 207–208, 221
insurance
    health, and retirement, 895
    and intergenerational economic links, 210
        transactions cost approach, 230–233
interdependent utility functions within families,
    60–62
    intergenerational, 62–66
    and Pareto optimality, 66–68
    sustainability of, 68–71
interfamily transfers in intergenerational links,
    206–211
intergenerational and interhousehold economic
    links, 5, 189–238
    altruism in, 189–212
        economic linkages, 199–206
        egoistic model, 198, 209
        general equilibrium, 217–222
        and human capital, 222–227
        interfamily transfers, 206–211
        life-cycle model, 192–193
        and marriage, 202
        simple model, 191–196
        transfers, 196–199
        two-sided, 212–217
    in long-run economic development, 1226–
        1228
    transactions cost approach, 228–234
        demonstration effect, 233–234
        insurance and credit, 230–233
        paternalistic preferences, 233–234
        production, 228–230
intergenerational utility interdependent within
    families, 62–66
interhousehold links *see* intergenerational and
    interhousehold economic links
internal migration
    in developed countries, 10–11, 647–720
        age and, 655–656
        cross-national comparisons, 651–655
        defined, 650–651
        determinants, 658–707

decision to migrate, 688–707
   family considerations, 702–707
   individual returns to, 688–702
   life-cycle considerations, 702–707
distance, 660, 666–668
employment status, 681–688
   national, 687–688
   personal, 683–687
   regional, 681–683
gravity models, 660–661, 663–666
place characteristics, 659–663
theoretical perspectives, 668–681
   disequilibrium, 669–673
   equilibrium, 673–681
education and, 655–656
trends, 656–658
in developing countries, 10–11, 721–798
flows and selectivity, 730–756
   capital, role of, 746–748
      financing migration, 746–747
      tied rents, 747–748
   context of migration, 753–755
   displaced persons, 755–756
   family strategies, 749–753
   income streams, 730–731
   job search, 731–738
      informal–formal mobility, 736–
         737
      informal–formal pay, 737
      initial unemployment, duration,
         735–736
      Todaro hypothesis, 731–735, 737–
         738
      urban jobs, frequency, 736
   labor market opportunities, 738–743
      earning differentials, 739–742
      industrial employment, 738–739
      networks and information, 743–
         746
      unemployment, 742–743
patterns, 722–730
   database, 723–724
   rural–urban migration, 728–729, 729–
      730
   temporary and circular migration,
      729–730
   urbanization, 724–728
permanent migration, 748–749
policy isues, 775–785
   education, 784–785
   industrial location, 780–782
   infrastructure investment, 782–784

mobility, controls on, 775–777
rural development, 778–780
   intent versus reality, 778–779
   schemes, 779–780
urban pay and labor costs, 777–778
and productivity, 756–775
   dynamic models of, 768–769
   and income distribution, 769–775
      movers and stayers, 769–774
      rural sector inequality, 774–775
   rural labor markets, 756–760
      nutrition wage, 758–759
      remittance, risk and new technol-
         ogy, 759–760
      sharecropping, 757–758
      surplus labor, 757
   urban labor markets, 760–768
      collective bargaining, 764–765
      efficiency wage models, 765–766
      government intervention, 760–764
      shadow wages, 766–768
      wage setting, 764–766
return migration, 748–749
sharecropping and, 757–758
temporary migration, 748–749
and residential mobility, 652–653
international migration
economic impact of, 11, 799–850
   assimilation of immigrants, 827–840
      estimates of, 833–837
      language proficiency, 837–840
   chain migration, 807, 811
   geographical concentrations, 803–805
   labor market adjustment to, 807–808,
      817–827
      econometrics of, 821–827
      effects of, 819–821
      gains and losses, 817–819
   social welfare transfers, 840–842
   source and receiving countries, 801–817
      controls, enforcing, 812–814
      determinants, 807–808
      impact of regulations, 810–812
      incentives to migrate, 805–807
      magnitude and characteristics, 801–
         805
      from receiving countries, 814–817
      regulation of, 808–810
      undocumented aliens, 812–814
   transfers and fertility, 842–844
   transfers and tax payments, 844–846
efficient volume of, 868–871

and international trade, 11–12, 851–887
  gains and losses, 871–873
  global population dispersion, 868–871
  income distribution, 880–884
  labor mobility and capital mobility, 865–867
  labor mobility and good mobility, 856–864
    complementarity, 861–864
    substitution, 857–861
  and productivity levels, 867
  and wage rigidity, 871–880
    rigid wages, 878–880
    wage flexibility, 871–878
international trade
  and GDP, growth of, 854–855
  and international migration, 11–12, 851–887
    gains and losses, 871–873
    global population dispersion, 868–871
    income distribution, 880–884
    labor mobility and capital mobility, 865–867
    labor mobility and good mobility, 856–864
      complementarity, 861–864
      substitution, 857–861
    and wage rigidity, 871–880
      rigid wages, 878–880
      wage flexibility, 871–878
intertemporal arbitrage conditions, 1154
intertemporally consistent preferences in consumer behaviour, 63
intervivo gifts in intergenerational links, 190, 206
intrahousehold allocations, 4–5, 125–187
  consensus parental preference models, 128–146
    with active children, 144–146
    with passive children, 129–144
      returns to schooling, 142–144
      separable earnings-transfers (SET) model, 137–142
      wealth model, 130–137
  nonconsensus models, 172–179
    income pooling, 174–176
    Nash bargaining models, 172–174
    Pareto-efficient collective household models, 176–179
  single period consensus parental preference models, 146–172
    endowment reinforcement or compensation, 151–162

    schooling allocation, 158–162
    SET model estimates, 152–154
    in subsistence economy, 154–157
    gender and birth-order effects, 163–167
      child health and gender inequality, 166–167
      health and nutrition variations, 164–166
      SET model estimates, 163–164
    prices and individual endowments, 147–151
      India mortality differentials, 148–149
      schooling prices, 149–151
    sibling differences, 167–172
Intrauterine Device (IUD), 287, 288–289
Ioannides, Y.M., 191, 221
Ireland: residential mobility, 653–654
Iron Law of Wages, 1066, 1070, 1076
Islam, M.N., 696, 700
Israel: residential mobility, 653
Italy
  immigrants, stock of, 802
  social expenditure by age, 1000

Jaeger, K., 1225
Jagannathan, V., 748
James, J., 1263
James, W.E., 780
Japan
  internal migration in, 655, 657
  residential mobility, 653–654
  social expenditure by age, 1000–1001
Jappelli, T., 223
Jasso, G., 811
Jaynes, G.D., 568
Jensen, L., 842
Jevons, W.S., 466, 1228
Jha, R., 768
Jha, S.C., 1183, 1195–1196, 1264, 1266
Jianakoplos, N.A., 933
Jimenez, E., 373, 377, 389, 1008
job search and internal migration in developing countries, 731–738
  informal–formal mobility, 736–737
  informal–formal pay, 737
  initial unemployment, duration, 735–736
  Todaro hypothesis, 731–735, 737–738
  urban jobs, frequency, 736
Jodha, N.S., 1190
John, A.A., 1228, 1245, 1269–1270
Johnson, G., 1050
Johnson, H.G., 769

Johnson, N., 583
Johnson, W., 117
joint output, maximizing in marriage, 84, 91
Jones, A., 601
Jones, C., 179
Jones, D.R., 581–582
Jones, E.L., 1256
Jones, L.E., 1254, 1257
Jones, R., 1086
Jones-Lee, M., 70–71
Jorgenson, D.W., 255–256, 1193, 1235
Joyce, T., 333
Ju, A., 601
Judd, K.L., 201, 223, 626
Juhn, C., 833
Julia, D., 451
Juster, F.T., 39, 109, 211, 600

Kadane, J., 599
Kaestner, R., 333
Kahn, H., 584
Kalbfleisch, J.D., 613
Kaldor, N., 1255
Kamien, M.I., 1229, 1238
Kanaye, S., 65
Kanbur, S.M.R., 742, 747, 774
Kane, T., 308, 582, 600, 610
Kaneko, M., 48
Kannappan, S., 734
Kaplan, E.L., 613
Kaplan, G.A., 584
Kaplan, R., 607
Kaprio, J., 582, 585
Kapteyn, A., 256, 260, 263
Karoly, L.A., 1050
Kasir, N., 808
Kates, R.W., 1086
Katz, E., 745–746, 750, 752, 767
Katz, L.F., 1050
Kau, J.B., 665, 691
Keane, M., 513, 623, 625–626
Keeler, E., 1237
Keeley, M., 109
Kelley, A.C., 379, 785
    on population dynamics, 1068, 1072, 1100–
        1101, 1104
    on population growth, 1183, 1186, 1263–
        1265
Kelly, A., 706
Kelly, W.R., 388
Kemeny, J.J., 65
Kenkel, D., 580

Kennickell, A.B., 196
Kentucky: fertility studies, 329–330
Keyder, C., 465
Keyfitz, N., 54, 1090–1091, 1104, 1183–
    1184
Keynes, J.M., 1100, 1184, 1220, 1236
Khan, M.A., 763
Kiker, B.F., 691
Kikuchi, M., 729, 1262
Killingsworth, M., 359, 579
Kim, J.M., 456, 471
Kimball, M.S., 60, 64–65, 191, 1227
Kind, P., 606
King, G., 466
King, M., 933
King's Law, 466
Kintner, H., 523–524, 535
Kirk, D., 650
Kitagawa, E., 568, 579, 580–581, 598, 612
Klaassen, L.H., 711
Klein, R.W., 623
Klerman, J.A., 6, 15, 275–347
Klinov-Malul, R., 983
Kliss, B., 599
Knapp, T.A., 676–677
Knight, J., 565
Knight, J.B., 766
Knodel, J., 1065, 1096, 1185
    on infant and child mortality, 490, 515–516,
        523–524, 535, 553
Knoer, E., 48
Knowles, J.C., 381, 383
Knudson, A., 565
Koch, M., 804–805
Kocher, J., 1048
Kolstad, C.D., 1234
Komlos, J., 463
Kontuly, T., 656
Koo, H., 1039–1041, 1043
Koopmans, T.C.
    on the family, 46–47, 63
    on population growth, 1177–1178, 1198,
        1218, 1228–1229, 1235, 1273, 1277
Korea
    birth ratios by birth order, 388
    circular migration, 729, 749
Korenman, S., 85, 109, 549
Kornhouser, L., 116
Kossoudji, S., 837, 839
Kostenvuo, M., 585
Kotlikoff, L.J., 88, 1107
    on aging, 903, 905, 917–918, 923, 936

on household linkages, 198, 202, 206–207, 219, 228–229, 231
on population aging, 992, 997–999, 1006–1007
Kotwal, A., 758
Kouame, A., 381
Krautkraemer, J.A., 1234, 1274, 1277
Kravis, I.B., 395
Kreig, R.G., 701
Kremer, M., 1262
Krueger, A., 585, 1260
Krueger, A.B., 764, 1194
Krueger, A.O., 866
Krugman, P., 868
Krumins, J., 565
Krumm, R.J., 706
Kuh, E., 409
Kunitz, S.J., 439
Kurz, M., 207, 924, 1219
Kusnic, M., 1033–1034
Kuuluvainen, J., 1242
Kuznets, S., 414, 662, 1032–1033, 1067, 1186, 1262
Kuznets curve, environmental, 1189, 1194–1195, 1196, 1244
Kuznets cycles, 1100
Kydland, F., 587

Laber, G., 698
labor
 and internal migration in developing countries
  costs of, 777–778
  rural labor, 757
 mobility of
  international trade and migration
   and capital mobility, 865–867
   and good mobility, 856–864
    complementarity, 861–864
    substitution, 857–861
 productivity of
  and nutrition, 468–470
  and population growth, 1263
 supply, 3
  in family, 96–97, 99, 119
  and income inequality, 1047, 1050
  and population size, 1064–1065, 1070
labor force participation
 and age distributions fluctuations, 1103
 decline in, 892–893, 896
 and disability, 610–611
 and fertility, USA, 291–292

and population aging, 992–993
 women, and income inequality, 1025–1026, 1028–1029
labor markets
 Cuban emigration to USA, 826–827
 and international migration, 817–827
  econometrics of, 821–824
   evidence, 824–827
  effects of, 819–821
  gains and losses, 817–819
 and intrahousehold allocations, 127, 130, 147, 148–149, 158
 and migration in developing countries
  rural, 756–760
   nutrition wage, 758–759
   remittance, risk and new technology, 759–760
   sharecropping, 757–758
   surplus labor, 757
  urban, 760–768
   collective bargaining, 764–765
   efficiency wage models, 765–766
   government intervention, 760–764
   shadow wages, 766–768
   wage setting, 764–766
 opportunities and migration in developing countries, 738–743
  earning differentials, 739–742
  industrial employment, 738–739
  networks and information, 743–746
  unemployment, 742–743
 and population aging, 989–994
  lifetime wage profiles, 990–991
  seniority promotion, 993–994
  unemployment and labor force participation, 992–993
  wages and marginal products, 991
Labrousse, C.E., 466
Lachler, U., 768
Laitner, J., 5, 13, 144, 1204
 on the family, 63–64, 66
 on household linkages, 189–238
Lal, D., 1262
Lalonde, R.J., 11, 799–850
Lam, D., 14–15, 103, 307, 381, 990, 1264
 on the family, 24, 55–56
 on income equality, 1015–1059
Lampman, R., 201
Lancaster, K., 298
Lancaster, T., 337, 374–375, 613
Land, K., 580
Landes, D.S., 469, 470

Lane, J., 1218–1219, 1225, 1235
Lang, K., 766
Langer, W.L., 387, 439
Langsten, R.L., 1082
language proficiency of immigrants, 837–840
Lansing, J.B., 697, 702
Lapham, R.J., 377, 402
Laquian, A.A., 722
Larson, U., 1082
Latin America
    economic crises on vital rates, 1080, 1082–
        1084
    life expectancy and infant mortality, 563
lattice property in stable marriage assignment, 46
Lauby, J., 751
Lavy, V., 381, 383
Layard, R., 864, 878, 1029
Lazear, E., 87, 903, 992
LeBrun, F., 445
Ledent, J., 655, 657
Lee, B.S., 384
Lee, E., 662, 783
Lee, L.-F., 621, 623–5
Lee, O.-J., 728, 749
Lee, R.B., 374
Lee, R.D., 15, 377, 974, 1047
    on population change, 1122, 1132
    on population dynamics, 1063–1115
    on population growth, 1197, 1263, 1265–
        1266
Lee, W.R., 439
Leff, N., 1101, 1103–1104
Lehrer, E., 1027
Leibenstein, H., 758, 1076, 1161, 1246, 1267
Leibenstein, H.A., 355
Leininger, W., 1227
Leonard, J., 611
Lerman, S., 618, 621
Lery, A., 516
Lesthaeghe, R., 120
Leung, S.F., 387
Levhari, D., 749
Levi-Strauss, C., 1282–1283
Levison, D., 1021–1022
Levy, M.B., 743, 747
Lewbel, A., 251, 253–254, 256
Lewis, A., 1261
Lewis, G., 363
Lewis, H.G., 143, 294–297, 489
Lewis, R.G., 695, 1246
    on endogenous population change, 1142–
        1144

Leyden approach to cost of children, 260–263
Leyfitz, N., 1005
Li, R.M., 776
Li, T., 583
Lichentenberg, F.R., 416
Liese, K., 571
life-cycle hypothesis of consumption, 923–931
    consumption data, 938–939
    wealth data, 931–935
life-cycle models
    and decision to migrate, 702–707
    of family outcomes, 356
    of fertility, 308–321
        and contraception, 321
        features of, 308–317
            child services, output of, 300–304
            child services, production, 310–311
            control of fertility, 312–313
            household budget constraint, 313–314
            human capital investment, 315
            intertemporal optimization problem,
                315–317
            maternal time constraints, 312
            preference structures, 310–311
        first birth, optimal timing, 317–319
        spacing of births, optimal, 319–321
    of intergenerational links, 192–193, 194, 196,
        220, 223
    and internal migration, 658, 676
    in population aging, 994–1000
        limitations of model, 998–1000
        and saving
            in general equilibrium, 997–998
            in partial equilibrium, 996–997
        two-period, change in, 995–996
life-cycle savings
    and fertility in low income countries, 379
    in intergenerational links, 206–207, 209, 219
life expectancy
    at age 65, 894
    by age cohort, 564
    developed countries, 1185
    distribution of, 564
    by gender, 567
    and GNP, 566
    and health demand models, 593
    and nutrition, 472
    period measures, world's regions, 355
    and public health expenditure, 569, 602
    by race, 565, 567
    rise in, world, 562–563
    in USA, 972

life history studies of internal migration, 706–707
life insurance in life-cycle hypothesis of consumption
    earnings, 946
    and social security, 947
life tables: mortality in elderly, 611–613
lifestyle and health risk factors, 583–586
lifetime utility function, 493–494, 496
likelihood function of mortality risk, 506–507
Lillard, L., 113
Lillian, D., 902
Lindahl equilibrium in households, 67
Lindahl–Samuelson rule of private and public
    consumption, 869, 871
Lindauer, D.L., 762
Lindbeck, A., 36, 214
Lindert, P., 1023, 1047
Lindert, P.H., 247, 383, 1070–1071, 1184
    on mortality and nutrition, 439, 449, 461, 469
Lindsay, B.G., 617
Linear Expenditure demand system, 255
linear programming assignment
    of marriage, 46–47
    of utility possibility frontier, 30–31
Linn, J.F., 781
Linneman, P., 665, 668, 704–705
Lipton, M., 450, 756, 774
liquidity constrained households, 222
Liu, I.Y., 610
Livi-Bacci, M., 439
Lobdell, R.A., 759
local capital in decision to migrate, 690
Locay, L., 88, 1077
Lockheed, M.E., 784
London: causes of death in, 439
Long, L.H., 648, 652–655, 657, 703
Lotka, A.J., 53, 247, 434, 437
Loury, G.C., 191, 221, 224
low income countries, demand for children in, 7,
    349–430
    births and deaths, regional trends, 351–355
    child mortality, 384–386
    cross-program effects, 390–393
    fertility
        and child mortality, 398
        contraception
            price of, 407–408
            unpredictable failures of, 364
        family planning, 402–407
        findings, 397–402
        inter-country comparisons, 393–417
        macroeconomics of, 377–380

        credit, security and savings, 379
        mobility and marriage, 379–380
        overlapping generations, 378–379
        time-series changes, 408–413
    household economic models, 355–377
        birth control and family planning, 376–377
        birth spacing, 373–376
        demands for children, 365–368
        elasticity of demand, 361
        fertility, production–demand model, 361–363
        fertility and mortality, 368–370
        general demand framework, 357–360
        production functions, 370–372
        quantity and quality of children, 363–365
        time-series changes, 372–373
    population growth and vital rates, 352–353
    sex preference of parents, 386–388
    technical and institutional change, 388–390
    wages and nonhuman capital, 380–384
    see also developing countries
Lowry, I.S., 671
Lucas, R.E. Jr, 10–11, 867, 1123
    on endogenous population, 1139–1141
    on household linkages, 219, 232
    on internal migration, 721–798
    on population growth, 1199, 1258, 1266–1267, 1270
Lucas–Romer model of economic growth in
    endogenous population change, 1139–1141
Lui, F.T., 1253, 1267
Lumsdaine, R., 911–912
Lundberg, S., 38–39, 44, 99, 173, 280
Lundborg, P., 763
Lutz, W., 1185
Lydall, H., 923
Lyons, R.K., 1257

Mabbut, J., 1191
MacDougall, G.D.A., 865
MacGregor, I.A., 455
MacKellar, F.L., 1188
MacLeod, W.B., 49
Macunovich, D.J., 1085
MaCurdy, T., 579
Madans, J.H., 568, 599
Maddala, G.S., 695
Maddison, A., 469
Maglad, N.E., 381, 384
Makower, H.J., 660–661, 687

Malathy, R., 391
Mäler. K.-G., 1190–1279 *passim*
malevolent preferences in competitive equilibrium in households, 67–68
malnutrition
  and diet, 446
  and mortality, extent and significance, 445–460
    caloric consumption, England & France, 449–452
    energy cost accounting, 445–449
    stature and body mass indices, 452–460
Malthus, T., 120, 434–435, 1044, 1177, 1184
  on endogenous population change, 1118, 1132–1139
  on mortality and morbidity, 572
  and population dynamics, 1064–1066, 1080, 1092, 1107
Malthus–Boserup model of economic growth in endogenous population change, 1132–1139, 1168
Malthusian cycles, 1184
  long-run population fluctuations, 1087
  population renewal, internal dynamics of, 1092–1097
Malthusian theory of population and growth, 1118, 1177, 1261
  support for, 1184
mandatory retirement age, 992
Mankiw, N.G., 223, 396, 1100–1104, 1139
Manne, A.S., 1192–1194
Manove, M., 748
Manser, M., 24, 32, 37–38, 42, 44, 95, 172–173
Manski, C., 618, 621
Manski, D.F., 575, 692
Manton, K.G., 573, 584, 609, 612, 614–616
Manuelli, R., 1254, 1257
Mare, D., 102
marginal product of capital in international trade, 865–866
marginal propensity to consume and costs of children, 249
marginal survivors and population aging, 982
marginal utility of childbearing, 491, 494
Mariger, R., 223
marital capital, 83, 110, 112
marital childbearing, USA, 283–287
  trends in, 286
marital endowment, 101–102
marital output, 89–90, 91, 101–102, 105
  matrix, 100

marital sorting and income inequality, 1024–1031
  assortative mating, 1030–1031
  other countries, 1029–1030
  in USA, 1027–1029
marital status in health risk factors, 582–583
market goods, family purchase of, 22
Markus, G.B., 364, 374
Markusen, J.R., 857, 864
Marmot, M.G., 472
Marr, W.L., 699
Marrewijk, C. van, 1244, 1269
marriage, 4
  age distributions, 1105
  altruism in intergenerational links, 202
  childbearing, out-of-wedlock, 305–308
  comparative advantage in, 84, 117
  decision, 105, 109
  economic reasons for, 82–89
    division of labor, 82, 102
    imperfect credit market, 82, 85–86
    increasing returns, 83–85
    risk pooling, 83
    risk sharing, 87–89
    sharing collective goods, 82, 86–87
  and fertility in low income countries, 379–380
  gains from, 83–85
    collective goods, 86–87
    division of, 101, 109–110
  and household membership, 45–59
    and age, 53–57
      classical population theory, 53–54
      transferable utility, 55–56
      two-sex mating theories, 54–55
      women and older men, 56–57
    alternative household structures, 57–59
      polygyny, 57–58
      unwed parents, 58–59
    household allocation, 49–53
      divorce as threat, 50–51
      equilibrium without perfect information, 50
      gifts, commitment and divorce, 49–50
      outside options, 51–53
    models, 45–49
      Gale–Shapley, 45–46
      linear programming assignments, 46–47
      stable matching, 48–49
      transferable utility, 47–48
  as insurance, 88, 98

as investment, 83
matching process, 104, 114–115
   and divorce, 110, 112, 114–115, 117
   quality of, 105, 107–108, 110, 112
sorting in, 102, 112–113
marriage markets, 99–110
  gains from, division of, 101, 109–110
  household allocation and, 49–53
    divorce as threat, 50–51
    equilibrium without perfect information, 50
    gifts, commitment and divorce, 49–50
    outside options, 51–53
  and income inequality, 1024–1025
  intrahousehold allocations, 127, 130, 158
  nontransferable utility, 103–104
  search in, 104–108
    intensity, 105
    value of, 105–106
  stable matching, 100–103
marriageable individuals and unwed parenthood, 59
Marshak, J., 36
Marshall, A., 692, 694, 1066
Marshall, T.H., 436
Marshallian demand functions, 1143
Martin, L.G., 532
Martorell, R., 452, 455–456, 458, 573
Maskin, E., 105
Mason, A., 1103, 1265
Masson, P., 997
Masters, S.H., 698
mate selection, 30–31
maternal age at birth, 487, 523, 525–526, 529, 542–543
Matheisen, P.C., 484
Mathios, A.P., 691
Mauldin, W.P., 402–403
Maurer, K., 368
Maurer, S.B., 1263
Mauskopf, J., 505–506, 508, 517–518
Maxwell, N.L., 706
Maynard, R., 327
Mazumdur, D., 737
McAlpin, M.B., 1079
McCall, J.J., 625
McCann, J.C., 484
McClements, L.D., 253
McCool, T., 763
McCormick, B., 685
McCoy, J., 569
McCulloch, C., 337–339, 374–375

McCulloch, R., 770
McDermed, A.A., 902
McDonald, I.M., 764
McDonald, J., 1085
McDowell, J.M., 650, 800
McElroy, M., 98, 172–174, 177
  on demand for children, 356, 360, 380
  on the family, 24, 32, 37–38, 42, 44
McEvedy, C., 1086
McFadden, D., 596, 618, 621–624
McFarland, D., 54
McGarry, K., 593, 600
McGue, M., 586
McKenzie, L., 68
McKeown, T., 437–439, 485
McMahon, S.F., 449
McManus, W., 837–839
McMaster, I., 679
McNeill, W.H., 1089, 1181–1182, 1245, 1280
McNicoll, G., 1183, 1264–1265
McRae, I., 253
Meade, J.E., 1214–1215, 1217–1218, 1220, 1225–1226, 1235, 1245
Meadows, D.H., 378, 1177, 1187
Medicaid (USA), 331, 332, 568, 842, 920, 957
Medicare (USA), 568, 573–575, 609, 920, 953, 957
Meeker, E., 439
Meerman, M.K., 1033
meetings and marriage, 105, 107
Meier, P., 613
Meisenheimer, J., 802–803
Melenberg, B., 263
melting pot, USA as, 828
Menchik, P.L., 169–170, 205–208, 221, 569, 924
Menken, J., 1080, 1083, 1086
Mennell, S., 451
Mensch, B., 415
merit goods in marriage, 94
Merrick, T.W., 381
Meuvret, J., 440–441
Mexico
  emigration to USA, 812–814
  immigrants in USA, 834
  life expectancy and infant mortality, 563
  migration in, 742, 755
Meyer, A., 1251
Meyer, M.B., 547
Michael, R., 87, 120, 321
Michel, P., 1225
Migot-Adholla, S., 1240
migration, 3, 9–12

age selectivity of, 687
circular, in developing countries, 729–730
decision to, 688–707
    amenities in, 689–690
    biases in, 689–692
    family considerations, 702–707
    household models, 673–674
    individual returns to, 688–702
    life-cycle considerations, 702–707
    local capital in, 690
    multiple migrations, 690–691
    reference groups in, 689
    sample selection, 692–697
    time scale and timing, 690
    training and experience, 690
distance elasticity of, 667
income–distance trade-off in, 672–673
information in
    cost of, 666
    networks, 743–746
internal *see* internal migration
international *see* international migration
mortality and morbidity and, 571–572
refugees, 755–756
return
    in developing countries, 748–749
    international, 815–816
and social class, 684
transport costs and, 666–667
Miller, A.R., 662
Miller, E., 672, 691
Miller, P., 836, 838–840
Miller, R., 311, 314, 320–321, 341, 374, 625
Miller, T., 1266
Millerd, F.W., 699
Mills, E.S., 782
Milne, W.J., 649, 687
Mincer, J., 293, 299, 355, 367, 701–704, 806
    on income inequality, 1020–1201, 1025,
        1027
Mira, P., 492, 513
Mirer, T., 923, 933, 935
Mirrlees, J.A., 881
Mishkin, F.S., 223
Mitchell, J., 577
Mitchell, O.S., 607, 903, 905, 912
Mitchison, R., 435
Mitra, T., 1235
Mnookin, R., 116
mobility
    controls on internal migration in developing
        countries, 775–777

and fertility in low income countries, 379–
    380
goods *see* goods mobility
intergenerational, and income inequality,
    1035–1044
    intergenerational, and differential fertility,
        1038–1043
    population growth, mathematics of,
        1036–1038
    welfare implications of, 1043–1044
in labor market and population aging, 992–
    993
labor *see* labor, mobility
Modi, J.R., 781
Modigliani, F., 192, 206–207, 373, 936
Moffitt, R.A.
    on aging, 901–902, 912, 915–916
    on fertility, 311, 319–320
    on mortality, 587, 607, 623
Mokyr, J., 1246, 1256, 1260, 1263
Moldevanu, B., 51
Molho, I., 681, 687
Moll, P.G., 766
Molyneaux, J.W., 413
Mont, D., 703
Montfort, A., 618
Montgomery, M.R., 359, 381, 413, 511
Moock, J.L., 390
Mookherjee, D., 1022
Moore, D., 582
Moore, J., 1281
Moore, R., 903
Morawetz, D., 1045
morbidity
    in elderly *see* elderly
    and nutrition, 452–460
    see also mortality
Morduch, J., 165
Moreland, R.S., 753
Morell, M., 449
Morgan, J.N., 697
Morley, S.A., 1022
Morris, C.T., 1035, 1045
Morris, J., 228–229
Morris, J.N., 581
Morrison, A.R., 739
Morrison, P.A., 689, 692
Morse, C., 1188
mortality
    declining
        developing countries, 1184–1185
        Europe, 1184

and population aging, 972–975
  production and consumption, 981–983
economic crises on, 1081–1082
in elderly, 9, 559–643
  data sources, 598–601
  and economic development, 563–565
  and gender, 565–567
  and health status, 601–611
    aging and disability, 609–611
    quality of life, 601–604
    self-assessed health, 604–609
  and infant mortality, 569–571
  and migration, 571–572
  public policy on, 573–575
  and race, 565, 568–569
  trends and variations, 562–575
in endogenous population change, 1119
and income per capita, 1185
iso-mortality curves, 457–458
and nutrition *see under* nutrients/nutrition
statistical and numerical techniques on, 611–626
  alternative estimators, 623–626
  classical MLE, 621–623
  life tables, 611–613
  survival hazard models, 613–621
    competing risk, 616–617
    proportional hazard, 614–616
    semi-nonparametric, 617–618
    simulation methods, 618–621
technical change and population growth, 1246–1250
  and infrastructure, 1253
on wages, 1074
  and population size, 1064–1066
Mortensen, D., 108, 112
Mossey, J., 601
mother's age at first birth in USA, 281–283
mother's time intensity in production–demand model of fertility, 361
Moumouras, A., 1274
Moynihan, D., 836
Mroz, T.A., 508, 511, 519–520, 538
Muellbauer, J., 23, 248–250, 252–253, 255–256
Mueller, E., 246–247, 366, 383, 702, 1073
Mueller, W.H., 458
Mueser, P., 668
Mukhopadhyay, S., 381–382, 390
multistate models in household production functions, 375
Mundaca, B., 169
Mundell, R.A., 861

Murdock, G.P., 57
Murphy, K.M., 130, 367, 577, 590, 990, 1050
Murray, C., 602, 604
Murray, J., 584
Murray, M.P., 781
Mussa, M., 785
Muth, R., 23
Muurinen, J.M., 577, 589–591, 597
Muvandi, I., 355
Myers, N., 1191
Myers, R., 573

Nag, M., 383
Nagar, A.L., 253
naive strategies of consumer behaviour, 62
Nakosteen, R.A., 699
Nam, C.B., 651
Narayana, N.S.S., 778–779
Narveson, J., 1215–1216
Nash bargaining models
  in household demand models, 359–360
  of intrahousehold allocations, 172–174
  on marriage, 37–39
Nash equilibrium
  in intergenerational links, 192, 203–204
    and human capital investment, 225
    and transaction costs, 229
    two-sided altruism, 214–215
  open-loop, and child to parent transfers, 1170
Nash product, generalized in noncooperative bargaining theory, 44
National Academy of Sciences, 1188, 1192
National Research Council, 377, 1183, 1191, 1263
national unemployment and internal migration, 687–688
Navratil, F.J., 683
Neal, L., 1100
Neel, J., 585
Neher, P., 1161–1163, 1172, 1247
Nelson, C., 577
Nelson, J.M., 724, 729, 730, 748–749, 753
Nelson, P., 666
Nelson, R.R., 1076, 1267
neonatal deaths and fertility, 523–524
Nerlove, M., 15–16, 881, 1027, 1078
  on endogenous population, 1117–1174
  on population growth, 1201, 1212, 1247, 1249, 1251, 1266
Nerlove, M.A., 243, 368, 391, 409
Nestel, G., 611
net maternity function, 1090, 1093

net reproduction rate, 1090
Netherlands
  internal migration, 685
  residential mobility, 653
  stature and nutrition, 456–458
Neumark, D., 85
New Home Economics theory of fertility, 1077,
  1119
new technology and internal migration in devel-
  oping countries, 759–760
New Zealand: residential mobility, 653–654
Newbery, D.M.G., 758
Newhouse, J.P., 573
Newman, J., 319–320, 337–339, 356, 374–375,
  385, 511
Ng, Y.-K., 1197, 1213
Nicaragua: marriage and migration, 751
Nicholson, J.L., 248
Nickell, S., 878
Nicoletti, G., 1005
Niehans, J., 1122, 1130–1132, 1167
Niehans model of economic growth, 1130–1132
Niemi, A.W. Jr., 698
nightlight example of transferable utility, 36
Nishimura, K., 1151, 1168
Nolan, P., 565
non-accelerating inflation rate of unemployment
  (NAIRU), 1103
non-paternalistic preferences in families, 60
non-wage income in marriage, 94, 96, 98–9, 102
nonaltruism and endogenous fertility, 1246–
  1247, 1250
nonaltruistic transfers in intergenerational links,
  196–199
nonbenevolent preferences in competitive equilibrium in households, 67–68
nonconsensus models of household behaviour,
  172–179
  income pooling, 174–176
  Nash bargaining models, 172–174
  Pareto-efficient collective household models,
  176–179
noncooperation in family decision-making, 95–
  96
noncooperative bargaining theory, 42–44
noncooperative Nash equilibrium, 41–42
nonmalevolent preferences in families, 60
nonmarital childbearing, USA, 283–287
  trends in, 286
nontransferable utility in marriage market, 103–
  104
Nord, E., 604

Nordhaus, W.D., 1187, 1192–1193, 1273
Norgaard, R.B., 1276
normal retirement age (USA), 983
normative budgets and cost of children, 245–
  246
North, D.C., 1259, 1262, 1280
Norway
  height of men, 458–459
  mortality, decline in, 453–455
Nozick, R., 1214
Nugent, J.B., 389, 1167, 1247
nutrients/nutrition
  in endogenous population change, 1121
  and fertility, 401
  health risk factors, 580–581
  intrahousehold distributions in subsistence
  economies, 154–157
  and morbidity, 572–573
  and mortality, 8, 433–481
  implications for policy, 470–473
  malnutrition, extent and significance,
  445–460
  caloric consumption, England &
  France, 449–452
  energy cost accounting, 445–449
  stature and body mass indices, 452–
  460
  and population theory, 460–470
  and body size variations, 460–466
  and European famines, 466–468
  labor productivity, 468–470
  secular decline in, 434–445
  and famine, 440–445
  initial explanations, 435–437
  McKeown on, 437–440
  variations in subsistence economies, 164–166
nutrition wage and internal migration, 758–759
Nyamete, A., 381

Oberai, A.S., 750, 776–777
obesity and life expectancy, 583
O'Brien, P., 465
occupation as health risk factor, 581–582
Oddy, D.J., 449
Odink, J.G., 250
Ogawa, N., 1048
O'Hara, D.J., 370, 489–490
Ohlsson, R., 445
Oken, B., 376
Okojie, C.E.E., 381, 384
old-age dependency, 977–979
old age security, 493, 1147

Olsen, R., 285, 614
  on demand for children, 374, 384–385
  on mortality and health, 503–550 *passim*
one-sex population theory, 53–54
one-sided altruism and fertility, 1249–1250
O'Neil, J.A., 671
Oppenheimer, V., 108
opportunity costs
  of children, 247–248, 299
    and demand for children, 361, 367
  of migration, 666
optimal population in long-run development
  in finite lifetimes, 1225–1226
  infinitely-lived agents, 1211–1220
    dynamic analysis, 1217–1220
    static analysis, 1211–1217
  renewable resources, 1236
Orcutt, G., 356
Organization for Economic Cooperation and
  Development (OECD), 246, 263, 1194
Orshansky, M., 246
Ortega-Osona, J.A., 1082
Ortiz, V., 599
Osmani, S.R., 452, 573
Osmond, C., 471–472
Ostrom, E., 1180, 1239
Otomo, A., 655
Otten, M.W., 569
outside options in noncooperative bargaining
  theory, 43
overlapping generations
  and discounting, 1275–1276
  and ethics of equal sharing, 1161
  model
    of fertility, 378–379
    in intergenerational links, 192–193
    optimal population, 1125–1126
  and population growth, 1121–1125

Paffenberger, R., 584
Paglin, M., 1022
Pakes, A., 596, 618, 621–624, 625
Palloni, A., 532, 536
Pappas, G., 583
parent-to-child transfers, within-family intergenerational relations, 1006–1007
parents
  altruism, 1141
    nonrecursive formulation, 1149–
      1150
    recursive formulation, 1150–1155
  child sex preference of, 386–388

fertility choices, price and income effects,
  322–333
offspring conflict within families, 72
Pareto efficiency
  of collective household models of allocation,
    176–179
  decision-making in the family, 40–42
  of marriage, 89, 92, 95
Pareto optimality
  in interdependent utility functions within
    families, 66–68
    sustainability of, 68–71
  and utility possibility frontiers, 25–27
Parfit, D., 1215–1216, 1276
Parikh, K., 1273
parity progression ratio and infant mortality, 514,
  516
Park, C.B., 387
Parker, G., 1088
Parker, H., 245–246
Parker, J.R., 524
Parks, R., 68
Parsons, D.O., 102, 610–611, 1281
part-time work in retirement models, 901, 907–
  910
Partridge, E., 1276
Pasek, J., 1213
Pashardes, P., 255
Passel, J., 812
Passmore, D.L., 577
paternalistic preferences in intergenerational
  links, 233–234
paupers, 469
Pearce, D., 60, 61, 69
Pebley, A.R., 532, 537
Peccenino, R., 1269–1270
Pechman, J., 169
Peck, A., 471
Peck, J.M., 816
Peller, S., 437
pensions
  and age distributions fluctuations, 1104
  and economics of fertility, 377
  eligibility, 916–917
  evaluation of, 903–904
  and retirement, 902–905
    effects of, 916–919
Perloff, H.S., 671
permanent migration in developing countries,
  748–749
Perrenoud, A., 439, 572
Perrings, C., 1276

personal unemployment and internal migration, 683–687
Persson, T., 1264
Peru: migration in, 742
Pessino, C., 744, 771
Pestieau, P., 1077, 1225
Peters, E., 113, 119
Pezzey, J., 1237, 1273–1274
Phelan, C., 911, 916
Phelps, C.E., 594
Phelps, E.S., 63, 1205, 1209
Phelps, M., 763–764
Phelps-Brown, E.H., 1067–1068
Philippines
    earnings and transfers, 171
    migration in, 744, 751–752, 754
Phillips, D., 568
Phlips, L., 255
Pindyck, R.S., 1235
Pines, D., 868
Pingali, P.L., 1262
Pischke, J.-S., 832, 836
Pissarides, C.A., 679, 681, 685, 687–688
Pitchford, J.D., 1217
Pitt, M.M., 381, 386, 571, 625, 784
    on intrahousehold and the family, 154, 156, 164–166
Plane, D.A., 655
pluralistic households, decision-making in, 37–44
    children's well-being, 40–42
    cooperative Nash bargaining, 37–39
    noncooperative bargaining, 42–44
    and Pareto efficiency, 40–42
    private-goods consumption, 39–40, 42
    proportional sharing rules, 37
Poe, G., 598
Pogue-Guile, M., 583
Polemarchakis, H.M., 1221
Pollack, R., 88, 128, 173, 234
    on costs of children, 244, 253–255, 258–260, 262
    on demand for children, 356, 358, 380
    on the family, 22–23, 38–39, 44, 54–55, 62–63
    on fertility economics, 304
Pollak, R.A., 190, 228, 1228
Pollak and Wales critique of consumer demand systems, 258–260
Pollard, D., 596, 618, 621–624
pollution, 1194–1195, 1237
Polyani, K., 1192

polygyny in marriage markets, 57–58
Popkin, B.M., 571
population
    aging *see* population aging
    dynamics of, 15, 1063–1115
        equilibrium, 1064–1078
            classical population theory, 1064–1066
                Europe, consequences, 1066–1073
                evidence, 1066–1074
                model for, 1075–1076
                vital rates, 1073–1074
            modern theories of, 1076–1078
        fluctuations, response to, 1097–1107
            behavioural effects, 1104–1107
            compositional effects, 1100–1104
            consequences of, 1099–1100
        response to shocks, 1078–1089
            long-run, 1086–1089
            short-run, 1079–1086
    global, efficient volume of, 868–871
    renewal, internal dynamics of, 1089–1097
        generational cycles, 1090–1092
        Malthusian cycles, 1092–1097
    size
        and demand for labor, 1064–1065
        on economy, pre-industrial Europe, 1067–1068, 1070–1073, 1261
        endogenous economic growth, 1260–1269
            analytical models, 1267–1269
            and economic development, 1260–1265
            and endogenous fertility, 1266–1267
            and social welfare, 1265–1266
        and income, 1065, 1068–1069
        and private and public goods, 868–871
    theory of
        classical theory, 53–54, 1064–1066
            Europe, consequences, 1066–1073
            evidence, 1066–1074
            model for, 1075–1076
            vital rates, 1073–1074
        and nutrition, 460–470
            and body size variations, 460–466
            and European famines, 466–468
            labor productivity, 468–470
population aging, economics of, 13–14, 967–1014
    determinants, 969–977
        immigration, 975–977
        sources of, 970–975

fertility, declining, 971–972, 972–975
  mortality, declining, 972–975
forecasts, 969–970
in life-cycle model, 994–1000
  limitations of model, 998–1000
  and saving
    in general equilibrium, 997–998
    in partial equilibrium, 996–997
  two-period, change in, 995–996
production and consumption *see* consumption; production
social security and government programs, 1000–1006
  age and life-cycle saving, 1001–1003
  and demographic change, 1003–1005
  dependency ratios, 1000–1001
  political economy of, 1005–1006
within-family intergenerational relations, 1006–1008
  child to parent transfers, 1007–1008
  parent to child transfers, 1006–1007
see also aging
population density and economic development, 1186–1187
population growth and change, 16–17, 1175–1298
  age structure and, 979–981
  and discounting, 1275–1278
  and economic development, 1186–1187
  endogenous, 15–16, 1117–1174
    Becker–Lewis model, 1142–1147
    human capital investment, 1147–1155
    Lucas–Romer model, 1139–1141
    Malthus–Boserup model, 1132–1139, 1168
    Niehans model, 1130–1132
    old age pension motives, 1161–1168
      ethics of equal sharing, 1161–1163
      imperfect capital markets, 1163–1168
    as old-age security motive
      old age pension motives, 1161–1168
    old age security motives, 1160–1168
    parental altruism, 1147–1155
      nonrecursive formulation, 1149–1150
      recursive formulation, 1150–1155
    Solow–Swan model, 1124–1130
    survival probability, 1155–1160
      basic model, 1156–1158
      investment in health care, 1159–1160
      and population growth, 1158–1159
    two-sided altruism, 1168–1171

and environmental degradation, 1189–1190, 1195–1197
fluctuations, consequences of, 1099–1100
and income inequality, 1019
  mathematics of, 1036–1038
  and wages, 1044–1049
    empirical evidence, 1046–1049
    relative wages, 1044–1046
increasing returns of, 1140
and infant and child mortality, 488
long-run development *see* economic development, long-run
Lucas and Romer on, 1139–1141
past and present, 1183–1187
positive checks on, 1118
preventative checks on, 1118
and resource use, 1187–1197
  exhaustible resources, 1187–1188
  population, role of, 1195–1197
  renewable resources, 1188–1195
    global problems, 1192–1195
    local phenomena, 1190–1192
and sustainable development, 1272–1275
and technical change *see* technical change
and uncertainty, 1278
and vital rates, world, 352–353
world
  historically, 1183–1184
  modern, 1185
Porell, F.W., 680
Post, J.D., 468
post-neonatal deaths and fertility, 523–524
Postan, M.M., 1067
Postel, S., 1191
Postgate, R., 451
Poterba, J., 610, 982
Potter, J., 1035
Potter, R., 372
poverty
  age distribution, 956–958
  and fertility, 1179–1180
  fertility and income inequality, 1042–1043
  and late marriage, 1184
  and life expectancy by race, 568
  and population growth, 1264
  and resource over-use, 1179
Prais, S.J., 251–252, 254
Prais–Houthakker procedure on demand systems, 254
Pramaggiore, M., 610
pre-industrial societies
  economic crises on vital rates, 1080–1082

population growth in Europe, 1184, 1261
population size in Europe, 1067–1068, 1070–1073, 1261
pregnancy
   and abortion, rate of, 290
   weight gain and infant mortality, 545
prenatal care
   and fertility, 525, 527, 529, 533
   and infant mortality, 540–542
Prentice, R.L., 613
Prescott, E., 587
Preston, S.H., 440, 485, 509, 1006, 1072, 1158, 1263
   on internal migration, 725–727, 739
   on mortality and morbidity, 565, 572, 574, 599
price effects of fertility choices, 322–333
price elasticity of food and famine, 466–467
prices
   and migration, equlibrium models, 676–677
   related to individual endowments, 129, 147–151
Primary Insurance Amount (PIA), 897, 899
prisoners' dilemma game in marriage, 49
Pritchett, L.H., 1182
private goods
   consumption, 39–40, 42
   and marriage, 86, 92–93, 95, 97
   and population size, 868–871
   and transferable utility, 28–29
private transfers in intergenerational links, 201–202
private wealth accumulation and intergenerational links, 206
production
   in intergenerational links, 228–230
   and population aging, 977–994
      age structure and population growth, 979–981
      and labor market, 989–994
         lifetime wage profiles, 990–991
         seniority promotion, 993–994
         unemployment and labor force participation, 992–993
         wages and marginal products, 991
      morbidity and mortality, 981–983
      sustainable in model with capital, 983–989
      youth and old-age dependency, 977–979
productive matrix in interdependent utility functions, 61

productivity
   and internal migration in developing countries, 756–775
      dynamic models of, 768–769
      and income distribution, 769–775
         movers and stayers, 769–774
         rural sector inequality, 774–775
      rural labor markets, 756–760
         nutrition wage, 758–759
         remittance, risk and new technology, 759–760
         sharecropping, 757–758
         surplus labor, 757
      urban labor markets, 760–768
         collective bargaining, 764–765
         efficiency wage models, 765–766
         government intervention, 760–764
         shadow wages, 766–768
         wage setting, 764–766
   slowdown in aging population, 1009
Projector, D., 923
promotion and seniority and population aging, 993–994
property rights, 1239
proportional hazard models of mortality in adults and elderly, 614–616
Pryor, F.L., 1263
public goods
   in divorce, 110, 114
   in families, 23–24
      and children's well-being, 40–42
      transferable utility of, 29–30
      utility possibility frontiers, 25–27
   in marriage, 86–87, 90, 92–94, 97–99, 102–103
   and population size, 868–871
public health, 1121
   expenditure
      and life expectancy, 569, 602
      and mortality, 573–574
      on research, 575
public institutions and environment, 1179, 1180
   and endogenous technical change, 1259–1260
public water supply and mortality, 437
Puffert, D., 1004
Pullar, P., 451

quality of life and health status in elderly, 601–604, 607
Quality of Well-Being (QWB) index, 607–609
quality–quantity model

economic growth in endogenous population
  change, 1141, 1142–1147
of economics of fertility, 294–298
and endogenous fertility, 1246, 1247
in household demand model, 364
substitution elasticity between children, 1146
quasilinear utility with private goods, 29–30
Quenouille, M.H., 447, 460
Quetelet Index, 453
Quinn, J., 912
Quisumbing, A.R., 171, 380

Rabianski, J., 682
race
  and education of immigrants, USA, 804
  and fertility, USA, 281–282, 283, 284, 286
  and household income inequality (USA),
    1027
  and infant mortality, 487, 544, 570
  and internal migration, 697–698
  life expectancy by, 565, 567
    and poverty, 568
    public health expenditure and, 569
  and mobility of labor supply, USA, 826
  mortality and morbidity and, 568–569
  see also ethnicity
Rader, T., 23
Radner, D.B., 948, 953, 956
Radner, R., 36, 1205
Raines, F., 207–208
Ram, R., 1048, 1104
Ramos, F., 817
Ramsey, F.P., 220, 1220, 1236, 1276
Randolph, S., 772
Rangarajan, A., 327
Ransom, M.R., 625
Ransom, R., 893
Rao, V., 109
Rathwell, T., 568
rational addictions in health demand, 590–591
Raut, L.K., 15–16, 1044
  on endogenous population, 1117–1174
  on population growth, 1201, 1212, 1247,
    1249, 1254, 1257, 1269
Ravallion, M., 1079–1080
Ravenstein, E.G., 649, 659–661
Rawls, J., 1212, 1213
Ray, D., 759, 1227, 1246
Ray, R.J., 255–256
Razin, A., 11–12, 374, 378, 1148
  on international migration, 851–887
  on population growth, 1246–1247, 1249

Razzell, P.E., 439, 1261
Rebaudo, D., 442
Rebelo, S., 1269
Reder, M., 802, 826
reduced-form demand equations in household
  demand models, 360
refugees and migration in developing countries,
    755–756
Regets, M.C., 836
regional unemployment and internal migration,
    681–683
Reher, D.S., 572, 1082
Rehnberg, R.D., 785
Reilly, J., 1193
remarriage, 50–51
remittances
  and internal migration in developing coun-
    tries, 759–760
  and international migration, 806
Rempel, H., 759
Rendall, M.S., 578
renewable resources and population growth,
    1188–1195
  global problems, 1192–1195
  local phenomena, 1190–1192
  in long-run development, 1236–1244
Repetto, R., 1023, 1048, 1180, 1198
replacement strategy and infant mortality, 486,
    492, 498, 500–506, 508, 510–511
  child mortality, 384
  estimates of, 514–520
    approximate decision rules, 519–520
    birth and death history data, 514–517
    total births and deaths, 517–519
residential mobility and internal migration, 652–
    653
resources, 4
  inefficient use of, 1179–1180
  and population change
    endogenous, 1123
      technical change, 1250–1253, 1271–
        1272
  and population growth, 1187–1197
    exhaustible resources, 1187–1188
    long-run development, 1228–1245
      exhaustible resources, 1229–1235
      finite lives, 1236
      international issues, 1245
      optimal population, 1235
      renewable resources, 1236–1244
    renewable resources, 1188–1195
      global problems, 1192–1195

local phenomena, 1190–1192
  in long-run development, 1236–1244
substitution of, 1177–1178
and technical change
  discounting, 1277
  endogenous growth, 1269–1270
  with endogenous population change,
    1250–1253
    and infrastructure, 1253
    local complementarities, 1252–1253
    natural resources, 1271–1272
  uncertainty, 1278
Restrepo, H.A., 562
Retherford, R., 566
retirement, 892–919
  consumption and saving following, 919–
    948
    bequest motive for saving, 939–947
    by couples, 927–931
    life-cycle model, 923–931
      consumption data, 938–939
      wealth data, 931–935
    by singles, 924–927
    wealth change, 935–938
  evidence on, 912–919
    pensions, 916–919
    social security, 912, 913–916
  explanations, 893–895
  hazard rates, 892, 897, 913, 918
  and intergenerational economic links, 209,
    211
  models of, 905–912
    budget set nonlinearities, 906–907
    full- and part-time work, 901, 907–910
    uncertainty, 910–912
  pensions on, 902–905
  social security on, 893, 895–902
return migration
  in developing countries, 748–749
  international, 815–816
returns to scale
  constant, and child to parent transfers, 1164
  in international trade, 866
reverse Gorman specification on demand systems, 254
Ricardian equivalence in intrahousehold allocations, 127, 146
Ricardian neutrality in intergenerational links,
  200
Ricardo, D., 1044, 1065
Rich, W., 1048
Richards, T., 445

Richardson, H.W., 783
Richels, R.G., 1192–1194
Richman, J., 436
Ridker, R., 390
Ridner, R.G., 246
Riley, J., 572, 614
Rios-Rull, J.-V., 1107
risk
  in economic models of health, 579–586
    genetic factors, 583–586
    human capital, 579–580
    lifestyle, 583–586
    marital status, 582–583
    nutrition, 580–581
    occupation, 581–582
  in internal migration in developing countries,
    759–760
  pooling in marriage, 83
  sharing
    in intergenerational economic links, 230–
      231
    in marriage, 87–89
Roback, J., 676, 680
Robbins, H., 617
Roberts, K.D., 754
Robertson, P., 768
Robinson, C., 696, 699
Robinson, D., 762
Robinson, J.A., 16, 1175–1298
Robinson, S., 773–774, 1036, 1043
Robinson, W., 1263
Rochford, S., 51
Rodgers, G., 1048–1049
Rodgers, G.B., 758
Rodriguez-Clare, A., 1254
Rodrik, D., 1264
Roemer, J.E., 1240
Rogers, A., 731
Rogers, R., 569
Rogerson, P.A., 657
Rogot, E., 581, 583–584, 599, 612
Romaguera, P., 766
Romer, P., 1123
  on endogenous population, 1139–1141
  on population growth, 1199, 1254–1258,
    1269
Rose, E., 166
Rose, M.E., 451
Rosen, S., 576, 579, 580, 582, 599, 676
Rosenberg, H., 574
Rosenberg, N., 1258
Rosenzweig, M.R., 1–17, 88, 228, 232

on demand for children, 357–405 *passim*
on fertility economics, 321, 326, 334
on internal migration, 729, 748, 750–751, 756–759, 783–784
on international migration, 811
on intrahousehold distribution, 148–149, 164–166
on mortality
    and health, 489, 522, 524, 527, 533–535, 537, 541–542, 548–553
    and morbidity, 571, 576, 577, 580, 591, 597, 614
on population dynamics, 1080
Ross, S., 375
Roth, A., 45–46, 48, 50, 104
Rothbarth, E., 165, 248–249
Rotten Kid Theorem
    decision-making in, 35–37
    in models of intrahousehold allocations, 128, 144–146
Roumasset, J., 780
Rousseau, J.-J., 120
Roy, A.D., 694, 695
Roy, N., 413, 417
Rozental, M., 562
Rubinstein, A., 42–44, 52–53, 107
rural development and internal migration in developing countries, 778–780
    intent versus reality, 778–779
    schemes, 779–780
rural sector inequality in developing countries, 774–775
rural–urban migration in developing countries, 727, 728–729
    and job search, 732
Rust, J.P., 513, 625, 911–912, 916, 936
Ruttan, V.W., 1262
Ruud, P., 621, 624
Ryder, N.B., 374

Sabot, R.H., 733, 739, 742–743, 762, 766
Sadka, E., 11–12, 851–887, 1246–1247
Sah, R.K., 370, 384, 490, 492, 1247, 1253
    on endogenous population change, 1156–1158, 1172
    on mortality and health, 487, 490, 492, 495
Sahn, D.E., 580–581
Saint-Paul, G., 873
Sala-i-Martin, X., 1254, 1259
Salvatore, D., 742, 773
Samaritan's Dilemma
    in household allocations, 146

in intergenerational links, 215
in transferable utility, 36
Samuelson, P., 192, 378, 1096
    on the family, 26, 31, 32, 34, 37, 62, 70
    on international trade, 857–859
    on population growth, 1221–1222, 1225, 1264
Samuelson condition, 26
Sanchez, N., 390
Sandefur, G.D., 706
Sandell, S.H., 705
Sanders, R.D., 736
Sanders, R.L., 754
Sanderson, W., 304
sanitation as environmental issue, 1189
Santiago, C.E., 737
Sargent, T.J., 588
savings
    and age distributions fluctuations, 1103–1104
    following retirement, 919–948
        bequest motive for saving, 939–947
        by couples, 927–931
        life-cycle model, 923–931
            consumption data, 938–939
            wealth data, 931–935
        rates, after-tax income, 939
        by singles, 924–927
        wealth change, 935–938
    life-cycle, and fertility in low income countries, 379
    and population aging
        in general equilibrium, 997–998
        in partial equilibrium, 996–997
    and population growth, 1264–1265
Scandinavia: mortality decline in, 436
Schirm, A.L., 599, 1027, 1029
Schlottmann, A.M., 684–687, 708
Schmalensee, R., 1192
Schmidt, C.M., 836
Schmidt, R.M., 1186, 1263
Schmitz, J.A. Jr, 1254
Schneider, E., 983
Schoeni, R., 57
Schoeni, R.F., 600
Schoening, N.C., 687
Schofield, R., 486
    on mortality
        and morbidity, 572
        and nutrition, 439, 442, 445, 452, 466–467
Schofield, R.S., 1067
schooling *see* education and schooling

Schultz, P., 98
Schultz, T.P., 7, 1120, 1158, 1265
  on demand for children, 349–430
  on the family, 39–42
  on fertility economics, 321, 326, 329
  on income inequality, 1032, 1034–1035
  on internal migration, 664, 723, 731, 742,
    755, 783–784
  on intrahousehold distribution, 148–149, 175
  on mortality and health, 522, 524, 527, 533–
    535, 537, 541–542, 549, 552
  on mortality and morbidity, 571, 576, 580,
    597, 614
Schultz, T.W., 356, 363, 380, 669, 1181
Schultze, C., 1139
Schutjer, W.A., 1074, 1263
Schwartz, A., 666, 744
Schwartz, N.L., 1229, 1238
Schwartz, S., 228
Schwartz, W., 574
Scott, D.W., 621
Scott, M.F., 767, 1255
Scott, W.J., 706
Scrimshaw, N.S., 436, 452, 572
Scrimshaw, S.C., 387
search in marriage market, 104–108
  intensity, 105
  value of, 105–106
Seckler, D., 456
second birth, timing of, 284
Second Welfare Theorem, 68–71
Sedjo, R.A., 1191
Seifer-Vogt, H.G., 749
self-assessed health in elderly, 604–609
Seltzer, J., 116
semi-nonparametric models of mortality in adults
    and elderly, 617–618
Sen, A.K., 126, 148, 467, 757
  on mortality and morbidity, 563, 565
  on population dynamics, 1079–1080, 1082
  on population growth, 1184–1185
Sender, J., 565
seniority and promotion and population aging,
    993–994
separable earnings-transfers (SET) model of
    intrahousehold distribution, 137–142
  endowment reinforcement or compensation,
    152–154
  gender and birth-order effects, 163–164
  returns to schooling and child quality in,
    142–144
Serageldin, I., 1189

sex preference of parents in low income coun-
    tries, 386–388
Shaked, A., 51
Shammas, C., 449
Shapiro, E., 601
Shapiro, S., 472, 529
Shapley, L., 30, 45–47, 103–104
sharecropping and internal migration in devel-
    oping countries, 757–758
sharing
  ethics of equal in child to parent transfers,
    1161–1163
  rule in marriage, 86–87
Shaw, A., 750
Shaw, R.P., 667, 671, 708
Shepherd's Lemma, 250, 255
Sheps, M., 1083
Shishido, H., 780
Shleifer, A., 1266
shocks, population response to, 1078–1089
  long-run, 1086–1089
  short-run, 1079–1086
Shorrocks, A.F., 933, 1022
Short, K., 383, 1073
Shoven, J.B., 585, 951
Shryock, H.S., 651, 662
Shubik, M., 30, 46–47
Shukla, V., 780–781
siblings
  correlations, 126
  earnings differences, 167–172
  and intergenerational linkages, 1227–1228
  and schooling allocations, 162
  schooling prices of, 149–151
  similarities in intrahousehold allocations,
    149–151
Sickles, R.C., 9, 559–643
Sidgwick, H., 1214–1215, 1217–1218, 1220,
    1225–1226, 1235, 1245
Siegel, J.S., 651
Sikora, R.I., 1216
Silver, M., 568, 579, 1085
Silvers, A., 681
Simmons, A., 722, 775–776
Simmons, G.B., 377
Simmons, P., 1234
Simon, A., 599
Simon, J.L., 378
  on international migration, 801, 802, 844–
    845
  on population growth, 1186–1187, 1218,
    1262–1263, 1265, 1269

simulation methods on mortality in adults and elderly, 618–621

Sincich, T., 649

Singer, B., 338–339, 374, 519, 612, 614–617

Singh, B., 253

Sirmans, C.F., 665, 691

Sjaastad, L.A., 669–670, 673, 730, 732, 805

Skeldon, R., 728

Skinner, J., 117

Slade, F., 611

Slade, M.E., 1182, 1188, 1235

Slesnick, D.T., 255–256

Slicher Van Bath, B.H., 466

Slutsky conditions in marriage, 96–97

Smeeding, T.M., 201, 262

Smith, A., 1044

Smith, D.S., 441

Smith, J.P., 359, 600

Smith, K., 569, 583

Smith, S.K., 649

smoking
and infant mortality, 529, 545, 547
and life expectancy, 566
as mortality risk, 584–586, 590

Smulders, S., 1269

social expenditure by age, 1000

social security
and fertility in low income countries, 379, 388
pay-as-you-go system, 1167
and population aging, 999, 1000–1006
age and life-cycle saving, 1001–1003
and demographic change, 1003–1005
dependency ratios, 1000–1001
political economy of, 1005–1006
replacement rate, 1002
and retirement, 893, 895–902
effects of, 912, 913–916

social welfare
functions
in basic dynastic economy, 1203, 1210–1211
and optimal population, 1213, 1217
technical change and population growth, 1265–1266
transfers and international migration, 840–842

soil degradation, 1237

Soligo, R., 770

Solon, G.R., 221

Solow, R.M., 764, 1044, 1076

on endogenous population change, 1122, 1124, 1126–1128, 1130–1132, 1139–1140, 1167
on population growth, 1177, 1198, 1200, 1212, 1228–1229, 1254, 1257, 1273–1274

Solow–Swan model of economic growth, 1123, 1124–1130

Song, L., 565

Sonic, A., 626

sophisticated strategies of consumer behaviour, 62–63

Sorlie, P., 581, 599

Sotomayor, M., 45–46, 48, 104

South America
life expectancy and infant mortality, 563
urban growth, 725–726

Spady, R.H., 623

Spain: immigrants, stock of, 802

Speare, A. Jr, 578

Spencer, G., 472

Spivak, A., 88, 231, 1007

Squire, L., 734

Srinivasan, T.N., 16, 387, 763, 866, 871
on endogenous population change, 1122, 1140–1141, 1168
on mortality and morbidity, 581
on population growth, 1175–1298

stable marriage assignment
Gale–Shapley model, 45–46
and marriage market, 100–104

stable matching in marriage
in marriage market, 100–103
models of, 48–49

stable populations
and age structure
and income inequality, 1018
and population growth, 979–981
fertility, declining, 972–975
mortality, declining, 972–975

Stadler, G.W., 1106–1107

Stafford, F.P., 39, 109

Staiger, D., 308, 577

Stallard, E., 616

Stapleton, D.C., 1030

Stark, O., 1–17, 88, 92, 1008, 1036, 1043
on cost of children, 214–215, 217, 225–226, 232, 234
on demand for children, 373, 379
on the family, 60, 75–76
on internal migration, 650, 729–781 *passim*

on international migration, 803, 806–808, 815

on population growth, 1226–1227, 1247–1248

Starrett, D., 1239–1240

Startz, R., 577

static lifetime fertility model, 488–491

stationary preferences in consumer behaviour, 63

stature

and malnutrition, 452–460

and mortality, 572–573

Stavins, R., 1071

steady-state economies, 1162

Steckel, R.H., 456, 471

Stein, G., 561

Steinmeier, T.L., 581, 903, 907, 912, 915–915

Stern, J., 1079, 1085

Stern, N.H., 758

Stern, S., 621, 625, 911

Stewart, A., 601

Stigler, G.J., 372, 449

Stiglitz, J.E., 733–735, 747, 758, 1228–1229, 1234

stochastic dynamic programming in retirement models, 911–912, 916

Stock, J.H., 577, 911–912, 919

stock adjustment equations in household production functions, 374

Stokes, C.S., 1074

Stokey, N.L., 219, 588, 1151, 1241

Stolnitz, G.J., 369, 435, 437

Stolper, W.F., 858–859

Stone, J.A., 679

Stone, L., 255

Stoto, M.A., 616

Strauss, J., 165, 372, 399–400, 580–581, 601

Stretton, A., 748

Streufert, P.A., 1246

Strotz, R.M., 62–63, 1276

Strupp, P.W., 532, 537

Stunkard, A., 583

stunting and nutrition, 453, 455–456, 471

Stys, U., 362, 381

Subramanian, S., 165

subsistence economies

health and nutrition variations, 164–166

intrahousehold distributions in, 154–157

subsistence levels and nutrition, 465, 467

Summers, L.H., 610, 764, 923, 936

on aging, 982, 999, 1007

on household linkages, 196, 206–207, 220

Summers, R.A., 866

Sumner, L.W., 1215

Sundstrom, W., 1247

superbenevolent utility, 62

support ratios and dependency, 977, 981–983, 984

survival hazard models in adults and elderly, 613–621

competing risk, 616–617

proportional hazard, 614–616

semi-nonparametric, 617–618

simulation methods, 618–621

survival probability in endogenous population change, 1155–1160

basic model, 1156–1158

investment in health care, 1159–1160

and population growth, 1158–1159

survival rates and birth rates, 489–491

sustainable development and economic growth, 1272–1275

and discounting, 1276

Sutch, R., 893

Sutton, J., 43, 51

Suzman, R., 600

Swamy, S., 1036

Swan, T.W., 1200

on endogenous population, 1122, 1124, 1126–1128, 1130–1132, 1139, 1167

Sweden

demographic transition in, 484–485

fertility studies, 329

height of men, 459

immigrants, stock of, 802

internal migration, 685–686, 687

mortality, decline in, 436

residential mobility, 653

Sweetland, D.P., 667

Swick, K., 1095–1096

Switzerland: residential mobility, 653

Tabbarah, R.B., 372

Tabellini, G., 1264

Taber, C.R., 617

Tahvonen, O., 1242

Tainer, E., 839

Tait, A.A., 762

Tamura, R., 1151

Tanner, J.M., 455, 456

Tansel, A., 580

target fertility model, 488–491

Tarisan, A.C., 375

Taubman, P., 9, 150, 153, 163, 559–643, 1093

on mortality and morbidity, 559–643

Tauchen, H., 583
Taussig, M.K., 1033, 1065
taxation
  on children, 1142
  and international migration, 844–846
Taylor, J.E., 232, 743–744, 747, 755
Taylor, W.E., 409, 412
technical change and population growth, 1245–1272
  endogenous economic growth
    population size and, 1260–1269
      analytical models, 1267–1269
      and economic development, 1260–1265
      and endogenous fertility, 1266–1267
      and social welfare, 1265–1266
    resources with, 1250–1253, 1269–1270
      and infrastructure, 1253
      local complementarities, 1252–1253
      natural resources, 1271–1272
    theories of, 1253–1260
  and fertility, 1246–1250
    endogenous, 1266–1267
  and mortality, 1246–1250
Teilhet-Waldorf, S., 737
temporary migration in developing countries, 729–730, 748–749
Thailand: migration in, 745
Thaler, R., 576
Thatcher, A.R., 612
Theil, H., 255, 294, 364, 393
third birth, timing of, 285
Third World: economic crises in, 1080, 1082–1084
Thomas, B., 1100
Thomas, D., 40–41, 98–99, 165, 174–175, 355
  on mortality and morbidity, 571, 580–581
Thomas, D.S., 661–662, 1085
Thomas, R.H., 1262, 1280
Thompson, E.P., 469
Thompson, J., 619–620
Thompson, W.S., 437
Thorbecke, E., 737
Thornthwaite, C.W., 661
threat points
  in household demand models, 359–360
  in marriage, 38, 39, 106–107
    divorce as, 39, 50–51
Tienda, M., 532, 536, 599, 814, 842
Tilly, C., 451
time allocation and demand for children, 298–305

time budget constraints in household economic
    models, 356
Tirole, J., 1170
Tobin, J., 219, 1105–1106
Todaro, M.P., 805
  on internal migration, 650, 681, 724, 727,
    732–735, 737–738, 753, 760, 767
Toman, M., 1273–1274
Tomes, N., 696, 699, 944
  on household linkages, 191, 199, 201, 205,
    207–208, 221, 226, 230
  on intrahousehold distribution, 128, 130–133,
    135–137, 144, 151, 167, 169–170
Topel, R.H., 11, 367, 799–850
Tornell, A., 1260
Torrance, G.W., 601, 604
total fertility rates
  inter-country comparisons, 398, 404, 408,
    411–412
  in USA (1900–1993), 278, 281
Toutain, J., 449–450
Townsend, P., 246
Townsend, R., 98
transactions cost approach to intergenerational
    links, 228–234
  demonstration effect, 233–234
  insurance and credit, 230–233
  paternalistic preferences, 233–234
  production, 228–230
transferable utility
  in family, 89–91, 97, 104–105
    and altruism, 93
    and divorce, 112, 117
    and stable matching, 100
  in households, 27–31
    and decision-making, 33–34
    and mate selection, 30–31
    with private goods, 28–29
    with public goods, 29–30
  and marriage assignments, 47–48
    and age, 55–56
transfers
  in intergenerational linkages, child to parent,
    1126
  and international migration
    and fertility, 842–844
    social welfare, 840–842
    and tax payments, 844–846
  in intrahousehold allocations, 127, 129–137
    and sibling differences, 167–172
  private, in intergenerational links, 201–202,
    203, 207–208

and human capital investment, 226–227
within-family intergenerational relations
    child to parent, 1007–1008
    parent to child, 1006–1007
Translog demand system and costs of children,
    255
transport costs and migration, 666–667
Trayham, E.C., 691
Trejo, S., 841–842
Treyz, G.I., 679, 682
Trivers, R., 72
Truchon, M., 27
truth telling in stable matching, 48
Tryon, R., 997
Trzcinski, E., 772
Tsiatis, A., 616–617
Tsoulouhas, T.C., 1070–1071
Tucker, G.S.L., 1261
Tuljapurkar, S., 1096
Tunali, I., 696, 699
twins, 151, 161–162, 163, 168
    and economics of fertility, 333–335
    in household demand model, 364, 369
    smoking and mortality in, 585–586
two-sex mating theories, 54–55
two-sided altruism, 64–65
    and economic growth, 1141, 1168–1171
    and intergenerational linkages, 1226
    in intergenerational links, 212–217

Udall, A.T., 782
Udry, C., 179, 1249
Ulph, D., 173
uncertainty
    in environmental issues, 1278
    in health demand models, 593–596
    in marriage, 98
        and divorce, 110, 113–114
        of income, 87
    in retirement, 910–912
undernutrition, 446
undocumented aliens, 812–814
unemployment
    and age distributions fluctuations, 1103
    and income inequality differential in devel-
        oping countries, 1048
    and internal migration
        in developed countries, 660, 684
            heads of family, 705
            national, 687–688
            personal, 683–687
            regional, 681–683

in developing countries, 742–743
    duration of, 735–736
and population aging, 992–993
unitary models of decision-making, 32–37
    with household social welfare function, 34–
        35
    with Rotten Kid Theorem, 35–37
    with transferable utility, 33–34
United Auto workers: pensions, 917
United Kingdom *see* Great Britain
United Nations, 435, 437, 445, 650
United States
    Easterlin cycles in, 1092–1093
    fertility, economics of, 277–292
        age-specific fertility rates, 282
        childlessness, 280–281
        cohort total rates, 278
        completed family size, 278–280
        contraceptive practices, 287–291
        first birth
            mother's age at, 281–283
            probabilities, 283
        and labor force participation, 291–292
        marital and nonmarital childbearing, 283–
            287
            trends in, 286
        second birth, timing, 284
        third birth, timing, 285
    global warming, impact of, 1193–1194
    immigration
        assimilation of, 833–835
        education of, 803–804
        fertility of, 843–844
        flow of, 802, 852–853
        and labour supply, 819–820
        language proficiency of, 838–839
        regulation of, 808–809, 812
        welfare participation, 841
    income inequality in, 1049–1052
        age structure and, 1019–1021
        and marital sorting, 1027–1029
    infant mortality, 570–571
    internal migration in, 661–663, 678–679,
        697, 701–702
        distance elasticities, 667–668
        and education, 655–656
        and employment, 682, 683–684, 685
        trends, 656–657
    life expectancy in, 562–563
        by age cohort, 564
        by gender, 567
        by race, 567, 568

and poverty, 568
median age, 969–970
mortality and morbidity in, 562–575
    and economic development, 563–565
    and gender, 565–567
    and infant mortality, 569–571
    and migration, 571–572
    and nutrition, 572–573
    public policy on, 573–575
    and race, 568–569
residential mobility, 653–654
social expenditure by age, 1000
undocumented aliens in, 812–814
unwed parents, 58–59
urbanization/urban areas
    immigrants in, USA, 804
    and income inequality differential in devel-
        oping countries, 1048
    internal migration in developing countries,
        724–728
        rates of growth, 724–727
        role of migration, 727
        selectivity in, 728
    wages and internal migration in developing
        countries, 777–778
US Bureau of Census, 472
US Nat. Cent. Health Stat., 450
Usher, D., 589, 1097
utility functions
    of childbearing, 491, 494, 499
    of marriage, 85, 90, 96
        altruistic, 93, 98
        of family, 94–95
utility in equilibrium models of migration, 674–
    675
utility possibility frontiers, 24–27
    with public goods, 25–27
Utterström, G., 437, 1088
Uzawa, H., 1258

Vallin, J., 516
value of life in benefit-cost analysis, 70
Van Arkadie, B., 1239
van de Ven, W., 587
van de Walle, E., 440, 572
van der Gaag, J., 587, 1027
van der Ploeg, F., 1200, 1242
Van der Sar, N.L., 260–262
Van Dijk, J., 685, 704
Van Imhoff, E., 250
Van Praag, B.M.S., 5–6, 241–273
Van Wieringen, J.C., 457–458, 472

Vanderkamp, J., 672–673, 701
Varian, H., 28, 34, 174
Vaughan, D.R., 601
Vaupel, J.W., 472, 573, 586, 614
Vedder, R.K., 667
Venezuela: migration in, 742
Vergoossen, D., 655, 658
Verry, D.W., 780
Vickrey, W.S., 1213
Vijverberg, W., 311
Vijverberg, W.P.M., 771
Vining, D., 656, 1188
Visaria, P., 1032–1033
Viscusi, W.K., 573, 594
vital statistics, historical, 436–437
Vlachonikolis, I., 610
Von Weizsäcker, R.K., 562
Vousden, N., 1229, 1274

Waaler, H.T., 573
Waaler surfaces and curves, 434, 453, 457, 472
Wachtel, P., 997
Wachter, K., 1095–1096
Wachter, M., 22–23, 304, 358
Wade, A., 973
Wadsworth, J., 681, 685, 687–688
Wadycki, W.J., 666, 682, 744, 747
wage gap, Eastern Europe, 856
wages
    and fertility, 1073–1074
    and full- and part-time work, 907
    and health demand models, 591–592
    and immigration, 817–821, 825
    and income inequality
        age structure and, 1023–1024
        population growth, 1044–1049
            empirical evidence, 1046–1049
            relative wages, 1044–1046
    and internal migration
        collective bargaining, 764–765
        efficiency wage models, 765–766
        nutrition wage, 758–759
        shadow, 766–768
        subsidies, 762–763
        wage setting, 764–766
    and migration, 668
        in equilibrium models, 675–676, 680
    and mortality, 1074
    and opportunity costs of children, 367, 368,
        381, 383
    and population aging, 991
    and population size, 1064–1066

Europe, 1068–1069, 1070–1073
in production-demand model of fertility, 361
and retirement, 895
rigidity in international trade and migration,
    871–880
    rigid wages, 878–880
    wage flexibility, 871–878
Wagstaff, A., 1079, 1085
on mortality and morbidity, 563, 579, 594
Waidman, T., 611
Waite, L., 113, 120
Waitzman, N., 583
Waldman, M., 36, 146, 214–215
Waldorf, W.H., 737
Waldron, I., 566
Wales, T.J., 244, 253–255, 258–260, 262, 624
Walker, J., 338–339, 375
Wallace, T.D., 505–506, 508, 517–518
Waller, H.Th., 452–453, 456
Walter, J., 439, 445, 1193
Wang, D., 945
Ward, M., 1078–1080, 1085
Ward, M.P., 372
Ware, J., 601
Warnaar, M.F., 5, –6241–273
Warren, R., 812, 816
Warshawsky, M.J., 197, 231, 924
water
    clean, as environmental issue, 1189
    shortages, Africa, 1191
Watkins, S., 1080, 1086, 1183
wealth
    change, in saving following retirement, 935–
        938
    distribution of
        in intergenerational links, 217, 220
        in retirement, 922
    of elderly
        comparisons, 959
        and mortality, 578
    in life-cycle model of retirement, 931–935
        annuitized and total, 946
        average bequeathable, 935
        one-year change, by age and health, 937
        real, average change, 941
        relative bequeathable, 932
        ten-year changes, 934
wealth model of intrahousehold allocations, 130–
    137
Weibull, J., 36, 214
Weil, D.N., 13–15, 378
    on population aging, 967–1014

on population dynamics, 1100–1104
Weil, P., 191, 1204, 1227
Weir, D., 1068, 1070, 1072, 1080, 1280
    on infant and child mortality, 508, 511, 519–
        520, 538
Weir, D.R., 445, 452
Weiss, A., 758, 765
Weiss, C., 923
Weiss, L., 697
Weiss, Y., 41, 305–306, 424
    on marriage and divorce, 81–123
Weitzman, M.L., 1244, 1278
Weizsäcker, R. von, 993
Welch, F., 386–387, 990, 1050
welfare
    and differential fertility, 1043–1044
    in sustainable development, 1273–1274,
        1275
Wellisz, S., 768
Wertheimer, R.F., 698
Whalley, J., 873
Wheaton, W.C., 780
Whelpton, P.K., 437
White, B.B., 923, 999
White, H., 614
Whiteford, P., 246, 265
Wicksell, K., 1213
Wilbraham, A., 451
Wilcoxen, P.J., 1193
Wildasin, D.E., 868
Wilhelm, M., 170, 927, 944
Wilkinson, M., 1100
Williams, A.D., 490
Williams, J., 584
Williams, R.M., 568
Williamson, O.E., 190
Williamson, J.G., 697, 1047, 1068, 1072, 1264
    on internal migration, 725, 739, 785
    on mortality and nutrition, 440, 449, 461, 469
Willis, K.G., 711
Willis, R., 1077
Willis, R.J., 6, 16, 143
    on demand for children, 361, 362–365, 373
    on endogenous population change, 1156,
        1163, 1172
    on the family, 24, 41, 58
        formation and dissolution, 109, 111–114,
            116
    on fertility economics, 275–347
    on mortality and health, 493, 511
    on population growth, 1247, 1265
Wilson, C., 376

Wilson, C.A., 451
Wilson, W.J., 59, 110, 305, 308
Winegarden, C.R., 1022–1023, 1048–1049
Winter, J.M., 439
Winter, S., 60, 68
Wise, D.A., 606
  on aging, 903, 905, 911–912, 914, 917–919
Wissoker, D., 113
Withagen, C., 1229, 1242
within-family intergenerational relations, 1006–1008
  child to parent transfers, 1007–1008
  parent to child transfers, 1006–1007
Wold, H.O., 356
Wolf, D., 1008
Wolfe, B.L., 372, 381, 545, 611, 751
  on mortality and morbidity, 571, 576, 580, 590–591
Wolfe, J.R., 577
Wolff, E.N., 932
Wolinsky, A., 52–53, 106
Wolpin, K.I., 8, 228, 1044, 1080, 1157
  on demand for children, 363–364, 368–369, 374, 378, 385, 391, 405
  on fertility, 320, 334, 340
  on internal migration, 748, 783–784
  on mortality
    and health, 483–557
    and morbidity, 576, 594, 614, 625–626
women
  fertility, USA, 291–292
  income inequality, 1025–1026, 1028–1029
  and internal migration, 703–705
    as tied movers, 702–703
  marrying older men, 56–57
  maximum children possible, and survival probability, 1159
  mortality and morbidity in, 565–567
  opportunity costs of children, 247–248
  see also gender
Wood, D.O., 1235
Woodland, A.D., 624
Woolley, F., 38–39, 40–41
work

at home, 109, 118–119
in market, 84, 86, 109, 117–119
World Bank, 165, 379, 403, 449, 451, 1016–1017, 1068, 1121
  on mortality and morbidity, 562, 607
  on population growth, 1178, 1180, 1183–1185, 1189–1191, 1194, 1252, 1262, 1264, 1280
World Health Organization (WHO), 156, 157
Wrigley, E.A., 1067
  on mortality and nutrition, 439, 441–442, 445, 452, 461, 465–467
Wu, D.M., 399, 401, 407

Yaari, M.E., 198
Yap, L.Y.L., 740, 743–745, 771
Yarri, M.E., 924, 943
Yashin, A.I., 616
Yazbeck, A., 594
Years of (Potential) Life Lost (YLL), 602
Years of Productive Life Lost (YPLL), 604
Yellen, J.L., 770
Yitzhaki, S., 754, 1036, 1043
Young, A.A., 1140
youth dependency and population aging, 977–979
Yugoslav equivalence scales in cost of children, 264–265

Zabalza, A., 1029
Zajonc, R.B., 364, 374
Zarate, A., 710
Zeira, J., 224
Zeldes, S., 223
Zeng, Y., 387, 413
Zhang, J., 387, 1168
Zick, C., 569
Zimmer, M., 699
Zimmerman, D.J., 221
Zimmermann, K.F., 1081
Zopf, P., 566
Zucker, A., 1188
Zvidrins, P., 565